CHILDREN AND ADOLESCENTS WITH EMOTIONAL AND BEHAVIORAL DISORDERS

Vance L. Austin

Manhattanville College

Daniel T. Sciarra

Hofstra University

Merrill

Boston   Columbus   Indianapolis   New York   San Francisco   Upper Saddle River
Amsterdam   Cape Town   Dubai   London   Madrid   Milan   Munich   Paris   Montreal   Toronto
Delhi   Mexico City   Sao Paulo   Sydney   Hong Kong   Seoul   Singapore   Taipei   Tokyo

Library of Congress Cataloging-in-Publication Data

Austin, Vance L.
 Children and adolescents with emotional and behavioral disorders / Vance L. Austin, Daniel T. Sciarra.
  p. cm.
 ISBN-13: 978-0-205-50176-2
 ISBN-10: 0-205-50176-1
  1. Mentally ill children—Education—Textbooks.   2. Problem children—Education—Textbooks.
3. Behavior disorders in children—Treatment—Textbooks.   4. Child psychopathology—Textbooks.
5. Adolescent psychopathology—Textbooks. I. Sciarra, Daniel T. II. Title.
 LC4165.A87 2010
 371.94—dc22

                                                                                                    2008051991

Vice President and Executive Publisher:
 Jeffery W. Johnston
Executive Editor: Ann Castel Davis
Editorial Assistant: Penny Burleson
Senior Managing Editor: Pamela D. Bennett
Project Manager: Kerry J. Rubadue
Project Coordination: Ravi Bhatt/Aptara®, Inc.
Art Director: Candace Rowley
Cover Image: FotoSearch

Cover Design: Ali Mohrman
Senior Operations Supervisor: Matthew
 Ottenweller
Operations Specialist: Laura Messerly
**Vice President, Director of Sales &
 Marketing:** Quinn Perkson
Marketing Manager: Erica Deluca
Marketing Coordinator: Brian Mounts

This book was set in Garamond by Aptara®, Inc. It was printed and bound by Bind-Rite Graphics.
The cover was printed by Bind-Rite Graphics.

Pearson® is a registered trademark of Pearson plc
Merrill® is a registered trademark of Pearson Education, Inc.

Pearson Education Ltd., London
Pearson Education Singapore Pte. Ltd.
Pearson Education Canada, Inc.
Pearson Education–Japan
Pearson Education Australia PTY, Limited

Pearson Education North Asia, Ltd., Hong Kong
Pearson Educación de Mexico, S.A. de C.V.
Pearson Education Malaysia Pte. Ltd.
Pearson Education Upper Saddle River, New Jersey

Merrill
is an imprint of

PEARSON

www.pearsonhighered.com

10 9 8 7 6 5 4 3
ISBN-13: 978-0-205-50176-2
ISBN-10:   0-205-50176-1

To my dear wife Theresa and my son Jimmy, who have given my life meaning and purpose; to my mother Lois, who taught me how to walk in the world . . .

       VA

. . . and to my grandchildren Alex and Alondra, whose childhood innocence manifests the wonder of all children.

       DS

PREFACE

This book is an introductory text that describes the enigmatic and challenging world of emotional and behavioral disorders for a target audience that includes nascent general and special education teachers, as well as veteran teachers and related services providers who simply want to know more about their affected students and how to work with them more successfully.

The approach we have adopted is to provide information that promotes greater understanding of specific emotional and behavioral disorders by examining the characteristics, causes, assessments, and current evidenced-based interventions for each of them. We accomplish this by using real-world case examples and practical, classroom-based approaches that target the behavioral issues presented in each of these cases. We believe that the duality of our very different experiences and expertise provides the reader with the benefit of two different perspectives that encompass both current theory and best practice.

Many textbooks address issues that are relevant to maladaptive behaviors and behavior management techniques in school-age children, but few, if any, provide the reader with a field-tested repertoire of classroom interventions. Using effective functional behavioral assessments that have been developed from authentic case examples, this book tries to remedy that deficiency. Furthermore, in accordance with the *Individuals with Disabilities Education Act* (IDEA) and the *No Child Left Behind Act* (NCLB), we provide the latest research on many of the disorders that affect student behavior and learning. In conjunction with a fundamental understanding of all aspects of a specific disorder, we also present scientifically developed interventions. Short of actual classroom experience, these chapters strive to provide the preservice and novice teacher with the most realistic simulations possible. This feature should be of great value to college and university instructors who want to provide the most relevant, authentic course experiences for their students. To that end, this book also addresses the latest requirements of *IDEA* and issues relevant to students with emotional disturbance, as well as the emphasis placed on functional behavioral assessment and its implications in the development of tenable behavioral intervention plans.

The structure of the book provides easy-to-use information that is organized according to emotional and behavioral disorders identified in field-based and professional journals. The 11-chapter format complements a 15-week semester: Three of the chapters encompass sufficient topical material for two college sessions, allowing for course evaluation during the fifteenth and final session.

Although the book is primarily designed for preservice teachers, the currency of material and the emphasis on assessment and related intervention strategies make it equally relevant for novice and veteran teachers, related services personnel, and school administrators who simply want to work more knowledgeably and successfully with this population.

Each chapter in the book begins with a series of key "Focus Questions" that are revisited near the chapter's end together with suggested responses. In addition, each of the content chapters concludes with a concise summary and a section called "Tips for Teachers," which offers easy-to-implement practice-based strategies that teachers can use to work more successfully with students who express the disorder in question. Each chapter is also enhanced with a "From the Field" feature, in which professionals and stakeholders share relevant experiences and suggestions with the reader.

Chapter 1 addresses the traditional challenges inherent in defining emotional and behavioral disorders, the profile of a "typical" student with an emotional or behavioral disorder (EBD), how to develop an effective functional behavioral assessment (FBA) and its application to treatment and intervention, as well as caregiver approaches that are generally effective or not effective in working with students with EBDs.

Chapters 2, 3, and 4 focus on students who have disruptive disorders, examining what are, arguably, the most challenging populations that teachers face in the classroom and that, statistically, represent the cause most frequently cited for teacher attrition. Chapter 2 describes *conduct disorder,* introducing it with a real-world case example that provides an authentic connection to practice. The chapter discusses the characteristics, causes, assessments, and treatments for conduct disorder, as well as school-based interventions to help the reader understand the disorder. Similarly, Chapter 3 examines *oppositional defiant disorder* and discusses the controversial notion that it may be a precursor to conduct disorder, thus emphasizing the importance of effective preemptory intervention. Chapter 4 introduces one of the most pervasive disruptive disorders affecting school-age children today—*attention-deficit hyperactivity disorder* (ADHD). This chapter includes a guide for students and teachers that outlines a recommended evaluation process, as well as effective treatment options, including a chart of current medications.

Chapters 5, 6, and 7 examine the most prevalent anxiety disorders in children and youth. Again, each of these anxiety disorders is introduced with a case example and is then described in a systematic way that educates the reader about characteristics, causes, current methods of assessment, and recommended treatment strategies to enhance clarity and ensure complete understanding of the disorder. Then, school-based interventions are provided to help teachers work more successfully with students who manifest these behaviors.

Chapter 5 explores *specific phobias, separation anxiety disorder,* and *social anxiety disorder,* and, once more, employs case examples to help connect the reader with classroom practice and the realistic "feel" of working with students who possess each of these disorders. In a similar fashion, Chapter 6 continues the study of the most prevalent anxiety disorders, examining *posttraumatic stress disorder, generalized anxiety disorder,* and *obsessive-compulsive disorder,* following the format employed throughout this book. Lastly, Chapter 7 investigates *eating disorders,* a source of growing concern among parents and teachers alike, because of their increased identification in today's schools and affecting, in some cases, girls as young as 10 years of age.

Chapter 8 considers mood disorders, including *depressive disorders* and *bipolar disorder,* and their high correlation with *suicide.* These disorders are thoroughly discussed in Chapter 8, which also follows our formula, effectively blending theory and practice, and incorporating the chapter features described earlier. An important part of this chapter deals with adolescent suicide; discussing assessments and warning signs, and providing additional teacher resources.

Chapter 9 discusses one of the most enigmatic disorders among school-age children today: *autistic spectrum disorders* (ASDs). These disorders, diagnosed in increasing numbers of children today, have received widespread attention in recent years, thanks, in part, to coverage in the media. The U.S. Department of Education, as well as the education departments of many states, have demanded an increased focus on ASDs in teacher preparation programs in response to the surge in the identification of new cases. Teachers must now be familiar with the diagnostic features of ASD and its various iterations, including *autistic disorder* (AD) and *Asperger syndrome* (AS), as well as with recommended interventions.

Chapter 10 explores four major types of risk for students possessing emotional and behavioral disorders: *substance abuse, at-risk sexual behavior, school violence and bullying,* and *gang membership and related activities.* Again, chapter features include authentic case examples and anecdotes, as well as effective school-based interventions. As a special education teacher and a child psychologist, respectively, both authors are acutely aware of the critical importance of the areas of risk identified in this chapter and their implications for youth possessing emotional and behavioral disorders. Thus, we have provided coverage significantly more extensive than comparable textbooks in the field. We believe that our readers need and will appreciate such thorough coverage of these serious risk factors.

Finally, Chapter 11 provides a conclusion and overall summary. We discuss current issues that affect our work with students who have EBD. Some of the chapter features include the implications of the new *IDEA* guidelines for students who have EBD, the benefit of technology and meaningful instruction in helping these students learn, the importance of celebrating diversity and its relevance to instruction and intervention, and the importance of professional and family collaboration. This last feature acknowledges the need for parents and legal guardians to be included and empowered as allies in the successful treatment of their children.

We would like to acknowledge the invaluable assistance and insightful suggestions provided by our developmental editor at Pearson, Christien Shangraw. Likewise, we offer special thanks to our editor, Virginia Lanigan, who was able to share our vision and commitment to this project, and was able to see beyond its developmental imperfections and grasp its worth. Similarly, we wish to thank our editorial assistant Penny Burleson, whose patience, focus, and attention to detail helped us move efficiently to production; and Ann Davis, our new editor, who provided generous support, especially with the esthetics of the textbook, and who was instrumental in helping us reach the "finish line." Also, we would like to acknowledge the exceptional work of our copy editor, Lynne Lackenbach, whose meticulous editing contributed significantly to the coherence and readability of our manuscript. A word of thanks also to our production coordinator at Aptara, Ravi Bhatt, who energetically kept us on schedule.

We also would like to thank those esteemed colleagues who committed their time, energy, and expertise to reviewing our manuscript and whose insightful suggestions helped make this a better textbook: Andrea Allen, *Barry University*; Ellyn Arwood, *University of Portland*; Joe Blackbourn, *University of Mississippi*; Luis Conde, *Barry University*; Corine Frankland, *Western New Mexico University*; David Gordon, *University of Wisconsin—Whitewater*; Beverley Johns, *MacMurray College*; Gwendolyn Jones, *Fairmont State University*; Kim Killu, *University of Michigan—Dearborn*; Louis Lanunziata, *University of North Carolina—Wilmington*; Festus Obiakor, *University of Wisconsin—Milwaukee*; Conn Thomas, *West Texas A & M University*; Johnna Westby, *Minot State University*; and Richard Williams, *Northwestern State University.*

Finally, we would like to thank our family members, Brenda, Theresa, Jimmy, and Lois, whose unconditional love, forbearance, and encouragement made all this possible and worthwhile.

Vance L. Austin
Daniel T. Sciarra

CONTENTS

Presentation on 11/1

Chapter 1

Introduction

Peggy Gans

FOCUS QUESTIONS

1. Why is it so difficult to provide a comprehensive definition for "emotional disturbance," and what are some of the contributing factors?

2. Is there a behavioral profile of a child that warrants the classification "emotionally disturbed"? If so, what are the characteristic traits?

3. What is a functional behavior assessment, and how is it applied to classroom intervention?

4. What are some typical nontherapeutic teacher responses to misbehavior in the classroom, and how can these be positively transformed?

5. How can teachers avoid conflict and help build a sense of community or shared responsibility in the classroom?

DEFINING EMOTIONAL AND BEHAVIORAL DISORDERS

Providing a comprehensive definition for emotional and behavioral disorders (EBD) is very difficult, primarily because of the following factors:

1. Subjectivity in determining abnormal behavior, that is, what constitutes an atypical level of severity (intensity), duration, and frequency, and how we differentiate between abnormal behavior caused by abnormal or mitigating circumstances and abnormal behavior exhibited under normal or near-normal circumstances

2. Effects of developmental change on the behavioral and emotional stability of an individual

3. The tendency of federal and state education agencies to exclude children and youth who are considered "socially maladjusted" or who are "court adjudicated"

4. The controversy surrounding certain diagnoses whose presenting characteristics are not deemed to be primarily emotional or behavioral (e.g., ADHD, autism spectrum disorder)

5. The amorphous nature of the field and special education, in general

6. The inclusion or exclusion of schizophrenia and other psychiatric diagnoses, depending on the predisposition of a particular state.

Subjectivity in Determining Abnormal Behavior

The recommendation of experts in the field of EBD is to develop a profile of what normal behavior is under a certain set of circumstances and then to compare it to the behavior of a child in question. If there is a significant disparity, then we are can justifiably conclude that the child's behavior is abnormal and in need of remediation. Similarly, some researchers (e.g., Kauffman, 2005) have recommended analyzing the child's behavior according to three evaluative criteria: (1) duration, (2) intensity, and (3) frequency. However, problems exist in the interpretation of what constitutes an excess in these three areas of analysis. In other words, "how long is too long?" in the case of a child who is depressed, for example, or what level of a behavior is "too" intense and indicates abnormality. Finally, how many times must a behavior be evident over a period of time to be considered "too" frequent? What are the lines or levels that demarcate unacceptable from acceptable behaviors, and can or should there be constant measurements for all behaviors and emotions or must they be adjusted according to the different types of emotions and behaviors?

The Effects of Developmental Change on the Behavioral and Emotional Stability of an Individual

Equally confounding to the identification of EBD are the effects of physiological development that are particularly evident in preadolescence and adolescence. In fact, most children experience significant emotional and behavioral instability during this developmental metamorphosis. Kauffman (2005) pointed out that most adolescents engage in some form of delinquent behavior and commit what might be referred to as "status" offenses. This mercurial state associated with adolescent development further complicates and obscures the notion of what constitutes "normal" behavior at this stage. For example, most adolescents engage in some form of risk-taking behavior that may include smoking cigarettes, underage drinking, early sexual activity, truancy, driving a car without a license or outside the restrictions imposed by the license, and the recreational use of controlled substances, to name but a few. Because a majority of youth participate in one or more of these "delinquent" behaviors, they compose the profile of normal behavior for adolescents. Thus, a young person who engages in or exhibits these behaviors should *not* be considered aberrant or "emotionally disturbed."

The Tendency of Federal and State Education Agencies to Exclude Children and Youth Who Are Considered "Socially Maladjusted" or Who Are "Court Adjudicated"

Youth who are considered to be **socially maladjusted** characteristically evidence behavior that conforms with conduct disorder. Many experts in the field have argued that if children and youth commit chronic acts of vandalism, property destruction, and violence in the community and display no concern for laws or the rights of others, such behavior is pathological and therefore evidence of an emotional disturbance. Indeed, it seems rather paradoxical to imagine that such egregious behavior could be confined to expression in only one setting or social context.

The Controversy Surrounding Certain Diagnoses Whose Presenting Characteristics Are Not Deemed to Be Primarily Emotional or Behavioral (e.g., ADHD, Autism Spectrum Disorder)

When experts in the field of special education consider appropriate classification, they usually evaluate the pathological characteristic that profoundly affects learning. Accordingly, some have argued for the inclusion of students who have attention-deficit hyperactivity disorder (ADHD), predominantly hyperactive-impulsive type, as well as more severe levels of autism spectrum disorder, because

SOCIALLY MALADJUSTED

An ambiguous term used frequently to describe children or youth who engage in delinquent acts in the school or community. Occasionally, the term is used interchangeably with the term *emotionally disturbed,* which is problematic because some states exclude students adjudged "socially maladjusted" from eligibility to receive special education services.

the behavior of children with these disorders tends to impede learning as well as socialization.

The Amorphous Nature of the Field and Special Education, in General

The field of EBD continues to be anomalous because of the varied and often discrepant views of its researchers and expert stakeholders regarding the requisite characteristics of its constituents. This lack of unanimity is evident when one reviews the major textbooks available on the subject. There appears to be significant variation in what types of disorders are included or excluded. Perhaps what is needed is a more concise universal federal definition of what are the essential criteria of an EBD. The absence of such a definition has resulted in confusion in diagnosis and treatment, as well as in the determination of incidence and prevalence rates.

The Inclusion or Exclusion of Schizophrenia and Other Psychiatric Diagnoses, Depending on the Predisposition of a Particular State

SCHIZOPHRENIA

Psychotic disorder characterized by distorted thinking, abnormal perception, and bizarre behavior and emotions observed for at least six months.

LABILITY

Unstable, mercurial, or volatile emotional state.

Several states do not recognize psychiatric disorders, such as childhood-onset **schizophrenia**, as appropriate for inclusion in the category of "emotionally disturbed." Those states that do so hold that, in particular, because of its emotional **lability** and behavioral volatility, schizophrenia is appropriately included in this category.

THE IMPLICATION OF INCLUDING SOCIALLY MALADAPTIVE STUDENTS

JUVENILE DELINQUENTS

Minors who engage in antisocial or illegal behavior or who commit crimes and misdemeanors.

As mentioned earlier, many experts (e.g., Cullinan, 2002; Jensen, 2005; Jones, Dohrn, & Dunn, 2004; Kauffman, 2005) have regarded the exclusion of socially maladaptive students from the category of "emotionally disturbed" as counterintuitive because these students display pathological behavior in the community and are often referred to as "**juvenile delinquents**." The fact that these students, either through truancy or expulsion, are not well represented in schools does not obviate the fact that they are "emotionally disturbed." In fact, the antisocial and maladaptive behaviors they display in the community are the same as those that characterize oppositional defiant disorder and conduct disorder, two subtypes of EBD that are found in students receiving special education services in the school.

Some advocates and educators contend that one reason for the exclusion of students deemed "socially maladjusted" may be a response to rising school budgets and the need for greater fiscal restraint fueled by sharp constituent criticism. Investigators have suggested that including students who are currently considered "socially maladjusted" would increase the number of students receiving special education services significantly, resulting in a substantial increase in school budgets. However, others have noted that simply not acknowledging the real social problem these delinquent youth represent is to deny the reality of our present situation, tantamount to "hiding one's head in the sand."

The fact remains that, in states where children and youth deemed "socially maladjusted" are currently excluded from classification as "emotionally disturbed," they become constituents of another and far more costly system—the penal and corrections complex. A comparison of the two systems reveals that the educational one has a far better rehabilitation rate than the juvenile justice system (U.S. Department of Justice, Bureau of Justice Statistics, 2004). In addition, the estimated per-student cost of educating a child with special education services ranges between $6,000 and $10,000 per year, depending on the school district. The estimated cost to incarcerate an individual in a state correctional facility or juvenile detention center is $25,000 per year, and the recidivism rate is roughly 62 to 75 percent. This high rate of return to custody is due, in part, to the poor job of rehabilitation done by these correctional facilities. In fact, experts suggest that incarcerating a youth in one of these facilities for a minor offense accomplishes one thing with certainty: The individual will learn "criminal" behaviors and emerge more likely to offend again (Correctional Association of New York, 2002; Frederick, 1999).

In contrast, there is evidence that, if effective school-based and family-based interventions are applied early for children and youth deemed "socially maladjusted" or "delinquent," these individuals gain the academic and social skills necessary to avoid engaging in criminal behavior and can lead socially productive lives (New York State Division of Criminal Justice Services, 2003). Therefore, if we include "socially maladjusted" youth in the category of emotional disturbance, we increase the probability that these individuals will be contributors to society rather than wards of it. In the long run, this proposition will almost certainly prove more cost-effective as well; we don't want to be guilty of being short-sighted or "penny wise and pound foolish" when it comes to the lives of children and youth and the betterment of society as a whole.

A GROWING FIELD

Even with the exclusion of socially maladjusted children and youth from the category, the number of students classified as "emotionally disturbed" is increasing significantly (Office of Special Education Programs, 2006). Part of this remarkable growth is a result of the increase in the identifications of children and youth with anxiety disorder; specifically, eating disorders, obsessive compulsive disorder, and posttraumatic stress disorder (Office of Special Education Programs, 2006). The rise in the number of students affected by these disorders is a result, in part, of the increase in environmental stressors, such as the perceived proliferation of terrorism, the elevated toxicity levels in air, water, and foods, and the increase in society's use of food as a means of control, escape, a measure of self-esteem, and as a reinforcement.

Likewise, the number of students diagnosed with various types of pervasive developmental disorder, especially autism spectrum disorder, has risen sharply in the last decade (CureAutismNow.org, 2008). Though part of this is explained by more precise diagnostic identification criteria, some researchers have pointed to rising levels of environmental toxins and related genetic factors (Rimland, 1998).

Furthermore, the increase in the number of students who have attention-deficit hyperactivity disorder has arguably contributed to the increase as well, particularly the "combined type" and "hyperactive-impulsive type" subcategories. The reasons attributed to the increase in the number of children and youth diagnosed with ADHD are controversial; however, most experts agree that there are many more bona-fide cases of the disorder identified per capita today than there were 10 years ago (CHADD.org, 2008).

Finally, perhaps the fastest-growing contributors to the growing incidence of EBD are those described as "defiance disorders" or "antisocial" behaviors. Principal among these is "conduct disorder" and its precursor, "oppositional defiant disorder." Most clinicians and experts agree that these disorders are closely correlated with ineffective parenting behaviors and family factors, such as abuse and neglect on the part of parents or guardians. Some research findings have pointed to the increase in single-parent households, which often imply diminished supervision, loss of same-sex role models, and decreased income and financial resources, as a principal contributor to the rise in conduct disorder among children and youth (Coleman & Webber, 2002; Walker, Ramsey, & Gresham, 2004). In addition, investigators have noted that the higher cost of living experienced nationwide, necessitating dual incomes and reduced child supervision, may also factor into the increase in the incidence of antisocial behaviors in children and youth in the United States.

PROFILE OF A CHILD WITH AN EMOTIONAL OR BEHAVIORAL DISORDER

EXTERNALIZED BEHAVIORS

Acting-out behavior, such as fighting, typical of students diagnosed with conduct disorder or another "disruptive disorder."

INTERNALIZED BEHAVIORS

Behavior typically associated with social reticence, as in the case of a child identified with an anxiety or mood disorder.

Most of the disorders associated with the category of emotional/behavioral disorder can be organized into two types: **externalized behaviors**, which describes those that are overtly displayed, and **internalized behaviors**, defining behaviors that are more difficult to observe. Subtypes of EBD that are predominantly externalized are those whose characteristics involve observable actions or behaviors that are antisocial, that is, impulsive, aggressive, disruptive, destructive, and in violation of the laws and rules or norms of society. Subtypes of EBD in which behaviors are primarily internalized and thus not as readily apparent include mood disorders such as depression, anxiety disorders such as posttraumatic stress disorder, and thought disorders/psychiatric diagnoses such as schizophrenia.

A typical profile of an individual with an "externalized" EBD is "Jack," an adolescent with a conduct disorder. Jack, a tenth-grader at a local high school, comes from a very abusive household. His father is currently serving time in a state correctional facility for assault with a deadly weapon. He has a history of abuse towards Jack's mother, and there is some suspicion that he has physically abused Jack as well. Since his father's incarceration, Jack's mother has had to work two jobs to make ends meet, leaving Jack to fend for himself.

At school, Jack is the classic "bully," threatening and intimidating other students and staff with his size and propensity for violence. He has been suspended twice so far this year, both times for fighting with other students on school grounds. His behavior in the community has been equally violent. In one instance, Jack fought with an older man who claimed Jack had intentionally damaged his car. Jack did not deny the charge, but he severely "beat up" his accuser in retaliation for the man's "bad attitude." The assault-and-battery case is awaiting trial, and if he is found guilty, Jack may do "hard time" in an adult prison.

Jack's behavioral profile fits that of an individual with conduct disorder, an "externalized" type of emotional/behavioral disorder. He represents a real challenge for his teacher and administrators, some of whom would like to see him "locked up."

THE FUNCTIONAL BEHAVIORAL ASSESSMENT AND ITS APPLICATIONS

The term **functional behavioral assessment (FBA)** refers to a systematic process used in identifying the "function" or purpose of a specific misbehavior or inappropriate action. According to Skinner (1969) and other behaviorists, all behaviors serve a purpose for the "actor." Therefore, if practitioners and caregivers can successfully identify that purpose, a relevant and effective intervention can be developed. The danger in not understanding the purpose or root cause of an undesirable behavior is to inadvertently compound the problem by either reinforcing the pathological behavior or wasting time and resources treating a misidentified one.

Throughout the chapters in this book, the authors provide a model of how a FBA is conducted relative to a representative case example. In each case, the FBA exemplar is used to develop an effective **behavioral intervention plan (BIP)**. Because identification of the root cause of a misbehavior or, more accurately, the function that a misbehavior serves for an individual is critical to the development of an effective behavioral intervention, it is important to establish a valid and reliable process for conducting a FBA (Gresham, Watson, & Skinner, 2001).

Several studies have demonstrated the efficacy of a well-executed FBA in the development of effective behavioral interventions (Hoff, Ervin, & Friman, 2005; Ingram, Lewis-Palmer, & Sugai, 2005). The need for a research-based behavioral assessment process that can be effectively employed by the classroom teacher has prompted the authors to employ a model that conforms to the recommendations of this research and includes critical elements identified in these studies. Our model is derived from the recommendations proffered by Barnhill (2005) as well as Sugai, Lewis-Palmer, and Hagan-Burke (2000) and includes the following important steps: (1) identify and describe the problem behavior, (2) collect baseline data and academic performance information, (3) describe the environmental and setting demands, (4) complete a direct observation, (5) develop a hypothesis, and (6) test the hypothesis by assessing the effectiveness of the behavior intervention plan in reducing the undesirable behavior and increasing the more appropriate behavioral response (see Figures 1.1 and 1.2).

FUNCTIONAL BEHAVIORAL ASSESSMENT (FBA)

Refers to a systematic process used in identifying the "function" or purpose of a specific misbehavior or inappropriate action.

BEHAVIORAL INTERVENTION PLAN (BIP)

Refers to a relevant, individualized treatment or approach designed to address and mitigate the adverse effects of a specific maladaptive behavior or series of related behaviors, based on the determination of the functional behavioral assessment.

FIGURE 1.1 Functional
Behavioral Assessment
Worksheet

Student Name: _____

Date: _____

Target Behavior: Operationally define the behavior that most interferes with the student's
functioning in the classroom. Include intensity (high, medium, or low), frequency, and
duration.

_____

_____

_____

_____

When, where, with whom, and in what condition is the target behavior *least* likely to occur?

_____

_____

Setting Events or Context Variables (i.e., hunger, lack of sleep, medications, problems on bus):

_____

_____

Immediate Antecedents and Consequences

Antecedents	*Problematic Settings*	*Consequences*
__ Demand/request	__ Unstructured setting	__ Behavior ignored
__ Difficult task	__ Unstructured activity	__ Reprimanded
__ Time of day	__ Individual seat work	__ Verbal redirection
__ Interruption in routine	__ Group work	__ Time-out (duration: _____)
__ Peer teased/provoked	__ Specials	__ Loss of incentives
__ No materials/activities	__ Specific subject/task	__ Physical redirection
__ Could not get desired item	__ Crowded setting	__ Physical restraint
__ People _____	__ Noisy setting	__ Sent to office
__ Alone	__ Other _____	__ Suspension
__ Other _____	__ Other _____	__ Other _____

What function(s) does the target behavior seem to serve for the student?

____ Escape from: __ demand/request __ person __ activity/task __ school __ other

_____

____ Attention from: __ adult __ peer __ other _____

____ Gain desired: __ item __ activity __ area __ other _____

____ Automatic sensory stimulation: _____

Hypothesis:

When _____ occurs in the context of

_____ (antecedent) (problematic setting)

the students exhibits _____ in order to

_____.

(target behavior) (perceived function)

This behavior is more likely to occur when

_____

_____.

(setting event/context variables)

Replacement or competing behavior that could still serve the same function for the student:

_____

_____

Is the replacement behavior in the student's repertoire, or will it need to be taught directly?

_____

If so, how will it be taught?

_____

List some potential motivators for student:

_____

_____

Source: Barnhill, G. P. (2005). Functional behavioral assessment in schools. _Intervention in School and Clinic, 40_(3), 131–143.

FIGURE 1.1   (continued)

A successful behavioral assessment depends on collaboration among the student's teachers, parents, and related service providers, and their willingness to collect accurate baseline data. In addition, the multidisciplinary team (or Individualized Education Plan [IEP] team) must prioritize problem behaviors and target the most serious for change. Furthermore, the student, when appropriate, should be an active participant, both in the FBA process, as well as the development of a viable BIP. Finally, the target behaviors identified by the FBA must be ones that can be readily addressed by a BIP in both the school and home environments; they must be measurable and regarded as "high priority." In short, the more painstakingly and thoroughly the FBA is conducted by teachers or caregivers, the more effective the BIP will be, because the most debilitating behavioral obstacle will have been identified and targeted (Shippen, Simpson, & Crites, 2003).

FIGURE 1.2   Functional Assessment Steps

1. Identify the problem behavior.
2. Describe the problem behavior.
3. Collect baseline data and academic information.
4. Describe the environment and setting demands.
5. Complete a functional assessment form and/or behavior rating scales.
6. Conduct a direct observation.
7. Develop a hypothesis.
8. Hypothesis testing (experimental manipulation).
9. Write a behavioral intervention plan (BIP).
10. Implement the BIP.
11. Collect intervention behavioral data.
12. Conduct a follow-up meeting and revise plan as needed.

Source: Barnhill, G. P. (2005). Functional behavioral assessment in schools. _Intervention in School and Clinic, 40_(3), 131–143.

DEVELOPING AN EFFECTIVE BEHAVIORAL INTERVENTION PLAN

According to Gresham (2004), most school-based behavioral interventions can be conceptualized using four broad theoretical categories: (1) applied behavioral analysis, (2) social learning theory, (3) cognitive behavior therapy, and (4) neobehavioristic stimulus–response (S-R) theory. A brief discussion of each approach follows.

replace behaviors.

1. ***Applied Behavioral Analysis.*** The applied behavioral analysis (ABA) approach fits quite nicely within the framework of a functional behavioral assessment. The goal of ABA is to determine the function that a problem behavior serves for an individual and then to replace that dysfunctional behavior with a more socially appropriate one.

2. ***Social Learning Theory.*** Social learning theory is based on the notion of reciprocity between the behavior of an individual and the environment (Bandura, 1986). The concept of "modeling" really emanates from this approach, and modeling is effective in teaching/generalizing desired behaviors to students who have not learned appropriate responses to ambiguous situations.

3. ***Cognitive Behavior Therapy.*** The essence of the cognitive behavior therapy (CBT) approach is the assumption that behavioral responses to the environment are mediated by the thoughts or thinking of an individual. Thus, teaching more effective or self-affirming ways of thinking about one's environment can positively affect the way an individual behaves within/toward it. Techniques such as self-talk, self-evaluation, problem solving, and self-instruction all emanate from this approach and are used primarily as therapeutic interventions with students who experience anxiety and mood disorders.

4. ***Neobehavioristic Stimulus–Response Theory.*** Neobehavioristic S-R theory is based on classical conditioning as presented by Skinner (Powers & Franks, 1988). In essence, the individual, through behavioral conditioning based on an environmental stimulus, learns a new and more appropriate behavioral response that will continue indefinitely in the presence of the stimulus. Systematic desensitization and exposure-based treatments are derived from this learning model.

MALADAPTIVE BEHAVIORS

Behavior that represents a pathological or antisocial set of actions designed to achieve a desired goal. Such behaviors are often habituated and learned from a high-stakes peer or role model who engages in them.

Some of the **maladaptive behaviors** displayed by students who have EBD might be more effectively addressed by one of the aforementioned models, whereas others might be better served by a multisystem approach. For teachers and school personnel, the important consideration is ease of application, or practicality, and the effectiveness of a particular intervention in the classroom setting. The potential for misuse of interventions by teachers is high, because research has suggested that, frequently, teachers continue to use techniques that are easy to employ but may not be effective (Walker et al., 2004).

Gresham (2005) examined the efficacy of matching the intensity of the intervention to the severity of the problem, which involves organizing the intervention into three levels: primary, secondary, and tertiary. The purpose of

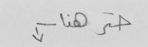

intervention at the primary level is preemptive; at the secondary level it is to reverse the deleterious affects of maladaptive behavior; and finally, at the tertiary level, intervention serves to contain the damage inflicted by the misbehavior and reduce harm.

Furthermore, Gresham (2004) identified three levels of "intervention intensity:" (1) universal intervention, (2) selected intervention, and (3) targeted/intensive intervention. Universal interventions are described as being directed toward all students in the same manner and under similar conditions. Examples of such plans include school-wide discipline plans, district-wide zero-tolerance plans, and social skills training provided consistently within a school system. Selected interventions are those that apply to noncompliant students, at-risk individuals, and, generally, those for whom the universal interventions were ineffective. Finally, targeted or intensive interventions refer to those extraordinary measures that target a very small percentage of students who cause the majority of behavioral disruptions and that require intensive treatments.

The goal of universal intervention is to facilitate the student's academic and social development. Selected interventions are intended to significantly change ineffective or undesirable behaviors or behavioral responses through reinforcement, that is, behavior modification. Similarly, the purpose of targeted interventions is to decrease the frequency and intensity of very serious behaviors and, hopefully, teach the individual more appropriate alternative ones.

According to Gresham (2004), an effective way to determine which of the three intervention levels is most appropriate for a student is through a decision-making model referred to as **response to intervention (RTI)**. In essence, the RTI model uses a student's lack of response to a seemingly appropriate research-based intervention as the starting point for revising or modifying it. If an initial behavioral intervention does not produce a measurable improvement in a student's behavior within a reasonable time period, it should be carefully reviewed using a functional assessment model, such as applied behavioral analysis (ABA), appropriately revised, and then reassessed to determine its overall effectiveness.

Buck, Polloway, Kirkpatrick, Patton, and McConnell Fad (2000) noted that the systematic response to behavioral problems as described in the federal Individuals with Disabilities Education Act (IDEA, U.S. Department of Education, 1997) is predicated on two key assumptions:

1. Behavior problems are best addressed when their cause is known, and that cause is most effectively determined/identified through a functional behavioral assessment.
2. Behavior interventions that involve positive reinforcements are more effective than punitive ones, and those behavior interventions, to be effective, need to be thoughtfully designed, systematically implemented, and periodically evaluated to ensure that they are successful.

Once the FBA has been completed, the resulting deductions inform the design of an effective behavioral intervention plan . Fad, Patton, and Polloway (1998) recommended five procedures in the development of a viable BIP. These procedures include: (1) review of the behavior targeted in the FBA; (2) identification of

RESPONSE TO INTERVENTION (RTI)

Refers to a process that emphasizes how well students respond to changes in instruction. The essential elements of an RTI approach are the provision of scientific, research-based instruction and interventions in general education; monitoring and measurement of student progress in response to the instruction and interventions; and use of these measures of student progress to shape instruction and make educational decisions.

the behavioral goal that will cause an increase or decrease in the frequency of a targeted behavior; (3) determination of individualized and appropriate intervention strategies, and the designation of the individual or individuals responsible for their implementation; (4) determination of the dates for its review and evaluation; and (e) selection of appropriate evaluation methods and criteria.

The rubric in Figure 1.3 provides an example of a behavioral intervention plan template that can be easily used by the classroom teacher to record and evaluate behavioral data relative to a target behavior and its executor.

FIGURE 1.3   A Behavioral Intervention Plan Template

Behavioral Intervention Plan

Name of Student _____   Start Date _____

Age____

Grade ___

Homeroom Mr./Ms._____

Specific Behavioral Goals:

1.

Oversight _____

2.

Oversight _____

3.

Oversight _____

For each goal above:

1. What antecedents, events, and consequences can I change to increase/decrease the behavior?

2. What strategies, curricular adaptations, and physical design modifications can I use to increase/decrease the behavior?

3. Which of these changes are most likely to be effective?

Evaluate the Plan:

How is it working? If it is not working, what changes or modifications are needed to make it work?

_____

ELEMENTS OF BEHAVIOR SUPPORT PLANS

Horner, Sugai, Todd, and Lewis-Palmer (1999–2000) have identified six key elements that are integral to an effective BIP: (1) learn how the student perceives
or experiences events in his or her environment; (2) invest in preventing occur-
rences of problem behavior; (3) teaching is the most powerful behavior support
strategy available in schools; (4) avoid rewarding problem behavior; (5) reward
positive behaviors; and (6) know what to do in the most difficult situations (see
Table 1.1).

*six
elements
of
behavior
support
plans.*

TABLE 1.1   Behavior Support Plan Checklist

Student: _____

When developing and implementing behavior support plans, judge the
degree to which each of the following has been considered:
G = Good, O = Okay, P = poor, N = not applicable

Date: _____

Functional assessment:
Develop understanding of problem behavior.
1. Describe problem behavior in operational terms.
2. Identify problem routines.
3. State complete functional assessment hypothesis.
4. Collect data to confirm hypothesis statement.

Foundations:
Consider factors that go across routines.
1. Health and physiology.
2. Communication.
3. Mobility.
4. Predictability.
5. Choice.
6. Social relationships.
7. Activity patterns.

Prevention:
Make problem behavior irrelevant.
1. Modify activity schedule.
2. Adapt curriculum.
3. Modify design of instruction.
4. Adapt instructional procedures.
5. Add prompts for appropriate behavior.
6. Precorrect for typical problem.

(continued)

TABLE 1.1   Behavior Support Plan Checklist (continued)

Teaching:
Make problem behavior less efficient.
1. Teach specific replacement skills.
2. Teach adaptive social skills.

Extinction:
Make problem behavior less effective.
1. Minimize positive reinforcement for problem behavior.
2. Minimize negative reinforcement for problem behavior.

Reinforcement:
Make appropriate behavior more effective.
1. Select range of effective positive reinforcers.
2. Maximize schedule of positive reinforcement for appropriate behavior.

Crisis Intervention Plan:
Prevent injury.
1. Arrange environment and practice procedures to prevent crisis and emergency situations.
2. Arrange environment and practice procedures to respond to crisis and emergency situations.

Ensure Contextual Fit:
Match intervention to social and treatment context.
1. Consider values and expectations of adults.
2. Assess skill level and fluency of adults.
3. Determine budget.
4. Assess time requirements.
5. Secure administrative support system.
6. Give priority to best interests of student and family.

Evaluation and Assessment:
Make plan more effective, efficient, and relevant.
1. Specify what questions need to be answered.
2. Specify information to be collected.
3. Develop measurement system.
4. Establish schedule for collecting data.
5. Collect and evaluate data.
6. Use data to improve plan.

Source: Horner, R. H., Sugai, G., Todd, A. W., & Lewis-Palmer, T. (1999–2000). Elements of behavior support plans: A technical brief. *Exceptionality, 8,* 205–215.

Learn How the Student Perceives or Experiences Events in His or Her Environment

Teachers should take the time to ascertain medical, physiological, and social factors that might affect the way in which a student is experiencing the classroom.

Invest in Preventing Occurrences of Problem Behavior

Be aware of antecedents that trigger misbehavior. Some of the more typical of these include: (a) poor or deficient communication skills, (b) mobility challenges and poor ambulation, (c) lack of or familiarity with a clear routine, (d) lack of choice in daily activities, (e) social isolation, (f) access to a limited number of activities, and (g) does not receive positive reinforcement, attention, or acknowledgment. In addition, teachers should be aware of and be willing to alter or remove environmental or aversive events and facilitate the attainment of perceived rewards, as appropriate.

Teaching Is the Most Powerful Behavior Support Strategy Available in Schools

Teaching new, adaptive skills is considered by many to be the single most effective behavioral intervention. Often, students engage in misbehavior simply because they do not know a more appropriate way to achieve their goals. Thus, an integral part of every effective behavior intervention plan should be explicit strategies for teaching pro-social behaviors, such as social skills instruction, with informative corrections, and high-frequency positive reinforcement for displays of desired alternative behavior.

Avoid Rewarding Problem Behavior (Malcontingency)

It is important that teachers clearly understand the process of identifying the problem or target behavior and only reward behaviors that approach the more appropriate replacement behavior. Preferably, teachers should design BIPs that alter the environment so that undesirable behaviors are unattainable.

Reward Positive Behaviors

Skilled and effective teachers need to identify "motivators" or incentives that encourage extra effort on the part of students to try to achieve an academic or behavioral goal. Students should receive positive acknowledgments for engaging in appropriate learning and social skills. However, positive reinforcement and praise to reward student effort needs to be meaningful and therefore should reference a concrete, viable achievement.

Know What to Do in the Most Difficult Situations

A good behavior intervention plan should describe, in detail, the appropriate response by teacher and family members to instances of severe misbehavior or misconduct. In addition, teachers and parents must be prepared for the possible reoccurrence of this behavior, because the most reliable predictor of severe misbehavior in a child is the evidence of such behavior in the past.

MONITORING AND EVALUATION

Teachers and caregivers who design and implement a behavior intervention plan have an obligation to monitor its effectiveness through systematic evaluation. Those with oversight of the BIP should always be observing the plan and the individual for whom the plan was designed, to ensure a good contextual fit among the elements of the plan, the skill level and motivation of the plan implementers, and the quality of environmental support. For a BIP to be implemented effectively, stakeholders must be involved in the development of the BIP, have the skills and knowledge to implement it, have sufficient time and resources to accomplish the plan's objectives, and, most important, believe that the plan can and will be effective.

TYPICAL NONTHERAPEUTIC TEACHER-CAREGIVER RESPONSES

Without proper training and preparation, teachers, parents, and community members will respond inconsistently to inappropriate or maladaptive behaviors of school-age children and youth. How they respond will depend on several personalogical factors, such as (1) perceived competence in behavior management, (2) tolerance of or predisposition/sensitivity to the offending behavior, (3) personal and professional management of stress, (4) perceived "goodness of fit" between the student of concern and the classroom or school culture, (5) the caregiver's affinity for or intuitive "connection" with the child, (6) school, community, or family policy regarding the type and severity of the misbehavior, and (7) the notion that behavior management is *not* the purview of teachers (Coleman & Weber, 2002; Cullinan, 2002; Jensen,2005; Kohn, 1996; Lane, Gresham, & O'Shaughnessy, 2002; Mendler, 1992; Rosenberg, Wilson, Maheady, & Sindelar, 2004; Wicks-Nelson & Israel, 1997). Each of these factors will be discussed, in brief, in the following.

Perceived Competence in Behavior Management

Many teachers and parents complain that they feel unprepared to deal effectively with problem behaviors and therefore abdicate responsibility for dealing with them or direct the student to someone they perceive to be better trained or more capable, such as a special educator, building administrator, or school counselor (Baker, 2005; Lane et al., 2002).

Tolerance of Predisposition/Sensitivity to the Offending Behavior

Despite efforts to the contrary, teachers and parents are often subjective in their consideration of misbehavior, as well as in their tolerance of certain personality types in children. For each of us, there is that one child who seems to be proficient at "getting under our skin." Even with the objectivity that should be provided by a systematic screening process, teachers and parents who respond subjectively or reactively often exacerbate the misbehavior by inadvertently reinforcing it. Occasionally, teachers and parents allow themselves to be drawn into a game of escalating threats and counter-threats, which can negatively affect their authority and influence (Coleman & Webber, 2002; Cullinan, 2002; Jensen, 2005; Wicks-Nelson & Israel, 1997).

Personal and Professional Management of Stress

The effects of personal and/or job-related stress on a teacher's or parent's tolerance level is often overlooked. Today's teachers and parents are under a significant amount of stress caused, in part, by high expectations imposed by each of these roles. For example, teachers are typically involved with more than academic instruction; they are frequently role models, unofficial social workers, and occasionally surrogate parents for their students. These additional unofficial responsibilities, combined with the pressures imposed by standardized tests and increased state and local certification requirements, place a daunting burden on the classroom teacher. Likewise, parents are often struggling with the increased demands of work, the high cost of living, and the pressures imposed by their sense of guilt at not spending enough "quality time" with their children. All of these personal and professional pressures, as well as many others, combine to create a potentially volatile psycho-emotional state for teachers and parents, one that provides little room for patience and tolerance toward misbehaving students (Cavin, 1998; Rosenberg, Wilson, Maheady, & Sindelar, 2004).

Perceived "Goodness of Fit" Between the Student of Concern and the Classroom or School Culture

Some studies have demonstrated the importance of "goodness of fit" in relation to the successful inclusion of a student into a preexisting classroom or school culture. Typically, students who exhibit atypical behaviors, such as those observed in students who have emotional or behavioral disorders, are ostracized by both their classmates and their teacher (Jones et al., 2004). In fact, one study indicated a tendency of students to eschew classmates who were disliked by their teacher (Sachs, 1999). Many students who have behavioral disorders exhibit oppositional and sometimes defiant behaviors, and it is very difficult for parents and teachers to treat them with equanimity; nevertheless, teachers who exhibit consistent intolerance and negativity toward these students invariably escalate the problem (Wicks-Nelson & Israel, 1997).

The Caregiver's Affinity for or Intuitive "Connection" with the Child

Occasionally, some teachers and parents display preferential treatment toward particular students, even ones who present behavioral challenges. The reason they sometimes give for this exclusive treatment is an "intuitive" connection or empathy for a particular child. This discriminatory treatment is inconsistent with professionally sound, research-based practice and can result in inconsistent treatment of misbehavior, depending on the teacher's or parent's predisposition toward a particular student. Best practice, of course, requires the teacher to conduct a functional assessment and then to develop an appropriate intervention based on the findings of that **nondiscriminatory assessment** (Barnhill, 2005).

NONDISCRIMINATORY ASSESSMENT

Refers, simply, to a comprehensive individual assessment that is free from bias and is used to determine eligibility for special education services.

ZERO TOLERANCE

Refers to the policy of schools, developed during the last decade in response to a series of violent acts on school grounds, to impose mandatory and, in some cases, severe punishments for infractions of school regulations relative to the health and safety of students and school personnel.

School, Community, or Family Policy Regarding the Type and Severity of the Misbehavior

Many schools and school districts have adopted "**zero tolerance**" policies in the aftermath of the Columbine tragedy (Austin, 2003b). In addition, some community and family cultures are less tolerant of students who display emotional or behavioral disorders. This low tolerance often results in indiscriminant rejection, alienation, or prescriptive punishment of individuals who engage in aberrant or antisocial behavior. Schools, communities, and families that hold conservative views regarding rule-breaking behavior, and that support the punishment of misbehavior as an effective deterrent, typically have a low tolerance for children and youth who engage in such behavior. Teachers and other caregivers within these social organizations tend to recommend punishments that are swift and severe, albeit usually ineffective.

The Notion That Behavior Management Is *Not* the Purview of Teachers

There is a pervasive notion among some teachers that behavior management is somehow outside their job description. In other words, these individuals insist that their mandated responsibilities begin and end with teaching and that behavior management is the responsibility of parents, administrators, school counselors, and sometimes the special educator. This flawed perception has led some to abdicate responsibility for managing misbehavior, like the ostrich burying its head in the sand, through planned ignoring. Unfortunately, this attitude sends the wrong message to children and youth with emotional or behavioral disorders. The message it conveys is, essentially, "I don't care about you enough to challenge you to correct your misbehavior." In addition, it allows students to escape the consequences of misbehavior and, in so doing, inadvertently reinforces it (Baker, 2005).

DEVELOPING THE RIGHT APPROACH: SOME TIPS FOR REDUCING MISBEHAVIOR AND BUILDING COMMUNITY IN THE CLASSROOM

This book is not intended to be a "how to" panacea that provides prescriptive responses to specific behavioral problems. On the contrary, we present research-based practices and interventions that provide teachers with valuable tools and approaches to help students with EBD be more successful in the classroom and, consequently, in life. To a degree, however, the book has been written from a constructivist perspective in that the authors firmly believe that all students, including those with EBD, affect and are affected by their social milieu. It is critical to our philosophy of behavioral intervention that, to the greatest extent possible, any intervention developed enhance the individual's ability to be a viable member of his or her community, whether that community be a classroom or society at large.

Furthermore, it is our contention that if behavioral interventions ostracize or alienate a student from his or her teachers or classmates, they will prove ultimately ineffective. Behavioral interventions must therefore be carefully developed to preserve the student's sense of "belongingness" to the **community in the classroom**. Such membership is critical in the development of a sense of shared ownership in the classroom and the social responsibility that is created. Likewise, ownership and responsibility within the classroom community fosters a sense of self-empowerment, which obviates the "learned helplessness" that springs from the external locus of control that is characteristic of most students who have EBD.

It can be argued that many students who engage in antisocial behavior do so because they feel alienated from society. They are often expressing anger, internally or externally, at being excluded, just as many adults express anger toward the government when they feel ignored. Although including these students as viable members of the classroom community will not act as a panacea for their deep-seeded emotional or behavioral problems, it will go a long way toward building trust and relationship, both of which are fundamental criteria for meaningful behavior change. Like the old joke that asks, "How many psychiatrists does it take to change a light bulb?" and replies with the punch line, "Only *one,* but the light bulb has to *want* to change," the student who has EBD must acknowledge the detrimental effects of his or her ineffective behavior and *want* to change it. Such an epiphany and resulting transformation can be best achieved in the presence of two antecedents: (1) a community that welcomes the student and whose memberships he or she values and (2) the use of a behavioral intervention that is research-based, relevant, and effective.

The latter of these predispositions will be carefully explored in the subsequent chapters in relation to specific emotional or behavioral disorders; the former was nicely encapsulated in the work of Kohn (1996), and some of its key elements are described next.

In his book, *Beyond Discipline: From Compliance to Community,* Kohn (1996) identified five criteria that are crucial to building community among students and teachers in the classroom. The first of these is a relationship with the adults. Kohn (1996) suggested that, far too often, teachers isolate themselves from their students, believing the old teacher adage that "teachers should not smile at their students until winter vacation." Instead, Kohn suggested, teachers should ask students what they think about a topic and then care about the answers the students give. Teachers who form truly caring relationships with students are both helping to meet those students' emotional needs and setting a powerful example. A teacher who listens patiently to student responses or "news," apologizes for a misperception or misinformation, or shows genuine concern for the problems expressed by a stranger is modeling the civil behavior

COMMUNITY IN THE CLASSROOM

A term used by Kohn (1996) to describe a classroom climate that fosters and sustains "belongingness;" one wherein each student, including individuals with emotional and behavioral disorders, is a valued constituent.

that demarcates a caring community. Many children with EBD have no such models and have rarely experienced such civility.

A second criterion suggested by Kohn (1996) relates to building connections between students. Kohn suggested that teachers provide opportunities for students to interact with every other student in the classroom across a variety of experiences and situations. Teachers, Kohn asserted, should provide activities that promote an understanding of another's perspective. Feshbach (1983) suggested that an appreciation for another person's point of view is the foundation of community building.

Third in Kohn's list of criteria was the promotion of class-wide and school-wide activities. He elaborated on this statement by explaining that students in classrooms and schools should be encouraged to meet *en masse* and discuss issues of relevance and importance to them and their well-being.

Kohn's fourth criteria involves the use of community-building activities to facilitate academic instruction. He suggested that skillful teachers can integrate academic lessons with group activities. A prime example of this assertion is the cooperative learning approach, whereby a small group of students (no more than four or five) work together on a project such as a report on the practice of medicine in ancient Egypt. A way to promote an equitable division of labor in these endeavors is to employ Kagan's (1990) "numbered heads together" approach. In this model of cooperative learning, each student in the various small groups is able to choose a specific task that is integral to the cooperative assignment, and that individual must share her results with the group as a whole and, ultimately, participate in a presentation to the entire class. She is supported in this endeavor by the rest of her group and receives the same evaluative score as the other members of the team. This type of activity promotes cooperation and teamwork, both essential elements in community-building.

Finally, Kohn (1996) extolled the value of decision making. He asserted that this aspect promotes autonomy and self-efficacy, both of which are important factors in character development and the promotion of good citizenship. In short, students in the classroom should be given the autonomy to make responsible, informed choices about the design and development of their classroom community. Research has long advocated the importance of choice for students who have EBD, for whom choice is typically not an option (Cullinan, 2002; Jensen, 2005; Kauffman, 2005). The opportunity to participate in the decision-making process is both empowering and community-building because it implies ownership and requires collaboration. In truth, autonomy and community membership are both essential elements of democracy, and the inclusion of students who have EBD in these processes will encourage their responsible participation and positive contribution to society (Kohn, 1996).

In conclusion, although we use the disability model as elaborated in IDEIA (2004) and the American Psychiatric Association's *Diagnostic and Statistical Manual of Mental Disorders, Text Revision* (4th ed.) (DSM-IV-TR, 2000), we use it only as far as it provides us with a way of understanding emotional and behavioral disorders and enables us to help the children affected by them.

We do not view children and youth as "labels" or "broken toys" that need to be fixed, nor do we recommend a "one size fits all" approach to behavioral intervention.

The purpose of this book is simply to help teachers work effectively with students who behave in ways that are detrimental to their learning and general well-being. The strategies described are research-based and have been shown to be effective in the classroom, and they are presented in a way that we think is clear and understandable, with real-world examples that suggest their most effective application. Further, we acknowledge that, although our approaches represent those currently recommended in the literature, it is very likely that they will not be effective every time for every student who has a particular disorder. There are, we recognize, no "magic bullets" in this business. The most powerful and effective intervention protocol is *you*, the teacher, and your thorough *understanding* of each of your students' needs allied with the positive *rapport* you have established with *each* of them.

Fundamental to our approach is our firm belief in the importance of valuing all individuals, appreciating their unique characteristics, and establishing a caring, respectful relationship with them. Furthermore, we recognize the importance of using a systematic and thoroughgoing approach in identifying both the problem behavior and, most important, the function it serves for these individuals. In addition, we strongly advocate the use of research-based interventions that are *appropriate* for an individual, given his or her specific behavioral characteristics and needs, and that these interventions must be periodically reevaluated and, if necessary, modified to ensure their positive effect.

Finally, in concert with the tenets of inclusion, we believe that each of our students is a constituent in our classroom and will benefit from the autonomy derived from choice and the responsibility of "belonging" inherent in that membership. In short, all of our students must be so empowered, and all of our students must feel valued.

The subsequent chapters in this book examine nine categories of EBD. Each begins with a description of a relevant case example and is followed by a discussion of the characteristics, prevalence, etiology, and research-based interventions that are relevant to the disorder. Then, in accordance with IDEIA (2004) and our research-based approach, we use the real-life case study to develop a relevant functional behavioral assessment from which we design an effective behavioral intervention plan. We conclude each chapter with a concise summary, a section called "Tips for Teachers" that offers easy-to-implement practice-based strategies, and study questions with recommended responses.

You will find that this format follows a logical progression and provides a practical application predicated on the real-life case example. It is our hope that this text will help you develop your own individualized behavioral intervention plans that are effective and easily implemented in your classroom. We believe your students will benefit from this research-based, programmatic approach that can and should be tailored to the needs of *your* students.

FROM THE FIELD

George Giuliani, J.D., Psy.D.

George Giuliani is a child psychologist, a legal expert on special education, executive director of the National Association of Special Education Teachers (NASET), and an associate professor and director of the Graduate School Program in Special Education at Hofstra University.

What is the "state-of-the-art" in special education today? Can you tell us about innovations or modifications that, in your opinion, have had the biggest effect on the field?

The state of the art in special education today centers around the concept of inclusion. The focus of our work in the field is primarily about how we can include children with special needs in the general education setting as opposed to segregation. The field is not that old, with the first federal law of P.L. 94-142 only enacted in 1975. But the major principles of this law still stand true. And two, the concept of "zero reject" and "least restrictive environment," has led to the idea that children with disabilities should be educated with their non disabled peers to the maximum extent appropriate. As the field of advances, these concepts become ever more important.

What do you think are the most important things a special education teacher should know about IDEIA (2004) and NCLB (2001, 2006)?

I think the answer lies in the question. So many teachers would be better served if they really understood what both laws represented and what they actually do to protect children with disabilities. Too often, we as professionals forget that almost everything we do in special education is primarily guided by federal law. Teachers need to be aware of what the laws allow for, as well as not. Ultimately, teachers need to understand the general principles of each law, and then be able to apply it to their classrooms. The question needs to be "How do these laws impact me as a teacher in my classroom?" "How

do they affect the children in my class?" "How do they affect the school in which I teach?" "How do they affect the overall state of education?" Only when teachers really understand the impact of the laws can they better be served by them.

What would you say about the importance of making and understanding the distinctions between students with emotional disorders, students who have behavioral disorders, and socially maladjusted students?

I think that the most important thing for teachers to understand is that each child is unique. Some children will exhibit only "symptoms" of behavioral problems, while others will be classified as students with an emotional disturbance. Regardless, the key lies in understanding why the children do what they do, and then what you, as a teacher can do about it. Teachers need to understand behavior, as well as the antecedents and consequences behind it. Furthermore, they have an obligation to learn about the disorders that exceptional children have in their classroom. The reality of "emotional disturbance" is that it tells us very little. It is probably the "vaguest" of all the disabilities. Does the child have depression, anxiety, conduct disorder, schizophrenia, etc? The list is endless. So, telling me a child is classified with ED, only tells me that the child has emotional/behavioral issues. But what does it really mean? In the end, teachers need to understand each child as a unique entity and learn what motivates the child.

What sort of advice would you offer a new teacher about creating functional behavioral assessments? What sort of advice would you offer a new teacher about creating effective intervention plans?

I have combined these two questions because I believe that the answer is the same. No one expects teachers to be able to write an FBA or BIP on their own. It's not their sole responsibility. Their primary role is to implement whatever is prescribed by the FBA and/or BIP. Teachers need to be very aware of what comprises these very important tools. They need to be giving the other special education professionals, especially the school psychologists, information that can make the plans as effective as possible. New teachers have so much on their plates, but the truth is that when you work with students in special education, you are going to have to work harder. That's the reality. The rewards are wonderful, but you will definitely have to work harder. Therefore, it is your responsibility to learn about FBAs and BIPs, look at models of effective ones, and really understand their rationale and purpose.

What sort of advice would you offer a new teacher about communicating with students with emotional disorders, students who have behavioral disorders, and socially maladaptive students?

The bottom line is: You need to be competent and confident. Working with children with ED or similar related disorders and disabilities requires a knowledge base in the field. You need to know how implement behavior modification plans, provide positive reinforcement, and know how to use punishment and discipline so as to be effective. Students with ED have often had very poor experiences in school. So, when they get a teacher or teachers who genuinely care about their well being and know that they are there for them 100 percent, they will often have great respect for them. It won't be easy, but the satisfaction in getting a child with ED to respond is often greater than any other teaching experience. But the only way it works is by understanding the student. You do this by becoming competent in the field, learning about what research has suggested works with children like the ones in your classes, and ultimately knowing how to teach them.

If you could impress something upon the readers of this book—something they often miss but that, if they understood it, would prepare them more effectively for their work—what would it be?

Never lose sight of the fact that you are teacher and the leader of the classroom. All students will look to your for leadership. Often times, teachers will say "I'm scared of working with those kids with behavioral problems." Well, if you are, then those students are almost assuredly going to recognize that fear. You need to feel good about working with students with ED. You want to be able to work with them and let them know that you understand and want them in your classroom. Students want to succeed, and want to feel like they are important. Too often, repeated failure inhibits children with ED to try at school. Your job is to find out what motivates these children and get them to reach their fullest potential.

What changes do you see on the horizon for special education? What do you think are the aspects of the field that most need changing?

The change in the field is definitely one of school districts moving towards inclusive classrooms. That's a given. We are taking students who used to be in special education classrooms for most/all of the day and now integrating them into the general education classroom for most/all of the day. So, the change is obvious. We as educators at the university and State levels need to give our general education teachers more courses and more professional development in working with exceptional children. Teachers will be much more effective if they are learning the latest state of the art research in the field. We need to level the playing field and educate all teachers in the field of special education so that they can feel competent when they are working with these children in the general education setting.

Focus Questions Revisited

1. Why is it so difficult to provide a comprehensive definition for "emotional disturbance," and what are some of the contributing factors?

A Sample Response

Providing a comprehensive definition for "emotional disturbance" is complicated by several key factors, including:

a. Subjectivity in determining abnormal behavior, that is, what constitutes an atypical level of severity (intensity), duration, and frequency, and how we differentiate between abnormal behavior caused by abnormal or mitigating circumstances and abnormal behavior exhibited under normal or near-normal circumstances.

b. Effects of developmental change on the behavioral and emotional stability of an individual

c. The tendency of the federal and state education agencies to exclude children and youth who are considered "socially maladjusted" or who are "court-adjudicated"

d. The controversy surrounding certain diagnoses whose presenting characteristics are not deemed to be primarily emotional or behavioral (e.g., ADHD, autism spectrum disorder)

e. The amorphous nature of the field and of special education in general

f. The inclusion or exclusion of schizophrenia and other psychiatric diagnoses, depending on the predisposition of a particular state

2. Is there a behavioral profile of a child that warrants the classification as "emotionally disturbed"? If so, what are the characteristic traits?

A Sample Response

Providing a general profile or set of characteristic traits to facilitate a classification of "emotionally disturbed" is virtually impossible; nonetheless, most of the disorders associated with this category of disability can be organized under two subcategories: "externalized," which describes behaviors that are overtly displayed; or "internalized," defining behaviors that are more difficult to observe. Subtypes of EBD that are predominantly "externalized" are those whose characteristics involve observable actions or behaviors that are antisocial, that is, impulsive, aggressive, disruptive, destructive, and in violation of the laws and rules or norms of society. Subtypes of EBD whose behaviors are primarily "internalized" and thus not as readily apparent include mood disorders such as depression, anxiety disorders such as posttraumatic stress disorder, and thought disorders/psychiatric diagnoses such as schizophrenia.

3. What is a functional behavior assessment, and how is it applied to classroom intervention?

A Sample Response

The term *functional behavioral assessment* (FBA) refers to a systematic process used in identifying the "function" or purpose of a specific misbehavior or inappropriate action. According to Skinner (1968) and other behaviorists, all behaviors serve a purpose for the "actor." Therefore, if practitioners and caregivers can successfully identify that purpose, a relevant and effective intervention can be developed. The danger in not understanding the purpose or root cause of an undesirable behavior is to inadvertently compound the problem by either reinforcing the pathological behavior or wasting time and resources treating a misidentified one.

4. What are some typical nontherapeutic teacher responses to misbehavior in the classroom, and how can these be positively transformed?

A Sample Response

Without proper training and preparation, teacher, parents, and community members may respond inconsistently to the inappropriate or maladaptive behaviors of school-age children and youth. All too often, untrained or unenlightened teachers react to maladaptive and disruptive behavior with a "knee-jerk" response, interpreting the misbehavior as intentional and vindictive and therefore assessing a "punishment" that is frequently subjective and counter-therapeutic. How they respond will depend on several personalogical factors, including: (a) perceived competence in behavior management, (b) tolerance of predisposition/sensitivity to the offending behavior, (c) personal and professional management of stress, (d) perceived "goodness of fit" between the student of concern and the classroom culture, (e) the caregiver's affinity for or intuitive "connection" with the child, (f) school, community, or family policy regarding the type and severity of the misbehavior, and (g) the notion that the task of behavior management is not the teacher's purview. Proper training in effective behavior management techniques can obviate many of these counterproductive teacher responses.

5. How can teachers avoid conflict and help build a sense of community or shared responsibility in the classroom?

A Sample Response

Kohn (1996) identified five criteria that are crucial in building community among students and teachers in the classroom, in and reducing conflict. The first of these is a relationship with the adults. Sec-ond, teachers should provide activities that promote an understanding of another's perspective. Feshbach et al. (1983) suggested that an appreciation for another person's point of view is the foundation of community building. Third, skillful teachers can integrate academic lessons with group activities. An example of this type of participative activity is represented in the cooperative learning approach. Fourth, students in the classroom should be given the autonomy to make responsible, informed choices about the design and development of their classroom community. Finally, research has long advocated the importance of choice for students who have EBD, for whom choice is typically not an option (Cullinan, 2002; Jensen, 2005; Kauffman, 2005). The opportunity to participate in the decision-making process is both empowering and community building, because it implies ownership and requires collaboration.

Chapter 2

Conduct Disorder

Photodisc/Getty Images

FOCUS QUESTIONS

1. What are the defining characteristics of a conduct disorder?

2. How can I effectively diffuse a behavioral crisis in my classroom that involves a student who has a conduct disorder?

3. Students who have conduct disorder can be defiant and verbally confrontational. What is the best way to deal with these behaviors when they occur in the classroom?

4. Because many students who have conduct disorder are co-diagnosed with ADHD, how can I deal effectively with their impulsiveness and off-task behavior?

Students who have been classified as *emotionally disturbed* typically receive counseling as a related service along with special education in either an inclusion or self-contained setting. In fact, teacher surveys have revealed that counseling is the preferred intervention for serious classroom problems (Walker, 1995). With the proliferation of the inclusive model in schools in the United States, increasing numbers of students who have emotional behavioral disorders (EBD), such as conduct disorder, oppositional-defiant disorder, and attention-deficit hyperactivity disorder (ADHD) are being educated in general education classrooms (Austin, 2001). This means that now both special and general education teachers may work with students who have EBD. Affected teachers will be required to participate in the development of these students' Individualized Education Plans (IEPs) and, where possible, coordinate with other service providers.

Unfortunately, because service providers are outside the classroom, there is little opportunity for the teacher to confer with them about issues relevant to a particular student. In addition, many teachers feel absolved of responsibility in providing meaningful interventions for these students because they believe that students who have emotional or behavioral disorders will change simply by gaining insight into the causes of their maladaptive/antisocial behavior (Walker, Ramsey, & Gresham, 2004).

Typically, service providers focus on helping students who have conduct disorder and other emotional or behavioral problems identify and understand the reasons for their maladaptive behavior and change it. Often, these students demonstrate an awareness of the inappropriateness of their behavior, but there is little empirical evidence to correlate awareness with behavior change (Dryfoos, 1990). Whereas awareness of a behavior problem and an understanding of its cause is a critical step in the process of behavior change, conscientiously applied, effective behavior change strategies, as well as cognitive behavior therapies must be practiced in the classroom, home, and community to ensure the permanence and generalizability of the results (Elliot, Witt, Kratochwill, & Stoiber, 2002).

This chapter addresses the need for greater reciprocity and collaboration between key stakeholders in the provision of services for students who have conduct disorder—specifically, the classroom teacher, related service providers, and the affected child. Each has an important role in providing therapeutic interventions and therefore all should strive to work together to optimize the treatment benefit to the student. To do this effectively, each stakeholder should clearly understand her role as well as that of her colleagues. This chapter provides the information necessary to begin this emerging collaborative process and begins with an overview of conduct disorder: its characteristics, causes, assessment issues, and treatment strategies. A case example follows that will serve as a paradigm for addressing a student who has conduct disorder in the classroom. Two further sections then divide interventions into instructional and behavioral approaches. The chapter ends with a question-and-answer format designed to address the most common problems faced by teachers in working with children and youth with conduct disorder.

CASE EXAMPLE: Michael

Michael ("Mike") is a fourteen-year-old boy who comes from an abusive home in a suburban area of New York City. He has been reported to the police by his mother twice for assaulting his younger brother and threatening to "kill" his older sister. In elementary and middle school, he was suspended for fighting with other students and threatening teachers. However, he was never referred for evaluation for special education services because he was considered "socially maladjusted," and such behavior is excluded from the current definition of "emotionally disturbed" (U.S. Department of Education, 2004). His mother fears his size and strength, as well as his volatility.

Mike is big for his age, standing 6 feet 2 inches in height and weighing 200 pounds. His antisocial behavior was first apparent in Grade 1. He would pick fights during recess and intimidate weaker children. When asked why he assaulted another student without provocation, Mike said, "That boy looked at me funny—I don't like him." This pattern of intimidation and aggression continued through the elementary grades and into middle school, despite a series of detentions, suspensions, and other punishments levied by the schools.

In Grade 7, Mike assaulted another student on the bus while returning home after school. Before the driver or the other student could stop him, he broke the student's nose and cheekbone, which resulted in a concussion. Consequently, Mike was expelled from the district. The high school he is now attending is in another district, his third new school in five years.

At home, Mike "rules the roost" in his father's absence. His father is currently serving three to five years in the state penitentiary for aggravated assault. According to his mother, Mike "comes and goes" as he chooses, disregarding her rules and restrictions. She feels intimidated by his size and explosive temper and is "powerless to stop him." As a freshman in a new high school, Mike has already developed a reputation for aggression and intimidation. Calling himself "The Enforcer," he has extracted money from several students. When confronted about this behavior, Mike insists the extracted monies are simply loans that he intends to repay once he gets a summer job.

In another incident that occurred less than a month after he had begun attending classes in the new high school, Mike had a disagreement with the computer teacher about appropriate use of computers. He was asked to sign off prematurely. Mike insisted that he had done nothing wrong and refused to sign off. When the teacher attempted to turn off his computer, Mike became enraged, picked up the computer monitor, and threw it against the wall. When the teacher called for security, Mike kicked out a second-story window and threatened to jump the two flights to the ground unless the security guards left. The school psychologist, with whom Mike had established a good rapport, as well as trust, was able to convince Mike to accompany her to the office. Subsequently, the principal called the police and charges were filed against Mike for assault and willful destruction of school property. Is Mike a student who should be referred to the juvenile justice system for punishment and incarceration, or should he be provided the emotional and academic supports he clearly needs, through the services of special education? In the actual case, Michael was eventually referred for evaluation to determine whether he qualified to receive special education services under the category of *emotional disturbance*.

CHARACTERISTICS OF CONDUCT DISORDER

Conduct disorder (CD), along with oppositional defiant disorder (ODD) and attention-deficit hyperactivity disorder (ADHD), is recognized as a major diagnostic category among disruptive behavior disorders (DBDs) in childhood and adolescence. CD is one of the most common reasons for referral of children and adolescents to mental health treatment centers (Finch, Nelson, & Hart, 2006; Scott, 2006). For every two to four children seen at child guidance clinics, at least one has a diagnosis of CD (Comer, 1995). Table 2.1 lists the diagnostic

---

TABLE 2.1 DSM-IV-TR Diagnostic Criteria for Conduct Disorder

A repetitive and persistent pattern of behavior in which the basic rights of others or major age-appropriate societal norms or rules are violated, as manifested by the presence of three (or more) of the following criteria in the past 12 months, with at least one criterion present in the past 6 months:

1. Often bullies, threatens, or intimidates others
2. Often initiates physical fights
3. Has used a weapon that can cause serious physical harm to others (e.g., a bat, brick, broken bottle, knife, gun)
4. Has been physically cruel to people
5. Has been physically cruel to animals
6. Has stolen while confronting a victim (e.g., mugging, purse snatching, extortion, armed robbery)
7. Has forced someone into sexual activity
8. Has deliberately engaged in fire setting with the intention of causing serious damage
9. Has deliberately destroyed others' property (other than by fire setting)
10. Has broken into someone else's house, building, or car
11. Often lies to obtain goods or favors or to avoid obligations (i.e., "cons" others)
12. Has stolen items of nontrivial value without confronting a victim (e.g., shoplifting, but without breaking and entering; forgery)
13. Often stays out at night despite parental prohibitions, beginning before age 13
14. Has run away from home overnight at least twice while living in parental or parental surrogate home (or once without returning for a lengthy period
15. Is often truant from school, beginning before age 13 years.

Source: From *Diagnostic and Statistical Manual of Mental Disorders, Fourth Edition, Text Revision* (pp. 98–99) by the American Psychiatric Association, 2000. Washington, DC: Author. Copyright by the American Psychiatric Association. Reprinted with permission.

criteria for CD. According to the *Diagnostic and Statistical Manual of Mental Disorders, Text Revision* (4th ed.) (DSM-IV-TR) (American Psychiatric Association, 2000), CD is "a repetitive and persistent pattern of behavior in which the basic rights of others or major age-appropriate societal norms or rules are violated" (pp. 98–99). The fifteen criteria listed in Table 2.1 reveal the basic symptomatology of CD. The DSM-IV-TR stipulates that at least three of the fifteen criteria must have been present during the last twelve months, and at least one criterion must have been present in the last 6 months, for a diagnosis of CD. In order to distinguish simple aggressive behaviors from CD, helpers need to consider the frequency, intensity, and degree of functional impairment, because it is estimated, for example, that 70 percent of adolescents participate in some delinquent behavior (Finch et al., 2006).

In order to distinguish conduct problems in general from CD in particular, researchers and theorists have developed various subtypes of aggression. The DSM-IV-TR distinguishes two subtypes based on age (childhood-onset type and adolescent-onset type) and three levels of severity (mild, moderate, and severe) based on the number of conduct problems presented. The case example of Michael at the beginning of the chapter provides a realistic profile of a student who has a more intense level of conduct disorder to better illustrate the characteristics as manifested in the home and at school.

Age of onset is a significant factor in determining the future course of CD. The adolescent type develops after age 10 years and usually with the onset of puberty. Well over 50 percent of those with early-onset (before age 8 years) continue with serious problems into adulthood, marked by disrupted and violent relationships, vocational problems, and substance abuse (Hinshaw, 1994b; Scott, 2006), and anywhere from 25 to 40 percent develop adult antisocial personality disorder (Finch et al., 2006). They are more likely to drop out of school. In contrast, about 85 percent of those with adolescent-onset type show an absence of antisocial behaviors by their early twenties (Scott, 2006).

Additional subtypes of conduct problems, though not included in the DSM-IV-TR include aggressive versus nonaggressive behaviors, reactive versus proactive aggression, and overt versus relational aggression (Kimonis & Frick, 2006). Nonaggressive behaviors, such as being stubborn, angry, defiant, and touchy, are more characteristic of ODD (see Chapter 3), whereas bullying, fighting, property violations, such as vandalism, cruelty to animals, and fire setting, are more indicative of CD. Overt aggression involves hitting, pushing, kicking, and threatening, in contrast to relational aggression designed to damage relationships and peer-group affiliations through gossiping and spreading rumors (Coie & Dodge, 1998, Crick et al, 1999; Kimonis & Frick, 2006). Research shows that children evidence either reactive or proactive aggression. Proactive aggression is carefully planned and designed with a clear purpose in mind—for example, to obtain some material benefit (robbery), power over others (bullying), or to increase one's social status (risk-taking behaviors) (Kimonis & Frick, 2006). Reactive aggression, on the other hand, is retaliatory and based on real or perceived threats (Kimonis & Frick, 2006). These children evidence deficits in social information processing, with a tendency to employ a hostile attribution bias to ambiguous situations (Crick & Dodge, 1996; Lochman, Powell, Whidby, &

Fitzjerald, 2006). A reactively aggressive child can turn a neutral encounter into a fight, often with deleterious consequences. Proactively aggressive children tend to have a more positive prognosis when it comes to decreasing the frequency of aggressive behaviors. A final subtype of children with conduct disorder behaviors is termed *callous* and *unemotional* (Caputo, Frick, & Brodsky, 1999; Frick, Bodin, & Barry, 2000; Silverthorn, Frick, & Reynolds, 2001). They tend to be more proactive in their aggression, suffer from an absence of guilt, like to participate in novel and exciting risk-taking behaviors, and are by and large insensitive to punitive consequences for their behaviors (Frick et al., 2003; Pardini, Lochman, & Frick, 2003).

PREVALENCE OF CD

Among community samples, the prevalence rate for CD is between 2 and 4 percent (Loeber, Burke, Lahey, Winters, & Zera, 2000). Difficulties in estimating prevalence rates for CD include the use of different criteria, the methods used to assess these criteria (child reports versus parent reports), and variations that occur at different ages and among different subgroups, such as males versus females (Hendren & Mullen, 2006). The ratio of prevalence for boys to girls ranges from 2:1 to 4:1 (Loeber et al., 2000; Shaffer, Fisher, Dulcan, & Davies, 1996). Childhood-onset CD is more common among boys; however, before the age of 5, rates are more or less equivalent for both sexes (Keenan & Shaw, 1997). Among a large urban sample, Loeber et al. (2000) found prevalence rates of 5.6, 5.4., and 8.3 for boys aged 7, 11, and 13, an indication that CD increases significantly during adolescence. In addition, researchers have found significant differences in rates of CD among ethnic groups. African American youth have higher rates of CD compared to White youth (Fabrega, Ulrich, & Mezzich, 1993; Lahey et al., 1995). Such differences may be contextual, because a greater percentage of children of color live in neighborhoods with higher rates of crime, poverty, and violence. Evaluator bias can also play a role in assessing clients of color more or less severely (Gushue, 2004; Gushue, Constantine, & Sciarra, 2008).

Comorbidities

Children and adolescents with CD often suffer from other disorders, the most frequent of which are ADHD, learning disabilities, anxiety, and depression. ADHD is the most common comorbid disorder with CD. Waschbusch (2002) found the rate of ADHD among community samples of those with CD to be 36 percent and as high as 90 percent among clinic samples. ADHD is more frequent among those diagnosed with childhood-onset CD, and this subgroup tends to display more chronic delinquency and more severely aggressive acts during adolescence (Loeber, Brinthaupt, & Green, 1990; Moffit, 2003), and more violent offenses in adulthood (Klinteberg, Andersson, Magnusson, & Stattin, 1993). It is not known whether the high rate of learning disability among those with CD is due more to the comorbid ADHD and less to the conduct problems. There is most likely an interaction effect, because some children with learning disabilities who do not have ADHD develop conduct problems later during adolescence.

Children with CD have high rates of anxiety and/or depression. Estimates are that anywhere from 15 to 31 percent of children with CD have depression. Among community samples, between 22 and 33 percent have an anxiety disorder, and this rate increases to between 60 and 75 percent among clinic samples (Kimonis & Frick, 2006; Russo & Beidel, 1994, Zoccolillo, 1993). Those who are depressed are at increased risk for suicidal ideation. Because children with CD have pervasive relationship problems, the high rates of anxiety and depression may be the result of interpersonal conflicts (Frick, Lilienfeld, Ellis, Loney, & Silverthorn, 1999).

ETIOLOGY OF CD

In general, the literature has divided the risk factors for developing CD into three categories: biological, psychological, and social. Multiple risk factors play a role in the development of CD. Kimonis and Frick (2006) suggested three methods for understanding the influence of multiple risk factors: cumulative, interactionist, and multiple pathways. In the *cumulative* method, one is concerned simply with the number of risk factors, and the more risk factors one has, the more likely one is to development CD. The *interactionist* perspective emphasizes the significance of certain risk factors interacting with others, and it is the combination rather than the accumulation of factors that result in CD. The *multiple* pathway method suggests that different causal processes are involved in the development of CD, and each involves a different set of risk factors. For example, childhood onset of CD has more to do with personality/depositional factors than adolescent onset, which may be the result of adolescent rebellion taken to an extreme (Moffitt, 2003).

Biological Factors

Biological factors can be subdivided into genetic, hormonal, neurotransmitter dysfunction, neurological, and prenatal toxin exposure factors (Hendren & Mullen, 2006).

GENETIC FACTORS   Studies examining a genetic link have found a high correlation for CD among twins (Eaves et al., 2000), and between family negativity and adolescent antisocial behavior (Pike, McGuire, Hetherington, Reiss, & Plomin, 1996). The most recent twins studies have examined the different subtypes of CD. Among those with adolescent-onset CD, family environment had more of an impact, in contrast to younger children with CD and comorbid ADHD, in whom the genetic influence was a more significant factor (Scott, 2006). Numerous studies have supported a strong association between parental antisocial behavior and preadolescent onset of CD (Elkins, Iacono, Doyle, & McGue, 1997; Frick et al., 1992; Lahey, Loeber, & Quay, 1998) and parental psychopathology, such as the mother's substance abuse, anxiety, or depression (Dierker, Merikangas, & Szatmari, 1999).

HORMONAL FACTORS   In general, studies have found hormone levels, particularly high levels of testosterone and its derivatives, to be associated with conduct disorder (Dimitrieva, Oades, Hauffa, & Egggers, 2001; Olweus, Mattsson, Schalling, & Law, 1988; van Goozen, Matthys, Cohen-Kettenis, Buitelar, & van Engeland, 2000). The van Goozen et al. (2000) study specifically mentioned boys with CD as having high levels of dehydroepiandrosterone (DHEAS), the precursor to testosterone, similar to boys with oppositional defiant disorder.

NEUROTRANSMITTER DYSFUNCTION   The role of neurotransmitter dysfunction has also been studied in the development of aggression in children, adolescents, and adults. Abnormal function of serotonin, the neurotransmitter implicated in the expression and regulation of affect and impulse control, has been found to play a role in aggression and lack of impulse control (Spoont, 1992), as have low levels of 5-hydroxyindoleacetic acid (metabolized serotonin) in the cerebrospinal fluid (Mehlman, Higley, Faucher, & Lilly, 1994, 1995). In addition, low levels of the neurotransmitter, serotonin, have been linked to aggression in children (Clarke, Murphy, & Constantino, 1999; Kruesi et al., 1990, 1992).

NEUROLOGICAL FACTORS   The relatively new research in neuroanatomy and CD has consistently shown frontal lobe damage in subjects who are prone to violence and aggression (Brower & Price, 2001; Giancola, 1995, Pliszka, 1999). Underarousal of the autonomic nervous system (i.e., slower heart rate) is associated with adolescent antisocial behavior (Mezzacappa et al., 1997) and later criminality (Raine, Venable, & Williams, 1990).

PRENATAL TOXIN EXPOSURE   Prenatal and perinatal complications, maternal smoking, and/or substance abuse during pregnancy have also been associated with behavioral problems (Loukas, Fitzgerald, Zucker, & von Eye, 2001; Raine, Brennan, & Mednick, 1997; Weissman, Warner, Wickramaratne, & Kandel, 1999). Finally, exposure to environmental toxins, such as lead, is also associated with delinquency and aggression (Needleman, Riess, Tobin, Biesecker, & Greenhouse, 1996).

In summary, there exists a host of biological factors for which empirical research has established a link not necessarily with CD in specific but with violence and aggression in general—the prominent characteristics of CD. A combination of these biological factors is more likely than any one factor alone to contribute to a diagnosis of CD.

Neuropsychological Factors

Burke, Loeber, and Birmaher (2002), in their review of the literature on CD, categorized psychological factors as temperament, attachment, neuropsychological functioning, intelligence and academic performance, reading problems, impulsivity and behavioral inhibition, social cognition, sociomoral reasoning, and pubertal/adolescent development. For many of these factors, contradictory findings exist. The more consistent and stronger associations with CD are neuropsychological deficits, especially in the area of **executive functioning**

EXECUTIVE FUNCTIONING

Refers to a set of high-level cognitive abilities that have to do with planning, organizing, strategizing, paying attention to, and remembering details. Those with good executive functioning are able to anticipate outcomes and adapt to changing situations. Concept formation and abstraction are also considered under the metaconstruct of executive functioning.

(Seguin, Boulerice, Harden, Tremblay, & Pihl, 1999), low achievement and school failure (Farrington, 1995; Frick, Kamphaus, et al., 1991), and reading problems (Maguin, Loeber, & LeMahieu, 1993; Sanson, Prior, & Smart, 1996). Intelligence level is mediated by other factors. For example, when controlling for ADHD, the relationship between IQ and CD is often insignificant (Hogan, 1999). Many of the functional factors may serve as pathways rather than predictors of behavioral disorders. Even the stronger associated factors appear to be mediated by confounding factors such as ADHD and early psychosocial factors discussed below. In general, children with CD have lower-than-average IQs (Martin & Hoffman, 1990) and, more specifically, have deficient verbal IQs (Moffit, Lynam, & Silva, 1994). Studies have also shown impairment in executive functions (concentration, attention, planning sequencing, and inhibition) (Moffit & Silva, 1988) along with deficits in reading (McGee, Williams, Share, Anderson, & Silva, 1986).

Psychosocial Factors

Among the most notable psychosocial factors in the development of conduct disorder are parenting (including abusive practices), peer effects, and neighborhood/socioeconomic determinants (Burke et al., 2002).

PARENTING   Poor family management (i.e., inconsistent and severe discipline, poor supervision, and failure to set clear expectations) is among the most powerful predictors of later delinquency (Capaldi & Patterson, 1996; Hawkins, Arthur, & Catalano, 1995; Mash & Wolfe, 2005; McCord, 1991). Another pathway to conduct disturbance seems evident: Children whose parents are hostile, negative, and neglectful are at risk for developing all sorts of mental health problems, which may in turn lead to patterns of antisocial and violent behavior (Steinberg, 2000). Undoubtedly, when children are exposed to violence in the home, they come to understand violence as an acceptable way of dealing with conflict and solving problems. Exposure to high levels of family and marital conflict increases the risk for later violence (Elliot, 1994; Farrington, 1989; Maguin et al., 1995). Mike, the student profiled at the beginning of the chapter, illustrates the deleterious effects of violence in the home on the emotional well-being of the developing child.

PEER EFFECTS   Peer-related factors in predicting conduct problems have been examined in terms of having delinquent siblings, delinquent peers, and gang membership. All three factors have been found to have a positive link to disturbances in conduct (Battin, Hill, Abbott, Catalano, & Hawkins, 1998; Farrington, 1989; Maguin et al., 1995; Minden, Henry, Tolan, & Gorman-Smith, 2000; Moffit, Caspi, Dickson, Silva, & Stanton, 1996).

NEIGHBORHOOD AND SOCIOECONOMIC FACTORS   The factors hypothesized as contributing to conduct disorder in youth are poverty, community disorganization, availability of drugs and firearms, neighborhood adults involved in crime (as was the case with Michael's father), exposure to violence and racial prejudice, and violence in the media. Maguin et al. (1995) found community disorganization (i.e., the presence of crime, drug selling, gangs, and poor housing), availability of drugs and firearms, and knowing adults involved in crime to be contributors to violence in youth.

Conclusions About Risk Factors

One of the difficulties in predicting CD is that most of the research has examined factors contributing to CD in conjunction with symptoms of other diagnoses, such as ODD and ADHD. Another problem is that most studies have looked at aggression and delinquency as outcomes and, for the most part, have left unexamined nonaggressive antisocial behaviors (Burke et al., 2002). Research is far from complete on youth violence and delinquency. More research is needed to study the interaction effects of different factors as predictors of other problems. The greater the number of risk factors, the more likely it is that a youth will have a diagnosis of CD. Farrington (1997) found that the percentage of youth convicted for conduct violations increased from 3 percent for those with no risk factors to 31 percent for youth with four risk factors. Helpers must be especially vigilant of those students who evidence more than one factor.

ASSESSMENT

Because many consider diagnoses such as CD to be overused, assessment needs to be both multimethod and multi-informant (Loney & Lima, 2003; Freeman & Hogansen, 2006). Most experts recommend at minimum the use of an interview, rating scales, and observational data (Loney & Lima, 2003).

Interviews

Interviews can be either unstructured or structured. The unstructured interview helps to build rapport, is used often by most clinicians (Barlow & Durand, 2005), but is questionable in terms of reliability and validity. The skilled provider, however, will know what questions to ask, intuit the client's capacity for victim empathy, and realize the degree of manipulation. Some adolescents who have conduct disorder actually don't mind talking about their egregious acts. Others refrain from talking because they see the sharing of information as giving up control.

Several semistructured interviews exist for diagnosing conduct problems. Sections on the *Child Assessment Schedule* (CAS; Hodges, Kline, Stern, Cytryn, & McKnew, 1982) and the *Schedule for Affective Disorders and Schizophrenia for School-Aged Children* (K-SADS; Spitzer, Endicott, Loth, McDonald-Scott, & Wasek, 1998) that deal with conduct problems can be helpful in recognizing and diagnosing CD. Reliability and validity of the K-SADS and the CAS are promising (Ambrosini, 2000).

Structured instruments (instruments that do not allow for any additional follow-up or probes) for assessing CD that use the DSM-IV criteria exist. Perhaps the most well known are the *Diagnostic Interview Schedule for Children* (DISC-IV; Shaffer, Fisher, Lucas, Dulcan, & Schwab-Stone, 2000) and the

Diagnostic Interview for Children and Adolescents (DICA-IV; Welner, Reich, Herjanic, & Jung, 1987). The disadvantage of the structured interview is that they are time consuming and often do not include normative data (Loney & Lima, 2003). Studies have shown both the DISC-IV and DICA-IV to have good reliability and validity (Lewczyk,Garland, Hurlburt, Gearity, & Hough, 2003; Reich, 2000).

Rating Scales

Numerous rating scales exist for the assessment of CD that are either self-reports or reports of significant others. Rating scales have the advantage of being relatively fast to administer and use normative data. One widely used measure is the Behavior Assessment System for Children (BASC; Reynolds & Kamphaus, 1992). It is a multi-informant measure for parent, child, and teacher that measures adaptive functioning and other clinical categories (e.g., depression, anxiety), as well as tapping into CD.

Self-reports are frequently used among adult populations. Their use with children and adolescents is questionable, because these populations often see themselves as not having a problem, and they can be poor historians. As a result, greater reliability is attached to reports from significant others. For parents of those suspected of CD, a frequently used measure is the *Eyeberg Child Behavior Inventory* (ECBI; Eyberg & Robinson, 1983), which primarily assesses problems at home, such as fighting and other oppositional behaviors. It also has a teacher-report form, the *Sutter-Eyeberg Student Behavior Inventory* (SESBI; Eyberg & Pincus, 1999). General, broad-band measures of psychopathology can also be used to confirm a diagnosis of CD. One of the most widely used for parents is the *Child Behavior Checklist* (CBCL; Achenbach, 2001a, 2001b). The CBCL also has a *Teacher Report Form* and a *School Behavior Checklist*, another widely used general measure of psychopathology. All of these instruments have favorable psychometric properties (Freeman & Hogansen, 2006).

Direct Observation

Behavioral observations are advantageous because they are less biased than child, parent, and even teacher reports. However, they can be time-consuming and complicated. Both the BASC and the CBCL have observation schedules for coding classroom and group interactions, in addition to the parent reports. After a designated time period, the observer completes a checklist of behavioral indicators. For example, the CBCL uses a 10-minute observation period and a checklist of ninety-six target behaviors rated on a Likert scale. Because many of the behaviors associated with CD are infrequent and covert in nature, some have called into question the reliability of direct observation to assess CD (Loney & Lima, 2003). Manipulation and deceit, often characteristic of CD, can reduce reliability in observation.

Direct observation of the parent and child together is also recommended for differentiating a diagnosis of CD. Typically, parent and child are observed in both a structured and an unstructured activity for communication patterns, positive parenting behaviors, and the child's response to parental demands. The three common approaches are free play, parent-directed play, and parent-directed chore situations (Roberts & Hope, 2001). For older children and adolescents, an argument-producing discussion topic or a problem-solving task can be substituted for play activity (Freeman & Hogansen, 2006). One of the more well known parent–child observation scales is the *Dyadic Parent-Child Interaction Coding System* (DPICS; Eyberg & Robinson, 1983). Research has shown that parent–child interactions can be coded reliably (Niec, 2004; Roberts & Hope, 2001).

Summary

The formal diagnosis of CD is not an easy task. Some symptoms can overlap with other diagnoses, and there is a high degree of comorbidity that may complicate the diagnostic picture. Because deceit forms a part of the symptomotology, even the more astute helper can be fooled. Therefore, assessment of CD should occur over time and should be multimodal. Helpers are encouraged to make every effort to gather as much information as possible through observation, both formal and informal, along with reports from parents, as well as academic and clinical records.

TREATMENT STRATEGIES

Effective treatment strategies for CD can be divided into four categories: individual cognitive-behavioral, family-based, multisystemic, and psychopharmacological. The following paragraphs describe and evaluate these four approaches to the treatment of CD.

Cognitive-Behavioral Treatment

Cognitive-behavioral treatment (CBT) focuses primarily on thought processes and employs behavioral techniques to change those processes that are seen as being responsible for the problematic behavior. The helper attempts to engage the client in new ways of thinking that will result in new ways of feeling and behaving. Because aggressive children tend to perceive neutral acts by others as hostile, the helper can work with the children on their perceptions and change some of their faulty thinking (Lochman, Powell, Jackson, & Czopp, 2006). The teaching of problem-solving skills and relaxation training can also form part of the treatment. Problem-solving strategies are a multistep process that involves:

1. A description of the problem and major goals for the solution
2. Generation of alternative solutions
3. Evaluation of these alternatives in terms of how well they will assist in the achievement of the goal
4. Selection and enactment of the best strategy identified
5. Evaluation of the degree of success of the outcome (Southam-Gerow, 2003, pp. 260–261)

Feindler developed a cognitive-behavioral program for CD that involves self-monitoring of one's triggers, self-talk to manage anger, planning ahead by

COGNITIVE-BEHAVIORAL TREATMENT OR THERAPY (CBT)

Refers to a therapeutic approach that teaches the individual to "think" about events in a different way, often from another's perspective, and provides strategies that facilitate this (e.g., using an acrostic or acronym such as "STOP" to remind the individual to use a set strategy).

using problem-solving skills, relaxation skills, and assertiveness skills (Feindler, Ecton, Kingsley, & Dubey, 1986). Lochman and Wells (2002) developed the *Coping Power Program,* which treats both child-level factors (poor decision-making skills, poor self-regulation, poor ability to resist peer pressure, and reading social skills appropriately) and contextual factors (poor parental caregiver skills and discipline). The skills imparted through the *Coping Power Program* are usually through a group modality.

Empirical studies over the years have found CBT to be moderately effective in treating CD and less effective than family-based and multisystemic treatments. For example, problem-solving skills have been found to be an effective treatment, but not as effective in combination with parent management training (Kazdin, Bass, Siegel, & Thomas, 1989; Kazdin, Esveldt-Dawson, French, and Unis, 1987; Kazdin, Siegel, & Bass, 1992). In 1998, a task force of the American Psychological Association concluded that child-focused CBT did not meet the criteria for well-established treatment status, in contrast to parent-focused interventions, which did (Brestan & Eyberg, 1998). By focusing on the child, CBT may not consider sufficiently family influences in the development and maintenance of CD (Snyder, Schrepferman, & St. Peter, 1997; Southam-Gerow, 2003; Strand, 2000).

Family-Based Interventions

Family-based interventions can be divided into two categories: those that focus on parenting and work exclusively with the primary caregiver(s) in terms of parent management training and those that work with the entire family system.

PARENT MANAGEMENT TRAINING   Parent management training (PMT) is used primarily for preschool and elementary school children who are evidencing conduct problems. The theoretical basis for PMT is the assumption that conduct problems are developed and sustained in the home by maladaptive parent–child interactions (Kazdin, 1995). The trainer works with the parents to alter their interaction with the child by teaching the parents to give clear rules and commands, positive reinforcement for compliance, time-outs and loss of privileges for noncompliance, negotiation, and **contingency contracting** with consistent consequences for unwanted behavior (Burke et al., 2002; Scott, 2006).

CONTINGENCY CONTRACTING

Refers to a prearranged system of consequences (reinforcers and punishers) designed to increase appropriate behavior and decrease inappropriate behavior.

PMT is perhaps the most empirically investigated technique for reducing symptoms of CD. Numerous studies have shown PMT to be effective in both the short and long term (see, for example, Kazdin & Wassell, 2000; Long, Forehand, Wierson, & Morgan, 1994; Miller & Prinz, 1990; Patterson, Dishion, & Chamberlain, 1993). Greater effects are associated with longer-terms programs. Programs with less than 10 hours of PMT produce negligible benefits. In spite of the overwhelming evidence in favor of PMT, parental resistance and psychopathology are impediments to treatment. The availability of numerous manuals makes PMT a simple and effective approach to treating CD, especially in younger children. If the helper can engage the parents into this form of treatment, it is likely that they will successfully reduce much of the problematic behaviors associated with CD.

FAMILY SYSTEMS THERAPY Treating the entire family (defined as those living together) for one member with CD results from the conceptualization that the identified symptom serves a systemic function. For example, a family counselor might view CD as the system's need to avoid interpersonal contact or distract the mother and father from their own relationship problems. Functional family therapy (FFT) consists of three phases: engagement and enactment, behavioral change, and generalization (Prinz & Jones, 2003). During the first phase, the provider meets with the family, knowing that within a short time the family will demonstrate its familiar ways of behaving. The provider is alert to patterns of communication, coalition, and boundaries being either too diffuse or too rigid. In the second phase, the provider begins to interrupt these familiar patterns and restore power and authority to the executive subsystem. In the third phase, the family members are taught to apply their new learning by anticipating problems, practicing, and preventing themselves from relapsing into old and familiar ways of relating.

The advantage of FFT is its short-term focus—anywhere form six to twelve sessions. Two disadvantages are the difficulty of engaging the entire family system and the lack of helpers sufficiently trained to work with the entire family. Over the years, family counselors have become known for their direct and sometimes confrontational style, which is often at odds with the traditional training one receives in working with individuals. Research evaluating FFT is rather sparse. A number of studies, however, have shown that FFT can be effective in reducing recidivism rates among adolescents with delinquent histories and improving the functioning of those with conduct problems (Alexander, Robbins, & Sexton, 2000; Friedman, 1989).

Multisystemic Treatment

More recently, **multisystemic treatment (MST)** for conduct disorder has shown the greatest success. MST goes beyond family treatment in that it considers the family system as important, but only one of a number of systems in which a child is embedded (Saldana & Henggeler, 2006). These other systems include peers, school, and neighborhood. Research has shown that not only family relations, but involvement with deviant peers, school difficulties, and neighborhood/community factors, are strong contributors to delinquency (Henggeler, 1991; Henry, Tolan, & Gorman-Smith, 2001; Le Blanc & Kaspy, 1998; Paschall & Hubbard, 1998). These studies suggest that successful treatment of CD must include these other systems.

At the family level, MST employs some form of FFT as outlined above. At the peer level, interventions attempt to diminish associations with deviant peers and replace those relationships with more positive ones by facilitating membership in organized athletics, after-school activities, and church youth groups (Borduin, Schaeffer, & Ronis, 2003). At the school level, the provider develops strategies to help parents monitor school performance by opening lines of communication between parents and teachers and structuring time at home to go over homework and other school-related activities. If biological factors are involved, MST employs the use of psychopharmacology, an intervention discussed

MULTISYSTEMIC TREATMENT

A multiple-system treatment approach to many emotional and behavioral disorders that typically combines family therapy with individual and peer-oriented therapies, acknowledging the importance of affecting behavior change in all these important milieus.

in a separate section later. MST is broad-based and flexible to consider and deal with any and all factors contributing to CD. For example, if a parent's stress because of unemployment complicates the task of effective parenting, this would also be addressed by the provider. Referring to the case example at the beginning of the chapter, family-based interventions would be difficult, if not impossible, to conduct because Michael's father, a key stakeholder, is currently incarcerated and is therefore unable to participate.

A number of MST programs operate nationwide, including Fast Track and Project LIFT. Research examining the effectiveness of MST has shown it to be superior to other forms of treatment for general delinquency (Henggeler et al., 1986; Ogden & Halliday-Boykins, 2004; Schaeffer & Borduin, 2005), violent and chronic offenses (Borduin et al., 1995; Henggeler, Melton, & Smith, 1992; Henggeler, Pickrel, & Brondino, 1999), substance use and abuse (Brown, Henggeler, Schoenwald, Brondino, & Pickrel, 1999; Henggeler et al., 1999; Henggeler et al., 1991), and sexual offenses (Borduin, Henggeler, Blaske, & Stein, 1990; Borduin & Schaeffer, 2001). In spite of its documented success, however, MST is not always the preferred mode of treatment for CD. One disadvantage is that MST is time-consuming, and practical concerns, such as insurance reimbursement for a provider's time spent outside the traditional therapeutic encounter stop, make it difficult for some clinics and programs to implement MST.

Psychopharmacological Intervention

As mentioned previously, recent literature has established a genetic and neurobiological link in the development of CD. This has led to a increased consideration of psychopharmacological intervention with this population. Although a number of different drugs have been shown to be effective, the difficulty of doing **randomized controlled studies (RCTs)** with children and adolescents caution circumspection in the use of drug therapy. The results from the few RCTs done with CD have been inconclusive and prevent generalizability because of small samples sizes (Burke et al., 2002; Kimonis & Frick, 2006).

Two RCTs (Campbell, Adams, Small, & Kafantaris, 1995; Malone, Delaney, Luebbert, Cater, & Campbell, 2000) found that lithium, when compared with a placebo, was both safe and effective in treating hospitalized youth diagnosed with CD. On the other hand, Rifkin, Karagji, Dicker and Perl (1997), in a similar study, found no such difference, although lithium had been administered for only 2 weeks. Other studies have found antipsychotic drugs to be effective in treating aggressive youth. These drugs include carbamazepine (Cueva, Overall, Small, & Amenteros,, 1996), molidine and thioridazine (Greenhill, Solomon, Pleak, & Ambrosini, 1985), and risperidone (Aman et al., 2005; Findling et al., 2000; Croonenberghs, Findling, Ryes, & Karcher, 2005).

The most-prescribed medications for conduct problems are stimulants, most especially methylphenidate (Ritalin being the most popular). Because CD is highly comorbid with ADHD, stimulants known to be effective in reducing the impulsivity associated with ADHD have effectively reduced conduct problems in children with both CD and ADHD (Connor, Glatt, Lopez, Jackson, & Maloni, 2002; Hinshaw, 1991; Pelham et al., 1993; Swanson et al., 2001). Even when ADHD was controlled for, stimulants helped in reducing symptoms of CD.

RANDOMIZED CONTROLLED STUDIES (RCTs)

Refers to the random allocation of interventions to different subjects. The most reliable RCTs are double-blind, where the researcher does not know to what intervention group a subject has been assigned. Double-blind studies are the best way to control for researcher bias.

There is some evidence for the effectiveness of several medications in reducing the symptoms of CD, but the support is far from conclusive. At most, medications are partially helpful, and more effective results require complementary treatment modalities. When psychosocial treatment is combined with medication therapy for conduct problems, the rate of improvement is far higher (Swanson et al., 2001). In addition, the benefits of medication must always be considered in conjunction with the cost of side effects.

Summary

In spite of studies showing the effectiveness for different interventions for CD, a number of challenges and limitations exist in achieving success with this population. A significant number of children do not improve. Improvement is difficult to sustain over time and across settings, and rarely does a child with CD reduce behaviors to a normative level. Children under the age of 8 years show the greatest improvement, which emphasizes the need for early intervention, and suggests that interventions with older children and adolescent are less effective (Kimonis & Frick, 2006). Because they work with children on a daily basis, schools that have developed school-based intervention programs for children with CD have the greatest chances of success in reducing aggressive behaviors.

SCHOOL-BASED INTERVENTIONS

Thorough coverage of the characteristics, prevalence, causes, assessments, and treatment strategies that are currently recommended concerning children and adolescents who have emotional and behavioral disorders is provided throughout this book. This information will provide the reader with a sound knowledge base from which to embark on the next phase of our investigation: the application of theory and research to classroom practice. This process involves two distinct stages: (1) assessing the problem and (2) developing an effective intervention plan, as required by the federal Individuals with Disabilities Education Act (IDEA, 1997, 2004). Both stages will be described in detail in the passages that follow, and a suggested intervention plan for Michael, the case example for this chapter, will be elaborated.

Assessing the Problem

The behavioral assessment, in this case a functional behavioral assessment (FBA), is based on the hypothesis that specific environmental factors are related directly to problem behavior, these variables or factors can be identified through assessment, and addressing these factors systematically can reduce the problem behavior and/or support the development of more functional, pro-social behavior.

In the case of a child or youth with a conduct disorder, this assessment approach is particularly useful to teachers, because it helps them identify the purpose the maladaptive behavior serves. The FBA can be direct, through actual teacher observation and recording of the target behavior, or indirect, through what other sources such as peers, family members, and others may say. A simple way of establishing a direct FBA assessment is through the use of an **A-B-C record sheet**. (**A = Antecedents; B = Behavior; C = Consequence**; see Figure 2.1.)

ANTECEDENT-BEHAVIOR-CONSEQUENCE (A-B-C) RECORD SHEET

Recognized as important information in assessing the purpose served by maladaptive behaviors, the A-B-C record sheet provides the teacher with a convenient and efficient means of identifying and recording the events that trigger the target (maladaptive) behavior, as well as the consequences of that behavior that serve to maintain it.

FIGURE 2.1 A-B-C Recording Form

Student's Name: _____ Date: _____ Class: _____

Teacher: _____ Consultant: _____ Time: _____

In the *Behavior* column, note codes for target behaviors as they occur. You can also record additional information about the behavior, such as the name of the student who was hit when the behavior "hitting" occurred.

In the *Antecedent* column, record the code for the classroom activity and any specific event that occured just before the student exhibited the target behaviour.

In the consequence column, record what occured just after the behaviour using codes or brief narration.

Antecedent	Behavior	Consequence

List codes and their definitions here:

_____

Source: Witt, J. C., Daly, E., & Noell, G. H. (2000). *Functional assessments: A step-by step guide to solving academic and behavioral problems.* Longmont, CO: Sopris West.

An example of the use of the A-B-C record sheet is for a child who consistently hits other children in class. The teacher records the incidents of hitting (the target behavior) over the course of the day and also pays close attention to the activities or specific events that occurred just prior to the target behavior. Next, the teacher records the events that occurred just after the target behavior, using codes or brief narration.

SETTING EVENTS

Refers to antecedent events that "trigger" or provoke the target or undesired behavior.

MAINTAINING CONSEQUENCES

Refers to consequences that facilitate the perpetuation of the target or undesired behavior.

The result of this behavior recording is the development of a hypothesis that should include: (1) **setting events**, (2) immediate antecedent events, (3) problem behavior, and (4) **maintaining consequences** (outcomes that help maintain the behavior—which may be positive or negative). For example, if it is hypothesized that the child hits to stop verbal antagonism from a classmate, the consequence might be that the antagonism stops, thus negatively reinforcing the hitting (i.e., an aversive, the antagonism, is removed by hitting). However, if the child derives gratification through the intimidation of peers by hitting, then the fear and intimidation produced in the victims serves as a positive reinforcement for the behavior (hitting).

In Michael's case, three types of assessment were used: (1) a formalized interview, the *Diagnostic Interview for Children and Adolescents* (DICA-IV; Reich, 2000), (2) rating scales, in this case the *Child Behavior Checklist* (CBCL; Achenbach, 2001a, 2001b), and three direct observations. As noted earlier, assessment of CD should occur over time and should be multimodal. The results of these assessments helped to confirm the diagnosis of conduct disorder and provided Michael with special education services under the classification, *emotionally disturbed.*

Based on extensive evaluation, Michael's behaviors "targeted" for treatment included: (1) physical and verbal intimidation and aggression, (2) unprovoked anger and hostility toward others, and (3) blatant disregard for the rights and property of others. The purpose or "function" served by these behaviors was hypothesized to be Michael's need to expiate his anger toward his father, as well as his own sense of alienation from society.

A behavioral intervention plan was subsequently developed to address these behaviors and their root causes. Michael's positive response to this plan confirmed the correctness of the functional hypothesis and therefore this behavioral intervention plan was incorporated into his IEP.

Developing an Effective Intervention Plan

Most teachers have few resources or the time to conduct elaborate behavioral assessments, despite the recommendations of some researchers. Often, these researchers fail to understand the complexities of today's classroom, which are often overcrowded (especially in urban schools), have insufficient resources, and include several children with special needs. To compound these concerns, typical preadolescent and adolescent students often engage episodically in delinquent, antisocial acts as a function of psychosocial and physiological development aggravated by environmental factors. In the real world of the classroom, teachers, in the moment of crisis, need strategies they can employ with reasonable effectiveness and immediacy given the time constraints of the typical class period. Unfortunately, many current books and "how-to" manuals have not been classroom-tested and do not take into consideration these limitations.

Because students who have conduct disorder often manifest aggressive, intimidating, and coercive behaviors and are therefore perceived as threats to safety and good order, they are often expelled during the middle or high school grades. This tendency underscores the importance of effective assessment at the earliest opportunity to determine the presence of challenging, antisocial behaviors as well as academic deficiencies. Students who exhibit these behaviors consistently are more likely to be removed from the school experience or withdraw voluntarily (Walker & Severson, 2002). Before a student can be provided an effective intervention, the teacher must gain an understanding of the interpersonal dynamics of the student, including academic and social strengths and weaknesses, as well as personal preferences. Next, teachers must take a personal inventory of their own prejudices toward this type of child and find the motivation to work with these students for the duration of the school year. Finally, the teacher must seek out and develop a support group consisting of other teachers who work successfully with students who exhibit maladaptive or antisocial behavior.

Recommended interventions for teachers who provide instruction for students who have conduct disorder can be divided into two categories: instructional and cognitive-behavioral. However, the first step in selecting an appropriate intervention is to establish a rapport with each of the students in the class. Taking the time to learn a little about the students and including them in decision making helps establish the trust necessary to ensure that an affected student will participate in an intervention. This alliance may, in some cases, obviate the need for a more formal intervention. An effective way for teachers to achieve the trust and respect of their students is to develop a sense of community in the classroom. A teacher can facilitate this goal by providing opportunities for meaningful student input and participation, teaching and practicing active listening skills, presenting the students with purposeful learning experiences, and promoting student choices (Kohn, 1996).

Instructional Approaches

All instructional approaches are designed to provide the student who has CD challenging and meaningful learning experiences. This presupposes that the student's academic strengths and weaknesses have been clearly identified.

MOTIVATION TO LEARN For students who have emotional and behavioral disorders, motivation is essential to learning. An effective model to use to increase a student's motivation to learn is the *expectation X value theory* (Feather, 1985). This theory postulates that the extent to which people become actively involved in an activity depends on (1) whether they believe they can be successful at a task and (2) the degree to which they value the rewards associated with successful task completion. A third component, *climate,* addresses the importance of relationships within the task setting experienced during task engagement. Students who have EBD are not likely to be motivated to learn unless all three components are present: (1) they must feel they can accomplish the task; (2) they find value in the task; and (3) they can complete the task in a climate that is supportive of their basic needs. Sometimes it is more expedient for the teacher to find other tasks than to try to motivate students to do tasks that do not meet these three criteria.

Some of the ways successful learning and the ensuing academic achievement can be accomplished include: (1) matching instructional methods and cultural styles to optimize student engagement; and (2) helping students understand what it means to be an effective learner (see Figure 2.2).

It is very important that students who have a CD understand and practice the behaviors associated with good attendance and successful learning (e.g., eyes focused on the speaker, asking questions, asking for help when needed, cooperating with others, etc.) (Jones, Dohrn & Dunn, 2004).

IDENTIFY STRENGTHS AND ABILITIES Teachers need to help students who have EBD understand their individual learning strengths or special abilities. For example, a student who has a conduct disorder may not have strengths in interpersonal or intrapersonal functioning, but he or she may have artistic/spatial aptitudes that provide unique opportunities to explore learning and develop

FIGURE 2.2 Defining a Successful Learner

Looks Like	Sounds Like
Eyes focused on speaker	Gives encouragement
Concentrates on their work	Uses appropriate voice level
Is well organized	Asks questions
Cooperates with others	Asks for help when needed
Follows classroom rules and procedures	Shares their ideas with others
Sets goals	Comments are on-task
Stays calm when having a problem	Is courteous to others
Uses time wisely	Uses problem solving
Learns from mistakes	
Shares materials	
Does not give up	

A successful learner is someone who works hard, cooperates with others, takes risks, sets goals, makes a good effort, asks for help if needed, doesn't give up, and learns from his or her mistakes.

Source: Vernon F. Jones and Louise S. Jones, *Comprehensive Classroom Management: Creating Communities of Support and Solving Problems,* Sixth Edition. Published by Allyn and Bacon, Boston, MA. Copyright Pearson Education.

knowledge. Also, understanding and accommodating the different learning styles of students who have EBD facilitates learning for them. Some students may learn most effectively when a passage of text is read to them, whereas they are unable to process information from a printed source. Thus, providing an opportunity for oral reading or reviewing a tape-recorded lecture or lesson will really help these students to learn. Further, allowing students to organize their learning environment to some degree may be helpful. For example, some students who have conduct disorder evidence a high degree of distractibility and prefer working in a "low-stimulus" environment. These students may prefer working in a study carrel, for example (Dunn, Thies, & Honigsfeld, 2001; Jones et al., 2004).

PROVIDE APPROPRIATE STRATEGIES   Many students who have conduct disorder do not seem to know how to learn, so providing them with suitable strategies to do so can be of great help. One such approach involves teaching these students some study skills. For example, cognitive interventions needed in accomplishing a specific task can be taught; examples of such skills include underlining, highlighting, using a mnemonic, outlining, and summarizing. Metacognitive interventions include selecting and monitoring one's use of strategies and determining when and under which circumstances one strategy is preferable to another. Finally, students who have conduct disorder should be taught learning behaviors that reflect the right attitude towards learning and ones that show a willingness to participate in the learning process and cooperate with the teacher (Hattie, Biggs, & Purdie, 1996). When teaching these learning skills, it is important to tie them to the lesson requirements of the day or week within a specific context, rather than to generalize skills.

PROVIDE REAL-WORLD LEARNING   Research with students who have conduct disorder and other emotional or behavioral impairments has suggested the importance of incorporating real-world learning in the academic curriculum. An example of this approach is "real-world problem solving," in which students work together to solve problems that are relevant to their lives and their communities. Students might work in small groups to identify a need within their school or community and develop a solution, in which they must participate or contribute. A derivation of this notion is the concept of "service learning" used in various colleges and universities as an extension of their course curricula. The intention here, as with the concept applied to schools, is to provide enriching experiences and constructive interactions between students and their community. A suggested checklist for developing such a program within a school curriculum might include: (1) choosing a problem to work on, (2) creating a vision, (3) studying the problem, (4) accepting the risks, (5) making a commitment, (6) planning the project, and (7) executing the plan (Jones et al., 2004).

ADAPTATIONS, ACCOMMODATIONS, AND MODIFICATIONS   Another important aspect of effective instruction that is especially relevant to students who have conduct disorder is the provision of adaptations, accommodations, and modifications. *Adaptations* are essentially changes made to the environment, curriculum, instruction, and/or assessment that help to ensure success for the learner. *Accommodations* are alterations in presentation and response format, timing, environment, and/or scheduling that do not affect level, content, or performance criteria, but do provide the student with equal access to learning, as well as demonstrating what is known. *Modifications* represent changes in instructional level, content, and performance criteria that provide students with an opportunity to participate meaningfully and effectively in learning experiences (Jones et al., 2004). Effective curriculum and environmental adaptations for students who have EBD are predicated on the following assumptions: (1) that such adaptations are for all students; (2) that the adaptation is not new; (3) that adaptations are best developed through collaborative problem solving; (4) that they start with individual pupil goals; (5) that they maximize the participation of the student in the standard curriculum; and (6) that they can be supported by instructional strategies (Deschenes, Ebeling, & Sprague, 1994).

Some specific areas that lend themselves to adaptation include: (1) the size of the task (e.g., the number of problems assigned may be reduced to relieve the perceived pressure and tedium associated with excessive work volume); (2) time allotted for learning, completion, or testing (e.g., allotted time can be increased); (3) level of support (e.g., students may be provided more individualized attention through peer tutoring or by an instructional aide); (4) input of information (e.g., students may be provided with more examples, or instructions can be repeated and reinforced); (5) difficulty of the skill, problem, or rule (e.g., students may have the skill or task broken down into more manageable segments or steps); (6) output, or how students can demonstrate mastery (e.g., students can provide evidence of mastery using a portfolio, project, graphic model, demonstration, report, etc.); (7) participation (e.g., students who cannot, because of their disability, participate in traditional ways, can do so by alternative methods; for example, they may help construct a model rather than write a report [Deschenes et al., 1994]).

IMPROVE COMMUNICATION SKILLS   Research suggests that many students who have EBD lack the basic skills to communicate effectively (e.g., Edwards & Chard, 2000). For students at the middle and high school level, a strategy-based approach has demonstrated effectiveness in improving language and literacy skills. The reason for this success is thought to be its focus on increasing metacognitive and metalinguistic skills. For example, students are taught how to learn, not just what to learn. One strategy that helps students comprehend unfamiliar words is called by the acronym DISSECT. The steps of the strategy are (1) Discover the content (skip difficult words); (2) Isolate the prefix; (3) Separate the suffix; (4) Say the stem; (5) Examine the stem; (6) Check with someone; (7) Try the dictionary (Lenz & Hughes, 1990).

A similar strategy, the LINCS technique, helps students focus on the key aspects of vocabulary and then use visual imagery, mnemonic devices, and self-evaluation to facilitate encoding and recall. Each letter of LINCS, accordingly, represents *L*ist the parts, *I*magine the picture, *N*ote a reminding word, *C*onstruct a LINCing story, and *S*elf-test. In teaching the strategy, students are asked to write the new vocabulary on the top half of an index card and the definition on the other side. Next, they are told to choose a reminding word and to write that word on the bottom of the of the front of the card (e.g., if the vocabulary word is "sari," the student might choose "sorry" as the reminder word), and create a sentence about the meaning of the vocabulary word. In the last step, *S*elf-test, the student says both the vocabulary word and the reminder word while thinking of the LINCing sentence and the image created, states the meaning of the new word, and checks for correct spelling (Ellis, 1992).

Cognitive-Behavioral Approaches

Walker (1995) recommended several principles to communicate to students who have conduct disorder that they have value and teachers care about them. Many of the following approaches may be helpful in working with students like Michael, the student profiled in the case example for this chapter.

ESTABLISH A POSITIVE CLIMATE   Kohn (1996) elaborated on the idea of establishing a positive climate in his assertion that the classroom is a community, which he described as "a place in which students feel cared about and are encouraged to care about each other. They experience a sense of being valued and respected; the children matter to one another and to the teacher" (p. 101). Given the antisocial nature of the student who has conduct disorder, whose experiences at home and typically at school are primarily of rejection and exclusion, a supportive, inclusive classroom may be critical to his or her rehabilitation.

CREATE HIGH EXPECTATIONS   A second principle that is relevant to teachers working with students who have conduct disorder is to establish and communicate high expectations in achievement and behavior for all students. Students who have conduct disorder are often very adept at manipulating teachers to lower standards, whether through intimidation, coercion, or negotiation. It is important that these students learn that these are ineffective approaches and they will be expected to produce consistently high-caliber work as is required of every student in the class.

STRUCTURED LEARNING ENVIRONMENT   Teachers should provide a structured learning environment in which students know what is expected of them and to whom to go to for assistance with social and academic issues. Research supports the importance of providing structure in the lives of students who have conduct disorder because, generally, their lives and families are in disarray, which increases their frustration and behavioral volatility (Kauffman, 2005).

COOPERATIVE LEARNING   Teachers are encouraged to employ cooperative learning strategies that permit small, diverse groups of students to interact, problem-solve, and develop collaborative skills. Most students who have conduct disorder adopt a "me against them" attitude in social situations. Assigning them to work with a small group of students who are congenial and empathetic can help the student who has CD feel valued and connected, and begin to develop necessary social skills.

POSITIVE REINFORCEMENT   Research and experience support the value of showing appreciation for the small behavioral gains made by students who have CD. Encouragement and praise, when related to a specific gain or accomplishment, are very powerful reinforcers because these students are more often criticized and admonished for failures and ineptitude. Teachers can demonstrate care for these students by communicating a genuine interest in their academic progress and personal development.

SOCIAL SKILLS TRAINING   Behavior-change programs have not had great success with students who have conduct disorder, but some social skills training programs have shown better results (Walker et al., 2004). In implementing any form of social skills training, it is important that the training be conducted in the natural environment. For example, if the targeted skill involves appropriate communication between students and authority figures, students should have an opportunity to practice the skill in authentic conversation with parents, teachers, and administrators. In addition, social skills training should encompass the following areas: (1) cooperation (e.g., helping others, following rules), (2) assertion (e.g., asking others for information), (3) responsibility (e.g., caring for property or work of self or others), (4) empathy (e.g., showing respect for others' feelings and ideas), and (5) self-control (e.g., responding appropriately to teasing and name-calling, compromising) (Walker et al., 2004). Likewise, selected social skills interventions should promote skill acquisition, enhance skill performance, remove or reduce competing problem behaviors, and facilitate the generalization and maintenance of the acquired social skills (Gresham, 2007).

Three key approaches used to teach appropriate social skills are **coaching, modeling**, and **behavior rehearsal**. Coaching involves teaching social skills in three consecutive steps: (1) presenting social concepts, (2) providing opportunities for practicing the targeted social skills, and (3) providing specific informational feedback regarding the student's performance. Essentially, coaching involves telling a student how to perform a specific social skill and providing oral feedback about the student's performance (Elliot & Gresham, 1991).

Modeling is based on the principles of observational learning and vicarious reinforcement (Bandura, 1977). In essence, observers (in this case, students who have CD) learn a behavior by being vicariously reinforced as they watch the model (teacher or caregiver) receiving reinforcement for effective social skills performance. The modeling should be conducted in a natural setting—when and where this behavior typically occurs. For example, the teacher can model appropriate respectful dialogue with an authority figure by asking the school principal to visit the classroom during a lesson and then soliciting a discussion about the nature of the exchange with the class afterwards.

Lastly, behavior rehearsal involves practicing a newly acquired social skill in structured role play. The advantage of this approach is that it provides students with an opportunity to practice the social skill without being concerned about negative consequences that might result from mistakes. This safeguard is particularly helpful in encouraging students who have conduct disorder to try out a new social skill without fear of negative social repercussions or rejection. Behavior rehearsal can be conducted in three ways: covert, verbal, and overt. In *covert rehearsal,* the student imagines or thinks through the use of the social skill in a specific situation. *Verbal rehearsal* requires that the student talk through the social skills application, and *overt rehearsal* requires that the student actually perform the social skill within a hypothetical situation (Gresham, 2007).

The behavioral intervention plan developed for Michael, based on the results of his functional behavioral assessment, focused primarily on learning strategies and cognitive-behavioral approaches. Concerning learning strategies, Michael's teachers were encouraged to provide him with reasonable academic goals, meaningful learning tasks, assignments that optimized success and thus increased self-confidence, alternative assessments, as well as "choices" in the selection of curriculum. The underlying assumption was that if Michael could be provided the opportunity to succeed academically, his self-esteem would also flourish. It was believed that much of Michael's aggression and hostility were fueled by his own lack of confidence and self-worth.

The cognitive-behavioral approaches employed by Michael's teachers included the use of positive reinforcement to encourage his participation in classroom social and learning activities. In addition, his teachers deliberately involved him in all aspects of classroom routine, from cooperative group activities to everyday duties and responsibilities. Lastly, Michael's teachers used the "teachable moment" to reinforce the social skills training that he is receiving in the Coping Power Program (Lochman & Wells, 2002), an after-school program that is part of Michael's multisystemic therapy. Michael's teachers are provided

COACHING

Coaching involves telling a student how to perform a specific social skill and providing oral feedback about the student's performance (Elliot & Gresham, 1991).

MODELING

Describes an intervention in which observers—in this case, students who have an emotional or behavioral disorder—learn a behavior by being vicariously reinforced as they watch the model (teacher or caregiver) receiving reinforcement for effective social skills performance. The modeling should be conducted in a natural setting—in other words, when and where this behavior typically occurs.

BEHAVIORAL REHEARSAL

Involves the practice of a newly acquired social skill within structured role play. The advantage of this approach is that it provides students with an opportunity to practice a social skill without concern for the negative consequences that can result from mistakes.

support from the school psychologist as they encounter behavioral challenges from Michael that exceed their capability. He has been a valuable resource in the implementation of the behavioral intervention plan.

 FROM THE FIELD

Lisa Goldberg, MSED.

Lisa Goldberg is a special education Teacher at a high school for students who have emotional and behavioral disorders.

Lisa, can you provide our readers with your "sense" of the typical student you work with who has been identified as having a conduct disorder?

Students who have conduct disorder tend to be smart, capable individuals who refuse to comply with classroom rules, school guidelines, or behave in a socially acceptable way despite intellectual ability. Frequently these individuals are identified as "bad kids" that are regularly in trouble. These students are commonly found to come from backgrounds that include abuse, traumatic experiences, haphazard parenting, and school failure. Typically these individuals have a history that includes initiating physically aggressive behavior towards others, bullying, threatening and intimidating behavior, property destruction, and show little empathy or concern for others, feelings, wishes or the well-being, and they blame others for their own behavior. They are the students who require a great deal of your attention and management. These students can be aggressive or act in a passive aggressive manner, rebelling against your every effort to effectually change, shape, and create new behavior patterns.

In your estimation, what are the greatest challenges these students pose to teachers and teaching?

These students frequently disrupt the regular pattern of the classroom, despite all of the behavior modification techniques you employ. These students generally attract a lot of attention from both classroom staff and peers alike. Frequently, students who have conduct disorder will employ any means they can to draw the attention of their peers in order to increase their own status and diminish the control of the teacher. Maintaining ongoing continuums of learning can be very challenging with these individuals in the classroom. In addition, these students have generally developed a history that includes ongoing fear and distrust of adults. All of this adds to a student's well-developed poor self-image. Their habit is to fail and be in trouble, and changing their normal, which is the heart of effectively teaching them new behaviors, is the greatest challenge a teacher faces when working with these individuals.

What are some potential "mistakes" that new teachers can make when working with a student who has conduct disorder?

New teachers may initially see the child's behavior as being personally about them and act in a reactionary manner. It is important for all teachers to be proactive and have interventions in place for handling a student's behavior. Educators need to maintain awareness that a student's oppositional behavior is frequently a way for that individual to manage his or her anxiety to perceived demands by the teacher and the school setting in general. These students are in desperate need of positive learning and success experiences. Recognition of this is key to changing the pattern of failure these students are accustomed to.

Can you provide a few of your most effective strategies for working successfully with these students? For, example, tips that you wish someone had given you when you started working with this population?

Being able to identify a child's "island of competence," that which they truly enjoy and do well, can be a huge factor in providing initial success experiences for these individuals. A proactive environment that is adaptable to the student's needs and provides short-term, somewhat easily achievable goals will give the student quick sense of success, which can be transferred, over time, to those behaviors that are targeted for change. It is extremely important to remember that in order to make long-term changes in these individual's behavior, specific target behaviors must be identified and worked on consistently. Consistent positive reinforcement will, over time, effect change in a more permanent manner than those behavior modification techniques that are merely disciplinary. Positive incentives may initially have to be tangible, as intrinsic values are not generally developed in these students, as they are uncommonly instilled in their at risk environment. Teachers and students should be working on goals that can be achieved over a relatively short time, providing near-immediate success initially, and over time, extend those goals to things that require a greater period to achieve, always keeping in mind that positive reinforcement, catching them doing something good and rewarding it, is going to be more effective than punishing these individuals. Punishment has been their whole world; it is our job to change that pattern and provide new experiences for them to relish.

Finally Lisa, could you share an anecdote from your teaching repertoire that highlights one of your most memorable successes in working with a student who has a conduct disorder?

Teaching students with conduct disorder has been one of the greatest challenges I have experienced, but it's yielded some of the most rewarding experiences I've had. While working in a residential treatment center for inner-city, court-mandated students who had piled up failure experiences and seen more of life's difficulties by 15 than others might see in a lifetime, *challenge* was the name of the game. I spent

years developing a program for students with significant gaps in their education, reading levels that were a minimum of 5 years below grade level, patterns of failure in the classroom, and experiences with court interventions and incarceration. Teaching these students, who were mainly but not totally male, ranging in ages from 15 to 21, required me to build a program that redeveloped success patterns, provided proactive interventions, taught them, through modeling, good examples and their own experiences, how to develop positive relationships with both peers and adults, and be ready to learn in a structured environment. Teaching my students to trust, for many of them the first time in their lives they had anyone they could trust, was a key factor in providing them with the initial success experiences necessary to breaking the pattern of failure that they had become so accustomed to. Accommodating all students, and individualizing curriculum, learning pace, and measurable expectations lay the groundwork for successful learning experiences such as these young people had not yet encountered.

Consistent positive reinforcement, rules, and—most importantly—consistent expectations eventually began to pay off. Students who, when they came to me, were nearing societal exile and a future that would almost definitely include incarceration, were able to learn acceptable behavior patterns that enabled them to participate in work study programs, off-campus jobs, and eventually graduate from high school, many with model of behavior that would allow them to be good citizens and members of the world community, not the burden they were bound to become prior to arrival in my program.

One of the most memorable of these students was Joey. Joey came to me at age 15, reading a K.9 level [Kindergarten, ninth month of the school year]. He did not recognize his own name in writing, did not know his address, and had already been incarcerated in high-level juvenile facilities prior to his arrival. Joey had spent much time in and out of school, because of his continued deteriorating pattern of behavior, as well as mere school avoidance. From his perspective, he was already so far behind that even a day or two was so overwhelming to face the huge task in front of him, in order of catch up with his peers, that he avoided school altogether and ran the streets instead. Joey was very accustomed to adults belittling him, reminding him of his failures, his inabilities, and intimidation had become his way of life.

Teaching Joey involved finding something that Joey would be able to focus on, that he did well, and even minimally could admit he enjoyed in order to provide him the immediate success experiences he so desperately needed. We quickly learned, although through discussion of his criminal escapades, that Joey was very automotively intuitive. Joey could tell you anything you needed to know about a car, inside out, diagnose and solve any problem he encountered related to the automobile. Identifying this "island of competence" was key in providing Joey with an initial increase in self-esteem, and identifying intact skills that we focused on transferring to other areas of the curriculum. In addition, modeling positive relationships was another key factor in Joey's reentering society in an effective manner.

Although students did not normally remain in our program for very long, Joey was with us for a little over two years. In that time, I was able to build a positive relationship with Joey, helped him improve his self-esteem, which in turn allowed him to risk venturing into areas that he had previously found overwhelming. I was also able to target key behaviors and begin the process of shaping them and extinguishing problem behaviors that Joey had developed during his many years of running the streets. Using behavior modification techniques like positive reinforcement, cost response systems, and tangible rewards, I was able to assist Joey in developing a series of successes, positive behaviors, and coping strategies for him to use when encountering situations that would otherwise have thrown him into old, well-formed habits.

At the end of Joey's stay in my program, Joey had grown to an individual who was able to read and write at a fourth-grade reading level, and hold down a job. He successfully stayed off of probation and no longer faced legal ramifications from his pattern of behavior. Three years after leaving my program, Joey came to visit with his mechanic's certification in hand, successfully holding down a job in a reputable station, maintained his own residence, and had become an effective member of the community.

Summary

This chapter began by providing an overview of conduct disorder, an emotional or behavioral disorder that creates challenging management situations for classroom teachers in particular and school personnel in general. The etiology of CD is more often than not mutlifactorial, and in clinical settings, a number of treatment modalities have been shown to be relatively effective. In the school setting, however, it is important to carefully determine the purpose served by the problem behavior as it pertains to the classroom and school environments in order to provide more relevant, effective interventions. This investigative process is referred to as a functional behavioral assessment or FBA (IDEA, 1997; 2004).

In working in the classroom with students who have CD, teachers can employ several effective interventions. The most helpful of these involve both instructional and cognitive-behavioral approaches such as those described in this chapter. It is also important that teachers find ways to establish rapport with these students. One way is to include them in all aspects of the classroom, accept and welcome them as constituents in the classroom "community," and engage them in meaningful learning activities.

Frustration, anger, and resentment are often the feelings that teachers use to describe the visceral effects produced by students who have conduct disorder. However, if teachers can better understand the nature of this disorder and have available a repertoire of effective, research-based interventions, they are much less likely to feel overwhelmed by the disruptive behaviors exhibited by affected students.

Tips for Teachers

Teachers are urged to keep in mind the following strategies to improve the quality of their interactions with students who have CD.

1. Build a sense of community and belonging that includes every student in your classroom.
2. Establish rules of conduct as a class, and include yourself and their expectations of you in the discussion.
3. Provide for choices—meaningful and appropriate ones.
4. Triage the crises: Some, such as a fist fight, require immediate attention; others, such as an epithet uttered under the breath, do not.
5. Provide *meaningful* praise and positive reinforcement. Connect the praise to a discrete accomplishment or behavior, *not* to some vague or future possibility.
6. Find a reason to appreciate every student in your class. There must be some quality the student possesses that can be viewed as a positive or strength.
7. Get to know the likes and dislikes, the hobbies and pastimes, the passions and dreams of your students—this will help build relationships, and no one can truly provide help without relationships. Similarly, a teacher cannot be simultaneously uncaring and effective—not with a student who has CD.
8. Provide meaningful learning experiences for your students; connect the lesson to real-life applications.
9. Ignore small annoyances and disruptions. Students who have CD will try to provoke their teacher—they expect to be disliked. Try not to fall into a contest of wills.
10. Be consistent and fair with each student. Treating each student fairly, especially those with CD, does not mean treating each student the same. Would it be fair to expect a student who has cerebral palsy to run competitively in a race with physically able students? Essentially, being consistent with rewards and consequences means just that (adapted from Cavin, 1998).

Although teachers have the most sustained contact with students in their classrooms who have a conduct disorder, teachers cannot provide the therapeutic interventions that have shown the greatest promise in treating CD. In fact, a multisystemic treatment strategy has demonstrated the greatest benefit for these students. This approach incorporates family systems therapy and takes into account other systems that affecting the students. School personnel are in a unique position to facilitate these interventions and to provide coordination of services with families and other social units. Lamentably, research has suggested that there is often little coordination between teachers and other helpers (Walker et al., 2004). Our hope is that the information provided in this chapter will facilitate collaboration between teachers and other professionals who play significant roles in the therapeutic process. Perhaps, then, students like Michael, who have a conduct disorder, will be provided a coherent, effective intervention plan that will help them experience success in school and in life.

Focus Questions Revisited

This final section of the chapter comprises a brief question-and-answer discussion of typical concerns raised by teachers who work with students who have CD. It may be particularly helpful for preservice and less experienced teachers to consider the behavioral profile of Michael, presented in the case example, while considering these questions.

1. What are the defining characteristics of a conduct disorder?

A Sample Response

The following represent the key characteristics that help to identify a conduct disorder: a repetitive and persistent pattern of behavior in which the basic rights of others or major age-appropriate societal norms or rules are violated, as manifested by the presence of three (or more) of the following criteria in the past twelve months, with at least one criterion present in the past 6 months:

1. Often bullies, threatens, or intimidates others
2. Often initiates physical fights
3. Has used a weapon that can cause serious physical harm to others (e.g., a bat, brick, broken bottle, knife, gun)
4. Has been physically cruel to people
5. Has been physically cruel to animals
6. Has stolen while confronting a victim (e.g., mugging, purse snatching, extortion, armed robbery)
7. Has forced someone into sexual activity
8. Has deliberately engaged in fire setting with the intention to cause serious damage
9. Has deliberately destroyed others' property (other than by fire setting)
10. Has broken into someone else's house, building, or car
11. Often lies to obtain goods or favors or to avoid obligations (i.e., "cons" others)
12. Has stolen items of nontrivial value without confronting a victim (e.g., shoplifting, but without breaking and entering; forgery)
13. Often stays out at night despite parental prohibitions, beginning before age 13
14. Has run away from home overnight at least twice while living in parental or parental

surrogate home (or once without returning for a lengthy period (DSM-IV-TR; APA, 2000).

2. How can I effectively diffuse a behavioral crisis in my classroom that involves a student who has a conduct disorder?

Sample Response A

One method that has been successful in many schools is the Life Space Crisis Intervention (LSCI) (Long, Wood, & Fecsur, 2001). This approach to a perceived or real crisis involving a student allows the teacher to use a classroom conflict to provide the student with insight into the problem, thus enabling him to regain emotional control and make rationale choices. LSCI is used to help students who are dealing with a crisis that is of such intensity they cannot be supported by the traditional tactics used by their teachers. LSCI can empower the teacher to turn a conflict into a meaningful learning experience for the student by determining what fuels his behavior and by defining the purpose served by the behavior (Long et al., 2001). According to Long and Morse (1996), LSCI can help the student discover that: (1) a crisis does not mean adult rejection or alienation; (2) an adult can still see potential for growth and positive attributes despite the student's loss of control during the crisis; (3) there is relationship between perception and behavior; (4) he exhibits a chronic pattern of nonproductive behaviors; (5) he can accept responsibility for his behavior; and (6) he can trust professional caregivers and teachers.

There are six stages in implementing a LSCI:

1. The student's crisis stage and the staff's deescalation stage (i.e., help define the child's irrational volatility)
2. The student's timeline stage and the staff's relationship skills (i.e., have the student develop a detailed, step-by-step narrative of the entire incident, beginning with events that preceded it)
3. The student's central issues stage and the staff's differential diagnosis skills (i.e., identify the central issue and determine whether the

issue represents a pattern or is merely an isolated episode)

4. The student's insight stage and the staff's clinical skills (i.e., carry out the appropriate intervention, which should provide the students and staff with insights regarding the undesired behavior, prompting a discussion of more effective and appropriate behavior alternatives)

5. The student's new skill stage and the staff's empowering skills (i.e., an opportunity for the teacher to present alternative pro-social skills)

6. The student's transfer-of-training stage and the staff's follow-up skills (i.e., establish expectations for the student to return to class and participate meaningfully) (Long et al., 2001)

This technique may have a viable application in a case such as Michael's when a student has physically or verbally assaulted another student, threatened a student or teacher, or damaged or destroyed school property.

Sample Response B

Another strategy that may be effective in addressing a serious crisis in the classroom, such as a fight between two students, is to isolate the combatants by insisting that other students leave the classroom. The teacher then asks one of the more responsible students to get help from the school's crisis intervention team. It is important to note that no teacher should attempt to break up a serious altercation between two adolescents without the assistance of other adults. Even physically smaller youth can cause serious injury to an adult (often the student who escapes restraint). One teacher, alone, can effectively restrain only one student (if the student is physically less powerful than the teacher), leaving the other student free to assault the restrained student without impedance. Teachers are cautioned that, ideally, two physically fit adults are required to safely restrain one typical adolescent. When the safety of staff and students cannot be assured, teachers should call for the assistance of law enforcement officers.

For crises that have not escalated to involve physical aggression or assault, but that have become seriously disruptive and antagonistic (e.g., verbal assaults, temper tantrums, verbal tirades,

oppositional defiance, and threats), once again, the authors recommend isolating the antagonist by asking him to leave the room. However, state and federal laws have established that teachers are responsible for the safety and supervision of all students assigned to them for the duration of the class period (see, e.g., Alexander & Alexander, 1992; Mawdsley, 1993). Thus, the teacher or teacher's aide should always accompany a student sent into the hall or to the office for corrective purposes. Nonetheless, if the angry, agitated, or hostile student can be calmed sufficiently, it is preferable to continue with the classroom activity, allowing the student the opportunity to sit calmly and regain composure. The nature and cause of the crisis should be addressed as soon as possible after class (perhaps employing a LSCI).

3. Students who have conduct disorder can be defiant and verbally confrontational. What is the best way to deal with these behaviors when they occur in the classroom?

A Sample Response

If a student who has CD or oppositional defiant disorder makes an offensive comment or uses patently offensive language, the best strategy is to ignore the behavior if possible. However, if the behavior persists and becomes disruptive to the learning environment, the student should be confronted firmly and calmly. One of the authors simply describes the offensive behavior and why it is so disruptive to the class, asks the offending student to refrain from the behavior, and reminds the student of the prescribed consequence if the behavior persists. The important aspects of this process are consistency and certainty: If the behavior is not curtailed, the student will incur the appropriate consequence. That the appropriate consequence will be administered by the teacher is certain—there can be no exceptions or deviations. However, it is important to note two things here: (1) the classroom rules of conduct should be meaningfully determined by the students and teacher in keeping with the desire to build community in the classroom; and (2) the teacher must, at all times, maintain composure and explain the rules and consequences in a matter-of-fact manner. Giving way to outrage, frustration, or fear will provide a student who has a conduct disorder an insight into the teacher's vulnerabilities, which he might exploit later.

4. Because many students who have conduct disorder are co-diagnosed with ADHD, how can I deal effectively with their impulsiveness and off-task behavior?

A Sample Response

It may be unreasonable to expect these students to remain seated, calmly working on a task for 45 minutes. One of the authors has established a "signal" whereby a student who exhibits hyperactivity and impulsive behaviors can obtain a pass to the bathroom or be assigned an "important" errand that will allow him legitimately to leave his seat and move around. Furthermore, providing meaningful and interesting learning tasks that can be completed in a 10 to 15 minute interval helps maintain student interest and provides the novelty and change the student needs to maintain focus. In addition, research has suggest that students who have CD and ADHD are seldom given options or choices; they are thus deprived of opportunities to participate in planning their learning experiences (Kauffman, 2004). Providing preselected choices or options for assignments or thematic units is a way to instill in these students a sense of ownership and thus empowerment. When provided such an option by one of the authors, one student seemed quite moved and stated, "I've never in my life been given a choice before, except do I want to be expelled or sent to Juvy [Juvenile Hall]."

Chapter 3

Oppositional Defiant Disorder

Photodisc/Getty Images

FOCUS QUESTIONS

1. Why is it so important that we address oppositional defiant disorder (ODD) behaviors observed in our students quickly and effectively?

2. What characteristic behaviors are symptomatic of ODD?

3. What does research say about the probable causes of ODD?

4. How is ODD appropriately assessed?

5. According to the best practice evidence provided in this chapter, which treatment option appears to be most effective? What are its principal strengths?

6. Suppose you have a student in your classroom who has ODD. What are some interventions you might employ to help him control and, ultimately, reduce his defiant behaviors while simultaneously increasing his pro-social ones?

7. What other professional support might you solicit in your efforts to help a student who has ODD?

Many researchers have regarded *oppositional defiant disorder* (ODD) as a term that identifies a separate category of emotional or behavioral disorder related to conduct disorder and attention-deficit hyperactivity disorder (ADHD) (e.g., Maughan, Rowe, Messer, Goodman, & Meltzer, 2004), whereas others have viewed it as an antecedent (Eaves et al., 2000). Students who have ODD display characteristic behaviors that often include (1) frequent loss of temper, (2) frequent arguing with adults, (3) refusal to comply with rules or requests of authority figures (adults), (4) exhibiting intentionally annoying behavior, (5) blaming others for his or her mistakes, (6) being easily annoyed by others, (7) being frequently angry or resentful, and (8) engaging in spiteful or vengeful behaviors (American Psychiatric Association, 2000, p. 102). Several of these behaviors are evident in the case example about "Jack Straw," which follows this introduction.

In this chapter we examine the characteristics, causes, and prevalence that delineate ODD, and, most importantly, we describe some of the most effective interventions that can assist teachers in working successfully with these individuals. Furthermore, we provide a research-based intervention plan predicated on a systematic assessment of the disruptive behavior in order to determine its ultimate purpose.

Students who have disruptive disorders, such as conduct disorder, ADHD, or oppositional defiant disorder, are unquestionably among the most challenging children to teach. Current studies on the cause of teacher attrition have indicated the primary cause to be the necessity of working with students who are defiant and disruptive. In addition, research on the academic performance of these students has shown that they typically perform poorly in school and have higher dropout rates than students who do not have these problems.

A search for causes, in most cases, points to ineffective parenting practices, such as lax supervision, inconsistent discipline, excessive punishment, volatile discipline, and inflexibility in discipline practices (Chamberlain & Patterson,

1995; Patterson, Reid, & Dishion, 1992). Logically, therefore, the most recommended interventions involve, to some degree, the parents of these children. For example, the three most popular treatment programs for individuals with ODD are Parent–Child Interaction Therapy (PCIT; Schuhmann, Foote, Eyberg, Boggs, & Algina, 1998), joint Problem Solving Skills Training (PSST) and Parent Management Training (PMT) (Kazdin, 2005), and the Incredible Years Training Series (IYTS) (Webster-Stratton & Reid, 2003), which includes a parent intervention training component.

Students who have ODD unquestionably represent a challenge to all teachers. They are often narcissistic, unpleasant to deal with, and disruptive to the lesson. However, contrary to the predictions of some of our colleagues, these students are not "lost causes," nor should we simply try to teach over, around, or in spite of them, as some teachers have suggested. These children often present oppositional defiant behaviors in the classroom because they feel "safe" to act out the accumulated frustrations acquired at home. For example, they know that most teachers typically will not react violently, as their parent might, or, conversely, provide inconsistent discipline. If we understand the underlying cause of the ODD, we will stop feeling "singled out" or exploited, stop feeling abused and indignant, and start to see that we are uniquely positioned to make a difference in the life of a very misunderstood and misrepresented child: For teachers, "the buck must stop here!"

CASE EXAMPLE: Jack Straw

Jack Straw is currently enrolled in a middle school in the southern United States. He has a history of disruptive behavior that dates back to the early elementary grades. Examples of this behavior include talking back to the teacher, using rude gestures when frustrated or angry with authority figures in the school, instigating fights with peers through verbal assaults, as well as chronic lateness to class and episodic truancy. His behavior has become so problematic that he has been recommended for evaluation for special education services under the classification of "emotionally disturbed." Jack's parents are very defensive when he is accused of disruptive behavior in the school. They state that they have never experienced or observed this type of oppositional defiant behavior at home and suggest that the teachers and administrators in the school are reactive and prejudiced. Jack's current behavior in class is typified by the following examples.

In September of this year, during Ms. Detmer's inaugural class in science, Jack turned to the student sitting behind him and proceeded to tell an off-color joke loud enough to be heard throughout the room. When Ms. Detmer asked him to turn around and pay attention to her lesson, Jack replied angrily that he would gladly pay attention if there was something worth paying attention to. Ms. Detmer asked Jack to apologize for the rude remark or leave the class. Jack looked defiantly at the teacher and said that his parents told him he had every right to stay in the class because they provide taxes that pay the teachers' salaries. Despite unsuccessful appeals for Jack to remove himself voluntarily from the class, Ms. Detmer finally called the office and had Jack escorted to the detention room. As he was leaving the room, Jack asserted that he would report this incident to his parents and they would call a lawyer and "have her job."

In another incident involving the language arts teacher, Mr. Ferris, Jack was accused of shooting "spitballs" at the teacher, whose back was turned, which Jack vehemently denied. Several of the other students corroborated the teacher's suspicions and Jack became outraged, hurling epithets at both the students who "ratted him out" and the teacher who "is always ragging on me." Once again, Jack needed to be escorted from the room because he refused to leave of his own accord. As Jack left the room, he repeated the threat that he would have the teacher "fired" for accusing him of something he did not do.

Perhaps the most serious episode occurred just last week in homeroom. Workmen were repairing the large plate-glass window on the back wall of the classroom. The homeroom teacher, Mrs. Blenkinsop, had just reminded her students to avoid going near the back wall, because of the precarious and dangerous condition of the large window. As an additional precaution, the workmen had boarded up the window and placed large signs around the structure warning students and staff to stay away from the window. Just as the bell rang, announcing dismissal to first-period class, Jack danced over to the window and said, "You can touch the stupid window, nothing's going to happen." He then proceeded to push at the windowsill, looking defiantly at the homeroom teacher, who lunged forward to stop him. Unfortunately, she was unable to reach him in time, and the entire window broke free and toppled to the sidewalk two stories below. Luckily, no one was directly below at the time, and the shards of glass plummeted harmlessly to the lawn below, leaving students and staff unscathed.

As a result of his impulsive act and blatant disregard for the directions of his teacher, as well as the safety of others, Jack was suspended for 5 days with an administrative hearing required before he was allowed to return to school. Jack's parents were outraged and are suing the school for requiring students to remain in a classroom with such hazardous conditions. His parents are also suing the homeroom teacher for negligence in endangering a minor by exposing their son to an environmental hazard. Upon his return from the 5-day suspension, Jack muttered under his breath, "Your days are numbered," as he passed Mrs. Blenkinsop's desk. When confronted by administrators about the alleged threat, Jack vehemently denied saying anything and contended, "Mrs. Blenkinsop was lying just to get me in trouble because she knows my parents will win [their lawsuit]."

Oppositional defiant disorder is one of three disorders in the more general category of disruptive behavior disorder (DBD), the other two being attention-deficit hyperactivity disorder (ADHD) and conduct disorder (CD). There has been considerable controversy over the years as to whether ODD and CD are separable disorders. The DSM-IV-TR (American Psychiatric Association, 2000) has maintained them as two distinct disorders, but does not allow that ODD be diagnosed in the presence of CD—an indication that ODD might be considered a precursor to CD. Table 3.1 presents the DSM-IV-TR diagnostic criteria for ODD. The various versions of the DSM have refined the symptom list for ODD to distinguish it from normal behavior. For example, the DSM-IV (American Psychiatric Association, 1994) eliminated swearing and using obscene language from the diagnostic criteria. This same version increased the diagnostic threshold from three to four symptoms to reduce the number of false positives (Lahey, Applegate, Barkley, & Garfinkel, 1994; Pardini & Lochman, 2003).

Research has been inconclusive as to whether ODD and CD should be considered separately or together. Eaves et al. (2000) found that they are components of the same underlying disorder, in contrast to Maughan, Rowe, Messer, Goodman, and Meltzer (2004), who found that the two disorders follow different developmental trends and differ comorbidly. Factor analytic studies of

TABLE 3.1 DSM-IV-TR Diagnostic Criteria for ODD

A. A pattern of negativistic, hostile, and defiant behavior lasting as least 6 months, during which four (or more) of the following are present:

1. Often loses temper
2. Often argues with adults
3. Often actively defies or refuses to comply with adults' requests or rules
4. Often deliberately annoys people
5. Often blames others for his or her mistakes or misbehavior
6. Is often touchy or easily annoyed by others
7. Is often angry and resentful
8. Is often spiteful or vindictive

Note: Consider a criterion met only if the behavior occurs more frequently than is typically observed in individuals of comparable age and developmental level.

B. The disturbance in behavior causes clinically significant impairment in social, academic, or occupational functioning.
C. The behaviors do not occur exclusively during the course of a Psychotic or Mood Disorder.
D. Criteria are not met for Conduct Disorder, and, if the individual is 18 years of age of older, criteria are not met for Antisocial Personality Disorder.

Source: From *Diagnostic and Statistical Manual of Mental Disorders, Fourth Edition, Text Revision* (p. 102) by the American Psychiatric Association, 2000, Washington DC: Author. Copyright by the American Psychiatric Association. Reprinted with permission.

ODD and CD have resulted in two separate factor loadings, although the factors are intercorrelated (Frick et al., 1991; Frick, Lahey, Applegate, & Kerdyck, 1994). What is clear, however, is that not all children and adolescents who are diagnosed with ODD progress to CD (Rowe, Maughan, Costello, & Angold, 2005). Approximately two-thirds of children diagnosed with ODD do *not* develop CD (Biederman, Faraone, Milberger, & Jetton, 1996; Hinshaw, 1994b), and there are adolescents who develop CD without having had an earlier diagnosis of ODD (Pardini & Lochman, 2003). The progression from ODD to CD appears to depend on three classes of risk factors: child characteristics, parenting practices, and family organization problems (Behan & Carr, 2000). Early onset, greater severity, frequent physical fighting, parental substance abuse, and low socioeconomic status are factors that increase the risk of ODD progressing to CD (Hendren & Mullen, 2006; Loeber, Green, Keenan, & Lahey, 1995).

PREVALENCE AND COMORBIDITY

Disruptive behavior disorders, in general, account for approximately 75 percent of the mental health disorders diagnosed in childhood and adolescence (Quay & Hogan, 1999). Prevalence rates for ODD range anywhere from 2 to 16 percent

(American Psychiatric Association, 2000). This wide range is due to the histori-cal lack of precision in diagnosing ODD and the difficulty in distinguishing mild ODD (e.g., tantrums, crying, screaming) from normal, developmentally appro-priate behavior (Greene, 2006). ODD is twice as common in boys as in girls, and it is most frequently diagnosed in children under age 8.

ODD rarely exists alone, and it is highly comorbid with ADHD and with anxiety and mood disorders. Approximately 80 percent of those diagnosed with ODD have ADHD, and about 60 percent of those diagnosed with ADHD have ODD (Greene et al., 2002). Several studies have examined the overlap between ODD and mood and anxiety disorders (see, e.g., Biederman et al., 1996; Geller & Luby, 1997; Wozniak, Biederman, Kiely, & Ablon, 1995). Greene et al. (2002) found that 80 percent of children diagnosed with major depression and 85 percent of those diagnosed with bipolar disorder also had a diagnosis of ODD. In this same study, 45 percent of youth diagnosed with an anxiety disor-der had a coexisting diagnosis of ODD, and more than 60 percent of those diag-nosed with ODD had a coexisting anxiety disorder. Studies have also indicated a strong association between language impairment and ODD (Gilmour, Hill, Place, & Skuse, 2004; Rogers-Adkinson & Griffin, 1999; Westby, 1999). Greene et al. (2002) found that 55 percent of youth diagnosed with a language disorder had also been diagnosed with ODD. Finally, because a defining characteristic of ODD is social impairment, studies have looked at the overlap between ODD and autism spectrum disorder (ASD). In one study, more than half of the chil-dren diagnosed with an ASD also met the criteria for ODD (Greene et al., 2002).

CHARACTERISTICS OF ODD

As the diagnostic label suggests, the defining characteristics of ODD are oppo-sition and defiance that follow a behavioral pattern and are developmentally in-appropriate, with high levels of negativistic, disobedient, and hostile behavior, especially toward authority figures.

> Specific behaviors associated with ODD include temper outbursts, persistent stubbornness, resistance to directions, unwillingness to compromise, give in, or negotiate with adults or peers; deliberate or persistent testing of limits; and verbal (and minor physical) aggres-sion. These behaviors are almost always present in the home and with individuals the child knows well, and they often occur simulta-neously with low self-esteem, mood lability, low frustration toler-ance, and swearing. (Greene, 2006, p. 285)

To gain more clarity about the diagnosis, differentiating ODD from ADHD and CD can be helpful. Although some symptoms of ADHD (interrupting oth-ers, blurting out, etc.) may overlap with those of ODD, the distinction lies in the purposefulness of the behavior. Such behavior in children with ADHD results from restlessness and is generally unintentional, whereas in children with ODD, the behavior is most often purposeful (Pardini & Lochman, 2003; Pillow, Pel-ham, Hoza, Molina, & Stultz, 1998). Children with ODD tend to have a hostile attribution bias (Behan & Carr, 2000) that causes them to react aggressively to otherwise neutral environmental stimuli. The aggression associated with ODD is often the result of a perceived threat or provocation. In contrast, the aggression associated with CD is more proactive (Kempes, Matthys, de Vries, & van Engeland, 2005), that is, one that anticipates a reward. Furthermore, social problems in children with ODD are, for the most part, with authority figures, whereas children with ADHD and CD have social problems that are more generalized.

ETIOLOGY OF ODD

Etiological factors in the development of ODD can be divided into biological factors, parenting and family factors, and the child's social-cognitive processes.

Biological Factors

Most etiological studies have focused on aggression in general and/or CD. Fewer studies have examined the causes of ODD as distinct from CD. For example, Miles and Carey (1997) found from twins studies and other investigations that 50 percent of the variability in aggression and disruptive behaviors can be attributed to genetics. On the other hand, most studies suggest that genetic factors interact with psychosocial and environmental factors to produce a diagnosis in the realm of disruptive behavior disorders (Burt, Krueger, McGue, & Iacono, 2001; Hendren & Muller, 2006; Steiner & Wilson, 1999). To our knowledge, the study of Comings et al. (2000) is the only one to mention ODD specifically, along with CD and ADHD, as having a strong association with **adrenergic genes**.

ADRENERGIC GENES

Hormonal genes that carry adrenalin.

    The same can be said for hormonal factors and their effect on adolescent behavior. In general, studies have found hormone levels, particularly high levels of testosterone and its derivatives, to be associated with conduct problems (Dmitrieva, Oades, Hauffa, & Eggers, 2001; Olweus, Mattsson, Schalling, & Low, 1988; van Goozen, Matthys, Cohen-Kettenis, Buitelaar, & van Engeland, 2000). The van Goozen et al. (2000) study specifically mentions boys with ODD as having levels of **dehydroepiandrosterone (DHEAS)** similar to those of boys with CD.

DEHYDROEPIANDROST-ERONE (DHEAS)

A natural steroid produced from cholesterol that undergoes conversion to produce testosterone in males and estrogen in females.

    The role of neurotransmitter dysfunction has also been studied in the development of aggression in children, adolescents, and adults. Abnormal function of serotonin, the neurotransmitter implicated in the expression and regulation of affect and impulse control, has been found to play a role in aggression and lack of impulse control (Spoont, 1992), as has low levels of **5-hydroxyindoleacetic acid** in the cerebrospinal fluid (Mehlman et al., 1994, 1995).

5-HYDROXY-INDOLEACETIC ACID

The principal metabolized form of serotonin.

    Minor neurological deficits have been found to correlate with conduct problems. For example, studies have shown a consistent association between low IQ and disruptive behavior (Moffitt, Gabrielli, Mednick, & Schulsinger, 1981; Moffitt & Silva, 1988a). To our knowledge, no study to date has examined the role of neurological deficits and their relationship specifically to ODD. The focus has been mostly on CD, for which studies have shown a relationship with reduced temporal lobe volume (Kruesi, Casanova, Mannheim, & Johnson-Bilder, 2004), resulting in deficits of executive function and inhibition (Kim, Kim, & Kwon, 2001).

Finally, studies have shown that prenatal toxins, such as nicotine and alcohol, have an association with disruptive behavior (Kelly, Day, & Streissguth, 2000; Wakschlag et al., 1997). In conclusion, few studies have examined the biological bases of ODD specifically. If, however, one accepts the position that ODD is a precursor to CD, then many of the biological bases for CD would logically apply to ODD. However, as mentioned earlier, only about one-third of those diagnosed with ODD progress to CD.

Parenting and Family Factors

Studies have consistently established a link between parenting and family characteristics and the development of ODD. Family dysfunction, lower levels of family income, higher levels of authoritarian parenting, lower levels of parental warmth and supervision, and inconsistent discipline have all been implicated in the development of ODD (Frick et al., 1992; Rey & Plapp, 1990; Simonoff, Pickles, Meyer, Silberg, & Maes, 1998). In addition, insecure attachment to the primary caregiver has also been associated with ODD (Speltz, DeKlyen, Greenberg, & Dryden, 1995). The most attention has been paid to patterns of parental discipline and the role of coercion in the development of ODD. The social interaction model (Chamberlain & Patterson, 1995; Patterson, Reid, & Dishion, 1992) developed a typology of parenting thought to be responsible for the development of ODD (see Table 3.2).

TABLE 3.2 A Typology of Parenting Based on the Social Interaction Model

1. *Inconsistent discipline* is parenting that involves a lack of follow-through with commands and consequences, as well as an indiscriminate response to positive and negative behaviors. The parent often gives in when the child argues and haphazardly changes the expectations and consequences for noncompliance.

2. *Irritable explosive discipline* is parenting that is marked by a high rate of commands, use of intense strategies, such as yelling, hitting, and threatening, as well as making derogatory and humiliating statements about the child. Such parenting practices augment the possibility of the child responding with defiant behaviors.

3. *Low supervision and involvement* is parenting that is disengaged. Parents who practice this type of parenting typically know very little about their children—their whereabouts, friends, performance at school, etc. They fail to provide supervision even when the child is participating in high-risk or delinquent activities.

4. *Inflexible, rigid discipline* is parenting that is very limited in its capacity to utilize various strategies. Such parents tend to rely on a sole means of discipline regardless of the severity of the transgression and fail to take into account contextual factors that may have caused the transgression. They tend to be poor listeners when it comes to their children and fail to provide rationales for their disciplinary actions.

Source: From "Discipline and Child Compliance in Parenting" by P. Chamberlain and G. R. Patterson, 2000 in M. H. Bomstein (Ed.), *Handbook of Parenting, Vol. 4: Applied and Practical Parenting* (pp. 206–209). Mahwah, NJ. Copyright 2000 by Lawrence Erlbaum and Associates. Adapted with permission.

Child Characteristics

Originally, the social interaction model placed almost exclusive emphasis on parenting practices as the cause for a child's conduct problems, without considering how child characteristics might contribute to parent–child interactions (Dishion, French, & Patterson, 1995; Patterson, DeBaryshe, & Ramsey, 1989; Patterson et al., 1992). More recently, experts have emphasized the need to pay greater attention to child characteristics such as the capacity for emotion regulation, frustration tolerance, adaptation, and problem-solving skills (Greene, 2006; Greene & Ablon, 2005; Greene & Doyle, 1999). The failure to possess such skills results in a lack of compliance, defined as the ability to delay one's own needs and wants in deference to those of an authority figure. If compliance is the result of having learned a complex set of social-cognitive skills, oppositional behavior (understood as a lack of compliance) can be understood as the child having a learning disability, that is, an inability to learn the skills needed for compliance (Greene, 2006; Greene & Ablon, 2005).

To further this argument, Greene (2006) pointed out that this lack of executive skills is also present in the psychiatric disorder that is most often comorbid with ODD (ADHD), leading to the conjecture that ADHD may "set the stage" for ODD. A deficit in the area of executive skills such as *working memory* (the ability to hold events in order to learn from them and act appropriately), *self-regulation* (the ability to regulate arousal to achieve a goal-directed action), *shifting cognitive set* (the ability to shift from rules and expectation in one situation to those of another situation), and *problem-solving* (the ability to generate possible solutions, choose the most appropriate, and enact a plan) can easily result in noncompliance. With regard to ODD, the child is not able to learn from past events nor anticipate the consequences of his or her actions (working memory), responds with a high level of emotion such as screaming or swearing (emotional regulation), has trouble responding immediately to adult requests (shifting cognitive set), and is limited in the repertoire of alternative responses (problem-solving skills) (Greene, 2006).

A similar argument is made for the high comorbidity between ODD and language disorders. "Those children compromised in the capacity to label emotions (such as frustration and anger) may have difficulty identifying and internalizing an adaptive repertoire of behavior strategies for responding to such emotions" (Greene, 2006, p. 287).

In addition to these cognitive deficiencies, studies have also identified **cognitive distortions** that tend to exist in children with ODD (Dodge, 1980; Dodge & Coie, 1987; Dodge, Price, Bachorowski, & Newman, 1990; Lochman & Dodge, 1994). Children with antisocial tendencies, when presented with ambiguous social situations, tend to attribute hostile intentions to others (Lochman & Dodge, 1994) and are more likely to support activities that are damaging to interpersonal relationships (Lochman, Wayland, & White, 1993). In contrast to proactive aggression, the reactive aggression often associated with ODD is the result of misinterpreting other's behavior as being hostile.

Perhaps the most significant deficit among those with ODD is in problem-solving skills. Children with ODD have trouble encoding social cues, generating alternative solutions, and choosing the most appropriate response (Matthys,

COGNITIVE DISTORTIONS

Refers to dysfunctional thinking.

Cuperus, & Van England, 1999). Their preferred means of solving conflicts is through aggression, because cognitively it is the only means available to them.

In summary, the etiological component of ODD has been investigated through two dimensions: parent/family characteristics and child characteristics. The controversy is around which is primary. Do child characteristics associated with ODD result from certain parenting practices, or the reverse? The most likely explanation is that there is an interaction effect between child and parent in which the parent's response to a lack of compliance can increase frustration and arousal in the child (Kochanska & Askan, 1995).

ASSESSMENT OF ODD

The assessment of ODD should come from multiple sources (Hendren & Muller, 2006). Clinicians and other professionals have relied on diagnostic interviews, rating scales, and reviews of school records to gather information en route to making a diagnosis of ODD. The *Diagnostic Interview Schedule for Children* (DISC) and *Child Behavior Checklist* (CBCL; Achenbach, 1991a, 1991b, 1991c, 1992) are two general instruments that have been used in the diagnosis of ODD. The information on the CBCL pertinent to ODD is relatively limited when compared to that for CD and ADHD, but nevertheless has proven useful in helping to diagnose ODD (Abolt & Thyer, 2003). Angold and Costello (1996) found that child reports of oppositional defiant symptoms were an important part of the assessment of ODD for research applications, clinical practice, and classroom management.

Rating scales specific to aggression have also been used in the diagnosis of ODD. The *Iowa Conners Aggression Factor* (Loney & Milch, 1985), the *Modified Overt Aggression Scale* (Kay, Wolkenfield, & Murrill, 1988), and the *Children's Aggression Rating Scale—Teacher Version* (Halperin, McKay, Grayson, & Newcorn, 2003) all have reported good reliability and validity. This last instrument, especially relevant to schools, distinguishes among various types and severity of aggression, which allows for a more accurate diagnosis of ODD.

The assessment of ODD must also take place across settings, people, and events. If the emergence of ODD is the result of a poor match between a child's behavior and the parent's response to that behavior, assessment must take into consideration information about the child, the parent, and environmental circumstances that contribute to the oppositional interactions (Greene, 2006). This is true for interactions that take place at home with the parent, as well as those that take place in the school with the teacher and other school personnel. Questions such as: "Who is the child interacting with when the behavior occurs?" "What is the child doing when the behavior occurs?" "Where do such behaviors tend to occur?" and "What are the precipitating events that result in oppositional episodes?" all need to be part of the assessment of ODD.

To complete the assessment of ODD, a thorough developmental, school, and treatment history should be gathered. The developmental history should focus on early temperament, attachment history, family history, and trauma history. The school history needs to ascertain the degree of oppositional behaviors across situations and teachers. The purpose of the treatment history is also to find out what behavioral interventions have been tried and to assess their effectiveness.

TREATMENT STRATEGIES

The effectiveness of different treatment interventions for conduct problems has garnered a great deal of attention in recent years. A number of research reviews exist (see, for example, Connor, 2002; Farmer, Compton, Burns, & Robertson, 2002; Kazdin, 1998, 2001; Neary, 2000). One difficulty has been that the majority of studies have been designed to assess the effectiveness of interventions for conduct problems in general and do not report findings disaggregated for a particular diagnostic group. Few studies have been limited to or report separately for ODD. To our knowledge, only two reviews focused on interventions for children who specifically met the diagnostic criteria for ODD exist: those of Behan and Carr (2000) and Bradley and Mandell (2005). What follows is a summary of these two reviews.

Reviews of Outcome Studies

In a meta-analytic review, Behan and Carr (2000) selected twenty-four studies divided into five categories:

1. Individually based behavioral parent training (eight studies)
2. Group-based behavioral parent training (four studies)
3. Behavioral parent training with a social support component (four studies)
4. Video modeling–based behavioral parent training (five studies)
5. Behavioral parent training combined with child-focused problem-solving skills (three studies)

All of the studies were conducted in the United States, except for two in Canada and two in Australia, and took place between 1977 and 1997. All of the studies contained treatment and control groups, but in only five of the twenty-four were the groups equalized in terms of comorbidity. Results indicated that all five of the different treatments were more effective than no treatment at all. Behavioral parent training combined with child-focused problem-solving skills training (Spaccarelli, Cotler, & Penman, 1992; Webster-Stratton, 1984, 1990, 1992) proved to be the most effective intervention for ODD and were more effective than either of these components alone. Such combined programs typically included thirty-five to forty sessions. Group-based behavioral parent training that included video modeling was as effective as individually based parent training programs (Bernal, Klinnert, & Schultz, 1980; Kent & O'Leary, 1976; McNeil & Nelson, 1991; Olson & Roberts, 1987; Patterson, Chamberlain, & Reid, 1982; Peed, Roberts, & Forehand, 1977; Wells & Egan, 1988; Zangwill, 1983). Both of these interventions were more effective than group-based parent behavioral training programs without video modeling (Christensen, Johnson, Phillips, & Glasgow, 1980; Cunningham, Bremner, & Boyle, 1995; Hamilton & MacQuiddy, 1984; Karoly & Rosenthal, 1977). Finally, in cases where the primary caretaker lacked the social support of his or her partner, intervention to enhance social support greatly increased the program's effectiveness (Dadds & McHugh, 1992; Dadds, Sanders, Behrens, & James, 1987; Firestone, Kelly, & Fike, 1980; Martin, 1977).

The Bradley and Mandell (2005) review included seven studies (August, Realmuto, Hektner, & Bloomquist, 2001; August, Lee, Bloomquist, Realmuto, & Hektner, 2003; Dadds & McHugh, 1992; Nixon, Sweeney, Erickson, & Touyz, 2003; Schuhmann, Foote, Eyberg, Boggs, & Algina, 1998; Webster-Stratton & Hammond, 1997; Webster-Stratton, Reid, & Hammond, 2004) that had to meet eight criteria:

1. Random assignment to treatment and control groups
2. The sample was school-aged
3. Children had a diagnosis of ODD
4. No requirement for residential or hospital treatment
5. Effects reported from at least one nonobservational outcome measure
6. The study reported effect sizes and their confidence intervals
7. The study was published between 1990 and 2004
8. The study was in English

The studies were conducted in the United States except for two that were conducted in Australia. Four of the seven studies used the child training component of the "Dinosaur School" developed by Webster-Stratton (Webster-Stratton & Reid, 2003a, 2003b). One study (Dadds & McHugh, 1992) targeted parents only; two studies (Webster-Stratton & Hammond, 1997; Webster-Stratton et al., 2004) targeted children only; and four targeted both children and parents (August et al., 2001, 2003; Nixon et al., 2003; Schuhmann et al., 1998).

For improving ODD symptoms at home, the largest effect sizes were for parent treatment only and a similar (slightly lower yet significant) effect size for child treatment only. Contrary to expectations, the effect sizes were small for interventions that targeted both child and parent. For symptoms at school, a small but insignificant effect was found for child-only and parent-only groups. A similar result was found for improving academic functioning. One study (Webster-Stratton & Hammond, 1997) found a small effect, but none of the studies indicated significant effects for improving academic functioning. With regard to social functioning, treating only children resulted in a medium yet significant effect, while interventions targeting both children and parents resulted in a small effect. For reducing parental strain or stress, interventions focused on the parents had the greatest impact, whereas interventions focused only on the child or on both parent and child had a small but not a statistically significant effect. In summary, the review by Bradley and Mandell (2005) indicated that interventions targeting parenting skills and/or child problem-solving skills significantly improved outcomes for children with ODD, with the greatest impact on the child's behavior at home. There was little support for interventions to improve academics or behavior at school.

INCREDIBLE YEARS TRAINING PROGRAM

The three most popular treatment programs for ODD are *Parent-Child Interaction Therapy* (PCIT) (Schuhmann et al., 1998), joint *Problem Solving Skills Training* (PSST) together with *Parent Management Training* (PMT) (Kazdin, 2005), and the *Incredible Years Training Series* (IYTS) (Webster-Stratton, 1992;

Webster-Stratton & Reid, 2003c). This last program has a teacher training component, and PCIT has been found to generalize to school settings (Funderburk et al., 1998). Although all three programs enjoy empirical support, the IYTS is perhaps the most well known and has the most empirical support. Its use of videotaped modeling has proven especially effective, and the fact that it has a teacher training component makes it especially attractive to those who work or plan to work in schools with young children, especially children ages 6 through 10, for whom the program was designed. It can, however, be adapted to older children. The IYTS has three different types of programs: one for parents, one for children, and one for teachers.

Parent Intervention Training Program

The goal of parent training is to increase competency and strengthen families. Table 3.3 lists the six objectives for parent training.

The basic parent training is videotaped-based, whereby participants watch vignettes of modeled parenting skills, a total of 250 vignettes that last from 1 to 2 minutes and shown in parent groups of eight to twelve members. They are designed to demonstrate social learning and child development principles and to teach parents the use of child-directed interactive play, praise, and incentive programs. Parents learn through discussion of the vignettes under the facilitation of a trained therapist. The program takes approximately 26 hours to complete over the course of thirteen to fourteen weekly 2-hour sessions.

TABLE 3.3   Six Objectives of Parent Training in the Incredible Years Training Program

---

- Increase parents' positive parenting, nurturing relationships, with their children, and general self-confidence about parenting.
- Replace critical and physically violent discipline with positive strategies, such as ignoring, natural and logical consequences, redirecting, monitoring, and problem solving.
- Improve parents' problem-solving skills, anger management, and communication skills.
- Increase family support networks and school involvement/bonding.
- Help parents and teachers work collaboratively to ensure consistency across settings.
- Increase parents' involvement in children's academic-related activities at home.

Source: From C. Webster-Stratton, and M. J. Reid, The Incredible Years Parents, Teachers and Children Training Series: A Multifaceted treatment Approach" (pp. 225–226) in *Evidence-Based Psychotherapies for Children and Adolescents* by A. E. Kazdin & J. R. Weisz (Eds.), 2003. New York: Guilford Press. Copyright 2003 by Guilford Press. Reprinted with permission.

There is also an advanced parent training program that consists of four-teen sessions based on watching sixty videotaped vignettes that emphasize the following three components:

1. ***Personal self-control.*** Parents are taught to substitute coping and positive self-talk for their depressive, angry, and blaming self-talk. In addition, parents are taught specific anger-management techniques.
2. ***Communication skills.*** Parents are taught to identify blocks to communication and to learn effective communication skills for dealing with conflict.
3. ***Problem-solving skills.*** Parents are taught effective strategies for coping with conflict with spouses, employers, extended-family members, and children (Webster-Stratton & Reid, 2003c, p. 226).

In addition, a school parent training component is designed to help parents promote their children's self-confidence at school, foster good learning habits, deal with their children's discouragement, participate in homework, use teacher–parent conferences to advocate for their children, and how to discuss a school problem with their child.

Teacher Training Intervention Program

As mentioned previously, children with ODD have problems with peer socialization and authority figures in the school. Often, teacher reactions exacerbate the difficulties of disruptive children. For this reason, the IYTS includes a teacher component that consists of a 4-day (32-hour) training component that is appropriate for teachers, school counselors, and psychologists. The goals of the training are to increase teachers' use of effective classroom management strategies for dealing with disruptive behaviors, promote positive relationships with difficult students, strengthen social skills in the classroom and beyond, and strengthen collaboration between teachers and parents (Webster-Stratton, 2000; Webster-Stratton & Reid, 2003c). School personnel are also taught effective problem-solving strategies to help children with ODD improve their peer relationships and, at the same time, help their peers respond more effectively to those with ODD.

Child Training Intervention

Table 3.4 lists the goals of the child training program. The program runs for 22 weeks, during which the children meet weekly for 2 hours in groups of six and watch over 100 hours of videotaped vignettes that teach problem-solving and social skills in response to real-life conflict situations at home and in school. Ideally, the parent training program runs concomitantly.

All three training programs are video-based, a unique aspect of the IYTS, and research supports the effectiveness of the program. Although the IYTS also makes use of role play, practice activities, and live feedback, videotape "provides a more flexible method of training than didactic instruction or sole reliance on role play; that is, we could portray a wide variety of models and situations" (Webster-Stratton & Reid, 2003c, p. 230). Models used in the videotapes reflect a diversity of age, culture, socioeconomic status, and temperament.

TABLE 3.4	The Goals of the Child Training Program in the Incredible Years Training Program

- Strengthening children's social skills and appropriate play skills (turn taking, waiting, asking, sharing, helping, and complimenting)
- Promoting children's use of self-control strategies such as effective problem-solving and anger management strategies
- Increasing emotional awareness by labeling feelings, recognizing the differing views of oneself and others, and enhancing perspective taking
- Boosting academic success, reading, and school readiness
- Reducing defiance, aggressive behavior, and related conduct problems, such as noncompliance, peer aggression and rejection, bullying, stealing, and lying
- Decreasing children's negative cognitive attributions and conflict-management approaches
- Increasing self-esteem and self-confidence

Source: From C. Webster-Stratton and M. J. Reid, "The Incredible Years Parents, Teachers, and Children Training Series: A Multifaceted Treatment Approach" (pp. 229–230) in *Evidence-Based Psychotherapies for Children and Adolescents* by A. E. Kazdin and J. R. Weisz (Eds), 2003. New York: Guilford Press. Copyright 2003 by Guilford Press. Reprinted with permission.

Models are often unrehearsed and show both the right and wrong approaches to interacting effectively with children with ODD. All presentations of video-taped vignettes are followed by focused discussions designed to promote learning and mutual support among members of the group. The inclusion of training for different constituencies (parents, children, and teachers) results from the premise that the origin of ODD and its maintenance is the result of a complex interaction in which outcome depends on the interrelationships among children, parents, teachers, and peers (Webster-Stratton & Reid, 2003c).

SCHOOL-BASED INTERVENTIONS: JACK STRAW

The first step in developing an effective school-based intervention that will be appropriate for Jack is to determine the purpose or "function" of his oppositional defiant behaviors. This determination needs to be made for each specific behavior described in the case example at the beginning of the chapter. One way to conduct such an informal assessment is to (1) determine specific *antecedents,* events that preceded the disruptive or defiant behavior, (2) operationally describe the *behavior* itself (in measurable terms), and then (3) identify the results or *consequences* of the misbehavior that serve to reinforce it. This process is referred to as the *A-B-C approach* to identifying the purpose served by the target behavior, in this case Jack's defiant behavior. Ideally, this approach will facilitate the development of hypotheses regarding the functions served by Jack's engagement in these problem behaviors and thereby help his teachers construct an effective behavioral intervention plan.

Assessing the Problem

From the scenario presented in the case example, it appears that the behaviors that most seriously affect Jack's classroom performance include: (1) talking back to the teacher, (2) using rude gestures when frustrated or angry with authority figures in the school (we need to identify these), and (3) instigating fights with peers through verbal provocation (again, we need to know more about the phrases or words he uses to incite his classmates). Jack's chronic lateness to class and episodic truancy are really secondary issues that are potentially related to his oppositional behaviors.

When working with a student, like Jack, who presents an array of problem behaviors, it is necessary to prioritize them according to their impact on learning and classroom performance. Consequently, based on what we know about Jack's classroom conduct, the primary target behaviors to address are (1) insubordination (talking back or speaking disrespectfully to the teacher), (2) displaying rude gestures to convey anger or frustration to authority figures and/or peers, and (3) instigating fights through verbal provocation. These target behaviors have to be **operationally defined** to facilitate their identification and recording.

OPERATIONALLY DEFINED

Refers to target behaviors that must be carefully delineated to ensure consistent identification for recording purposes.

ANECDOTAL DATA

Behavior recording consisting of written observations of the targeted behaviors identified within a specific time frame.

To provide the necessary baseline data for each of these target behaviors, Jack's teachers, in conjunction with the multidisciplinary evaluation team, are asked to provide **anecdotal data** consisting of written observations of the targeted behaviors identified within a specific time frame, as well as event recording, noting the frequency with which the target behaviors occur (see Figures 3.1 and 3.2). In addition, these teachers are asked to conduct systematic observations of the target behaviors relative to a specific situation (e.g., second-period social studies class), across various settings (e.g., content-area classes, specials, extracurricular activities and postschool events), and at different times of the day (e.g., homeroom, before lunch, lunch, after lunch, dismissal, and departure).

Once the baseline for each of these behaviors has been established, Jack's teachers need to deduce the following:

1. The circumstances in which the behavior appears most likely to occur.
2. Various contributing factors.
3. The consequences of the specific behavior for the student or the benefits derived by the student from engaging in the problem behavior.
4. Circumstances in which the student is least likely to engage in the problem behavior.
5. Any other contributing factors (Lewis-Palmer & Sugai, 2005).

Subsequently, Jack's teachers, in coordination with the multidisciplinary evaluation team, will determine the primary function or purpose served by each of the target behaviors and design an intervention plan that will address each one effectively. A behavioral intervention plan (BIP) should be carefully derived from the child's functional behavioral assessment and address:

1. Short-term prevention
2. Teaching of alternative skills
3. Responses to problem behaviors
4. Long-term prevention (Barnhill, 2005)

FIGURE 3.1 Scatterplot

Student Name: _____

Target Behavior(s): _____

_____

Put an "X" in the space that corresponds to the time and date of each observed behavior. If plotting more than one behavior, use another letter.

Dates: _____ _____ _____ _____ _____

Monday	Tuesday	Wednesday	Thursday	Friday	Comments
8:30					
8:45					
9:00					
9:15					
9:30					
9:45					
10:00					
10:15					
10:30					
10:45					
11:00					
11:15					
11:30					
11:45					
12:00					
12:15					
12:30					
12:45					
1:00					
1:15					
1:30					
1:45					
2:00					
2:15					
2:30					
2:45					

Source: Barnhill, G. P. (2005). Functional behavioral assessment in schools. *Intervention in School and Clinic, 40*(3), 131–143.

FIGURE 3.2 Functional Behavioral Assessment Worksheet

Student Name: _____

Date: _____

Target Behavior: Operationally define the behavior that most interferes with the student's functioning in the classroom. Include intensity (high, medium, or low), frequency, and duration.

_____
_____
_____
_____

When, where, with whom, and in what condition is the target behavior *least* likely to occur?

_____
_____

Setting Events or Context Variables (i.e., hunger, lack of sleep, medications, problems on bus):

_____
_____

Immediate Antecedents and Consequences

Antecedents Problematic Settings Consequences

__ Demand/Request __ Unstructured setting __ Behavior ignored

__ Difficult task __ Unstructured activity __ Reprimanded

__ Time of day __ Individual seat work __ Verbal redirection

__ Interruption in routine __ Group work __ Time-out (duration: _____)

__ Peer teased/provoked __ Specials __ Loss of incentives

__ No materials/activities __ Specific subject/task __ Physical redirection

__ Could not get desired item __ Crowded setting __ Physical restraint

__ People _____ Noisy setting __ Sent to office

__ Alone __ Other _____ Suspension

__ Other _____ Other _____ Other _____

What function(s) does the target behavior seem to serve for the student?

___ Escape from: __ demand/request __ person __ activity/task __ school __ other _____

___ Attention from: __ adult __ peer __ other _____

___ Gain desired: __ item __ activity __ area __ other _____

___ Automatic sensory stimulation: _____

Hypothesis:

When _____ occurs in the context of _____

(antecedent) (problematic setting) the students exhibits _____ in order to _____.

(target behavior) (perceived function)

This behavior is more likely to occur when _____.

(setting event/context variables)

Replacement or competing behavior that could still serve the same function for the student:

_____
_____

Is the replacement behavior in the student's repertoire, or will it need to be taught directly? _____

If so, how will it be taught? _____
_____

List some potential motivators for student:

_____

Source: Barnhill, G. P. (2005). Functional behavioral assessment in schools. *Intervention in School and Clinic, 40*(3), 131–143.

Developing an Effective Intervention Plan

Using the case example of Jack, we will develop an appropriate intervention plan as a model. First, we must clearly address each of our target behaviors in priority order. Let us begin with (1) *insubordination,* defined as *talking back or being disrespectful to the teacher or other authority figure.*

A. ***Short-term prevention.*** Oppositional defiance disorder, like conduct disorder and ADHD, does not appear to be affected in the short term. About the only immediate intervention that might provide some behavioral improvement would be the change in teacher attitudes and approaches relative to affected individuals, which are components of the teacher-training in the Incredible Years Training Series (IYTS) (Webster-Stratton, 1992; Webster-Stratton & Reid, 2003). This intervention is currently both the most popular and empirically supported of the treatment programs designed to help individuals with ODD.

Insubordination, distinguished by disrespectful speech and address, is characteristic of the child with ODD. The tone and quality of the teacher's response can do much to exacerbate or mitigate a potentially volatile situation. The Old Testament aphorism: "A gentle answer turns away wrath, but a harsh word stirs up anger" (Proverbs 15:1, New American Standard Version) still holds relevance; particularly for this situation. Remembering that the student who has ODD is often reacting to the position of power and control that the teacher holds and is rarely a personal attack can sometimes help the teacher maintain composure and provide the student a model of civility and respect—important attributes we want the student with ODD to acquire.

B. ***Teaching of alternative skills.*** The goals of the child training program component of the IYTS are clearly the teaching of alternative skills to replace the undesirable and antisocial ones associated with ODD. As outlined in the treatment section of this chapter, some of these substitute skills include: (1) strengthening children's social skills and appropriate play skills (turn taking, waiting, asking, sharing, helping, and complimenting), (2) promoting children's use of self-control strategies such as effective problem-solving and anger management strategies, (3) labeling feelings, recognizing the differing views of oneself and others, and enhancing perspective taking, and (4) increasing self-esteem and self-confidence (Webster-Stratton & Reid, 2003a, pp. 229–230).

C. ***Responses to problem behaviors.*** Research has supported the importance of providing immediate response to problem behaviors, especially those that involve verbal and/or physical aggression (Whelan, 1998; Kauffman, 2005). Because the roots of oppositional defiant behavior are generally found in ineffective and sometimes abusive caregiver relationships, it is important that the teacher establish a firm but caring and respectful rapport with the student who exhibits such behaviors. This does not mean that the student displaying ODD behaviors should be treated deferentially; on the contrary, evidence suggests that meaningful consequences should be swiftly applied. Students who have ODD need to know that insubordinate behavior will not be permitted in the classroom and will be met with consequences that are predictable and sure (Walker, Ramsey, & Gresham, 2004).

RESTITUTION

A behavioral consequence that involves a meaningful and substantive reparation on the part of the transgressor or perpetrator to help make amends to the victim, as well as to ensure that the transgressor takes responsibility for his or her behavior and acknowledges its destructive consequences.

D. **Long-term prevention.** **Restitution** should also be an integral part of any behavioral intervention plan for students who engage in ODD behaviors (Malley, Beck, & Adorno, 2001). Unlike the child with a conduct disorder, the child with ODD will most typically engage in verbal aggression and insult, or blatant disrespect expressed verbally. As a consequence, the insult or injury inflicted by these children tends to be felt on an emotional level. Restitution, in this case, typically means an apology, written and/or verbally expressed. The apology does not preclude additional consequences as in a case involving a physical threat, racist or sexually explicit epithets, or property damage that occurs inadvertently as a result of the oppositional or defiant behavior. However, the most effective responses to children who are disrespectful are ones that model respect and civility—the ones that display "grace under fire." Engaging in heated verbal exchanges with these children invariably escalates the frequency and intensity of the very behaviors we want to extinguish. Once again, there appear to be no "quick fixes" for behavior problems that have developed over time, incubated in an unhealthy or pathological home environment. The best deterrent for ODD behaviors is a teacher–student relationship that has been built on trust, has been time-tested, and is compassionate.

The next set of behaviors to address is Jack's (2) *display of rude gestures to convey anger, frustration, or disdain to authority figures and/or peers.* These exhibitions include (a) prominently displaying the middle finger, (b) making faces, and (c) making lewd and obscene gestures.

A. **Short-term prevention.** Similar to disrespectful behavior, the display of rude gestures is an expression of frustration and anger that may be misplaced but nonetheless must be swiftly and effectively addressed. Typically, the use of such antisocial communication is not tolerated in the classroom, and the guilty party is subject to some sort of established punishment or consequence. This level of deterrence is usually effective for most students, for whom such behavior is an anomaly; however, for students who have ODD, punishment is often ineffective because the acting-out behavior is frequently a demonstration of deep-seated anger that cannot be expressed to the child's parents. Once again, the Incredible Years Training Program (IYTP) (Webster-Stratton & Reid, 2003) provides effective intervention for this behavior set through promoting the use of self-control strategies, such as effective problem-solving and anger management techniques, increasing emotional awareness by labeling feelings, recognizing the differing views of oneself and others, and enhancing perspective taking. Likewise, the teacher-training component of IYTP equips the teacher with the skill set to allow the teacher to see beyond the antisocial, repugnant behaviors to the need for acceptance and affirmation on the part of the child with ODD.

B. ***Teaching alternative skills.*** This is an important component of the IYTP program. Depending on the age of the child exhibiting the problem behavior, the teacher can use the infraction to conduct a "social skills autopsy" (LaVoie, 2005). This may be a more effective approach for younger children because they are less constrained by image and peer pressure. In essence, the "social skills autopsy" involves on-the-spot analysis of the misbehavior to determine (1) the specific misbehavior and why it occurred, (2) its effect on the student and others, and (3) the socially appropriate behavior to be implemented "next time." In the case of the child's display of rude gestures, the student might be taught to use appropriate replacement behaviors, such as speaking with the teacher about situations that are perceived as stressful, frustrating, or provocative, using a pre-arranged signal to notify the teacher of the need to take a "time-out" from an activity that is becoming tedious or a situation that is exceptionally stressful. An older student might be asked to confer with the teacher immediately after the misbehavior to allow the student to "decompress" and also to permit the teacher to explain the negative consequences of the problem behavior, investigate possible antecedents, and collaborate to identify and implement an appropriate alternative behavior response for the future.

C. ***Responses to problems.*** In the case of a very challenging student like Jack, the teacher is often pushed to the limits of tolerance and, in that aggravated state, can behave unprofessionally toward the offending student. We know of several cases in which typically effective professionals have succumbed to the relentless provocations of a student like Jack. For a few, a careless and unprofessional response was a career-ender, whereas others, a bit more established and resilient, were able to weather the unpleasant repercussions. There is never a circumstance that is so dire that a teacher cannot ask a colleague for some assistance. All of us, at one time or another, reach "the end of our tether." The real professional wisdom is to acknowledge those moments and, however uncomfortable, ask for a few minutes of relief from an understanding colleague. However, at no time should the teacher engage the student in a power game of threats and counterthreats.

In any event, the correct response to the provocations of someone like Jack is always one tempered by restraint and reason: The reaction of the teacher should be swift, firm, and brief. For example, in response to rude gestures, the teacher might move to a position beside the offending student rather than in front, to avoid an escalation of the problem behavior. The teacher then should assume a lower body stance (i.e., squat or support himself on one knee) and quietly but firmly remind the individual that such behavior is unacceptable and will not be tolerated in the classroom. At this point, the student should be provided the opportunity to speak with the teacher about perceived antecedents outside the classroom or, if the improper behavior was unprovoked, the student should be reminded about relevant consequences. If the student persists in engaging in defiant, disruptive behavior, he needs to be escorted to a designated "time-out" room, and the incident should be anecdotally recorded.

D. **Long-term prevention.** Many times students who have ODD, like Jack, continue to engage in the same inappropriate or offensive behaviors because they simply don't know a better way to achieve the objective they want. There is evidence suggesting that if students who have ODD are simply taught more appropriate ways to attain those ends, many will stop behaving badly; they simply lack the skills repertoire that would offer them more socially acceptable options (Walker, Ramsey, & Gresham, 2004). Also, through treatment programs, such as the Incredible Years Training Program, students who have ODD learn self-control strategies such as effective problem-solving and anger management techniques, enhancing perspective taking, and conflict management approaches, all of which can ultimately lead to an increase in self-esteem and self-confidence.

The last of Jack's target behaviors that needs to be addressed in the classroom is (3) *instigating fights with peers through verbal provocation.* Clearly, this behavior contributes to Jack's isolation from his peers, as well as his own sense of alienation. The irony here is that, as much as children, like Jack, insist they don't care about being socially excluded by their classmates, the fact remains: They are deeply affected.

A. **Short-term prevention.** Students who have ODD, like Jack, simply don't have the self-awareness or the intrapersonal skills to understand and control their innate feelings of frustration and anger (Patterson, Reid, & Dishion, 1992). Whatever a teacher can do to help reduce the alienation brought about by the antisocial behavior of students like Jack may help break a vicious cycle and restore the child's sense of "belongingness" (Kohn, 1996). One technique that is used effectively in schools is **peer mediation**. This approach requires that both students involved in a fight or disagreement work through their problems with the aid of a trained peer mediator. A teacher, who has also been trained in the intervention, provides adult oversight; however, as long as the disputants comply with the rules of mediation, formal school sanctions are typically not applied.

B. **Teaching alternative skills.** The functional behavioral assessment conducted by the multidisciplinary team should identify a plausible purpose for Jack's provocative behaviors. This information is critical to his instructors and caregivers, who will be teaching and modeling alternative behaviors. Let's assume that, in Jack's case, these behaviors serve two primary purposes: to gain attention and recognition, albeit negative, from peers; and as retribution for being ostracized by his peers. In response, then, teachers must first model proactive rather than reactive responses to stressful events. For example, rather than shouting at Jack in reaction to his verbal outbursts, teachers should speak calmly and firmly, directing Jack away from the contentious situation and into a less stimulating environment, such as the hallway or designated "time-out" or "quiet" room.

PEER MEDIATION

An approach that requires both students involved in a fight or disagreement to work through their problems with the aid of a trained peer mediator. A teacher, who has also been trained in the intervention, provides adult oversight; however, as long as the disputants comply with the rules of mediation, formal school sanctions are typically not applied.

Once removed from the stressful situation and after Jack has regained his composure, the teacher can deconstruct the event and suggest ways that Jack might constructively handle similar situations in future. He might be taught a self-management technique to help him deescalate a potentially volatile situation, something as simple as POST: *P*ause, consider *O*ptions, *S*eek help, *T*ry a new way. If the situation is too volatile, the student might be provided a "signal" that will enable him to surreptitiously remove himself from the demands of the setting and relocate to a predetermined neutral location (Webster-Stratton & Reid, 2003).

C. ***Responses to problems.*** As in the case of Jack's other target behaviors, teachers need to remember to respond therapeutically, not overreacting or personalizing his defiant remarks. Teachers must understand that they are simply "safe" targets of opportunity, ones that will not reciprocate in kind. That does not mean that they cannot or should not confront the behavior, dispensing swift and sure consequences for the child's misbehavior. The important thing to remember is that, ultimately, the child must not feel that he or she has been disenfranchised; on the contrary, the child with ODD must understand that her membership in the class is inviolable.

D. ***Long-term prevention.*** Like the other two target behaviors, the most effective means of preventing a recurrence of peer aggression is through the child and her caregivers' participation in an effective intervention program such as the Incredible Years Training Program (IYTP). Specifically, the IYTP teaches the student effective strategies that help the affected individual reduce defiant behaviors, as well as related conduct problems such as noncompliance and peer aggression and rejection, among others. To reiterate, the eventual goal of any school-based intervention relative to the child who exhibits oppositional and defiant behavior is the effective replacement of those undesirable behaviors with ones that are pro-social and self-affirming.

 FROM THE FIELD

James Slavet, Ph.D.

James Slavet is a clinical psychologist at the Manville School, which is part of Judge Baker Children's Center in Boston, Massachusetts. He earned a Ph.D. from UMass–Amherst in 2004, where he focused on research and training opportunities with court-involved youth. He was an intern in the Department of Public Behavioral Health and Justice Policy at the University of Washington and a postdoctoral fellow at Brown University and the Rhode Island Training School. His current interests include the application of evidence-based practices to therapy with children and families.

You've worked with a large number of students who were both oppositional and defiant. How would you describe the typical behaviors of these children?

Typically, students diagnosed with ODD actively disobey rules and regulations, argue with authority figures, and disrupt teaching and classroom activities. Students presenting with oppositional and defiant behaviors are often struggling with other emotional and/or learning problems. It is important to generate hypotheses regarding the function of oppositional and defiant behaviors for an individual student (Why is he or she acting this way?). For example, some students may exhibit these behaviors while they are angry, others might act this way when they feel as though they have little control over their environment, and still others may be modeling behaviors of peers or siblings. Understanding the function of behavior can help you plan an appropriate intervention for an individual student.

In your experience, what is it about the oppositional-defiant child that presents the greatest challenge to the teacher and to teaching?

I think that the greatest challenge for teachers is forming a solid relationship with oppositional-defiant children. It can be extremely frustrating when a child defies classroom rules, disrupts the class, and is openly hostile towards the teacher, and it is very challenging not to take this behavior personally. If a teacher is able to disapprove of the behavior, while still showing that he or she cares about the student, it can go a long way to building respect and a positive relationship. This kind of positive teacher–student relationship is especially important with students who have oppositional and defiant behaviors. Typically, these students have been often punished both at school and at home, and have internalized these experiences into their identity. A positive relationship with an adult focused on their strengths and pro-social behaviors can be the key to shifting behaviors.

As a novice, I'm sure that you, like all of us, made a few mistakes with these students. For the benefit of the new and inexperienced teachers who are reading this, could you share one or two of these "missteps" with us so that we can be aware of and, hopefully, avoid them?

My biggest mistake has been trying to reason with a child who is exhibiting oppositional or defiant behavior. Rarely is a child available for a rational conversation when he or she is behaving this way. When I've tried to reason with students during an instance of problematic behavior, it has only led to an increase in the intensity of the problem. I remember one occasion, during my first year working at Manville School, a teacher and I debated the utility of school rules over and over again with a particular student. It turned out that this student ended up liking debating the rules with us much more than going to class. It took us a while to figure out that he was purposely acting out to get out of class so that he could get our attention!

Can you provide a few of your most effective strategies for working successfully with these students? For, example, tips that you wish someone had given you when you started working with this population?

I believe that the most important strategy in working successfully with students who are displaying oppositional defiant behavior is to shower them with positive reinforcement when they are not displaying problematic behavior. This is difficult and at times counterintuitive. People often say, "Why should I reward a kid for doing what he or she is supposed to do anyway?" It is important to realize that doing the "right" thing and the "effective" thing are sometimes different.

Ignoring problematic behavior is critical, but sometimes the behavior is so bad that a student needs to be removed from the class or "consequenced" in another way. But for these students, the way in which the consequence is handed out is just as important as the consequence itself. Whenever possible, giving a verbal consequence in front of the class in a pejorative tone should be avoided. Writing students a note clearly describing the consequence usually works pretty well; in my experience, they find it harder to argue with a clearly written statement!

Finally, could you share an anecdote from your teaching repertoire that highlights one of your most memorable successes in working with a student who has a conduct disorder?

Several years ago I was working with an adolescent girl who was incarcerated. Her behavior problems were among the most intense that I have worked with. When I first met her she refused to follow most of the staff rules, often fought verbally and physically with peers, and had conflictive relationships with most of her family members. In therapy, I was able to engage her in a discussion of her strengths, her goals, and, and her interpersonal relationships. We spent almost no time discussing her "bad behavior." I was also able to include her mother in therapy sessions. While we had intense discussions and talked about some important issues, she remained oppositional at times in therapy and had very little immediate behavior change outside of therapy. Therapy ended after she was transferred to a different facility, due mostly to her bad behavior. Months later, I received a letter from her thanking me for the work we had done together. She told me of the great changes that she had made in her behavior and her upcoming return to living in the community with her family. In the letter, she repeated back several phrases that I had used with her in therapy and she had seemed to internalize these concepts. She taught me the important lesson that people change their behavior on their own schedule, and while our work might not have led to an immediate change in her behavior, it ultimately did help her. Classroom teachers don't have the luxury of the time afforded by therapy, but they may still benefit from this lesson. As I mentioned earlier, a positive relationship with an adult who ignores negative behaviors as much as possible while focusing on and reinforcing strengths and pro-social behaviors can be the key to shifting behaviors.

Summary

Perhaps the most challenging students teachers must instruct are those with defiance disorders. Some researchers have suggested that oppositional defiant disorder is a precursor to its more serious manifestation, conduct disorder. If this is so, it then follows that teachers are in a unique position to intervene in the development of the disorder and prevent its pernicious evolution.

Prevalence rates for ODD range anywhere from 2 to 16 percent (American Psychiatric Association, 2000) because of the historical lack of precision in diagnosing ODD and the difficulty of distinguishing mild ODD from normal, developmentally appropriate behavior (Greene, 2006). ODD is twice as common in boys as in girls, and it is most frequently diagnosed in children under age 8. Moreover, ODD is highly comorbid with ADHD and with anxiety and mood disorders. Finally, because a defining characteristic of ODD is social impairment, some studies have looked at the overlap between ODD and autism spectrum disorder. In one study, more than half of the children diagnosed with ASD also met the criteria for ODD (Greene et al., 2002).

The principal characteristics of the ODD are opposition and defiance that have become a developmentally inappropriate pattern of behavior, with high levels of negativistic, disobedient, and hostile behavior, especially toward authority figures. These behaviors include temper outbursts, persistent stubbornness, resistance to following directions, unwillingness to compromise, give in, or negotiate with adults or peers; deliberate or persistent testing of limits; and verbal (and minor physical) aggression (Greene, 2006, p. 285). In addition, children with ODD tend to have a hostile attribution bias (Behan & Carr, 2000) that causes them to react aggressively to otherwise neutral environmental stimuli. The aggression associated with ODD is often the result of a perceived threat or provocation and is for the most part directed at authority figures, whereas children with ADHD and CD have social problems that are more generalized.

Etiological factors in the development of ODD can be divided into biological factors, parenting and family factors, and the child's social-cognitive processes. Studies have consistently established a link between parenting and family characteristics and the development of ODD. Family dysfunction, lower levels of family income, higher levels of authoritarian parenting, lower levels of parental warmth and supervision, and inconsistent discipline have all been implicated in the development of ODD (Boyle & Pickles, 1998; Frick et al., 1992; Rey & Plapp, 1990).

Researchers have agreed that the assessment of ODD should come from multiple sources (e.g., Hendren & Mullen, 2006). Clinicians and other professionals have relied on diagnostic interviews, rating scales, and reviews of school records to gather information en route to making a diagnosis of ODD. The assessment of ODD must also take place across settings, people, and events. If the emergence of ODD is the result of a poor match between a child's behavior and the parent's response to that behavior, assessment must take into consideration information about the child, the adult, and environmental circumstances that contribute to the oppositional interactions (Greene, 2006). This is true for interactions that take place at home with the parent, as well as those that take place in the school with the teacher and other school personnel. Finally, a thorough developmental, school, and treatment history should be gathered.

Lastly, in this chapter we identified several research-based interventions that have demonstrated success in mitigating the behaviors of ODD in school-aged children. One of the more popular of these is the Incredible Years Training Program (IYTP; Webster-Stratton & Reid, 2003c), which provides explicit training programs for all key stakeholders—teachers, parents, and affected children. Using a case example, we developed an assessment plan that helped identify target behaviors and their specific functions and, as a result, an effective intervention plan to address each of the problem behaviors.

Tips for Teachers

1. Do not allow the child to draw you into an argument that can escalate. Likewise, be careful not to use ultimatums (e.g., "If you say one more word, I will assign you a 30-minute detention," or "Get up out of your seat and leave the room at once—I want you out of here!"). These kinds of responses often force the child to choose between compliance (sometimes viewed as a sign of weakness) and insubordination that will invariably result in punishment.

2. Plan a regular conference time for the student during which his or her comments and expressed feelings will not be subject to censure or sanctions. This will show the student that there are socially appropriate times and places for expressing anger and frustration.

3. Investigate the causes of the student's agitation. Take immediate steps to provide relief from the source, and help the student select a more appropriate behavioral approach.

4. Praise the student frequently for making appropriate behavioral choices; remind the individual that, ultimately, he or she is responsible for both the good and bad ones.

5. Become an "expert" in identifying the verbal and nonverbal signals characteristic to the individual that precede a behavioral incident.

6. Say what you mean and mean what you say! If you must give the student a warning or an ultimatum, make sure that you follow through. Sometimes teachers feel compelled to give the student an "if, then" condition: "If you do this, or if you don't do that, then . . . (name a

consequence)." Occasionally, such an admonition is a reaction to what is perceived as "outrageous" behavior; frequently, it is simply a human response to what ostensibly is disrespect. Nevertheless, if you do assign a consequence, then you are duty-bound to deliver. The same is true for the promise of a reward. Students who have ODD are used to inconsistency in dealings with authority figures and the meting out of consequences, good or bad. This inconsistent treatment is often a factor in the development of their defiant behavior (Chamberlain & Patterson, 1995; Patterson, Reid, & Dishion, 1992).

7. Set boundaries around the inappropriate behavior. Speak privately with the child and, keeping in mind that defiance of authority is a sign not of strength but of a fragile ego, establish yourself as the benevolent authority. Explain that although you understand that the child may have underlying issues and that you will help him or her try to understand them, you will not tolerate the inappropriate behavior. Stress the seriousness of the situation and the consequences if it persists (Pierangelo & Giuliani, 2000a, 2000b, 2001).

8. Try to help the student understand why she is defiant. Encourage her to verbalize what she is feeling or why she does what he does. If she cannot give voice to her feelings, you may want to provide her with some descriptors. For example, you may want to say that you have seen other students defy authority because they felt they were not doing well in school, had problems at home, or felt

rejected by peers (Pierangelo & Giuliani, 2000a, 2000b, 2001).

9. If the defiant behavior follows a consistent pattern, confer with the student's parents to obtain information about any issues at home. Consult with the school counseling or social work staff or the school psychologist about developing a behavioral contract for the student. Parent involvement will be important. Finally, if the problem is severe and persists, consult the school's pupil personnel or child study team (Pierangelo & Giuliani, 2000a, 2000b, 2001).

10. Arrange for a safe and supervised "time-out" or "chill space." The purpose of such a place is to provide a neutral site where the student can "cool off" when he becomes aware that he is about to "lose it." Give him a laminated "chill pass" to show you before he leaves the room. Praise him for his self-awareness and good choice in removing himself from the classroom and taking a positive time-out rather than succumbing to his volatile and unpredictable emotions. If the student seems to abuse this privilege, discuss your concerns in a private conference and negotiate the number of times he may use the pass, encouraging him to reduce the frequency of its use as he learns to employ more appropriate coping strategies. Suggestion: Because students who exhibit defiance disorders often prefer to receive praise or criticism in private, avoid publicly "spotlighting" them with public display of praise and criticism (Pierangelo & Giuliani, 2000a, 2000b, 2001).

Focus Questions Revisited

1. Why is it so important that we address oppositional defiant disorder (ODD) behaviors observed in our students quickly and effectively?

A Sample Response

It is important that we address these defiant behaviors for two reasons: (a) because the defining characteristics, which can include temper outbursts,

persistent stubbornness, resistance to following directions, unwillingness to compromise, deliberate limit testing, and verbal aggression, make teaching these students very challenging, if not almost impossible; and (b) because a significant number of children with ODD often progress to the more serious diagnosis of conduct disorder (Eaves et al., 2000; Hendren & Mullen, 2006).

2. What characteristic behaviors are symptomatic of ODD?

A Sample Response

Characteristic behaviors include negativistic, hostile, and defiant behavior lasting as least 6 months, during which four (or more) of the following are present: (a) often loses temper; (b) often argues with adults; (c) often actively defies or refuses to comply with adults' requests or rules; (d) often deliberately annoys people; (e) often blames others for his or her mistakes or misbehavior; (f) is often touch or easily annoyed by others; (g) is often angry and resentful; and (h) is often spiteful or vindictive (American Psychiatric Association, 2000).

3. What does research say about the probable causes of ODD?

A Sample Response

Research has established a link between parenting styles—specifically, patterns of discipline and the role of coercion—and the integrity of the family unit in the development of ODD (e.g., Boyle & Pickles, 1998; Chamberlain & Patterson, 1995). Similarly, some investigators (Chamberlain & Patterson, 1995; Patterson, Reid, & Dishion, 1992) have identified specific parenting traits that may be instrumental in the genesis of ODD. These traits include: (a) inconsistent discipline, (b) explosive discipline, (c) low supervision and involvement, and (d) inflexible, rigid discipline. In contrast, other research has pointed to child characteristics—in particular, the capacity of the child for emotional regulation, frustration tolerance, adaptation, and problem solving. These studies regarded the affected child as simply unable to learn the skills needed for compliance (Greene, 2006; Greene & Ablon, 2005). A more popular explanation contends that ODD may be more accurately described as a recursive effect created by these two dynamic variables, that is, the interaction effect between child and parent (Kochanska & Askan, 1995).

4. How is ODD appropriately assessed?

A Sample Response

As is the case for all emotional behavioral disorders, assessment of ODD should come from multiple sources. Professionals should administer rating scales, conduct diagnostic interviews, review school records, and examine the structured and unstructured observations of teachers, parents, and other stakeholders to confirm a diagnosis of ODD (Hendren & Mullen, 2006). Furthermore, because the disorder is often linked to the quality of the child–parent interaction, the assessment process should investigate the nature of the parental relationships of the child in question (Greene, 2006).

5. According to the best practice evidence provided in this chapter, which of the treatment options appears to be most effective? What are its principal strengths?

A Sample Response

The most popular and well-supported intervention described in the chapter is the Incredible Years Training Series (IYTS; Webster-Stratton, 1992; Webster-Stratton & Reid, 2003). The principal strength of this program is its recognition of the importance of long-term commitment on the part of all three stakeholders: the parents, the child, and the teachers. For example, the goal of the parent intervention training component is to increase competency in parenting skills relative to the affected child, improve parent–child communication, and strengthen the family unit through the development of support networks that include collaboration with teachers and other professionals.

Similarly, the teacher training intervention component stresses the importance of increasing collaboration with parents. It also provides the teacher with training in effective classroom management techniques, especially those that address working with disruptive behaviors, promote positive relationships with difficult students, and strengthen social skills (Webster-Stratton & Reid, 2003).

Finally, the child training intervention component helps to strengthen the child's social skills, promotes greater self-control through the acquisition of problem-solving strategies, increases emotional awareness by enhancing perspective taking and teaching the child to label feelings, teaches conflict-management strategies, and helps to improve academic success by focusing on key skill areas, thereby reducing the child's innate sense of failure and increasing self-esteem and self-confidence (Webster-Stratton & Reid, 2003).

6. Suppose you have a student in your classroom who has ODD. What are some interventions you might employ to help him control and, ultimately, reduce his defiant behaviors while simultaneously increasing his pro-social ones?

A Sample Response

Acknowledging, of course, that every child is unique and will most assuredly present distinctive problem behaviors, the child with ODD will likely present one or two of the behaviors identified in the example case of Jack Straw. Of course, one must conduct a functional behavioral assessment, both to identify and confirm the target behaviors and to identify the purpose served by each one. Accordingly, the interventions employed must be research-based and address effectively the identified target behaviors and their functions.

Suppose, for example, that the student is similar in his expression of oppositional-defiant behaviors to the case example of Jack Straw. In such a case, the following approaches might be tried: (a) plan a regular conference time for the student during which his comments and expressed feelings are not subject to censure or sanctions, which will show him that there are socially appropriate times and places for expressing anger and frustration; (b) investigate the causes of the student's agitation and take immediate steps to provide relief from the source and help the student select a more appropriate behavioral approach; (c) praise the student frequently for making appropriate behavioral choices and remind him that, ultimately, he is responsible for both the good and bad ones; (d) become an "expert" in identifying the verbal and nonverbal signals characteristic to the individual that precede a behavioral incident; (e) set boundaries around the inappropriate behavior; (f) speak privately with the child and, keeping in mind that defiance of authority is a sign not of strength but of a fragile ego, establish yourself as the benevolent authority; and finally, (g) try to help the student understand why he is defiant and encourage him to verbalize what he is feeling or why he does what he does—if he cannot give voice to his feelings, you may want to provide him with some descriptors.

7. What other professional support might you solicit in your efforts to help a student who has ODD?

A Sample Response

If the defiant behavior follows a consistent pattern, confer with the student's parents to obtain information about any issues at home. Consult with the school counseling or social work staff or the school psychologist about developing a behavioral contract for the student. Finally, if the problem is severe and persists, consult the school's pupil personnel or child study team and solicit their help in addressing the difficulty.

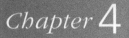

Chapter 4

Attention-Deficit
Hyperactivity Disorder

Peggy Gans

FOCUS QUESTIONS

1. Differentiate the three types of attention-deficit hyperactivity disorder (ADHD) as presented in the DSM-IV-TR. Which of the three poses the greatest challenge in the classroom and why?

2. As the teacher of a student who has ADHD, would you advocate for the use of a pharmacological intervention?

3. What can the teachers of a student suspected of having ADHD do to provide meaningful data to help inform the multidisciplinary team and thus facilitate the referral process?

4. Discuss the controversy surrounding the classification of ADHD. Based on your knowledge of the disorder, should ADHD be classified as an emotional/behavioral disorder, a health impairment, a learning disability, or is it distinctive and therefore deserving of a separate category?

5. Why do many "experts" contend that arriving at a correct diagnosis of ADHD is one of the most challenging tasks for clinicians?

6. After reviewing the section in the chapter on pharmacological interventions used in the treatment of ADHD, what are your impressions of its efficacy?

INTRODUCTION

A Brief Explanation

I [Vance Austin] would like to alert the reader at the start of this chapter that, unlike all the others, only one author's voice will be discernible: mine. Dan Sciarra has graciously acceded to my request to write this one alone. That request is predicated on the fact that the majority of the students with whom I work and have worked for the past 25 years have been diagnosed with attention-deficit hyperactivity disorder (ADHD) in one of its three forms or subtypes. Accordingly, I consider myself somewhat practiced in the identification, education, and treatment of ADHD in children and youth, and Dan has been kind enough to humor me in this conviction.

I am compelled to further advise the reader that whereas research presently contends that there are two *somewhat* distinctive "types" of the disorder, namely, *predominantly inattentive type* and *predominantly hyperactive-impulsive type,* a third type comprised of a combination of the characteristics of these two is becoming increasingly prevalent. However, all three subtypes of ADHD share the same purported etiologies, are assessed using the same instruments, and are similarly treated. Accordingly, this chapter begins with two case examples: Vincent, diagnosed with ADHD, predominantly hyperactive-impulsive type; and Brett, diagnosed with ADHD, predominantly inattentive type. A case example is not provided for the "combined" category because the behavioral characteristics of a child with this typology are clearly delineated in the other two cases.

Finally, I have included an extensive review of the use of pharmacological interventions in the treatment of ADHD. The coverage of this aspect of treatment may seem to be excessive, but the reason should be apparent given the ubiquity of **methylphenidate (Ritalin)** as the preferred treatment for the disorder.

METHYLPHENIDATE (RITALIN)

A prescription stimulant commonly used to treat attention-deficit hyperactivity disorder (ADHD). It is also one of the primary drugs used to treat the daytime drowsiness symptoms of narcolepsy and chronic fatigue syndrome. The drug is seeing early use to treat cancer-related fatigue.

Methylphenidate, the most widely prescribed drug for children, is also acknowledged to be among the most abused drugs by school-age children in the United States (Drug Enforcement Administration, National Drug Threat Assessment, 2008; National Institute on Drug Abuse. Fact Sheet, 2006; PBS *Frontline,* 2001). Furthermore, the prodigious lack of research concerning the effects of the prolonged use of methylphenidate has prompted me to ensure that the reader is fully informed both as to the potential for harm, as well as the recommended procedures for its prescription and use.

ADHD Introduced

ADHD has been described as the most common neurobiological disorder of childhood (Furman, 2005). Its cause is believed to be primarily a malfunctioning of **neurotransmitters** that facilitate the transfer of signals from one neuron to another. Specifically, there appears to be a deficiency in a specific neurotransmitter known as **dopamine** (Bower, 2003; Litner, 2003; Tannock & Martinussen, 2001). As a result, this inefficient neurotransmission in response to the reduced levels of dopamine impairs the executive functioning of the brain, which is reportedly focused in the **prefrontal cortex**. Although this perspective is debated, a majority of researchers support it (Furman, 2005).

Just as controversial is the classification of ADHD under the Individuals with Disabilities Education Improvement Act (IDEIA; U.S. Department of Education, 2004). Currently, many students who have been diagnosed with ADHD receive special education and related services under the category, "Other Health Impaired," whereas others, whose symptoms may not be as severe or affect their educational performance to a degree considered appropriate for classification under IDEIA (U.S. Department of Education, 2004) may receive accommodations under Section 504 of the Rehabilitation Act of 1973 (Smith, Polloway, Patton, & Dowdy, 2006). However, many practitioners still consider ADHD to be primarily an emotional/behavioral disorder given that its presenting symptoms appear to be principally behavioral. In contrast, other investigators have contended that ADHD affects the cognitive processing areas of the brain and should therefore be considered a learning disorder (Tannock & Martinussen, 2001). The following two cases provide helpful examples of actual students who have been diagnosed with ADHD.

CASE EXAMPLE: Vincent

ADHD, Predominantly Hyperactive-Impulsive Type

Vincent is an eighth-grader attending Parksdale Middle School. He was diagnosed with ADHD, predominately hyperactive-impulsive type, while in the third grade, and his behaviors have become more intense and pervasive of late. Vincent's parents report that his teachers and principal call frequently to complain about his "acting out" in school. They also have noted that his impulsivity is becoming more of a challenge at home, as well as in his after-school activities. His friends have ostracized him because of his volatility and mercurial temper. He recently punched one of his friends because he fouled Vincent accidentally in a basketball game. Vincent apologized and reportedly felt bad about his behavior, but he does not seem able to stop it.

Academically, Vincent continues to struggle in all content areas. He is receiving his instruction in self-contained special education classes because it was determined that he would not be provided sufficient help or structure in general education classes. Even with the additional support, Vincent is receiving grades of "incomplete" in English and social studies. Behaviorally, he is also in jeopardy. The principal has called for several meetings with the Committee for Special Education (CSE), as well as Vincent's parents, to discuss more effective approaches for dealing with his hyperactivity and impulsivity.

A recent incident is representative of Vincent's impulsive behavior. Following a class trip, Vincent was cavorting with two of his friends when suddenly, as his mother pulled her car in front of the school building to take him home, he slapped one of the boys "very hard" across the face. He then ran to his mother's car and they drove away, leaving the injured student crying in the foyer. An assistant principal, who witnessed the incident, ran outside to apprehend Vincent but was too late. On the next school day, Vincent was called to the office and the incident was reviewed. Vincent admitted "playfully" slapping the other student but insisted it was just in fun and that he and the other student frequently engaged in "play fighting." Nevertheless, the principal, in accordance with school policy, suspended Vincent for 2 days and called home to inform his parents and request a meeting with them about the incident.

His parents are convinced that some of Vincent's teachers as well as the school administration "have it in for him" because he is a bit active and "stands up for himself." This has created an adversarial relationship between Vincent's parents and school administrators that has adversely affected communication and cooperation.

Recently, Vincent's parents have taken him to an outside specialist, a psychiatrist who was recommended to them as an expert in diagnosing and working with students who have ADHD. The psychiatrist has determined that Vincent is appropriately diagnosed as having ADHD, hyperactive-impulsive type, and has recommended that, in addition to cognitive-behavioral therapy and family therapy, Vincent be prescribed a trial dose of Ritalin (methylphenidate). Vincent's parents support the CBT and family therapy, but they are uncomfortable with the pharmacological intervention recommended. They have expressed concern about the adverse affects produced by the medication and the impact of long-term use. Vincent, they say, has the skill to become a professional athlete, and they fear that his use of methylphenidate might impair his chances for success in basketball. The school administration, however, is strongly urging that Vincent comply with the psychiatrist's recommendations and begin the medication trial, citing its beneficial effect for students who have similar diagnoses.

Currently, as noted earlier, Vincent is receiving his instruction in self-contained special education classes for the content-area subjects. He participates in a general education gym class and has lunch in the cafeteria with all the students in his grade level at the school. His behavioral problems continue despite the extra support he receives in the special classes; however, he has made some academic gains in all of the core subjects. School administrators as well as his teachers share legitimate concerns about his successful transition to the high school next year, because of its size and reduced structure. Working with Vincent continues to be challenging.

CASE EXAMPLE: Brett

ADHD, Predominantly Inattentive Type

Brett's situation is unusual in that a formal diagnosis of ADHD, predominantly inattentive type, was not made until he was 12 years old. This may be explained, in part, by the fact that he was a very congenial, cooperative boy, who was willing to seek extra help to ensure academic success. He also had siblings who were older and academically proficient, who could and did provide him with remedial support. Also, Brett has always been very athletic and excels in basketball, having participated on both the JV and varsity basketball teams at school. In fact, Brett's diagnosis was so exceptional that his parents believed it might be better accounted for by a concussion he suffered as a result of a mid-court collision in a pick-up game in middle school. Extensive neurological tests, as well as magnetic resonance imaging (MRI), revealed no evidence of brain injury or trauma.

However, as Brett's teachers reviewed his academic records and quarterly teacher comments, a pattern of concern over episodic distractibility and occasional inattentiveness began to materialize. These episodes of inattention and disorganization began to increase in frequency during the middle school grades, prompting the recommendation that Brett be evaluated for special education services to address these areas of concern. An outside child psychologist with experience in diagnosing and treating children with ADHD determined that Brett had the disorder—specifically, ADHD, predominantly inattentive type. At school, the multidisciplinary referral team reviewed records and conducted tests such as the *Conners' Parent and Teacher Rating Scales—Revised* (Conners, 1997) and was satisfied that Brett had been appropriately diagnosed with ADHD and would benefit from special education services under the category of "Other Health Impaired." Currently, at age 16, Brett's treatment regimen includes, in addition to self-management techniques, the use of **dextroamphetamine (Adderall)**. Even his basketball coach has noted Brett's improvement on and off the court: his increase in focus and attention, and his improved self-confidence.

CHARACTERISTICS OF ADHD

ADHD is identified symptomatically in the *Diagnostic and Statistical Manual for Mental Disorders* (DSM-IV-TR; American Psychiatric Association, 2000) according to criteria for inattentiveness, hyperactivity, and impulsivity (see Table 4.1). In addition, some of those symptoms need to have been evident before age 7. Furthermore, some of the symptoms need to be observable in two or more settings (e.g., school, home, work, or in community activities). Similarly, the symptoms must significantly impair social, occupational, or academic performance, and they cannot be better accounted for as a mood disorder, anxiety disorder, disassociative disorder, or personality disorder.

ADHD comprises three subtypes: (1) predominantly inattentive, (2) predominantly hyperactive-impulsive, and (3) combined (types 1 and 2) (American Psychiatric Association, 2000).

ADHD, Predominantly Inattentive Type

Students who have ADHD, predominantly inattentive type, typically perform poorly in school, and 35 to 50 percent can be appropriately codiagnosed with a specific learning disability (Brown, 1996). These students typically make careless mistakes in school, and they have real difficulty staying on task and screening out irrelevant stimuli. An example of this type of ADHD is provided in the case example of Brett.

ADHD, Predominantly Hyperactive-Impulsive Type

Students diagnosed with ADHD, predominantly hyperactive-impulsive type, seem to have boundless energy and have great difficulty staying in one place

TABLE 4.1 DSM-IV-TR Criteria for ADHD

I. Either A or B:

A. Six or more of the following symptoms of inattention have been present for at least 6 months to a point that is disruptive and inappropriate for developmental level:

Inattention

1. Often does not give close attention to details or makes careless mistakes in schoolwork, work, or other activities.

2. Often has trouble keeping attention on tasks or play activities.

3. Often does not seem to listen when spoken to directly.

4. Often does not follow instructions and fails to finish schoolwork, chores, or duties in the workplace (not due to oppositional behavior or failure to understand instructions).

5. Often has trouble organizing activities.

6. Often avoids, dislikes, or doesn't want to do things that take a lot of mental effort for a long period of time (such as schoolwork or homework).

7. Often loses things needed for tasks and activities (e.g., toys, school assignments, pencils, books, or tools).

8. Is often easily distracted.

9. Is often forgetful in daily activities.

B. Six or more of the following symptoms of hyperactivity-impulsivity have been present for at least 6 months to an extent that is disruptive and inappropriate for developmental level:

Hyperactivity

1. Often fidgets with hands or feet or squirms in seat.

2. Often gets up from seat when remaining in seat is expected.

3. Often runs about or climbs when and where it is not appropriate (adolescents or adults may feel very restless).

4. Often has trouble playing or enjoying leisure activities quietly.

5. Is often "on the go" or often acts as if "driven by a motor."

Impulsivity

1. Often blurts out answers before questions have been finished.

2. Often has trouble waiting one's turn.

3. Often interrupts or intrudes on others (e.g., butts into conversations or games).

II. Some symptoms that cause impairment were present before age 7 years.

III. Some impairment from the symptoms is present in two or more settings (e.g., at school/work and at home).

IV. There must be clear evidence of significant impairment in social, school, or work functioning.

V. The symptoms do not happen only during the course of a Pervasive Developmental Disorder, Schizophrenia, or other Psychotic Disorder. The symptoms are not better accounted for by another mental disorder (e.g., Mood Disorder, Anxiety Disorder, Dissociative Disorder, or a Personality Disorder).

Based on these criteria, three types of ADHD are identified:

1. ADHD, *Combined Type:* If both criteria 1A and 1B are met for the past 6 months.

2. ADHD, *Predominantly Inattentive Type:* If criterion 1A is met but criterion 1B is not met for the past 6 months.

3. ADHD, *Predominantly Hyperactive-Impulsive Type:* If Criterion 1B is met but Criterion 1A is not met for the past six months.

Source: American Psychiatric Association (2000). *Diagnostic and statistical manual of mental disorders, fourth edition, text revision.* Washington, DC: American Psychiatric Association.

for an extended period of time: They cannot seem to sit still. In school, this often results in discipline referrals, which only exacerbate the problem. Paradoxically, as a result of the time spent out of class caused by frequent discipline referrals, students who have this type of ADHD tend to miss important aspects of the curriculum. Such absences seriously impact the affected students' academic performance and identify them as "troublemakers" as well.

In conjunction with the symptom of hyperactivity, students who have this type of ADHD also experience **disinhibition**. This suppression of the inhibitory response mechanism in the cerebral cortex often results in impulsivity (Myers, Collett, & Ohan, 2003; National Institutes of Health Consensus Statement, 1998). This impulsiveness can manifest in poor choices in the classroom—for example, affected students may blurt out answers in the classroom, they may intrude on or interrupt the activities of other children, and they experience real difficulty with turn taking (Schlozman & Schlozman, 2000). Vincent, the student profiled at the beginning of the chapter, is a classic example of a child with ADHD, predominantly hyperactive-impulsive type.

DISINHIBITION

Loss of inhibition, as through the influence of external stimuli, such as drugs or alcohol, or as a result of brain damage.

ADHD, Combined Type

Students displaying the characteristics of both hyperactivity-impulsivity and inattention represent the fastest-growing and most common diagnostic category of ADHD (Furman, 2005). They display, in varying degrees, several of the behaviors of hyperactivity-impulsivity, as well as inattention described in the DSM-IV-TR and, as a result, present teachers with a significant challenge to manage the unproductive behaviors associated with hyperactivity and impulsivity while helping the student stay focused (Austin, 2003; Kauffman, 2005).

UNIVERSAL CHARACTERISTICS

It is not surprising, based on these behavioral characteristics, that children and youth with ADHD experience significant academic challenges. Typically, these educational problems occur in strategic areas that include written expression, listening skills, reading, general knowledge, and social functioning (Bender, 1997). In addition, children with ADHD perform slightly lower on general intelligence tests than same-age peers, which may account, in part, for the increase in hyperactivity (Wicks-Nelson & Israel, 2005). Furthermore, it is estimated that 30 percent of children with ADHD repeat a grade at school, 30 to 40 percent are classified under IDEA to receive special education services, and approximately 56 percent need academic tutoring. Finally, between 10 and 35 percent of these students may fail to graduate from high school (Wicks-Nelson & Israel, 2005).

Cognitively, students who have ADHD evidence deficits in executive functioning that involves planning, organizing, inhibitory responses, mentally representing a task, switching strategies, and self-regulation.

Social skills deficits are consistently present in a majority of students who have ADHD. These are exacerbated by estimates that suggest that 50 to 70 percent of students who have ADHD have concomitant emotional or behavioral disorders, principally, conduct disorder (30 to 50 percent) and oppositional defiance disorder (35 to 70 percent), which are characterized by poor or deficient social skills (Johnston & Ohan, 1999; Kauffman, 2005). In addition, studies suggest that about 25 percent of these children also have anxiety disorder, which is also highly correlated with poor social skills development (e.g., Barkley, 1998; Jensen, Martin, & Cantwell, 1997). As a result of poorly developed social skills and undesirable behaviors exhibited by students who have ADHD—such as poor turn taking, lack of focus, hyperactivity, and forgetfulness—students who have ADHD are often the least popular and most disliked by peers and teachers (Barkley & Murphy, 1998; Hinshaw, 1994a; Schlozman & Schlozman, 2000).

Lastly, and perhaps most important, students who have ADHD pose significant problems for the family and its relationship to them. The principal problem seems to be one of perception: Mothers and fathers as well as siblings tend to view the inattentive, hyperactive-impulsive behaviors of the family member with ADHD as volitional—intentionally oppositional and defiant or adversarial. This leads to disaffection and alienation of the child with ADHD and a tendency to view her or him as the "black sheep" of the family. However, there is growing evidence that supports the heritability of ADHD, and thus many of the behaviors viewed as undesirable by the parents may, in fact, be shadowy reflections of their own behaviors (Barkley, 2003; Biederman, Faraone, & Lapey, 1992; National Institutes of Health Consensus Statement, 1998). In any event, family systems theory, popularized in the 1990s, suggests that dysfunction affecting one member of the family, in this case, the child with ADHD, invariably affects every member of the family to some extent (Wicks-Nelson & Israel, 2005).

In addition, a point of interest is the fact that, compared with control groups, children with ADHD experience significantly more accidental injuries. For example, 7 percent of students who have ADHD suffered accidental poisoning, compared with 3 percent of students who do not have ADHD; similarly, 23 percent had bone fractures, in contrast to only 15 percent of students who do not have ADHD (Pastor & Reuben, 2006; PBS *Frontline,* 2008).

PREVALENCE AND COMORBIDITY

Kauffman (2005) noted that the difficulty experienced by stakeholders in reaching a consensus about what are viewed as universal characteristics for ADHD makes it very difficult to estimate how many school-age children actually have ADHD. Estimates of prevalence of between 3 and 5 percent of school-age children qualify it as one of the most common reasons for referral for special education (Hallahan, Lloyd, Kauffman, Weiss, & Martinez, 2005; National Institutes of Health, 1998). Boys are identified three times as often as girls; this disparity may be explained, in part, by gender bias, but it may also be a function of fundamental behavioral differences between boys and girls (Kauffman, 2005).

ADHD is frequently comorbid with other types of emotional and behavioral disorders. For example, research has suggested that between 19 and 63 percent of children with ADHD could also be identified as having a learning disability. Barkley, DuPaul, and McMurray (1990) were perhaps the more conservative of these experts, whereas Silver (1998) believed that this overlap is far higher (30 and 50 percent), and McKinney, Montague, and Hocutt (1993) argued that it could be as high as 63 percent.

Another concomitant disorder is oppositional defiant disorder (ODD). According to DuPaul and Stoner (1994), more than half of children with ADHD have ODD as well, making it the most frequently identified comorbid condition.

Finally, Jordan (1998) and Weyandt (2001), among others, maintained that possibly as many as 65 percent of children whose primary diagnosis is ADHD could also be said to have conduct disorder. However, it has been our experience that most children with ADHD behave in a manner that is impulsive but in which the consequences of these behaviors are seldom malicious or premeditated. As we noted in Chapter 2, children with conduct disorder typically engage in behaviors that are disruptive or destructive with **intentionality**. Consequently, we find the high rate of comorbidity suggested by Jordan (1998), Weyandt (2001), and others to be counterintuitive.

ETIOLOGY OF ADHD

Although no single cause of ADHD has been identified or substantiated, there are several hypotheses concerning its etiology. The most popular cause of ADHD is believed to be neurological dysfunction or genetic predisposition (Kauffman, 2005); however, some researchers have posited other causative hypotheses. These include brain structure and activity, pregnancy and birth complications, poor nutrition and dietary concerns, environmental factors (e.g., lead exposure), and psychosocial factors (family factors).

Brain Structure and Activity

Some researchers have suggested that individuals with ADHD have brain abnormalities; that is, that the brains of these persons are anatomically different from those of persons without ADHD. For example, researchers in one study found that the total brain volume of boys with ADHD is 5 percent less than that of boys without the condition (Castellanos, Giedd, Eckburg, & Marsh, 1994; Castellanos & Swanson, 2002). Similarly, the corpus callosum and the cerebellum are sometimes smaller in individuals with ADHD. These anomalies would help account for the problems with motor coordination and certain kinds of memory recall experienced by individuals with the disorder. The most prevalent anomaly, however, is the measurably smaller right frontal area of the brain referred to as the caudate nucleus, as well as the globus pallidus (Barkley & Murphy, 1998; Tannock, 1998). Finally, investigators are now focusing on the role of neurotransmitters on brain functioning—specifically, **norepinephrine**, dopamine, and **serotonin** (Myers et al., 2003; Taylor, 1994).

Pregnancy and Birth Complications

There is evidence to support a correlation between low birth weight and attention problems, as well as increased activity and impulsivity. Similarly, maternal alcohol and substance abuse also correlate to increased activity level, attention deficits, and organizational problems in the developing infant. Medical investigators continue to hypothesize a connection between pregnancy and birth complications; to date, however, little evidence supports this contention (Wick-Nelson & Israel, 2005).

INTENTIONALITY

A behavior or act that is thoughtfully planned and executed; it is not carried out impulsively.

NOREPINEPHRINE

A stress hormone, norepinephrine affects parts of the brain where attention and responding actions are controlled. Along with epinephrine, norepinephrine also underlies the fight-or-flight response, directly increasing heart rate, triggering the release of glucose from energy stores, and increasing blood flow to skeletal muscle.

SEROTONIN

A hormone, also called 5-hydroxytryptamine, in the pineal gland, blood platelets, the digestive tract, and the brain. Serotonin acts as a chemical messenger that transmits nerve signals between nerve cells and also causes blood vessels to narrow. Changes in the serotonin levels in the brain can alter mood. For example, medications that affect the action of serotonin are used to treat depression.

Poor Nutrition and Dietary Concerns

In the 1970s, Benjamin Feingold and others posited a theory that linked **hyperkinesis** or hyperkinectivity to excess sugar and preservative intake on the part of children. Feingold (1975) claimed that 25 to 50 percent of children affected with chronic hyperactivity and learning disabilities could be effectively treated with nutritious diets that conscientiously excluded sugars, artificial dyes, preservatives, and salicylates. Subsequent research failed to support Feingold's claims, however (e.g., Spring, Chiodo, & Bowen, 1987).

HYPERKINESIS

A state of overactive restlessness in children. It is also a medical condition resulting in uncontrolled muscle movement, akin to spasms.

Environmental Factors

Researchers have also speculated as to the deleterious affects of environmental toxins such as lead (in lead paint and pipes) and air pollutants (e.g., fluorocarbons and CO_2). To date, however, no significant studies have supported the affects of teratogens as a viable cause of ADHD (May, 2000; Zala & Penn, 2004).

Genetic Factors

Research has supported a strong correlation between genetic transmission and ADHD. For example, recent studies have found that between 10 and 35 percent of immediate (first-degree) family members are likely to have ADHD, and the children of parents or a parent with ADHD are at higher risk of experiencing the disorder. Twins studies have indicated on average heritability of 0.80, thus, establishing a clear link between genetic heritability and ADHD transmission (Faraone & Doyle, 2003; Todd et al., 2002).

Psychosocial Factors (Family Factors)

Studies have found evidence to suggest a link between family factors, such as parental malaise, marital discord, adversarial child–parent relationship, as well as family adversity, and the development of ADHD (e.g., Goodman & Stevenson, 1989; McGee, Partridge, Williams, & Silva, 1991; McGee, Williams, & Silva, 1984). Similarly, incompatibility between mother and child also correlates with ADHD. Also, one study found that inconsistent, intolerant, and authoritarian parenting styles also were more predictive of ADHD in children (Campbell, 1995; Woodward, Taylor, & Dowdney, 1998). Another study pointed to characteristic depression and/or anxiety in mothers and ADHD diagnoses in fathers as strong predispositions for ADHD in their children (Nigg & Hinshaw, 1998). However, these studies must be interpreted with caution; for example, some of the negative parent behaviors may be attributed to their reaction to having a child with ADHD, not a cause of it. Likewise, teacher behaviors may affect a child's attentiveness or exacerbate preexisting conditions of hyperactive-impulsive behavior (Jerome, Gordon, & Hustler, 1994; Laine, 1991).

Despite all the research to understand and identify the etiology of ADHD, it appears that the most likely and defensible cause is in the area of the neurobiology of the child. Future research is needed to better understand the connection between neurology and the development of ADHD in order to advance new treatments that are more effective.

ASSESSMENT OF ADHD

Experts consider the process of arriving at a correct diagnosis of ADHD to be singularly difficult—in fact, perhaps one of the most challenging diagnoses to make. In order to ensure that the identification process is accurate, a sequence of steps is essential. These steps involve assessment instruments that have been normed and standardized, as well as parent, child, and teacher interviews, careful observations, and a thorough medical and psychological evaluation. Such a comprehensive process typically includes the following steps:

1. Administering and collecting rating scales from relevant persons
2. Orienting the family and the student to the evaluation
3. Interviewing the student
4. Administering normed tests such as IQ, achievement, and continuous performance tests
5. Conducting direct observations in several settings, including school, community, and home if possible
6. Interviewing the parent(s)
7. Conducting a medical evaluation
8. Integrating all the data
9. Giving feedback and recommendation to the team (Culatta, Tompkins, & Werts, 2003).

Typically, the school psychologist presides over the data collection process.

A similar sequence of assessment is suggested by the Council for Exceptional Children's Task Force on Children with ADHD (1992). The CEC guidelines are as follows.

Step 1 Document behavior observed by both parents and teachers that is indicative of ADHD.

Step 2 Reevaluate tests to determine whether they are accurate measures of potential or whether poor performance may be the result of attention problems. A physician may be consulted to see whether an identifiable physical condition is causing inattention or hyperactivity.

Step 3 Attempt classroom management to correct or control behavior leading to poor academic performance. If such attempts are unsuccessful, request a referral for ADHD placement.

Step 4 Conduct a psychological evaluation to see whether the student meets criteria for ADHD placement. Administer individual tests and behavioral rating scales. Review medication recommendations.

Step 5 Have the team, including the child's parents, plan for the special educational needs of the child.

Step 6 Implement the Individual Education Plan.

Checklists and rating scales are helpful in providing certain insights relative to a child's inattention or hyperactive behavior; however, the results are very subjective and provide only a "snapshot" of a limited behavioral domain.

The most commonly used checklist is the *Child Behavior Checklist* (Achenbach & Edelbrock, 1991). The *Connors' Rating Scale* (Conners, 1998) is another very popular instrument used in evaluating the problem behaviors associated with ADHD. It offers versions that are specifically tailored for administration to students, parents, and teachers. Another relevant instrument is the *Attention Deficit Disorders Evaluation Scale—3rd ed* (ADDES-3; McCarney, 2004), which has a parent and teacher version and identifies and differentiates the three types of ADHD as described in the DSM-IV-TR (American Psychiatric Association, 2000).

Systematic observation conducted in natural settings also provides valuable information in determining a diagnosis of ADHD. Direct observation should be conducted in various school settings, including the classroom, the playground, the lunchroom, and the hallways. In addition, careful daily records of academic performance should be maintained (Kauffman, 2005).

Similarly, interviews should be conducted with parents and teachers to facilitate the diagnostic process. These stakeholders typically have valuable information to pass on regarding the student's aberrant behaviors and academic deficiencies.

Lastly, the student assessment should include a complete medical examination to rule out medical or health causes for the behaviors that appear to be symptomatic of ADHD. For example, the hyperactive component of ADHD may be simply an adverse effect produced by medication to relieve the symptoms of a health problem such as asthma.

TREATMENT STRATEGIES

A number of interventions have been recommended in the treatment of ADHD. These include psychosocial training for parents and teachers, cognitive strategy training, pharmacological interventions, and multisystemic therapies. These interventions are usually more effective with young children and involve some form of positive reinforcement for the performance of desired behavior or, conversely, a negative consequence (punishment) such as response cost. A "time out" should never be used as a punishment; ideally, it represents the removal of all stimuli to facilitate the child's return to emotional "stasis." It is important that, to the extent possible, all behavioral interventions be conducted in the natural setting where the target behaviors are most likely to occur (Wicks-Nelson & Israel, 2005).

Psychosocial Training for Parents and Teachers

The goal of parent and teacher training is to help these key stakeholders learn to deal with the challenging behaviors of children with ADHD and to cope more effectively with their own nontherapeutic behaviors. Therapists or psychologists typically involve parents and teachers in an intervention plan that is generalized to the settings of the home and school. In addition, parents and teachers are taught to develop greater tolerance for the **perseverating behaviors** of the child with ADHD and are helped to understand that she or he is not displaying these disruptive behaviors willfully, but can, nonetheless, learn to

PERSEVERATING BEHAVIORS

Many children with severe disabilities, particularly those on the autism spectrum, perseverate. Perseverating means they do certain actions over and over again, such as repeating a phrase, shutting a door, twiddling fingers, lining up toys, rubbing their hands together, or spinning objects.

reduce their frequency and severity. This understanding can reduce the indifference that parents and teachers sometimes express toward students who have ADHD, as well as the tendency to blame these children for their disorder, thereby increasing tolerance and understanding. This change in appreciation and attitude on the part of teachers and parents can help affected children improve their self-esteem (Alberto & Troutman, 2003; Barkley, 2003).

Cognitive Strategy Training

Cognitive strategy training encompasses self-instruction, self-monitoring, self-reinforcement, and cognitive-interpersonal problem solving (Hallahan et al., 2005). Although research has not demonstrated significant benefit from these approaches in reducing the undesirable symptoms associated with ADHD, self-monitoring and self-instruction will be described because, in conjunction with behavioral approaches and pharmacological treatments, they can be beneficial.

Self-monitoring functions as a reminder by prompting the student to ask herself if she was "paying attention" to the lesson. Typically, the student is provided with a checklist of desirable target behaviors and, prompted by an audible signal at timed intervals, chooses "yes" or "no" in response. Ostensibly, over time, the student internalizes this external control and, hopefully, the desirable behaviors become part of the student's repertoire.

Self-instruction teaches students to "talk to themselves" about their behaviors in relation to a classroom task. At first, the teacher, who talks aloud, describing, for example, the steps in solving a math problem, models the procedure. Next, the student follows suit, verbalizing each step of the process. Later, the goal is for the student to employ the "self-instruction" techniques where needed, subvocally (Kauffman, 2005).

The use of mnemonics, another cognitive strategy, is helpful in providing the student who has ADHD a way of organizing information so that it can be effectively stored and easily retrieved later, when needed. Examples of mnemonic strategies include the use of the "silly story," "the Roman room," and acrostics designed to be spoken or sung that represent or include the target information. An example of one such acrostic, PEMDAS ("Please Excuse My Dear Aunt Sally"), represents the order of operations in solving algebraic equations.

Pharmacological Interventions[1]

A clinical expert who is a consultant in the school district on matters regarding ADHD diagnoses provided the families of Vincent and Brett with a brief explanation of the plausible relationship between various therapeutic drugs and ADHD symptoms. She explained that research on the effects of popular psychostimulants, such as Ritalin and Adderall, suggests that these drugs may accelerate the production of norepinephrine, an important neurotransmitter responsible

---

[1]Much of the material in this section is adapted from Austin, V. L. (2003). Pharmacological interventions for students with ADD. *Intervention in School and Clinic, 38*(5), 289–296. Copyright 2003 by Sage Publications. Adapted with permission.

for the transfer of "messages" from one part of the brain to another (Valente, 2001). Investigators have also established that the increased availability of these neurotransmitters improves brain function, which includes attention and focus, as well as the ability to control impulsivity (Brown, 2000; Kollins, Barkley, & DuPaul, 2001). Because some studies have pointed to a lack of dopamine and norepinephrine production as a possible cause of ADHD, the benefit of such stimulant drugs is evident (Kollins et al., 2001).

The procedure for determining which drug is right for an individual involves a process of elimination (Szymanski & Zolotor, 2001). For example, because methylphenidate (Ritalin) has demonstrated effectiveness in controlling undesirable symptoms such as inattentiveness and impulsivity for approximately 70 percent of the persons diagnosed with ADHD to whom it was prescribed, and is generally well tolerated, it is usually the first course of medication prescribed (Szymanski & Zolotor, 2001).

Typically, the initial dose is administered once daily, and the effects of this dose on predetermined behavioral and educational objectives such as focus, time on task, and impulse control are carefully monitored. If a higher dose is needed to achieve these treatment objectives, then the amount is increased incrementally until the desired outcomes are obtained. Because the effects of methylphenidate are of short duration (3 to 4 hours) and the length of the school day may exceed 6 hours, a second dose is often recommended to be taken at lunchtime. Occasionally, if undesirable behaviors develop after the noontime dose begins to wear off (a rebound effect); a third dose may be prescribed. Newer, slow-release preparations such as **Concerta** have been formulated to address the need for a longer-lasting, sustained dose (Greenhill, Halperin, & Abikoff, 1999).

If an individual is unresponsive to the effects of a particular psychostimulant such as Ritalin, another type, such as Adderall may be tried. However, if it appears that stimulants in general are ineffective in improving the effects of ADD, then tricyclic antidepressants such as buproprion hydrochloride (Wellbutrin) and venlafaxine (Effexor) may be used, both of which increase the availability of norepinephrine and dopamine. In addition, desipiramine and imipramine have demonstrated effectiveness in treating the symptoms associated with ADD, however, the potential for life-threatening side effects in children generally preclude their consideration as a treatment option (Greenhill et al., 1999).

Other medications, such as the alpha-blockers, clonidine (Catapres), and guanfacine (Tenex), help to reduce aggressive behaviors and feelings of hostility, anxiety, and frustration. Similarly, beta-blockers and low doses of antiseizure medications can be helpful, but when a comorbid condition such as conduct disorder is evident, or when tics become troublesome, major tranquilizers such as risperidone (Resperidol) may prove helpful (Szymanski & Zolotor, 2001).

It is important to acknowledge that any substance introduced artificially into the human biosystem presents the potential for adverse effects. Each of these popularly prescribed medications can produce some undesirable conditions ranging in severity from mild discomfort to death. Table 4.2 lists these drugs, the possible beneficial and adverse effects, and the typical dosage and duration of action.

CONCERTA

An extended-release central nervous system stimulant (methylphenidate) that is used to treat children and teens with attention-deficit hyperactivity disorder (ADHD). It can be prescribed to children who are more than 6 years old, although because it is a pill that must be swallowed, younger school-aged children may have problems taking it.

TABLE 4.2 Drug Specifications

Name of Drug	Dosage	Potential Benefits	Potential Adverse Effects
Methylphenidate (Ritalin)	2.5–20 mg	Reduction of hyperactivity, impulsivity, and inattentiveness	Loss of appetite, sleeplessness, rapid heartbeat, tics, risk of liver cancer
Methylphenidate SR 20 (sustained-release)	20 mg	Same as for methylphenidate	Same as for methylphenidate
Methylphenidate (Concerta) sustained-release	18 mg, 36 mg, 54 mg Duration: 10–12 hours	Same as for methylphenidate	Same as for methylphenidate
Mixed salts of a single-entity amphetamine product (Adderall)	5 mg, 7.5 mg, 10 mg, 12.5 mg, 15 mg, 20 mg, 30 mg Duration: 3.5–8 hours	Same as for methylphenidate	Same as for methylphenidate
Dextroamphetamine (Dexadrine, Dextrostat)	2.5 mg–10 mg Onset: 20–30 minutes Duration: 4–5 hours	Same as for methylphenidate	Same as for methylphenidate
Pemoline (Cylert)	18.75 mg, 37.5 mg, 75 mg Duration: 8–10 hours	Same as for methylphenidate	Potential for serious liver damage; frequent monitoring of liver function required
Imipramine and desipramine (Tofranil and Norpramin)	10 mg, 25 mg, 50 mg, 100 mg Onset: 1–3 weeks Duration: 24 hours (not abruptly stopped)	Low doses improve focus and control; higher doses may stabilize mood	Similar to methylphenidate; may produce arrhythmia and change blood count
Buproprion (Wellbutrin)	75 mg, 100 mg Duration: 6–8 hours	Same as for methylphenidate and helps relieve depression	Headaches and difficulty sleeping
Clonidine (Catapres)	Patches or tablets of 0.1 mg, 0.2 mg, 0.3 mg Duration: patch, 5–6 days; tablets, 4–6 hours (not abruptly stopped)	Improves hyperactivity and insomnia; may decrease facial or vocal tics; reduces hostility	Fatigue, dizziness, dry mouth, hyperactivity, and irritability
Guanfacine (Tenex)	1 mg tablet Duration: 6–8 hours	Reduces facial and vocal tics as well as hostility and oppositional behavior	Dizziness, dry mouth, hyperactivity, irritability, and other behavior problems

Source: CHADD (2000). Fact Sheet No. 3. Medical management of children and adults with AD/HD. Retrieved April 24, 2002, from http://63.102.85.98/fs/fs3.htm.

After presenting this information to Vincent and Brett's families and teachers, the consultant discussed the findings of several recent studies conducted to assess the efficacy of pharmacological interventions in the treatment of ADHD (Lyon, Cline, Zepetnek, Shan, & Pang, 2001; Northup, Gulley, Edwards, & Fountain, 2001; Riccio, Waldrop, Reynolds, & Lowe, 2001; Scahill, Chappell,

Kim, & Schultz, 2001; Wilens, Spencer, Biederman, & Girard, 2001). She did this in a very informal and practical manner to ensure that all the individuals present understood the benefits of medication in the treatment of ADHD as compared with other interventions. The principal study she described involved the largest and longest trial ever conducted with children diagnosed with ADHD: the Multimodal Treatment of ADHD (MTA) Study, sponsored by the National Institute for Mental Health (MTA Cooperative Group, 1999). Based on the results of this study, which involved over 500 school-age children diagnosed with ADHD conducted over 14 months, medication alone—specifically, methylphenidate—was found to be superior to behavioral and educational interventions, combined pharmacological and behavioral treatments, and treatment in the community (MTA Cooperative Group, 1999). Further studies recommended the value of a combined, multimodal approach involving behavioral, as well as pharmacological interventions (e.g., Kollins et al., 2001).

Unfortunately, as the consultant pointed out, in some cases, psychostimulants and other pharmacological interventions are being prescribed with little adherence to American Academy of Pediatrics (AAP) guidelines (Hyman et al., 1998; Livingston, 1997), which include the following important recommendations:

1. Primary care physicians should establish a management plan that recognizes ADHD as a chronic condition and should serve as a resource and clearinghouse for information, collaborating with children, families, teachers, nurses, psychologists, and counselors to develop child-specific treatment plans. Furthermore, physicians should maintain currency about new research on treatment efficacy and innovation.
2. The treating physician, family members, child, teachers, and psychologist should establish three to six treatment goals that encompass realistic and measurable outcomes that may include improvements in relationships, self-esteem, and school performance, as well as a decrease in disruptive behaviors.
3. The physician should recommend psychostimulant medication and/or behavior therapy as a first-line treatment, based on the overwhelming body of research that supports their effectiveness in the treatment of ADHD.
4. Individuals, families, and teachers should be informed that the long-term effect of stimulant use has not been determined.
5. The use of pemoline is not recommended because of rare, but potentially fatal, liver damage (hepatoxicity). In addition, second-line treatments include the tricyclic antidepressants (imipramine and desipramine) and buproprion (Wellbutrin).
6. Physicians are advised to adjust the dosage upward from an initial low dose until treatment objectives are met. Conversely, if side effects and no further benefits are experienced by the patient; the physician is encouraged to adjust the dosage downward in order to identify a dose that achieves the optimal treatment objectives with minimal adverse effects.
7. In the case of children taking stimulant medications such as Ritalin, a lack of success at the highest safe dose suggests considering another approved stimulant medication such as Adderall.

8. Concomitant behavior therapy should be employed whose goal is to adjust the physical and social environments to change behavior through positive reinforcement, with effective reinforcers acquired through response-cost inventories and/or token economies.

9. Family members, teachers, and other caregivers should be appropriately trained to implement these behavioral interventions.

10. If the multimodal intervention plan is ineffective, it may be the result of misdiagnosis, a misidentification of pertinent symptoms, the presence of a comorbid condition, a lack of adherence to the recommended treatment regimen, or treatment failure.

11. A systematic follow-up should be conducted periodically by the physician for the child with ADHD relative to the achievement of treatment objectives and presence of adverse effects, based on input from teachers, family members, and the child. (Chatfield, 2002)

Furthermore, the medical consultant cautioned the families and teachers of Vincent and Brett about the credibility of findings from studies funded by pharmaceutical companies such as Ciba-Geigy (manufacturer of Ritalin) and Shire Richwood, (manufacturer of Adderall) (Lan, 2001; Spencer, Biederman, Wilens, & Faraone, 2001). In addition, she explained that many of the studies used by pharmaceutical companies and others to support the efficacy and safety of a particular medication used to treat ADHD often involve small sample sizes of from twenty to thirty participants or fewer (e.g., Northrup, Gulley, Edwards, & Fountain, 2001). This limitation significantly affects the usefulness of the findings, yet to the inexperienced consumer, results so obtained can sound conclusive and authoritative. Finally, and most important, the consultant informed the families of Vincent and Brett as well as their teachers that no research has been conducted on the long-term effects of psychostimulants such as methylphenidate and dextroamphetamine (CHADD Fact Sheet No. 3, 2000; Kollins et al., 2001). She also noted that because these drugs affect and alter an individual's neurobiology, it is reasonable to predict that, if used consistently for 20 or 30 years, some adverse effects might develop.

In addition, the consultant assured the families and teachers that she was not an advocate of pharmacological intervention exclusively, but her professional experience, as well as much of the research on interventions for ADHD, supported the carefully monitored use of psychostimulants in conjunction with effective educational and behavioral approaches (e.g., Brown, 2000; Kollins et al., 2001; Valente, 2001). She also noted that, based on the information presented, the family members of one or both children might choose to forego pharmacological interventions in favor of psychosocial or behavioral ones. The important thing in determining interventions for Vincent and Brett, she stressed, was its endorsement by the families, the teachers, and the students themselves, as well as its effectiveness in helping each of these students achieve the desired treatment outcomes.

In concluding her recommendations concerning pharmacological interventions, the medical consultant asserted the importance of accurate information about the beneficial and adverse effects of the various medications used in the treatment of ADHD. She further elaborated best practices that teachers and families can use collaboratively to monitor and assess drug effects. The first of these is to ensure that the child has had a thorough physical and psychological examination that includes height and weight determination, the presence of any cardiological anomalies, the potential for behavioral side effects, any evidence of seizure disorders, tics, and tests of liver function (Kollins et al., 2001). In addition, families, teachers, and clinicians should assess the symptoms of ADHD using several of the following instruments: the *Child Behavior Checklist/Teacher Report Form* (Achenback & Edelbrock, 1991), the *ADHD-IV Rating Scale* (DuPaul, Power, Anastopoulos, & Reid, 1999), the *Disruptive Behavior Rating Scale* (Barkley & Murphy, 1998), and the *Conners Rating Scales—Revised* (Conners, 1997).

Also, researchers have suggested that, before making the decision to use medication, family members and teachers review the information provided by the answers to the following questions:

1. How old is the child? (Although psychostimulants are increasingly prescribed for pre-school-age children, methylphenidate [Ritalin, Concerta] has never been approved for children under the age of 6 [Leo, 2002].)
2. Have other interventions been tried, and if so, why were they ineffective?
3. How severe are the child's current symptoms?
4. Can the family afford the costs associated with pharmacological intervention?
5. Can family members adequately supervise the use of medication and prevent abuse?
6. What are the attitudes and cultural perspectives of family members toward medication?
7. Is there a substance-abusing family member in the home?
8. Does the child have concomitant disorders such as tics or mental illness?
9. Is the child overly concerned about the effects of the medication?
10. Does the physician seem committed to appropriate follow-up and monitoring?
11. Is the child or adolescent involved in competitive sports or planning on entering the military? (The medication will be detected as a "controlled substance" in the course of urinalysis.) (Kollins et al., 2001)

Families and teachers are also valuable monitors of the effectiveness of a particular medication as well as the dosage level. Researchers recommend a double-blind procedure whereby family members, teachers, and the student do not know the dose level of the prescribed medication or if it is in fact a placebo. Thus, their weekly reports using a teacher/family ratings scale as well as a side-effects questionnaire (Barkley & Murphy, 1998) will be more likely to reflect true drug effects than the phenomenon referred to as "practice effects." *Practice effects* refers to the tendency of family members and teachers to rate the behaviors of students receiving medication as significantly improved once the regimen has begun.

Similarly, teachers can assess the effects of medication in the treatment of ADHD with the use of continuous performance tests such as the presentation of a symbol (e.g., a letter or number) at varied intervals within a series (Riccio, Waldrop, Reynolds, & Lowe, 2001). Also, the use of restricted academic tasks has demonstrated validity in confirming optimal medication doses for children and may help to identify the effects of incremental medication changes and adjustments on carefully structured academic problem sets (Fischer & Newby,

1998). Moreover, research has suggested that a functional analysis of behavior may allow teachers to identify and control for antecedent and consequent events, which can help them assess the impacts of these conditions on the effects of medication as it relates to the child with ADHD (Northup & Gulley, 2001).

Finally, teachers can use curriculum-based measurement (CBM) to measure the effects of medication on behaviors that affect academic function (Shinn, 1995). When using CBM, students become their own controls, and comparisons are made between their performance on an academic task before and after treatment with medication. Significant changes in either a positive or negative direction are noted and reported to the physician as one indicator of the effectiveness of the medication and dosage level.

Multisystemic Therapies

Pharmacological treatment appears to be the single most effective therapy for children who have ADHD, but it often comes at a cost in the form of adverse side effects. Behavioral approaches also have drawbacks and require intensive, time-consuming monitoring. Similarly, cognitive-behavioral therapies have demonstrated limited success in reducing undesirable ADHD behaviors, perhaps because they require some level of executive function and self-control, qualifications that many children with ADHD simply do not seem to possess.

Thus, researchers have looked to a multisystemic treatment that combines pharmacological therapy with behavioral intervention. Some studies have supported the efficacy of multimodal therapy in maintaining treatment benefits over time (Ialongo et al., 1993). More recently, the National Institute of Mental Health (NIMH) conducted an investigation of a multisystemic treatment regimen that included medication plus psychosocial intervention consisting of tutoring, social skills training, organization training, parent training, counseling, and limited contingency management. Results of the study showed improvement in all outcome measures; however, when the participants were taken off medication, their behavior regressed (Hinshaw, Klein, & Abikoff, 1998). These findings engendered optimism about the use of multisystemic treatments. It is important to note, however, that this optimism is based on awareness that any such treatment regimen must be tailored to the specific needs of the individual with ADHD and that these needs vary greatly from individual to individual depending on the degree and type of ADHD.

SCHOOL-BASED INTERVENTIONS

After considering the preceding clinical review of ADHD, teachers can, in consultation with the school or child psychologist, develop a practical intervention plan for a student who has the disorder. Such an intervention plan, as we have noted, cannot be successfully designed without a thorough understanding of the root causes of the problem behavior—that is, what function or purpose the behavior serves for the child, if any, and what contingencies help maintain it. This section offers suggested approaches for the case examples of Vincent and Brett.

As with other emotional and behavioral disorders, the logical first step in developing an effective treatment or intervention plan is to identify and describe the presenting undesirable behavior accurately. The step-by-step process developed by Barnhill (2005) is one way to reach an effective intervention plan. We will use this process to develop behavioral intervention plans for Vincent and Brett, based primarily on the findings of their functional behavioral assessments.

Assessing the Problem: Vincent (ADHD, Predominantly Hyperactive-Impulsive Type)

IDENTIFY AND DESCRIBE THE PROBLEM BEHAVIOR Vincent's teachers and parents have observed and documented frequent episodes of hyperactivity and impulsivity that seem to be increasing in frequency and intensity. Examples of some of the more severe of these include physical aggression toward others, unsolicited and unwanted physical contact, mercurial and volatile temper, verbal abuse, concomitant academic failure, and inability to complete tasks and remain focused. These undesirable behaviors appear to be escalating despite the use of psychosocial interventions.

COLLECT BASELINE DATA AND ACADEMIC INFORMATION The school psychologist has administered the Brown *ADD Scale for Adolescents* (Brown, 1996), as well as the *Conners-Wells Adolescent Self-Report Scale* (Conners, 1998), which helped to confirm the diagnosis of ADHD, predominantly hyperactive-impulsive type. The psychologist obtained observation data from all of Vincent's middle school teachers, as well as his parents; teachers also provided completed child behavior checklists.

DESCRIBE THE CONTEXT IN WHICH THE BEHAVIOR IS OBSERVED Behavioral observations by teachers were made in the school and classroom. In a similar vein, Vincent's parents conducted observations in and around the home. Both contexts revealed similar behavioral characteristics: episodes of heightened activity, inattention and lack of focus, as well as impulsive behavior that included unsolicited touching and aggression.

COMPLETE A FUNCTIONAL BEHAVIORAL ASSESSMENT (FBA) AND/OR A BEHAVIOR RATING SCALE Both of these protocols were completed; the template for the FBA is shown in Figure 4.1.

CONDUCT A DIRECT OBSERVATION As mentioned earlier, direct observations were conducted by both Vincent's parents and teachers, and the recorded data were analyzed. The findings were used to help confirm the diagnosis and develop a viable treatment plan.

DEVELOP A HYPOTHESIS Based on the data from multiple assessments, Vincent's diagnosis of ADHD, predominantly hyperactive-impulsive type, was confirmed. Vincent clearly requires structure and guidance to be successful in the classroom. He tends to become unruly and uncooperative unless he is provided with stimulating, meaningful tasks. He also suffers from a lack of self-esteem, which is exacerbated when he "acts out" and is alienated from teachers and students. The

FIGURE 4.1 Functional Behavioral Assessment (FBA) Template and Corollary Behavioral Intervention Plan (BIP) Template

Functional Behavioral Assessment (FBA)

Student Name: _____ ID: _____ DOB: _____ HR: _____ SW: _____

Date: _____

Behavior Number(s)	Precipitating Conditions (Setting, time, or other situations typically occurring before the behavior)	Specific Behavior (Exactly what the student does or does not do)	Consequences (Events that typically follow the behavior)	Function of the Behavior (Hypothesized purpose(s) the behavior serves)

How was the Data Collected _____

Related Information/Considerations

Academic: _____

Family: _____

Social/Peer: _____

Other: _____

FIGURE 4.1 (continued)

Behavioral Intervention Plan (BIP)

Student Name: _____ ID: _____ DOB: _____ HR: _____ SW: _____

Date: _____

Describe the Behavior that interferes with learning	Expected Outcome(s)/ Goal(s)	Intervention(s) & Frequency of Intervention(s)	Person Responsible What Supports will be offered	Goal/ Intervention Review Notes

*Review Notes: (NP)-No Progress (LP)-Little Progress (SP)-Satisfactory Progress (GM)-Goal Met

Expected Review Dates _____ _____ _____

Participants: _____

107

multidisciplinary committee has recommended a multimodal approach that includes social skills training, cognitive-behavioral therapy, parent and teacher training, as well as titrated medication therapy (recommended but as yet untried).

TEST THE HYPOTHESIS AND MODIFY AS NECESSARY A behavioral intervention plan has been implemented for Vincent, but it has not yet been reviewed.

Developing an Effective Intervention Plan

Vincent's behavioral intervention plan, as recommended, will be multimodal and include cognitive-behavioral therapy, parent and teacher training, and a carefully monitored medication regimen.

Vincent's teachers will employ a cognitive approach that includes self-monitoring and self-instruction. To facilitate the first of these two strategies, his teachers have developed a list of desirable target behaviors that they provide to Vincent at the start of each class. They then start a small alarm mechanism, which is designed to give off an audible signal at timed intervals. When Vincent hears the alarm, he is prompted to check "yes" or "no" to indicate whether or not he performed or engaged in the desired behavior.

Vincent's teachers model self-instruction or "self-talk" by describing aloud the steps or procedures required to conduct an experiment in science class, for example. Vincent is encouraged to follow the same procedure for all the tasks that require steps or involve formulas. Eventually, the goal is for Vincent to internalize these steps.

A third cognitive approach that his teachers employ to help Vincent encode information to facilitate retrieval is the use of mnemonic devices and semantic webs or other graphic organizers. For example, to assist his recollection of the five Great Lakes as discussed in his social studies class, the teacher has taught him to use the acronym HOMES, in which each letter represents the first letter of the name of one of the Great Lakes (Huron, Ontario, Michigan, Erie, and Superior).

Vincent's teachers, directed by the school psychologist, also provide social skills training whenever possible, using the "teachable moment" as the pretext for such instruction. For example, Vincent wanted to ask a female classmate to accompany him to a middle school dance, but after offering the invitation, proceeded to comment on her acne and suggest some topical medication he uses. He was genuinely surprised when she took exception to his "well-intentioned" advice and declined his invitation. However, after an astute teacher explained how his forthright and unsolicited comments might be misperceived, he seemed truly remorseful and apologized to the young lady, who later accepted his invitation.

Some well-supported behavioral approaches that Vincent's teachers employ include increasing the use of positive reinforcement (McCluskey & Mc-Cluskey, 1999) and using a daily report card (Pisecco, Huzinec, & Curtis, 2001). With regard to positive reinforcement, it has been observed that many teachers are negatively predisposed toward students who have ADHD. This is not an indictment of their professionalism, because students who have ADHD, like Vincent, who exhibit extreme hyperactivity and often act impulsively, present a real challenge for teachers. However, research has shown that teacher comments toward and interactions with students who have been diagnosed with ADHD are significantly more negative than their comments and interactions with students who do not have ADHD (Reis, 2001). Clearly, such negative treatment is counterproductive and merely aggravates the undesired behaviors. Instead, Vincent's teachers employ positive verbal reinforcement such as "Wow, you've completed half the page, I know you'll get the rest done by the end of the period." Vincent responds well to these positive comments, as evidenced by his increased productivity as well as the improved quality of his work.

Pisecco et al. (2001) demonstrated the effectiveness of and teacher preference for the *daily report card* (DRC). The daily report card involves the collaboration of parents and teachers in first identifying from three to five problem behaviors. A "report card" is then developed that consists of daily goals that address each of the target behaviors in a positive manner. The student takes this report card home and earns rewards for meeting these daily goals both at school and at home. Ideally, there should be a seamless transition from the school to the home in the supervision and reinforcement of this valuable behavioral intervention.

In addition, Vincent's teachers work hard to provide viable connections between what Vincent already knows (has mastered) and new concepts being taught. Research has supported that providing such a "bridge" between the known and the new facilitates the student's ability to incorporate what he is currently studying and ensures that he will generalize the new information to related applications (Howell, Fox, & Morehead, 1993). Similarly, his teachers require that Vincent use *focus journals* to facilitate the application of concepts and principles learned in class to the reality of his daily life. One example of the use of a focus journal is to have Vincent write a brief reaction to a teacher's daily "journal focus" question that includes support for his response.

These various behavioral and cognitive interventions have been effective in helping Vincent maintain focus and reduce his off-task behavior and impulsivity; however, his therapist, the school psychologist, and his teachers feel that his hyperactivity, inattentiveness, impulsivity, and, most important, physical acting out and aggression would be greatly reduced with the administration of a carefully titrated pharmacological intervention such as methylphenidate. His parents' resistance to this treatment option represents a real roadblock to Vincent's ultimate success in overcoming the significant behavioral and academic challenges posed by his ADHD.

Assessing the Problem: Brett (ADHD, Predominantly Inattentive Type)

IDENTIFY AND DESCRIBE THE PROBLEM BEHAVIOR Brett displays distractibility and occasional inattentiveness both in school and at home. These episodes of inattention and disorganization began to increase in frequency during the middle school grades, prompting the recommendation that he be evaluated for special education services to address these areas of concern. An outside child psychologist with experience in diagnosing and treating children with ADHD determined that Brett has ADHD, predominantly inattentive type.

COLLECT BASELINE DATA AND ACADEMIC INFORMATION At school, the multidisciplinary referral team reviewed records and conducted tests, such as the *Conners Parent and Teacher Rating Scales—Revised* (Conners, 1998), and were satisfied that Brett had been appropriately diagnosed with ADHD and would benefit from special education services under the category of "Other Health Impaired."

DESCRIBE THE CONTEXT IN WHICH THE BEHAVIOR IS OBSERVED Behavioral observations by teachers were made in the school and classroom. Brett's parents conducted observations in and around the home. Both contexts revealed similar behavioral characteristics: periods of inattention, lack of focus, distractibility when not meaningfully engaged, and disorganization in terms of schoolwork and tasks he was asked to do at home.

COMPLETE A FUNCTIONAL ASSESSMENT FORM AND/OR A BEHAVIOR RATING SCALE The *Conners Parent and Teacher Rating Scales—Revised* (Conners, 1998) was administered during the referral process. In addition, the child psychologist Brett has been seeing administered several tests that helped confirm the diagnosis.

CONDUCT A DIRECT OBSERVATION As noted earlier, direct observations were conducted by both Brett's parents and his teachers, and the recorded data were analyzed. The findings were used to help confirm the diagnosis and develop a viable treatment plan.

DEVELOP A HYPOTHESIS Based on the data from multiple assessments, Brett's diagnosis of ADHD, predominantly inattentive type, was confirmed. Brett clearly requires structure and guidance to be successful in the classroom. He needs to use graphic organizers, daily and weekly planners, and memory enhancers; in addition, a laptop computer will enable him to record notes and important dates. His inability to focus and attend is being addressed through the administration of Adderall, a stimulant that is effective in improving focus and concentration.

TEST THE HYPOTHESIS AND MODIFY AS NECESSARY A behavioral intervention plan has been implemented for Brett, but it has not yet been reviewed.

Developing an Effective Intervention Plan

Brett's behavioral intervention plan will be multimodal and consist primarily of academic interventions that will be complemented by the use of Adderall. Because Brett's social and interpersonal skills are unaffected and represent areas of strength, behavioral interventions are considered unnecessary; however, cognitive-behavioral strategies such as self-management using checklists and "memory jogs," as well as mnemonics to improve information storage and retrieval, will be used and reinforced by his classroom teachers.

To assist Brett in developing organization and management skills, he goes to the resource room for one period each day. During this period he is taught various research-based organizational skills. For example, he uses the "silly story" memory technique to prepare for an upcoming term test in U.S. history. This technique features the pairing of a viable history term from the unit he is studying with an exaggerated or "silly" visual cue or image; Brett then creates a story that includes each of these embellished terms in a desired sequence. He is encouraged to use bizarre imagistic connections to help encode the data for easy retrieval later. This technique seems to be working well for him.

Another organizational approach that Brett has learned to use effectively involves a graphic organizer called a *semantic word web* or *mind map*. This technique involves the use of pictures or geometric shapes to create a chart or graph of the main ideas of a lecture, book chapter, or term paper outline. The shapes or graphic images help Brett, whose preferred learning modality is visual and tactual/kinesthetic, to "see" the structure of the learning task. He is then able to convert this graphic structure to the more abstract organization of print. Brett uses speech-recognition software to convert his speech to print. He has mastered this technology and can word-process more efficiently using this software. He finds that he actually enjoys subjects such as English and social studies that were previously anathemas because, thanks to this assistive technology, he can now be successful in them. He is thus able to explore topics he finds interesting and meaningful via the Internet and integrate the data he uncovers into his research projects.

Lastly, Brett has been taught to use a reading comprehension strategy called *reciprocal reading* (Palincsar & Brown, 1986; Palincsar & Klenk, 1992) to improve his comprehension of print and increase his ability to sustain focus and concentration. The technique is predicated on the effective use of a self-questioning strategy. The student is taught to ask four types of question concerning a written passage or story: literal types, clarifying types, predicting types, and summarizing types. An important component of the strategy is that the user must actually teach a familiar passage to a classmate using the questions types as prompts to enhance the partner's understanding of the passage. Brett has shown significant improvement in reading comprehension as a result of this strategy, and he is able to use it in all his subjects, even for math word problems.

 FROM THE FIELD

Vincent D'Amico, PsyD.

Vincent D'Amico, a clinical psychologist, doctor of integrative medicine, certified nutritional consultant, and interfaith minister, is an expert in the field of attention-deficit disorder (ADD)/ADHD. He is director of the ADD/ADHD Diagnostic & Treatment Center, the Family Stress Reduction Institute, and the Discovery Summer Program. He is in private clinical practice utilizing various treatment protocols that have been found to be safe and effective in working therapeutically with students who have these disorders. He is the author of *The Sacred Journey of Parenthood* (Frederick, MD: PublishAmerica, 2006) and *Renato's Quest* (Frederick, MD: PublishAmerica, 2005). He has conducted research on brahmi (*Bacopa monniera*), an herb, and its effect on attention, impulsivity, concentration, short-term auditory memory, working memory, and sympathetic nervous system arousal in ADHD children. Initial results are promising.

Discuss approaches that you have found successful in your practice relative to students diagnosed with ADD or ADHD.

Approaches that I have found useful in working with students diagnosed with ADD/ADHD are those that offer encouragement, empowerment, and self-control. Before I discuss the approaches/interventions, it is important to note that each individual is unique. I do not know of any single approach that works for everyone. It is critical to understand the students' individual and unique personalities—their unique strengths, weaknesses, and temperaments.

First and foremost, form a working, therapeutic relationship with the student. Without a working relationship based on mutual respect, most interventions are likely to fail. In an effective mentoring relationship, a student feels understood, not judged. He or she is more likely to benefit from feedback, a crucial factor in working therapeutically with ADD/ADHD students. Many students with ADD/ADHD suffer from low self-esteem, and can be terribly sensitive to criticism. An atmosphere of support, encouragement, and teamwork will likely help them to lower their defenses and be more receptive to feedback to help correct weaknesses. When we demonstrate our confidence in them, they begin to believe in themselves.

There are many interventions that I have found effective with students who have ADD/ADHD after a working relationship has been formed. These interventions empower the student. The goal is to expose the student to various interventions and help them to choose those that they like most. These can be included in a "virtual toolbox" and utilized as needed. Just as a mechanic, surgeon, carpenter, mason, computer software programmer, and plumber need tools to perform their respective tasks, ADD/ADHD students also require tools for success.

One such approach is to teach the student to develop an internal dialogue or "self-talk." This takes the form of "talking out loud" at first. Then, the dialogue becomes internalized so the student learns to work problems through in their mind. This helps to reduce impulsivity and anxiety and improve concentration. In modeling this type of problem-solving approach, coupled with words of inspiration and encouragement, the student learns to become their own coach.

Another approach is to find the optimal time interval that the student is able to attend and perform assignments. I recommend using a timer, such as the "TimeTimer," which has a large red dial that provides a visual reminder of the passage of time. The timer can be set at the optimal length of time (e.g., 10, 20, or 30 minutes). Then, when the time is up, the timer is set again for a rest break. Each student is unique, so the amount of time will have to be determined based upon their current ability to work effectively. Then, in time, the length of time can be increased.

Another tool that I have found effective in helping ADD/ADHD students to develop mental stamina is EEG biofeedback, also known as neurofeedback. The brain produces electrical patterns in the cerebral cortex called brainwaves. Brainwaves are measured in cycles per second (cps). The slower brainwaves (theta) are "daydreaming" brainwaves. The very fast brainwaves (high beta) are "hyperactive/frustration/anxiety" brainwaves. Sensory motor rhythm is a brainwave that is associated with attention, concentration, and peak performance. Therefore, different brainwaves are associated with different conscious states. Neurofeedback teaches students how to control their brainwaves. Brainwaves are electronically monitored, recorded, and analyzed by a computer. Visual and auditory feedback is provided by a simple video game. Success in the game is based on the student's ability to regulate the brainwave pattern. Through feedback, the brain learns how to produce more or less of the desired/undesired brainwave.

Another useful technique is progressive muscle relaxation (PMR) and diaphragmatic breathing. PMR is a way to self-monitor by training the body and mind to engage the body's relaxation response. It involves a series of exercises where different muscle groups are first made tense for several seconds, then the tension is released. At the same time, the student engages in deep, diaphragmatic breathing where inhalation takes place in the abdominal area. They are instructed to breathe in as if they are filling their belly like a balloon. Then, they exhale pulling their abdomen in, squeezing the air out. This is repeated throughout the exercise. Daily practice helps to reduce impulsivity and anxiety, while increasing attention, concentration, and overall mental stamina. Practicing this technique, combined with stretch and rest breaks during school hours, will likely increase academic achievement.

Effective communication is vital in working therapeutically with ADD/ADHD students. By the therapist/teacher's modeling ways to communicate clearly and concisely, the student is more likely to both understand directions and learn ways to communicate clearly. Here are some guidelines.

- Be brief and to the point.
- Keep it simple and address one issue/lesson at a time.
- Establish an interactive dialogue and avoid monologues.
- Ask questions and enlist their involvement in solving the "problem."
- Demonstrate that you are in this together, that you are on the same team.
- Be patient and avoiding strong reactions such as anger or disappointment, suspending judgment and being mindful of your own need to control and be effective.

Patience serves as a protection against wrong as clothes do against cold. For if you put on more clothes as the cold increases, it will have no power to hurt you. . . . Grow in patience when you meet with great wrongs, and they will then be powerless to vex your mind.

—Leonardo DaVinci

- Match language with maturity. Talk with, never down, to students. Never speak above or below the student's level of maturity. Ask them to paraphrase what you said to ensure that the message was understood the way you intended it to be. This is a way to identify and correct miscommunication/misunderstanding.

I'd also like to add a note about the importance of nutrition. The old adage, "You are what you eat," is profound wisdom. In order to function optimally, the absorption of proper nutrients is essential. Proper nutrition includes a balance of proteins, amino acids, healthy fats,

vitamins, minerals, and complex carbohydrates. Today's fast and highly processed foods have greatly depleted our bodies of essential nutrients. For example, sugar consumption in the United States has risen dramatically. Refined sugars stress the blood sugar control mechanism. It sets the student up for metabolic roller coaster rides that can include mood swings, excessive energy, fatigue, and concentration and memory difficulties. Sugar, in the short term, can have a stimulant effect. This then rebounds into an exaggerated fatigue response. Also, some ADD/ADHD students respond negatively to wheat (gluten) and dairy (casein). They may have food allergies/sensitivities. There are tests that a clinician can perform to determine this. A general rule of thumb is to eat fresh, organic fruits and vegetable, meats that are organic, and free-range and organic grains, dairy, and nuts.

What about approaches or interventions that you would not recommend for those working with students with ADD or ADHD?

I would not recommend approaches that create power struggles, such as authoritarian "do it or else" types of systems. Punishment is not effective in the long term; in time, it causes more harm than good. Resentment builds, and learning suffers. This does not mean that natural consequences are not built into the learning system. If homework is not handed in, certainly a consequence is appropriate. However, it is important it understand whether the homework was not completed due to boredom or lack of understanding. If the student grasps the concept, then giving less is better. If they do not understand the assignment, a review is needed until comprehension is mastered. A general rule of thumb with ADD/ADHD students is to give less homework but ensure comprehension.

What about success stories? Can you tell us a personal anecdote that illustrates a successful treatment experience?

One success story that stands out in my mind is a student I will call Bill (his name has been changed). I first saw Bill when he was a 15 years old and diagnosed with ADHD. He was failing nearly all his subjects, and he suffered from low self-esteem and social anxiety. He also suffered from inattention, impulsivity, limited concentration, poor organizational skills, and deficits in memory. He had been in cognitive-behavioral therapy for years with no observable improvement. He had also taken many different medications that included Ritalin, Adderall, Celexa, Prozac, Paxil, and Lexapro. I inherited Bill on my case load when I took over as director of an ADD/ADHD center.

As I looked over his chart before meeting him, I had doubts about his treatment. Reminding myself that a new person and different perspective can have a positive impact, I threw away the textbooks, so to speak, and began to get to know Bill. I created a supportive, empathic, safe environment where Bill could "say everything." Bill began to talk about his troubles at home and at school. He began to trust me with "secrets" he never told anyone before. He told me how he was bullied; how afraid he was to tell anyone; and how he suffered in silence. He described how difficult it was for him to keep track of assignments, and how frustrated he was with his poor academic performance.

After several months, Bill decided to make some changes. He showed interest in learning strategies to help him to focus and relax. He learned and practiced progressive muscle relaxation, diaphragmatic breathing, and visual imagery. These techniques helped him to quiet his mind enough to have the mental stamina necessary to focus and attend school. He also participated in EEG biofeedback (neurofeedback), which further helped him to pay attention and focus. After 2 years, he stopped taking all medication. He graduated high school and went to a community college, where he became interested in journalism.

He took an interest in diet and nutrition. He began taking vitamin/mineral supplements. He also took an herb called brahmi (*Bacopa monniera*), which he reported helped him to concentrate better. He graduated from the community college and was accepted to and earned a scholarship at a 4-year accredited university, where he graduated with nearly all As. He successfully participated in several internship programs, wrote articles for the school newspaper, and had articles published in several magazines. He is currently pursuing a master's degree in fine arts.

When Bill was asked what helped him most, he said, "All the things I learned from you were helpful; the visual imagery, neurofeedback, nutrition, the brahmi, and all that stuff. But from the beginning, I think what was most helpful was that you listened to me. You became a friend, a father-figure. You gave me advice my own father couldn't give me. You've been a great friend, and coach. You helped motivate me to help myself."

Never underestimate the power of listening. Listening is in itself therapeutic. If we listen deeply to our students, they will be more likely to learn from us. In my years of working with students, I have learned this: *Students choose their teachers.* You can place them in front of hundreds of "teachers," but they will choose who they will learn from. They are more likely to choose us if we listen to them. Our Creator gave us one mouth, but two ears. We need to talk less, and listen more.

What strategies or approaches would you recommend as an expert in the field that the teacher of a student who has ADHD might try to improve that student's academic success?

First, let the student know that you are on the same team. Make yourself available before and after school to meet with the student. During the day, place your hand on his or her shoulder when asking him to perform a task.

Second, utilize strategies that allow for movement in the classroom. This can take the form of stretching, simple yoga postures, deep breathing, and jumping in place. Also, give special tasks to the ADHD student. For example, ask him or her to assist in handing out materials, or cleaning up after an activity. Also, several "passes" can be given to the ADHD student for use when he or she needs a break. This increases the locus of control within the students. Often, students require less frequent breaks because they know they have a pass that they can use when they need to.

Third, ensure that all homework is written down. If the student is forgetful, recommend a checklist to review with you at the end of the day to ensure that all assignments are written down. Make sure to break large assignments into smaller, clear steps. Some children prefer auditory interventions. In this regard, a microcassette tape recorder can be suggested and assignments recorded verbally. If books are continuously forgotten, a second set of textbooks to keep at home can be made available.

Fourth, alternate creative tasks with structured ones. For example, after a lesson in social studies which the ADHD student might find boring, include a "guessing game" or a series of funny riddles or jokes during a 5-minute break. Also, make as many lessons as possible "hands on." If you're teaching the 50 states and their capitals, rather than simply reading and memorizing them from a book or sheet, use a large puzzle and have the AHDH student arrange the pieces together. This increases their attention, participation, and retention. Associate the name of the state and the capital with something humorous. For example, the capital of New York has many rabbits: "All Bunny" (i.e.,

Albany); the capital of New Jersey has ten people named "Trent" (e.g., Trenton); etc.

Fifth, utilize a vertical accordion file system to organize assignments by subject. Give each subject a different color sticker on the tab to help differentiate each one and to assist in organizing work.

Sixth, an academic incentive plan can be created between the teacher and student, and between the parents and student. For example, rewards can be given for completed assignments, grades, class participation, staying on task in the classroom, etc. The student can earn "time in," where he or she earns "free time" which can be taken at scheduled times during the day. Points, stickers, tokens (e.g., marbles, poker chips) can be earned and exchanged for "time in" where the student can choose something he or she likes to do for a period of time (e.g., listen to music, read a comic book, play cards, etc.). Parents can reward the student with other incentives (e.g., going out to a movie, a toy, money, etc).

Seventh, let the ADHD student know that you will call on him or her the next day to answer a question. Tell him the question, and let him be prepared to answer it the next day. This strategy helps improve attention, retention, and self-esteem, as the student is prepared when called upon to answer the question.

Eighth, avoid power struggles. Implement a collaborative teaching paradigm, treating the ADHD student as an equal partner in learning.

Summary

ADHD continues to be among the most challenging disabilities to diagnose and remediate. Current estimates suggest that from 3 to 5 percent of school-age children in the United States are affected by this disorder. Although there is no single definitive cause for ADHD, it appears to be primarily neurobiological and thus not attributable to poor parenting or as a convenient excuse for laziness, egocentricity, or incorrigibility.

The DSM-IV-TR (American Psychiatric Association, 2000) differentiates three subtypes of ADHD: (1) predominantly inattentive, (2) predominantly hyperactive-impulsive, and combined type (1 and 2). The DSM-IV-TR provides behavioral criteria for each of these subtypes, as well as several universal criteria, including that (1) behavioral characteristics are evident by age 7; (2) some of the symptoms are evident in two or more settings (e.g., school and home); and (3) the symptoms significantly impair social, occupational, or academic performance and cannot be better explained by a mood disorder, anxiety disorder, disassociative disorder, or a personality disorder.

Students who have ADHD, predominantly inattentive type, experience significant academic problems, and 30 to 50 percent may be codiagnosed with a learning disability. These students also have difficulty maintaining focus and screening out extraneous stimuli. In contrast, students who have ADHD, predominantly hyperactive-impulsive type, seem to have an inexhaustible supply of energy and have real difficulty staying in one place for an extended period of time. In addition, the disinhibition associated within the impulsivity of these children impels them to make rash choices that may cause accidents and result in disciplinary referrals.

Not surprisingly, the behaviors associated with ADHD create a host of social problems, resulting in stigmatization and, ultimately, alienation. This social isolation often leads to low self-esteem, poor self-efficacy, a heightened sense of loneliness, and "learned helplessness."

Because of the difficulty in accurately diagnosing ADHD, assessment needs to be thorough and employ valid and reliable instruments. The process involves several steps and is both time-consuming and costly. Typical instruments used in the diagnostic process include: checklists and rating scales; parent, teacher, and student interviews; direct observation of target behaviors by parents and teachers; and a complete medical examination to rule out medical or health-related causes for the symptoms.

Effective interventions include behavioral ones, such as contingency reinforcement schedules and daily report cards; cognitive ones such as self-monitoring and self-instruction; academic ones that provide organizational aids such as graphic organizers and semantic webs; as well as information-encoding/retrieval strategies such as mnemonics and memory enhancers. Finally, the single most effective intervention is the prescription of medication such as methylphenidate (Ritalin). Effective pharmacological intervention must follow stringent procedures and be closely monitored to ensure minimal adverse effects and optimal treatment benefits.

As we learn more about the causes of ADHD, we will be better prepared to develop more effective academic and behavioral interventions. Despite the controversy surrounding our current diagnostic protocols and interventions, new research is helping to illuminate the many misperceptions and mysteries surrounding this enigmatic and often controversial disorder. Although teachers are not typically involved in this research, they can influence and improve the academic and behavioral approaches used to help students who have ADHD achieve success in school and in life.

Tips for Teachers

1. Whenever possible, avoid steps with more than one instruction, and also avoid giving multipart assignments. Allow the child to finish one assignment or follow one direction at a time before offering the next.
2. Designate a specific location where the child should deposit completed assignments.
3. If the child is capable at this stage, teach her to keep a daily homework journal. Or prepare a copy of the homework assignments to give to the child at the end of the day.
4. Give shorter but more frequent assignments to increase success rates. Break long-term projects into short-term assignments. Reward the child for completing each step. Remember, confidence builds through repeated successful experiences.
5. Ask parents to help the child get organized each night before school. Encourage them to develop a checklist so the child's clothes, books, assignments, and so on, are ready for the next morning.
6. If necessary, have the child finish all assignments at school.
7. Require the child to clean out her desk each day.

8. Use boxes, bins, or other organizers to help the child separate and store various items.
9. Encourage the use of binders or individual folders to help keep schoolwork organized. Set up a special place for tools, materials, and books. Organization and routine are critical to success.
10. If possible, do not place the student near distracting stimuli, such as an air conditioner, heater, high-traffic areas, doors, or windows. Create a "stimuli-reduced" study area. Let all students be allowed to go to this area so that the student who has ADHD will not feel self-conscious or singled out.
11. Avoid planning numerous transitions and changes throughout the day. Clearly list and explain the daily schedule to help the child deal with change.
12. Stand near the student while lecturing. This is called *proximity control*.
13. Try to preempt the child's behavior, especially during changes in the schedule. Inform the child of the change about 5 minutes beforehand and define your expectations for appropriate behavior.
14. As appropriate to the age and situation, identify strengths in the child you can pub-

licly announce or praise. This will help the other students develop a more positive perception of the child.
15. If the child takes any mediation, protect her privacy (e.g., by avoiding publicly reminding her to go down to the nurse's office to take it).
16. Encourage the use of word processing, typing, spell checking, and other computer skills.
17. Create chances for peer interaction and cooperative learning for academic tasks that do not require sitting for long periods of time.
18. An effective management system concentrates on a few behaviors at a time, with new behavior patterns added when the student masters the first ones. Reinforce appropriate behavior with something the student is willing to work for (or to avoid). For example, give or remove points immediately, according to the behavior, so the child understands why he is or is not being rewarded. Although older children may be willing to work toward a deferred reward, younger children generally need more immediate reinforcement (Pierangelo & Giuliani, 2001).

Focus Questions Revisited

1. Differentiate the three types of ADHD as presented in the DSM-IV-TR. Which of the three poses the greatest challenge in the classroom and why?

A Sample Response

Essentially, the three are differentiated as follows:

• *ADHD, predominantly inattentive:* These students typically make careless mistakes in school, and they have real difficulty staying on task and screening out irrelevant stimuli.
• *ADHD, predominantly hyperactive-impulsive:* These students seem to have boundless energy and have great difficulty staying in one place for an extended period of time: They

cannot seem to sit still. In conjunction with hyperactivity, students who have this type of ADHD also experience disinhibition. This suppression of the inhibitory response mechanism in the cerebral cortex often results in impulsivity.

• *ADHD, combined type:* Affected students display the characteristics of both inattention and hyperactivity and impulsivity. Students diagnosed with the combined type may represent the greatest challenge in the classroom because, they display both of these detrimental characteristics.

2. As Vincent's teacher, would you advocate for the use of a pharmacological intervention?

Provide a rationale for your response based on his presenting behaviors.

A Sample Response

I would do so reluctantly, but only because Vincent appears to be unresponsive to all other interventions and research supports the stand-alone efficacy of stimulant medication, such as methylphenidate, in improving focus and reducing impulsivity.

3. What can the teachers of a student suspected of having ADHD do to provide meaningful data to help inform the multidisciplinary team and thus facilitate the referral process?

A Sample Response

In accordance with the steps suggested by Culatta et al. (2003), teachers can do the following in order to produce meaningful and informative data about a student during the referral process:

a. Administer and collect rating scales from relevant persons.
b. Orient the family and the student to the evaluation.
c. Interview the student.
d. Administer normed tests such as achievement and continuous performance tests.
e. Conduct direct observations in several settings, including school, community, and home if possible.
f. Interview the parent(s).
g. Recommend a medical evaluation.
h. Integrate all the data.
i. Give feedback and recommendation to the team.

4. Discuss the controversy surrounding the classification of ADHD. Based on your knowledge of the disorder, should ADHD be classified as an emotional/behavioral disorder, a health impairment, a learning disability, or, is it distinctive and therefore deserving of a separate category? Provide a justification for your position.

A Sample Response

Some investigators have expressed concern at the recent proliferation in the incidence of ADHD among school-age children in the United States, citing inadequate and faulty assessment practices or the lack of creditable science to make a case for a discrete category of ADHD. Others claim that it is a convenient construct that provides billions of dollars in profit to the pharmaceutical industry, which commissions flawed studies to justify its existence. I agree that ADHD is frequently misdiagnosed and overidentified, partly because of a lack of thorough assessment; however, I believe that a sufficient number of credible studies demonstrate its viability. I think, based on the behavioral nature of its most prominent characteristics, that it can appropriately be considered an emotional/behavioral disorder.

5. Why do many "experts" contend that arriving at a correct diagnosis of ADHD is one of the most challenging tasks for clinicians? What are some of the most perplexing factors? What are the potential ramifications of a misdiagnosis?

A Sample Response

The reason that experts consider ADHD to be among the most challenging diagnosis to make is due in no small way to the universality of its purported characteristics: many disorders and illnesses can "mask" as ADHD based on its identifying criteria. Also, ADHD is comorbid with several other and potentially more serious disorders. Clinicians are then faced with a task of triage: determining the most serious disorder and treating it first. The detrimental effects of misdiagnosis are the stigmatizing effects of the classification and the likelihood of providing ineffective treatment.

6. Review the case example of Brett. If you were the clinician, would you arrive at a similar diagnosis? Explain your answer.

A Sample Response

Yes, I would. The confirmatory data are the report card comments from elementary school that reveal the concerns of teachers early on regarding Brett's ability to focus and screen out extraneous stimuli. The results of extensive neurological tests ruled out the possibility of brain injury, which provides further support for the diagnosis of ADHD, predominantly inattentive.

7. What academic and/or behavioral accommodations would Brett need to be successful in your class or in your school?

A Sample Response

Brett would need to be provided the opportunity to use a laptop computer in class to facilitate note taking. He might benefit from a "study buddy" or peer tutor to ensure that his notes are organized and relevant and that he is clear on the requirements and time frame for assignments (use a pocket organizer of some type). Brett would likely require extended time and an alternate location, free of excessive stimuli, to enable him to be successful on major tests, exams, and assignments. He might benefit, as well, from the provision of a period in the resource room each day to help him stay current on all assignments and get help with his organization and management skills.

8. What academic and behavioral interventions would Vincent need to be successful in your class or in your school?

A Sample Response

Vincent appears to be relatively unresponsive to the behavioral interventions that have been provided him to date. I believe that he needs firm and consistent setting of limits, as well as a well-defined routine to enable him to succeed in the classroom. Of course, I believe he would respond most dramatically to the administration of medication; specifically, methylphenidate. Whether that is a viable option for him remains to be seen.

9. After reviewing the section in the chapter on pharmacological interventions used in the treatment of ADHD, what are your impressions of its efficacy? Are there students for whom it might be appropriately prescribed? Provide an example of one. What are some counterindications that make the decision to prescribe a pharmacological agent a very deliberate and painstaking one?

A Sample Response

Vincent seems to represent an exemplary case for the prescription of medication. His hyperactive-impulsive behaviors would clearly benefit from a drug that helps him focus, stay on task, and reduce impulsive behaviors. A medication such as Ritalin, which offers significant improvements in these areas, might be Vincent's best treatment option. Clearly, the adverse effects of any of the medications used in the treatment of ADHD are potentially very serious, as delineated in the Table 4.2. Consequently, even for Vincent, who might benefit from an optimal dose of Ritalin, the health risks, in both the short term and the long term, are real, and the decision to prescribe the drug, as well as determination of the optimal dosage-level, must be made only after carefully weighing these risks.

Chapter 5

Anxiety Disorders I: Specific Phobia, Separation Anxiety Disorder, and Social Anxiety Disorder

Photodisc/Getty Images

FOCUS QUESTIONS

1. Suppose a child who has a specific phobia, such as a morbid preoccupation with death, was assigned to your class. What might you do to facilitate his acceptance and integration?

2. List some specific fears experienced by children. What differentiates the pathological ones that characterize a phobia from those that are common to many children who are able to function successfully without special treatment?

3. How common is separation anxiety disorder in children? How can a teacher determine whether a child's symptoms represent a bona fide disorder or will simply disappear in time?

4. What can a classroom teacher do to help a child who is experiencing separation anxiety disorder?

5. How do you define social phobia or social anxiety disorder as it pertains to school-age children?

6. What are the five most feared situations for children who have social anxiety disorder, and how can a teacher facilitate the student's participation in them?

7. Describe the Social Effectiveness Therapy for Children (SET-C) cognitive behavioral intervention and identify its strengths in helping students who have social anxiety disorder.

Recently, much attention has focused on school-age children and phobias. In the aftermath of the disaster of September 11, 2001, thousands of children throughout the United States, but especially in the greater metropolitan area of New York City, suffered the debilitating effects of posttraumatic stress disorder (PTSD) and social anxiety disorder (SAD). The comprehensive media attention given to the threat of terrorism intensified the sense of foreboding and dread that permeated American society after the catastrophic events of 9/11. This continuing climate of fear may help account for the significant increase in the identification of social phobia and generalized anxiety disorders in children and adolescents. Similarly, chronic nonattendance at school is on the rise, especially among older children and adolescents, as a result of several psychosocial and environmental factors (Institute of Educational Sciences, U.S. Department of Education, 2006).

These sociocultural triggers and the corresponding increase in phobias among school-age children demand that teachers and related service providers be especially aware of and familiar with the characteristics of these disorders, as well as the most effective school-based interventions. This chapter offers a practical approach to identifying childhood phobias and the most effective school-based interventions. Where possible, case examples drawn from actual practice are used to provide teachers and related service providers with authentic applications of school-based interventions.

To facilitate clarity and understanding, the chapter examines the most prevalent phobias that affect school-age children: specific phobia, separation anxiety disorder, social anxiety disorder, and generalized anxiety disorder. Each of these diagnoses is introduced with a relevant case example, followed by an elaboration of the characteristics, causes, and recommended interventions for the specific disorder, and concluding with a behavioral intervention plan as required by the Individuals with Disabilities Education Improvement Act (IDEIA; U.S. Department of Education, 2004).

SPECIFIC PHOBIA

CASE EXAMPLE: Ricky V

Ricky V. is a 13-year-old boy who lives at a residential treatment facility for children and youth who are experiencing emotional difficulties. His case file provides a description of his presenting emotional/behavioral disorder, specific phobia (SP). His symptoms first emerged 4 years ago, at age 9, shortly after attending a late-night showing of a horror film with several other boys and a parental chaperone, on the occasion of a planned sleepover in celebration of his best friend's birthday. Ricky told his parents that he saw a film about "a guy that was buried alive" and was unable to sleep for fear he might wake up to find himself in a similar predicament. The protagonist in the movie suffered from a very rare form of narcolepsy in which vital signs were undetectable. Following a very acute episode, the protagonist was presumed dead and subsequently buried, only to awaken hours later to the excruciating realization that he was in a coffin. Ricky began to question his parents incessantly about the "condition" and the possibility that he might have it. His parents insisted that narcolepsy was not evident on either side of the family tree and that Ricky was overreacting to a fictional story whose sole purpose was to terrify the moviegoer and that had no basis in fact. Their explanations did nothing to alleviate Ricky's morbid preoccupation.

Ricky's fear of being buried alive persisted and, after a week of being unable to sleep despite the constant reassurance of his parents that he would not be buried alive, Ricky was taken to a psychiatrist for examination. The psychiatrist diagnosed a specific phobia related to this pervasive fear of premature burial and prescribed a sedative to help Ricky sleep. Ricky was initially fearful of the sleep-inducing medication and refused to take it, however, after his parents and the psychiatrist assured him that it would not prevent him from waking, he was persuaded to take the prescribed drug.

Because of the effects of sleep deprivation, Ricky missed a week of school and needed to make up a significant amount of work; this, too, created anxiety in Ricky. Although his teachers were notified of Ricky's psychiatric diagnosis and the precipitating events, they reported significant behavioral changes. Specifically, teachers observed that Ricky seemed extremely anxious whenever the subject of death or dying was mentioned, often asking to be excused to go to the bathroom. Moreover, Ricky began asking questions about the procedures followed during autopsies, and he remarked to teachers that he would want medical personnel to be absolutely sure he was dead before he was buried. His morbid preoccupation disturbed his teachers, who began, at the recommendation of the school psychologist, to record the gist of these conversations. On one occasion, Ricky remarked to his science teacher that he would "rather be cremated than buried" because "there's no way you could be alive after that, right?" Likewise, his classmates began to find his morbid fascination with death and burial to be "creepy," and they alienated him as a result. Ricky was encouraged to continue to see the psychiatrist, who specializes in treating phobias. After a thorough evaluation, a treatment plan was developed that would be implemented both at home and in school.

Characteristics of Specific Phobia

Specific phobia is a marked and persistent fear that is excessive or unreasonable, cued by the presence of anticipation of a specific object or situation (e.g., flying, heights, animals, receiving an injection, seeing blood) (American Psychiatric Association, 2004, p. 449). It rarely exists in isolation but is highly comorbid with other anxiety disorders, depressive disorders, and disruptive disorders. Studies have suggested comorbidity rates as high as 60 percent in general and as high as 75 percent specifically with other anxiety disorders (Last, Perrin Hersen, & Kazdin, 1992; Strauss & Last, 1993; Weems, Hammond-Laurence, Silverman, & Ferguson, 1997). Separation anxiety disorder is the most common comorbid disorder with SP. In addition, it is important to distinguish SP from normal fear, because all children have fears, considered part of the normal developmental process.

Marks (1969) articulated four distinguishing characteristics of a phobia:

1. It is out of proportion to the demands of the situation.
2. It cannot be explained or reasoned away.
3. It is beyond voluntary control.
4. It leads to avoidance of the feared situation.

Mark's definition did not distinguish between phobias in adults and children, but Miller, Barrett, and Hampe (1974) did so by adding three more characteristics to phobia in children:

5. It persists over an extended period of time.
6. It is unadaptive.
7. It is not age- or stage-specific.

These seven characteristics formed the basis of the DSM-IV-TR's (American Psychiatric Association, 2000) definition of a SP, which does allow for distinguishing characteristics in children, most notably its expression through crying, tantrums, freezing, or clinging.

The manifestation of specific phobia is through a triple response system: behavioral, cognitive, and physiological (Barrios & Hartmann, 1997; King, Muris, & Ollendick, 2004; King, Ollendick, & Murphy, 1997). The most common behavioral manifestation of SP in children is avoidance of the feared stimulus. Some examples include:

- Avoiding or escaping certain situations such as feared places in the home (e.g., the basement)
- Keeping the light on when sleeping or insisting on sleeping with parent(s) to escape darkness
- Avoiding eating for fear of choking
- Refusing to attend a doctor's appointment for fear of a needle

Cognitive responses usually include scary thoughts ("I'm afraid"), negative self-statements ("I can't do it"), and the expectation of some catastrophic result ("I'm going to die from the lightning"). Physiological responses include sweating, upset stomach, dry mouth, increased heart rate, shakiness, muscle tension, and even fainting associated with the blood/injection type of SP (American Psychiatric Association, 2000; Ginsburg & Walkup, 2004; Page, 1994).

Prevalence

Specific phobia is present in approximately 5 percent of nonclinical children and adolescents, but increases to 15 percent among clinical samples, an indication of the high comorbidity of SP. Evidence has suggested that girls have higher rates of SP than boys (Ollendick & King, 1994; Ollendick, Yang, Dong, Xia, & Ling, 1995), but differences across racial/ethnic groups are not significant. A diagnosis of SP is given only when other anxiety disorders have been ruled out, especially fear related to separation (separation anxiety disorder), social situations (social phobia), dirt/contamination (obsessive-compulsive disorder), a traumatic event (posttraumatic stress disorder), or fear of having an attack (panic disorder) (Ginsburg & Walkup, 2004). Developmentally, specific phobias are known to occur before the age of 7, especially those related to animals, darkness, insects, and blood/injury, whereas those of the natural-environment type more commonly begin around age 11 or 12.

Etiology of Specific Phobia

The etiology of childhood fears in not completely understood (Ollendick, King, & Muris, 2002). Previously, it had been thought that all fears in children came about through Rachman's (1976, 1977) pathways to fear acquisition: direct **classical conditioning**, **vicarious conditioning**, and information/instruction. More recent studies have suggested, however, that not all fears can be accounted for by an individual's learning history and that other factors (e.g., biological/genetic and parenting influences) must also be considered in the causality of SP.

LEARNING FACTORS The earliest thinking about phobia acquisition concentrated on aversive classical conditioning. A child would experience a trauma around a certain stimulus and then associate the same trauma with any future experience of the same stimulus. The well-known case of "Little Albert" (Watson & Rayner, 1920) concerned a boy who developed a fear of rats after pairing an aversive sound with the sight of the rat. Although trauma can certainly cause a phobia, it is not the only learning pathway to developing a phobia. Social learning factors can also play a part. A child may observe a phobic reaction in someone else (e.g., another child) or learn about the phobic reaction of others through reading and various media outlets (Ollendick et al., 2002). Most of the research on the etiology of phobias has been retrospective, i.e., investigating adult or adolescent reports many years after the development of their phobias. Relying on Rachman's tripartite theory of fear acquisition, Ollendick & King (1991) studied 1092 phobic Australian and American children (ages 9 to 14) and found the most common pathways to be vicarious and instructional rather than direct conditioning. Rarely was only one factor responsible for the development of the fear, and in most cases there was an interaction between two of the

CLASSICAL CONDITIONING

A paradigm in which an unconditioned stimulus is paired with a conditioned stimulus to evoke a conditioned response. For example, child who approached a dog and was bitten would learn to avoid all dogs and/or places where there might be dogs.

VICARIOUS CONDITIONING

An operant response that is strengthened or weakened as a result of consequences that are either reinforcing or punishing. For example, children's fears may get them what they want—care and comfort from their parents.

factors proposed by Rachman. In a study with parents of water-phobic children, Menzies and Clarke (1993) found that only 2 percent attributed the fears of their children to direct conditioning events; 26 percent attributed them to vicarious conditioning. Furthermore, the majority of parents (56 percent) believed that their child's fear of water was present from the very beginning and could not be attributed to any specific conditioning event. Findings such as these led theorists to conclude that although various forms of conditioning are important factors in the development of specific fears in children, they do not tell the whole story, and other causal factors must be considered. These other factors include heritability of phobias, biological-constitutional factors, and parenting influences (Ollendick et al., 2002).

HERITABILITY OF FEARS   Inherited phobia proneness is a controversial hypothesis that has escalated the debate about the causes of specific fears. The only heritability studies on specific fear have been done with adults (Carey, 1990; Kendler, Neale, Kessler, & Heath, 1992). Specific phobias, because of their early development, are considered to have the lowest heritability, as opposed to, for example, agoraphobia (fear of open spaces), considered to have the highest heritability because of its relatively late onset. Kendler et al. (1992) concluded that environmental factors account for twice as much variance as genetic factors in the development of phobias. Genetic factors play a part in the development of fears, but not an overwhelming one. The role of genetics appears to be more related to an individual's propensity to fear, and environmental factors play the part of manifesting this propensity in the form of a specific fear.

CONSTITUTIONAL FACTORS   Certain temperament characteristics (shyness, introversion, withdrawal, etc.) are thought to play a role in the development of childhood fears. Kagan, Reznick, and Gibbons (1989) used the term *behavioral inhibition* to describe a child who is constitutionally disposed to acquire phobias, and they estimated that 10 to 15 percent of U.S. children fit this description. In a study comparing inhibited versus uninhibited children, Biederman, Rosenbaum, Hirshfield, and Faraone (1990) found significantly different rates of phobic disorders for the inhibited group (31.8 percent) versus the uninhibited group (5.3 percent). Differences in the **sympathetic nervous system** activation responses of behaviorally inhibited children lend support to the neuropsychological basis of anxiety disorders in general and phobic disorders in particular (Biederman, Rosenbaum, Chaloff, & Kagan, 1995; McNaughton & Gray, 2000).

FAMILY INFLUENCES   Increased rates of behaviorally inhibited children born to parents with anxiety and phobic disorders raise the question not only of a genetic connection but also an environmental one. Children who are constantly exposed to the influence of anxiety-disordered parents may develop behavioral inhibition characteristics such as cautiousness, uncertainty, and fearfulness in new and different situations (Ollendick et al., 2002). Phobic parents may model avoidance behaviors, thwart risk-taking behaviors, and discourage exploration

SYMPATHETIC NERVOUS SYSTEM

A part of the autonomic nervous system that becomes more active during stress. It is responsible for the fight-or-flight response to fear-provoking situations.

by their children. Direct behavioral observations of the interaction between parent and child in stressful or difficult situations have confirmed that phobically inclined parents tend to use insulating and protective behaviors (Barrett, Rapee, Dadds, & Ryan, 1996; Whaley, Pinto, & Sigman, 1999).

In summary, the literature on the etiology of specific phobia suggests that it is multifactorial and that a number of factors, including genetics, temperament, parental psychopathology, parenting practices, and individual conditioning histories, interact in the development and maintenance of childhood phobias (Ollendick et al., 2002).

Assessment of Specific Phobia

Most experts on childhood phobia have agreed that its assessment needs to be multi-informant and multimethod (Ginsburg & Walkup, 2004; King, Muris, & Ollendick, 2005). There are three assessment approaches for diagnosis of phobias in children: diagnostic evaluation/interview, fear rating scales, and behavioral tasks with observation.

DIAGNOSTIC EVALUATION/INTERVIEW Interviews for the diagnosis of SP can be structured, semistructured, or unstructured. Structured interviews have the most reliability. Of all the structured interviews designed to asses psychiatric diagnosis in children, only one has been designed specifically to assess SP and other anxiety disorders in children: the *Anxiety Disorders Interview Schedule for DSM-IV, Child and Parent Versions* (ADIS-C/P; Silverman & Albano, 1996). Because the ADIS-C/P diagnoses other anxiety disorders in addition to SP, it is useful in cases of comorbidity. The interview process usually begins with the child and uses a time frame of the preceding year. The questions are organized around type (i.e., animal, natural-environment, blood–injection/injury, situational, and other type). Both the parent and child versions use a 0–8 Likert-scaled format to assess the degree of fear in relation to a specific object or event. To control for variability in language across subjects, the ADIS-C/P utilizes a "feelings thermometer" to help children rate the tasks. Extensive research has been done on the ADIS-C/P, and various studies have reported reliabilities anywhere form 0.84 to 1.0 (Rapee, Barrett, Dadds, & Evans, 1994; Silverman & Rabian, 1995; Silverman, Saavedra, & Pina, 2001).

FEAR RATING SCALES Fear rating scales are self-report, standardized measures that allow a child or someone else to rate the degree of fear in relation to a particular object or event. The most well known and widely used is the *Fear Survey Schedule for Children—Revised* (FSSC-R; Ollendick, 1983). The FSSC-R includes eighty items with a 5-factor underlying structure:

- Fear of the unknown
- Fear of failure and criticism
- Fear of minor injury and small animals
- Fear of danger and death
- Medical fears

Extensive research on the FSSC-R has shown it to have good reliability and validity (King, Gullone, & Ollendick, 1992). More recently, Gullone and King (1992) developed the *Fear Survey Schedule for Children and Adolescents* (FSSC-II), which consists of seventy-eight items with the same underlying factors structure as the FSSC-R but which includes more contemporary events such as nuclear war and AIDS (acquired immunodeficiency syndrome).

In addition to these instruments that measure a broad spectrum of fears, a number of instruments have been developed that asses a specific fear, such as fear of darkness (*Nighttime Coping Response Inventory and Nighttime Fear Inventory;* Mooney, 1985), snakes (*Snake Attitude Measure;* Kornhaber & Schroeder, 1975), tests (*Test Anxiety Scale for Children;* Sarason, Davidson, Lighthall, Waite, & Ruebush, 1960); medical procedures/hospitals (*Fears Schedule;* Bradlyn, 1982); and dental procedures (*Children's Fear Survey Schedule;* Melamed & Lumley, 1988).

Fear rating scales can be used for several purposes. They are helpful in determining a child's level of fear and therefore can be used to establish a baseline level of fear. Subsequent administration will determine the level of improvement. General fear rating scales can also determine the range of fears from which a child may suffer. Most of the scales are easy to administer, have good reliability, and can help to distinguish anxious from normal youth (Beidel & Turner, 1988; Ginsburg & Walkup, 2004). Fear rating scales, however, should not be used to make differential diagnoses, especially among children who have psychiatric disorders, as the **discriminate validity** of these scales has not been determined (Perrin & Last, 1992)

BEHAVIORAL TASKS   Another form of child phobia assessment instrument is the *Behavioral Avoidance Task* (BAT) (King et al., 2005; King, Ollendick, & Murphy, 1997). The BAT requires a child, under observation, to enter a room and approach the feared stimulus in gradual fashion. Assessment results from the determination of how close the child can get to the feared stimulus, at what point (if any) the child freezes and refuses to approach any closer, time spent in the presence of the feared stimulus, and the number of approach responses (Kazdin, 1973). Hamilton and King (1991), in a study with fourteen dog-phobic children, determined the **reliability** of the BAT through a test–retest procedure, to be 0.97. Ten of the fourteen subjects had identical scores on the two administrations of the BAT. On the other hand, the **external validity** of the BAT is questionable, because the controlled setting allows the child the nearby support of the researcher and a caregiver. In addition, the BAT usually employs fairly safe exercises. As a result, a child's fear may be assessed as lower than what corresponds to a real-life, everyday situation.

Treatment Strategies

Four methods have been used to treat children who have specific phobia: behavioral, cognitive-behavioral, psychodynamic psychotherapy, and medication. By far the most popular and researched methods have been behavioral and cognitive-behavioral, so we begin with those. Ollendick and King (1998) did a

DISCRIMINATE VALIDITY

A test's or scale's ability to discriminate a concept (e.g., fears) from another concept that is theoretically different and should not be similar.

RELIABILITY

The ability of a measure to produce consistent results. Test–retest is one way to determine reliability.

EXTERNAL VALIDITY

The ability of a test or experiment to generalize to the broader population and not be limited to the controlled, idiosyncratic settings in which the measure was administered.

seminal review of empirically supported behavioral and cognitive-behavioral interventions for children who have phobic and anxiety disorders. Their review utilized the guidelines of the American Psychological Association for the determination of psychological procedures into three categories: well established, probably efficacious, and experimental. We have relied heavily on this review to present an overview on treatment of childhood phobia.

SYSTEMATIC DESENSITIZATION Systematic desensitization is a counterconditioning behavioral intervention that has three forms: in vivo, imaginal, and emotive. First developed by Wolpe (1958), it is based on the theory that phobias are classically conditioned responses and therefore can be unlearned through counterconditioning procedures. Systematic desensitization basically has three parts: (1) induction of an incompatible response (e.g., muscle relaxation, imagery, and meditation); (2) presentation of a fear-producing hierarchy from least to most fearful; and (3) systematic, graduated pairing of items in the hierarchy with the incompatible response (Ollendick & King, 1998; Wolpe, 1958).

In-vivo systematic desensitization uses a real-life stimulus and an incompatible response. Ultee, Griffioen, and Schellekens (1982), in a study with water-phobic children, demonstrated the greater effectiveness of in-vivo systematic desensitization compared to imaginal and a no-treatment control group. Kuroda (1969) found similar results with feline-phobic children. Based on these and other studies, Ollendick and King (1998) concluded that in-vivo desensitization is probably efficacious in the treatment of child phobia. They reached the same conclusion about imaginal systematic desensitization, in which, in contrast to an in-vivo presentation, subjects are asked to imagine the feared stimulus. Studies by Kondas (1967), Barabasz (1973), Mann and Rosenthal (1969), and Miller, Barrett, Hampe, and Noble (1972) have all shown imaginal systematic desensitization to be more effective than a no-treatment control group. A third form of systematic desensitization is emotive, in which the participant, instead of an actual anxiety inhibitor, such as muscular relaxation or edibles, is asked to imagine something exciting or pleasant (e.g., the child's favorite hero). Based on studies by Lazarus and Abramovitz (1962), Cornwall, Spence, and Schotte (1997), and King, Cranstoun, and Josephs (1989), Ollendick and King (1998) concluded that emotive systematic desensitization should be accorded only experimental status at this point because, to date, only one study has shown it to be more effective than a no-treatment control group.

MODELING Based on Bandura's (1973) theory of social learning, modeling makes use of observational learning to reduce and/or eliminate childhood fears. Modeling can be symbolic (e.g., the child watches a film or studies a picture), live, or participating, in which the child is invited to engage in the same behavior as the model in relation to the feared stimulus. A number of studies have compared the different types of modeling (see, e.g., Bandura, Blanchard, & Ritter, 1969; Bandura & Menlove, 1968; Hill, Liebert, & Mott, 1968; Lewis, 1974; Mann & Rosenthal, 1969), and the results have been, for the most part, quite consistent. All types of modeling have been shown to be more effective than a nonintervention control group, and participant modeling was shown to be more effective than symbolic or live modeling without participation. This consistency led Ollendick and King (1998) to conclude that participant modeling enjoys well-established status as a psychological procedure with phobic children, whereas live and symbolic modeling should be considered probably efficacious.

CONTINGENCY MANAGEMENT   Based on the principles of operant learning, contingency management is a behavioral intervention designed to reduce childhood fears by managing consequences. The assumption is that the fear is being maintained and reinforced through consequences. Its elimination, therefore, must be based on the removal of reinforcers. A simple example is a child who is afraid of the dark and cannot fall asleep. As a result, the parents allow the child to sleep in their bed. This child's fear is being reinforced by getting him what he wants: closeness and connection with his parents. Under contingency management, the parents are instructed not to allow the child to sleep with them, to encourage the child to deal with the fear, and to reward the child with their presence every time the child is able to face the fear on his/her own.

To date, four between-group (intervention versus control) studies have been done to examine the effects of contingency management (Leitenberg & Callahan, 1973; Menzies & Clarke, 1993; Obler & Terwilliger, 1970; Sheslow, Bondy, & Nelson, 1983). In two of the studies (Leitenberg & Callahan; Obler & Terwilliger), contingency management proved more effective than no-treatment controls. The other two (Menzies & Clarke; Sheslow et al.) showed that contingency management was more effective than two other proven effective treatments—verbal coping skills and live (adult) modeling. Based on these results, Ollendick and King (1998) concluded that contingency management should be considered a well-established psychological procedure for dealing with childhood phobias.

COGNITIVE-BEHAVIORAL INTERVENTIONS   Cognitive-behavioral interventions include any intervention designed to alter the child's distorted, fear-producing cognitions through verbal self-instruction that generate positive self-statements. The main goal is for the child to develop a plan to deal with the feared stimulus through problem-solving strategies and relaxation. For example, children who are afraid of dogs might be taught to tell themselves, "I am a brave boy (girl)—I know I can take care of myself"; "Dogs can be fun to watch and play with—they do many interesting things." To date, two between-group studies have investigated the effectiveness of verbal self-instruction (Graziano & Mooney, 1980; Kanfer, Karoly, & Newman, 1975). Both studies demonstrated that verbal self-instruction was more effective than no treatment.

Silverman et al. (1999) compared the efficacy of three groups (self-control, contingency management, and an education/support control group) and found that all three resulted in positive outcomes. In their 1998 review, Ollendick and King did not have access to the Silverman et al. (1999) study. Based on the two previous studies (Graziano & Mooney, 1980; Kanfer et al., 1975), Ollendick and

King (1998) concluded that cognitive-behavioral interventions should be accorded "probably efficacious" status, because in at least two studies they had been shown to be effective in comparison to controls. It is not known whether or how the Silverman et al. (1999) study would have affected their evaluation, because that study showed no difference between cognitive-behavioral intervention and contingency management, an already well-established intervention for childhood phobia.

PSYCHODYNAMIC PSYCHOTHERAPY   Although psychodynamic psychotherapy and psychoanalysis have been used in the treatment of childhood phobia, Ollendick and King (1998) did not include them in their review because of a lack of rigorous evaluation of such treatments. In 2003, however, Muratori, Picchi, Bruni, Patarnello, and Romagnoli conducted a study with fifty-eight outpatient children (twelve of whom had a diagnosis of specific phobia) who received an 11-week psychodynamic psychotherapeutic intervention together with their parents. Assessed at baseline, 6 months, and at 2-year follow-up, significant improvement had occurred. More studies are needed to determine the effectiveness of psychodynamic psychotherapy for childhood phobias.

SELECTIVE SEROTONIN REUPTAKE INHIBITORS (SSRIs)

A class of drugs used in the treatment of depression and anxiety. They block the reuptake of serotonin, the neurotransmitter responsible for mood regulation, making it more available to the brain.

MEDICATION   Relatively little evidence exists for the effectiveness of pharmacological intervention for childhood phobia. Antidepressants and antianxiety medications have been used for the treatment of a number of anxiety disorders in children, but there are no reliable outcome studies for specific phobia (King et al., 2005; Ollendick & March, 2004). Among adults, **selective serotonin reuptake inhibitors (SSRIs)** have become the preferred class of drugs for dealing with phobias and other anxiety-related disorders. There is little evidence, however, of the effectiveness of SSRIs among children who have specific phobia (Ginsburg & Walkup, 2004).

STAGES OF TREATMENT   Silverman and Carmichael (1999) recommended a three-phase treatment for children who have specific phobia:

- An education phase
- The application phase
- A relapse-prevention phase

In the education phase, both the child and the parents are given information about fears, the key ingredient to overcoming them (i.e., exposure), and, especially for parents, an understanding of contingency management. In the application phase, the child learns relaxation training as part of systematic desensitization, cognitive restructuring, self-evaluation, and reward (King, Muris, & Ollendick, 2004). Finally, fears are not expected to be conquered once and for all, because most children will relapse after having made some progress. To minimize relapse, helpers should try to anticipate future events that might cause the child to become afraid. By creating "what if" scenarios, helpers work with the child in applying already-learned skills to future events.

School-Based Interventions

This section provides practical, effective strategies for working with students who have specific phobia. To make the recommended school-based interventions described in this section as real and pertinent as possible, we present both the assessment of the behavior and the appropriate behavioral intervention in relation to Ricky, the child described in the preceding case example.

ASSESSING THE PROBLEM   In this book, we address an array of emotional and behavioral disorders. Some of these involve primarily internalizing behaviors, which require extensive treatment protocols that engage the participation of all the child's caregivers, particularly the school psychologist. Remember that any purposeful assessment of problem behavior is essentially a problem-solving process conducted to identify the purpose of a behavior so as to develop a plan that will mitigate it effectively. The steps involved in any such plan should include: (1) identifying and describing the problem behavior, (2) collecting baseline data and academic information, (3) describing the context in which the behavior is observed, (4) completing a functional assessment form and/or behavior rating scales as appropriate, (5) conducting a direct observation, (6) developing a hypothesis, and (7) testing the hypothesis and modifying it as necessary (Barnhill, 2005). Once a viable hypothesis has been established, the teacher can develop a behavioral intervention plan (BIP). Teachers are required to provide such assessment as a precursor to the development of an effective BIP (IDEA, 2004). We will use the case example of Ricky, the 9-year-old boy with specific phobia related to being buried alive, to demonstrate an appropriate functional behavioral assessment. First, relative to *identifying and describing the problem behavior,* Ricky's teachers have agreed that the principal undesirable behavior he manifests involves his obsession with being buried alive. This perseverating behavior significantly impairs his social as well as his academic success.

Next, in terms of *collecting baseline data and academic information,* Ricky's teachers have begun to use a behavior checklist to record the number of times during the school day that Ricky talks about being buried alive or asks questions to assuage his worries. He is currently speaking about death and premature burial on average fifteen times per school day, as observed by his teachers. In addition, Ricky's grades have been declining significantly since he began to obsess about premature burial and narcolepsy. For example, his English language arts grade dropped from an A to a C+ in the quarter immediately following his "crisis." Furthermore, he is clearly sleep-deprived, and he dozes off in every class.

It is also beneficial to *describe the environments and setting demands* in determining the function served by a problem behavior. It appears that Ricky is indiscriminant about whom he shares his fears with. There does not seem to be a specific environmental "trigger" for his morbid disclosures. Ricky seems to initiate a morose conversation in an opportunistic way. He waits for a sympathetic listener and then "unloads" his phobic preoccupation.

Furthermore, a *functional behavioral assessment* and a *behavior rating scale* were completed in addition to annotated teacher-conducted behavioral observations that are ongoing.

After conducting a rigorous assessment to determine the function of the targeted maladaptive behavior, Ricky's teachers developed a hypothesis about its function as a prerequisite to developing an effective behavioral intervention plan. Based on the antecedent and current behavioral data, it seems logical to assume that Ricky will continue to obsess about being buried alive until an effective school-based intervention is identified and employed. Ricky is currently receiving therapy from an outside psychologist who specializes in the treatment of phobias and will share his treatment regiment with both Ricky's family as well as school personnel.

As a preliminary step, the proposed behavioral intervention plan will be implemented, monitored, and evaluated to ensure its efficacy. The multidisciplinary team, in conjunction with the outside psychologist, has recommended the implementation of what is hoped will be an effective school-based intervention. School personnel have just started to employ it, however, and they feel that more time is needed to assess its effectiveness in helping to mediate Ricky's obsession. If it is successful, the treatment plan will be written into Ricky's Individualized Education Plan (IEP) as a behavioral intervention plan.

A multidisciplinary team meeting with Ricky and his parents is scheduled for next month, to allow sufficient time before then for the newly instituted BIP to produce measurable results.

DEVELOPING AND EFFECTIVE INTERVENTION PLAN   The Individuals with Disabilities Education Act (IDEA, 1997, 2004) requires that school personal develop a behavioral intervention plan for students who experience significant emotional or behavioral problems in school (Buck, Polloway, Kirkpatrick, Patton, & McConnell Fad, 2000). This BIP should: (1) be research-based and relevant; (2) only be implemented after informed consent has been provided by the child's parents; (3) document the steps of the intervention plan, including who will be responsible, when and where it will occur, and for how long; (4) establish realistic and measurable goals; and (5) establish a method to measure progress. After the BIP has been implemented for a reasonable period of time, it should be evaluated to determine the extent of behavior change and, thus, the plan's overall effectiveness (Ryan, Halsey, & Mathews, 2003).

For Ricky, our case example, a research-based intervention developed in response to the results of the behavioral assessment will most likely be a behavioral and/or cognitive-behavioral one. Considering all the recommended interventions described earlier in the chapter, the most effective intervention plan for use in school will include: *contingency management* and *verbal self-instruction*. These two are preferred because they can be effectively and easily implemented and monitored in the classroom. The former technique was used initially in the classroom because it did not require training; the latter one was used after Ricky had been trained in verbal self-instruction.

Specifically, in Ricky's case, *contingency management* involved ignoring him when he began to perseverate about being buried alive. Teachers and students were instructed to "walk away" or immediately change the subject. Teachers also were requested to maintain a behavior checklist to record the frequency of the target behavior (i.e., talking about or asking questions about being buried alive) in order to monitor the effectiveness of *systematic ignoring.*

The cognitive behavioral management technique selected for use with Ricky involved a problem-solving strategy employing *verbal self-instruction* or *self-talk* as reinforcement. Explicitly, Ricky was taught to remind himself that narcolepsy is a very treatable disorder, doctors are trained to use very advanced technology to confirm the death of a patient, and there has never been a recorded case of premature burial in the United States in the past 100 years (1900–1970; U.S. Public Health Service, *Vital Statistics of the United States,* annual, Vol. I and Vol. II; 1971–2001, U.S. National Center for Health Statistics, *Vital Statistics of the United States,* annual; *National Vital Statistics Report* [*NVSR;* formerly *Monthly Vital Statistics Report*]). Initially, Ricky was told to reinforce himself perceptibly (aurally) so that teachers could monitor his use of this intervention. Ricky was taught that when intrusive, morbid thoughts about premature burial permeated his mind, he was to remind himself that people are not buried alive today, reciting the following facts: "Doctors use new devices that prevent a living person from being declared dead," "My parents and teachers would never let that happen," and "I am not going to be buried alive—these are just silly thoughts and I can control them." Teachers were asked to provide prompts if Ricky appeared somber or started to mention morbid topics. The prompt was *"Ricky, remember to use your reminders."*

Finally, teachers were provided with contingencies should Ricky's specific phobia relapse. In this eventuality, teachers were prepared to help Ricky reassert control over the fear induced by various stimuli. For example, in the future, Ricky will likely be exposed to death via the media, either through television programs, movies, or radio programs dealing with the subject. These exposures might result in a reemergence of fear-related behaviors, but Ricky can, once again, be reminded to use the strategies he has learned to regain control.

Tips for Teachers

1. Don't allow the student to perseverate about her fear.
2. Don't allow the student to monopolize your attention with her fearful obsession; instead, reinforce the prescribed intervention plan or use "planned ignoring."
3. Avoid deviating from the treatment plan by acceding to the student's requests to call home.
4. Provide established prompts if the student appears fearful or mentions feeling afraid.
5. Immediately change the subject if the affected student becomes preoccupied with her phobia.
6. Be prepared to provide a rational explanation to help allay the child's fear.

SEPARATION ANXIETY DISORDER

CASE EXAMPLE: Jimmy

According to his mother, Jimmy enjoyed going to school until the end of Christmas break in fourth grade. At the conclusion of the holidays, Jimmy seemed increasingly despondent and experienced frequent sleeplessness and nausea prior to returning to school for the third quarter. His mother, Anna M., reported that during the holidays, Jimmy appeared anxious around his cousins, who are of a similar age and whose company he usually enjoyed. Oddly, Jimmy would not leave his mother's side during their visits; if she was out of sight, he would abruptly stop whatever he was doing and frantically search the house until he found her.

Mrs. M. noted that, on occasion, Jimmy "barged" in on her while she was in the bathroom. Although she scolded him for this invasion of her privacy, he continued this behavior unabated. He said that he felt afraid that something "terrible" might happen to her while she was out of his sight—something that might be within his power to prevent. He also described the "panicky feelings" brought on by her absence and said that he felt his heart beating very fast—so fast that he feared it might "explode."

The morning of the first day at school after the holiday recess resulted in a "major meltdown." Mrs. M. explained, "He threw up in the bathroom and I took his temperature, but it was normal . . . he didn't have a fever. He began pleading with me not to make him go to school, that he felt something terrible would happen to him if I left him there." Nevertheless, Mrs. M. insisted, hoping his fear would subside once he was back among familiar surroundings and classmates. Unfortunately, this was not the case. As they approached the school in her car, Jimmy began screaming at the top of his lungs: "Please don't make me go in—I can't stay there without you—I'm going to be sick—I'm going to die, and you don't even care!"

The assistant principal and a teacher's aide tried to help Mrs. M., who was by now struggling with Jimmy in a vain attempt to get him physically up the front steps and into the school. Despite their attempts to reassure Jimmy that all would be well and that he could call his mother at lunchtime, Jimmy was intractable and would not enter the building. He began to tantrum and scream so loudly that the assistant principal feared that the classes now in session would be disrupted by the commotion.

At this point, feeling embarrassed, angry, and frustrated, Mrs. M. relented and took Jimmy home, admonishing him for his "immature" behavior. As soon as his mother conceded and began to drive him home, Jimmy stopped crying and acted as though nothing had happened: He was *clearly* relieved, and his hysteria abated.

Characteristics

Separation anxiety disorder (SAD) is the only anxiety disorder in the DSM IV-TR that is included in the section, "Disorders Usually First Diagnosed in Infancy, Childhood, or Adolescence." The focal point of SAD's symptomatology is a child's excessive fear and anxiety related to being away from home and/or attachment figures, and tremendous worry that harm will come to themselves or their parents while they are separated. Many children have fears of separation; therefore, it is important to distinguish between normal separation anxiety and that which constitutes a disorder. The differential diagnosis is made according to the type, severity, duration, and impact of symptoms on the child's functioning.

Most children who suffer from SAD develop symptoms between the ages of 8 and 12 years. Social phobia is more prevalent in adolescents than in children, but the reverse is true for SAD (Breton et al., 1999). Symptom expression differs across age groups: Adolescents with SAD tend to report physical complaints on schools days; older children (ages 9 to 12) tend to report excessive distress upon separation, and younger children (ages 5 to 8) tend to report nightmares about separations (Francis, Last, & Strauss, 1987).

Among clinical samples, SAD is highly comorbid with other anxiety disorders especially generalized anxiety disorder and specific phobia. About half of children who have SAD are also diagnosed with one of these two disorders, and about a third are diagnosed with depression (Hewitt et al., 1997). To a lesser extent, SAD is comorbid with obsessive-compulsive disorder (Valleni-Basile, Garrison, Jackson, & Waller, 1994) and gender identity disorder (Zucker, Bradley, & Sullivan, 1996). Refusal to attend school is often a symptom of SAD but can have many other causes and should not be considered an automatic indicator of the disorder (Heyne, King, & Tonge, 2004). In a study of sixty-three school-refusing children, Last & Strauss (1990) found that the most common primary diagnoses were SAD (38 percent), social phobia (30 percent), and simple phobia (22 percent). Heyne et al. (2002) studied sixty-one school refusers, and their results indicated the following diagnoses: adjustment disorder with anxiety (39 percent); anxiety disorder, not otherwise specified (15 percent), SAD (10 percent), social phobia (10 percent), generalized anxiety disorder (3 percent), specific phobia (3 percent), obsessive-compulsive disorder (2 percent), panic disorder with agoraphobia (2 percent), and agoraphobia without panic disorder (2 percent).

When compared to other anxiety disorders in children, SAD has been found to have one of the highest recovery and lowest stability rates (Cantwell & Baker, 1989; Last, Perrin, Hersen, & Kazdin, 1996). With the proper interventions, the prognosis of children who have SAD is very good. There has been some suspicion that SAD may be linked to the development of panic disorder and/or agoraphobia in adulthood (Manicavasagar, Silove, Curtis, & Wagner, 2000). Although some adults with panic and agoraphobia report retrospectively the existence of SAD in childhood, this is not true in all cases. It is also possible that SAD in children can persist into adulthood, albeit at very low rates. Such persistence is most likely the result of biological factors and/or the experience of continued insecurities in primary attachments (Manicavasagar et al., 2000).

Prevalence of SAD

Separation anxiety disorder is one of the most common anxiety disorders among children, estimated to constitute about a third of all anxiety disorders. Prevalence rates are estimated to be between 3 and 5 percent in children and adolescents. A fairly recent study found the prevalence rate to be 3.6 percent (Briggs-Gowan, Horwitz, Schwab-Stone, Leventhal, & Leaf, 2000). A number of studies have found higher rates of SAD in girls (Compton, Nelson, & March, 2000; Costello et al., 1996), whereas other studies have found equal frequency in boys and girls (Bird, Gould, Yager, Staghezza, & Canino, 1989; Last, Perrin, Hersen, & Kazdin, 1992). Compton et al. (2000) found higher rates among girls in a community sample, but higher rates among boys in a clinical sample. It may be that boys who show symptoms of SAD are more likely to be referred to treatment than girls (Perwien & Bernstein, 2004). In contrast to other anxiety disorders, for which children tend to come from middle- to upper-middle-class families, 50 to 75 percent of children who have SAD come from low-socioeconomic-status families (Last et al., 1992).

Etiology of SAD

Silverman and Dick-Niederhauser (2004) identified six developmental pathways for SAD: biological factors, cognitive factors, family processes, parental anxiety/depression, and caregiver stress. Following is a brief explanation along with empirical support for each of these factors.

BIOLOGICAL FACTORS   Overall, genes appear to play less of a role in the development of SAD than environment. Topolski, Hewitt, Eaves, and Silberg (1997), in the Virginia Twin Study, found that genetics accounted for 4 percent and environment for 40 percent of the variance in the development of SAD. There was, however, a marked gender difference among the same sample in the heritability of SAD, with a zero estimate for boys and a 75 percent estimate for girls (Eaves et al., 1997). A substantial gender difference in genetic contribution to SAD was also found by Silove, Manicavasagar, O'Connell, and Morris-Yates (1995). Borrowing Kagan et al.'s (1989) concept of the behaviorally inhibited child, Biederman, Rosenbaum, Bolduc-Murphy, and Faraone (1993) found higher rates of SAD among this population than among uninhibited children. To date, no other study has examined this relationship, and more research is needed to establish a link between the development of SAD and temperament.

COGNITIVE FACTORS   In general, children who have anxiety disorders manifest more negative thinking than nonanxious comparison groups, and children who have SAD are no exception. Research has not discovered any cognitions that would distinguish children who have SAD from children who have other anxiety disorders.

FAMILY PROCESSES   Family dynamics and parenting styles have long been studied as factors in the development of SAD. One long-standing consideration has been an enmeshed relationship between mother and child, the result of a dysfunctional marital relationship that forms a coalition between the two against father. Other psychodynamic explanations include the sexually inhibited mother who prefers the affective fulfillment she receives from the relationship with her child to that provided by her husband. The lack of research to support such hypotheses has turned attention away from psychodynamic explanations to the investigation of parenting styles. The conceptualization of parenting styles is fourfold:

- Secure
- Insecure-avoidant
- Insecure-ambivalent
- Insecure-disorganized (Ainsworth, Blehar, Waters, & Wall, 1978)

Insecure-disorganized is the parenting style that poses the greatest risk for the development of anxiety disorders in children and is usually associated with unresolved loss and trauma (Cassidy, 1995; Warren, Huston, Egeland, & Sroufe, 1997). No specific link to SAD, however, has been established (Silverman & Dick-Niederhauser, 2004).

According to Manassis (2001), two possible parenting pathways can lead to the development of SAD. The first is the pairing of a difficult child with an ambivalent caregiver who is only sporadically available to the child. This heightens the child's insecurity, who then seeks to attach him/herself to the caregiver in order to attain comfort.

This exaggerated effort to seek comfort from a parent reduces the possibility of the child's exploration, and the child becomes unaccustomed to dealing with new and different situations. In addition, the parent becomes anxious in dealing with the difficult child; the child picks up on this anxiety and seeks to comfort the parent by attaching himself to her. This increases the parent's anxiety, setting up a cycle of reinforcement for attachment behaviors.

The second pathway proposed by Manassis (2001) is the parent's inability to provide a consistent model for dealing with stress. Often, this parent is ill, and the child becomes preoccupied with the health and well-being of the parent and eventually develops SAD. Several studies shave shown support for an insecure-preoccupied attachment style and the development of anxiety disorders in children (see, e.g., Boer, 1998; Hudson & Rapee, 2002; Rapee, 1997). No study, however, has been conducted to show the linkages between parenting style and the development specifically of SAD.

PARENTAL ANXIETY AND DEPRESSION Children who have SAD are known to come from families with a high incidence of anxiety disorders and depression. In one study (Last, Phillips, & Statfeld, 1987) of mothers of children who have SAD, 68 percent had an anxiety disorder and 53 percent had depression. Children whose parents have panic disorder are three times more likely to develop SAD, and they are ten times more likely if their parents have panic disorder plus depression (Leckman et al., 1985).

CAREGIVER STRESS Caregiver stress, whether caused by the marital relationship or something outside the family, is known to result in insecure attachment between parents and their children (Jacobson & Frye, 1991). Some studies have sought to examine maternal employment and placement in daycare with insecure attachment (Fein, Gariboldi, & Boni, 1993; Stifter, Coulehan, & Fish, 1993). No study, though, has been able to show a direct link between the mother's employment status and attachment style. Parent background variables (age, degree of support, education) are more predictive of anxiety in mothers than employment status. Mothers who were younger, less educated, and received less support were found to be more anxious and have more insecure attachment styles (Fein et al., 1993).

Assessment of SAD

Assessment of SAD is done through diagnostic interviews, clinician rating scales, and self-report measures.

DIAGNOSTIC INTERVIEWS   Diagnostic interviews may be either structured or unstructured. A structured interview, specific to the diagnosis of SAD, does not exist, but can be accomplished using more general interview formats:

- *Schedule for Affective Disorders and Schizophrenia for School-Age Children* (K-SADS; Ambrosini, 2000)
- *Diagnostic Interview Schedule for Children* (DISC-IV; Schaffer, Fisher, Lucas, Dulcan, & Schwab-Stone, 2000)
- *Child and Adolescent Psychiatric Assessment* (CAPA; Angold & Costello, 2000)
- *Interview Schedule for Children and Adolescents* (ISCA; Sherrill & Kovacs, 2000)
- *Children's Interview for Psychiatric Symptoms* (ChIPS; Weller, Weller, Fristad, Rooney, & Schecter, 2000)
- *Anxiety Disorders Interview Schedule for Children* (ADIS; Silverman & Albano, 1996)

A separate category of diagnostic interviews is pictorial in nature. Valla, Bergeron, and Smolla (2000) developed the *Dominic-R* for White children and the *Terry* for African American children. There is also the *Pictorial Instrument for Children and Adolescents* (PICA-III-R; Ernst, Cookus, & Morovec, 2000). A computer version also exists for the *Dominic-R,* and it has been translated into Spanish, German, and French. The PICA-III-R serves a broader range of children (ages 6 to 16) than the *Terry* or the *Dominic-R.* Most of the instruments mentioned above generally have good psychometric properties in relationship to the diagnosis of SAD and can be used with a degree of confidence.

CLINICIAN RATING SCALES   There are three clinician rating scales appropriate for assessing levels of anxiety: the *Anxiety Rating Scale for Children—Revised* (ARC-R; Bernstein, Crosby, Perwien, & Borchardt, 1996), the *Pediatric Anxiety Rating Scale* (PARS; Walkup & Davies, 1999), and the *Hamilton Rating Scale* (HARS; Hamilton, 1959). All three measures yield overall anxiety scores, and none is designed to diagnose SAD specifically. The ARC-R, however, does have a separation anxiety item: "When you're not with your folks, are you afraid or worried about something bad happening to them?" It is recommended that clinician rating scales be used in conjunction with other assessment techniques.

SELF-REPORT MEASURES   There are a number of self-report measures that specifically assess for separation anxiety symptoms. The *Multidimensional Anxiety Scale for Children* (MASC; March, Parker, Sullivan, Stallings, & Conners, 1997) has a 9-item separation anxiety subscale with high internal consistency and test–retest reliability. Validity, both convergent and discriminate, has been supported by comparison with other anxiety and depression measures. The

Screen for Child Anxiety Related Emotional Disorders (SCARED; Birmaher, Khetarpal, Brent, & Cully, 1997) has both child and parent versions with an 8-item separation anxiety subscale. It also has good psychometric properties. Lastly, the *Spence Children's Anxiety Scale* (SCAS; Spence, 1998) has a 6-item SAD subscale, which has been shown to have adequate reliability and validity.

The use of self-reports as a screening tool and a first step toward the diagnosis of SAD is appropriate. These measures, however, suffer from the problems of all self-report measures: Participants may want to present themselves in a favorable light (Perwein & Bernstein, 2004). These measures should always be used in conjunction with other forms of assessment.

The differential diagnosis of SAD can be problematic. Social phobia and school refusal due to other causes can complicate the diagnostic picture, as can the high comorbidity rates between SAD and other anxiety disorders. Assessment should rule out any medical conditions that might simulate SAD, be multi-informant (child, parent, and teacher), and be multimethod (interview and at least one rating scale).

Treatment Strategies

As mentioned previously, cognitive-behavioral therapy (CBT) is the treatment of choice for anxiety disorders in children and enjoys the most empirical support and investigation. Often, CBT is used in conjunction with other interventions, such as educational support, family management, and group therapy. Few studies have had a pure separation anxiety sample (Perwien & Bernstein, 2004), but a number of well-designed studies of the treatment of anxiety disorders are relevant to SAD. For example, Last, Hansen, and Franco (1998) investigated a sample of children who have school phobia, some of whom received twelve sessions of CBT with graduated in-vivo exposure plus the teaching of coping self-statements and the nonexposure intervention of educational support during which children discuss and learn about their fears. Both groups increased their school attendance, and there were no significant differences between the two groups. The children diagnosed with SAD, however, showed more improvement in school attendance than those diagnosed with other anxiety disorders.

Mendlowitz et al. (1999) studied the effects of a 12-session group intervention on children who have anxiety disorders. Participants were assigned to one of three groups: child-only intervention, parent-only intervention, and parent-and-child interventions. Parent groups were basically psychoeducational, and the child groups incorporated a number of CBT interventions, such as relaxation training, teaching of coping self-statements, and self-reinforcement. All three groups showed a decrease in anxiety-related symptoms, but the parent-and-child intervention groups improved the most. These results are consistent with other studies (see, e.g., Barrett, 1998; Barrett, Dadds, & Rapee, 1996) that support the added benefits of a parent component.

In the Barrett et al. (1996) study, 6- and 12-month follow-up revealed that 70 percent of those who received a CBT workbook intervention did not meet the criteria for an anxiety disorder, compared to 96 percent of those who received the CBT intervention plus family management. Flannery-Schroeder and Kendall (2000) investigated a group CBT intervention by comparing it to an individual CBT intervention for a group of children aged 8 to 14. After an 18-week workbook intervention, a significant number of children in both groups (73 percent of the individual modality versus 50 percent for the group modality) no longer met the criteria for an anxiety disorder when compared to a control group, in which only 8 percent did not meet the criteria.

Research has not supported a consistent significant difference between group and individual treatment for anxiety disorders in children. Both are effective, and some studies have shown one to be more effective than the other. Schools that have a number of children who have anxiety disorders can use a group intervention, knowing that research supports its effectiveness. Keep in mind, however, that the addition of a parent component has been shown to be the most effective together with either group or individual treatment.

PHARMACOLOGICAL INTERVENTION   Over the years, tricyclic antidepressants (e.g., imiprimine), benzodiazepines (e.g., Buspar, Xanax), and selective serotonin reuptake inhibitors (SSRIs; e.g., Prozac, Luvox) have all been used and studied in the treatment of SAD. Bernstein et al. (2000) compared two groups of school-refusing children who had been diagnosed with anxiety or depression. One group received imipramine plus CBT; the other CBT plus placebo. After 8 weeks, the imipramine-plus-CBT group improved their school attendance significantly, but this was not true for the placebo group (70 percent versus 28 percent rate of school attendance). Several studies have examined SSRIs and children who have anxiety disorders (Birmaher, Waterman, Ryan, & Cully, 1994; Fairbanks et al., 1997; Research Units on Pediatric Psychopharmacology [RUPP] Anxiety Study Group, 2001). RUPP (2001) studied the effects of Luvox for 128 children, 59 percent of whom had SAD, compared to a placebo. Both groups received supportive psychotherapy. The Luvox group had a greater reduction in anxiety-related symptoms. More studies are needed to assess the risk/benefit ratio of medication and the use of medication in combination with CBT interventions.

In summary, successful treatment of SAD is usually multimodal, consisting of some combination of individual and or group CBT, family therapy and psychoeducation, consultation with teachers, and possibly medication for the more dysfunctional cases. Presently, the first choice of medication appears to be the SSRIs. For SAD, as for many of the other anxiety disorders in children, training in contingency management for parents and school personnel is also necessary. Reinforcement for SAD symptoms must be eliminated and reserved for the successful management of anxious feelings.

School-Based Interventions

Teachers who have students diagnosed with SAD in their classes can, in collaboration with the school psychologist, develop effective behavioral interventions for the disorder. As we have consistently recommended, such intervention plans cannot be successfully developed without a thorough understanding of the root causes of the problem behavior; that is, what purpose is served by the behavior, and what contingencies help maintain it. This section offers a suggested for Jimmy, the child described in the case example.

ASSESSING THE PROBLEM The following are the outcomes of the behavioral assessment for Jimmy, a child who has SAD, organized according to the steps recommended by Barnes (2005).

In terms of *identifying and describing Jimmy's problem behavior,* based on observation, that would be best described as his constant desire to be with his mother, as manifested dramatically by his refusal to attend school. He also exhibits the following symptoms associated with SAD when he is, or thinks he will be, separated from his mother: having tantrums and crying; resisting separation attempts or "clinging"; physiological symptoms such as nausea; and psychological symptoms that include a pervasive sense of impending calamity.

Relative to *data collection,* Jimmy's mother and the school psychologist have begun to work on a plan to facilitate his gradual reintroduction to school. Baseline data and academic information are currently unavailable because of Jimmy's high rate of absenteeism. As Jimmy is able to stay in school for progressively longer periods without panicking, his teachers will be able to provide duration recordings of his on-task behavior and length of time in school. Teachers will also maintain accurate records of Jimmy's academic performance, starting from his first day back in school, noting improvement or regression.

In describing the demands exerted by *environment and setting,* Jimmy's SAD symptoms are exacerbated by any attempt to separate him from his mother. Proximity to the school building and perceived "abandonment" there create the acute symptoms of anxiety.

A *functional assessment form* was completed after Jimmy's first week back at school. In addition, *behavioral assessment measures* that included the *Multi-dimensional Anxiety Scale for Children* (MASC; March, Parker, Sullivan, Stallings, & Conners, 1997), as well as the *Screen for Child Anxiety Related Emotional Disorder* (SCARED; Birmaher et al., 1997) were administered to Jimmy during his first trial week back in school (half-day schedule). The results from these self-report measures correlated highly with separation anxiety and provided a first step toward formal diagnosis.

Research has indicated the importance of a multimethod assessment that includes teacher and parent observations as well interviews conducted with the child, parent, and teacher. Observations of Jimmy during the modified trial return to school revealed three "phases" of behavior: (1) initial separation anxiety characterized by hysteria, physiological symptoms such as nausea, and persistent requests to be allowed to call his mother; (2) a gradual cessation of these symptoms followed by a willingness to be distracted and attempts to reengage in school work; and (3) a gradual escalation of the earlier symptoms of anxiety that seemed to "magically" disappear when his mother returned to the school to take him home.

From a review of the precipitating event, as well as antecedent and consequent stimuli, it appears that Jimmy has developed SAD, cause unknown. A systematic research-based approach must be developed and implemented to get Jimmy back in the classroom and ensure that he stays there.

In cooperation with parents and related services providers, Jimmy's teachers will implement the behavioral intervention plan that has been developed by the multidisciplinary team. After sufficient time has elapsed, the effectiveness of the plan will be assessed and, if indicated, it will be modified accordingly. If the intervention plan is revised or modified, the improved plan will be trialed; this process will continue until the desired results have been achieved.

DEVELOPING AN EFFECTIVE INTERVENTION PLAN Recommended treatments for children who have SAD are multivariate. Cognitive-behavioral therapy, which involves various self-management techniques, which may include relaxation training, teaching of coping self-statements, and self-reinforcement, appears to be the single most effective intervention, as well as the one most easily employed by the classroom teacher.

Jimmy's therapist has developed an effective CBT to help reduce and regulate his separation anxiety and assist him in resuming a normal school routine. This intervention has been developed to be effectively implemented and monitored during the school day. Jimmy's teachers have received training in supporting his treatment plan, which will be implemented both in school and at home.

As part of this plan, his teachers encourage Jimmy to use coping self-statements such as "I am here with teachers who care about me and I'll see Mom at 3:30 P.M.," and "All the other kids love and often miss their mothers, but they can wait until school is over to see them," and finally, affirming statements such as "School is cool. I can learn new things and spend time with my friends." When these self-talk strategies are ineffective, such as during times of high stress and anxiety, Jimmy can call his mother at a prearranged time and speak with her for a maximum of 5 minutes. This option is only available in an emergency, when Jimmy is feeling out of control. His teachers must confirm this exceptional circumstance.

In addition, his teachers are advised to remind Jimmy of his mother's admonishment to him, that "Your [Jimmy's] job is to attend school Monday to Friday all day, from 8:30 A.M. until dismissal at 3:30 P.M. If you feel sick or anxious during the day, you need to follow the plan." The plan specifies that if Jimmy is truly ill, he will be referred the school nurse, who will determine the severity of his illness and call his mother, who will then come and pick him up at her earliest opportunity. Jimmy is to remind himself or be reminded that his mother must work to provide the money they need to live; he can't stay home alone but must attend school. There are no other options.

The teaching staff and related services providers in the school are supportive of this plan. Jimmy's mother has agreed to comply with the plan and insist that he attend school for the full day. Thus, a coordinated plan that provides consistent reinforcement is in place both at school and at home. Parents and teachers have recourse to meet if some part of the behavioral intervention plan is not working or the plan needs to be revised.

Tips for Teachers

If you have a child like Jimmy in your class, consider the following strategies.

1. Show support and encouragement, and provide positive reinforce for even small achievements, such as going through the school day without a panic attack, emotional outburst, or request to call home.
2. Maintain a firm position relative to the child's requests to call a parent or be sent home. The child will only begin to accept school attendance as compulsory if there are no alternatives.
3. Give the child encouragement, let her know you truly care about her and are committed to her success in school. Help her feel valued and to have a sense of belonging.
4. Encourage the child who has SAD to make friends in class. Provide cooperative learning opportunities, consider pairing the student with a peer tutor or "study buddy."
5. If the student is absent for any reason, let her know when she returns that she was truly missed.
6. If the student is absent for any reason, call home to let the child know you missed her and want her to return as soon as possible.
7. Never shame or punish the child for an emotional outburst. Instead, try to comfort and isolate the student until she can regain her composure.
8. Hold the student accountable for all work missed because of absence; the student must take responsibility for her school performance.
9. Ensure that you understand the behavioral intervention plan instituted for this child and participate in it as directed. For example, if the key intervention is CBT, know the self-statements or prompts and encourage the student to use them; provide reinforcement where possible.
10. Develop an effective rapport with the child's parents or guardians to enhance collaboration and facilitate the exchange of relevant information concerning the student's target behavior.
11. Speak to your other students before the child who has SAD returns to your classroom, to help them understand their classmate's challenges and solicit their support.
12. Perhaps most important to the success of a school-based intervention is the individualization of treatment. For the teacher, this means making a special effort to develop a positive relationship with the child. Research has supported the importance of this individualized approach in the reduction of SAD behaviors (Ollendick & King, 1999).

SOCIAL ANXIETY DISORDER (SOCIAL PHOBIA)

CASE EXAMPLE: Jody

Jody, a 12-year-old African American girl, has recently developed a generalized fear of public "exposure" that involves speaking, reading, or performing in front of a group of people—even engaging in a conversation with two or more people. Her parents recently divorced after 14 years of marriage, but her mother insists that was not a factor in the development of Jody's social anxiety disorder.

The implications of this phobia as it affects her ability to engage others in social settings are profound and far-reaching. Jody was previously very active in music and dance, as well as the youth choir in her church. She is unable to participate in these activities as a result of her social phobia. Similarly, Jody, traditionally very gregarious and popular in school, has become almost reclusive, preferring solitary activities to group ones. Her best friends report really missing their once personable friend's contributions to their social activities. Jody had been a very popular student who was twice elected class representative to the student council.

Jody's mother told the school psychologist that the family had moved seven times in the last 12 years, because the father is a professional musician who has played in several traveling bands in different regions of the country. Jody seemed to adjust well to the new environments and schools until recently. Her mother also reports that Jody experienced puberty early and that the experience was a difficult one for her.

Jody's teachers are very concerned about her recent withdrawal from activities and people she used to love; this reticence is clearly affecting her school performance. Her teachers want to be supportive and sensitive to her needs, but they are not sure what to do to help her regain her former confidence and reverse her academic downturn.

Characteristics of Social Anxiety Disorder

The child who suffers from social phobia is often referred to as "shy." Much of the research on social phobia has been done with adults. Approximately 1 percent of the adult population is diagnosed with social phobia, but most experts agree that social phobia has its precursors in childhood, and the prevalence rate is likely the same or higher in children. Unlike some of the other anxiety disorders, the most common age of onset for social phobia is adolescence (Wittchen, Stein, & Kessler, 1999), particularly early to middle adolescence. Beidel, Turner, and Morris (1999) studied fifty children (age range 7 to 13 years; average age 10 years) with social anxiety disorder and reported their five most feared situations to be

1. Reading in front of the class
2. Musical or athletic performance
3. Joining in on a conversation
4. Speaking to adults
5. Starting a conversation

Approximately 60 percent of socially distressing events occur at school. When they are distressed, children who have social phobia manifest physical symptoms, such as heart palpitations, shakiness, flushes, chills, sweating, and nausea. Social anxiety can be distinguished from other forms of social withdrawal when it is ego-distonic, that is, the child recognizes a problem and wishes that he or she were not that way. The socially anxious child wants to engage socially and feels distressed at not being able to do so. In a sample of preadolescent children who have social anxiety, Beidel et al. (1999) found that 60 percent also had another disorder: generalized anxiety disorder (10 percent), attention-deficit hyperactivity disorder (10 percent), specific phobia (10 percent), selective mutism (8 percent), separation anxiety disorder (6 percent), obsessive-compulsive disorder (6 percent), depression (6 percent), panic disorder (2 percent), or adjustment disorder with anxious and depressed mood (2 percent).

In adolescence, the disorder may take the additional forms of poor social networks, underachievement in school and work, and poor social skills. Age of onset appears to be the strongest predictor of recovery from social anxiety. In retrospective studies with adults, those who reported developing social anxiety after the age of 13 were nine times more likely to recover than those who reported an onset before the age of 7 (Davidson, 1993; DeWit, Ogborne, Offord, & McDonald, 1999).

Etiology of Social Anxiety Disorder

Most experts agree that the development of social anxiety disorder is multifactorial. Two studies (Hayward, Gotlib, Schraedley, & Litt, 1999; Hayward et al., 2000) found that the risk of developing social anxiety during high school increased with the number of factors. These factors included behavioral inhibition as a child, a history of parental separation and divorce, early pubertal maturation in females, and ethnic-group identification other than White, Latino, or Asian. Among those with three or more risk factors, approximately 33 percent developed social anxiety disorder, compared to less than 5 percent with no risk factors. Chartier, Walker, and Stein (2001) studied those with social phobia between the ages of 15 and 64 and found risk factors to include:

- Lack of a close relationship with an adult
- Not being the first born (males only)
- Marital conflict in the family of origin
- Parental history of mental disorder
- Moving more than three times as a child
- Childhood physical and sexual abuse
- Juvenile justice and child welfare involvement
- Running away from home
- Failing a grade
- Special education before age 9
- Dropping out of school

Traditionally, risk factors have been categorized as either psychological or biological.

PSYCHOLOGICAL FACTORS Among the psychological factors, direct conditioning, social learning, and information transfer are considered pathways for the development of social phobia (Beidel, Morris, & Turner, 2004). Stemberger, Turner, Beidel, and Calhoun (1995) found that 44 percent of adults attributed their social phobia to a direct traumatic event. Although it may be a risk factor, direct conditioning is not sufficient to explain the development of social phobia, for two simple reasons: A significant number who reported a conditioning event did not develop social phobia; and, among those who developed social phobia, a significant number reported no such conditioning event. Having a parent who is shy, reticent, or avoidant of social situations is also considered a risk factor because of the modeling and social learning it provides to the child (Masia & Morris, 1998). More research is needed to determine the significance of this risk factor.

Information transfer, the third psychological factor in the etiology of social anxiety disorder, refers to family communication patterns through which the child may have received messages emphasizing shame and/or an exaggerated concern for the opinions of others (Bruch & Heimberg, 1994). Current research is focusing on parent–child interactions to determine the significance of information transfer in the development of social anxiety and avoidance behavior (Turner, Beidel, Roberson-Nay, & Tervo, 2003).

BIOLOGICAL FACTORS As in the case of other anxiety disorders, genetic disposition and temperament are thought to play a role in the development of social anxiety. Many experts believe there is an interaction effect between biological and environmental factors. If a child is behaviorally inhibited by temperament, a parent may feel compelled to protect the child from challenging social situations and therefore reinforce what is a genetic disposition.

Assessment of Social Anxiety Disorder

Many children shy away from strange situations until they gain a sense of comfort, which makes the assessment of clinical levels of social anxiety somewhat challenging. Therefore, when assessing for social anxiety, the developmental age of the child must be taken into consideration. For example, younger children have stranger anxiety, which normally decreases as the child gets older. Another difficulty is differentiating social anxiety disorder from other disorders, particularly generalized anxiety disorder. The key to differentiation is the *theme* of the child's anxiety. With social anxiety, fears are limited to a negative evaluation, rejection by others, or humiliating oneself in front of others (Albano & Hayward, 2004). Some children may suffer from clinical levels of social anxiety, which can be explained by environmental factors, such as living in a high-crime neighborhood, coming from an abusive home, and so on. An investigation into the child's school history may help to distinguish anxiety that is more reactive to environmental stimuli as opposed to being a long-standing part of the child's presentation. With these considerations in mind, many of the self-report and behavioral assessment scales recommended previously to diagnose clinical levels of anxiety can also be used to diagnose social anxiety disorder.

Treatment Strategies

Many of the empirically supported treatments for children who have social anxiety disorder have very small sample sizes, because they are usually part of a much larger sample of those with anxiety disorders in general.

INDIVIDUAL/GROUP TREATMENT   Albano, Marten, Holt, Heimberg, and Barlow (1995) were the first to develop a cognitive-behavioral therapy program (known as Group Cognitive-Behavioral Treatment for Adolescents, or GCBT-A) designed specifically for socially phobic children. In a design of five case studies, Albano et al. (1995) found that after treatment, four children had subclinical levels of social anxiety. Hayward et al. (2000) compared GCBT-A with a no-treatment control group and found that after treatment, 45 percent of those treated for social phobia did not meet the clinical criteria, compared to 4 percent in the control group. One year later, however, there were no differences between the treatment and the control groups. Beidel, Turner, and Morris (2000) studied sixty-seven children with social phobia who received either Social Effectiveness Therapy for Children (SET-C) or active, nonspecific, control interventions. SET-C consists of group social skills training, peer-generalization experiences, and individual in-vivo exposure. Posttreatment follow-up revealed that 67 percent of SET-C groups no longer met the criteria for social phobia, compared to 5 percent of the nonspecific control group.

FAMILY TREATMENT   As with other anxiety disorders, parent education and contingency management for children who have social phobia can be an important part of the treatment process. Spence, Donovan, and Brechman-Toussaint (2000) studied CBT interventions for children who had social phobia plus a parent component. At posttreatment, 87.5 percent of the CBT-plus-parent involvement group, 58 percent of the CBT no parent involvement group, and 7 percent of no-treatment controls met the diagnostic criteria for social phobia. More studies on family treatment with children whose primary diagnosis is social phobia are needed.

PHARMACOLOGICAL TREATMENT   Like many of the CBT studies, pharmacological studies use samples of children who have a variety of anxiety disorders. It is difficult in some of these studies to decipher drug effectiveness specifically for children who have social anxiety. Compton et al. (2001) studied fourteen children and adolescents (mean age 13.57 years) who participated in a 4-week trial of setraline (Zoloft). At posttreatment, 76 percent were considered responders while 36 percent were partial responders. There was no control group. Two trials from the RUPP Anxiety Study Group (2001) examined the effectiveness of alprazolam (Xanax) in twenty children (ages 8 to 16) with social anxiety. After a 6-week initial trial, six of the twenty children were considered moderately improved in overall status. More pharmacological research, specifically designed for children who have social anxiety disorder, is needed to determine more convincingly the preferred use of SSRIs with this population.

School-Based Interventions

Once again, after carefully reviewing the information provided in the previous section about the characteristics of and recommended treatment strategies for this disorder, teachers and caregivers should conduct a systematic evaluation as a precursor to developing an effective behavioral intervention. The intervention process is therefore two-staged, consisting of a data-based assessment and a relevant research–based intervention based on the target behavior identified in the assessment.

ASSESSING THE PROBLEM As with any case involving a child who exhibits inappropriate or unproductive behavior, teachers should conduct an analysis of behavior. A hypothetical analysis based on Jody's case is provided below.

The first step in the evaluative process is to *identify and describe the problem behavior.* Jody had recently begun to avoid "public" situations, ostensibly fearing criticism and rejection. This has had a negative affect on her school performance because she is unwilling to participate in group activities such as peer-assisted learning, which is the preferred instructional format in most of her seventh-grade courses. Jody has also lost interest in the performing arts, which her teachers believe was instrumental in helping her develop and maintain self-esteem. As a result of these behavioral changes, Jody has become excessively self-conscious and introverted.

A second step in the process is for teachers to collect behavioral and academic information. Accordingly, Jody's teachers report that she is unable to participate in public events, becoming panicky and complaining of nausea. She expresses a palpable fear of being criticized or judged for her ineptitude. This pervasive fear of social situations generalizes to classroom as well as extracurricular activities and includes interactions with peers as well as with teachers and other adults.

Jody's refusal to participate in small-group or cooperative activities has negatively affected her academic performance in several of her classes. Prior to the onset of the disorder, for example, Jody consistently earned an A in Social Studies and English; afterwards, her grades in both these favorite subjects dropped to C−. Moreover, her withdrawal from and avoidance of social situations has adversely affected her self-esteem and eroded her confidence.

The third stage in the process entails *describing the environmental and setting demands.* Jody seems very uncomfortable presenting or reading in front of the class. Similarly, she has dropped out of the school chorus and drama club, explaining to the program coordinators that she has to "make up school work." In addition, her teachers and mother report that she appears to be very uncomfortable speaking with adults: She "clams up," responding with one- or two-word utterances when asked a question. Classmates, too, have noticed a significant change in Jody—from gregarious and outgoing to shy and retiring, except in the presence of her mother or very close friends.

As the next step in the assessment process, a functional behavioral assessment was completed in October of last year. In addition, the school psychologist administered a self-report measure, the *Spence Children's Anxiety Scale* (SCAS) (Spence, 1998), as well as the *Fear Inventory—Children* (Esonis, Esonis, & Cautela, 1996). The results of these tests confirmed the diagnosis of social anxiety disorder or social phobia. The data from these assessments provided the information necessary to develop an effective behavioral intervention plan.

Jody's mother and teachers maintained anecdotal records based on observations of anxiety displayed by the child in social situations. These observations revealed a child who has experienced a dramatic behavioral change, moving from gregarious and outgoing to guarded and fearful in social situations. They further confirm the results of behavior rating scales, as well as Jody's own expressions of fear and social anxiety.

After reviewing the data as well as identifying the environmental "triggers," it appears that Jody has developed social anxieties in relation to classroom and extracurricular "performance" that necessitates public speaking. This condition is further aggravated by the need to speak to adults or a group of persons. Based on this hypothesis, it seems prudent to identify and implement an effective school-based intervention as soon as possible.

In response to the development of the hypothesis described above, it is critical that Jody's caregivers select an appropriate, research-based intervention that will help reduce her fear of participating in social situations. In response to this need, a behavioral intervention plan will be developed and implemented for a prescribed duration, long enough to be able to assess its effectiveness. Necessary modifications will be made, if warranted, after evaluating the success of the plan.

DEVELOPING AN EFFECTIVE INTERVENTION PLAN   Horner, Sugai, Todd, and Lewis-Palmer (2000) have identified the following key components of any effective behavioral intervention plan:

1. Learn how the student perceives or experiences events in his or her environment.
2. Invest in preventing reoccurrences or problem behavior.
3. Include instructional objectives, realizing that teachers can and should provide relevant social skills instruction in class.
4. Always reward positive behavioral responses.
5. Develop contingency plans that cover most "emergencies" relating to the problem behavior and the individual responsible.

After reviewing recommended interventions for adolescents and children who have social phobia, two were identified as most appropriate for Jody and, subsequently, implemented: a *group cognitive-behavioral intervention* and *family treatment*. The first intervention selected was social effectiveness therapy for children (SET-C), which consists of group social skills training, peer-generalization experiences, and individual in-vivo exposure. In conjunction with this intervention, Jody joined a group of adolescents who shared similar social phobias and participated in public speaking events, presentation activities with the support of peers, and practiced speaking to adults, as well as initiating conversation. Jody's teachers played a significant role in this treatment strategy by providing supported and "safe" opportunities for her to engage in rehearsed class discussions and debates.

The SET-C intervention was conducted in conjunction with family treatment that involved Jody's mother. This extracurricular intervention involved teaching Jody's mother about the causes and characteristics of social phobia, as well as relevant contingency management and the identification and avoidance of malcontingencies. Here, too, Jody's teachers played an important role by inviting her mother to classroom presentations or public speaking events that involved her daughter. In addition, they encouraged Jody's mother to share her insights and offer suggestions regarding Jody's performance in the classroom and behavior at home. This bimodal treatment plan has achieved measurable success in helping Jody overcome her social anxiety. To date she has made significant progress in initiating conversations with adults and groups of peers. Jody is also able to read in front of a small group of classmates. Her progress has been steady and consistent, and her therapist and teachers, as well as her mother and friends, have expressed delight at her newfound confidence.

Tips for Teachers

Classroom interventions that may be helpful to a student who has social phobia, like Jody, include the following.

1. Assign the individual a "study buddy" to help him with coursework and projects.
2. Encourage the student to participate in small-group discussions of four to six students.
3. Encourage the individual to find outlets for nonacademic skills and interests, typically ones that involve membership in after-school programs and extracurricular activities.
4. Make a point of speaking to the student every day in both academic and social contexts, to desensitize the student and demystify the experience of speaking with an adult or authority figure.
5. Help the student identify school- or community-based clubs that help individuals who are socially withdrawn or "shy" gain self confidence and poise (e.g., the toast masters club, the school debating society, the speakers' bureau).
6. Teachers might consider presenting a unit or a series of lessons on verbal and nonverbal communication skills that would benefit all students in the class, especially a student who has social phobia.
7. Teachers should avoid embarrassing the student or inadvertently creating anxiety by arbitrarily calling on the student without advance notice. Teachers should consider "rehearsing" a planned question with the student before class, to allow the individual to prepare and then be able to respond with confidence. Similarly, the teacher and student might establish a nonverbal "cue" that would signal the teacher's intention to ask the student to respond. The student could then signal her willingness to do so, or decline surreptitiously and thereby avoid embarrassment.

FROM THE FIELD

Justin R., Student

Justin is an 18-year-old white male from a major metropolitan area in the Northeast. He has been attending the Apex School, a private residential treatment facility for adolescents experiencing learning and adjustment difficulties, for the past 2 years. Justin has clearly benefited from the services offered as well as the relationships formed during his stay at Apex, and, with graduation imminent and having been accepted to a prestigious university, he shares some of his insights regarding this experience.

Justin, can you provide a brief overview of the challenges you faced in public school and your referral for special education services?

In public high school, I suffered from clinical depression and anxiety. The depression was not diagnosed until fifth grade and the anxiety not until late middle school. I would refuse to attend school because I was terrified to attend, but for no legitimate reason.

What circumstances led you to choose or be referred to a special school for your high school education?

After being sent to Restwell, a psychiatric facility, for having thoughts of suicide, I was sent to multiple alternative high school settings. After that, I was sent to the psychiatric ward of Saint Peter's Hospital twice for the same suicidal desires. I was held back in eighth grade because my mom didn't think I was ready for high school, and after half a year in public high school, along with other attempts at alternative settings, I was sent to Apex School, a residential treatment facility.

Can you provide a brief description of life at this special high school? What is a typical day like, for example?

We are woken up at 7:30 A.M. by the staff member that stayed in our cottage (or dorm) overnight. At around 8:00 breakfast opens downstairs, and we are required to be out of our rooms by 8:30. Homeroom begins at 8:45, first period at 9:00. We have 50-minute periods, seven a day, with school ending at 2:55. We have a point system, boys starting with three points at the beginning of the day. If you misbehave or break a rule, a staff member will remove points from your point sheet and the staff members in your cottage will impose appropriate penalties. At 3:00 we return to our cottages and get settled. By 3:15 we should be out of our rooms and attending one of the various activities around the campus. Activities generally close at 5:00, and the different cottages have dinner at different times, the earliest being 5:00, the latest being 6:30. After dinner, we have a 45-minute "quiet time" where we are required to stay in our rooms. If we aren't up-to-date in our classes, we have "double quiet time," requiring the student to be in his room for an hour and a half. We are allowed to stay out of our cottages until 9:00 and must be in our rooms by 10:45. Lights out is at 11:00 P.M.

In your opinion, what are the major drawbacks to receiving a high school education in this setting?

There are many restrictions set in place that greatly limit the enjoyment of daily life. For instance, we are only allowed to be off-campus until 5:00 P.M., but it takes about 15–30 minutes to get into town or to the mall, allowing for only about an hour or so to ourselves. My cottage is given specific shower times which becomes problematic when I have very limited time to spend with some friends. I must shower at my shower time or suffer consequences, even though I know I will be responsible and can be accountable to shower on my own. Also, we must attend dinner. I usually don't eat the food served at dinner (I'm a very picky eater), but I must go down and sit with my cottage for 15 minutes, regardless of whether I am eating there or not. In my experience, most drawbacks are in the residential aspect, though there are academic drawbacks, as well. As an example, there are very few teachers to teach any specific subject, meaning that if you don't get along with any given teacher, or maybe you aren't suited to that teacher's teaching style, you are limited in your ability to switch classes.

By way of contrast, can you share the major benefits of such an educational experience?

The limitations described prior are not entirely negative. I, as a senior, have overcome most of the challenges I faced earlier in my attendance. When I first arrived at Apex, I still suffered from depression and didn't care much about myself or my appearance. I wouldn't shower regularly because I didn't think that people realized or cared that I didn't clean myself. After the shower times were implemented, I began to shower regularly, and started to pay more attention to other people that didn't clean themselves. It allowed me to understand the importance of taking care of myself and the effect it has on how people view me and treat me.

It would be very helpful for our readers if you could provide representative examples of each of the following:

a. A teaching approach or approaches that you found counterproductive or unhelpful

With such small class sizes, teachers are able to cater to individual students that may not understand the material. While this is in a sense a positive thing, the students that are able to learn faster or grasp the concepts of a certain study better that others are the ones now "left behind," so to speak. They are un-

able to proceed through the class as quickly as they would be able to or would like to.

b. A teaching approach or approaches that you found very helpful in improving your social and academic experience at this high school

One of the first things students need to get used to at Apex is the fact that we are on a first-name basis with nearly every teacher. The teachers here are not only our teachers; they are our friends. At a public high school, things are very formal. Sometimes students are reluctant to ask for assistance from a teacher. Maybe they're embarrassed to do so. Asking a friend for help is much easier. It also eases tension in the classrooms. Students also feel more obliged to do work for their friends than for their teachers.

Finally, nothing is more instructive than an anecdote or personal story that highlights an individual's most significant life experiences. Could you take a moment to reflect on and share such an experience from your life as a student at this high school?

I would say that the school as a whole was a significant life experience. I can't put my finger on one specific event that had some profound effect on me, but I know that this school definitely provided me with an experience that I would not have received in a public high school. For instance, living exclusively with students that are generally more difficult to live with than many, if not most, of the students that I will encounter in college has prepared me for the worst, so to speak. My transition to college will be easier because I'm used to living away from home, as well. But most importantly, it has provided me with the ability to graduate. This in and of itself is reason enough for me to appreciate the time I have spent there.

Summary

In this chapter we have examined three of the more prevalent childhood phobias; specific phobia, separation anxiety disorder, and social anxiety disorder. Our three real-life case examples provided vicarious experiences to use in applying appropriate identifying criteria, becoming familiar with effective assessments used in diagnosis, learning about recommended research-based interventions, and, most important, gaining practice in the development of relevant behavioral intervention plans predicated on the results of purposeful behavioral assessments. In each case, the most effective treatments turned out to be behavioral and cognitive-behavioral interventions, but the critical factor in effective intervention must always be the teacher's familiarity with the specific behavioral needs of the child. This knowledge is best determined through the application of a thorough behavioral assessment that will ensure the development of an effective behavioral intervention plan.

Ricky's specific phobia expressed in a morbid fear of being buried alive, Jimmy's sudden and seemingly inexplicable panic at the possibility of being separated from his mother, and Jody's dread of social situations after her parents' divorce are examples of childhood phobias that teachers will encounter in their classrooms today. Indeed, children are bombarded every day with the fears and stressors exerted by a world that is increasingly perceived as less safe, one in which their country is at war with "terror," and media that constantly reinforce these fears with news and images of impending disaster. Under these conditions, it is inevitable that many children will develop phobias as they are affected by the proliferation of our adult fears.

In response to the anticipated increase in students who are diagnosed with phobias, it is incumbent on today's teachers to be equipped to help identify and treat these insidious disorders as they arise in the classroom.

Focus Questions Revisited

1. Suppose a child who has a specific phobia, such as Ricky, who has a morbid preoccupation with death, was assigned to your class. What might you do to facilitate his acceptance and integration?

A Sample Response

I would invite the school psychologist to explain and discuss phobias and anxiety disorders with the class and then advise them that a student who has a specific phobia will be joining them shortly. Depending on the maturity of the students in my class, I might describe the characteristics of Ricky's phobia. I would also provide strategies that have been effective in helping Ricky control his fears and solicit their support. It might be beneficial to ask for a volunteer to act as a class partner or peer mentor to

assist Ricky in acclimating to the classroom. Last, I would point out that we all experience fears and anxieties that others might regard as silly or unnecessary; nevertheless, to those affected, these seemingly inconsequential stimuli can be very troubling. We should, therefore, be understanding and supportive of other's struggles to overcome fears.

2. List some specific fears experienced by children. What differentiates the pathological ones that characterize a phobia from those that are common to many children that are able to function successfully without special treatment?

A Sample Response

Some fears might compel a child to avoid or escape certain situations—for example, avoiding places in the home (e.g., the basement) that are perceived as "scary," keeping the light on when sleeping or insisting on sleeping with parent(s) to escape darkness, avoiding eating for fear of choking, refusing to attend a doctor's appointment for fear of a needle, and so on. Cognitive responses usually include scary thoughts ("I'm afraid"), negative self-statements ("I can't do it"), and the expectation of some catastrophic result ("I'm going to die from the lightning"). Although most children experience these feared events to some extent and at some time, the degree to which they prevent the child from engaging in daily activities such as school and home routines, as well as experiencing a sense of well-being, demarcates a phobia.

3. How common is separation anxiety disorder in children? How can a teacher determine whether a child's symptoms represent a bona fide disorder or will simply disappear in time?

A Sample Response

Separation anxiety disorder is one of the most common anxiety disorders among children, estimated to constitute about a third of all anxiety disorders. Prevalence rates have been estimated to be between 3 and 5 percent in children and adolescents. A recent study found the prevalence rate to be 3.6 percent (Briggs-Gowan, Horwitz, Schwab-Stone, Leventhal, & Leaf, 2000).

As with any emotional or behavioral disorder, the identification of a bona fide disorder is accomplished by examining the anxiety associated with leaving a caregiver or the security and comfort of home that is typical of children who are the same age as the individual of concern. If that child's anxiety is significantly greater (intensity), experienced much more frequently (frequency), and has been manifest for a significantly long time (duration)—e.g., 6 months or longer—then a teacher will have reasonable cause to suspect an anxiety disorder and suggest to the parents that they consider having the child evaluated by a qualified clinician (psychologist or psychiatrist).

4. What can a classroom teacher do to help a child who is experiencing separation anxiety disorder?

A Sample Response

As with any behavioral intervention, the classroom teacher must comply with the plan developed by the IEP Committee incorporating the recommendations of the school psychologist. To the extent feasible, the classroom teacher should implement this plan to help the affected child in the classroom. In general, teachers working with students who are experiencing SAD should provide good instruction and engage them in meaningful work. In addition, students who have SAD should not be allowed to call home other than at previously arranged times that do not interfere with instruction or the students' class schedule. The teacher should provide clear expectations that the individual will remain and participate in classroom activities for the duration of the school day. In the event of tantrums or more severe behavioral manifestations, a prearranged emergency plan should be initiated. Such a plan might include sending the student to the school psychologist's office or to the school nurse to help the individual to regain self-control and "decompress."

5. How do you define social phobia or social anxiety disorder as it pertains to school-age children?

A Sample Response

Children who have social phobia manifest physical symptoms when under distress, such as heart palpitations, shakiness, flushes, chills, sweating, and nausea. Social anxiety can be distinguished from other forms of social withdrawal when it is ego-distonic. The socially anxious child wants to engage socially and feels distressed at not being able to do. The child who suffers from social phobia typically may be referred to as "shy." In adolescence, the disorder may take the additional forms of poor social networks, underachievement in school and work, and poor social skills. Age of onset appears to be the strongest predictor in recovery from social anxiety. Unlike some of the other anxiety disorders, the most common age of onset for social phobia is adolescence (Wittchen et al., 1999), particularly early to middle adolescence.

6. What are the five most feared situations for children who have social anxiety disorder, and how can a teacher facilitate the student's participation in them?

A Sample Response

Beidel et al. (1999) studied fifty children (age range 7 to 13 years; average age 10 years) with social anxiety disorder and reported their five most feared situations as

1. Reading in front of the class
2. Musical or athletic performance
3. Joining in on a conversation
4. Speaking to adults
5. Starting a conversation

Taking reading in front of the class and starting a conversation as examples, a teacher might facilitate the student's participation in them in the following ways.

1. **Reading in front of the class.** One way to facilitate this desired participative goal is to have the student read to a friend to develop the self-confidence to take the next step, which would involve reading to a small group of select peers who are supportive of the individual's goal. Finally, after the individual expresses sufficient confidence, he or she would be scheduled by the teacher to read a rehearsed passage in front of the entire class. The teacher would also prepare the class by apprising them of the student's fear and enlisting their support in being an attentive, sympathetic audience.

5. **Starting a conversation.** The student could be provided with a set of generic "conversation starters," questions that require more than a "yes/no" response. These could include questions about the weather, such as "How are you enjoying the lovely weather?," or about some common themes relative to school, e.g., "What do you think about the new principal?," "How are you coming with the history paper?,"

or sport- or activity-related ones, e.g., "What do you think of the Yankees' chances of winning the World Series this year?" Once the individual is adept at starting a conversation, she should then be taught ways to sustain one by asking probing questions that elicit voluntary elaborations. These kinds of questions should be ones that encourage the social partner to share some personal information. This provides opportunities to extend the dialogue and facilitates reciprocity, the hallmark of true conversation.

7. Describe the Social Effectiveness Therapy for Children (SET-C) cognitive behavioral intervention and identify its strengths in helping students, like Jody, who have social anxiety disorder.

A Sample Response

SET-C consists of group social skills training, peer-generalization experiences, and individual in-vivo exposure. The focus of this intervention is to expose the individual with SAD to controlled, "safe" group experiences. Students like Jody, who lack confidence and become anxious when faced with social situations that carry risk, such as when public speaking or performing, can "practice" with a sympathetic audience that consists of students who are similarly affected. Once the individual feels comfortable speaking or performing in front of the peer group, she is ready to engage in a similar real-life experience, with the support of her therapist and group members. To ensure success, the initial experience or trial should be well rehearsed and brief. For example, Jody might choose to read a favorite short poem to the class, demonstrate a simple dance step, or play an abbreviated selection on the piano as a first step. Emboldened by this success, Jody's next public experiences would involve incrementally greater risk and longer public exposure; ideally, in time, her self-confidence would be fully restored.

Chapter 6

Anxiety Disorders II: Posttraumatic Stress Disorder, Generalized Anxiety Disorder, and Obsessive-Compulsive Disorder

Photodisc/Getty Images

FOCUS QUESTIONS

1. Which related services providers and other knowledgeable persons can provide critical advice and support to the teacher of a child who has posttraumatic stress disorder (PTSD)?

2. How would you, as the teacher of a child diagnosed with PTSD help that child succeed in the classroom?

3. What are some plausible causes of PTSD in school-age children in U.S. schools today? Which of these, do you think, would be most typical and why?

4. How can you, as a classroom teacher, differentiate between a student who is simply "overanxious" or a "worry wart" by nature and a student who has generalized anxiety disorder? What diagnostic "tools" do you have at your disposal?

5. What could you, as a classroom teacher, do to reduce the maladaptive behaviors represented by (a) perfectionism and (b) excessive fear of perceived threats in one of your students diagnosed as having generalized anxiety disorder?

6. If you were assigned a child who has obsessive-compulsive disorder (OCD), what might you do to help him feel valued and included in your classroom?

7. What might be some good questions to ask the school counselor or school psychologist about a child in your class who has been diagnosed with OCD? Similarly, what questions might you ask family members to help you work more effectively with this child in your classroom?

Posttraumatic stress disorder, generalized anxiety disorder, and obsessive-compulsive disorder are becoming more prevalent among school-age children and youth. These anxiety disorders can have a significant effect on a student's academic performance, to say nothing of their impact on the individual's well-being. The reasons for the increase in identification are, to a significant degree, attributable to environmental factors that include increased stress in our society because of the proliferation of drugs, violence in the media, instability in the home and parental anxiety, and a pervasive climate in response to a perceived increase in the incidence of fear of crime and terror.

These disorders can be ameliorated, to a great extent, by effective behavioral intervention applied by teachers in the classroom. This chapter provides an understanding of these disorders, as well as recommended research-based interventions that are effective in reducing the undesirable behaviors associated with these anxiety disorders, which can be easily implemented in the classroom.

Similar to the other chapters in this book, we begin our discussion of each of these disorders with a real-life case example that typifies a student who has the disorders, followed by an elaboration of characteristics, causes, and research-based interventions. We then provide a fully developed functional behavioral assessment and relevant behavioral intervention plan (BIP) appropriate to the student profiled in the introductory case example. This feature should prove particularly helpful for teachers of students diagnosed with any of these disorders, because behavioral intervention plans may be integral to the Individualized Education Plans (IEPs) of these students and, likewise, a thorough understanding of the construction and implementation of a BIP is expected of these teachers.

POSTTRAUMATIC STRESS DISORDER

CASE EXAMPLE: Sandy

Sandy's father was a New York City firefighter assigned to a station in Lower Manhattan. His unit was the first to respond to the 911 call from Tower 2 of the World Trade Center on September 11, 2001. Tragically, Lieutenant G. was inside the tower when it collapsed. Sandy and her family received the news shortly before noon as they, like most American families, were watching events of the tragic day unfold on television.

Mrs. G., Sandy's mother, reports that initially Sandy seemed uncharacteristically subdued, "almost as if she was in a trance and needed to be told what to do." For example, Sandy, who was 11 years old and in sixth grade at the time, was by nature a very extroverted, outgoing student. The abrupt change in Sandy's personality was at first attributed to the traumatic loss of her father, with whom she had enjoyed a very close relationship. When she remained despondent and reclusive after the Christmas holiday, her mother took her to a psychologist at the suggestion of the school counselor. The psychologist whom Sandy began seeing specialized in working with children and adolescents who had experienced traumatic events. In terms of the DSM-IV-TR (American Psychiatric Association, 2000) criteria for posttraumatic stress disorder (PTSD), Sandy had experienced a qualifying event, was having nightmares about the event, refused to fly or go into Manhattan or enter tall buildings, and was having difficulty sleeping, resulting in chronic fatigue and poor academic performance.

In her diagnostic assessment, the clinician administered the *PTSD Schedule for Children and Adolescents* (CAPS-CA; Nader, Blake, Kringler, & Pynoss, 1994). The results of this instrument supported the diagnosis of PTSD. The psychologist has elected to use trauma-focused cognitive-behavioral therapy (CBT) to treat Sandy's PTSD, which seems to be helping in reducing Sandy's depression, anxiety, and the behavioral symptoms associated with the disorder.

Although Sandy is manifesting fewer of the symptoms of PTSD in class, she is still affected by recurring memories associated with the 9/11 tragedies. Some of these behaviors are negatively affecting Sandy's academic performance and social integration. For example, Sandy worries excessively about her mother's well-being, fearing that she, too, might experience an "accident" or a terrorist attack. Sandy will not watch network television for fear of seeing broadcast pictures of the World Trade Center or other events of 9/11. She also refuses to attend classes that are not on the first floor of her school building, fearing an inability to get out of the building during a terrorist attack. Furthermore, Sandy, a previously accepting and nondiscriminatory person, has become very fearful of and prejudiced toward students and teachers from Muslim countries or of Arab descent. This has presented some very real challenges, because the school is situated in a part of the city with a large Muslim population. Sandy's family cannot afford the differential cost to place her in another district.

In the classroom, Sandy has difficulty concentrating for more than a few minutes and complains of frequent headaches and nausea. After several referrals to the school nurse, Sandy was given a thorough physical examination that revealed no neurological or gastrointestinal anomalies. Finally, Sandy must be removed from the school building during fire drills, because they remind her of her father's occupation and horrific death. Likewise, she becomes quite emotionally "overcome" for no apparent reason. She explains that this melancholia results from spontaneous thoughts about her father and the realization that he will never be coming home to his "little girl," and that she was unable to say "goodbye" to her father.

Characteristics of PTSD

Most experts agree that PTSD has been widely overlooked in children. Incidents of sexual abuse, physical assault, domestic violence, serious illness, accidents, and natural or man-made disaster can easily result in PTSD in children. These children may become avoidant, amnestic, drug-abusing, and engage in other self-destructing behaviors to numb their emotional pain. Hyperarousal is also a common reaction and may include:

> . . . angry outbursts, irritability, sleep disturbance, difficulty concentrating, shortened attention span, feeling jittery or displaying motor hyperactivity, somatic complaints such as stomachaches or headaches, increased startle response and hypervigilance. (Cohen & Mannarino, 2004, p. 406)

Terr (1991) distinguished between two types of trauma, type I and type II.

- Type I includes sudden, unexpected, and unpredictable single-incident stressors.
- Type II includes expected, repeated, and chronic stressors such as child abuse, bullying, etc.

Distinguishing between these two types of traumatic events can help to develop more appropriate treatment plans.

Prevalence and Comorbidity

Among the adult population, it is estimated that 70 percent have experienced a traumatic event (Kessler, Sonnega, Bromet, Hughes, & Nelson, 1995). Among a school sample, Giaconia et al. (1995) found that 40 percent of children had experienced a PTSD qualifying trauma before the age of 18. Jenkins and Bell (1994) studied more than 1,000 middle and high school students in Chicago and found that:

- 25 percent had seen someone killed;
- 39 percent had seen a shooting;
- 35 percent had seen a stabbing; and
- 46 percent had been the direct victim of a violent crime.

Although it is clear that children quite commonly experience events that can cause PTSD, it is less clear just how many children actually are diagnosed with PTSD. Those who experience a life-threatening event are more likely to develop PTSD. Other variables in developing PTSD include physical proximity to the event (Pynoos, Frederick, Nader, & Arroyo, 1987), disordered cognitive processing during the event and, with regard to type II traumas, the duration of the experience.

PTSD in children has significant comorbidity with other disorders. Depressive spectrum disorders have especially high comorbidity. Giaconia, Reinherz, Silverman, & Pakiz (1995), found that 41 percent of adolescents with PTSD also met the criteria for major depression by the age of 18, compared to 8 percent of those without PTSD. Children who develop PTSD in response to child abuse are more at risk for developing major depressive disorder. Researchers have also found a high rate of anxiety disorders in children who have PTSD (Brent, Perper, Moritz, & Liotus, 1995; Clark, Bukstein, Smith, & Kaczynski, 1995; McCloskey & Walker, 2000). La Greca, Silverman, & Wasserstein (1998), in a study of children who experienced Hurricane Andrew, found that anxiety levels had a significant effect on the development of PTSD. Those with higher anxiety levels were more predisposed to developing PTSD.

ADHD is frequently diagnosed in children who have been exposed to a traumatic event. A number of researchers found that trauma-exposed children more frequently present with ADHD before PTSD (DeBellis et al., 1994; Looff, Grimley, Kuller, & Martin, 1995). It is not clear what this finding means. Because hyperarousal is also a symptom of ADHD, it may be that PTSD children are misdiagnosed with ADHD or that children who have ADHD are more disposed to traumatic experiences. More research is needed to understand the relationship between ADHD and PTSD. Besides ADHD, other disruptive disorders (such as oppositional-defiant disorder and conduct disorder) have been found in children who have PTSD (Ford et al., 2000; McCloskey & Walker, 2000). One hypothesis concerning this relationship is that children who develop PTSD from violent PSTD-qualifying events are more likely to develop anger and behavioral problems than children who experience nonviolent events.

Substance abuse also has been found to have a significant relationship with PTSD. Research has suggested that adolescents with PTSD turn to drugs as a form of self-medication, because exposure to a traumatic event without the development PTSD did not lead to substance abuse, nor did preexisting substance increase the risk of developing PTSD (Chilcoat & Breslau, 1998). Data also exist that documents comorbidity between PTSD and **dissociative disorders** (Carrion & Steiner, 2000) and **borderline personality syndrome** (Stone, 1990). This is especially true for adolescents who have been physically or sexually abused.

The differential diagnosis of PTSD can be complicated. A child may present with the symptoms of PTSD but a traumatic-qualifying event cannot be identified. Even when a traumatic event is identified, one must distinguish the symptoms of PTSD from other disorders, either premorbid or developing after

DISSOCIATIVE DISORDERS

Disorders that result in disassociation (disconnection or interruption) of waking consciousness. A person may lose consciousness of his or her own identity or past.

BORDERLINE PERSONALITY SYNDROME

A personality disorder marked by long-standing and pervasive instability in mood, relationships, behavior, and self-image. It is commonly thought to result from the lack of early bonding with the primary caretaker.

the traumatic event. Stress from a traumatic event can cause any preexisting disorder to reappear. A careful history might also reveal that the child had PTSD symptoms before the event. Many children are exposed to a PTSD-qualifying event without developing PTSD. There could be any number of reasons for this. Children may be more resilient, underdiagnosed, or develop symptoms related to another preexisting disorder. As children mature, they are more likely to manifest a wider range of PTSD symptoms. Very young children may report only a very few PTSD symptoms and may resemble children who have generalized anxiety disorder (Cohen & Mannarino, 2004). Again, some experts believe that the lack of qualifications in the DSM-IV-TR for PTSD in children make it an inappropriate diagnostic tool for this population. A differential diagnosis must be based on a thorough premorbid history, as well as the development of symptoms after experiencing the traumatic event.

Etiology of PTSD

For a diagnosis of PTSD in adults and children, the DSM-IV-TR has established four criteria:

1. Exposure to a PTSD-qualifying event
2. A reexperiencing of the traumatic event
3. Persistent avoidance of stimuli associated with the trauma along with a numbing of general responsiveness
4. Persistent increased arousal

If symptoms last for more than 3 months, the PTSD is labeled "chronic"; if they last less than 3 months, "acute"; and if the onset of symptoms is at least 6 months after the event, "with delayed onset." Most of the criteria require children to describe internal states and experiences, a requirement that is developmentally more appropriate for adults (Scheeringa, Zeanah, Drell, & Larrieu, 1995).

Reexperiencing can included intrusive memories, thoughts, and perceptions of the event, recurring dreams, flashbacks, and distress over exposure to cues that recall the traumatic event. It is not uncommon for children who have PTSD to engage in traumatic play and reenactment behaviors (McKnight, Compton, & March, 2004; Terr, 1990). Avoidance can be:

- Cognitive—thoughts, feelings, or conversation associated with the trauma
- Behavioral—people, places, or activities that recall the trauma
- Amnestic—inability to recall aspects of the trauma
- Emotional—feelings of detachment and restricted range of emotion along with a sense of foreshortened future.

More than feelings of numbness, children who have PTSD often report feelings of aloneness or even wanting to be alone to keep their emotions in check (McNight et al., 2004). Hyperarousal includes sleep disturbance, irritability, difficulty concentrating, hypervigilance, and exaggerated startle response. The child with PTSD may constantly seem "on alert."

Assessment of PTSD

A difficulty in assessing PTSD is the unreliability of children's self-reports and, in cases of domestic violence and child abuse, that of the parents or alleged perpetrator. Evaluator suggestibility and the inadequacy of childhood memory create the need for evaluations that are independent of both child and parent (Cohen & Mannarino, 2004). In many areas, for example, sexual abuse response teams exist that allow the children to recount their story one time before a team of experts who observe from behind a one-way mirror. This is in contrast to previous methods of evaluation, when children were forced to tell their story multiple times to different constituencies that often resulted in different and contradictory versions of the event.

Once the reliability of the reported traumatic event has been determined, the next step in the assessment of PTSD is the evaluation of symptoms. The clusters used by the DSM-IV-TR can help structure the assessment interview. There are two widely used structured assessment instruments for PTSD (both require that the parent and child be interviewed separately): the *Clinician Administered PTSD Schedule for Children and Adolescent* (CAPS-CA; Nader, Blake, Kriegler, & Pynoos, 1994) and the PTSD section of the *K-SADS* (Kaufman, Birmaher, Brent, & Rao, 1997). In addition, numerous child and parent self-reports exist to evaluate the symptoms of PTSD in children. Some of these include the *PTSD Reaction Index* (Pynoos, Goenjian, & Steinberg, 1998), the *Child PTSD Symptom Scale* (Foa, Johnson, Feeny, & Treadwell, 2001), and the *Children's PTSD Inventory* (March, 1999). All three have good psychometric properties and, because of their brevity, are especially appropriate for the school setting.

As mentioned previously, both the overdiagnosis and underdiagnosis of PTSD is a real problem. Overdiagnosis is the result of the evaluator simply discovering a traumatic event in the life of the child and then looking for symptoms of PTSD. On the other hand, some evaluators are reluctant to pursue questioning about trauma because of the discomfort it can generate in both the child and the parent. Further complicating the assessment of PTSD with children is the DSM-IV-TR requirement that symptoms exist across clusters that some experts feel may be mutually exclusive. For children who are manifesting avoidant and numbing responses to the trauma, the assessment might conclude, for example, that they are not being affected by the trauma, when in reality these symptoms are simply hiding more positive PTSD symptoms (Arroyo & Eth, 1995). To make a diagnosis of PTSD in children, some have suggested different, less stringent criteria (Scheeringa, Peebles, Cook, & Zeanah 2001). At least one study has suggested no difference in the functional impairment of children diagnosed with partial versus full-blown PTSD (Carrion, Weems, Ray, & Reiss, 2002). The same treatment strategy, therefore, might be appropriate for both populations (Cohen & Mannarino, 2004).

Treatment Strategies

Compared to other anxiety disorders in children, less research has been done on treatment effectiveness for children who have PTSD. Treatments that have been studied include cognitive-behavioral therapy, eye movement desensitization and reprocessing (EMDR), nondirective supportive therapy, psychological debriefing, and pharmacotherapy (Cohen & Mannarino, 2004). CBT is the treatment that has been most supported by empirical studies.

TRAUMA-FOCUSED COGNITIVE-BEHAVIORAL THERAPY Trauma-focused CBT includes many of the basic interventions, such as gradual exposure, cognitive processing of the event, psychoeducation, and stress reduction through positive self-talk and relaxation (Cohen, Berliner, & Mannarino, 2000). Deblinger, Lippmann, and Steer (1996) found CBT to be more efficacious than nondirective supportive therapy and standard community care regardless of whether treatment was given only to the child, only the parent or both. Studies have supported the superiority of CBT to nondirective supportive treatment for 3- to 7-year-olds who were sexually abused (Cohen & Mannarino, 1996, 1997). Cohen, Deblinger, Mannarino, & Steer (2004) conducted a multisite treatment study and found CBT to be more effective than child-centered **Rogerian therapy** for improving depressive, anxiety, and behavioral symptoms associated with PTSD. Studies have also found CBT to be efficacious in treating children who have PTSD when compared to no-treatment controls (Chemtob, Hamada, & Nakashima, 1996; Goenjian et al., 1997).

March, Amaya-Jackson, Murray, & Schulte (1998) developed an 18 week treatment protocol called Boss Back for children diagnosed with PTSD. "Boss back" means helping children feel they have some control as opposed to feeling controlled by PTSD. See Table 6.1 for a session outline for the Boss Back program.

PSYCHOLOGICAL DEBRIEFING In recent years, **psychological debriefing** has come under scrutiny for both adult and child populations, but its effectiveness with child and adolescent populations still needs to be determined (Stallard & Law, 1993). How, when, where, and with whom are variables that can determine the effectiveness of psychological debriefing. Helpers should not consider this intervention as an automatic first-line approach to treatment for children who have PTSD (Cohen & Mannarino, 2004).

EYE MOVEMENT DESENSITIZATION AND REPROCESSING EMDR is a newer treatment and a form of exposure therapy that has been used to treat a variety of populations, including children, who have experienced a traumatic event. Two studies have supported its efficacy with children. Jaberghaderi, Greenwald, Rubin, Dolatubadim, and Zand (2002), in a study of Iranian sexually abused children, found EMDR and CBT to be comparably efficacious. Chemtob, Nakashima, and Carlson (2002) studied hurricane-event children who received four sessions of EMDR and showed significant improvement in anxiety-related symptoms when compared with wait-listed controls.

EMDR is a relatively brief form of treatment. After a history taking, assessment, and educational phase, the intervention consists of imaginal exposure, verbalization of the negative cognition, and attention to physical sensations. Exposure is limited, as little as less than 1 minute to the most disturbing part. During this time, the client is instructed to visually track the helper's index finger as it moves back and forth rapidly and rhythmically across the client's line of vision for anywhere from twelve to twenty-four times. The client is instructed to block out any negative experience, breathe deeply, and express what he or she is imagining,

ROGERIAN THERAPY

A form of therapy in which the client, not the counselor, directs the counseling process. Named for its originator, Carl Rogers, and also known as client-centered, person-centered and nondirective counseling.

PSYCHOLOGICAL DEBRIEFING

Usually done with a group of victims, psychological debriefing attempts to recreate a traumatic event by having participants talk about what happened, as well as their thoughts and feelings about the event. There is also discussion of strategies to deal with the stress resulting from the experienced trauma.

TABLE 6.1 Session Outline of Boss Back Program for Children Diagnosed with Posttraumatic Stress Disorder (PTSD)

Session 1	Overview of treatment, information gathering,
Session 2	and "bossing back PTSD" by giving it a silly nickname
Session 3	Anxiety management: muscle relaxation
Session 4	Anxiety management: diaphragmatic breathing
Session 5	Anxiety management: use of the fear thermometer to manage distress
Session 6	Anger control: monitor self-statements and perspective taking
Session 7	Anger control: conflict resolution through role play
Session 8	Boss back PTSD: positive self-talk and realistic risk-appraisal
Session 9	Boss back PTSD: positive self-talk and PTSD
Session 10a	Overview of exposure and response prevention
Session 10b	Individual pull-out exposure sessions
Session 11	Narrative exposure: each member tells his or her story to the group
Session 12	Imaginal exposure
Session 13	Introduce in-vivo exposure
Session 14	Exposure targets through verbalizing "worst moment" possible
Session 15	Exposure targets through verbalizing "worst moment" possible
Session 16	Confront dysfunctional beliefs and substitute helpful beliefs
Session 17	Relapse prevention and generalization: how to keep bossing back PTSD
Session 18	Graduation party

Source: From "Cognitive Behavioral Psychotherapy for Children and Adolescents with Posttraumatic Stress Disorder after a Single-Incident Stressor," by J. S. March, L. Amaya-Jackson, and A. Schulte, 1998, *Journal of the American Academy of Child and Adolescent Psychiatry, 37,* p. 587. Copyright 1998 by Lippincott, Williams, & Wilkins. Reprinted with permission.

thinking, and feeling (Corey, 2008). The second part of the treatment, known as the installation phase, focuses on replacing the negative cognition with the positive one identified by the client. Once installed, the client is instructed again to imagine the traumatic event, but this time with a positive cognition and scan the body for any tension. The goal is to experience as little bodily tension as possible.

PHARMACOLOGICAL TREATMENT To date, there have been no randomized clinical trials with placebo controls for the use of medication for children who have PTSD. Horrigan (1998), in a study of eighteen children who had full-blown PTSD who were medicated with the dopamine-blocking agent risperidone (Risperdol), found that thirteen of the sample experienced a remission of PTSD symptoms. Seedat et al. (2002) found the selective serotonin reuptake inhibitor (SSRI) citalopram (Celexa) to be effective in decreasing PTSD symptoms in children and adolescents. The paucity of research in pharmacotherapy for children who have PTSD requires that such an intervention be used sparingly, as a last resort, and monitored very carefully.

Summary

The importance of assessing and monitoring children for PTSD cannot be overemphasized. Child abuse, domestic violence, natural disasters, and accidents continue to occur and maintain their frequency in the lives of today's children. In addition, the 9/11 attacks and the ever-present possibility of other attacks increase the need to be vigilant for partial and full-blown indications of PTSD in children. Assessment and diagnosis is difficult and can often be overlooked in view of the unreliability of self-reports. If the presentation is not clear or not sufficient to make a formal DSM-IV-TR diagnosis, a rule-out diagnosis of PTSD can be recorded, and the child can be monitored and assessed again at a future point in time. CBT treatment for children who have PTSD has proved efficacious, making help for these children readily available.

School-Based Intervention

Armed with the information we have provided about the characteristics, causes, and recommended treatment strategies for students with PTSD, you, the classroom teacher, are ready to learn an effective model for (1) identifying key or target behaviors that you wish to change in a student who has this disorder, and (2) developing an effective behavioral intervention plan to address target behaviors so identified.

ASSESSING THE PROBLEM   Again, the most effective approach in determining a school-based intervention is a systematic assessment of the behaviors of concern and the function they serve for the student. As noted earlier, the function of some maladaptive behaviors may be symptomatic of a specific disorder and therefore be difficult to assess using a functional behavioral assessment protocol. For example, an individual with a psychiatric disorder such as schizophrenia may exhibit bizarre behaviors that preclude learning and can be occasionally harmful to that individual or others. Conducting a functional behavioral assessment for behaviors produced by disordered thinking processes would be fruitless, because the undesired behavior is driven by a biochemical imbalance. Nevertheless, for Sandy, an older child with PTSD, a functional behavioral assessment would be appropriate in identifying target behaviors that could be changed or modified with the application of a behavioral intervention plan. Such a functional behavioral assessment might conform to a model like the one developed by Barnhill (2005), which consists of seven steps that are considered important for the development of an effective behavioral intervention. As a reminder, these steps are (1) identifying and describing the problem behavior or behaviors, (2) collecting baseline data as well as academic information, (3) describing the context in which the behavior is observed, (4) completing a functional assessment form and/or behavior rating scales, (5) conducting a direct observation, (6) developing a hypothesis, and (7) testing the hypothesis to confirm effectiveness or modify accordingly.

Let's apply this investigative model to Sandy's case. Accordingly, the first step is to *identify and describe the problem behavior*. Sandy's teachers have indicated concerns about her distrust of her Muslim American peers and teachers, as well as her frequent inability to focus in class and her emotional volatility.

Next, we systematically *collect baseline data and academic information.* For example, Sandy's academic performance has dropped significantly in all subject areas because of her lack of ability to focus. Using a behavior checklist, her teacher reports that she is off-task approximately 50 percent of the allotted class time. She must also excuse herself at least two times per week, because of an emotional outburst. She usually misses the entire period of instruction. When this occurs, her school performance and, consequently, her grades are affected. For instance, before 9/11, Sandy was averaging a B+ in all her subjects; after her father's death, her grades dropped significantly. Currently, her overall average hovers around the C− level.

Third, we need to *describe the environment and setting demands* that affect Sandy's behavior. Sandy is affected by several stimuli in the classroom environment, including (1) the sound of a fire alarm or fire engine, (2) anything or anyone who frustrates her, (3) sudden noise or movement around her, which triggers a panic response, (4) the anniversary of September 11, 2001, and (5) televised news reports about terrorism or the ongoing war in Iraq and Afghanistan.

Fourth, we should complete a *functional assessment form and/or behavior rating scale.* Both of these have been completed with regard to Sandy's presenting behavioral concerns.

The next step recommended by Barnhill (2005) is to *conduct a direct observation.* To this end, Sandy's teachers and caregivers have conducted several direct observations over time, and they have consistently revealed a girl who is constantly fearful and anxious. Sandy appears tentative and unsure of herself in class and always "looks like she expects imminent disaster," according to her homeroom teacher, Mrs. Mansfield.

Ultimately, we must *develop a hypothesis* and then test its validity through an assessment of the efficacy of the interventions we employ. Based on the data and observations, Sandy's PTSD seems to have been exacerbated by events related to terrorism and the World Trade Center disaster. Furthermore, it seems that trauma-focused CBT, as described earlier in this chapter, will be the most effective school-based intervention.

Teachers who have used the trauma-focused CBT intervention with Sandy report that it seems to have helped, citing her positive response to the cognitive processing of the event, as well as to the use to self-talk. These techniques will be discussed in greater detail in the next section of this chapter. This treatment approach has been added to Sandy's behavioral intervention plan, which is integral to her IEP. Recent examination of the behavioral data revealed a significant reduction in her trauma-related fears and anxieties. This reduction in symptoms is credited to the effectiveness of the interventions.

DEVELOPING AN EFFECTIVE INTERVENTION PLAN   As mandated by the federal Individuals with Disabilities Education Act (IDEA; 1997, 2004; U.S. Department of Education, 1997, 2004), the multidisciplinary team has developed a behavioral intervention plan based on trauma-focused CBT. This approach involves gradually exposing the child to the traumatizing situation and cognitive processing of the event, in which the individual revisits the event and is coached through the more unsettling, traumatizing aspects. Her teachers have been taught to assist Sandy with positive self-talk, whereby she is able to verbally rationalize the fear-inducing event and acknowledge the inability of this imagined fear to affect her safety and well-being in the present. In addition, Sandy has been encouraged to use relaxation techniques, including controlled breathing, visualizing a favorite place and activity, and, in extreme circumstances, going to a "safe place" within the school (i.e., the school psychologist's office) to sit and discuss her feelings, look at a favorite movie, or listen to relaxing music.

Once Sandy feels ready to rejoin class activities, she is encouraged to do so in order to minimize time away from studies. She is expected to make up missed work and is responsible for getting notes from her "study partner," another student who has been assigned to help Sandy remain up to date in her schoolwork. The classroom teacher keeps a record of the frequency, duration, and intensity of Sandy's "panic attacks" or episodes of extreme anxiety, as well as the time she spends out of class. This information is shared with the school psychologist, Sandy's mother, and the multidisciplinary team. Presently, these interventions are proving effective in helping Sandy cope with her bouts of anxiety and fear and to remain in class. Her teachers hope that, eventually, Sandy will internalize the CBT techniques and no longer require time away from the classroom.

Tips for Teachers

Teachers may employ the following strategies in the classroom to help students like Sandy who have PTSD symptoms.

1. Ensure that the child feels safe and supported in the classroom.
2. Consider assigning a classmate to act as a study partner or "study buddy" to take notes and collect assignments and handouts for the child with PTSD when the individual is absent from class.
3. Follow the strategies prescribed in the behavioral intervention plan in the student's IEP.
4. Speak with the child's counselor to provide updates on the individual's classroom behaviors. Also, be sure that you know how to apply the recommended techniques, such as trauma-focused CBT.
5. Stay in close contact with the child's parents to monitor changes in behavior at home and to apprise them of the student's classroom performance.
6. Maintain a record of the student's behaviors relative to PTSD, noting the intensity, frequency, and duration of each episode.
7. Try to avoid including or emphasizing stimuli that trigger an anxiety attack or phobic reaction in the child (e.g., showing graphic film clips of battles, using detailed accounts of tragic events, or realistic descriptions of scenes that depict a traumatic event).
8. Provide positive reinforcement, such as praise, when the child displays resilience in the presence of an anxiety-provoking stimulus. Always model a confident and rational demeanor when helping the student process a fearful event.

GENERALIZED ANXIETY DISORDER (OVERANXIOUS DISORDER)

CASE EXAMPLE: Jerry

Jerry is a 14-year-old freshman in high school who is generally regarded as a "worry wart." His parents note that he has "always been this way." They offer an anecdote from his childhood to support this observation: "When Jerry was 6 years old, we were driving upstate to spend our summer vacation in a cabin on a relatively secluded lake. Out of the blue, Jerry asked, 'Are there wolves in these woods? Is there poison ivy?' For the next 10 days, all he did was obsess about these perceived dangers. It really detracted from the adventure and fun of discovery, because one of us had to stay around the cabin with Jerry, who refused to venture beyond the limits of the yard and boat docks. We had to constantly reassure him that he wouldn't encounter any of these perceived 'dangers' in this part of the state."

Jerry's parents recounted several more incidents from his childhood that were similar to the "wolves and poison ivy" anecdote, except that they involved different fears. Similarly, Jerry's teacher described him as a "very cautious young man who doesn't like to take risks." This is especially apparent in gym class, in which he refuses to participate in most of the sports and activities, claiming that they are "too dangerous." His classroom teacher also notes that he is a perfectionist and, as a result, does not hand in assignments on time. He is always revising them for fear of producing a less-than-perfect product. Furthermore, Jerry has a difficult time accepting criticism, believing it to be a confirmation of his self-perceived ineptitude and failure. Currently, the school psychologist is working with Jerry and his teachers to help him view feedback as positive and to be less self-critical and demanding. Similarly, Jerry's classmates find him difficult to work with because he is so critical and is never satisfied with an assignment product. One of his classmates refers to him as "a little old man" because of his tendency to be overcautious and "play it safe."

As a result of his generalized anxiety and hypercritical nature, Jerry is at risk for academic failure. He typically receives three or four "incompletes" on his report card and, unless these are soon resolved, he will not be given credit for these courses.

Characteristics of Generalized Anxiety Disorder

The anxiety disorders discussed so far have all been relatively focused. Generalized anxiety disorder (GAD) is more pervasive and is marked by excessive worry in any number of areas—for example, health, safety, performance, the safety of others, the future, keeping to schedules, family finances, and relationships (Flannery-Schroeder, 2004; Kendall, Pimentel, Rynn, Angelosante, & Webb, 2004). Perfectionism is another sign of GAD, which can result in an overwhelming reaction to a small mistake or refusing to do anything that might be evaluated publicly (go to the board, read aloud, etc.). To defend against their anxiety, children who have GAD may adhere rigidly to social norms, be eager to please, and behave like adults, often creating an illusion of maturity that allows the adults around them to appreciate some of their behaviors (Kendall et al., 2004). When they are stressed, children who have GAD can become oppositional. A common symptom is somatic complaints, such as headaches, stomach upset, muscles aches, and sleep disturbances for which there are no known medical causes (Kendall & Pimentel, 2003). Older children tend to have more symptoms than younger children. When compared to nonanxious youth, children who have GAD made more negative self-statements, but the two groups may not differ in the number of positive self-statements (Treadwell & Kendall, 1996).

The greatest challenge in making a diagnosis of GAD is differentiating it from other anxiety disorders. For example, some of the social problems associated with GAD are similar to social phobia. However, as indicated previously, the anxiety in social phobia is confined to social interactions, which is not true in GAD. Similarly, in specific phobia, the fear is limited to a specific object or situation. The anxiety produced by GAD is not related to obsessions and compulsions, as it is in obsessive-compulsive disorder. Finally, in order to make a diagnosis of GAD, the excessive fear or worry must be present for at least 6 months.

Prevalence of Generalized Anxiety Disorder

Using strict diagnostic criteria, the prevalence rates for GAD among all youth range from 2 to 4 percent (Canino et al., 2004). These rates increase to about 14 percent among those children in psychiatry clinics and to anywhere from 14 to 58 percent among those referred to anxiety clinics (Kendall, Panichelli-Mindel, Sugarman, & Callahan 1997). In children ages 9 to 13, there are no gender differences in the diagnosis of GAD. There is, however, a marked gender difference among older adolescents. In the general population of adolescents, prevalence rates range from 3.7 to 7.3 percent (Kashani & Orvaschel, 1990; Whitaker, Johnson, Shaffer, & Rapoport, 1990). Girls in the age range from 14 to 20 are diagnosed with GAD at the rate of 14 percent, compared to boys in the same age group, who are diagnosed at a rate of 5 percent.

GAD is highly comorbid, especially with other anxiety disorders. Anywhere from approximately 33 to 50 percent of those diagnosed with GAD have a secondary diagnosis of another anxiety disorder (Last, Hersen, Kazdin, Finkelstein, & Strauss, 1987; Last, Strauss, & Francis, 1987). The type of comorbidity is often related to age: Younger children tend to be also diagnosed with separation anxiety disorder or ADHD, whereas older children tend to be diagnosed concurrently with simple phobia or major depression (Brady & Kendall, 1992). Even if they do not meet the clinical criteria for major depression, children who have GAD often have low self-esteem and suicidal ideation.

Etiology of Generalized Anxiety Disorder

Etiological factors in the development of GAD are no different than those of other anxiety disorders in children: attachment issues, temperamental characteristics (e.g., behavioral inhibition), parental anxiety, and parenting characteristics that reinforce avoidant behaviors. Recent research has often focused on cognitive-processing variables, such as negative self-talk, expectations of danger, and self-questioning (Kendall, 1991).

Assessment of Generalized Anxiety Disorder

Circumspection must be used to avoid the overdiagnosis of GAD, because a certain amount of fear and worry is normal in children and adolescents. As with other anxiety disorders, assessment should focus on cognitive, behavioral, and physiological symptoms. Clinical interview, clinician rating scales, and self-reports are all recommended for the assessment of GAD. Many of the instruments designed to diagnose anxiety disorders in general and mentioned previously in this chapter are appropriate for use in diagnosing GAD. The recent emphasis on cognitive processing factors in the etiology of GAD has generated measures of anxious cognitions. Two measures specifically designed to assess cognitive processing in children are the *Negative Affectivity Self-Statement Questionnaire* (NASSQ; Ronan, Kendall, & Rowe, 1994) and the *Coping Questionnaire for Children—Child (or Parent) Version;* CQ-C, CQ-P) (Kendall, 1994; Kendall et al., 1997). The NASSQ is designed to measure negative affect, as well as cognitions of anxiety and depression. It has an underlying 4 factor structure: depressive self-statements, anxiety/somatic self-statements, negative-affect self-statements, and positive-affect self-statements (Lerner et al., 1999). The NASSQ can be a valuable diagnostic tool in that it distinguishes between anxious and depressive self-talk.

BEHAVIORAL AVOIDANCE TASKS

Children are exposed to various anxiety-producing stimuli and assessed for their degree of avoidance.

The CQ-C and CQ-P are designed to assess a child's perceived ability to cope with anxiety in certain situations. The CQ-P offers the advantage of gathering data from other sources. Teacher reports are also important, and the teacher version of the *Child Behavior Checklist* (Achenbach, 1991a) can be used. Structured observations using **behavioral avoidance tasks** are also important in the diagnosis and assessment of GAD. As with other anxiety disorders, the assessment of GAD needs to be multi-informant and multimethod. If there is suspicion that the cause of the child's anxiety lies in family functioning, the evaluator can use family assessment tools such as the *Family Environment Questionnaire* (FEQ; Caster, Inderbitzen, & Hope, 1999) or the *Family Adaptability and Cohesion Evaluation Scale II* (FACES-II; Olson, Bell, & Portner, 1982).

Treatment Strategies

A number of studies (e.g., Eisen & Silverman, 1993, 1998; Kane & Kendall, 1989; Kendall, 1994; Kendall et al., 1997) have shown CBT to be effective with children diagnosed with GAD. Education and skill building are two fundamentals in the treatment of GAD, which can begin with the development of the 4 step FEAR plan as outlined in Table 6.2. The FEAR plan is designed for children ages 8 to 13 and is adapted from the *Copy Cat Workbook* (Kendall, 1992). The child's primary caregivers need to be included in the treatment so they can extend the child's practice at home of newly taught or acquired skills.

School-Based Interventions

This section discusses school-based interventions for students who have GAD using the case example of Jerry described earlier.

ASSESSING THE PROBLEM An assessment of Jerry's problem behaviors, conducted by the multidisciplinary team, revealed the following information organized according to the steps we have been using consistently throughout this book.

First, with regard to *identifying and describing the problem behavior,* Jerry's most challenging behaviors seem to be organized in two areas: his generalized

---

TABLE 6.2 **The 4 Step FEAR Plan for the Treatment of Generalized Anxiety Disorder**

- *Feeling frightened?* The helper works with the child to develop awareness of her anxious responses and to use such awareness to begin relaxing.
- *Expecting bad things to happen?* The child is taught how to identify cognitions that result in anxiety and modify those cognitions through rehearsal, social reinforcement, and role playing.
- *Attitudes and actions.* The child learns problem-solving skills and develops a plan for coping with anxiety. The counselor helps the child to brainstorm and evaluate the consequences of alternative behaviors.
- *Results and rewards.* Together, the child and helper evaluate the plan and make any necessary adjustments. The child also learns how to reward herself for successfully managing her anxiety.

Source: From *Copy Cat Workbook* (p. 50), by P. C. Kendall, 1992, Ardmore, Pennsylvania: Woodstock Publishing. Copyright by P. C. Kendall. Adapted with permission.

---

fear of things he perceives as a threat; and his desire to be liked and accepted, especially by adults, which he associates with perfect performance.

Next, teachers need to *collect baseline data and academic information.* In performing this task, Jerry's teachers have provided assessment data that substantiate the frequency of Jerry's refusal to participate in physical education activities, as well as the number of incomplete assignments in all core subjects.

Relative to the *generalizability of environment and setting demands,* Jerry's anxieties occur across settings—that is, at home and in the community, as well as in school. School appears to be a catalyst for the appearance of performance anxiety and perfectionism. Academic assessment and homework assignments present the possibility of failure or, at minimum, substandard performance, which in turn generates extreme anxiety in Jerry.

As required by the IDEA (U.S. Department of Education, 2004), a *functional behavioral assessment* was conducted relative to Jerry's anxiety in school, and the results confirmed the diagnosis of GAD and pointed to parental factors in the development of the disorder (e.g., his mother was diagnosed with GAD as a child). In the same way, both the *Negative Affectivity Self-Statement Questionnaire* (NASSQ) and the *Family Environment Questionnaire* were administered to Jerry and his family to provide further data to inform the diagnosis and possible treatments.

In addition, Jerry's teachers conducted systematic observations to identify the frequency, duration, and intensity of the behaviors related to his anxiety. An examination of these observations revealed a student who is overanxious and a perfectionist; as one teacher observed about Jerry's in-class behavior, "He is afraid of his own shadow." Similarly, another teacher reported that, while observing Jerry write an essay in English, she noticed that he became easily frustrated and destroyed several pages of work because he considered it substandard. As a result, he was unable to complete written assignments on time. In some instances, the teacher would actually retrieve his discarded draft from the waste can and provide a grade based on the preliminary draft; otherwise, Jerry would not have completed the revision in time to receive *any* grade.

The next stage in the assessment process is to *develop a hypothesis* or *supposition* about the purpose that the problem behavior serves for Jerry. According to the data from direct observation, as well as his academic performance, it appears that environmental triggers or catalysts induce Jerry's chronic anxieties. Based on this understanding, it seems that his generalized anxiety may be best addressed through cognitive-behavioral training, such as the FEAR plan (Kendall, 1992), as outlined in Table 6.2.

The final confirmatory step involves testing the validity of the hypothesis. If our initial guess is accurate, Jerry's anxious behaviors should diminish significantly with the application of CBT. Similarly, observing Jerry's response to the use of praise, encouragement, and positive reinforcement to help generalize appropriate replacement behaviors will further confirm the accuracy of our hypothesis.

DEVELOPING AN EFFECTIVE INTERVENTION PLAN   The behavioral intervention plan for Jerry involves the following school-based treatment approach and includes his primary caregiver. Research supports the effectiveness of instituting a 4 step FEAR plan (Kendall, 1992). The plan will be fully explained to Jerry's teachers by the school psychologist and then will be incorporated into their classroom routines.

The first step in the FEAR plan involves asking the student whether she or he is feeling frightened. If the answer is "yes," the teacher asks whether the student expects bad things to happen. If the student affirms this, the teacher can briefly explore the specific negative expectations and provide a rationale that will help expel them while simultaneously replacing them with positive ones.

Next, the teacher, following the recommendation of the school psychologist, will help Jerry employ problem-solving skills to help reduce anxiety. For example, if Jerry procrastinates on handing in an assignment for fear that it is substandard and might receive a failing grade, the teacher can (1) edit the rough draft without grading it, (2) provide Jerry with an example of acceptable work as a guide as well as an assessment rubric, or (3) break up the larger assignment into more manageable components and grade each of these components separately, ultimately providing a cumulative grade for the entire project (Salend, 2005; Smith, 2007; Smith, Polloway, Patton, & Dowdy, 2006).

Lastly, the teacher should evaluate the plan with Jerry, make necessary adjustments, and provide positive reinforcement for overcoming or managing the fear. For example, Jerry might be rewarded for completing and submitting an assignment, regardless of its quality. This reward might be in the form of bonus points that can be exchanged for a desired secondary reinforcement at a later time or, preferably, an additional assessment component that will provide points for assignment completion (Pierangelo & Giuliani, 2000a).

Tips for Teachers

1. Consult with the school psychologist in developing the behavioral assessment and intervention plan and apply the intervention plan conscientiously.

2. Always provide the affected student in your class with a safe, structured environment in which to learn.
3. Provide consistent praise and positive reinforcement for every effort the student makes to control the targeted behaviors.
4. Never demean or disparage a student who has GAD for expressing "unreasonable" fears.
5. Get to know *all* of your students. Building positive relationships with your students is the single most important step in the development of an effective school-based intervention plan.
6. Read the student's case file and become knowledgeable about the behavioral and academic goals described in the student's IEP.

OBSESSIVE-COMPULSIVE DISORDER

CASE EXAMPLE: Nikolas

Nikolas is an 11-year-old boy in fifth grade who has been diagnosed with obsessive-compulsive disorder (OCD). The disorder first appeared 2 years ago and may have been triggered by his parents' insistence that he wash his hands thoroughly, hoping to avoid a particularly severe outbreak of influenza in the schools. Thereafter, Nikolas developed a habit of washing his hands, at first only after using the toilet; later, after any contact with other children, adults, or frequently touched surfaces. Nikolas's parents became concerned that his preoccupation with germs might be obsessive when they noticed that he was using up two bars of soap each day and his hands were becoming cracked and raw. Lately, they have noticed that Nikolas has started to engage in "checking" behaviors (e.g., turning the light switches on and off three times, locking and unlocking doors three times, and checking the faucet handles frequently to be sure they are closed. Nikolas's teachers also have reported observing these rituals.

The "last straw" occurred several months ago, however, when Nikolas's mother observed him perform a routine before dressing each morning over the course of a week. The ritual, she reports, consists of counting each article of clothing three times aloud before putting it on, then "patting" the garment three times as though to confirm its existence. Nikolas's parents decided to take him to a child psychologist who specialized in diagnosing and treating children who have OCD and other related anxiety disorders. Dr. Attwood ultimately diagnosed Nikolas as having OCD.

The most debilitating effect of Nikolas's obsessive-compulsive behaviors is their effect on his regularity in attending school and making appointments. Nikolas's mother sends a note to school with him every day explaining that his chronic lateness is due to compulsive behaviors associated with OCD. For example, most mornings Nikolas is an hour late for school because his morning dressing and personal hygiene rituals take him at least an hour to complete. Attempts to encourage Nikolas to hurry up, even those involving threats and punishment, have so far been ineffective.

Nikolas also demonstrates a compulsion to sort his things. For example, he arranges his textbook and notepad as well as the pens and pencils on his desk in a very distinctive order. Any disruption of this arrangement creates anxiety for Nikolas and compels him to restore the original order to reestablish his sense of security and well-being. Other students have observed this compulsion and occasionally take his pencils or purposefully disrupt his orderly desk arrangement to provoke him. This teasing has occasionally provoked angry outbursts from Nikolas so severe, in fact, that on several occasions he had to be escorted from the classroom.

Characteristics of Obsessive-Compulsive Disorder

To receive a diagnosis of OCD, a child must have either obsessions or compulsions or both. The DSM-IV-TR defines obsessions as "recurrent and persistent thoughts, impulses, or images that are experienced, at some time during the disturbance, as intrusive and inappropriate and that cause a marked anxiety or distress" (American Psychiatric Association, 2000, p. 217). Compulsions are "repetitive behaviors (e.g., hand washing, ordering, checking) or mental acts (e.g., praying, counting, repeating words silently) that the person feels driven to perform in response to an obsession, or according to rules that must be applied rigidly" (American Psychiatric Association, 2000, p. 217). A compulsion is designed to neutralize an obsession. What distinguishes OCD from a thought disorder is that the person recognizes that the obsession and compulsions are unreasonable and senseless. This recognition requirement, however, is waived for children because of the understanding that children, more than adults, may see OCD symptoms as somewhat reasonable.

Rapoport et al. (2000) conducted the most comprehensive study of youngsters with OCD and reported on the most frequent obsessions and compulsions in children, as listed in Table 6.3. Many children who have OCD have more than one obsession and compulsion, and symptoms most likely will change over time. Because most young children have some obsession or compulsion (e.g., a bedtime ritual), it is important to distinguish between OCD and normal developmental behaviors. Most experts have agreed that timing, content, and severity are the most important considerations (Leonard, Goldberger, Rapoport, & Cheslow, 1990; March, Franklin, Leonard, & Foa, 2004). Normal obsessive-compulsive behaviors occur early in childhood, do not interfere with everyday functioning, and are appropriate to the developmental need for mastery and control over the child's environment.

Prevalence of Obsessive-Compulsive Disorder

Obsessive-compulsive disorder affects about 1 percent of the child and adolescent population at any given time and has about a 2 percent lifetime prevalence rate (Rapoport et al., 2000). Among younger children, boys outnumber girls; but by adolescence there appears to be no gender difference (March et al., 2004). The mean age of onset is around age 10; however, some children develop the disorder as early as age 7. Among adults with OCD, one-third to one-half developed the disorder during childhood (Rasmussen & Eisen, 1990). OCD is highly comorbid, with only 26 percent of children and adolescents having OCD as the sole disorder (Rapoport et al., 2000). The most common comorbid disorders are other anxiety disorders, ADHD, developmental disabilities, conduct and oppositional disorders, substance abuse, and depression (Rapoport & Inoff-Germain, 2000). Tourette syndrome or other tic disorders also commonly occur with OCD (Leckman, Grice, Boardman, & Zhang, 1997).

TABLE 6.3   Most Common Obsessions and Compulsions in Children

	Percent Reporting Symptom
Obsessions	
Concern with dirt, germs, or environmental toxins	40
Something terrible happening (fire, death, or illness of self or loved one)	24
Symmetry, order, or exactness	17
Scrupulosity (religious obsessions)	13
Concern or disgust with bodily wastes or secretions (urine, stool, saliva)	8
Lucky or unlucky numbers	8
Forbidden, aggressive, or perverse sexual thoughts, images, or impulses	4
Fear of harming oneself or others	4
Concern with household items	3
Intrusive nonsense sounds, words, or music	1
Compulsions	
Excessive or ritualized hand washing, showering, bathing, tooth brushing, or grooming	85
Repeating rituals (going in and out of a door, up or down from a chair)	51
Checking (doors, locks, appliances, emergency brake on car, paper route, homework)	46
Ritual to remove contact with contaminant	23
Touching	20
Measures to prevent harm to self or others	16
Ordering or arranging	17
Counting	18
Hoarding or collecting rituals	11
Rituals of cleaning household or inanimate objects	6
Miscellaneous rituals (such as writing, moving, speaking)	26

Source: From "The Biology of Obsessions and Compulsions," by J. L. Rapoport, 1989, *Scientific American, 260(3),* p. 84. Copyright 1989 by Scientific American, Inc. Rerpitned with permission.

Etiology of Obsessive-Compulsive Disorder

Early psychoanalytic and learning theories about the etiology of OCD have given way to the understanding of OCD as a neurobiological condition. Imaging studies have shown the areas of the brain most affected in those who manifest symptoms of OCD: the orbital frontal cortex, the anterior cingulated areas, and the head of the caudate nucleus (Insel, 1992). Pharmacological and genetic studies have furthered the understanding of OCD as a neurobiological disorder.

The strongest evidence implicates the neurotransmitter serotonin, because drugs that block the reuptake of serotonin have been very effective in reducing symptoms of OCD (March et al., 2004). It is estimated that serotonin dysfunction explains approximately 50 percent of the variance in OCD (Pauls, Mundo, & Kennedy, 2002). The other neurochemical hypothesis involves the neurotransmitter **dopamine**: There is evidence suggesting that some forms of OCD are related to **Tourette syndrome**. Drugs that control the level of dopamine in the body have been effective in reducing Tourette and associated OCD symptoms (Pauls, Alsobrook, Goodman, & Rasmussen,1995).

The relatively strong relationship between OCD and tic disorders (TDs) led to the discovery that OCD and TD symptoms can arise or worsen with group A beta-hemolytic streptococcal infection (GABHS), a strep infection. Leonard and Swedo (2001) labeled this combined symptomatology "pediatric autoimmune neuropsychiatric disorder associated with strep" (PANDAS). An exacerbation of OCD symptoms is also found in pediatric patients with Sydenham chorea, a neurological variant of rheumatic fever (March et al., 2004). Five criteria must be met for a diagnosis of PANDAS to be made:

1. The presence of OCD, a tic disorder, or both
2. Prepubertal onset
3. Episodic course of symptom severity
4. Association with GABHS
5. Association with neurological abnormalities (Swedo et al., 1998)

When dealing with children who show symptoms of OCD, helpers need to rule out the existence of PANDAS, which can be done though a review of the medical history.

Finally, twins and family studies have suggested that OCD has a strong genetic component. Nedstadt et al. (2000) found that among 326 first-degree relatives of people with OCD, 11.7 percent also met the criteria for OCD, compared to 2.7 percent of controls. Twins studies have suffered from methodological flaws and variability in the use of criteria, but, in general, they have shown higher rates of OCD among monozygotic (identical) twins compared to dyzogotic (fraternal) twins (Andrews, Stewart, Allen, & Henderson, 1990).

Assessment of Obsessive-Compulsive Disorder

A number of the general scales use to assess anxiety disorders can also be used for OCD (e.g., the ADIS-C, the MASC). There are, however, a number of assessment instruments designed specifically for OCD, for instance, the *Children's Yale-Brown Obsessive Compulsive Scale* (CY-BOCS; Seahill, Riddle, McSwiggin-Hardin, & Ort, 1997), which can be administered with or without a parent present. The authors caution that, especially in the case of sexual obsession, a child or adolescent might feel uncomfortable giving accurate information in the presence of a parent. The *Children's PCD Impact Scale* (COIS; Piacentini, Jaffer,

---

DOPAMINE

A hormone and neurotransmitter that is responsible for critical brain functions, such as controlled movement and pleasure. It is a precursor to adrenaline.

TOURETTE SYNDROME

A neurological disorder characterized by repetitive, stereotyped, involuntary movements and vocalizations called tics.

Bergman, McCracken, & Keller, 2001) can be used to assess the degree of functional impairment in an individual with OCD.

Treatment Strategies

As with most other anxiety disorders, CBT is the nonpharmacological treatment of choice for children who have OCD.

COGNITIVE-BEHAVIORAL TREATMENT The two fundamentals of treatment are exposure and response prevention (Franklin, Rynn, Foa, & March, 2004; March et al., 2004). Exposure is based on the principle that repeated and sustained contact with the feared stimulus will reduce the associated anxiety. A child, who obsesses about dirt or germs might be instructed to touch something dirty. Response prevention consists of blocking the habitual response (i.e., the compulsion). For example, the child is prevented from washing his or her hands, and the provider helps the child to work though the anxiety that otherwise would be mitigated through hand washing. This working through is done through constructive self-talk, cognitive restructuring, and minimizing the effects of thought suppression. Exposure to the feared stimulus is either gradual or flooded (an extreme form of exposure), because both have been shown to be effective (Franklin, Rynn, March, & Foa, 2002). The final part of treatment focuses on generalization and relapse prevention.

Franklin, Foa, and March (2003) developed a 12 week, 14 visit protocol for working with children who have OCD. Visits 1 through 4 include psychoeducation about OCD, cognitive training, and understanding the stimulus hierarchy (most feared to less feared). Sessions 5 through 12 provide the intervention exposure and response prevention, and the last two sessions deal with generalization and relapse prevention. Parents are involved in sessions 1, 7, and 11. They are given homework assignments to help with response prevention at home and to provide positive reinforcement. Successful treatment depends on the presence of rituals, the motivation to eliminate them, compliance with treatment, the child and/or parents' ability to report symptoms accurately, and the absence of severe comorbid disorders (March et al., 2004; Steketee, 1994).

Comprehensive studies on the effectiveness of CBT in cases of OCD are currently underway. Other studies have found CBT to be an effective short-term treatment for OCD (see, e.g., Albano, Knox & Barlow, 1995; March & Mulle, 1995; March, Mulle, & Herbel, 1994). In many of these studies, CBT was combined with pharmacological intervention in the form of selective serotonin reuptake inhibitors (SSRIs). Only one study (de Haan, Hoogduin, Buitelaar, & Keijsers, 1998) directly compared CBT with drug therapies, and it found that CBT was superior to clomipramine (Anafranil), a chemical cousin of trycyclic antidepressants that is commonly used in the treatment of OCD. At this time, there is limited evidence of the effectiveness of CBT as a stand-alone treatment for OCD.

PHARMACOTHERAPY Today, SSRIs have overtaken Anafranil as the drug treatment of choice for OCD. All the SSRIs except for Celexa and Lexapro have been shown to be efficacious in the treatment of pediatric OCD (Geller et al., 2001;

March et al., 1998; Riddle et al., 2001). However, Luvox and Zoloft are the only SSRIs that have U.S. Food and Drug Administration (FDA) approval for the treatment of child and adolescent OCD. Based on a number of studies on SSRIs in the treatment of OCD, March et al. (2004) reached the following conclusions.

1. SSRIs result in about a 30 percent reduction of OCD symptoms.
2. Effects appear in as early as 2 to 3 weeks and level off at between 10 and 12 weeks.
3. There is no **placebo effect** in OCD as there is in depression.

PLACEBO EFFECT

A measurable, observable, or felt improvement in health or behavior that is not attributable to a medication or treatment that has been administered.

In summary, there is less research available on treatment effectiveness with OCD than with other anxiety disorders. More controlled studies are needed that compare the stand-alone effectiveness of SSRIs and CBT and that compare combined treatments to a stand-alone treatment. In the meantime, there is sufficient evidence to encourage helpers to use CBT with OCD children and adolescents.

School-Based Interventions

After studying the preceding clinical review of OCD, teachers can, in collaboration with the school psychologist, develop a practical behavioral intervention plan for a student who has the disorder. As we consistently recommend, such an intervention plan cannot be successfully designed without a thorough understanding of the root causes of the problem behavior—that is, what purpose the behavior serves for the child and what contingencies help maintain it. This section provides a suggested approach relative to Nikolas, the child described in the case example.

ASSESSING THE PROBLEM   As a preliminary step in developing a behavioral intervention plan to be implemented in the classroom, teachers must conduct a data-based behavioral assessment. A viable behavioral assessment for Nikolas should be conducted systematically in accordance with standard protocols similar to that described in the following.

The first step in any such process is to *identify the target or problem behaviors.* The principal concerns that affect Nikolas's academic performance are the compulsive behaviors he uses to "neutralize" his obsessions, which result in chronic tardiness, difficulty completing assignments on time, and an inability to participate in physical education classes. These target behaviors include excessive hand washing and showering, "checking" behaviors, counting, and avoidance.

For Nikolas, these target behaviors include constantly asking to use the bathroom to wash his hands, and taking 40 minute showers after gym class, which often causes him to miss the next class period entirely. In addition, he painstakingly checks over assignments, which often results in a lower grade for late submission. Sometimes, his checking behaviors become a source of embarrassment and humiliation. For example, several weeks ago he was asked by the classroom teacher to turn off the lights in preparation for a video presentation; in complying with the teacher's request, he performed his usual "counting" behavior, turning the lights on and off three times, to the amusement of his classmates. In another instance, a teacher who was not familiar with his problem behaviors asked him to make copies of an assignment. After 2 hours, the teacher found Nikolas meticulously counting each page of each copy three times before stapling the pages together.

As before, the next step in the process involves *establishing a baseline and collecting relevant data*. Nikolas's teachers have been asked to keep records of the frequency of his checking, counting, and ordering behaviors as they occur in their classrooms. In addition, they record each time Nikolas asks to use the bathroom, presumably to wash his hands. The teachers try to pair the bathroom request with Nikolas's contact with a "contaminant," such as a door-knob, another student's hand, a "borrowed" pen or pencil, a classroom text-book, or the keys on a computer keyboard.

As a matter of procedure, the school maintains records of Nikolas's tardi-ness as well as the number of classes missed in courses that follow a gym period.

Nikolas's compulsive behaviors do not appear to be affected or influenced by a specific *environment* or *setting*: His home, school, and community all present stimuli that engage his obsessions and fuel his compulsions. The conditions that trigger Nikolas's OCD behaviors include: (1) opportunities to contact contami-nants; (2) any routine situation that he associates with a potential for danger or that might jeopardize him or a loved one (e.g., unplugging an electrical appli-ance, or turning off the gas for a burner in the science lab, or turning off the stove in life skills class); (3) his own ritualized beliefs associated with the protec-tion provided by counting to three that are integral to his daily routine; or (4) ob-jects, especially his own, that are out of order, which can occur in any setting.

A *functional behavioral assessment form* was completed at the start of the school year by the coordinator of the multidisciplinary team. Moreover, the school psychologist conducted two behavioral assessments for OCD, one using the *Children's Yale-Brown Obsessive Compulsive Scale* (CY-BOCS; Scahill et al., 1997), and the other using the *Children's PCD Impact Scale* (COIS; Piacentini et al., 2001), which is used to determine the level of impairment of persons with OCD. The results of these tests confirmed the diagnosis of OCD for Nikolas and helped to provide the information necessary to develop an effective behavioral intervention plan.

In conjunction with the more formal, objective assessments, Nikolas' teachers, counselor, and parents provided anecdotal evidence concerning his obsessive-compulsive behaviors. These observations followed the usual prac-tice of identifying the frequency, intensity, and duration of targeted behaviors. After reviewing these observation reports, it was evident that Nikolas's aca-demic and social success is significantly affected by his obsessive-compulsive behaviors.

The next stage in the assessment process involves the development of a *hypothesis* regarding the function of the identified problem behaviors. After re-viewing the data produced by interviews with caregivers, teachers, and Nikolas himself as well as observations of his behaviors at home and at school, it ap-pears that Nikolas is significantly affected by the following obsessions and com-pulsions: (1) a concern with dirt and germs, resulting in excessive hand washing, (2) a subconscious or habitual connection between checking behaviors and the prevention of dreaded or undesirable consequences, (3) a sense of well-being derived from symmetry and order in his environment, (4) a subconscious or innate correlation between counting and a sense of security. These obsessions must be mitigated by the corresponding compulsive behaviors for Nikolas to be able to function in the classroom and elsewhere.

The development of an effective behavioral intervention plan predicated on the carefully formed hypothesis will help to confirm or disconfirm its accuracy. An effective behavioral intervention plan must address each of the key concerns identified in the hypothesis and, most important, be easily administered by classroom teachers. After implementing the initial behavior plan, its success or failure will determine whether modifications are warranted and, specifically, which ones.

DEVELOPING AN EFFECTIVE INTERVENTION PLAN   Following the recommendations of Horner, Sugai, Todd, and Lewis-Palmer (2005), an effective behavioral intervention plan for Nikolas should address the following concerns:

1. ***How Nikolas perceives or experiences events in his environment.*** Nikolas appears driven to perform his compulsive behaviors because of perceived threats to his safety and well-being, as well as that of his loved ones.
2. ***How invested Nikolas and the other stakeholders are in preventing or preempting reoccurrences of the problem behaviors (compulsions).*** Nikolas has shared on numerous occasions his desire to control his obsessive thoughts and ensuing compulsive behaviors. His teachers and other caregivers have indicated their commitment to helping him achieve this challenging goal.
3. ***Teachers should always include instructional objectives and provide relevant social skills instruction in class.*** When it is feasible, Nikolas's teachers should incorporate behavioral goals in their instructional objectives relative to his disorder.
4. ***Teachers should always reward positive behavioral responses and approximations.*** When Nikolas employs a therapeutic intervention or coping strategy to avoid engaging in a compulsive behavior, he should receive immediate praise or some other form of positive reinforcement. He should never be punished for exhibiting compulsive behaviors; these should be ignored, when possible.
5. ***Develop contingency plans that cover most "emergencies" relative to the problem behavior.*** Although it is not so far apparent in Nikolas's behavioral repertoire, should he become hysterical or exhibit destructive or violent behaviors, a plan to remove him to a "time-out" room or "cool-down" facility should be in place.

Based on a thorough review of Nikolas's functional behavioral assessment, and the treatment plan instituted by the school psychologist, the following represents an appropriate school-based approach to his behavioral concerns.

1. Nikolas has been receiving therapy from a child psychiatrist outside the school, who has prescribed a minimal treatment dose of Zoloft, an SSRI that has been shown to be effective in reducing OCD symptoms.

2. By adhering to the treatment plan developed by the school psychologist in collaboration with the private therapist, Nikolas's teachers help block the habitual responses (compulsions) associated with his OCD. Nikolas's teachers, for example, do not permit him to wash his hands after touching a "contaminant," such as a classmate's hand, a desk top, or someone else's pen or pencil. Instead, his teachers provide a consistent rationale that helps him realize the irrationality of compulsive hand washing. They prompt him to consider the reality of the actual consequences of not washing by pointing out the probability that he will "survive" contact with a contaminant, while acknowledging the prudence of not placing his fingers in his mouth and of washing his hands thoroughly after using the toilet.

3. Similarly, they do not permit him to engage in repetitive counting or checking behaviors, providing a similar rationale. For example, after preventing him from turning on and off the light switch three times, the teacher asks Nikolas what he thinks he might have accomplished in so doing, and what might happen if he does not. The teacher then provides concrete examples that expose the inaccuracy of his prediction and the lack of validation for his fears.

4. Nikolas's teachers maintain a checklist that records the frequency of each of the targeted behaviors. The resulting data will be evaluated in approximately 8 to 10 weeks to confirm the effectiveness of the behavioral intervention plan. If the plan fails to produce a significant behavior change in Nikolas, another behavioral assessment will be conducted to suggest improvements to the current behavior plan or recommend a different approach altogether.

Tips for Teachers

1. Never demean or punish a student for his or her obsessive-compulsive behaviors.

2. Develop a climate of support and understanding in your classroom. Educate your students about OCD and ways they can help students who have OCD.

3. Follow the treatment approaches outlined in the student's behavioral intervention plan conscientiously and maintain accurate records as directed.

4. Find ways to reduce stress in your classroom. Be flexible with assignment completion time, model tolerance of "different" behaviors, and practice patience.

5. Provide support for parents and other caregivers. They can and do experience "burnout" from overexposure to their child's perseverating behaviors.

6. Be clear and firm about expectations relative to timely assignment completion and acceptable classroom behavior.

7. Provide the student who has OCD with a sense of structure and routine in your classroom. This will increase the student's feeling of security and predictability; both of these factors are critical in helping students who have OCD control their compulsive behaviors.

FROM THE FIELD

Mitch Abblett, Ph.D.

Mitch Abblett, a clinical psychologist, is Clinical Director at The Manville School at Judge Baker Children's Center, in Boston, Massachusetts. The Manville School is a therapeutic day school serving children aged 5 to 15 who have emotional and behavioral disorders as well as learning difficulties. In addition to direct clinical services and administrative oversight of clinical services at the school, a primary focus of his work at Manville is consultation with the teaching staff.

Dr. Abblett, can you provide our readers with your sense of the typical student you work with who has been identified as having an anxiety disorder?

At Manville School, students vary widely depending on which specific anxiety disorder fits their diagnostic profile. A common feature for any of our students struggling with anxiety is their experience of significant emotional distress in certain situations, and that they will often show behaviors aimed at avoiding these situations. For example, some of our students suffer significant anxiety in response to social situations (such as during lunch or recess). Due to their levels of distress in these settings, these kids will actively avoid social interactions with peers, and look to either isolate themselves, or spend time with adults. Other students might have significant anxiety reactions to being challenged academically, and will exhibit problematic behaviors as a result. Some kids have more significant trauma histories, and fit criteria for posttraumatic stress disorder. Many of these children have a highly disrupted ability to trust that others will not cause them further harm or upset, and experience a great deal of impairment in their daily lives. Again, the nature of the anxiety varies by the student, based on what has sparked the anxiety reaction in the first place.

By your estimation, Dr. Abblett, what are the greatest challenges these students pose to teachers? And to themselves?

By avoiding the situations that cause them anxiety, many of these children miss out on opportunities to develop their social and academic potential. These kids can pose difficulty in the classroom because, in order to "escape" the anxiety that the classroom environment might create for them, they may become disruptive to other students, making a teacher's job more difficult. Sometimes, anxiety-disordered students require a lot of one-to-one support, and often a lot of redirection, in order to stay on task and complete their academics.

What are some potential "mistakes" that new teachers can make when working with a student who has an anxiety disorder?

First, I think it's important to say to new teachers that you *will* make mistakes, but it's very unlikely that you're going to make a mistake that is not "fixable." Mistakes are best thought of as learning opportunities for you as the teacher, and for the student as well. Some of my best progress clinically with students has been after I've made a mistake, owned up to it, and authentically worked to improve myself as a therapist. Certainly teachers with the right willingness will benefit from this same process of making mistakes, learning from them, and improving as a result.

In terms of common mistakes that new teachers might make, I would say that, particularly with anxiety-disordered students, it's tempting to consider students who repeatedly avoid their work, and might even seem to be "whiny" in doing so, to be lazy and possibly lacking in ability. It's very common to develop a negative view of these students, to view them as intentionally trying to get out of doing their work. These negative views can get in the way of providing the best teaching and behavior management interventions that will help these kids make progress. Research studies have shown that if teachers form negative expectations of students and their capabilities, students will "live down" to these expectations and perform beneath their ability levels. Children who have anxiety disorders don't *want* to fail. Just like a diabetic needs insulin, or a short-sighted kid needs glasses, children who have emotional and anxiety difficulties need behavioral and emotional supports in order to meet their potential.

We know that these students are often very needy and can absorb a great deal of emotional energy from teachers. What can teachers do to prevent "burn-out" and get the help they may not know they need?

I would say it's very important for all teachers to pay a lot of attention to keeping themselves physically healthy and emotionally "sharp." Any teacher or clinician working with anxiety-disordered children will eventually experience emotional strain. A self-care and rejuvenation routine is very helpful as a preventative tool. For me, it's writing, and running or working out. I find these activities crucial to keeping myself emotionally fit. The most effective teachers are aware of themselves emotionally, know their limits, and develop their own emotional skills in order to make themselves resilient, yet open and accessible individuals.

Working with kids who are emotionally distressed and who might act out as a result requires that teachers have a great deal of supervision and support from colleagues. It's important to talk out one's feelings and not let things "fester" such that they get in the way of effective work, as well as drain away one's enjoyment of teaching. It also helps reduce the stress of working with anxiety-disordered kids to develop skills for behavior management. If disruptive anxiety-related behaviors receive clear, firm, yet supportive limits, things will be much less likely to escalate, and teachers will feel more in control and confident in managing their classrooms. As a result of such effort on the part of teachers in developing their behavior management and self-care skills, burn-out becomes much less likely.

Can you provide a few of your most effective strategies for working successfully with these students? For example, tips that you wish someone had given you when you started working with this population?

One thing I learned early on is to be flexible to the needs of students, but consistent in managing their behavior. Anxious kids feel out-of-control, and unable to structure their daily lives; they need an adult "anchor." Teachers who can create consistent emotional support, but the behavioral limits kids need to nudge them forward, are most likely to have classrooms with an atmosphere of growth and academic/social progress. Teachers should look for ways to bring out the strengths in children; to champion these for the kids and help them feel successful and valued. A good relationship with a teacher gives an anxious child the confidence they need to risk change and face their fears.

Remember, these children are not intentionally trying to fail. They didn't wake up in the morning with a plan of disrupting your classroom. They have disorders that need support and treatment. You are allowed to "hate" the behavior, just not the kid.

Finally Dr. Abblett, could you share an anecdote from your practice in working with these students as well as providing support for their teachers that highlights one of your most memorable successes?

Last year, I supervised a trainee—let's call her Jane—who did an impressive job of creating the supports necessary for a student whom we'll call Jonathan with significant social anxiety to make progress and adjust to the school environment at Manville. Jane sought supervision and was flexible enough to take the advice she got from us about how to "shift gears" in order to strike a balance between supporting Jonathan emotionally (allowing him to set the pace of change) and nudging him toward facing his anxiety and attempting interactions with peers. Jane worked closely with Jonathan's classroom teaching staff, to help them understand the student's emotional needs, and how to best respond to his anxiety. Jonathan started his year at Manville hating school and wanting to avoid his peers, but he ended the year feeling as though he belongs at school, and that he can be successful there. A motivated caregiver such as Jane, or a dedicated teacher, can make that happen.

Summary

In this chapter we have examined generalized anxiety disorder (GAD), posttraumatic stress disorder (PTSD), and obsessive-compulsive disorder (OCD) as they pertain to school-age children and youth. The real-life case examples of Sandy, Jerry, and Nikolas provided practical insights about the challenges these students present to the classroom teacher. To further prepare the teacher to work more effectively with students who experience these disorders, the chapter has provided a research-based overview of each disorder, including a definition, key characteristics, causes, and recommended interventions.

   Consistent with the most effective school-based interventions for phobias, students who exhibit these anxiety disorders appear to benefit from cognitive-behavioral therapies. As for any emotional or behavioral disorder that affects school-age children and youth, an individualized behavioral intervention plan that is tailored to the specific circumstances and needs of the affected child is essential. For Sandy, a child with posttraumatic stress disorder, the recommended approach was trauma-focused CBT, which involves gradual exposure to the traumatizing situation with teacher support in processing the more "unsettling" aspects, along with positive self-talk and relaxation techniques including controlled breathing, visualization, and the establishment of a "safe place" within the school. In Jerry's case, involving a student who has generalized anxiety disorder, the school-based approach involved the use of a 4-step FEAR plan (Kendall, 1992); and lastly, for Nikolas, a student who has obsessive-compulsive disorder, a response-prevention cognitive-behavioral treatment plan was instituted. By blocking the habitual response and providing a consistent rationale that helps Nikolas understand the irrationality of his compulsions, his teachers are helping to reduce the frequency of these deeply entrenched behaviors.

   This chapter has shown once again that classroom teachers, when properly prepared, can successfully implement a behavioral intervention plan that has been instituted by the multidisciplinary team. These school-based interventions are critical in providing the student who has an emotional or behavioral disorder an integrated and effective treatment plan. Thus, teachers must ensure that they understand the behavioral dynamics of these anxiety disorders and the most effective ways to address them in the classroom.

Focus Questions Revisited

1. Which related services providers and other knowledgeable persons can provide critical advice and support to the teacher of a child, such as Sandy, who has posttraumatic stress disorder?

A Sample Response

The classroom teacher should be encouraged to speak with the school psychologist, as well as Sandy's parents, to gain a better understanding of how to accommodate her in the classroom.

2. How would you, as one of Sandy's classroom teachers, help her succeed in the classroom?

A Sample Response

I would encourage Sandy to use positive self-talk to help rationalize the fear-inducing stimulus and acknowledge the inability of this imagined fear to affect her safety and well-being in the present. In addition, I would prompt her to use relaxation techniques, including controlled breathing, visualizing a favorite place and activity, and, in extreme circumstances, going to a "safe place" within the school to sit and discuss her feelings or listen to relaxing music.

Once Sandy feels ready to rejoin class activities, I would encourage her to do so, to minimize time away from studies. I would also remind Sandy that she is responsible to make up missed work and get notes from her study partner. In addition, I would record the frequency and duration of Sandy's anxiety episodes, as well as her time out of class. This information would be shared with the school psychologist, Sandy's mother, and the multidisciplinary team.

3. What are some plausible causes of PTSD in school-age children in U.S. schools today? Which of these, do you think, would be most typical and why?

A Sample Response

Clearly, the effects of the terrorist attacks of September 11, 2001, as well as media coverage of subsequent terrorist acts and the graphic coverage of the war in Iraq and Afghanistan have accounted for much of the recent increase in PTSD identification among school-age children and youth. In addition, the heightened awareness and identification of child abuse, at the hands of both strangers and caregivers, appears to have risen sharply in the last decade, accounting for many new cases of PTSD. In the first instance, children view many hours of television each day, which will inevitably include news coverage of acts of terrorism and warfare. The latter of these two "plausible causes" appears to be proliferating because, in part, of increased attention to the problem given by the media and justice system. Statistically, the incidence of child

sexual and physical abuse is increasing annually, and the likely causes are embedded in the perpetuation of poor parenting practices, as well as the deleterious effects of poverty.

4. How can you, as a classroom teacher, differentiate between a student who is simply "overanxious" or a "worry wart" by nature and a student who has generalized anxiety disorder? What diagnostic "tools" do you have at your disposal?

A Sample Response

The classroom teacher should not circumvent the school clinician (school psychologist) in diagnosing a student perceived to have GAD. However, teachers should familiarize themselves with several of the instruments that are typically used by psychologists in identifying bona-fide cases of GAD. Similar to other emotional and behavioral disorders, the three broad criteria used to differentiate GAD from the anxiety that affects many school-age children and youth are frequency of manifestation, intensity of symptoms, and the duration of the "problem" (Walker, 1995).

Many of the instruments designed to diagnose anxiety disorders in general are appropriate for use in diagnosing GAD. The recent emphasis on cognitive processing factors in the etiology of GAD has generated measures of anxious cognitions. Two measures specifically designed to assess cognitive processing in children are the *Negative Affectivity Self-Statement Questionnaire* (NASSQ; Ronan, Kendall, & Rowe, 1994) and the *Coping Questionnaire for Children—Child* (or *Parent*) *Version* (CQ-C, CQ-P; (Kendall, 1994; Kendall et al., 1997).

5. If Jerry were one of your students, how might you address his inability to complete assignments? What incentives might you employ?

A Sample Response

If Jerry is unable to complete or hand in an assignment, possibly because of his fear of receiving a substandard or failing grade, I could (a) edit the rough draft without grading it; (b) provide Jerry with an example of acceptable work as a guide as well as an evaluation rubric; or (c) break up the larger assignment into more manageable components and grade each of these separately, ultimately providing a cumulative grade for the entire project.

In accordance with recommendations in the chapter, I would discuss this plan with Jerry, make necessary adjustments, and provide positive reinforcement for overcoming or managing the fear. For example, Jerry might be rewarded for completing and handing in an assignment, regardless of its quality. This reward might be in the form of bonus points or, preferably, a built-in assessment component.

6. What could you do, as a classroom teacher, to reduce the maladaptive behaviors represented by (a) perfectionism and (b) excessive fear of perceived threats in one of your students diagnosed as having generalized anxiety disorder?

A Sample Response

As the classroom teacher working with a child who has GAD and exhibits both perfectionism and excessive fear, I would address each concern as follows.

a. *Perfectionism:* Assign work that must be completed in class and within a time frame that encompasses a class period or two. Display flexibility in not penalizing for lack of neatness and spelling. Offer to edit major written assignments and simply have the student incorporate those edits in revising the paper to produce a final draft.

b. *Excessive fear:* Cognitive-behavioral therapy (CBT) is especially effective in providing a child with GAD new ways of think about and dealing with fear-inducing circumstances. An example of an effective CBT strategy is the 4-step FEAR plan, which includes the following components:

- *Feeling frightened?* The child is helped to develop an awareness of her anxious responses and to use such awareness to begin relaxing through controlled breathing, thinking of a happy experience, and realistically appraising the perceived threat in order to minimize its emotional impact.

- *Expecting bad tings to happen?* The child is taught how to identify cognitions that result in anxiety and modify those cognitions through rehearsal, social reinforcement, and role playing.

- *Attitudes and actions.* The child learns problem-solving skills and develops a plan for coping with anxiety. The teacher or caregiver helps the child to brainstorm and evaluate the consequences of alternative behaviors.

- *Results and rewards.* Together, the child and helper evaluate the plan and make any necessary adjustments. Children also learn how to reward themselves for appropriate responses to minimize the effects of fear.

Teachers can learn to use strategies like FEAR plan in the classroom under the guidance of the school psychologist to help the student generalize the techniques of the intervention to the classroom and thus provide the student with consistency.

7. If you were assigned a child like Nikolas, who has obsessive-compulsive disorder, what might you do to help him feel valued and included in your classroom?

A Sample Response

I might use some or all of the following strategies to help a child with OCD in my classroom:

a. Never demean or punish the student for his or her obsessive-compulsive behaviors.

b. Develop a climate of support and understanding in my classroom. Educate my students about OCD and ways they can help other students who have OCD.

c. Find ways to reduce stress in my classroom. Be flexible with assignment completion time, model tolerance of "different" behaviors, and practice patience.

d. Be clear and firm in my expectations about assignments and classroom behavior.

e. Provide the student who has OCD with a sense of structure and routine in my classroom. This will increase the student's feeling of security and predictability, both of which are critical in helping students who have OCD control their compulsive behaviors.

8. What might be some good questions to ask the school counselor or school psychologist about a child in your class who has been diagnosed with OCD? Similarly, what questions might you ask family members to help you work more effectively with this child in your classroom?

A Sample Response

A teacher who is concerned about working with a student who has recently been diagnosed as having OCD might ask the school counselor or psychologist the following questions.

a. What strategies would you recommend to help reduce off-task behaviors associated with OCD?

b. What are recommended responses to classmates who tease and mistreat this student?

c. How do I address bizarre or more severe behaviors such as excessive requests to use the bathroom, inappropriate sexual obsessions, bizarre rituals, and "mantras" that are distracting to others?

d. What do I do if an obsession or compulsion that is verbalized or enacted by the student might have serious or even criminal outcomes? For example, an adolescent touches another student inappropriately; a student threatens to harm someone or himself, etc.

9. Suppose you had a child with a behavioral profile similar to Nikolas's in your classroom. Would it ever be appropriate to punish this student? Explain your response.

A Sample Response

Yes, insofar as the misbehavior violates established classroom or school rules and was not a characteristic of his disorder. IDEA (U. S. Department of Education, 2004) has elaborated the process to ensure that a student who has a disability is not being "punished" for a behavioral manifestation of his disorder; such a process is referred to as a manifestation determination. For example, if a characteristic behavior of autism disorder is behavioral volatility due, in part, to sensory overstimulation, and a child with autism suddenly tantrums in your classroom, it would be inappropriate to punish her as you might if she was able to control such a reaction. On the other hand, if a student with OCD brought a weapon or drugs to school, or caused physical harm to a teacher or classmate, that student would be liable for punishment in accordance with school policy regardless of whether these behaviors were manifestations of OCD.

Eating Disorders

Photodisc/Getty Images

FOCUS QUESTIONS

1. How are anorexia nervosa and bulimia nervosa currently differentiated, and what do researchers think about the relationship between these two eating disorders?

2. Describe the diagnostic criteria for identifying a binge eating disorder.

3. Imagine that you are a classroom teacher in a local middle school and you notice that one of your female students refuses to eat lunch with her classmates and routinely uses the bathroom immediately after lunch. Concerned students ask to speak with you privately and confide that they have witnessed this student "throwing up" on numerous occasions after lunch, which confirms your suspicions. What should you do, as a concerned teacher, to help this individual?

4. What are some things you could do, as the teacher of a student who has anorexia nervosa who insists that she is fat when it is obvious that she is seriously underweight?

5. Suppose that you had a student who was grossly overweight and was a binge eater, constantly hoarding and consuming high-calorie, non-nutritious foods. What could you do to help this student?

In the course of the last decade, eating disorders have gone from being a "dirty little secret" to a growing phenomenon of Western industrialized societies, preeminent among them, the United States. Thirty years ago, the death of a celebrity, such as the highly successful singer and drummer Karen Carpenter, who suffered from anorexia nervosa, was an anomaly. The fact that perhaps thousands of girls and young women attending schools and colleges in the United States, Canada, and other economically prosperous nations were struggling with the same disorder was suppressed and underreported. Many viewed the problem as an ephemeral one, the product of diet- and body-image-obsessed females that could be corrected with improved self-image and the infusion of some common sense (National Institute of Mental Health Home Page, 2007; Striegel-Moore & Bulik, 2007).

Nevertheless, high-profile cases, like that of Karen Carpenter, helped to focus medical attention on a growing national problem among girls and young women. Although teachers cannot be expected to provide therapeutic interventions for their students suspected of having an eating disorder, they can learn the danger signs that warn of the presence of one. As we will learn in this chapter, there are some misperceptions about the typical cause of eating disorders. Contrary to popular belief, they are not simply the product of a young woman's desire to be fashionably thin and therefore attractive to men. In fact, research has suggested that often these disorders are attempts to take control of one's life in an area over which the individual has absolute control—that is, the consumption of food.

During the last 30 years, eating disorders have come to the forefront of emotional and psychological concerns facing the school-aged adolescent population. Although starvation has been a subject of inquiry since the fourth century, it was not until the 1970s that clinical studies led to a reexamination of eating disorders, away from unconscious conflict based on psychoanalytic thought and toward a more developmental, family and socioenvironmental perspective. More recently, biological factors have been studied in the causality of eating disorders. The 1970s also began the distinction of different kinds of eating disorders, namely, *anorexia nervosa* and *bulimia nervosa*. In addition to anorexia nervosa and bulimia nervosa, the DSM-IV-TR (American Psychiatric Association, 2000) lists a third diagnostic category: *eating disorder, not otherwise specified* (ED-NOS). In more recent years, clinicians have discovered that binge eating can occur in the absence of purging, leading most to consider it a fourth and separate category. In the DSM-IV-TR, *binge eating disorder* is considered a "tentative diagnostic category, worthy of further study" (Terre, Poston, & Foreyt, 2006, p. 779) and, at the present time, must be classified as an ED-NOS. This chapter considers the characteristics of eating disorders, differential diagnosis and comorbidity, epidemiology and prevalence, and developmental course, etiology, assessment, treatment, and prevention.

ANOREXIA NERVOSA

CASE EXAMPLE: Siobhan

Siobhan, at first glance, seems like many other 16-year-old adolescent girls. Despite being very slim, she is pretty, on level academically, personable, articulate, and enjoys dressing fashionably. The thing that separates Siobhan from many of her peers is that, for the last 2 years, she has been enrolled in a residential treatment program for adolescents with emotional or behavioral disorders and is receiving treatment for anorexia nervosa, a condition she was diagnosed with in 2004.

Family members first noticed the early stages of the disorder when Siobhan was in middle school. Siobhan's mother noted that Siobhan would comment about the thin and attractive bodies of models she saw on television and in magazine ads. She was also very envious of the body types of thinner friends, to whom she constantly compared herself. Despite encouragement from family members and friends, Siobhan's preoccupation became increasingly severe, which prompted her mother to seek the help of a psychologist who specializes in the treatment of eating disorders.

In conversations with her therapist, Siobhan denies wanting to be thin, but instead insists that her motivation for limiting food intake is simply to maintain health and vitality and to "look good." Currently, Siobhan's condition is a classic example of the more typical *restricting type* of anorexia, which has been historically more responsive to treatment than the *binge eating/purging type*. However, she insists that she needs to lose 10 to 15 pounds to look and feel her best and is compulsive about her restricted dietary choices, claiming that she "feels full" after only a few bites of a meal. At the present time her condition is not serious enough to require hospitalization, but the school psychologist, as well as her therapist, have asked that a nutritionist supervise both the preparation and her consumption of meals to ensure that she is receiving sufficient nutrients to prevent severe weight loss. This latest treatment mandate has become a real bone of contention for Siobhan and her family. Sometimes caregivers must sit with and observe Siobhan's meal consumption for upwards of 2 hours to ensure that she has ingested the minimum number of calories. These supervised meal sessions can resemble the old-fashioned "eat everything on your plate before you're dismissed" exhortations typically reserved for finicky young children. Understandably, Siobhan finds this process humiliating and degrading, but left to her own devices, Siobhan would never eat enough to meet the minimum nutritional requirements necessary to sustain her target body weight (at least 85 percent of normal body weight by age).

Siobhan's parents and therapist have appealed to her teachers to provide supervision during lunchtime to ensure that she consumes enough food. This has become a real challenge for her teachers, who have only a 30 minute lunch period and must commit the services of a teacher's assistant for this duty, which regularly takes more than 1 hour. This allocation of critical human resources has strained the relationship between school personnel and Siobhan, who is sometimes seen as "attention-seeking" and self-absorbed. In addition, the extended lunch period has negatively affected Siobhan's academic progress in Math, the class she has right after lunch. Because she often misses this class entirely, Siobhan receives after-school tutoring in Math; however, her Math grade continues to suffer, contributing further to her negative self-image.

Characteristics of Anorexia Nervosa

Although the DSM allows for a wide range of symptomology, three critical components must be present for the diagnosis of an eating disorder: The problem must be related to eating, include behavioral and psychological symptoms, and result in significant dysfunction (Lock & le Grange, 2006).

Table 7.1 lists the diagnostic criteria for **anorexia nervosa (AN)** according to the DSM-IV-TR (American Psychiatric Association, 2000). The core symptom

ANOREXIA NERVOSA (AN)

A serious, often chronic, and life-threatening eating disorder defined by a refusal to maintain minimal body weight within 15 percent of an individual's normal weight. Other essential features of the disorder include an intense fear of gaining weight, a distorted body image, and amenorrhea (absence of at least three consecutive menstrual cycles when they are otherwise expected to occur).

TABLE 7.1   DSM-IV-TR Criteria for Anorexia Nervosa

A. Refusal to maintain body weight at or above a minimally normal weight for age and height (e.g., weight loss leading to maintenance of body weight less than 85 percent of that expected; or failure to make expected weight gain during period of growth, leading to body weight less than 85 percent of that expected)

B. Intense fear of gaining weight or becoming fat, even though underweight

C. Disturbance in the way in which one's body weight or shape is experienced, undue influence of body weight or shape on self-evaluation, or denial of the seriousness of the current low body weight

D. In postmenarcheal females, amenorrhea, i.e., the absence of at least three consecutive menstrual cycles (A woman is considered to have amenorrhea if her periods occur only following hormone, e.g., estrogen, administration.)

Specify type:

Restricting type: During the current episode of anorexia nervosa, the person has *not* regularly engaged in binge eating or purging (i.e., self-induced vomiting or the misuse of laxatives, diuretics, or enemas).

Binge eating/purging type: During the current episode of anorexia nervosa, the person has regularly engaged in binge eating or purging behavior (i.e., self-induced vomiting or the use of laxatives, diuretics, or enemas).

Source: From *Diagnostic and Statistical Manual of Mental Disorders, Fourth Edition, Text Revision* (p. 589), by the American Psychiatric Association, 2000, Washington, DC: Author. Copyright 2000 by the American Psychiatric Association. Reprinted with permission.

of AN is a morbid desire to be thin and a fear of becoming fat (Terre et al., 2006; Steinhausen, 2006). It is common for those with AN to insist that they are too fat even if they are dangerously underweight. This distorted body image interferes with their body sensations. The individual may never feel hungry or may feel satiated after eating even a morsel of food. Excessive exercise and purging may also be part of the symptomatic picture. In fact, the DSM-IV-TR classifies AN into two types: the binge eating/purging type and the restricting type, the classic form of the disorder. The bulimic features of the former type are associated with longer-term negative outcomes (Steinhausen, Boyadjieva, Griogoroiu-Serbanescu, & Neumärker, 2003) and demand a different treatment approach than the latter type.

Anorexia nervosa tends to begin in adolescence, between the ages of 14 and 18. The DSM-IV-TR diagnostic criteria pose some challenges when working with adolescents. The criterion of body weight of less than 85 percent of expected is problematic because adolescents are still growing, may be unusually tall, or may not have experienced the onset of menses (Lock & le Grange, 2006). It is not uncommon for menstrual cycles in adolescents to be irregular. Therefore, the diagnostic criterion of "the absence of at least three consecutive menstrual cycles" can be misleading (Macera &,Mizes, 2006; Robin, Gilroy, & Dennis, 1998). Rather than being fat-phobic or wanting to lose weight, many adolescents report a strong desire to be healthy. Another problem with the DSM-IV-TR criteria is their specifically female orientation, as there is no substitute for amenorrhea in males.

BULIMIA NERVOSA

CASE EXAMPLE: Michele

Michele is an attractive, outgoing high school senior who has already received acceptance letters from three colleges. Michele is pursuing acting lessons privately and reportedly has appeared in several regional television advertisements.

Michele is currently receiving treatment for bulimia nervosa from a psychologist who works exclusively with young people who struggle with eating disorders. She is very private about this fact, however, and only her family, teachers, and closest friends are aware of her diagnosis.

Michele was first diagnosed with the disorder last year, when she was a junior. Her friends noticed that she always used the bathroom immediately after lunch and, when they entered the washroom after her, they noted the distinct odor of vomit. Similarly, her parents noticed that she began to purchase large quantities of high-calorie "junk food" that she often secreted away. She was sometimes observed eating the snacks very late at night, and when she was confronted about this unhealthy habit, she would become very defensive and say that she liked a little "sweet treat" now and again. Her weight has remained constant despite her binging, and this constancy can only be explained by subsequent recourse to purging, which she has reluctantly acknowledged to her therapist and parents.

The seriousness of Michele's eating disorder was recently highlighted when her mother found a large stash of uneaten and partially eaten snack foods that included Twinkies, chocolate bars, peanut M&Ms, marshmallows, various types of potato chips and corn chips, peanut butter, saltines, cheese spread, icing, chocolate chip cookie dough, and chocolate-covered mini-doughnuts. The cache was hidden above ceiling tiles in Michele's closet. When her mother confronted her with this discovery, Michele flew into a rage and then broke down crying. The final straw came when Michele disclosed that she had been using the drug Ipecac to help her purge after binging, despite a warning from her physician about the potential for serious adverse effects posed by its abuse. Michele's therapist informed Michele and her parents, during a recent family session, that this most recent disclosure represented a serious setback for Michele, because in abusing a potentially dangerous drug like Ipecac, she was, subconsciously choosing "thin" over "life" and might need to be hospitalized to reestablish homeostasis (stable internal physiological conditions) and ensure her continued health and safety.

Characteristics of Bulimia Nervosa

Table 7.2 lists the DSM-IV-TR criteria for **bulimia nervosa (BN)**. The core characteristic of BN is a recurrent, out-of-control pattern of binge eating episodes characterized by the consumption of large quantities (1,000 to 2,000 calories) of high-calorie food over a short period of time (Levine & Piran, 2005). The eating

BULIMIA NERVOSA (BN)

An eating disorder in which the subject engages in recurrent binge eating followed by feelings of guilt, depression, and self-condemnation. The sufferer then engages in compensatory behaviors to make up for the excessive eating, which are referred to as "purging." Purging can take the form of vomiting, fasting, the use of laxatives, enemas, diuretics, or other medications, or overexercising.

TABLE 7.2   DSM-IV-TR Criteria for Bulimia Nervosa

A. Recurrent episodes of binge eating. An episode of binge eating is characterized by both of the following:

 1. Eating, in a discrete period of time (e.g., within any 2 hour period), an amount of food that is definitely larger than most people would eat during a similar period of time and under similar circumstances

 2. A sense of lack of control over eating during the episode (e.g., a feeling that one cannot stop eating or control what of how much one is eating)

B. Recurrent inappropriate compensatory behavior in order to prevent weight gain, such as self-induced vomiting; misuse of laxatives, diuretics, enemas, or other medications; fasting; or excessive exercise.

C. The binge eating and inappropriate compensatory behaviors both occur, on average, at least twice a week for 3 months.

D. Self-evaluation is unduly influenced by body shape and weight.

E. The disturbance does not occur exclusively during episodes of anorexia nervosa.

Specify type:

Purging type: During the current episode of bulimia nervosa, the person has regularly engaged in self-induced vomiting or the misuse of laxatives, diuretics, or enemas.

Nonpurging type: During the current episode of bulimia nervosa, the person has used other inappropriate compensatory behaviors, such as fasting or excessive exercise, but has not regularly engaged in self-induced vomiting or the misuse of laxatives, diuretics, or enemas.

Source: From *Diagnostic and Statistical Manual of Mental Disorders, Fourth Edition, Text Revision* (p. 594), by the American Psychiatric Association, 2000, Washington, DC: Author. Copyright 2000 by the American Psychiatric Association. Reprinted with permission.

episodes occur in conjunction with compensatory behaviors of either the purging or nonpurging type. Those with BN often also present with a history of AN, and vice versa. The current preference is to understand eating disorders as existing along a continuum and not as mutually exclusive categories (Terre et al., 2006). The onset of BN is usually in late adolescence or early adulthood (Levine & Piran, 2005). Those with BN can be either underweight or overweight. Males with BN often have a history of overweight or obesity (Muise, Stein, & Arbess, 2003).

BINGE EATING DISORDER

CASE EXAMPLE: Aaron

Aaron is a boy who has been diagnosed as having *eating disorder, not otherwise specified,* which has been tentatively categorized as *binge eating disorder* (a proposed diagnostic category for possible inclusion in DSM-V, 2012). According to the information about binge eating disorder provided earlier in this chapter, Aaron's case may be viewed as slightly unusual because he is not an adult, but a 17-year-old adolescent. Aaron's binge eating began much before the present, however. While he was enrolled in a special residential treatment program for students who have emotional and behavioral disorders, at the age of 13, Aaron was discovered up past curfew, rummaging through the dumpster used by the kitchen staff to dispose of kitchen waste. He had eaten a significant amount of refuse that, fortunately for Aaron, had been only recently discarded and therefore was not yet bacteria-ridden.

At present, Aaron's food intake is carefully monitored, and his room and person are frequently checked for concealed food items; at least twice a day, the searches disclose prohibited foods. Although Aaron's parents are affluent and can provide him with a substantial allowance, the residential staff must carefully disperse his cash allotment to prevent his buying junk foods at the corner deli. Recently, Aaron was intercepted in the act of attempting to bribe a younger student to purchase food at the deli for him and secrete it in a bookbag that Aaron would later insist contained only school-related materials.

To illustrate the extent of his eating compulsion, a few weeks ago, Aaron voluntarily remained at the school over a scheduled home-visit weekend. While "a confederate distracted his cottage staff," Aaron sneaked into the nearby town, eluding on-duty personnel for an hour. After an extensive search of the town, Aaron was found, comfortably seated on a bench in the local park, devouring a cherry pie. In a nearby plastic bag, his counselor found numerous food wrappers, three empty pie containers, a package containing eight cinnamon buns, an empty economy-size bag of potato chips, a partially eaten frozen pork-pie, several candy bar wrappers, and an empty two-liter soda pop container.

At age 17, Aaron is grossly overweight, and for health reasons has been placed on a calorie-restricted diet. In fact, obesity runs in his family; both his parents and two of three siblings meet the American Medical Association's criteria for obesity (American Medical Association, 2005). Furthermore, concomitant medical problems such as atherosclerosis and diabetes are prevalent in his family, and both grandfathers died prematurely as a result of heart attacks caused by congenital heart ailments exacerbated by obesity.

Aaron's obsession with food has begun to affect both his social life and his academic progress. Classmates are repulsed by his poor table manners and gluttonous behavior at meals and, consequently, refuse to socialize with or befriend him. He has also become increasingly inattentive in school, clearly distracted by his obsession with food. Several times a day, teachers confiscate food items he has sneaked into class and subtly consumed or tried to consume without being caught. If confronted, he is very reluctant to surrender the food item to teachers and has become belligerent and even physically aggressive on occasion, causing him to be removed from the classroom and placed in the in-school suspension room.

Characteristics of Binge Eating Disorder

Binge eating disorder (BED) is currently classified in the DSM-TR-IV "Criteria Sets and Axes for Further Study." This means that it is a proposed diagnostic category, and there are guidelines for evaluating the usefulness of the category. Most experts agree, however, that BED is a valid diagnostic category and predict that it will become such in the DSM-V scheduled to be published in 2012. Presently, BED has to be coded as an **eating disorder, not otherwise specified (ED-NOS)**. It appears to be a common phenomenon in people who are obese and who have little or no concern about their weight. Table 7.3 lists the DSM-IV-TR research criteria for BED. Similar to BD, the core characteristic of

---

TABLE 7.3 DSM-IV-TR Research Criteria for Binge Eating Disorder

A. Recurrent episodes of binge eating. An episode of binge eating is characterized by both of the following:

  1. Eating, in a discrete period of time (e.g., within any 2 hour period), an amount of food that is definitely larger than most people would eat during a similar period of time and under similar circumstances

  2. A sense of lack of control over eating during the episode (e.g., a feeling that one cannot stop eating or control what of how much one is eating)

B. The binge eating episodes are associated with three (or more) of the following:

  1. Eating much more rapidly than normal

  2. Eating until feeling uncomfortably full

  3. Eating large amounts of food when not feeling physically hungry

  4. Eating alone because of being embarrassed by how much one is eating

  5. Feeling disgusted with oneself, depressed, or very guilty after overeating

C. Marked distress regarding binge eating is present.

D. The binge eating occurs, on average, at least 2 days a week for 6 months.

  (**Note:** The method of determining frequency differs form that used for bulimia nervosa; future research should address whether the preferred method of setting a frequency threshold is counting the number of days on which binges occur or counting the number of episodes of binge eating.)

E. The binge eating is not associated with the regular use of inappropriate compensatory behaviors (e.g., purging, fasting, excessive exercise) and does not occur exclusively during the course of anorexia nervosa.

Source: From *Diagnostic and Statistical Manual of Mental Disorders, Fourth Edition, Text Revision* (p. 787), by the American Psychiatric Association, 2000, Washington, DC: Author. Copyright 2000 by the American Psychiatric Association. Reprinted with permission.

BINGE EATING DISORDER (BED)

A newly recognized condition that probably affects millions of Americans. People with binge eating disorder frequently eat large amounts of food while feeling a loss of control over their eating. This disorder is different from binge-purge syndrome (bulimia nervosa) in that people with binge eating disorder usually do not purge afterward by vomiting or using laxatives.

EATING DISORDER, NOT OTHERWISE SPECIFIED (ED-NOS)

A diagnostic category that is frequently used for people who meet some, but not all, of the diagnostic criteria for anorexia nervosa or bulimia nervosa. For example, a person who shows almost all of the symptoms of anorexia nervosa, but who still has a normal menstrual cycle and/or body mass index, may be diagnosed with ED-NOS.

BED is eating an excessive amount of high-calorie food within a short period of time. What distinguishes BED from BN is the lack of compensatory behaviors. The frequency of binge eating episodes required by the DSM-IV-TR may be more applicable to adults than to adolescents, whose behaviors may be more intermittent and have various periods of intensity (Lock & le Grange, 2006)

GENERAL CHARACTERISTICS OF EATING DISORDERS

Given the strict diagnostic criteria for eating disorders in the DSM-IV-TR, many adolescents do not meet the criteria for either AN or BN, but still have behaviors that can be considered an eating disorder and fall into the category of ED-NOS. In spite of the diagnostic difficulties, all individuals with eating disorders share common characteristics that are useful to understanding eating disorders in adolescents:

- An abnormal attitude or set of beliefs about food, weight, and/or shape
- A degree of emotional, social, or behavioral dysfunction that results from these behaviors and attitudes (significant problems with school, work, social, or familial functioning)
- Evidence that these behaviors and attitudes are unlikely to change without intervention (Lock & le Grange, 2006, p. 486)

EPIDEMIOLOGY, PREVALENCE, AND DEVELOPMENTAL COURSE OF EATING DISORDERS

Most studies have estimated the point prevalence rate for AN in adolescent girls to be 0.5 percent, or 1 in 200 girls (American Psychiatric Association, 2000; Hoek & van Hoeken, 2003; Lucas, Beard, O'Fallon, & Kurland, 1991). Incidence rates for AN have risen continuously. In the 1980s, the incidence rate of AN for women between the ages of 15 and 24 was 74 per 100,000. The rise in cases of AN has eliminated social class as a major predictor. It is not clear whether this rise is a true one or simply the result of improved detection, screening, and heightened awareness in both the professional and general populations. Prevalence rates for BN are higher and have been estimated to be anywhere from 1 to 3 percent (American Psychiatric Association, 2000; Hoek & van Hoeken, 2003). Subclinical cases of BN are considerably more common. It is estimated that anywhere from 4 to 19 percent of young women may engage in less severe bulimic-type behaviors. BN is also on the rise especially among younger age groups. Adult women, however, have the highest prevalence rate, estimated to be about 2 percent (Hoek, 1993). Epidemiological data for BED is rather scant, given the definition of this disorder and its tentative status as a diagnostic category. Preliminary estimates of the prevalence rate for BED range from less than 1 percent to 4 percent in the general population and perhaps as high as 50 percent among clinical samples (American Psychiatric Association, 2000; Hoek & van Hoeken, 2003; Striegel-Moore & Franko, 2003).

With regard to gender, all three eating disorders have higher prevalence rates among girls than among boys. For AN, the prevalence rate is 19:2, female to male, and for BN it is 29 to 1 per 100,000 (Hoek, 1993). In general, adolescent and adult males comprise approximately 10 percent of clinically diagnosed cases of eating disorders (American Psychiatric Association, 2000; Garfinkel, Goering, & Spegg, 1995). Some believe that eating disorders are significantly underdiagnosed in males because of a prevailing bias toward seeing such disorders as exclusively female. In addition, some symptoms, such as binge eating, may be more socially accepted in men than in women, and men may be less likely than women to seek clinical intervention for their disordered eating. One study found that whereas 53 percent of women with BN sought treatment, only 16 percent of men did so (Olivardia, Pope, Mangweth, & Hudson, 1995). Further research is needed to determine more accurately the prevalence of eating disorders in males. Muise et al. (2003) found that 2 to 24 percent of boys suffered from acute levels of anxiety about being either too fat or insufficiently muscular. To what degree these symptoms approach subclinical and clinical problems warrants further investigation.

Developmental Course of Eating Disorders

Anorexia nervosa and bulimia nervosa appear to have different developmental courses, with the former being the more serious in terms of morbidity and mortality (Lock & le Grange, 2006).

ANOREXIA NERVOSA   Anorexia nervosa typically develops in early adolescence, around the age of 13 or 14, with the individual beginning a diet to either lose weight, eat healthier, or improve performance in some activity such as sports or dancing. The dieting usually begins with cutting out a small number of foods, such as desserts, but as time goes on the food choices become more narrowed, with an emphasis on consuming smaller quantities. Food preparation can become quite elaborate, accompanied by an obsession over not consuming a morsel of food that is contraindicated. Often, the individual will prefer to eat by herself. As food consumption decreases, rigid adherence to an exercise regimen increases. Through self-induced vomiting, the individual progresses to purging herself of even a small quantity of consumed food and may also resort to diet pills and laxatives. At some point during the process, as body fat declines, menstruation ceases in postmenarcheal females, though this varies according to the individual. Some develop amenorrhea early in the process, whereas others continue to menstruate in spite of being very underweight (Lock & le Grange, 2006). This variability has led some to lobby for the removal of amenorrhea as a required diagnostic criterion for AN (Garfinkel, Lin, Goering, & Spegg, 1996). As malnutrition sets in, a number of medical problems begin to develop, which may include:

- Lowered body temperature
- Decreased blood pressure and heart rate
- Changes in skin and hair texture, including lanugo (the development of fine body hair)
- Hypogonadism, causing ovary malfunction

- Cardiac dysfunction
- Brain abnormalities
- Gastrointestinal difficulties (Lock & le Grange, 2006)

Some of these problems can become life-threatening. The most common chronic medical problems among those with AN include growth retardation and bone mass reduction (Fisher, Golden, Katzman, & Kreipe, 1995).

Outcomes for persons with AN vary, as some make a complete recovery while others suffer from long-term weight gains and losses, which may lead to the development of BN (Eddy et al., 2002; Fairburn et al., 2003). Less than a third of those with AN develop BN (Eddy et al., 2002). Some never recover and follow a deteriorating course that may result in death. Mortality rates for those with AN range from 3 to 10 percent; and half of these deaths are the result of suicide (Herzog et al., 2000; Lee, Chan, & Hsu, 2003), while the rest are from medical complications. Agras (2001) determined the aggregated mortality rate of AN to be approximately 5.6 percent per decade, making the mortality rate associated with AN higher than that for any other psychiatric disorder. The longer the illness exists, the greater is the chance of death.

BULIMIA NERVOSA In comparison to AN, BN develops later in adolescence, with most cases beginning around the age of 18. Prior to its development, individuals typically have a history of preoccupation with their weight, and many of them suffered from mild to moderate obesity in childhood (Lock & le Grange, 2006). Their histories often include failed attempts at weight reduction, and many report that their binge eating is the result of denying themselves food through fasting and dieting. The cycle includes guilt over binging and the consequential purging to avoid gaining weight. The most common form of purging is vomiting, but the use of laxatives, diuretics, and exercise is also common. As the illness progresses, these individuals organize their lives around opportunities to binge. Because binging is done in private, they may withdraw from family and friends, show declines in their schoolwork, and suffer from depressed mood. In addition to binging, those with BN may participate in other impulsive behaviors, such as drug use and stealing (Lock & le Grange, 2006). Although the weight of those with BN may fluctuate rather significantly, it rarely approaches the dangerously low levels of those with AN. Common medical problems, mostly the result of purging, include:

- Low potassium levels
- Tears in the esophagus
- Gastric abnormalities
- Dehydration
- Severe changes in heart rate and blood pressure

There are no mortality data for those with BN, but it should be noted that any of the medical problems associated with BN can become severe enough to cause death. Without treatment, bulimics can sustain a regimen of binging and purging for many years. Many patients are treated successfully, with about 50 percent becoming asymptomatic and another 20 percent significantly improved (Wilson & Fairburn, 2002).

COMORBIDITY AND DIFFERENTIAL DIAGNOSIS OF EATING DISORDERS

Conditions that are comorbid with eating disorders can be both psychological and medical. The most common DSM-IV-TR disorders that are comorbid with eating disorders are mood, anxiety, substance use, and personality disorders (American Psychiatric Association, 2000; deZwaan, 2001; Dingemans, Bruna, & van Furth, 2002). Depression is the most frequent comorbid condition for both AN and BN.

As a result of starvation, an individual with AN may exhibit many symptoms of depression (e.g., insomnia, irritability, fatigue, dysphoria, psychomotor retardation, and social withdrawal) (Sansone & Sansone, 2005). When proper weight is restored, many of these symptoms tend to disappear. It is therefore recommended that assessment for depression take place when the individual is within 10 percent of normal weight. The most frequent personality disorders associated with AN, restricting type, are:

- Obsessive-compulsive (22 percent)
- Avoidant (19 percent)
- Borderline or dependent (10 percent)

In contrast, the most frequent personality disorders in those with AN, binge eating/purging type, are:

- Borderline (25 percent)
- Avoidant or dependent (15 percent)
- Histrionic (10 percent)

Borderline is also the most frequent comorbid personality disorder for those with BN (28 percent), followed by dependent (20 percent), and histrionic (20 percent) (Sansone & Sansone, 2005).

One of the more difficult differential diagnoses is between AN and obsessive-compulsive disorder (OCD). Those with AN limit their obsessive-compulsiveness to food and weight. For full-blown OCD to exist, the obsessive-compulsiveness must include aspects beyond food and weight. Anxiety disorders may coexist with eating disorders and AN in particular, but a drive for thinness and extreme fear of becoming fat should not be confused with phobias and other anxiety disorders (Steinhausen, 2006). The high comorbidity between eating disorders and depression should be a major concern. However, depression is given as a separate diagnosis only if the depressive symptoms appear to be unrelated to the consequences of the eating disorder, such as starvation, sleep disturbance, low energy, and poor concentration (Macera & Mizes, 2006). Overeating can be a symptom of depressive disorders but is distinguished from overeating in BN by the absence of compensatory behaviors (First, Frances, & Pincus, 2002). Similarly, weight loss associated with depression is not accompanied by intense fear of becoming fat, a critical sign of AN (American Psychiatric Association, 2000). The same may be said for body dysmorphic disorder, which is characterized by an excessive preoccupation with defects in general appearance that is not limited to body shape and size, or the fear of becoming fat.

TABLE 7.4   Medical Conditions Comorbid with Eating Disorders

1. Structural brain abnormalities
   - Brain atrophy
   - Deficits in gray matter
   - Altered serotonin levels
   - Altered blood flow to the brain
2. Dental and dermatological abnormalities
   - Dental erosion
   - Skin lesions
   - Alopecia
3. Endocrinological abnormalities
   - Osteopenia
   - Osteoporosis
   - Metabolic irregularities
4. Gynecological abnormalities
   - Amenorrhea
5. Gastrointestinal abnormalities
   - Bleeding
   - Peptide release
   - Gastric emptying
   - Gastric capacity

Source: From "Eating Disorders," by L. Terre, W. S. C. Poston, and J. P. Foreyt in *Treatment of Childhood Disorders* (3rd. ed., pp. 783–784) by E. J. Mash and R. A. Barkley (Eds.), 2006, New York: Guilford Press. Copyright 2006 by Guilford Press. Adapted with permission.

Medical conditions that are comorbid with eating disorders are numerous and are listed in Table 7.4. Most of these medical conditions will subside with an increase in nutrition, though some (e.g., growth stunting and long-term risk of fractures) may persist even after a return to normal weight (Abella et al., 2002; Lantzouni, Frank, Golden, & Shenker, 2002; Modan-Moses et al., 2003).

ETIOLOGY OF EATING DISORDERS

Etiological factors in the development of eating disorders can be divided into biological, psychological, familial, and sociocultural factors.

Biological Factors

The role of genetics has been investigated as a cause of eating disorders. Studies have found higher rates of both AN and BN in first-degree relatives of those with these disorders (Stein et al., 1999; Strober, Lampert, Morell, Burroughts, & Jacobs, 1990; Walters & Kendler, 1995). Twins studies have revealed higher concordance rates among monozygotic (identical) twins than among dyzogotic (fraternal) twins: 50 percent versus 14 percent (Lamberg, 2003; Wade, Bulik, Neale, & Kendler, 2000). The unraveling of shared and nonshared environments in the causality of eating disorders remains a work in progress, and the contribution of genetic versus environmental influences remains unclear (Bulik, Sullivan, Wade, & Kendler, 2000; Jacobi, Hayward, de Zwann, Kraemer, & Agras, 2004; Kendler, 2001). The lack of longitudinal studies also complicates the etiological picture (Lock & le Grange, 2006). Furthermore, although some genetic influence may be apparent, it is not clear exactly what is being genetically transmitted (Sansone & Sansone, 2005). For example, is a genetically inherited temperament or personality trait(s) responsible for the development of an eating disorder? The answer to this question is not really known. The safest thing that can be said about the role of genetics in the causation of eating disorders is that girls, especially girls who grow up in families in which either the mother, father, or a sister have an eating disorder, are very much at risk for developing an eating disorder of their own (Bulik, 2004).

Investigators have also considered the role of neurobiological factors, most especially differences in serotonin activity, among those with eating disorders. Low levels of serotonin have been found in those with BN (Steiger et al., 2001), and antidepressants that increase levels of serotonin have been efficacious in the treatment of those with BN (Brewerton, 1995; Ericsson, Poston, & Foreyt, 1996; Kaye & Weltzin, 1991). If binge eating of high-calorie foods plays a role in mood regulation (i.e., increases levels of serotonin), an antidepressant regimen may very well decrease the desire for such foods. In contrast, it has been hypothesized that that those with AN may suffer from an overactivity of serotonin, which would decrease the desire for food intake (Brewerton, 1995). Though studies have shown an association between serotonin activity and eating disorders, a definite causal link has not been established (Terre et al., 2006). It is possible that the differing levels of serotonin could also be the result of an eating disorder rather than the cause (Bailor & Kaye, 2003). Because serotonin activity seems to play a role in numerous other disorders, it may a be a common pathway rather than a specific link to eating disorders (Ericsson et al., 1996).

Recently, some research has investigated prenatal, perinatal, and early childhood complications as possibly having a role in the development of eating disorders (Terre et al., 2006). Perinatal factors in the development of AN include preterm birth (less than 32 weeks of gestation), low birth weight, and birth trauma (Cnattingius, Hultman, Dahl, & Sparen, 1999), as well as pediatric infectious disease (Powers & Santana, 2002; Sokol, 2000). To date, few of these finding have been replicated, and they should be regarded as tentative (Terre et al., 2006).

Psychological Factors

PERSONALITY For many years, the role of personality patterns has been considered an important factor in the development of eating disorders. Those with AN often exhibit premorbid personality patterns of compliance, perfectionism, dependence, social inhibition, emotional restraint, obsession, self-hate, and guilt

(Berghold & Lock, 2002; Sohlberg & Strober, 1994; Steinhausen, 2006; Wonderlich, 1995). Other studies have found those with AN to be low in novelty seeking, high in harm avoidance, and high in reward dependence (Cloninger, 1986, 1988). Personality patterns among those with BN are less consistent (Terre at al., 2006). Depression, poor impulse control, acting-out behaviors, low frustration tolerance, affective lability, difficult temperament, and inhibition have all been posited as personality traits that are common in those with BN (Wonderlich, 1995; Vitousek & Manke, 1994). More recent research has examined the role of attentional biases in the development of eating disorders (Dobson & Dozois, 2004; Zonnevijlle-Bender, van Goozen, Cohen-Kettenis, van Elburg, & van Engeland, 2002).

EARLY TRAUMA Another line of research in the development of eating disorders is the experiencing of early trauma in the form of separation and loss (Jacobi et al., 2004; Johnson, Cohen, Kasen, & Brook, 2002), family discord and divorce, parental death, dysfunctional parental behavior, parental illness, sibling or parental pregnancy, and other types of family difficulties (Jacobi et al., 2004; Johnson et al., 2002). Childhood sexual abuse has received special attention as an etiological factor (Everill & Waller, 1995; Jacobi et al., 2004; Wonderlich, Brewerton, Jocic, Dansky, & Abbott, 1997; Waller, 1998). Studies have produced mixed results. The greatest continuity has been between sexual abuse and BN. In their meta-analysis, Smolak & Murnen (2002) concluded that there was a small yet positive relationship between eating disorders and sexual abuse. It may be that sexual abuse has more of an indirect effect because of its association with other risk factors and is part of a complex interaction (Jacobi et al., 2004; Terre et al., 2006). The relationship between traumatic events and eating disorders has extended to sexual harassment (Levine & Piran, 2005). Studies have found a significant relationship between disordered eating and the experience of sexual harassment (Harned, 2000; Harned & Fitzgerald, 2002; Piran & Thompson, 2004).

ADOLESCENT DEVELOPMENTAL PATTERNS Adolescent developmental patters have also been seen as playing a major role in the development of eating disorders. Adolescence can be a time of great insecurity, especially about one's physical appearance. Pubertal changes, especially those that result in weight gain, can leave some adolescents feeling negatively about their bodies. Some are victims of teasing. This can create a desire to be thin, especially in light of the emphasis on fashion in our society. An exaggerated focus on weight and shape may lead some adolescents to engage in extreme and various weight-loss measures (Lock & le Grange, 2006). Studies have found that as many as 45 percent of children express a desire to be thinner and approximately 37 percent engage in some form of dieting or other weight-loss strategy (Maloney, McGuire, & Daniels, 1988; Schur, Sanders, & Steiner, 1999). These rates increase in middle and high school, with some estimates being as high as 70 percent of high school girls engaging in some form of weight loss strategy. Engaging in measures that are extreme and harmful is a significant risk factor in the development of an eating disorder (Patton, Selzer, Coffey, Carlin, & Wolfe, 1999; Steiner et al., 2003).

Sociocultural Factors

For many years, Western society's pressure for thinness has been held responsible for the development of eating disorders. As our society becomes more obese, thinness also becomes a rare and valued commodity (Sansone & Sansone, 2005). Its connection with fashion, success, and beauty is constantly reflected in the media and, most especially, in magazines and television shows that are popular among adolescents. Femininity and self-worth are defined in terms of body size (Bulik, 2002). This bombardment can easily result in some adolescents resorting to extreme weight-loss measures. For males, the media's portrayal of muscularity and low body fat as an indication of real manhood can contribute to body dissatisfaction and increased concerns about weight (Leit, Pope, & Gray, 2001; Ricciardelli & McCabe, 2004; Robb & Dadson, 2002). Concern is high for those who come from other cultures. In an effort to increase their acculturation and social acceptance in their new environment, they internalize the cultural messages about weight, which could result in disordered eating (Gowen, Hayward, Killen, Robinson, & Taylor, 1999; Gunewardene, Huon, & Zheng, 2001).

Cross-cultural studies seem to support the notion that the drive for thinness and fat phobia are culture-specific in their relationship to the development of eating disorders (Gilbert & Thompson, 1996; Lee, 1995). AN also exists in non-Western cultures where the emphasis on thinness is absent. It appears, then, that eating disorders are not culture-bound syndromes, but that etiological factors vary across cultures (Simpson, 2002).

Family Factors

Serious attention has been given to family dysfunction as a possible cause of eating disorders. Those with eating disorders have been found to come from families that are enmeshed, conflict-avoidant, and inflexible (Minuchin, Rosman, & Baker, 1978), controlling (in cases of AN) (Humphrey, 1986, 1987), chaotic, critical, and conflicted (in cases of BN) (Humphrey, 1987). High incidences of weight problems, eating disorders, physical illness, affective disorders, obsessive-compulsive disorders, and alcoholism in families have all been considered risk factors in the development of eating disorders (Steinhausen, 2006). Two things must be said about these kinds of family dysfunction and eating disorders, however. First, not all those with eating disorders come from families with these kinds of dysfunction. Second, these types of family dysfunction have also been linked to numerous other emotional disorders. Therefore, it is difficult to isolate a family factor(s) as having a direct etiological link to eating disorders. At best, they may play an indirect role and be part of the pathway to the development of an eating disorder. According to most studies, general family environment and family dynamics do not predict disordered eating (Jacobi et al., 2004; Stice, 2002). On the other hand, parents and family members who tend to tease, criticize, and offer weight-loss advice to a family member have been shown to contribute to negative body image and unhealthy weight-control measures (Stice, 2002; Thompson, Heinberg, Altabe, & Tantleff-Dunn, 1999).

Summary

From the above description, it seems certain the causality of eating disorders is multidetermined, and that antecedents to the disorder vary from one individual to another (Sansone & Sansone, 2005). In recent years there has been a bias in favor of biological and genetic factors. Eating disorders are most likely the result of a genetic/biological predisposition to the disorder that interacts with a number of cognitive, psychological, and environmental variables to result in symptoms as outlined in the DSM-IV-TR. Future research needs to examine more carefully these interacting factors to determine perhaps the pathway(s) of an eating disorder. This will help shed some light on what is currently understood as a complex and, to some extent, undetermined etiology of eating disorders.

ASSESSMENT OF EATING DISORDERS

As for many other disorders, the assessment of eating disorders needs to be comprehensive and multimodal (Devlin, 1996; Foreyt & Mikhail, 1997; Terre et al., 2006) and should include a medical evaluation, an interview with the adolescent, an interview with the parents, consultation with a dietician, and, if necessary, the administration of a standardized assessment instrument(s).

Medical Evaluation

Any individual with an eating disorder (or suspected of having one) should undergo a thorough medical evaluation by a pediatric specialist or internist (Steinhausen, 2006). Careful attention needs to be paid to signs of malnutrition, such as tooth erosion, dehydration, and lanugo (Lock & le Grange, 2006). Blood tests are performed with special attention to liver, kidney, and thyroid functioning to rule out other illnesses that might be responsible for weight loss. In addition, an examination of endocrinological/metabolic, cardiovascular, gastrointestinal, dermatological, and pulmonary systems is necessary (Leonard & Mehler, 2001; Mcgilley & Pryor, 1998; Terre et al., 2006). Electrolyte imbalance, the result of purging, can manifest through complaints of weakness, tiredness, constipation, and depression and should not be overlooked. The medical evaluation is a key element in determining whether hospitalization is necessary for those whose lives might be in danger because of the consequences of having an eating disorder.

Interview with the Adolescent

Engagement of adolescents with eating disorders can be difficult, as they are often in denial about their condition. The interviewer must be both empathic and challenging to break through the denial. The existence of a precipitating event should be investigated:

- Onset of menses
- Family conflicts
- Starting middle or high school
- Dating

- A romantic breakup
- Knowing others in and outside the family who might be dieting

Second, the interviewer should obtain a detailed history of efforts to lose weight, such as counting calories, restricting consumption of fats, fasting, skipping meals, not drinking, restricting consumption of meat and protein, increased exercise, binge eating, purging behaviors (exercise, laxatives, diuretics), and use of stimulants and diet pills (both over-the-counter supplements and illegal products) (Lock & le Grange, 2006, p. 492). Because both those who have AN and those who have BN engage in binge eating, this must also be assessed. The difference between the two disorders is that those who have AN may refer to eating a normal amount of food as binging, whereas for those who have BN, the binging usually involves eating excessive amounts of high-calorie food. The interviewer should pay attention to possible physical symptoms, such as dizziness, headaches, fainting spells, weakness, poor concentrations, stomach and abdominal pain, and loss of menses (Lock & le Grange, 2006). These symptoms are often the result of binging and purging behaviors.

Interview with the Parents

There are several purposes to the parent interview, which both parents should attend if both are involved in the life of the adolescent. The first purpose is to assess the adolescent's development history:

- Pre-, peri-, and postnatal complications
- Early feeding history
- Transition into preschool and elementary school
- Quality and differences of attachment to mother and father
- Early temperament
- Family problems
- Relationships with siblings and peers (Lock & le Grange, 2006)

The interviewer should also pay careful attention to signs of overprotectiveness, communication problems, and conflict-resolution strategies, which have all been implicated in the development of eating disorders (Casper & Troiani, 2001; Shoebridge & Gowers, 2000; Terre et al., 2006). The family's history of eating and weight-related behaviors such as dieting and whether the adolescent was a victim of insults or teasing concerning issues of weight (Fairburn & Harrison, 2003) also needs to be assessed. The parent interview may also be used to assess interpersonal difficulties outside the family, because eating disorders are known to impede psychosocial development.

Consultation with a Dietician

The main purpose of this assessment is to determine the adolescent's body mass index (BMI) and to establish a weight range for recovery (Lock & le Grange, 2006) based on proper nutrition. The consultation is necessary for both the adolescent and the parents who are in charge of monitoring their child's nutrition. The dietician or nutritionist's scientific knowledge may help to challenge faulty beliefs about food that usually develop in those with an eating disorder. For example, if an adolescent accepts the idea of eating a bagel but objects to eating a poppy-seed bagel because of its additional calories, the dietician might be able to deal with such obssessiveness by providing accurate information about the additional calories in a poppy-seed bagel.

Standardized Assessment

Numerous formal instruments can be used for the assessment of eating disorders. It is beyond the scope of this chapter to discuss all of them. The majority of these measures are designed to assess cognitions and behaviors either through self-report or a diagnostic interview. Others assess outcomes expectancies associated with dieting and other eating behaviors, dietary restraint (those who have dieted many times and failed), body image, and appearance. All of the instruments listed in Table 7.5 have been published since 1988 and have sound psychometric properties.

TREATMENT OF EATING DISORDERS

Depending on the possible need for hospitalization, treatment for eating disorders differs according to where the treatment takes place. Inpatient treatment is typically multidisciplinary, with the goal of restoring the patient to a noncritical weight.

Inpatient Treatment

Many good specialized inpatient treatment centers exist for eating disorders. Weight that is 15 to 25 percent below average, significant medical problems, psychiatric emergencies (e.g., a suicide attempt), and the failure of outpatient treatment may all be cause for hospitalization (Lock, Reisel, & Steiner, 2001; Williamson, Thaw, & Varnado-Sullivan, 2001). A typical inpatient team includes a psychiatrist, a psychologist, a medical consultant, and a dietician or nutritionist. The primary goal of inpatient treatment is refeeding, with an initial goal of 1,000 to 1,600 calories per day, gradually increased to 3,000 to 3,600 calories per day (Anzai, Lindsey-Dudley, & Bidwell, 2002). Forced feeding through gastric tubing is rare, and the patient is encouraged to participate as much as possible in planning meals (Breiner, 2003; Cummings et al., 2001). Along with the goals for caloric intake, there are also goals for weight gain of anywhere from 1 to 3 pounds per week (Weltzin & Bolton, 1998). Patient denial, comorbid conditions (e.g., depression and other medical problems), and the feeling of loss of control inherent in any hospitalization may all delay or hinder successful inpatient treatment (Terre et al., 2006).

In recent years, the length of hospital stay for eating disorders has been trending downward (Anzai et al., 2002; Wiseman, Sunday, Klapper, Harris, & Halmi, 2001). The typical hospitalization ranges anywhere from 7 to 26 days (Kaczynski, Denison, Wiknertz, Ryno, & Hjalmers, 2000; Striegel-Moore, Leslie, Petrill, Garvin, & Rosenheck, 2000). In some programs, patients transition to less intensive care before being fully discharged. Discharge

TABLE 7.5   Assessment Measures for Eating Disorders

Purpose	Domain/Construct	Instrument	Authors
Diagnostic interview	Assess severity of eating preoccupation and rituals	Yale-Brown-Cornell Eating Disorder Scale (YBC-EDS)	Mazure et al., 1994
	Frequency and severity of eating behaviors and attitudes	Eating Disorder Examination (EDE, 12th ed.)	Fairburn & Cooper, 1993
Self-report of behavioral symptoms	Frequency and severity of eating behaviors and attitudes	Eating Disorder Questionnaire (EDE-Q)	Fairburn & Belgin, 1994
	Severity of symptoms associated with AN and BN	Eating Disorder Inventory-2 (EDI-2)	Garner, 1991
	Bulimia symptoms, DSM-IV criteria	Bulimia Test—Revised (BULIT-R)	Thelen, Mintz, & Vander Wal, 1996
	Symptoms of eating disorders, DSM-IV criteria	Eating Attitudes Test (EAT)	Lavik, Clausen, & Pederson, 1991
	Children's symptoms of eating disorders	Children's Eating Attitudes Test (ChEAT)	Maloney et al., 1989
	Symptom checklist for bulimia and binge eating	Eating Questionnaire—Revised (EQR)	Williamson, Davis, Bennett, & Goreczny, 1989
	DSN-IV criteria for diagnosing AN, BN, and binge eating disorder	Survey for Eating Disorders (SEDs)	Gotestam & Agras, 1995
	DSM-IV criteria for diagnosing eating disorders	Questionnaire for Eating Disorder Diagnoses (QEDD)	Mintz, O'Halloran, Mulholland, & Schneider, 1997
	DSM-IV criteria for diagnosing AN, BN, and binge eating disorder	Eating Disorder Diagnostic Scale (EDDS)	Stice, Telch, & Rizvi, 2000
	Eating disorder cognitions and behaviors	Stirling Eating Disorder Scales (SEDS)	Williams, Power, Miller, & Freeman, 1994
	Cognitions associated with eating disorders	Mizes Anorectic Cognitions Questionnaire (MAC-R)	Mizes et al., 2000
Assess expectancies	Expectancies related to dieting practices and losing weight	Weight Loss Expectancy Scale (WLES)	Allen, Thombs, Mahoney, & Daniel, 1993
	Cognitive expectancies for eating	Eating Expectancy Inventory (EEI)	Hohlstein, Smith, & Atlas, 1998
	Cognitive expectancies for dieting and thinness	Thinness and Restricting Expectancy Inventory (TREI)	Hohlstein et al., 1998
Assess dietary restraint	Caloric restriction and disinhibited eating	Restrain Scale	Lowe, 1993
	Cognitive aspects of restrained eating	Dutch Eating Behavior Questionnaire—Revised (DEBQ-R)	van Strien, Frijters, Bergers, & Defares, 1986
	Cognitive aspects of restrained eating	Factor Eating Questionnaire—Revised (FEQ-R)	Stunkard & Messick, 1985
Assess body image	Dysfunctional beliefs about implications of one's appearance	Beliefs About Appearance Scale (BAAS)	Spangler & Stice, 2001
	Body image attitudes	Multidimensional Body-Self Relations Questionnaire (MBRSQ)	Cash, 1994

Source: From "Assessment of Eating Disorders and Obesity," by R. L. Collins and L. A. Ricciardelli in *Assessment of Addictive Behaviors* (pp. 326–327) by D. M. Donovan and G.A. Marlatt (Eds.), 2005, New York: Guilford Press. Copyright 2005 by Guilford Press. Adapted with permission.

is recommended when the patient has achieved a stable and suitable weight, is medically stable, and has identified psychological and family factors that need to be addressed in outpatient treatment (American Psychiatric Association, 1996).

Individual Counseling

Individual approaches to those with eating disorders have included behavioral therapy, cognitive-behavioral therapy (CBT), and interpersonal therapy. Research has failed to identify an overwhelmingly more effective approach for treating all eating disorders. The one exception appears to be the use of CBT as an initial treatment for BN (Agras et al., 2000; Grave, Ricca, & Todesco, 2001; Fairburn & Harrison, 2003; Thompson-Brenner, Glass, & Western, 2003).

BEHAVIORAL THERAPY Techniques used in the behavioral approach to treating eating disorders include response prevention, operant conditioning, response delay, self-monitoring techniques, and stimulus control.

Response Prevention In response prevention, the individual is prevented from vomiting. Because for these individuals, vomiting reduces anxiety, the hypothesis is that those with eating disorders will not binge if they are prevented from vomiting. However, there is little empirical support for the efficacy of response prevention in treating eating disorders (Bulik, Sullivan, Carter, McIntosh, & Joyce, 1998; Carter, McIntosh, Joyce, Sullivan, & Bulik, 2003; Wilson, Eldredge, Smith, & Niles, 1991).

Operant Conditioning Operant conditioning (the use of positive and negative environmental contingencies) has been used primarily in impatient settings. Research has shown that when it is used within a comprehensive treatment plan, operant conditioning can be helpful (Steinhausen, 1995; Wilson & Fairburn, 1993).

Response Delay Response delay is designed to have the client delay the impulse to binge by participating, for example, in an alternative activity. The technique is based on the hypothesis that if the response can be delayed, the sequence of events can be altered (Terre et al., 2006). Response delay is a commonly used and well-accepted technique in the treatment of eating disorders in spite of the absence of studies that support its effectiveness.

Self-Monitoring Techniques As part of a comprehensive treatment plan and not as a stand-alone treatment, self-monitoring techniques have proven useful in helping with eating disorders (Agras, Schneider, Arnow, Raeburn, & Telch, 1989; Fairburn, 1980). This intervention requires careful monitoring by the individual of his or her thoughts, feelings, and behaviors, both before and after the problematic behavior. This information is then used in counseling, with the goal of manipulating the antecedents that lead to the behavior.

Stimulus Control Stimulus control involves environmental engineering to remove or reduce opportunities to participate in problematic eating. For example, favorite high-calorie foods, the preference of many binge-eaters, are not kept in the home. Replacement strategies might include removing all candy and substituting fresh fruit. Little research has been done on the effectiveness of stimulus control, specifically. It is, however, very much a part of CBT programs, because logic suggests that reducing the opportunities to binge-eat makes sense.

COGNITIVE BEHAVIORAL APPROACHES   The primary goal of CBT is the use of techniques to restructure an individual's distorted cognitions about body image and his or her faulty beliefs that equate thinness with worthiness, strength, and success (Fairburn, Shafran, & Cooper, 1999; Terre et al., 2006), in conjunction with some of the behavioral techniques described earlier. Empirical support for the use of CBT, especially with bulimia nervosa, is very strong (Anderson & Maloney, 2001; Grave et al., 2001; Fairburn & Harrison, 2003; Thompson-Brenner et al., 2003; Wilson & Pike, 2001). Studies have also found CBT and pharmacological intervention to be superior to drugs alone in the treatment of BN (Casper, 2002; Mitchell, deZwaan, & Roerig, 2003). With anorexia nervosa, CBT has been shown to be helpful in relapse prevention in adults (Pike, Walsh, Vitousek, Wilson, & Bauer, 2004), and other studies have reported promising results (Bowers, 2001; Serfaty, Turkington, Heap, Ledsham, & Jolley, 1999). However, the use of CBT with adolescents who have AN has not been studied empirically to any systematic extent (Lock & le Grange, 2006). Studies have shown that CBT can also be effective in treating binge eating disorder (Ricca, Mannucci, Zucchi, Rotella, Faravelli, 2000; Wilfley et al., 2002.)

INTERPERSONAL COUNSELING   Interpersonal counseling focuses on the client's relationships, based on the hypothesis that maladaptive relationships have either a direct or an indirect effect in the development of eating disorders. Research has found that this approach is as effective as CBT in treating BN, but results are obtained more slowly (Agras et al., 2000; Fairburn et al., 2003; Wilfley et al., 2002). Interpersonal counseling has not been found to be effective with BED (Agras et al., 1995).

Family Counseling

Based on the hypothesis that maladaptive patterns of family interaction play an important role in the etiology of eating disorders, family counseling has long been a preferred mode of treatment. Family counseling is often used as a component of a comprehensive treatment package. Interventions range from simply providing education to the family about the disorder to changing a family's structural patterns. The latter approach is based on *structural family therapy* (SFT) (see Minuchin et al., 1978) and results from the hypothesis that those with eating disorders come from families that are overly enmeshed, overprotected, and conflict-avoidant. The goal of counseling is to effectuate a gradual disengagement from the family that allows the adolescent appropriate separation and autonomy. Families are helped to establish boundaries that are neither too rigid nor too diffuse.

A different approach utilizes the family as a resource in the treatment by eliciting their help in refeeding, consistent application of eating patterns, and meeting the developmental challenges of adolescence (Dare & Eisler, 1997; Dare & Szmukler, 1991; Lock & le Grange, 2001). In some ways, the family's role is similar to that of a nurse in that it provides parental control over eating until the adolescent is able to maintain consistent and appropriate eating alone. Though some studies have supported the effectiveness of this approach (Krautter & Lock, 2004; Robin, Siegel, Koepke, Moye, & Tice, 1994; Russell, Szmukler, Dare, & Eisler, 1987), others have not shown it to be more effective than individual treatment (Eisler et al., 2000; Robin & Siegel, 1999). It seems that using the family as a resource may be more effective in weight restoration, but less effective than individual treatment, in dealing with some of the psychological variables responsible for the disorder. For example, Eisler et al. (2000) found that those with eating disorders who came from families that were highly critical did better when they and their parents were seen separately. The effectiveness of family versus individual approaches may also depend on age, with older adolescents and adults doing better with individual treatment (Russell et al., 1987). One thing, however, remains clear: Whether they are seen together with or separately from their adolescent son or daughter, parents need to be involved in the treatment of eating disorders, and this is especially true for those who develop eating problems at a younger age.

Group Counseling

Over the years, group work has been used more with BN and BED and less so with AN. Until the adolescent is medically stabilized, group work is not recommended for those who have AN. Recent studies, however, have shown promising results after stabilization (Gerlinghoff, Gross, & Backmund, 2003; Waisberg & Woods, 2002; Williamson, Duchman, Barker, & Bruno, 1998). Group interventions commonly employ either a feminist and/or psychoeducational perspective. In the former, participants are given the opportunity to discuss the conflicting demands placed on women. They are helped not to turn over their self-definition as women to the sexist elements of society. The psychoeducational approach basically provides information about the disorder, and the group members act as coaches and sources of support for each other. Although it is not suitable for everyone, the psychoeducational group approach offers efficient and cost-effective treatment (Stice & Ragan, 2002; Wiseman, Sunday, Klapper, Klein, & Halmi, 2002).

Pharmacological Treatment

In general, the use of psychotropic medications for those with eating disorders is not effective and, most especially, in cases of AN (Terre et al., 2006). Some have argued that certain medications can help to stimulate appetite, whereas others have argued that lack of appetite is rarely the cause of AN (Andersen, Bowers, & Evans, 1997). Medication is more indicated to prevent relapse after the individual has reached a healthy weight (Attia, Mayer, & Killory, 2001; Casper, 2002; Mitchell, Myers, Swan-Kremeier, & Wonderlich, 2003). In cases of comorbidity with obsessive-compulsive disorder and depression, the use of a selective serotonin reuptake inhibitor (SSRI) should be considered (Sansone & Sansone, 2005).

The use of SSRIs and other antidepressants has been more common in treating BN, based on the theory that the disorder is the result of decreased levels of serotonin in the brain. Two studies, albeit with small sample sizes, have shown fluoxetine (Prozac) to have short-term effectiveness in reducing binge eating and vomiting when compared to placebo (Goldstein, Wilson, Thompson, Potvin, & Rampey, 1995; Walsh & Devlin, 1995). However, research comparing fluoxetine only and CBT only treatments showed the latter to be more effective, whereas the combination of the two treatments was only slightly better than CBT alone (Goldbloom et al., 1997; Walsh, Wilson, Loeb, & Devlin, 1997).

Based on the current literature, the use of antidepressants can be useful for the short-term treatment of BN, but medication alone is associated with more relapse and less overall effectiveness than CBT (Bacaltchuk, Hay, & Mari, 2000; Fairburn & Harrison, 2003; Zhu & Walsh, 2002).

Treatment Outcomes

Outcome literature on eating disorders reveals that about one-third of patients experience poor outcomes (Ben-Tovim et al., 2001; Herpertz-Dahlmann et al., 2001; Herzog et al., 1999; Steinhausen et al., 2003). Factors related to poor outcomes for those with AN are hospitalizations, longer duration of illness, very low weight during illness, and the presence of bulimic symptoms, such as vomiting and laxative abuse. Favorable factors include early age of onset, high socioeconomic status, good parent–child relationships, short interval between onset and treatment, histrionic personality, and short duration of inpatient treatment without readmission (Steinhausen, 1995). In more recent reviews of the outcome literature, Steinhausen (2002, 2006) concluded the following with regard to those diagnosed with AN:

- The mortality rate in AN averages around 5 to 6 percent.
- Full recovery occurs in only about 45 percent; 33 percent improve, and 20 percent develop a chronic course.
- A large proportion of patients evidences other psychiatric disorders throughout life (e.g., mood, anxiety, substance abuse, obsessive-compulsive, and personality disorders).
- About one-third do not achieve normal employment and education, and only a minority enter marriage or a stable relationship.

In general, those diagnosed with BN tend to have better outcomes than those diagnosed with AN or those who have AN and BN. A significant number can continue with subclinical features of BN. In a recent review, Steinhausen (2006) concluded the following with regard to outcome for those diagnosed with BN:

- Full recovery occurs in about 47 percent; 26 percent improve; and 26 percent are chronic cases.
- Mortality rates are less than 1 percent.
- Many have other psychiatric disorders: mood disorders (25 percent), substance abuse (15 percent), and anxiety (13 percent).

Conclusion

Eating disorders are complex, have a multifactorial etiology, and require a comprehensive treatment plan to heighten the probability of a favorable outcome. The research on eating disorders is relatively sparse, and many of the studies that have been done had small sample sizes and suffer from a lack of replication. There is a need for greater understanding of eating disorders in diverse populations to assess more clearly the cultural dimension in the etiology of these disorders. Even less research exists for younger populations who suffer form eating disorders. The lack of clinical trials prevents us from discovering consistently effective methods of treatment for adolescents. The little research that exists suggests that family intervention should be part of a comprehensive treatment plan based primarily on a CBT approach. Those who work in schools should be adept at recognizing an adolescent who shows signs of an incipient eating disorder. The more quickly treatment can begin, the better is the prognosis. And those who are already working with students diagnosed with an eating disorder need to know and maintain the pathways for these adolescents to access and participate in a comprehensive treatment plan.

SCHOOL-BASED INTERVENTIONS

As with any emotional or behavioral disorder, before an effective school-based intervention can be identified and implemented, a functional assessment needs to be conducted. The purpose of the assessment is to determine the frequency, intensity, and duration of the problem behavior—in this case, the eating disorder—as well as the function or purpose it serves for the affected individual.

To ensure the thoroughness and reliability of the assessment, it is recommended that multidisciplinary team members employ a strategic approach that includes (1) identifying and describing the problem behavior; (2) collecting baseline data as well as information about academic performance; (3) describing the context in which the behavior is observed; (4) completing a functional assessment form and/or behavior rating scale as appropriate; (5) conducting a direct observation; (6) developing a hypothesis; and (7) testing the hypothesis and then modifying it as necessary (Barnhill, 2005). Once a valid hypothesis has been established, the multidisciplinary team can develop an appropriate behavioral intervention plan (BIP) and have reasonable confidence in its likelihood of success.

Because anorexia nervosa, bulimia nervosa, and eating disorder, not otherwise specified, can have different etiologies and behavioral manifestations, we will provide an individual assessment and intervention plan for each of our three representative case examples.

Assessing the Problem: Siobhan

In the case involving Siobhan, a student diagnosed with anorexia nervosa, our assessment is as follows.

IDENTIFYING AND DESCRIBING THE PROBLEM BEHAVIOR   The most serious effect of Siobhan's AN in the classroom is its negative impact on her academic progress, particularly in Math, because of her extended lunch period, which causes her to miss the Math period entirely. A secondary but clearly related problem is the resentment created by the allocation of scant faculty resources to provide supervision to ensure she attains a minimum caloric intake.

COLLECTING BASELINE DATA AND ACADEMIC INFORMATION   During the preceding two-quarters, Siobhan has missed 85 percent of her Math classes, which has negatively impacted her grades in the course, despite efforts to make up the work after school. Before the institution of supervised lunch, with a required minimum caloric consumption, Siobhan's average grade in Math was a B+. After the imposition of supervision, Siobhan's grade in Math drop to a D. Furthermore, her Math teacher, as well as her homeroom teacher and teacher's assistant, have become resentful, not of Siobhan personally, they insist, but of the inequitable allocation of the teacher's assistant's time relative to Siobhan's mealtime supervision and monitoring. To illustrate the extent of this problem, Ms. S., the teacher's assistant assigned to Siobhan's homeroom, keeps a log of the time Siobhan takes to consume sufficient calories at lunch. She estimates that, on average, Siobhan takes 1 hour 25 minutes to eat her lunch. This is almost three times the lunch period allocation for other students. Furthermore, Ms. S. notes, the time Siobhan needs to consume her minimum number of calories has actually increased over the course of the school year.

DESCRIBING THE CONTEXT IN WHICH THE BEHAVIOR IS OBSERVED   Siobhan's problem behavior related to her eating disorder manifests only at mealtimes, specifically, at lunch, as it affects the school staff. Siobhan is on a strict high-calorie diet that is monitored and enforced by the school nurse. She and her parents have contracted with the school to promise that she will comply with the prescribed minimum calorie intake at lunch. A school representative, in this case the homeroom teacher's assistant, monitors her compliance in this matter. Although Siobhan is generally cooperative, the process of consuming food is nonetheless painstaking, sometimes lasting an hour and a half. After months of this tedious routine, the teacher's assistant is becoming impatient and resentful, and this is creating a very tense lunch-time atmosphere for both Siobhan and the teacher's assistant.

COMPLETING A FUNCTIONAL ASSESSMENT AND/OR BEHAVIOR RATING SCALES AS APPROPRIATE   A daily log is maintained by Siobhan's lunch monitor that documents both the start and end times for her lunch, determined by the time needed to achieve her target calorie intake. The monitor also provides an anecdotal entry describing Siobhan's demeanor and disposition throughout the meal. Periodic reviews of the log reveal changes in eating behavior and are used to plan or adjust treatment approaches, as well as target calorie intake levels. Siobhan is weighed daily at school by the nurse to monitor weight loss and gain, and to be sure that her body weight does not drop below the minimum level prescribed as "acceptable."

CONDUCTING A DIRECT OBSERVATION Because the lunch period is the only context in which the target behavior is observed and that observation is carefully recorded by Siobhan's lunch-time monitor, further direct observation is unnecessary.

DEVELOPING A HYPOTHESIS Siobhan does poorly in Math class because, to ensure sufficient food intake, she requires an extended lunch period that frequently extends past the time allocated for Math. She clearly needs either to take Math in a different time slot or receive a make-up lesson for each of the lessons she misses because of her extended lunch period. Furthermore, it is hoped that, as her treatment plan proves effective in helping her overcome her fear of gaining weight and her concern about maintaining a subnormal body weight, Siobhan will take less time to attain her target calorie level, thus enabling her, at some point, to complete her meal within the standard lunch period. Finally, we postulate that once Siobhan has demonstrated improvement toward achieving this goal, the resentment of staff will diminish and, ultimately, be replaced with a more positive, supportive attitude toward her.

TESTING THE HYPOTHESIS AND MODIFYING IT AS NECESSARY This aspect of the assessment can only be addressed once an appropriate behavioral intervention plan has been developed and implemented. Such a plan, once employed, will confirm or disconfirm the validity of the hypothesis.

Developing an Effective Behavioral Intervention Plan for Siobhan

According to the sound protocols established by Ryan, Halsey, and Mathews (2003), an effective BIP should address the following criteria: It should be (1) research-based and relevant; (2) only be implemented after informed consent has been given by the individual's parents; (3) document the steps of the intervention plan, including who will be responsible, when and where it will occur, and for how long; (4) establish real and measurable goals; and (5) establish a method to measure progress.

In Siobhan's case, the treatment plan established by her doctor and therapist involves a bi-modal approach consisting of a prescribed antidepressant, fluoxetine, and cognitive-behavioral therapy. Although teachers have no direct part in the administration of medication, they can provide important anecdotal observations about Siobhan's response to the prescribed medication in terms of weight gain, a reduction in obsessive thoughts about food, improved mood, and reduced abnormal eating behavior. Furthermore, teachers can record instances during the school day, and particularly during her supervised lunch period, when Siobhan monitors her thoughts, feelings, and behaviors, to track her assumptions about expressing emotions, forming close relationships, and the significance of a low body weight.

The behavioral goals for the school staff in conjunction with Siobhan's BIP are (1) a significant reduction in expressed and observed obsession with specific low-calorie foods as well as calorie totals, (2) an increase in positive statements about her body and a greater acceptance of clinically normal body weight, and (3) a less perfectionist and critical view of herself and others, leading to greater acceptance of others and improved interpersonal connections.

A secondary target goal is a significant reduction in the time required for Siobhan to consume the number of prescribed calories during lunch; ultimately, Siobhan should be able to do so within the standard time allotted for lunch. An indirect benefit of this goal would be Siobhan's ability to attend the full Math period every day, thus obviating the need for extracurricular tutoring.

Finally, an ancillary goal is the improvement of the aversive attitudes of the lunch monitors toward Siobhan. Clearly, as she is able to eat her lunch more quickly in compliance with standard time allocation, school personnel will not be spending an inordinate amount of time performing what they consider "menial" tasks, that is, observing Siobhan eat.

Teachers and other school staff are encouraged to support the treatment plan at every opportunity by providing positive reinforcement when Siobhan displays an appropriate perception of body image, as well as a healthy attitude toward food. Furthermore, staff members are encouraged to reinforce any expression that suggests acceptance of less than perfect performance on Siobhan's part, as well as for her tolerance of the imperfections of others. Lastly, teachers should also support Siobhan's efforts to socialize and communicate with peers and school staff.

Assessing the Problem: Michele

In the case involving Michele, a student diagnosed with bulimia nervosa, our assessment is as follows.

IDENTIFYING AND DESCRIBING THE PROBLEM BEHAVIOR   Michele is very careful to avoid eating in front of others at school. In fact, she restricts her snacking, as well as lunch to her car, which she is allowed to bring to school and intentionally parks in an isolated space far away from other students. She has been observed on several occasions dumping plastic bags, presumably containing food wrappers and containers, into the school's trash dumpster. An additional concern for teachers and administrators are reports that, immediately after lunch, Michele uses the bathroom. Female classmates consistently notice the unmistakable odor of vomit after she leaves the bathroom.

Thus, the concerns are twofold: (a) that Michele seems to be binging in secret, in violation of her treatment plan, and (b) that frequently, immediately after eating, she may be purging in the girls' bathroom.

COLLECTING BASELINE DATA AND ACADEMIC INFORMATION   Michele's teachers have been asked to closely monitor the frequency with which she goes to her car, as well as the number of times she is observed discarding trash bags. According to these observers, she unobtrusively goes to her car an average of three times during the school day, always providing a plausible explanation to her teachers. A woman teacher's assistant has been assigned to confirm the likelihood that Michele has purged after consuming food, and she reports the frequency of this as concurrent with the number of trips Michele makes to her car—on average, three times during the school day.

DESCRIBING THE CONTEXT IN WHICH THE BEHAVIOR IS OBSERVED Michele's binging and purging behavior occurs in secret; while in her car in the school parking lot, or in a bathroom cubicle. She is very discrete and painstaking in disguising these behaviors; for example, after purging, she brushes her teeth and gargles with mouthwash she brings in her handbag, and she covertly disposes of the plastic garbage bag she uses to discard food wrappers and containers.

COMPLETING A FUNCTIONAL ASSESSMENT AND/OR BEHAVIOR RATING SCALES AS APPROPRIATE A functional assessment has been conducted that identifies the purposes served by Michele's binging and purging as being beyond the scope of school-based interventions; however, teachers can support Michele's treatment plan by monitoring her bathroom visits after lunch or snacks and ensuring that she eats with her classmates and is not permitted an opportunity to isolate herself or be unaccounted for during lunchtime and breaks.

CONDUCTING A DIRECT OBSERVATION Several teachers and teacher's assistants have observed Michele binge-eating in her car, and both a woman teacher and the teacher's assistant have entered the girls' bathroom on several occasions while she was purging.

DEVELOPING A HYPOTHESIS Although the reasons for Michele's binging and purging are complex and multivariate, the important thing about this behavior that teachers should know is that it involves both an obsession with weight loss and food, as well as a feeling of disgust with her overeating and relief produced by purging—a chronic cycle of self-abuse.

TESTING THE HYPOTHESIS AND MODIFYING IT AS NECESSARY The hypothesis has been confirmed by clinical practitioners after careful and reliable assessments.

Developing an Effective Intervention Plan for Michele

As discussed previously, Michele's maladaptive behaviors are symptomatic of her diagnosed condition, bulimia nervosa. The behavioral intervention plan that was developed for implementation in the school involves the following components. In order to ensure that Michele does not engage in binge eating during the school day, a one-to-one aide is assigned to ensure that she does not leave the school building, access her locker, or use the snack machines. Furthermore, she is restricted to two snacks and a specific lunch menu that has been prepared by the school dietitian to meet Michele's unique nutritional requirements. The aide sits with her during lunch to ensure she consumes sufficient calories and adheres to the prescribed diet. In addition, the aide ensures that Michele does not use the washroom for at least 1 hour after eating lunch, to allow for the absorption of nutrients; after the compulsory 1 hour wait, the aide accompanies Michele to the bathroom to prevent her purging.

Assessing the Problem: Aaron

Our third case example involves Aaron, a student who has a binge eating disorder.

IDENTIFYING AND DESCRIBING THE PROBLEM BEHAVIOR   Aaron is a compulsive eater, who is obsessed with thoughts of food and an irresistible desire to consume. His obsession with food has negatively impacted his ability to make friends as well as his academic progress, which is compounded by his frequent removal from class.

COLLECTING BASELINE DATA AND ACADEMIC INFORMATION   Teachers have recorded each time Aaron was found eating in class or stashing food in his desk or backpack. Similarly, teachers have noted the scores of tests taken in all content areas, and these provide continuous evaluations of his academic performance throughout the escalation of his binge eating behavior.

DESCRIBING THE CONTEXT IN WHICH THE BEHAVIOR IS OBSERVED   Aaron is compulsive in his eating behavior, taking advantage of any opportunity to consume food, even attempting to consume snack foods in class. Driven by his compulsion, Aaron will consume available food until it is gone. He does not have the behavioral controls to stop, and this excessive behavior is negatively impacting his academic performance, as well as his social life.

COMPLETING A FUNCTIONAL ASSESSMENT FORM AND/OR BEHAVIOR RATING SCALES AS APPROPRIATE   The underlying function of Aaron's binge eating behavior is multifaceted and thus very complex, but it is clear that the consumption of food provides a powerful oral gratification that produces a feeling of mild euphoria and satisfaction. The results of assessments such as the *Survey for Eating Disorders* (SCOS; Gotestam & Agras, 1995) and the *Eating Disorder Diagnostic Scale* (EDDS; Stice et al., 2000), when compared with the behavior checklist completed on a daily basis by Aaron's teachers, underscore the severity and detrimental effects of his binge eating.

CONDUCTING A DIRECT OBSERVATION   Aaron's teachers have been careful to record any observed binge eating, defined as attempts, successful or not, to consume food during class or outside of the lunchroom.

DEVELOPING A HYPOTHESIS   Aaron's eating is clearly the result of his disorder, which causes him to obsess about food and compels him to consume it without restraint. The goal for school-based intervention is to employ teachers as external controls to help reduce, if not stop, Aaron's binge eating while in school.

The task facing the multidisciplinary team is precisely how best to help Aaron control his compulsive eating during school. With the help of the school psychologist, Aaron's therapist, the school dietitian, and the input of Aaron's pediatrician, the team has developed an intervention plan that they believe will prove effective in reducing the frequency of Aaron's binge eating, as well as provide a replacement behavior to mitigate the frustration caused by the restrictions placed on Aaron's food intake.

Developing an Effective Behavioral Intervention Plan for Aaron

While Aaron is engaged in the treatment plan developed by his therapist, which involves cognitive-behavioral approaches and self-monitoring techniques, the recommended intervention to be employed by teachers and school staff involves (1) response delay (Terre et al., 2006) and (2) stimulus control (Bowers & Andersen, 2007).

In the response-delay intervention, the teacher simply determines an alternative activity to substitute for the impulse to binge, or at least help to delay the impulse. Such alternative activities should be ones that elicit high interest on the part of the affected student. In Aaron's case, his teachers have determined that providing a box of Lego building blocks or a drawing pad and pencil stimulates him sufficiently to delay the compulsion to eat. The Lego blocks are preferred because Aaron is able to focus on schoolwork while creating structures with the blocks.

The use of stimulus control is another effective measure adopted by the multidisciplinary team as a school-based intervention. Aaron's teachers have determined that he typically craves sweets, such as candy bars, M&Ms, marshmallows, and toffee candy. On the recommendation of the school dietitian and with parental support, Aaron receives dried fruit as a nutritious, low-fat substitute for the sweet snacks he craves. Periodically, teachers will distribute a small, pre-measured plastic bag of dried fruit that Aaron can consume discreetly in class, without reservation or guilt, thus significantly reducing conflict and emotional outbursts while helping to curb Aaron's impulse to binge on high-calorie, non-nutritious snacks.

Thus far, these two interventions seem to be helping to reduce the target behaviors, identified as impulsive binging on unhealthy snack foods and the emotional outbursts and consequential physical restraint and removal from class that frequently results when Aaron is denied these snacks.

 FROM THE FIELD

Leah DeSole, Ph.D.

Leah DeSole is a licensed clinical psychologist and an expert in the field of eating disorders. She is affiliated with the New York City Eating Disorder Resource Center, and she is a member of the editorial board of *Eating Disorders: The Journal of Treatment and Prevention*. She also has served as adjunct faculty at Columbia University and Hunter College. In her private practice, she advocates a multidisciplinary team approach incorporating, as needed, the support of specialists in the fields of nutrition, medicine, acupuncture, and psychiatry. Together with clients, she advocates creating a personalized plan to move toward recovery utilizing cognitive-behavioral therapy and psychodynamic psychotherapy. Dr. DeSole is the author of *Making Contact: The Therapist's Guide to Conducting a Successful First Interview* (Boston: Allyn & Bacon, 2006). Dr. DeSole's responses here benefited from the help of David Steinmetz, a family systems therapist with a private practice in New York City. Dr. Steinmetz earned degrees in Family Constellations at The Bert Hellinger Institute, USA, Redding, Connecticut, and in Integrated Kabbalistic Healing at A Society of Souls, Lebanon, New Jersey. He has extensive training in "voice dialogue" with Dr. Jodi Prinzivalli at The School of Energetic Psychology, Ramsey, New Jersey; "visualization/imagery techniques and dream work" with Dr. Catherine Schainberg at The School of Images, New York, New York; and "object relations and psycho-spiritual development" with Drs. Alexis Johnson and Judith S. Schmidt at the Center for Intentional Living, South Salem, New York.

The problem of eating disorders appears to be growing exponentially among adolescent and preadolescent girls in schools, a trend you must be seeing in your practice. To what do you ascribe this alarming increase?

Epidemiological research cannot confirm the problem of eating disorders is growing exponentially in society. However, it can be stated with certainty that more cases of eating disorders are being reported nationwide among adolescent and preadolescent girls. Let me add that I believe the fact that more cases are being reported nationwide reflects success in the field. It suggests that there is greater community awareness regarding the signs and symptoms of eating disorders among students, teachers, and administrators in schools. It also suggests that the stigma associated with eating disorders, such as binge eating disorder, bulimia nervosa, and anorexia nervosa, is beginning to lessen. Word is spreading that eating disorders are legitimate illnesses, effective treatment is available, and recovery is possible. Whether or not it can

be proven that the problem of eating disorders is growing exponentially in a sense is a moot point: *What matters most is that people who need help increasingly are getting help.*

One of the most widely-discussed theories regarding why we are seeing more adolescent and preadolescent girls presenting with symptoms of eating disorders argues that it results in no small part from societal pressure. We are living in a society that progressively has placed greater emphasis on "beauty," or appearance, as an essential aspect of one's well-being. In common parlance, "To look good is to feel good." Moreover, increasingly, people who are viewed as beautiful are also seen as "better people" than those who deviate from society's standard beauty ideals. They are seen as smarter, more competent, and more successful than their physically less attractive counterparts. Making matters worse is society's shifting definition of what constitutes beauty. Over the years, it has steadily shifted to a more and more slender figure for preadolescent and adolescent girls alike. Paralleling the development of this new, narrower beauty ideal has been development of a $50 billion diet industry and an exponential rise in the popularity of plastic surgery. As a matter of fact, weight-loss competitions, plastic surgery challenges, and modeling contests are currently listed among the nation's top-rated television shows. Shows like these simply did not exist in prior generations.

Why the alarming increase of eating disorders specifically among preadolescent and adolescent girls in the schools today? Preadolescents and adolescents are keenly aware of society's current beauty ideal. They watch these top-rated, nationally televised shows. Furthermore, they are the primary consumers of women's fashion magazines. The majority of articles and advertisements in these magazines concern dieting, exercising, and how to become more attractive (hence "happy") girls. As a consequence, preadolescent and adolescent girls are exposed to messages regarding their bodies and beauty at an intensity (and of a kind) unknown to prior generations.

And preadolescent and adolescent girls are, unfortunately, particularly susceptible to these messages. They come at a time in their development when their bodies are changing and they are just beginning to establish a sense of personal identity. Their bodies may represent a ready canvas on which they can express themselves. For some, their bodies are the sole area in which they feel autonomous and in control: What they eat and how much they exercise is within their power. Societal messages regarding not only the importance of beauty for women but also a beauty ideal that is unhealthy set the stage for the development of eating disorders. Indeed, I fear that they may have become a socially acceptable way for adolescent girls to alleviate anxiety, enact their desire for control, and elevate their sense of self-esteem.

Could you provide an abbreviated profile of the "typical" girl that you treat for an eating disorder?

I am tempted to say there is no "typical" girl that I treat for an eating disorder. I think it is all too easy to lose sight of the distinctiveness of each person who suffers from an eating disorder by describing anyone as typical. Nonetheless, I see commonalities among my patients with distinct eating disorders such as anorexia nervosa or bulimia. These may be most easily described according to a biopsychosocial model, one that conceptualizes a person across three specific domains: biological, psychological, and sociological.

My sense is that many of the girls I see in my practice possess a particular cognitive set. One such cognitive set is a kind of chronic dissatisfaction and self-critique of their bodies. Typically, this is coupled with a constant fear of becoming fat, regardless of their size. Another common cognitive set I observe involves an intricately woven notion of expectancies such as: "If I reach a 103 pounds, fit into the jeans I wore 3 years ago, and consume only 700 calories a day, I will be happy, admired, and

successful—both in relationships and at school." Given that these expectancies tend to be unrealistic, failure is likely. And this highlights another tendency I observe in my practice among adolescent girls with eating disorders. There is a tendency for patients to think in dichotomous terms: The world is black and white; there is no gray. This thinking is epitomized by the firmly held belief, regularly voiced by persons with eating disorders, that "there are good foods and there are bad foods."

In addition to these cognitive sets, I observe that girls with eating disorders tend to manifest distinct temperaments. In my own practice I can say that it is not uncommon to observe anorexic girls whom parents and teachers alike describe as having "controlling personalities." These girls are disciplined in their social activity, oriented toward achievement in school, and seek comfort in routine. They want to be "good girls," and they describe feeling strong and competent when they restrict what they eat. Often, they do not seek out self-gratification or pleasure, and they are not sexually active. In contrast, the bulimic girls whom I see in my practice more commonly describe themselves as feeling "out of control." All the while, their parents and teachers still describe them as "being controlling." Outwardly they may appear as disciplined as their anorectic peers; inwardly they are aware of being overwhelmed by feelings, craving intense relationships, and behaving impulsively. What I observe among both groups are difficulties identifying feelings, tolerating intense states of arousal, and adequately soothing themselves without the use of food.

The typical girl whom I see in my practice is white and middle-to-upper class. That said, I am increasingly seeing Latino and Asian patients, as well as young men. Religion and ethnicity often vary as well. However, within this variation I have found that most of my patients seem to identify as "American" rather than with any particular religious or ethnic group. Moreover, few of them have a spiritual practice in their lives. With regard to family, my observation is that often an extreme exists: Either the girl is very attached to her family (i.e., "My mother is my best friend") or notably detached (i.e., "We never talk"). Patients often report that one or both of their parents have body image issues and engage in behaviors such as chronic dieting or compulsive overeating. Lastly, it is not un-common for parents to openly discuss their chil-dren's bodies and/or eating habits. The discussion may be praise or criticism. Neither seems to matter. What matters most is that the patient experiences a kind of conditional love, i.e., "I like you more when you are a size 4," which is felt although it may be unsaid.

How is an understanding of the character-istic behaviors of an individual with an eating disorder helpful to the treatment process?

To understand the characteristic behaviors of an individual with an eating disorder is to un-derstand the patient herself. It is crucial: It is the basis for empathy and comprehension of the patient's struggle, and forms the foundation of the relationship between the patient and therapist—all good treatment begins from this relationship. Adolescents often come to treat-ment reluctantly. Many are not ready to change their behaviors, let alone allow another person (the therapist) into their world and actually tell someone what they are thinking, feeling, and doing on a daily basis. Often, they will not offer information about their disordered eating patterns unless they are specifically asked.

Knowing what to ask is very important. What may be less obvious is the importance of *knowing how to ask*. For example, I do not ask an anorexic adolescent, "Do you take diuret-ics?" I may say, "I know girls sometimes take water pills or diuretics when they feel bloated; how often will you take something like that? Several times a day or week?" Eating disorder specialists will know to ask the appropriate questions in a way that is most likely to yield accurate information. And people with eating disorders, especially adolescents, may be reluc-tant to be truthful. They may fear criticism. They may worry that they will anger their par-ents, and they will be punished. They may not

be ready to change or they may worry that if they speak truthfully they will be pushed to change at a rate that is unacceptable to them. They also may be unaware of their behavior, and unless they are asked questions about their behavior directly *and* in a nonthreatening man-ner, this information may not be available to their consciousness. This knowledge is the key to guiding treatment and establishing achiev-able goals for recovery.

Are you ever asked to provide information to schools, since many of the individuals you treat are school-age?

While I don't, several of my colleagues at The New York City Eating Disorder Resource Center with which I am affiliated are strong advocates for education regarding eating disorders and speak regularly at schools. The Center, itself, also maintains a website listing nationwide re-sources for individuals, families, and organiza-tions (www.edrcnyc.org). In addition, there are several national organizations that provide these services in a variety of educational settings across the country. These organizations include NEDA (The National Association for Eating Dis-orders), EDreferral.com (Eating Disorder Referral and Information Center), and AED (The Acad-emy for Eating Disorders), to name a few.

What would you like to share with teach-ers, administrators, and school clinicians that might assist them in identifying and working with affected students? Could you share any caveats that might help teachers and administrators avoid making costly mistakes in working with students who have eating disorders?

These questions are important. I, myself, err on the side of caution in response. I do not believe that teachers and administrators should work with students who have been diagnosed with an eating disorder *around their eating disor-dered behavior*. I think the efforts of teachers and administrators should remain in the do-main of academic guidance and not in the provision of psychological services to their students. In my experience, the psychological health of students is best left to trained professionals in the field. Teachers and administrators can avoid making costly mistakes by routinely making referrals to them for evaluation and treatment.

School clinicians can be an excellent resource in this regard. They are the ideal members of the school administration to refer students who may have an eating disorder for evaluation. Given their clinical training, they will know the community resources that are available, and they will know how to communicate the school's concerns to a student in a compassionate manner. In addition, my sense is that they are more likely to reach out to an affected student and be heard, since they do not grade or discipline students.

I believe schools would serve their students well by targeting their efforts at the prevention of disordered eating attitudes. Intervening after an eating disorder has developed is far too challenging and costly.

Recent studies point to an increase in the identification of what is currently termed "binge eating disorder." Based on your clinical experience, do you think this is a legitimate disorder? Why is it proliferating, and what can teachers and administrators do to help prevent its growth and provide assistance to affected students?

I do consider binge eating disorder (BED) a legitimate disorder. BED is characterized by recurrent binge episodes of binge eating without the compensatory behaviors of bulimia nervosa such as purging, laxative use, or excessive exercise. A binge may be defined by several factors, such as a loss of control of one's eating (or eating more than one intended at one sitting), eating in secret, and eating while distracted or agitated. Feelings associated with BED include significant anxiety, distress, shame, and sadness.

There is a lot of speculation about why binge eating is proliferating in society. It has been suggested that two trends are responsible for this development: increased availability of high-calorie food and the development of the fast-food industry. Perhaps unwittingly, the government supports these trends by subsidizing the production of high-calorie, non-nutritious foods rather than healthier alternatives. Indeed, a paradox exists: More government money goes to support the production of food which we are supposed to eat less of, such as meat, dairy, and high-fructose corn syrup, rather than food we are supposed to eat more of, such as fruits, grains, and vegetables. The net result is that less nutritious food is not only more available but also cheaper than more nutritious alternatives. Furthermore, research reveals that these less nutritious foods may trigger binge eating, as well as overeating in general, thus contributing to the current proliferation of BED.

As with other eating disorders, I believe teachers and administrators can serve an important role in the prevention of BED by providing education. In addition, schools can make a significant impact by *monitoring the foods they make available to students* in the hallways, as well as the school cafeteria. In school cafeterias, some administrators have elected to eliminate the use of deep fryers in food preparation. More and more schools are consulting with nutritionists in the preparation of healthy lunches. Some even have opted to provide students with breakfast, out of a growing recognition that having breakfast improves students' concentration and mood. Likewise, some administrators have decided to eliminate candy and soda machines in school hallways. Studies suggest that having these machines in school invites snacking, binging, and ultimately overeating. The susceptibility of preadolescents and adolescents, in particular, to these foods and beverages has come under increasing public scrutiny. It has been proposed that once children's taste buds become accustomed to sweet, salty, high-fat foods, it is difficult for them to enjoy other foods. Only now is research being done to asses how eating these foods may contribute to the development of

BED, as well as be harmful to the physical development of growing adolescent bodies.

Although current research indicates that eating disorders primarily affect girls and young women, there is growing evidence that this trend might be changing to include more boys and young men. Can you speak to this recent development from your experience as a practitioner?

Increasingly I see boys and young men in my private practice who are affected by eating disorders. These include the full spectrum of eating disorders from anorexia nervosa and bulimia nervosa to binge eating disorder. I attribute this development to many factors, but essentially they all boil down to one: shifting societal norms. Just as there is for girls and young women, there is growing public scrutiny of the bodies of boys and young men. Narrowly defined standards of attractiveness based on weight that once applied only to women are now being applied to men as well.

Men, conventionally, were thought to be "protected" from developing eating disorders. According to a traditional chauvinist maxim, "Men are evaluated by the size of their wallet; women by the size of their dress." This has shifted, and males are being judged by their size as well. It has become a measure of one's worth and a reflection of one's character. Thin, fit boys and young men are seen as more competent, healthy, and successful than boys and young men of a larger size. For example, male models are venerated by the current generation of boys, in stark contrast to the past, in which it was thought to be an embarrassment to be a male model. In recent decades, men's magazines have proliferated. And they are not just talking about news, sports, and sex—now they contain articles and advertisements concerning diet, exercise, and sculpting various body parts. Such topics would have been an anathema in the past for men, much like ordering a light beer in a bar in front of one's friends or date.

These shifting social norms encourage young boys and men to be conscious of their weight, shape, and appearance. Sadly, the "protection" that they once had from developing eating disorders has eroded. Should a young boy with a biological predisposition for an eating disorder experience a stressful event, current American culture will do little to discourage him from turning to his body to provide a release from tension and sense of self-esteem. This is what I have observed in my practice. Adolescent boys who become overly reliant on controlling their weight in order to relieve tension and increase their self-confidence are at a high risk of developing a serious eating disorder.

Finally, would you share a "success story" from your practice that offers hope and underscores the benefits of good practice in treating school-age children and youth affected by these debilitating disorders?

I have had several "success stories" in my practice. The one I will share here is a composite of three patients, each of whom shares similar histories, as well as paths to recovery. I will call this patient Isabelle.

Isabelle was referred to me by her medical doctor, a specialist in adolescent medicine. Her presenting problem was anorexia nervosa (AN). At the time, Isabelle was 16 years old and attending a private school in Manhattan. She was 5' 8" and 110 pounds. Like many AN sufferers, she was a white, middle/upper-class "American" girl who did not identify with a particular ethnicity or religion.

My overall approach to treatment in this case was twofold. I began with cognitive-behavioral therapy (CBT) and subsequently provided supportive psychotherapy. CBT methods focus on the thoughts and behaviors of the patient. I find that it offers much needed relief from the initial experience of symptoms. I used supportive psychotherapy in later sessions, primarily to address relapse prevention. In my experience, supportive psychotherapy is necessary to tackle underlying stressors such as managing relationships with friends and family. It also enables patients to cope with the myriad of feelings that arise in recovery around weight gain and body image issues. In addition to using CBT and supportive psychotherapy, I take a team approach: I coordinate care with medical doctors, nutritionists, the patient's parents, and anyone else involved in treatment.

Isabelle realized that she did not really know how to convey her feelings appropriately. Indeed, she was accustomed to smiling unless she was under great duress, such as in the session with her mother. We talked about where she learned to smile all the time and how she might find ways to express her emotions without feeling overwhelmed by them. We also discussed how "fat is not a feeling," but that the associations that she makes with being fat *are feelings*: sadness, anxiety, and fear. Likewise, I encouraged her to discuss the feelings she associated with gaining control over her eating disorder, such as feeling powerful and responsible. Subsequently, we widened our discussion of feelings beyond the realm of food and eating to

her relationships with others. It was apparent that as she became less preoccupied with her weight, she had more time to attend to others. Later sessions increasingly focused less on food and more on the people in her life: friends, boyfriends, teachers, and family members.

Isabelle's weight eventually stabilized around 118 pounds. By that time, she was back on the track team. She no longer was weighed by her medical doctor, and she saw the nutritionist whenever she wished. We began to meet every other week. Eventually, we met once a month. I often joked, "Use me as needed, like aspirin." When problems arose, she would come in more often. One summer, between her freshman and sophomore year of college, she came in weekly. By then, she had the normal struggles that we all have. I consider her recovered from AN; however, it may always be her Achilles heel. During times of difficulty, it may be the way her frustration first becomes evident. Over time, I remain hopeful that one day this too may "heal."

Summary

The increase in the last few decades of identification of school-aged children and youth who have eating disorders has been alarming. Despite the temptation to ascribe this increase to the preoccupation with "thinness" on the part of many girls and young women in Western industrial societies, the real reasons that these young people engage in this self-destructive behavior are complex and multivariate.

Regardless of the cause or causes, the fact that many girls and young women, and, to a lesser but ever-increasing degree, young men, are affected by one or more of these disorders compels school staff to become involved. Although there are clearly characteristics that are common to *all* eating disorders—namely, a preoccupation with eating, concomitant behavioral and psychological effects, and significant dysfunction in patterns of daily living, as well as quality of life (Lock & Le Grange, 2006)—there presently appear to be three distinct subtypes: anorexia nervosa, bulimia nervosa, and binge eating disorder or, as it is currently referred to, eating disorder, not otherwise specified (Striegel-Moore & Bulik, 2007).

The most lethal of these disorders, anorexia nervosa, is typically characterized by a pathological drive to be thin and a fear of becoming fat. This obsession with being thin results in a severely restricted diet that may be exacerbated by extreme exercise and purging. If left untreated, AN can result in death as a result of organ failure (Rome & Ammerman, 2003; National Institute of Mental Health Home Page, 2007).

Bulimia nervosa is a prevalent eating disorder that affects both adolescents and young adults. It can be comorbid with AN, which is consistent with the current views of eating disorders as a continuum of symptom progression from less serious to more serious. The core symptom of BN is described as re-current, compulsive binge eating episodes involving large quantities of high-calorie food, followed, most typically, by purging (Levine & Piran, 2005).

The third, recently proposed subtype, is binge eating disorder (currently classified as ED-NOS). The defining characteristic of binge eating disorder is eating excessive amounts of high-calorie food within a short period of time. Individuals diagnosed with this disorder are typically obese but seemingly unconcerned about their excessive weight (Lock & Le Grange, 2006).

Various causes have been hypothesized for eating disorders. Some of the more investigated ones include biological factors, psychological factors, familial factors, and sociocultural factors. Of these four, biological and genetic factors have been best supported by research; it has been shown that girls who grow up in a family in which one or both parents or a sibling have an eating disorder are much more predisposed to develop one. It is further suspected that individuals who have eating disorders may suffer from over-activity of serotonin, which would decrease their appetite for food. In any event, a review of the research suggests that the cause of an eating disorder is multidetermined and varies greatly across individuals, suggesting that several causative variables may be in play.

The assessment of eating disorders typically involves a medical evaluation to determine the cause of weight loss, malnutrition, and electrolyte imbalance, as well as an interview with a clinical psychologist. Further evaluation can be conducted by a dietitian to determine the kinds of foods and quantities an individual suspected of having an eating disorder consumes. In addition, many standardized assessments can be used by clinicians to confirm a diagnosis.

Treatments for eating disorders range from hospitalization, in extreme cases in which the individual is health-compromised and at risk for serious health complications or death, to cognitive-behavioral therapy, which may help the affected individual reframe faulty perceptions of body image—for example, equating extreme thinness with beauty. The two treatments we have discussed in the chapter that are most easily adapted to classroom use are response delay and stimulus control.

To conclude, as the number of students diagnosed with an eating disorder continues to increase, classroom teachers will inevitably work with an affected individual. Understanding the characteristics of eating disorders, their causes, developmental course, and treatment interventions, will prove invaluable to the classroom teacher in preparing to work effectively with these students.

Tips for Teachers

For students who have anorexia nervosa:

1. Avoid commenting on the individual's thinness.
2. Find things that you can genuinely compliment in the student (e.g., attractive dress, academic performance relative to a real accomplishment, pleasant demeanor).
3. Give the student as much of your attention and positive reinforcement as possible; give generously!
4. Model healthy eating practices, eat good food, and consume healthy portions.
5. Display pictures of "real" people in the classroom; these should include individuals who

are full-figured, of various shapes and sizes, doing everyday things. Avoid reinforcing the student's obsession with "perfectionism."
6. Accept less-than-perfect work. Remind everyone in your class that learning new skills takes time and most of life consists of working through processes; ideally, we improve as we practice.
7. Avoid bringing food for the individual or suggesting that she "needs to eat more" to look healthy (the student who has AN will be unlikely to eat the food and will feel embarrassed at being the focus of attention).

Remember that for the student who has AN, eating is a very private ritual.

8. Keep students engaged in interesting, meaningful work; hopefully they will "discover" avocations or activities that help them enjoy life more and be more accepting of themselves as they learn that they can engage in rewarding activities and share these experience with others.

9. Stay in close contact with parents and the school counselor, dietitian, and psychologist and be ready to support the treatment plan as appropriate and where feasible.

10. Keep parents and clinicians informed of any significant behavior or changes in behavior observed in the classroom (e.g., melancholia or depression, lack of interest in others or schoolwork, a morbid preoccupation with death, expressed disgust with body weight or image).

For students who have bulimia nervosa:

1. Praise the student for some legitimately laudable quality.

2. Celebrate the normal body type. Avoid displaying pictures of ultraslim celebrities or models.

3. Model healthy eating and stress the importance of good nutrition.

4. Compliment the individual's wardrobe or "look." You can honestly say, "Those colors really make your eyes stand out," or "I really like the way you've styled your hair," etc.

5. Be alert but don't overreact to the student's requests to use the bathroom.

6. Support the treatment plan developed by clinicians as appropriate and feasible within the framework of the classroom and school (e.g., don't let the student cajole you into letting her use the bathroom immediately after lunch if the treatment plan prohibits it, even though the student insists that she really "has to go," unless she can be provided with one-on-one supervision).

7. If the student's behavioral intervention plan calls for you or your assistant to supervise her during lunch, make it an enjoyable experience for both of you and really "enjoy" your food.

8. Make sure that the student is included in class discussions and activities and provide frequent opportunities for her to choose assignments and projects. Providing choices is empowering.

9. Create cooperative groups when possible and ensure that the student has opportunities to make relevant contributions to the group process.

10. Ask the student for her input in class debates and discussions. Make her feel valued by reinforcing the importance you place on her contributions to the learning process and the classroom community.

For students who have binge eating disorder:

1. Avoid shaming the student for his impulsive eating.

2. Substitute tactual/kinesthetic activities such as engagement in a preferred craft, such as model building, or a board game such as chess, during breaks in the academic routine, as a distraction from the compulsion to eat.

3. Keep a container of dried fruit or sugar-free candy as a healthier, low-calorie substitute for traditional high-calorie snacks when the student craves a treat.

4. Avoid making comments about the student's weight and ensure that the student's classmates do likewise. Instead, invite the individual to go for a walk around the school grounds with you or a peer during lunch.

5. Prohibit or restrict access to snack and soda machines, and lobby the administration to allow only ones that dispense healthy beverages and snacks, such as fruit juices, water, pretzels, popcorn, and trail mix.

6. Avoid eating in the classroom; restrict food consumption to the cafeteria or staff room.

7. Similarly, don't permit students to eat in the classroom; encourage them to eat in the cafeteria or outside the school building.

8. Avoid discussing favorite foods and meals with the student, as this will only serve as a stimulus for the desire to snack.

Focus Questions Revisited

1. How are anorexia nervosa and bulimia nervosa currently differentiated, and what do researchers think about the relationship between these two eating disorders?

A Sample Response

The diagnostic criterion for identifying AN is the insistence of the affected individual that she is overweight, and the most typical response to this concern is a severe reduction in caloric intake. In contrast, the individual diagnosed with BN eats impulsively, consuming a great quantity of food at one time, afterwards feeling intense shame and disgust, which is mitigated by purging.

2. Describe the diagnostic criteria for identifying a binge eating disorder.

A Sample Response

Binge eating disorder is characterized by excessive consumption by an affected individual of high-calorie foods within a short period of time. As the disorder affects the adolescent, periods of excessive food consumption or binging may be intermittent. Furthermore, unlike individuals diagnosed with AN and BN, persons with BED appear to be unconcerned about their weight and do not engage in purging after excessive eating.

3. Imagine that you are a classroom teacher in a local middle school and you notice that one of your female students refuses to eat lunch with her classmates and routinely uses the bathroom immediately after lunch. Concerned students ask to speak with you privately and confide that they have witnessed this student "throwing up" on numerous occasions after lunch, which confirms your suspicions. What should you do, as a concerned teacher, to help this individual?

A Sample Response

As the teacher of this young adolescent, I would seek the help of the school psychologist. I would also contact the girl's parents to see whether they were aware of the possibility that their daughter might have an eating disorder, and whether they had observed similar behavioral characteristics, such as binging and purging, at home. If a treatment plan is already in place, I would follow it conscientiously; however, if none had been developed, I would convey my concerns to the school's multidisciplinary team and request a preliminary evaluation. Finally, once a diagnosis had been confirmed and a treatment plan developed, as in the case of Michele, I would ensure that she received supervision during the lunch period and restrict bathroom use to at least an hour after lunch, also monitoring her bathroom visits.

4. What are some things you could do, as the teacher of a student who has anorexia nervosa (like Siobhan) who insists that she is fat when it is obvious that she is seriously underweight?

A Sample Response

I would follow the treatment plan as developed by the student's psychologist or physician to the extent possible. Such a plan would likely require that the individual's teachers maintain a record of eating-related behaviors, including episodes of binging, preoccupation with calorie counting, and perceived body image. In addition, I would avoid making comments about weight and extolling thinness and I would point out examples of healthy body types, as well as the importance of consuming healthy foods in quantity. If requested, I would monitor the student during lunch to ensure that sufficient calories were consumed. On the other hand, I would avoid passing judgment about the individual's acute thinness or exhorting her to eat more and gain weight. Furthermore, I would find meaningful ways to provide positive reinforcement for the student's achievements, affording her opportunities to make choices in the classroom and take "reasonable risks" while deemphasizing the need to be "perfect." Finally, I would ensure that the student feels accepted and valued in my class and that this acceptance is unconditional.

5. Suppose that you had a student who was grossly overweight and a binge eater, constantly hoarding and consuming high-calorie, non-nutritious foods both inside and outside of your classroom. What could you do to help this student?

A Sample Response

I would provide nutritious, low-calorie snacks such as trail mix, whole-wheat pretzels, and dried fruit for distribution to students both as a reward, and, in the case of the student who has BED, as a healthy alternative to "junk food." In addition, I would avoid embarrassing or shaming the student by making comments about his impulsive eating or his excessive weight. In contrast, I would try to model healthy eating habits by selecting nutritious foods, enjoyed during scheduled breaks outside of the classroom. Finally, I would provide alternative activities to replace the student's cravings for food; such as, a doodle pad, a favorite board game, Lego blocks, or similar tactual/kinesthetic materials that could be played with during class breaks, lunch period, or other free time.

Chapter 8

Depressive Disorders, Bipolar Disorder, and Suicide Prevention in School-Age Children and Youth

Photodisc/Getty Images

FOCUS QUESTIONS

1. How would you differentiate between a student who has major depression and one who has dysthymia?

2. What are the characteristics of bipolar disorder II, and how might they affect a student's academic and social performance?

3. What steps would you take if you suspected that a child in your class might be clinically depressed?

4. What related services personnel might be important resources to you as the classroom teacher of a child with a mood disorder? How might these personnel provide support and/or assistance?

5. Which of the models of depression would be most helpful to you as a classroom teacher? Provide a rationale for each of your selections.

6. How is knowing about comorbidities (e.g., between bipolar disorder and attention-deficit hyperactivity disorder) potentially helpful to you as the classroom teacher of a child or adolescent who has a mood disorder?

7. What observation protocol might be helpful to classroom teachers in providing relevant data for a child assigned to them who is suspected of having a mood disorder?

8. What are some of the warning signs you would look for in assessing a student's risk of suicide?

PARASUICIDE

An apparent attempt at suicide, commonly called a suicidal gesture, in which the aim is not death—for example, a sublethal drug overdose or wrist slash. Previous parasuicide is a predictor of suicide. The increased risk of subsequent suicide persists without decline for at least two decades.

Mood disorders, which include major depressive disorder and bipolar disorder, are clearly more prevalent among school-age children and youth today (Geller, Zimerman, Williams, Bolhofner, & Craney, 2001; Kowatch, Emslie, & Kennard, 1997; Reichart, 2005). The reasons for this increase in identification may include, in part, the improved screening instruments developed within the last decade, as well as a better understanding and delineation of the characteristics that define these disorders (Reichart, Wals, & Hillegers, 2004). Correspondingly, suicide and **parasuicide**, the two most pernicious outcomes connected with mood disorders, are also on the rise among children and adolescents (Minino, Arias, Kochanek, Murphy, & Smith, 2002; Office of Statistics and Programming, National Center for Injury Prevention and Control, Center for Disease Control, 2006).

In this chapter we provide current, research-based information about depressive disorders, bipolar disorder, and suicide prevention, and a model of assessment and recommended interventions using real-life case examples and anecdotes for each. After this thorough introduction, enhanced by illustrative cases, we offer further suggestions for effective intervention and review. We believe it is vital to the effectual integration of students who have these debilitating disorders that their teachers are knowledgeable about the characteristics and research-based interventions that can enhance their chance for success in school and in society.

CASE EXAMPLE: Emily

Emily had always been "daddy's little girl." Everyone close to her family noted the bond between Emily and her father; her mother admits being envious of their relationship. At school, Emily performed well, scoring in the 90th percentile and above on most tests and exams. She was also very active in school and extracurricular activities such as concert band and the science club. Similarly, Emily was a proficient soccer player, as well as a talented first base player in the girls' softball league. Neighbors and teachers remember her as an energetic, gregarious child who was always smiling, but that all changed the year Emily was in seventh grade—the year her father and "best friend" was diagnosed with pancreatic cancer.

As treatment after treatment proved unsuccessful in slowing the disease and her father's prognosis was assessed as grave, a coincidental change became evident in Emily. She stopped eating, her demeanor changed from ebullient to somber, her grades declined precipitously, she lost interest in her many school and extracurricular activities, and she withdrew socially. These profound behavioral changes climaxed with the death of her father in February of Emily's seventh-grade year. Her mother notes that, at her father's funeral, Emily seemed emotionally detached and that she subsequently withdrew from all social activities, finding even attending school an arduous task.

Family members remarked at the fact that, despite the close relationship between father and daughter, they never observed Emily displaying emotion over her father's death. Her mother and other relatives consigned this lack of emotional response to Emily's grief process and were sure that, in due time, she would rebound and return to being the "Emily" they all knew and loved. However, things did not change; in fact, they seemed to get worse. As the months wore on, Emily began to withdraw more and more, as if she were retreating into some dark tunnel in which she felt safe and secure. When, a year after her father's death, Emily's emotional state remained unchanged, Mrs. Helm, Emily's mother, contacted the school's psychologist, who in turn referred her to a psychiatrist who specializes in cases involving children and adolescents with mood disorders. This clinician diagnosed Emily with major depression and prescribed a multimodal treatment regimen consisting of cognitive-behavioral therapy, medication, and family therapy. In addition, the school psychologist scheduled a meeting with Emily's teachers and school administrators to explain the treatment process; the relevant aspects of the cognitive-behavioral therapy, and the beneficial and adverse effects of the medication prescribed.

CHARACTERISTICS OF MOOD DISORDERS

Mood disorders, also known as affective disorders, are abnormalities and disturbances in the regulation of mood. There are basically two types of mood disorders: depressive disorders, characterized by periods of sadness and bipolar disorders, characterized by alternating moods of sadness and mania. The consideration and diagnosis of mood disorders in children has had a historical development. Before the 1960s, when the field of psychology was dominated by psychoanalysis, children were considered incapable of being in a state of depression because of insufficient formation of personality structure (Sabatino, Webster, & Vance, 2001). In the 1960s, Glasser (1965) advanced the idea of *masked depression* in children, whose manifestation of depression, in contrast to adults, can be irritable, agitated, and disruptive.

By the 1980s, the prevailing opinion was that childhood depression was not all that separate from adult depression but did have some singular characteristics such as conduct problems and school refusal. Some even put forth the idea that childhood and adult depression are mirror images of each other (Sabatino et al., 2001). Today, the prevailing view seems to be a research-based cognitive developmental view of child and adolescent depression. Depression exists across the life span, but its diagnosis requires age-level consideration because symptom manifestation is different for different age groups.

MAJOR DEPRESSIVE DISORDER (MDD)

A depressive disorder in which symptoms cause significant impairment in social and/or occupational/school functioning.

The highs rates of comorbidity for children and adolescents with **major depressive disorder (MDD)** raises the question of whether this high rate "is the result of the lack of a well-developed exclusionary criteria in this age group or whether it represents true comorbid disorders" (Kowatch, Emslie, Wilkaitis, & Dingle, 2005, p. 144). There are many psychiatric disorders (e.g., anxiety, learning disabilities, personality disorders, substance abuse, eating disorders, and disruptive disorders) that have symptoms that overlap with MDD but do not meet the full diagnostic criteria. In such cases, the child or adolescent must be monitored to assure that what may be depressive symptoms do not evolve into a more serious disorder.

PREVALENCE OF DEPRESSIVE DISORDERS

DYSTHYMIA

A mood disorder on the depressive spectrum. It is considered less severe than major depression but is of a more chronic nature. It is explained more fully later in the chapter.

The DSM-IV-TR (American Psychiatric Association, 2000) divides depressive disorders into three types: major depression; **dysthymia**; and depressive disorder, not otherwise specified. This last category is used for those who do not quite meet the criteria for major depression. Major depression occurs in approximately 2 percent of children and 5 percent of adolescents, and dysthymia in 2 percent of children and 4 percent of adolescents (Muriel, Bostic, & Dolan, 2002). In childhood, girls and boys are equally likely to be diagnosed with depression; but by adolescence, girls are twice as likely to become depressed. Among clinical adolescent samples, however, the gender effects of having a diagnosis of a MDD are insignificant, although there are gender differences in symptom presentation. Girls have more mood symptoms such as feeling sad and depressed, whereas boys have higher rates of irritability (Weller, Weller, & Danielyan, 2004a).

Most experts believe that depression in childhood and adolescence is underdiagnosed, and there are several reasons for this. As mentioned previously, the manifestation of symptoms can be different than what is typically thought of as depression (e.g., vegetative states of psychomotor retardation, loss of appetite, excessive sleep). Another factor is that children do not have the capacity to express in verbal terms their emotions and may present with dubious somatic complaints—just "not feeling well" (Weller, Weller, & Danielyan, 2004b). Because it is highly comorbid with other disorders, underlying depression may often be overlooked. Studies have estimated the cumulative percentage of depression by late adolescence range from 10 to 20 percent (Kessler, McGonagle, Zhao, & Nelson 1994; Lewinsohn, Rohde, & Seeley, 1998; Shaffer, Fisher, Dulcan, & Davies, 1996).

MAJOR DEPRESSIVE DISORDER

According to the DSM-IV-TR (American Psychiatric Association, 2000), a child or adolescent diagnosed with MDD has had one or more major depressive episodes without ever having a manic episode. Table 8.1 lists the features of a depressive episode. Depressed or irritable mood must be present during a 2 week period along with four or more of the associated features. Although the DSM-IV-TR uses the same criteria to diagnose depression in adults and children, it does allow irritable mood to be substituted for depressed mood when dealing with children and adolescents. Depressed children and adolescents can differ in their clinical presentation. Children tend to show more symptoms of anxious and somatic complaints, whereas adolescents tend to have sleep or appetite disturbances, suicidal thoughts or behavior, and social or school impairment. Coyle et al. (2003) suggested that, in prepubertal depression, environmental factors are more a primary influence, in contrast to adolescent depression, in which genetic factors play a more primary role.

TABLE 8.1   Features of a Depressive Episode

Discriminating Features

1. Depressed mood or loss of interest or pleasure
2. Change from usual functioning
3. Not due to substances or a medical condition

Consistent Features

1. Appetite and sleep disturbances
2. Impaired social or academic functioning
3. Absence of use of mood-altering substances
4. Absence of physical condition that alters mood

Variable Features

1. Irritability
2. Weight loss or weight gain
3. Insomnia or hypersomnia
4. Psychomotor agitation or retardation
5. Fatigue or loss of energy
6. Feelings of worthlessness and inappropriate guilt
7. Impaired concentration and change in school performance
8. Suicidal ideation
9. Diurnal variation, with worsening of symptoms in the morning
10. Unexplained somatic complaints
11. Sleep–wake cycle reverse

Source: From "Mood Disorders" by R. A. Emslie, G. J. Wilkaitis, and A. D. Dingle in *Child and Adolescent Psychiatry* (p. 134) by S. B. Sexon and R. B. David (Eds.), 2005, Malden, MA: Blackwell Publishers. Copyright 2005 by Blackwell Publishers. Adapted with permission.

Course of MDD

MDD is an episodic condition that can recur. If it does recur after a 2 month interval, the diagnosis is MDD, recurrent (American Psychiatric Association, 2000), and what occurs during the interval is important. Several studies (Kovacs & Paulaukas, 1984; McCauley, Myers, Mitchell, & Calderon, 1993; Strober, Lampert, Schmidt, & Morrell, 1993) found that more than 90 percent of children and adolescents recover from an initial episode of MDD within 1 to 2 years of onset. After recovery, however, children and adolescents have high rates of relapse. Studies have found a cumulative relapse rate of 72 percent within 5 years (Birmaher, Ryan, Williamson, & Brent, 1996; Kovacs & Paulaukas, 1984), 45 percent within 2 years (Asarnow & Carlson, 1988), 54 percent within 3 years (McCauley et al., 1993), and 39 percent within 2 year (Emslie et al., 1998). A summary of the research on the development and course of MDD appears in Table 8.2.

Comorbidity and Differential Diagnosis of MDD

Comorbid diagnoses among children and adolescents with mood disorders are more the rule than the exception (Weller et al., 2004b). Studies have revealed that anywhere from 40 to 70 percent of depressed children and adolescents have a comorbid psychiatric disorder (Angold & Costello, 1993; Rohde, Lewinsohn, & Seeley, 1991). In addition, a variety of medical conditions can produce symptoms of depression, including:

- Malignancy
- Brain injury
- Infection
- Endocrine disorders
- Metabolic abnormalities
- Acquired Immune Deficiency Syndrome (AIDS)
- Multiple sclerosis
- Chronic fatigue syndrome

TABLE 8.2   A Summary of Research on the Development and Course of Major Depressive Disorder (MDD)

1. The rate of mood disorders in adulthood in significantly higher for those diagnosed with MDD during childhood or adolescence.
2. A minority of children and adolescents who have MDD develop manic or hypomanic episodes.
3. In adolescent, the course of MDD appears similar for boys and girls.
4. Comorbid nonaffective disorders predict a more severe course of depression.
5. The rate of anxiety disorders in adulthood is higher for those with MDD in childhood or adolescence than those without.

Source: Adapted from "Mood Disorders in Adolescents," by E. B. Weller, R. A. Weller, and A. K. Danielyan in *The American Psychiatric Textbook of Child and Adolescent Psychiatry* (3rd ed., p. 439) by J. M. Wiener and M. K. Dulcan (Eds.), 2004, Washington, DC: American Psychiatric Publishing.

A thorough physical examination is a perquisite for making a diagnosis of MDD in children and adolescents. The most common comorbid diagnoses are dysthymic disorder, anxiety disorders, personality disorder, disruptive behavior disorders, and substance abuse.

Among a community sample, Lewinsohn, Rohde, Seeley, and Hops (1991) found that 33 percent of those with MDD also had a diagnosis of dysthymic disorder, but only 7 percent of those with dysthymic disorder had MDD. Those with this so-called double depression (dysthymia plus MDD) have been found to have more severe and longer episodes of depression, high rates of comorbidity, greater social impairment, and more *suicidality* (suicidal thoughts or ideas, not a completed suicide) (Ferro, Carlson, Grayson, & Klein, 1994; Kovacs, Akiskal, Gatsonis, & Parrone, 1994). Anxiety and depression are highly comorbid even among adult samples. It may be difficult at times to decide on a primary diagnosis because individuals can become depressed about their anxiety and vice versa. A good history-taking to decide what came first is necessary to make a primary diagnosis.

Kutcher and Marton (1989) found that 60 percent of adolescents with MDD have a personality disorder, and borderline personality accounted for 30 percent of all personality disorders associated with MDD. Conduct disorder and oppositional defiant disorder are also highly comorbid with MDD. Those who have both MDD and an externalizing disorder have been found to have worse short-term outcome and to suffer more rejection by their peers (Cole & Carpentieri, 1990). Depressed adolescents tend to have an earlier onset of substance abuse than substance abusers who do not have a history of MDD (Rao, Ryan, Birmaher, & Dahl, 1995). It is quite possible that adolescents turn to drugs to self-medicate for their depression. One must also rule out a substance-induced depression, in which the use of substances has actually caused the depression. This differential diagnosis is made by taking a careful history and assuring that no depressive episodes occurred before the use of substances. A substance-induced mood disorder usually results from long-term abuse.

Etiology of MDD

There is no one specific cause of MDD. A number of interacting factors can result in a child or adolescent suffering from depression. These factors are biological, genetic, and environmental. McWhirter, McWhirter, Hart, and Gat (2000) divided the suspected causes of depression into five models: biological, psychodynamic, behavioral, cognitive, and family systems.

BIOLOGICAL MODELS Biological models of depression are of two types: genetic and biochemical (McWhirter et al., 2000). The genetic model derives from research that found that genetic factors account for approximately 50 percent of the variance in mood disorders (Birmaher et al., 1996). A child who has a depressed parent is about three times more likely to experience depression than one who does not (Weissman, Kidd, & Prusoff, 1982). Having a depressed parent is one of the strongest predictors of depression in children and adolescents (Beardslee, Versage, & Gladstone, 1998). Concordance rates of depression are much higher in monozygotic (identical) twins (54 percent) (McGuffin & Katz, 1989) than in dizygotic (fraternal) twins (24 percent) (Carlson & Abbott, 1995).

Biochemical models of depression explain depression as a hormonal imbalance (Puig-Antich, 1985; Puig-Antich, Perel, Lupatkin, & Chambers, 1987; Hart, 1991). There is some evidence that depressed children and adolescents secrete unusually large amounts of growth hormone (Jensen & Garfinkel, 1990; Ryan, Dahl, Birmaher, & Williamson,, 1994). Sleep studies in which the secretion of growth hormone has been observed, however, have been inclusive and even contradictory (Birmaher et al., 2004; Emslie, Weinberg, Rush, & Adams, 1990; Emslie et al., 1997; Emslie, Kennard, & Kowatch, 1995). Some have argued that biochemical imbalances may be less the cause and more a result of depression (Geddes & Butler, 2002; Hazell, 2002).

This same argument can be applied to the neurotransmitters (norepinephrine, serotonin, and acetylcholine) that are believed to play a part in the regulation of mood and consequently in the development of clinical depression. The antidepressants that regulate neurotransmitters in the brain—monoamine oxidase inhibitors (MAOIs), tricyclic antidepressants (TCAs), and selective serotonin reuptake inhibitors (SSRIs)—have all been shown to be effective in treating depression in adults.

PSYCHODYNAMIC MODELS   Traditional psychoanalytic theory described depression as anger turned inward—toward the self—and connected to a judging and controlling superego. Because the superego is still forming in children and adolescents, Freudian theorists reasoned that depression was not possible in these age groups (Hart, 1991). More-recent psychodynamic models have described depression among the young in terms of a loss that stems from childhood helplessness and the disruption of emotional bonding with the primary caregiver. The result is a loss of self-esteem. The child or adolescent has no internal sense of self-worth, relying instead on external sources for confirmation of his or her self-worth; when those external sources are lost, the child or adolescent becomes depressed (Capuzzi & Gross, 2000).

BEHAVIORAL MODELS   Behaviorists argue that depression is produced by the lack of positive reinforcement for behaviors that are considered more normal. As time goes on, the depressed youngster manifests behaviors that are less likely to elicit positive reinforcement but that do draw attention to the child and give him or her a sense of control. The symptoms of depression, then, are both cause and consequence of the lack of positive reinforcement. The key for helpers is not to reinforce the depressed behaviors, to reserve praise and encouragement for those behaviors that show improvement in both task and social functioning (Bauer, 1987).

Seligman's (1974) *learned helplessness* model of depression is based directly on research with behavioral reinforcement. Learned helplessness is a response to a series of failures to solve a problem or to improve a situation. In time, the individual becomes convinced that nothing he or she does or tries makes a difference. People who have learned helplessness have an external locus of control (their life is controlled by external forces) and an internal locus of responsibility (they blame themselves). Their feelings of hopelessness generalize to most of life's situations. For children and adolescents, learned helplessness often revolves around schoolwork. The student has made numerous attempts and tried numerous means to improve his or her schoolwork but without success. So the student gives up, and depression sets in. Schloss (1983) recommended several strategies to help students overcome learned helplessness:

1. Help the child avoid a sense of constant failure by providing work tasks in small incremental steps that give the child a sense of mastery and success.
2. Neutralize helplessness by providing opportunities for choice and power (as in selecting work assignments or self-rewards).
3. Provide increased verbal feedback and explanations to the depressed child, who may lack the ability to see cause and effect.
4. Encourage depressed children to identify behaviors and outcomes themselves, for a growing sense of confidence. (Quoted in S. L. Hart, 1991, p. 284)

COGNITIVE MODELS According to cognitive theorists, depression is the direct result of negative or irrational thoughts. Beck (1967) was the first to develop a cognitive theory of depression; some years later, he and his colleagues described a cognitive triad that they believed is characteristic of people who are depressed (Beck, Rush, Shaw, & Emery, 1979). The triad consists of three negative thought patterns: of self, of the world, and of the future. Over time, these thought patterns develop into *schemas,* frameworks so much a part of the individual's cognitive makeup that they are like personality traits. Environmental stimuli are filtered through these schemas and distorted to conform to the individual's negative view of self, world, and future. Even the most positive experiences are distorted. For example, a depressed child might respond to praise for a good grade with "The teacher probably felt sorry for me." Depressed children often making negative comments about themselves: "I always fail," "I'm not good at anything," "No one likes me."

In the cognitive model, the first step in helping a student who is depressed is to teach the student to substitute positive self-talk for negative self-statements. The helper usually gives the student a homework assignment: "Every time you say to yourself, 'I'm a bad person,' I want you to correct that statement by saying, 'I'm a good person.'" Other school-based interventions include guidance lessons that teach the relationship between thoughts and feelings, and role-play activities that focus on the problems and symptoms of childhood depression (peer rejection, feelings of guilt and failure) (Clarizio, 1985).

Another cognitive model, Rehm's (1977) *self-control model,* explains depression as the product of deficiencies in three cognitive processes:

- *Self-monitoring:* The child pays attention only to negative events.
- *Self evaluation:* The child frequently makes negative self-judgments. He or she sets high standards for positive self-evaluation and low standards for negative self-evaluation.

• *Self-reinforcement:* The child has a negative attribution style: Events are beyond his or her control because external forces control them or because he or she has some sort of internal deficiency.

The broad goal of intervention in this model is to help the student gain a greater sense of self-control. Helpers should begin by assigning the student small, manageable tasks and provide positive reinforcement when those tasks are accomplished. Also, there is some evidence that group interventions in schools can increase students' sense of self-control (Omizo & Omizo, 1987).

THE FAMILY SYSTEMS MODEL   Family systems theorists believe that children's behavior—even behavior that is symptomatic of depression—maintains balance (homeostasis) in the family system. Family systems theorists would not approve of treating just the child; they would argue that the family must be treated. The helper should consider family dynamics in working with a student who is depressed and should consult with the parents about their child, looking for signs during the meeting that the parents are using their child's depression in some way. For example, a child's illness allows parents to focus their psychic energy on the child instead of on other difficulties they should be resolving. If there is evidence that the child's depression is serving some function in the family, the school should facilitate a referral for family counseling.

Dysthymia

Dysthymia occurs in approximately 2 percent of children and 4 percent of adolescents (Muriel, Bostic, & Dolan, 2002). High rates of comorbidity between dysthymia and MDD that have led some to question whether these are two distinct disorders (Weller et al., 2004b). Early onset of dysthymia is considered a gateway to the occurrence and reoccurrence of mood disorders. Kovacs et al. (1994) found that 70 percent of children diagnosed with MDD had underlying dysthymia.

Dysthymia is less intense and more prolonged than MDD. For a diagnosis to be made, symptoms in children must have persisted for at least 1 year (American Psychiatric Association, 2004). Children who have dysthymia "characteristically have good days and bad days, or they may have many mixed days, but they do not have good weeks" (Kowatch et al., 2005, p. 135). Features of dysthymic disorder can be found in Table 8.3. According to the DSM-IV-TR (American Psychiatric Association, 2000), two or more of the variable features must be present before making a diagnosis of dysthymia.

Assessment of Depressive Disorders

Because of high comorbidity and confounding symptoms, the assessment of a mood disorder in children must include a number of strategies and constituencies. In addition to interviewing the child and parents, teachers and even peers should be included in the assessment.

Most experts agree that the best method for diagnosing depression in children and adolescents is through the clinical interview. There are, however, a

TABLE 8.3 Features of Dysthymic Disorder

Discriminating Features

1. Dysphonic or irritable mood for at least 1 year

Consistent Features

1. Symptoms not severe enough to diagnose a major depression

2. Absence of a psychotic illness

3. Absence of a physiological mood-altering condition

5. Impaired social and academic functioning

Variable Features

1. Poor appetite or overeating

2. Insomnia or hypersomnia

3. Low energy or fatigue

4. Low self-esteem

5. Poor concentration or difficulty making decisions

6. Feelings of hopelessness

Source: From "Mood Disorders" by R. A. Emslie, G. J. Wilkaitis, and A. D. Dingle in *Child and Adolescent Psychiatry* (p. 136) by S. B. Sexon and R. B. David (Eds.), 2005, Malden, MA: Blackwell Publishers. Copyright 2005 by Blackwell Publishers. Adapted with permission.

number of self-report measures that are used for screening and to obtain additional information (Kowatch et al., 2005).

SELF-REPORT MEASURES   The *Children's Depression Inventory* (CDI; Kovacs, 1985) is perhaps the most widely used self-report measure. It consists of twenty-seven items that deal with affective, cognitive, and behavioral aspects of depression. Participants are asked to choose which of three alternatives best describes them during a 2 week period. Research on the CDI has supported good psychometric properties (Reynolds & Johnston, 1994).

Reynolds (1987) developed the *Reynolds Adolescent Depression Scale* (RADS) for adolescents ages 13 to 18. The scale consists of thirty items derived from symptoms of depression and dysthymia. Responses—"Almost never," "Hardly ever," "Sometimes," "Most of the time"—are weighted from 1 to 4 points, which means that scores on the RADS can range from 30 to 120. Higher scores indicate higher levels of depressive symptoms. The RADS takes 5 to 10 minutes to complete. According to Ramsey (1994), the RADS is easy to administer and "provides an efficient and economical method for individual, small, or large group prevention screening (p. 258)".

The *Reynolds Child Depression Scale* (RCDS; Reynolds, 1989) was designed for use with children in grades 3 to 6. There is only a slight difference between the formats of the RCDS and the RADS. The last item in the RCDS is a series of faces showing different emotions, from happy to sad. This item is marked on a 5-point scale, so scores on the RCDS can range from 30 to 121. Like the RADS, the RCDS is easy to administer and takes about 10 minutes to complete.

The *Beck Depression Inventory* (BDI) is designed to assess the severity of depression in adolescents and adults (A. T. Beck & Steer, 1993; A. T. Beck, Ward, Mendelson, Mock, & Erbaugh, 1961). The current BDI (it was revised in 1993) consists of twenty-one items, each a statement related to an affective, cognitive, motivational, or physical symptom of depression. Test takers are asked to rate each item a 0, 1, 2, or 3 on a severity scale. Scores can range from 0 to 63, with 0 to 9 indicating minimal depression, 10 to 16 mild depression, 17 to 29 moderate depression, and 30 to 63 severe depression. The BDI can be administered individually or in a group, in oral or written form, and it can be scored by hand or by computer.

PEER RATINGS   Lefkowitz and Tesiny (1980) developed the *Peer Nomination Inventory for Depression* based on the theory that peers are sometimes the best sources for recognizing a troubled child. The inventory asks children to nominate peers who fit certain descriptions, such as "Who often plays alone?" "Who often sleeps in class?" There are twenty items in total: fourteen load on a depressed score, four on the happiness score, and two on the popularity score.

OBSERVATION   Over the years, a number of observational and performance-based measures have been developed to aid in the diagnosis of depression in children. Many of these are time-consuming and require special training to learn different coding systems. Garber and Kaminski (2000) developed the following categories that are depression-related and should be observed in social-interaction tasks:

- *Emotions:* smiling, frowning, crying, happiness, sadness, anger, fear
- *Affect regulation:* control or expression of affect
- *Problem solving:* identifying problems, proposing solutions
- *Nonverbal behaviors:* eye contact, postures
- *Conflict:* noncompliance, ignoring, demanding, negotiating
- *Cognitive content:* criticism, praise, self-derogation
- *Speech:* rate, volume, tone of voice, initiation
- *Engaged or disengaged:* enthusiasm, involvement, persistence
- *On- or off-task behavior*
- *Physical contact:* threatening, striking, affection
- *Symptoms:* depression, irritability, psychomotor agitation, retardation, fatigue, concentration

Observational data should be gathered across several domains: the child's play, interaction with caregivers and treatment providers, and in both familiar and unfamiliar environments.

Treatment Strategies for Depressive Disorders

The treatment of depressive disorders can be divided basically into two categories: psychopharmacological and psychosocial. Psychosocial treatments include cognitive-behavioral therapy (CBT), interpersonal psychotherapy (IPT), and family counseling. The goal of treatment is to shorten the duration of the mood disorder, decrease the negative consequences of depression, and restore the child or adolescent to optimal functioning (Kowatch et al., 2005).

COGNITIVE-BEHAVIORAL THERAPY Meta-analytic studies have shown CBT to be effective in treating child and adolescent depression (Marcotte, 1997; Reinecke, Ryan, & DuBois, 1998). Two structured programs for treating adolescents with depression are Primary and Secondary Control Enhanced Training (PASCET; Weisz, Southam-Gerow, Gordis, & Connor-Smith, 2003) and the Adolescent Coping with Depression (CWD-A) course (Clarke, DeBar, Lewinsohn, Kazdin, & Weisz, 2003; Lewinsohn, Clarke, Hops, & Andrews, 1990).

The PASCET was initially tested among children in grades 3 to 6 who showed signs of mild to moderate depression. It is an 8 session program in which participants meet in small groups and emphasizes control skills. Children are helped to identify activities that enhance their mood, change maladaptive thoughts, and learn relaxation and positive imagery. End-of-treatment and 9 month follow-up evaluations showed a significant decrease in depressive symptoms than a no-treatment control group.

In the initial study of the CWD-A (Lewinsohn et al., 1990), participants included fifty-nine high school students (ages 14 to 18) who met the diagnostic criteria for depression and were randomly assigned to one of three groups: wait-list controls, the CWD-A with parent intervention, or the CWD-A alone. Treatment included fourteen 2 hour group sessions over a 7 week period that focused on social skills, communication, problem-solving, relaxation training, identifying and modifying negative thoughts, and pleasant-event scheduling. Parents attended seven 2 hour sessions that gave an overview of the skills their children were learning. At the end of treatment and at 24 month follow-up, both treatment groups showed significant improvements with low rates of relapse. There was no difference between the CWD-A–only group and the CWD-A with parent intervention except in terms of parent perception. A second clinical trial (Lewinsohn, Clarke, & Rhode, 1994; Lewinsohn, Clarke, Rohde, Hops, & Seeley, 1996) utilized a revised version of the CWD-A in which adolescents attended sixteen 2 hour sessions over 8 weeks and parents attended nine 2 hour sessions in the same time frame. Results showed that 67 percent of those who attended the CWD-A course no longer met the diagnostic criteria for depression at the end of treatment, compared to 48 percent of those on the wait-list. And at 24 month follow-up, 98 percent had recovered (Clarke, Rohde, Lewinsohn, Hops, & Seeley, 1999; Lewinsohn et al, 1996; Lewinsohn, Gotlib, & Hautzinger, 1998).

In a comparison study, Brent, Roth, and Holder (1996) compared individual CBT, systemic behavior family therapy, and a nondirective supportive treatment for 107 adolescents (ages 13 to 18) who met the diagnostic criteria for major depression. At the end of treatment, more adolescents from the CBT group were in remission than among those from the family and supportive treatment groups. However, a 2 year follow-up assessment found no differences among the three groups.

INTERPERSONAL PSYCHOTHERAPY Interpersonal psychotherapy treats depression through improving interpersonal functioning and enhancing communication skills in relationships with significant others. Studies (Mufson & Fairbanks, 1996; Mufson, Weissman, Moreau, & Garfinkel, 1999) have supported the effectiveness of IPT. IPT addresses four areas of interpersonal functioning:

- Interpersonal deficits
- Interpersonal role conflicts
- Abnormal grief
- Difficult role transitions

Parents are involved in all phases of the treatment. Among fourteen clinically depressed adolescents (ages 12 to 18) who received twelve weekly 45 minute sessions (the standard treatment for IPT), 90 percent were no longer depressed at posttreatment, and only one of nine met the criteria for mood disorder at 1 year follow-up assessment (Mufson & Fairbanks, 1996). Similar results were found in a sample of forty-eight adolescents who met the criteria for MDD (Mufson et al., 1999).

FAMILY COUNSELING   Family counseling is also recommended for the treatment of depression in children and adolescents. Based on the structural model of family therapy, Minuchin (1974) hypothesized that enmeshed relationships between children and parents were responsible for depression because they prevented appropriate levels of attachment and separation. Unfortunately, except for the comparison study by Brent et al. (1996), mentioned previously, no treatment-outcome studies on family counseling of depressed adolescents have been published. Many individual approaches to depression in adolescents include a parent-education component, but at this time it is not clear how much the parent component contributes to the overall effectiveness of treatment. Two studies (Clarke et al., 1999; Lewinsohn et al., 1990) reported that parent participation contributed no improvement in adolescent depressive symptoms. A limitation of these studies, however, was that parents' attendance at the sessions was very inconsistent.

PSYCHOPHARMACOLOGY   Over the years, a number of medications have been used to treat depression in children and adolescents. These fall into three groups: selective serotonin reuptake inhibitors (SSRIs), trycyclic antidepressants (TCAs), and monoamine oxidase inhibitors (MAOIs). Today, without a doubt, the SSRIs are the first-line pharmacological treatment for depression. Though they are still popular, the SSRIs are used with precaution in children and adolescent because there has been some evidence of an increased rate of suicidality (Bridge et al., 2007; Olfson, Marcus, & Shaffer, 2006). At the present time, the U.S. Food and Drug Administration (FDA) has approved only fluoxetine (Prozac) for use with children and adolescents.

Fluoxetine (Prozac)   Emslie, Rush, Weinberg, and Gullion (1997) conducted the first double-blind, placebo-controlled study of the use of Prozac in children and adolescents. A sample of ninety-six outpatients (ages 7–17) with MDD were treated with 20 mg of Prozac for eight consecutive weeks. Results showed that 56 percent of those taking the medication were rated "much" or "very much" improved, compared to 33 percent of those receiving a placebo. Complete remission, however, occurred in only 31 percent of the Prozac-treated patients, compared to 23 percent of those taking a placebo.

Paroxetine (Paxil)   Keller et al. (2001) compared Paxil with placebo, and imiprimine, a TCA, with placebo, and found that Paxil was more effective than placebo on some but not all outcome measures of depression, whereas the response to imiprimine was not significantly different from placebo on any outcome measures.

Setraline (Zoloft)   In a study including fifty-three adolescent outpatients who had MDD on a trial of setraline, Ambrosini et al. (1999) found that all severity scores showed significant differences from baseline within 2 weeks and continued through 10 weeks. A study conducted by Wagner et al. (2003) including 376 children and adolescents (ages 6 to 17) who had MDD found that 63 percent were "much improved" or "very much improved," compared to 53 percent on a placebo.

Citalopram (Celexa)   In a multisite, double-blind, placebo-controlled study including 174 children and adolescents (ages 7 to 17), Wagner et al. (2004) found that citalopram was no better than placebo on measures of global improvement.

Other Uses of Psychopharmacological Agents   With the advent of SSRIs, TCAs and MAOIs are rarely used in the treatment of depression among children and adolescents. Little has been written about the effectiveness of these drugs with this population. There are special concerns regarding TCAs because of possible cardiovascular risk, after reports of sudden death in five children who were taking TCAs (Weller et al., 2004b).

In spite of the high regard for the combination of medication and psychotherapy, only one study to date has examined the combination of treatments in adolescents who have MDD. The Treatment for Adolescent with Depression Study (TADS, 2004) compared fluoxetine, CBT, combination treatment, and placebo in 439 adolescents (ages 12 to 18) who had MDD. Based on global improvement scores, results showed that 71 percent of those on combination responded positively, compared to 61 percent on fluoxetine only, 43 percent receiving CBT only, and 35 percent receiving placebo.

School-Based Interventions

We will now use the knowledge we have gained about the characteristics, causes, and recommended treatment strategies for MDD to develop an effective behavioral intervention for Emily, our case example. To ensure that our treatment approach is precisely tailored to Emily's needs, we must first conduct a careful assessment to determine both what the problem behaviors are and what function or purpose they serve for Emily. Once this has been accomplished, we will be able to develop an individualized behavioral intervention plan to help her deal successfully with these behavioral challenges.

ASSESSING THE PROBLEM   To determine effective ways to improve Emily's participation in school, as well as her self-esteem, the multidisciplinary team will conduct a behavioral assessment. This process will ensure that all stakeholders thoroughly understand the circumstances surrounding Emily's disability, as well as the things that exacerbate it. Furthermore, the information provided through this problem-solving process will assist her teachers and other educational professionals in developing school-based interventions to help Emily succeed academically and socially. These school-based interventions will complement the treatment plan prescribed by Emily's psychiatrist.

A thorough behavioral assessment for Emily should include the following components.

The first step is *identifying and describing the problem behavior.* Emily, is withdrawn in class and participates in activities with great reluctance and only when required. In addition, she seems morose all the time. This behavior is a recent development that has been observed to coincide with the death of her father.

The second step of the assessment process involves *collecting baseline and academic information.* Emily's teachers have been instructed by the school psychologist to use three measurements to assess her emotional state in the classroom: (1) The *Reynolds Adolescent Depression Scale* (RADS), (2) peer ratings using the *Peer Nomination Inventory for Depression* (Lefkowitz & Tesing, 1980), and (3) observations of Emily's behavior in the classroom according to depression-related categories developed by Garber and Kaminski (2000).

The results of the RADS produced a score of 115 (the mean score on the RADS can range from 30 to 120, with higher scores indicating higher levels of depression). The *Peer Nomination Inventory for Depression* administered to Emily's classmates showed that, in the estimation of the majority of these students, Emily was nominated for the fourteen items that are associated with depression. The cumulative outcome of these data supports the diagnosis of major depression for Emily.

The third stage of the assessment process involves *describing the environment and setting demands.* Emily is clearly avoiding any social situation that might trigger memories of her father or his death. She seems unable to cope with this loss and is insulating herself from the pain of this reality through self-imposed exile and emotional disconnectedness.

Next, where appropriate, affected professionals should *complete a functional behavioral assessment form and/or behavior rating scale.* On Emily's behalf, a functional behavioral assessment form was completed in September of Emily's eighth-grade year. In addition, the RADS and *Peer Nomination Inventory for Depression* were administered in the same month, with results as described above.

Another important element in the assessment process is *direct observation of her classroom performance.* Therefore, Emily's teachers conducted numerous systematic observations, focusing principally on the categories developed by Garber and Kaminski (2000) as described earlier in the chapter. Their observations helped to confirm the diagnosis of major depression.

A final step in the process involves *developing a hypothesis about the function or purpose of the problem behavior,* including what causes and sustains it. In Emily's case, the cause appears to be self-evident: the untimely death of her father. It is unclear what function her depressive symptoms serve; according to researchers, the causes are multifactorial (McWhirter, McWhirter, Hart, & Gat, 2000). The symptoms are likely an organic response to mitigate the pernicious effects of a stressor or stressors. The various assessments conducted by school and clinical staffs have supported a diagnosis of major depression for Emily. Her depression can be treated using a research-based, multimodal approach that combines cognitive-behavioral therapy with pharmacological intervention.

The hypothesis developed in the functional behavioral assessment will be *confirmed* after the treatment plan has been implemented for a reasonable period of time. If the symptoms of Emily's depression are sufficiently suppressed, the hypothesis will be confirmed and the behavioral intervention plan will be continued. If, however, the plan produces results that are less than desirable (i.e., does not meet minimally acceptable goals), then the plan will be modified to achieve these objectives.

DEVELOPING AN EFFECTIVE INTERVENTION PLAN   In accordance with the assessment data provided by Emily's teachers, peers, and family members, as well as the clinical diagnosis of Dr. D'Amico, her therapist, a treatment plan has been developed. The plan consists of a recommended, research-based approach that involves both cognitive-behavioral therapy, as well as pharmacological intervention. Specifically, Emily will begin an after-school course with several other students who have also been diagnosed with depression. The program, the Adolescent Coping with Depression course (CWD-A) (Lewinsohn et al., 1996) involves fourteen 2 hour group sessions over a 7 week period and includes training in social skills, communication, problem solving, relaxation, identifying and modifying negative thoughts, as well as desirable-event scheduling. In addition, Emily's mother will attend seven 2 hour sessions that provide an overview of the skills Emily is acquiring.

The second component of this multimodal intervention plan involves prescribing fluoxetine (Prozac), a selective serotonin reuptake inhibitor (SSRI), which is FDA-approved for use with children and adolescents. Fluoxetine has been demonstrated to produce significant improvements in the symptoms of depression in patients to whom it was prescribed, and combined treatment appears to have an even greater therapeutic effect.

Emily's teachers can help by continuing to monitor her emotional state, using the depression-related categories developed by Garber and Kaminski (2000) and systematically recording any changes. They should also report any physiological changes such as visible weight gain or other adverse effects that may be attributed to the use of the SSRI. In addition, her teachers should note any increase in social activity, as well as self-initiated interpersonal communication.

BIPOLAR DISORDER

CASE EXAMPLE: Calvin

Calvin is a 14-year-old high school freshman who is active in varsity sports, specifically, baseball and basketball, and has recently been referred to a psychologist for evaluation for bipolar disorder (BPD). His mother and great aunt have both been diagnosed with the disorder.

Calvin began to exhibit the behavioral symptoms of BPD at the onset of puberty; about the time he turned 13. Family members and close friends noted that Calvin appeared to be talking "very fast" and was uncharacteristically overbearing in social interactions.

Likewise, he seemed to be more egocentric in his conversation and in his relationships. His parents noticed that Calvin began staying up later, despite their protests, yet was able to get up at the usual time in the morning. He would also perseverate about some goal or idea, seeming to have a "one-track mind" about his current passion. These periods of frenetic activity and singular focus would last for 3 or 4 days, after which he would appear to lose some of his initial enthusiasm and actually seem a bit depressed or melancholy.

These behaviors steadily intensified through eighth grade, culminating in several bizarre episodes. The first of these occurred early in eighth grade, when Calvin was playing on the modified basketball team. Although he was one of the weaker players on the squad, in the last half of a game as his team was losing badly, Calvin ran up to the coach and insisted he be "subbed in." "I know I can help us win coach," he shouted, "just let me get the ball . . . give me a chance!" Realizing that his team could not win, and with only minutes left in the game, the coach acceded to Calvin's persistent appeals and sent him in to play. However, despite his confidence and enthusiasm, Calvin was unable to receive a pass, let alone take a shot, and the game ended, as predicted, with Calvin's enthusiasm undaunted.

In contrast, in social studies, Calvin offered to be the team leader for an important and challenging term project. Once again, as the deadline loomed and the pressure to complete the project mounted, Calvin succumbed, stating he felt "overwhelmed," and had to pass the leadership role onto another student. As a result of this "failure," Calvin became slightly depressed, chiding himself for ever thinking he could accomplish such a difficult task.

Finally, in an episode at the close of eighth grade, Calvin decided to ask one of the most popular girls in the middle school to accompany him to the end-of-year dance. He told friends that he was convinced she would go with him because he was "smart" and a "jock," and he had read somewhere that often the most popular girls were overlooked because everyone assumed they already had a date. While his enthusiasm was commendable and his rationale seemed plausible, he was refused outright and was actually threatened by the girl's "steady" boyfriend. Calvin was devastated and withdrew from social contacts for a week, appearing mildly dysthymic. Despite the coaxing of his friends, Calvin refused to attend the function and instead spent the evening by himself in his room playing video games.

After a year of this "cycling behavior," alternating between periods of high energy and euphoria and depressive episodes, behavior that was profoundly uncharacteristic for Calvin, his parents and teachers requested a formal evaluation to determine the cause.

Characteristics of Bipolar Disorder

Bipolar disorder is typically characterized by the alternating presence of both depressed and euphoric moods. The DSM-IV-TR (American Psychiatric Association, 2000) distinguishes three types of bipolar disorder: bipolar disorder I, bipolar disorder II, and cyclothymic disorder. Difficulties in diagnosis make it challenging to report accurate prevalence rates. It is widely accepted that BPD occurs in about 1 percent of adolescents (Lewinsohn, Klein, & Seeley, 1995). Peak onset appears to be between 15 and 19 years of age (Wicks-Nelson & Israel, 2006).

The diagnosis of *bipolar I disorder* requires the presence of a manic episode or manic and depressive episodes. The DSM-IV-TR symptomatology for

---

TABLE 8.4 DSM-IV-TR Symptomotology for a Manic Episode

1. Persistent elevated, expansive, or irritable mood

2. Inflated self-esteem

3. Decreased need for sleep

4. Being more talkative than usual

5. Feeling of thoughts racing

6. Distractibility

7. Increased goal-directed activity or psychomotor agitation

8. Excessive pleasurable activity that can lead to negative consequences (e.g., buying sprees, sexual indiscretions)

Source: From *Diagnostic and Statistical Manual of Mental Disorders, Fourth Edition, Text Revision* (pp. 362) by the American Psychiatric Association, 2000, Washington, DC: Author. Copyright 2000 by the American Psychiatric Association. Adapted with permission.

a manic episode is listed in Table 8.4. Bipolar I can also include a mixed episode as long as there is evidence of a previously occurring manic or depressed episode, manic or mixed episode. A *mixed episode* is defined as meeting the criteria for both a manic and a major depressive episode. In addition, bipolar I can include a hypomanic episode as long as there is evidence of a previously occurring manic or mixed episode. *Hypomania* is defined as a distinct period of persistently elevated, expansive or irritable mood that is not as severe as mania by not causing significant impairment in functioning and lasts at least 4 days. If hypomania occurs with evidence of only a depressive episode, the diagnosis is *bipolar II disorder.* Bipolar II is two to three times more common than bipolar I in children and adolescents (Kowatch et al., 2005). If hypomania occurs only in conjunction with periods of depressive symptoms insufficient to meet the criteria for a major depressive episode during the course of 2 years, the diagnosis is *cyclothymic disorder.*

There are few data on the development and outcome of children and adolescents with BPD. Geller, Tillman, Craney, and Bolhofner (2004) followed eighty-six prepubertal and early adolescent patients with bipolar I and found that during a 4 year period, they spent 57 percent of the time in hypomania, 39 percent in mania, and 47 percent with depressive features. After a 4 year period, the recovery rate was 87 percent, but the relapse rate was 64 percent. Early onset of BPD may have a markedly different presentation than in adults. Rapid cycling (i.e., alternating often from mania to depression in the course of a single day) is more common. The mean age of onset for the first episode reported by adolescents with BPD was 11.8 years, which was significantly earlier than the first episode (15 years old) reported by those diagnosed with MDD (Geller & Luby, 1997).

Assessment of Bipolar Disorder

The diagnosis of BPD is complicated by two factors: a high rate of comorbidity and the difficulty of distinguishing manic and hypomanic symptoms from typical childhood behaviors. Table 8.5 presents the estimated rates of disorders that are frequently comorbid with BPD.

TABLE 8.5 Estimated Rates of Disorders Frequently Comorbid with Bipolar Disorder

Disorder	Prepubertal	Adolescent
Attention-deficit hyperactivity disorder	70–90%	30–60%
Anxiety disorders	20–39%	30–40%
Conduct disorder	30–40%	30–60%
Oppositional defiant disorder	60–90%	20–30%
Substance abuse	10%	50–70%
Learning disabilities	30–40%	30–40%

Source: From "Mood Disorders" by R. A. Emslie, G. J. Wilkaitis, and A. D. Dingle in *Child and Adolescent Psychiatry* (p. 144) by S. B. Sexon and R. B. David (Eds.), 2005, Malden, MA: Blackwell Publishers. Copyright 2005 by Blackwell Publishers. Reprinted with permission.

Attention-deficit hyperactivity disorder (ADHD) is by far the most common comorbid disorder, with some studies estimating the rate to be as high as 98 percent (Wozniak, Biederman, Kiely, & Ablon, 1995) and 97 percent (Geller et al., 1998). Furthermore, the symptoms of ADHD (distractibility, irritability, increased talkativeness, risk-taking behaviors) can mimic those of mania. A differential diagnosis will be based on severity, occurrence, and age of onset. The symptoms of mania are more severe, occur episodically, and more often occur after the onset of puberty. The symptoms of ADHD are less severe, chronic, and begin typically in the preschool or early elementary school years (i.e., before the age of 7). The child who has ADHD may have difficulty sleeping, but the child with mania has less need for sleep. The overactive child with mania is goal-directed, in contrast to the child who has ADHD, in whom the overactivity is often disorganized and haphazard (Weller, Weller, Fristad, Rooney, & Schecter, 2000). The rate of substance abuse among those diagnosed with BPD is slightly higher than among normal adolescents, estimated to be about 40 to 54 percent (U.S. Department of Health and Human Services, 1999). Though many adolescents are sexually active, the hypersexuality that accompanies a manic episode can lead to risky sexual behaviors. Often not in control of their thoughts and actions, hypersexualized adolescents with BPD will not take the necessary precautions to avoid sexually transmitted diseases. Bipolar adolescents are at increased risk for suicide, a topic that is treated in depth later.

Measures to assess BPD in children and adolescents are much less developed than those for depression. Structured diagnostic interviews, such as the K-SADS, have been used to gather information for making a diagnosis of BPD (Wick-Nelson & Israel, 2006). Rating scales for mania are all adult versions that have been adapted for children. These include the *Young Mania Rating Scale* (Young, Biggs, Ziegler, & Meyer, 1978; Youngstrom, Findling, & Calabrese, 2004) and the *General Behavior Inventory* (Depue, Krauss, Spoont, & Arbisi, 1989). Interviews and observational data are still the recommended methods for diagnosing mania and hypomania in children and adolescents.

Psychopharmacological Treatment of Bipolar Disorder

Lithium, anticonvulsants, and atypical antipsychotics have all been used in the treatment of children and adolescents with BPD. Unfortunately, few published double-blind, placebo-controlled studies exist for the efficacy of any medication for BPD with this population.

LITHIUM Lithium is the first-line medication for BPD and the only one approved by the FDA for the treatment of BPD in adolescents, ages 12 to 18 (Kowatch et al., 2005). Geller et al. (1998) did the only double-blind, placebo-controlled study on lithium use with adolescents dually diagnosed with BPD and a substance dependency disorder (marijuana or alcohol). In a sample of twenty-five adolescents, those who received lithium for a period of 8 weeks, 46 percent showed significant improvement in global assessment functioning, compared to 8 percent in the placebo group. In an open-label lithium study including one hundred adolescents ages 12 to 18, Kafantaris, Coletti, Dicker, Padula, and Kane (2003) found that sixty-three responded positively, and after 4 weeks, twenty-six were in full remission. In a follow-up study of thirty-seven adolescents hospitalized with BPD and started on lithium, 92 percent of those who discontinued lithium at 18 months relapsed, compared to 38 percent who were still taking lithium. Poor response to lithium has been associated with pre-pubertal onset and co-occurrence of ADHD (Strober et al., 1998).

ANTICONVULSANTS Two anticonvulsants, sodium divalproex and carbamazepine, have been used to treat mania in children and adolescents, especially for cases of mixed states and rapid-cycling BPD (Weller et al., 2004a). Response rates for sodium divalproex ranged from 53 to 82 percent (DelBello et al., 2002; Wagner et al., 2002). It is sometimes used in combination with lithium. Findling et al. (2003), in an open-label study of ninety patients under the age of 18 who were medicated with both lithium and sodium divalproex, found they all showed improvement in all outcome measures by week 8, and forty-two had achieved full remission. In a comparison study, Kowatch et al. (2000) found that all three mood stabilizers, lithium, divalproex, and carbamazepine, showed strong effects in the treatment of forty-two acutely manic or hypomanic children. The largest effect size was for divalproex (1.63), followed by lithium (1.06), and then carbamazepine (1.00).

ATYPICAL ANTIPSYCHOTICS In recent years, antipsychotics (e.g., clozapine, risperidone, olanzapine, and quetiapine) have been used extensively in the treatment of BPD in adults, and there is evidence suggesting that they may be equally effective in treating children and adolescents with BPD. DelBello et al. (2002) conducted the only controlled study of the use of antipsychotics, enrolling thirty adolescents, ages 12 to 18, who had been diagnosed with either manic or mixed bipolar I disorder. Results indicated that those medicated with a combination of quetiapine and divalproex showed statistically more significant improvement of overall functioning than the group medicated solely with divalproex. More studies are ongoing to determine the effectiveness of antipsychotics in children and adolescents diagnosed with BPD. Many of the pharmacological agents used to treat children and adolescents who have BPD are associated with significant weight gain. These children must be monitored closely for obesity and the development of type 2 diabetes mellitus.

School-Based Interventions

Equipped with the preceding information, teachers who have a student who has BPD should assess the problem behavior with a focus on the conditions that induce and maintain it. The following intervention plan for Calvin, our case example, serves as an exemplar. A systematic approach that involves sound data collection methods and research-based interventions is recommended. Such an approach provides the best chance for success in helping a student cope with BPD in the school environment.

ASSESSING THE PROBLEM The purpose of conducting a behavioral assessment in the context of the school environment is to establish the cause or function of the target behavior and its effect on learning. To ensure consistency and thoroughness, the multidisciplinary team should follow a well-conceived protocol, such as the one recommended in this textbook (Barnhill, 2005). For Calvin, an effective one would consist of the following components.

The first step is *identifying and describing the problem behavior.* Accordingly, Calvin's parents and teachers have observed a significant behavioral change in him during the past academic year. Calvin, who in the seventh grade displayed normal preadolescent behaviors and was stable and predictable, has recently evidenced extreme polarity of behaviors, cycling fairly rapidly from periods of euphoria and frenetic activity to episodes of depression and fatigue. His emotional volatility is negatively impacting his educational performance, as well as his social life. Calvin, once an A student, is now in danger of failing.

The second step is *collecting baseline data and academic information.* Calvin's parents and teachers have provided anecdotal data that documents his mood swings and behavioral aberrations. The school psychologist has asked that Calvin's teachers complete the *Young Mania Rating Scale* (Young et al., 1978; Youngstrom et al., 2004), which helps distinguish manic episodes. His teachers have also been encouraged to address each of the eleven categories that are depression-related (Garber & Kaminski, 2000) in their written observational reports. Also, Calvin's teachers have compiled a report that consists of a summary of his grades and test scores for the past academic year, during which the disordered behavior was manifest, to compare with his academic performance records from previous years.

Next, from *examining the environment and setting demands,* there does not appear to be a particular environment or setting that precipitates Calvin's emotional polarity. Indeed, the impetus for these changes seems to be better explained by neurobiological factors as opposed to environmental ones.

The next step in the assessment process involves *completing a functional assessment form and/or behavior rating scales.* To this end, the functional assessment form was completed at the end of the fourth quarter of Calvin's eighth-grade year, and the *Young Mania Rating Scale* (Youngstrom et al., 2004), described earlier in the chapter, was completed at the same time.

Teachers and caregivers were encouraged to conduct direct observations of Calvin's behavior in the classroom and at home. In response to this recommendation, Calvin's teachers and parents conducted ongoing behavior observations, noting the frequency, duration, and intensity of both his depressive and manic episodes. In addition, as recommended by the school psychologist and his private therapist, Calvin's teachers also described his depressive behavior in accordance with the eleven descriptive categories developed by Garber and Kaminski (2000).

As a final step in the process, teachers formulated a hypothesis regarding the cause of the aberrant behavior, as well as its purpose. Based on the behavioral data collected by Calvin's teachers, parents, and therapist, a formal diagnosis of bipolar II disorder was hypothesized and, ultimately, confirmed. The organic nature of this disorder precludes the determination of a purpose or function for the behaviors that are symptomatic of this condition.

Subsequent behavior consistent with the diagnosis of bipolar II disorder was observed in Calvin that was sufficiently intense, and of significant duration, to confirm the correctness of the preliminary diagnosis. The multidisciplinary team will meet as soon as possible to develop an Individualized Education Plan (IEP) for Calvin that will include an effective intervention plan to address Calvin's academic and social-emotional needs.

DEVELOPING AN EFFECTIVE INTERVENTION PLAN   In accordance with IDEA (2004) and in conformity with the model developed by Buck et al. (2000) and Ryan et al. (2003), a behavioral intervention plan was developed for Calvin that involves multimodal treatment plan consisting of appropriate cognitive-behavioral therapy, a parent-education component, and a psychopharmacological intervention.

Calvin's teachers, while not directly involved in these treatment regimens, nevertheless should be familiar with them and continue to provide observational data to help identify and document behavioral changes that may be associated with one or more of the treatments. In addition, these teachers should continue to provide Calvin with a supportive and structured classroom environment and quickly notify his parents and the school psychologist and/or counselor if they observe any sudden or significant behavior changes. They should also be informed about the type of medication prescribed for Calvin's disorder and its possible beneficial and adverse effects. Likewise, there should be a contingency plan in place in the event that Calvin requires emergency care relative to his bipolar II disorder. Lastly, as with any child affected by depression, teachers should be educated about the warning signs of suicide, as well as suicide-prevention techniques. A comprehensive examination of the warning signs of adolescent suicide and suicide assessment is provided in the following sections.

ADOLESCENT SUICIDE

CASE EXAMPLE: A Personal Anecdote

As one of the authors of this textbook, I (Vance Austin) would like to share a personal experience involving the suicidal death of one of my students some years ago. Marcia (not her real name) was a student assigned to my tenth-grade special education class in a rural school district. She was one of those students who easily "slips under the radar" because she was quiet, self-composed, and cooperative in a class of mostly boys who were anything but quiet and cooperative.

Marcia had a reading disability but was otherwise a model student. In fact, she was mainstreamed in all her courses except English 10. Nonetheless, because she worked hard and completed all her assignments, eagerly revising her written work to achieve a better grade, she was my most successful student.

She was so pleasant to have in class that she quickly became a favorite of mine, as well as of many of her other teachers. I think we all missed the tell-tale signs of impending suicide because she was so good, the "*least* of our worries." In retrospect, I think we were all lulled into complacency by her congeniality and compliance.

However, tragically, at 5:00 A.M. on the last Monday of the marking period in June, I received the phone call that is every teacher's nightmare: a call from the principal informing me that Marcia had committed suicide in the early morning hours on Sunday. I was asked to come in an hour early to help support students who might have already heard the news and to be prepared for the emotional fallout when the announcement of her loss was made by the principal during homeroom that morning.

The impact on the students was similar to the detonation of a bomb. Students and teachers who were affected by the news were invited to go to preset locations to receive grief counseling; clearly, I wasn't the only one who was blind-sided by this "unimaginable" tragedy. Nevertheless, I kept asking myself how I had missed the cues, the warning signs. Surely, they must have been evident. The one question that plagued me for weeks and months afterwards was, "Could I have been instrumental in preventing Marcia's death if I had been more observant and identified the signs? But what were those "signs?" I was ashamed to admit, I wasn't sure.

A few months after the tragedy, I attended a meeting with several of my colleagues, as well as the principal, to discuss the issue of adolescent suicide and risk assessment. Instead of an adversarial gathering of faculty, administrators, and parents that involved finger pointing and blame, the tone of the meeting was refreshingly cathartic. We came away determined to research the subject of adolescent suicide and develop effective inservice training, as well as a fluid, responsive contingency plan.

My coauthor, Dan Sciarra, and I hope the following information will prove useful to teachers, related services providers, and administrators in developing an effective plan to help prevent and, if necessary, cope with the crisis of suicide.

Prevalence of Adolescent Suicide

Every year in the United States, 1,900 individuals between the ages of 10 and 19 are victims of suicide (Anderson & Smith, 2003). Suicide is the second leading cause of death for people between the ages of 15 and 19, and the third leading cause of death for those between the ages of 15 and 24. There are approximately 100 to 200 suicide attempts for every youth who actually commits suicide. Approximately 85 percent of the people who commit suicide in this country each year are between ages 15 and 19. Although suicide rates among

TABLE 8.6	Suicide Rates for Males and Females from 1980 to 2001 for Two Different Age Groups		
	1980	**1995**	**2001**
Ages 10–14			
Males	1.21	2.61	1.90
Females	0.29	0.83	0.60
Ages 15–19			
Males	13.79	17.41	12.90
Females	3.02	3.11	2.70

Note: Rates are per 100,000.

Source: Anderson, R. N., & Smith, B. L. (2003) Death: Leading causes for 2001. *National Vital Statistics Report, 52*(9).

younger children are relatively low, they increased more than 200 percent from 1980 to 2001 for those between the ages of 10 and 14.

Table 8.6 breaks down suicide rates for males and females from 1980 to 2001 for two different age groups. The group with the highest suicide rate by far is white adolescent males (Metha, Weber, & Webb, 1998). When gender is removed as a variable, Native American adolescents have the highest rate of attempted and completed suicide, nearly twice the rate of any other racial or ethnic group—an alarming 27.7 per 100,000 for males in the age range from 15 to 19 years (Anderson & Smith, 2003)—although there is a great deal of variability across tribes. Asian Americans and Hispanic Americans have the lowest suicide rates compared with Native Americans, Whites, and African Americans.

Not all adolescents who commit suicide are depressed, but a large number of them are. That makes recognizing the symptoms of adolescent depression and helping students who manifest those symptoms all the more crucial.

The Warning Signs of Adolescent Suicide

For adolescents who complete or attempt suicide, killing themselves is the only way out of an untenable situation (Peach & Reddick, 1991). Although teenagers may not come right out and ask for help, they almost always hint at their desperation in words or behavior. It is critical that teachers and other providers be attuned to these cues. One caution though: No determination that a youngster is suicidal can be made on the basis of one event, statement, or behavior. When adolescents attempt suicide, several of these variables have come together, convincing them that suicide is the only way out.

VERBAL CUES Actually, some adolescents do communicate their suicidal intent directly ("I'm going to kill myself"; "I just want to die"), but most communicate their intentions subtly, often using metaphorical language (Capuzzi & Gross, 2000; Kalafat, 1990):

- "I'd like to go home."
- "I won't be around much longer."

- "They'll be sorry for what they did to me."
- "I'm very tired."
- "I wonder what death is like."
- "They'll see how serious I am."
- "Things are never going to get any better."
- "I'll always feel this way."
- "Nobody cares."
- "People would be better off without me."

These are just a few examples; there are many others. The point is that when a student says something that strikes the helper as odd or that can be interpreted in a number of ways, the helper should be quick to ask the student for clarification: "Can you help me understand a bit better what you mean when you say, 'They'll be sorry'?"

School personnel also need to be sensitive to themes that might communicate what an adolescent is thinking. Table 8.7 lists nine themes that signal thoughts of suicide on the part of adolescents. Each of these nine motivations can be categorized into one of the three primary functions of suicide: to avoid a difficult situation, to take control of one's life, or to communicate pain. All suicides serve one of these three functions.

BEHAVIORAL CUES School personnel must also pay attention to certain behaviors that could signal the intention to commit suicide. Capuzzi and Gross (2000) identified a number of behaviors that are cause for concern.

> ***Lack of concern about personal welfare.*** At times, adolescents reveal their suicidal tendencies by putting themselves at risk—for example, by driving recklessly, accepting dares from friends, or marking or cutting

---

TABLE 8.7 Nine Themes That Signal Thoughts of Suicide on the Part of Adolescents

- Wanting to escape from a difficult situation
- Wanting to join someone who has died
- Wanting to attract the attention of family and friends
- Wanting to manipulate someone
- Wanting to avoid punishment
- Wanting to be punished
- Wanting to control when and how death will occur (especially for adolescents who have a chronic or terminal illness)
- Wanting to end a conflict that seems irresolvable
- Wanting revenge

Source: From "I Don't Want to Live: The Adolescent at Risk for Suicidal Behavior," by D. Capuzzi and D. R. Gross in *Youth at Risk: A Prevention Resource for Counselors, Teachers, and Parents* (3rd ed., p. 328) by D. Capuzzi and D. R. Gross (Eds.), 2000, Alexandria, VA: American Counseling Association. Copyright 2000 by the American Counseling Association. Reprinted with permission.

themselves. School personnel should understand that these individuals may be in pain but unable to express that pain.

Changes in social patterns. Helpers should notice sudden changes in students' behavior: a socially active student becomes withdrawn and isolated, a normally compliant student become argumentative and rebellious, a student leaves one group of friends and joins another group whose members are more daring or more rebellious.

A decline in school achievement. Helpers should be aware of any good student who suddenly loses interest in schoolwork, itself a symptom of depression in this population. If a student is vague or refuses to talk about the problem, the helper should not be put off: "For some kids, going from A's to C's means they're giving up. Are you giving up? Have you ever thought about or considered hurting yourself?"

Difficulties concentrating and thinking clearly. Again, these difficulties are symptomatic of depression. They also can indicate that the student is focusing his or her energies on planning a suicide.

Altered patterns of eating and sleeping. Although there can many causes for disturbances in eating and sleeping, depression and suicidal tendencies are clearly among them. The helper should watch for a dramatic loss or gain of weight and should ask teachers to watch for students who are nodding off in class.

Attempts to put personal affairs in order or to make amends. An adolescent's efforts to put his or her affairs in order could signal that the youngster is preparing to die. Before a suicide attempt, adolescents often repair a broken relationship, call old friends, impulsively finish a project that had been put off, or give away important personal items.

Alcohol or drug use or abuse. Many adolescents experiment with alcohol and drugs, but sustained use, which leads to abuse, diminishes some of the psychological defenses that protect youngsters from thoughts of suicide. Substance abuse can increase impulsivity and at the same time decrease the adolescent's communications skills. For the substance-abusing adolescent, then, suicide may appear to be a viable option at a particular moment in time.

Unusual interest in how others are feeling. As a defense against their own pain, suicidal adolescents may show exaggerated interest and responsiveness to the problems of others. A preoccupation with others serves a dual purpose: It helps suicidal adolescents focus on something other than their own problem; and, paradoxically, it helps them communicate their own pain.

Preoccupation with themes of death and violence. This kind of preoccupation is quite common in suicidal adolescents. Certainly, many youngsters are drawn to violence in the media; but when violence becomes a major interest, the school helper needs to be concerned. Movies, books, music, video games, drawings, and writings that focus on destruction, death, and dying could signal suicidal tendencies. Teachers might become aware of such activity through a student's drawings or parents who notice a change and an extraordinary interest in such themes.

Sudden improvement after a period of depression. Students who show a sudden improvement after a period of depression may be at risk for suicide. Having made the decision to go ahead with the suicide, they are mobilizing themselves to carry out the plan. This is not the gradual improvement that signals a depression is lifting; this is a sudden and drastic change.

Sudden or increased promiscuity. Experimentation with or escalation of sexual activity can be an adolescent's way of diverting attention from suicidal thoughts and feelings. The consequences of promiscuity—for example, an unwanted pregnancy or feelings of guilt—can augment the adolescent's suicidal tendencies.

The Suicide Interview

Assessment of suicide risk should cut across four dimensions: ideation, volition, plan, and history. The following outline is a practical guide for assessing students' risk for suicide.

1. ***Suicidal ideation.*** Variability in terms of frequency, duration, and intensity of suicidal thoughts is one indicator of risk level. When a student's thoughts of suicide are frequent, last a long time, and interrupt the student's routine, the student is at increased risk of hurting himself or herself. To determine the frequency, duration, and intensity of suicidal ideation, the helper should ask the following questions:
   a. In the course of a single day, how often do you think about hurting yourself?
   b. When the idea of hurting yourself comes to mind, how long does the idea stay with you? How long do you dwell on it?
   c. When these thoughts come to you, are you able to continue with what you're doing, or do these thoughts get in the way of your everyday activities?

   If the suicidal ideation is not frequent (e.g., just once a day) and does not last long (several minutes), and the student is able to continue with his or her routine, then the student's risk of suicide is low. In this case, the helper should simply alert the child's parents and give them a list of symptoms to watch for—for example, increased isolation, moodiness, the child's locking himself or herself in a room. When suicidal tendencies remain at the level of ideation, the risk of suicide generally is low.

2. ***Suicidal volition.*** The key question here is "Do you want to hurt yourself?" Most students answer no, they are only thinking about it. When adolescents say they want to hurt themselves, the risk of suicide automatically increases to moderate at least. The helper must immediately alert the parents, ask them to come to the school, and direct them to take their child to the nearest medical center for a psychiatric evaluation.

3. ***Suicide plan.*** Having a plan increases the risk of suicide. The question the helper needs to ask is "If you did hurt yourself, how would you do it?" If the adolescent answers, "I don't know" or "I haven't really thought about it," the risk is lower than if the student is able to give concrete details about how and when he or she plans to commit suicide. Another

factor here is the lethality of the method (a gun, for example, versus pills). Volition plus a plan increase the risk of suicide to high. The helper should notify the parents immediately and, after letting the principal know what's going on, should call 911 to have the student taken for an immediate psychiatric evaluation. In extreme cases, when the helper has determined that the risk of suicide is imminent, the call to the parents can be made after the student is en route to the hospital.

4. *A history of attempted suicide.* A history of attempted suicide automatically increases the student's present risk. Spirito, Plummer, Gispert, and Levy (1992) found that 10 percent of those who attempted suicide did so again within a 3 month period. The helper should always ask, "Have you ever tried to hurt yourself in the past?" Here, too, the lethality of the earlier attempt should be investigated. There's a significant difference between taking a few pills and ending up in the hospital with a serious injury. Even in the absence of volition, if a suicidal student has made a serious attempt at some earlier time to hurt himself or herself, the helper should consider the current risk to be moderate.

This outline will help school personnel to cope in an orderly and professional manner with a suicidal crisis. The goal is to stabilize the situation by choosing an appropriate intervention based on an informed assessment of the risk to the student.

 FROM THE FIELD

Michelle Zagrobelny, Special Education Educator and Administrator

Michelle Zagrobelny began her career as a special education teacher and transition coordinator in Culpeper County, Virginia, after which she spent several years as an academic administrator in a residential school for students who have special needs. For the past 9 years, she has served as chairperson for both the Committee on Special Education and the Preschool Committee on Special Education in New York State public school districts.

Michelle, you've been a special education professional for over 15 years, and you've worked with many children and youth with mood disorders such as depression and bipolar disorder. We know that children who have these diagnoses are be- **coming more prevalent in our special education population. How would you account for this increase?**

I would approach answering that question in two parts. The first part is attempting to address the argument/debate of whether children are being overdiagnosed, misdiagnosed, or prematurely diagnosed versus the idea that families are reaching out more to mental health professionals to finally discover an appropriate name for why their child behaves or feels they way they do. I have known numerous children who were given a mental health diagnosis with a prescribed pharmaceutical treatment plan on their first visit to a medical physician who didn't specialize in mental health treatment. This is very frustrating to educational staff, especially when their input was not requested or considered. Unfortunately, it isn't unusual for a child to suddenly have a behavioral diagnosis yet have no issues at all in educational settings. However, I have also worked with other families and educational teams who finally understand, or begin to understand, why a child is the way they are because their emotional needs are appropriately being treated. We can't always get away with saying children who behave poorly in school are only angry, purposely delinquent, or have poor parenting outside of school.

Now, the second part of the question is why are children who have mood disorders becoming more prevalent in special education specifically? When I was growing up, special education services were for children who have mental retardation, physical disabilities, learning disabilities, etc. Children who have emotional or behavioral problems didn't always get to stay in school: They were sent away, suspended or expelled, or quit school. Since then, federal and state education laws and regulations have widened educational doors for these students and have increased the protection of parental and children rights. In addition, as an understanding of mental health needs increases in our general population, more children, as well as adults, are receiving these diagnoses. Consequently, these children are in school and may experience interruptions in education. Special education has expanded classifications to include mental health mood disorders and the appropriate supports that can be recommended and provided in the educational environment.

What are schools, such as the ones you've worked in, doing to help children affected by these debilitating conditions?

I've seen in an increase in school counselors added to schools' faculties. I'm not referring to guidance counselors. Typically, schools used to have the standard guidance counselors for mostly educational planning support. With the increase of children who have mood disorders, guidance counselors' responsibilities have increased at times to a point where neither guidance nor counseling can be effective. Thus,

counselors are hired to support just the children who have mental health needs.

Schools and outside resources, such as youth advocacy programs, mental health workers, and even social services at times, are reaching out more to one another to support these children and their families. These interventions can be very helpful, however, much improvement and efficiency is needed to make them truly beneficial to children. Lack of funding or and personnel (in rural areas) are the biggest obstacles.

I have also seen an increase in educational staff awareness through training and communication about mood disorders. The teaching staff works directly with these children more than any other school-based professional. If they are unaware and insufficiently educated about these children, then educational success can be significantly impeded.

As a former special education teacher and the current chairperson for the Committee on Special Education in your school district, what can you share with our readers that might help them work more successfully with students affected by depression?

I would encourage teachers to increase their education and training to include how to work with and understand children who have depression or other mood disorders. The days have long gone by that teachers just teach in their specialty area. For some students to progress through school successfully, they need to be surrounded by educational staff in all learning areas that are aware and may at times allow appropriate exceptions for atypical behaviors and learn how to better accommodate these children in their classrooms. I'm not implying an unfair advantage should be provided, but they deserve at least a fair chance to be successful with an increased awareness.

What are some common pitfalls new teachers might hope to avoid as they work with

these students, and how would you advise them to do so?

Quickness to judge is a common pitfall. In our everyday lives, we all either do this or really try hard not to. Also, if you are aware of a student who has mental health needs, don't assume you are able to address those needs by yourself. Always communicate with other educational or administrative staff and counseling support staff regarding specifics about the child. Don't presume that those two psychology classes you took as an undergrad qualify you to diagnose or treat what it takes trained professionals weeks to see. Even the best intentions may cause more harm then good, especially if something were to happen with a child and you may not have communicated "red flag" information to other staff or attempted your own treatment or intervention without proper input and guidance.

Finally, on a positive note, could you share a "success story" from your experience as either a teacher or administrator that highlights the benefits of effective practice relative to children and youth who have a mood disorder?

After 15 years, I struggle to think of a single success story that is worthy of a made-for-TV movie. In real life we deal with the situations as they appear, and children who have any type of disability or mental health disorder move through school like any others. If we are truly successful, the students move on to live productive lives and feel no reason to return to say thanks. It's not because they aren't grateful but rather because the system was so effective that the practice was commonplace: That's success.

Summary

Mood disorders in children and adolescents continue to be among the most challenging conditions to diagnose and treat. This larger category encompasses major depression, dysthymia, and bipolar disorder, and the diagnosis of each of these is complicated by their high rate of comorbidity with other disorders (e.g., ADHD, learning disabilities, oppositional defiant disorder, conduct disorder, and anxiety disorders).

Major depression is characterized by a major depressive episode that typically involves appetite and sleep disturbance, impaired social or academic functioning, depressed mood or loss of interest or pleasure, and change from usual functioning that is not due to the use of chemical substance or medical condition. Dysthymia is a condition quite similar to major depression but is distinct in degree of severity. For example, its discriminating feature is the presence of a dysphonic or irritable mood in the individual for at least a year. The alternating presence of both depressed and manic or euphoric moods distinguishes bipolar disorder.

The etiology of each of these mood disorders is not relegated to a specific cause. Rather, the cause may be more accurately attributed to the interaction of several factors, including the biology of the individual, the genetic makeup of the individual and her predisposition to the disorder, and environmental factors that include family structure and learned behaviors. Furthermore, assessment of depression and mania are primarily accomplished through observation, structured interview, and self-report measures.

Typically, observations are conducted using performance-based measures, such as the depression-related categories developed by Garber and Kaminski (2000). Experts have contended that the clinical interview continues to be the most effective method for diagnosing depression in children and adolescents (Kowatch et al., 2005). Self-report measures provide additional confirmation and are relatively easy to administer. Some of the more popular of these include the *Children's Depression Inventory* (CDI; Kovacs, 1992), the *Reynolds Adolescent*

Depression Scale (RADS; Reynolds, 1987), and the *Peer Nomination Inventory for Depression* (Lefkowitz & Tesiny, 1980). A recommended scale to measure mania in children is the *Young Mania Rating Scale* (Young et al., 1978; Youngstrom et al., 2004).

The most serious potential effect of depression in children and adolescents is suicide. Indeed, suicide is the second leading cause of death for individuals between the ages of 15 and 19, and has increased significantly in the past 20 years. What is more, a significant number of these suicides were committed by youth who were clinically depressed, which makes the treatment of depression a very important step in reducing the alarming number of these tragic and preventable deaths. Warning signs are often precursors to parasuicide and suicide and include (1) verbal cues (e.g., "I won't be around much longer"; "They'll be sorry for what they did to me"; "I'm very tired"; "Nobody cares"; and "People would be better off without me") and (2) behavioral cues (e.g., lack of concern about personal welfare, changes in social patterns, attempts to put personal affairs in order or to make amends, alcohol or drug use or abuse, and a sudden improvement after a period of depression).

Research on the treatment of mood disorders recommends a multimodal approach, typically involving a cognitive-behavioral therapy such as the Adolescent Coping with Depression (CWD-A) course (Lewinsohn, Clarke, Hops, & Andrews, 1990; Clarke et al., 2003), family therapy, and psychopharmacological treatment. Fluoxetine, an SSRI, is currently the only such medication approved for use with children and adolescents by the FDA. Similarly, lithium is the recommended medication for the treatment of bipolar disorder in children and adolescents and, once again, the only one approved by the FDA for use with this population.

Although mood disorders continue to be among the low-incidence disorders in school-age children; nonetheless, the potential for catastrophic consequences compels teachers, clinicians, and family members to be vigilant in identifying and painstaking in assessing suspected cases. Furthermore, teachers and parents need to be well informed regarding diagnostic procedures, as well as thoroughly familiar with current, research-based interventions. Each of these stakeholders plays a critical role, in collaboration with clinicians, in the journey to wellness for students who have a mood disorder.

Tips for Teachers

1. Become thoroughly familiar with the characteristics, assessment procedures, and recommended interventions for students suspected to have or diagnosed with a mood disorder.

2. Maintain accurate and detailed anecdotal records for any student in your class who has been diagnosed with a mood disorder. This information will be invaluable in helping medical personnel determine the effects of psychopharmacological and other cognitive and/or behavioral interventions.

3. Provide a structured curriculum and establish a predictable classroom routine for students who have been diagnosed with a mood disorder. Stability that comes from routine is comforting to students who may be experiencing mood cycles, dysthymia, or a depressive episode. Their world may seem

"out-of-control," but your classroom may provide a "safe haven" of predictability, understanding, and support.

4. Don't try to "make it all better" or "cheer up" a student who is depressed. Provide encouragement and support and alert parents, clinical professionals, and administrators if significant changes in behavior are observed.

5. Familiarize yourself with the warning signs of adolescent suicide. Carefully review the recommendations provided in this chapter, and make sure that you communicate your concerns about the student's well-being to the student, her parents, clinicians, and administrators. Experts suggest that it is important to maintain communication regarding suicidal ideation, threats, or intuited "warning signs" among caregivers and stakehold-

ers and to "stay connected" with the student of concern.

6. Avoid looking for causes for the student's dysphoria or depressed state. Usually the student does not understand the reason for her depression—it may be biochemical and therefore beyond anyone's power to "cure."

7. Most important, be firm, compassionately firm. Don't accept the student's depression as an excuse for not trying or completing an assignment. Of course, teachers need to be flexible and accommodating if the student has been absent as a result of treatment for depression or hospitalization, but it is important to help the student return to a sense of "normalcy" and routine as quickly as possible.

8. If the student's depression is associated with a "trigger" or precipitating event, try to structure the classroom environment and activities so as to avoid exposing him to evocative stimuli.

9. Consider reducing the student's workload. For example, provide fewer problems on a test or reduce the number of questions to be answered on a homework assignment. Similarly, provide alternative projects or assessments and give the student a choice. Finally, give the student and extension of the due date of an assignment, because many students who have mood disorders have difficulty with organizational tasks and meeting stringent deadlines—be flexible!

10. Provide the student who has a mood disorder with a "study buddy" or peer tutor. This can serve two purposes: provide needed social interaction; and help the student stay on task and not feel overwhelmed by the demands of the curriculum. Finally, always include the student who is depressed in all classroom activities, and ensure that he knows he is a valued member of the classroom community.

Focus Questions Revisited

1. How would you differentiate between a student who has major depression and one who has dysthymia?

A Sample Response

Dysthymia is less intense and more prolonged than major depressive disorder. Children who have dysthymia tend to exhibit irritability, but while this is similar to those for MDD, it is far less severe. Children who have dysthymia do not evidence a psychotic illness, nor do they exhibit a physiological mood-altering condition. Typically, they have good days and bad days, or they may have many mixed days, but they do not have good weeks. For a diagnosis to be made, symptoms must have persisted for at least 1 year (American Psychiatric Association, 2000).

2. What are the characteristics of bipolar disorder II, and how might they affect a student's academic and social performance?

A Sample Response

A student who has bipolar II disorder displays the characteristics of hypomania, defined as a distinct period of persistently elevated expansive or irritable mood that is not as severe as mania and lasts at least 4 days, as well as a depressive episode. Logically, a student who has this disorder will experience a loss of motivation and energy during the depressive episode that will impair academic and social performance. In addition, the hypomanic phase might prompt the student to take on too much in terms of academic workload or a social commitment, which might cause the individual to feel overwhelmed and therefore simply "shut down."

3. What steps would you take if you suspected that a child in your class might be clinically depressed?

A Sample Response

I would first alert the school psychologist or a school counselor and express my apprehension to the student. It might be prudent as well to convey my concerns to the family members of the child, who might also have noticed behaviors that suggest the individual is unhappy or despondent. Upon the recommendation of the school psychologist and with the consent of the child's parents, I would initiate prereferral interventions. If, after a reasonable period of time, these measures proved ineffective in improving the student's disposition, I would recommend that the individual be evaluated by the multidisciplinary team to determine the appropriate provision of special education services.

4. What related services personnel might be important resources to you as the classroom teacher of a child with a mood disorder? How might they provide support and/or assistance?

A Sample Response

The appropriate related services personnel in this instance would be the school psychologist and/or school counselor. These individuals are professionally qualified to develop effective treatment plans that can generalize to the classroom, which may involve a cognitive-behavioral strategy or a multimodal treatment approach. They also serve as consultants to the teacher regarding specific interventions that might be used in the classroom.

5. Which of the models used in treating depression would be most helpful to you as a classroom teacher? Provide a rationale for each of your selections.

A Sample Response

Clearly, the cognitive model offers teachers a practical approach to helping students who have MDD by encouraging students to monitor their own behavior and reinforce desired outcomes. The other models require clinical training or are simply too involved to be of benefit to the classroom teacher.

6. How is knowing about comorbidities (e.g., between bipolar disorder and attention-deficit hyperactivity disorder) potentially helpful to you as the classroom teacher of a child or adolescent who has a mood disorder?

A Sample Response

The interaction of the two disorders typically results in a more involved constellation of behaviors and clearly complicates all aspects of the treatment process: from assessment to the development of an effective behavioral intervention plan. Thus, the more the teacher knows about the diagnosis and treatment of both disorders, the better prepared she will be to provide effective interventions that address both the distractibility, irritability, increased talkativeness, and risk-taking behaviors associated with ADHD, as well as the mania and hypermania that are characteristic of bipolar disorder.

7. What observation protocol might be helpful to classroom teachers in providing relevant data for a child assigned to them who is suspected of having a mood disorder? Describe its benefits.

A Sample Response

It would be very helpful if teachers used the list of characteristic behaviors developed by Kowatch et al. (2005) and organized under three headings: discriminating features, consistent features, and variable features. These characteristics include:

Discriminating features such as

1. Depressed mood or loss of interest or pleasure
2. Change from usual functioning
3. Not due to substances or medical condition

Consistent features such as

1. Appetite and sleep disturbances
2. Impaired social or academic functioning
3. Absence of use of mood-altering substances
4. Absence of a physical condition that alters mood

Variable features such as

1. Irritability
2. Weight loss or weight gain
3. Insomnia or hypersomnia
4. Psychomotor agitation or retardation
5. Fatigue of loss of energy
6. Feelings of worthlessness and inappropriate guilt

7. Impaired concentration and change in school performance
8. Suicidal ideation
9. Diurnal variation, with worsening of symptoms in the morning
10. Unexplained somatic complaints
11. Sleep–wake cycle reverse

Of course, as with all emotional and behavioral disorders, several of these characteristics should be observed in the individual of concern, and these should be clearly evident as intense, frequent, and of significant duration (exceeding 6 months). This list of typical or characteristic behaviors should be organized as a checklist that can be easily used by the classroom teacher to record the frequency, duration, and intensity of the behaviors observed. The completed daily or weekly checklists could then be compared with those distributed to all the student's teachers and assessed to identify behavioral trends. This aggregated data would be instrumental in determining the need for formal screening and evaluation.

8. Consider the case example of Emily. Do you think she might develop suicidal ideations? Justify your response. What are some of the warning signs you would look for in assessing Emily's risk of suicide?

A Sample Response

It seems very likely that Emily has at least contemplated suicide as a means of escaping from her pain over the loss of her father and "best friend." Unless the treatment regimen is successful, there is, I think, a very good chance that Emily will need help in dealing with thoughts of suicide and will need to be closely supervised. Some of the "warning signs" to look for in Emily's case include verbal cues, such as:

a. "I'd like to go home."
b. "I won't be around much longer
c. "They'll be sorry for what they did to me."
d. "I'm very tired."
e. "I wonder what death is like."
f. "They'll see how serious I am."
g. "Things are never going to get any better."
h. "I'll always feel this way."
i. "Nobody cares."
j. "People would be better off without me."

and Behavioral cues that include the following:

a. Lack of concern about personal welfare.
b. Changes in social patterns.
c. A decline in school achievement.
d. Difficulties concentrating and thinking clearly.
e. Altered patterns of eating and sleeping.
f. Attempts to put personal affairs in order or to make amends.
g. Alcohol or drug use or abuse.
h. Unusual interest in how others are feeling.
i. Preoccupation with themes of death and violence.
j. Sudden improvement after a period of depression.
k. Sudden or increased promiscuity.

Chapter 9

Autism Spectrum Disorder

Photodisc/Getty Images

FOCUS QUESTIONS

1. Suppose you are going to be the new classroom teacher of a student who has an autistic disorder (AD). What would you want to know about the child's classroom performance and about her learning and behavioral needs as provided by her current teacher?

2. What would be important for you to know about the classroom performance of a student who has Asperger syndrome (AS) to be fully prepared to help him learn and develop?

3. Describe the *theory of mind* and what insights it provides about the functional understanding of students who have autistic disorder?

4. As the teacher of a student who has an autistic disorder, what are some important academic considerations to facilitate his acquisition of skills?

5. Explain discrete trial training.

6. What is paradigm/pivotal response training (PRT), and why is it often preferred over more structured techniques such as discrete trial training?

7. Describe video modeling and what its therapeutic implications are for children who have AD or AS.

8. What are "social stories," and how are they used to help students who have Asperger syndrome or higher-functioning autism (HFA) acquire strategies for appropriate social conversation and emotional regulation?

9. List the key behavioral characteristics of students who have autism spectrum disorder.

Few behavioral disorders that affect children and youth are more enigmatic or challenging to teachers than autism spectrum disorder (ASD). The reason for this is apparent in the principal diagnostic criteria for the disorder, which describe a child who appears both disinterested in and inept at socialization and communication. Because most people are, by nature, social creatures, this apparent lack of interest in other people on the part of most children who have ASD creates confusion and frustration in most caregivers.

Equally disconcerting is the fact that the number of children diagnosed with ASD continues to grow exponentially each year. Unless this trend abates, predictions are that, within a decade, ASD may be among the most prevalent disorders affecting school-age children. In 1992 there were 15,580 cases of ASD identified in the United States among school-age children; by 2003 that number had increased to 163,773, representing a growth rate of 393 percent (National Center for Health Statistics, 2007). Recent statistics have revealed that the number of identified cases has almost doubled in the last 3 years and, currently, the number of school-age children assessed with ASD is approximately 300,000 (IDEAdata.org., 2007). An examination of incidence rates in the United States supports this exponential growth in identification. For example, in 1992 there were 1,925 new cases of ASD reported; in 2003, a total of 9,486 new cases were identified. Furthermore, an examination of incidence rates from 1992 to 2003 reveals a consistent 20 percent increase in the number of new cases identified each year (National Center for Health Statistics, 2007).

These alarming statistics, together with the challenging behaviors displayed by children who have ASD underscore the importance of educating teachers about its characteristics and effective treatment practices. Teachers must be prepared to work effectively with students who have been diagnosed with ASD because they are compelled by IDEA to do so and, like physicians, they too are bound by a higher imperative: to help all students in their classroom to learn. Working effectively with students who have ASD requires methodical preparation both in understanding autism spectrum disorder and in providing effective remediation for those whose academic and social development have been affected by it.

This chapter will help to prepare teachers and other education professionals to do just that. The authors anchor the clinical presentation of characteristics, etiology, and research-based interventions with practical examples, based on real-life cases. By the end of the chapter, the reader should understand the nature of ASD, as well as the learning needs of individuals so diagnosed. In addition, readers will be provided examples of functional behavior assessments (FBA), as well as a behavioral intervention plans (BIPs) developed to address real-life case examples of students who have ASD. It is hoped that these examples will provide the reader with an effective process by which to address the behavioral problems that most typically affect individuals with ASD.

Finally, readers are provided with a set of strategies to facilitate working with students who have ASD, as well as relevant study questions and suggested responses to ensure their grasp of the chapter content and familiarity with effective school-based interventions.

CASE EXAMPLE: Carmen

The Stewarts report that Carmen seemed like any other infant after his birth, and he achieved developmental milestones on schedule through his third year of life. It wasn't until he was about 3½ years of age that his parents noticed something amiss: Carmen seemed disinterested in people and, most disturbingly, in his own parents. At the same time, he seemed to regress in his ability to communicate. He had developed a limited vocabulary typical for toddlers and young children of 2 or 3 years of age, but it almost seemed that he was losing it, like air rushing from a punctured balloon. By 3 years of age, Carmen was essentially nonverbal and gesticulated or resorted to tantrums to communicate his needs. Occasionally, even these nonverbal modalities produced unclear messages, and without affective response or eye contact, his parents sometimes failed to understand him. This lack of response on the part of Carmen's parents resulted in "acting out" or tantruming behavior from Carmen.

At this point, the Stewarts decided to have their son evaluated by a psychologist who specializes in evaluating and working with children who have pervasive developmental disorders, in particular, autism spectrum disorder. The psychologist used the *Autism Diagnostic Observation Schedule* (ADOS; Lord, Rutter, DiLavore, & Risi, 1999), which permits assessment through direct observation by the practitioner and is designed for use with preschool children who have little or no expressive language. In addition, the psychologist interviewed Mr. and Mrs. Stewart, inquiring about their recollection of Carmen's attainment of developmental milestones, such as walking, social speech, gaze, initiation, joint attention, and affective development. He noted the parents' concern over Carmen's apparent regression in all of these developmental areas, and that this was a recent occurrence. The clinician readily observed Carmen's impairment in social and communication skills, and a diagnosis of autistic disorder (AD) was easily confirmed.

Dr. Stilman, the child psychologist who made the diagnosis, was encouraging, citing the success of several local programs and noting that an early diagnosis increased Carmen's chances to acquire the necessary social, academic, and adaptive behavior skills to enable him to live relatively independently. The psychologist recommended immediate placement in an early-intervention program called Rainbow Riders, which was developed exclusively for young children with AD, and referred the Stewarts to an organization in the community that provided respite care for children like Carmen and in which the staff were trained in the techniques of discrete trial training used in the Rainbow Riders program.

These early interventions proved quite successful in helping Carmen acquire both communication and social skills. By the time Carmen was 6 years old, Mr. and Mrs. Stewart were sufficiently familiar with both AD and the accommodations provided for children affected by it under the federal Individuals with Disabilities Education Act (IDEA, 2004) that they were able to have Carmen classified under the category of autism. Because their school district does not have a self-contained program for children with AD, the Stewarts were successful in substantiating Carmen's need for an out-of-district placement paid for by the district. Carmen was placed in the Metamorphosis School, a magnet school for children and youth who have autistic disorder that, like the Rainbow Riders program, used an intensive "discrete trial training" approach in teaching social and communication skills. In addition, the Metamorphosis program used picture exchange communication systems (PECS) to facilitate the communication of daily tasks and agendas. For more advanced students, the program incorporated the concept of "social stories" to help teach social skills and enable children who have AD to appreciate another person's perspective. This latter technique is predicated on an approach referred to as the "theory of mind" (Garfinkle, 2000).

Carmen, currently enrolled in third grade, has made significant progress in the areas of social skills development, communication, and adaptive behavior skills. At this point, his parents are very pleased with his growth in these areas and are understandably optimistic about his prognosis.

Autistic disorder (AD), Asperger syndrome (AS), and pervasive developmental disorder, not otherwise specified (PDD-NOS), also known as atypical autism, are three DSM-IV-TR (American Psychiatric Association, 2000) diagnoses considered to form a continuum now known as autism spectrum disorder (ASD). Rhett disorder and childhood disintegrative disorder (CDD), both very rare, complete the category of pervasive developmental disorder (PDD) in the DSM-IV-TR. The almost phenomenal rise in the rates of ASD in the last 10 years has captured the interest of many. Whether the fact that more cases are being identified represents a real increase is a subject of controversy. Changes in definition and diagnostic criteria articulated in the DSM-IV-TR, better diagnosis at both ends of the spectrum, a growing awareness of the condition, and labeling needed for appropriate educational services may have contributed to this rapid rise (Volkmar & Klin, 2005). This has led some to conclude that the rise in autism diagnoses is not a real one but results from the necessity of accessing special services. In spite of this confusion, numerous epidemiological studies have been done in recent years on ASD and PDD.

CLINICAL FEATURES OF AUTISTIC DISORDERS

The DSM-IV-TR lists three categorical symptoms for autistic disorder: impairment in social interaction, impairments in communication, and restricted repetitive and stereotyped patterns of behavior. For Asperger syndrome, the categories are the same except for impairments in communication. In this section, we also discuss school adjustment, academic achievement, and some of the unique features of AS.

Impairments in Social Interactions

Children, adolescents, and adults with AD have deficits in more than one aspect of social functioning. These deficits are in the areas of gaze, social speech, joint attention, imitation, play, attachment, peer relations, and affective development (Carter, Ornstein-Davis, Klin, & Volkmar, 2005).

GAZE Normally developing infants are predisposed to establish social relationships with the primary caregiver that begins with their ability to gaze toward faces (Farroni, Csibra, Simion, & Johnson, 2002). Gazing and making eye contact are the modes of communication between the preverbal child and the primary caretaker and provide the basis for socialization (Adamson, 1995). Infants who have AD are not able to enter into mutual gazing with the primary caretaker. This feature distinguishes AD from those with developmental delays and mental retardation who are able to establish patterns of gaze. Close to 90 percent of parents of children who have AD often report retrospectively their child's inability to eye gaze (Volkmar, 1987).

SOCIAL SPEECH Normally developing infants show an attraction to the human voice, especially that of the mother, over other sounds. The reverse exists for children with AD, who prefer other kinds of sounds rather than speech. Preverbal vocalizations are atypical, and there is a limited use of communication behaviors (Sheinkopf, Mundy, Oller, & Steffens, 2000). This lack of interest in social speech denies the child the ability to establish interpersonal patterns, leading to later problems in communication.

JOINT ATTENTION Problems in gaze and social speech leads to interference in *intersubjectivity*, "the coconstruction of shared emotional meaning between parent and caregiver" (Carter et al., 2005, p. 319), which leads in turn to the failure of joint attention. *Joint attention* is the ability to share with another person an object or event (Shaffer, 1984). For example, infants often point to something (e.g., a toy) that is attractive and look back at the primary caretaker. Children who have AD are not able to establish these kinds of exchanges—an inability that appears unique to autism and is not part of the clinical presentation of other developmental disorders. If children who have AD do engage in joint attention (e.g., pointing), it is usually for functional purposes—to get something, but not to engage the interest of another person.

IMITATION   Various forms of imitation are part of the developing child and allow the child to engage in symbolic activities. This imitation usually begins with the parental behaviors. The child who has AD does not spontaneously imitate parental actions (Meltzoff & Gopnik, 1994) and has particular difficult imitating body movements and those involving objects (Stone, Ousley, & Littleford, 1997), such as playing patty-cake and pick-a-boo.

PLAY   The play of a child who has AD is distinctly different, marked by a lack of social engagement, a lack of symbolic play, and a manipulation of objects, which tends to be repetitive and stereotyped (Stone, Lemanek, Fishel, Fernandez, & Altemeier, 1990).

ATTACHMENT   At the end of the first year of life, normally developing infants have learned an array of social behaviors designed to maintain closeness with the primary caregiver, whose absence causes extreme distress (Bowlby, 1969). Insecure attachment is a feature of AD. A recent meta-analytic study, however, found no difference in attachment between those with high-functioning autism (HFA) and typically developing peers (Rutgers, Bakermans-Kranenburg, van Ijzendoorn, & van Berckelaer-Onnes, 2004). With regard to object attachment, young children who have AD prefer objects that are hard in nature as opposed to soft and cuddly ones (Volkmar & Klin, 1994).

PEER RELATIONS   Children who have AD rarely engage in mutual or cooperative play; they prefer to be alone and to engage in activities that are self-stimulating (Carter et al., 2005). Achieving typical peer relationships is very rare (Koning & Magill-Evans, 2001; Orsmond, Krauss, & Seltzer, 2004). When they do approach others, children who have AD prefer adults rather than other children (Jackson et al., 2003). In a sample of 235 adolescents and adults who had AD and were living at home, 46.4 percent were reported to have no peer relationships (Orsmund et al., 2004). As they reach adolescence, and with the help of interventions, some of those who have AD make significant gains in social skills, but their difficulty understanding and complying with social rules and conventions remains (Church, Alisanski, & Amanullah, 2000; Seltzer et al., 2003).

AFFECTIVE DEVELOPMENT   By age 3, typical children develop the capacity to understand and name their own and others' emotional states. Children who have AD have great difficulty doing so. Their disengagement and aloofness restricts emotional expression. When they do express emotion, children who have AD often do so in inappropriate or unusual fashion (Kasari, Sigman, Baumgartner, & Stipek, 1993). A lack of empathy is the consequence of their inability to recognize emotional expression; therefore, it might be typical for a child who has AD to react indifferently to someone who is in pain (Bacon, Fein, Morris, Waterhouse, & Allen, 1998).

It is important to note that although the above-mentioned social features exist with some consistency, there is still a great deal of variability among individuals who have AD with regard to social functioning. Much of this variability has been observed in laboratory settings, and it is not clear at this point to what degree such variability exists in natural settings. Along with the absence of relatedness in individuals who have AD, it is also important for future research to examine the kind of relatedness that might be typical in autism.

Language and Communication

Problems in speech are usually the first signs to parents that something is not quite right in their child's development. Language problems present a differential challenge because they overlap with many other disorders. Most children who have AD, in contrast to those who have AS, begin to speak late and develop speech at a slower rate (Le Couteur, Bailey, Rutter, & Gottesman, 1989). IQ can account for some differences in language development. In some cases, those who have higher IQ have better language development (Howlin, Goode, Hutton, & Rutter, 2004), and those who have very low verbal IQ do not achieve functional language (Tager-Flusberg, Paul, & Lord, 2005).

For those who do speak, articulation is often normal and even advanced, and those who have HFA can score quite well on standardized vocabulary tests (Kjelgaard & Tager-Flusberg, 2001). Social-emotional words cause notable difficulty for those who have AD (Eskes, Bryson, & McCormick, 1990). Echolalia, the repetition with similar tone of words or phrases that someone else has said, has always been considered a classic symptom of AD. Not all children who have AD, however, engage in echolalia, and it can be present with other disorders. Echolalia can serve any number of communicative and protective functions for the child who has AD: turn taking, assertions, affirmative answers, requests, rehearsal to aid processing, and self-regulation (Prizant & Duchan, 1981).

Another salient characteristic in language use among those who have AD is confusion about the use of personal pronouns. For example, a child may manifest a desire for ice cream by saying, "Do you want some ice cream?" Such confusion is not limited to children who have AD, but it does exist more frequently in this population. A plausible explanation for pronoun confusion is that individuals who have AD have difficulty distinguishing self from other (Lee, Hobson, & Chiat, 1994). Intonation can also be peculiar: Children who have AD often speak in a monotonous tone, devoid of any feeling or emotion. Most children who have AD make attempts at communication, albeit limited, but they rarely initiate spontaneous communication (Stone & Caro-Martinez, 1990). The most common difficulties in language use among those who have autism spectrum disorder include listening, talking to self, following rules of politeness, and making irrelevant remarks (Tager-Flusberg et al., 2005). Some studies have shown that unusualness of speech increases with the amount of speech (Caplan, Guthrie, Shields, & Yudovin, 1994; Volden & Lord, 1991).

Reading comprehension among those who have AD is often commensurate with overall ability. Many will learn to read words without any direct instruction, and some will manifest an early and exaggerated interest in letters and numbers (Loveland et al., 1997). A small number of children who have AD will manifest *hyperlexia*, indicated by superior word recognition and compulsiveness about reading letters or writing (Nation, 1999; Tager-Flusberg et al., 2005). Hyperlexia can be considered a **savant skill** and, like other savant skills, fails to connect to overall intelligence and function.

SAVANT SKILL

A special brilliance, ability, or expertise in a particular areas(s) that is in contrast to the individual's overall intelligence.

Recent literature has investigated the narrative storytelling capacities of verbal children who have AD. Their stories tended to be less complex, shorter, have more grammatical errors (Bruner & Feldman, 1993), be less likely to have a resolution or introduce new characters (Tager-Flusberg, 1995), be less likely to reveal mental states of the characters (Baron-Cohen, Leslie, & Frith, 1986), often include **neologisms** and idiosyncratic expressions (Loveland, McEvoy, Tunali, & Kelley, 1990), and lacked identification of the causes of their characters' internal states (Capps, Losh, & Thurber, 2000).

Stereotyped, Repetitive, and Ritualistic Behaviors

This is the third categorical symptom in the DSM-IV-TR, and these behaviors occur in both children and adults. There has been less research into these symptoms compared to social development and language. One difficulty is distinguishing the stereotypes and ritualistic behaviors of AD from obsessive-compulsive disorder (OCD). There appears to be a development around such behaviors for those with AD as they go from repetitive sensory motor activities at an early age to more complex and elaborate activities similar to those of OCD (Militerni, Bravaccio, Falco, Fico, & Palermo, 2002). These more developed symptoms are often maintained through adulthood. Some have argued that the stereotypes of ASD can be distinguished from those of OCD because their forms are less organized, less complex, and more **egosyntonic** (i.e., acceptable and desirable) (Swedo et al., 1989), whereas others have argued that those with OCD also may regard their ritualistic behaviors as egosyntonic (Insel & Akiskal, 1986).

Stereotypes and ritualistic behaviors also occur in other disorders, such as mental retardation, schizophrenia, and neurological conditions such as Tourette syndrome and Parkinson disease. At least among adults with AD, the compulsions, stereotypy, and self-injury are more frequent and more severe (Bodfish, Symons, Parker, & Lewis, 2000). Among other age groups with AD, this cluster of symptoms varies greatly and appears to be related to the developmental level of the individual.

School Adjustment and Academic Achievement

Because of difficulties in social development, the school environment can be particularly challenging for children who have AD, as they find it difficult to regulate their own behaviors and understand the expectations of their teachers and peers. These deficits can result in tremendous confusion and bewilderment. Any changes in routine can be especially difficult because of their cognitive rigidity and inflexibility (Loveland & Tunali-Kotoski, 2005). Impairments in executive functioning along with attention/concentration deficits can make it very difficult for students who have AD to organize their time, complete homework and tests, and so on. They are also known to exhibit symptoms of hyperactivity, which can interfere with learning. Often, their nonverbal skills are more developed than their verbal skills (in contrast to those who have AS). Among those with HFA, mechanical reading, computational tasks, and spelling pose fewer challenges. There is a great deal of variability in the academic challenges for those who have

NEOLOGISMS

Newly coined words, usages, or expressions. Individuals who have ASDs may use neologisms that have no meaning to others.

EGOSYNTONIC

An individual's feelings, attitudes, and behaviors are consistent with the needs of the ego and one's self-image.

AD, and the best educational placement will be those that are sensitive to each individual's needs.

ASPERGER SYNDROME

CASE EXAMPLE: James

James is a 15-year-old high school sophomore enrolled in a residential treatment program for youth who have learning and adjustment difficulties. He is currently attending the program as a day student. James was recently diagnosed with Asperger syndrome (AS), but he was originally treated for major depression. It now appears that the depression may have been a by-product of the acute social alienation and rejection James experiences as a result of his AS.

James presents as a very loquacious young man who is passionate about politics, specifically, U.S. politics and the Democratic Party. He appears to be very knowledgeable about these subjects, based on the volume of information he shares with often unresponsive audiences, and he is constantly reading newspaper articles, as well as books that are politically focused. As a result of his extensive reading, he has developed some very strong opinions regarding the current political climate in the United States and the world. He is eager to share his amassed knowledge and his perspective with anyone who will listen; however, his inability to pick up on social cues and his pedantic, unidirectional style is "off-putting." Ironically, James is very sensitive to this "rejection" and experiences depression as a result of his perceived alienation and his inability to attract and retain friends. These bouts of acute depression have caused James to be hospitalized for suicidal ideation and expressed threats to harm himself.

Recently, James has begun participating in group therapy with other students diagnosed with AS. The focus of this group is the development of social communication skills and competence in interactions with social partners. Because people with AS typically have strong verbal abilities, eliciting conversation is not a problem; the challenge is helping these individuals understand the emotional states of social partners and their perspective, as well as recognizing social conventions relative to context. In addition, the group facilitator, Dr. Edwards, has formed a "buddy skills training program" that helps nondisabled peers learn about AS and its characteristics, as well as effective communication interventions predicated on the use of concrete, unambiguous speech. Many individuals who have AS are very literal in their interpretation of language, missing the subtleties of irony and sarcasm. For these persons, it is important that communication partners use concrete language and avoid the ambiguities inherent in sarcasm and figurative speech. For example, the therapist uses the anecdote about the father who observes his son, lounging on the patio beside the overgrown lawn and idle lawnmower, and remarks, "I guess I'll be saving some money this week." The counselor then asks the group participants to explain the sarcasm in the father's remark. At the start of the program, none of the participants could identify and explain the nuance; however, after three sessions, all the group members could do so.

In addition, the therapist uses "social stories" to enhance James's appreciation of social context, appropriate behavioral response, and the perspective of a social partner. His participation in the group sessions, as well as his rehearsal and use of the skills taught by the counselor, has succeeded in increasing James's self-confidence in social situations and thus reducing the incidence of depression. Helping James "fit in" and become more socially accepted is the ultimate goal of this cognitive approach. For students like James, successful social integration is the key to a productive, satisfying life.

Characteristics of Asperger Syndrome

One of the distinguishing features of AS is the absence of any significant delays in language acquisition, cognitive development, and self-help skills (Klin, McPartland, & Volkmar, 2005). In fact, language acquisition is often precocious and may have a pedantic, teaching quality to it. During the preschool years, attachment patterns, unlike those of individuals who have AD, seem unremarkable to parents. These children are not isolated or withdrawn, and they do tend to approach others, albeit in an inappropriate or eccentric fashion. Because they are able to acquire a wealth of facts and information related to some interest, individuals who have AS will often engage in one-way conversation by communicating a lot of information related to their interest while being insensitive to someone who does not share the same interest. These awkward approaches result in others' wanting to distance themselves and explains why the child who has AS may have few friends.

With regard to communication patterns, Klin (1994) distinguished three aspects that are helpful in diagnosing AS. The first is poor and restricted range of inflection and intonation, even though it may be less rigid than is found in AD. Poor modulation of rate, volume, and fluency may also be evident. The second aspect is that the language content is often circumstantial and tangential, with loose associations and even incoherence. Third, an individual who has AS is often verbose and capable of carrying on lengthy and monotonous monologues about a favorite subject independent of the listener's interest.

Circumscribed interests is another diagnostic feature of AS. People who have AS are capable of acquiring huge amounts of information about a particular topic of interest. These topics can change. What does not change is that other family members find themselves immersed in listening for long periods of time. Typically developing children also can have exaggerated interests. What distinguishes the child who has AS, however, is that these interests interfere with their learning by absorbing the child's capacity for attention and motivation and negatively affecting socialization (Klin et al., 2005). Motor difficulties may also be part of the presentation of those who have AS. They often have difficulties with coordination and in learning sophisticated motor skills associated with athletic activities.

Comorbidity is high among those who have AS, with the most significant conditions being anxiety and depression. Depression is often the result of repeated failures at socialization, and anxiety results from the demands for socialization. Often, parents of children who have AS pressure them into socializing and force them into situations that provoke anxiety. Comorbidity rates of anxiety and/or depression may be as high as 65 percent (Ghaziuddin, 2002). Some case reports have suggested that because of their lack of empathy, people who have AS are at risk for violent and criminal behavior, but there is little empirical support for this hypothesis. Although lack of empathy is a defining characteristic of AS and a consequence of poor insight into the emotions of other people, such individuals do manifest concern and compassion for others (Klin et al., 2005). Because of their social clumsiness, children who have AS are more likely to be victims than victimizers. In early reports on AS, schizophrenia was another suggested association, but research has not supported such an association. The suggestion is most likely the result of the tendency of those who have AS to engage in long, sometimes incoherent and disorganized, monologues about their special interest. Although disorganized thinking can be a feature of AS, it rarely meets the criteria for a thought disorder.

PREVALENCE OF AUTISM SPECTRUM DISORDERS

Between 1966 and 1993, eighteen epidemiological surveys for autistic disorder were conducted and yielded a median rate of 4.7 per 10,000, in contrast to surveys completed between 1994 and 2004, which yielded a median rate of 12.7 per 10,000. Little doubt exists that the diagnosis of AD has increased dramatically. The reporting, however, of a more specific current prevalence rate for AD is not an easy task. Twenty-eight surveys published since 1987 show an average prevalence rate of 16.2 per 10,000, with a median rate of 11.3 per 10,000. According to Fombonne (2005), a conservative estimate for the current rate of AD is somewhere between 10 per 10,000 and 16 per 10,000 with a midpoint of 13 per 10,000, and this is considered to be good estimate of the current rate of AD. Many epidemiological surveys have also reported medical conditions associated with AD, and these are summarized in Table 9.1.

Prevalence rates for Asperger syndrome are even more difficult to establish, because it is a relatively recent diagnostic category with a paucity of epidemiological surveys. What we do know about the rates for AS is derived from surveys on AD. In almost all surveys, the rate for AS was lower than for AD. A conservative estimate is that the ratio of AD to AS is about 5:1 which translates into a prevalence of 2.6 per 10,000 for AS based on the above-mentioned prevalence of 13 per 10,000 for AD.

Epidemiological surveys have consistently yielded a higher rate for PDD-NOS than for AD. Between 1966 and 2004, fourteen studies yielded separate

TABLE 9.1   Medical Conditions Associated with Autism

	Number of Studies	Median Rate/10,000	Range
Cerebral palsy	7	1.4	0–4.8
Fragile X	9	0.0	0–8.1
Tuberous sclerosis	11	1.1	0–3.8
Phenylketonuria	8	0	0–0
Neurofibromastosis	7	0	0–1.4
Congenital rubella	11	0.0	0–5.9
Epilepsy	12	16.7	0–26.4
Hearing deficits	8	1.3	0–5.9
Visual deficits	6	0.7	0–11.1

Source: From "Epidemiological Studies of Pervasive Developmental Disorders," by E. Fombonne in *Handbook of Autism and Pervasive Developmental Disorders: Vol 1. Diagnosis, Development, Neurobiology, and Behavior* (3rd ed., p. 50) by F. R. Volkmar, R. Paul, A. Klin, and D. Cohen (Eds.), 2005, New York: Wiley. Copyright 2005 by Wiley Publishers. Reprinted with permission.

estimates for PDD-NOS (or a similar category) with a ratio range of 0.44 to 3.33 and a mean ratio of 1.6 for PDD-NOS to AD. Based on a 13/10,000 rate for AD, this translates into a prevalence of 20.8 per 10,000 for PDD-NOS.

Combining the prevalence rates for AD, AS, and PDD-NOS yields a combined rate of 36.4 per 10,000, considered a very conservative estimate. More recent surveys have indicated a combined prevalence rate as high as 60 per 10,000. Considering these two rates as low and high endpoints, it is estimated that currently in the United States anywhere from 284,000 to 486,000 individuals under the age of 20 suffer from a pervasive developmental disorder. Disaggregating the data along the lines of race, ethnicity, social class, and immigrant status have failed to produce any significant differences.

ETIOLOGY OF AUTISM SPECTRUM DISORDERS

In recent years, research on the causes of autism spectrum disorders has focused on genetics, neurochemistry, neurology, and brain functioning. Other risk factors, mostly environmental in nature, such as obstetrics and vaccinations, have also been studied.

Genetic Influences

Two major twins studies have been done on autism: the Scandinavian Twin Study (Steffenburg, Gillberg, Hellgren, & Andersson, 1989) and the British Twin Study (Bailey, Le Couteur, Gottesman, Bolton, 1995). Both these studies showed a huge disparity in the concordance rates between monozygotic (MZ) and dizygotic (DZ) twins—60 percent for the former versus 5 percent for the latter. Quantitative analysis on these studies resulted in estimating the **heritability index** for autism at 90 percent (Rutter, 2005). The significant discrepancy in these studies between MZ and DZ twins strongly supports genetics as a factor in the etiology of ASD and, at the same time, suggests a broader **phenotype** because only about 1 in 10 of DZ pairs were concordant in terms of social and cognitive deficits. Family studies have attempted to determine the rate of autism in siblings and parents. Bolton, Macdonald, Pickles, and Rios, (1994) found the rate of autism in siblings of autistic individuals to be 3 percent, and an additional 3 percent showed symptoms along the spectrum.

HERITABILITY INDEX

A number that expresses the influence of heredity on a property or attribute. A high heritability index means that environmental factors are less important than genetic factors.

PHENOTYPE

The observed qualities of an organism, as opposed to genotype, which refers to the genetic basis of an organism, which may or may not be observed.

Neurochemical Risk Factors

The behavioral, emotional, and cognitive features of ASDs indicate that the central nervous system (CNS) is different in people who have ASD. Studies have focused on three neurotransmitters (serotonin, dopamine, and norepinephrine) and on hypothalamic–pituitary (HPA) function.

NEUROTRANSMITTERS

Serotonin Most of the interest in neurotransmitters as an etiological factor has focused on serotonin (also called 5-hydroxytryptamine, or 5-HT) because of its role in perception and a small number of treatment studies that have indicated a positive therapeutic effect for selective serotonin reuptake inhibitors (SSRIs) in persons with ASDs. Dating back to the 1960s (see, e.g., Schain & Freedman, 1961), it has been generally accepted that blood levels of 5-HT are elevated in individuals with autism. In a recent study, Mulder et al. (2004) found that 5-HT was bimodally distributed (there are two distinct peaks in the distribution curve) in autism and PDD. It is now recognized that about half of the individuals who have PDD also have *hyperserotonemia,* which is a group of symptoms caused by severely elevated serotonin levels in the body (Anderson & Hoshino, 2005). Whether high or low, abnormal levels of serotonin are well documented in individuals with PDDs.

Dopamine Dopamine has also generated a good deal of interest in the causality of autism because of its regulatory role in motor function, cognition, and hormone release dopamine blockers have been shown to be effective in treating some aspects of autism (Anderson & Hoshino, 2005). Early studies supported the tendency of dopamine levels to be lower in children with autism when compared to normal samples (Cohen, Caparulo, Shaywitz, & Bowers, 1977; Cohen, Shaywitz, Johnson, & Bowers, 1974). Later studies, however, found that only 50 percent of the autism samples had elevated levels of homovanillic acid (HVA) (the principal metabolite of dopamine) in the cerebrospinal fluid (Gillberg & Svennerholm, 1987; Gillberg, Svennerholm, & Hamilton-Hellberg, 1983). Other studies found no significant elevations in the group that had autism when compared to controls (Narayan, Srinath, Anderson, & Meundi, 1993; Ross, Klykylo, & Anderson, 1985). As a result of these studies, the dopamine hypothesis as an etiological factor in ASDs remains controversial, and more research is needed. "Taken together, the CSF [cerebrospinal fluid] studies do not appear to provide strong support for the idea that central DA [dopamine] turnover is increased in autism" (Anderson & Hoshino, 2005, p. 457).

Norepinephrine The same may be said for norepinephrine (NE), a neurotransmitter that is crucially related to processes of arousal, anxiety, stress responses, and memory. NE operates in both the CNS and the **sympathetic nervous system (SNS)**. The NE causal hypothesis is based on the indication that in some individuals who have autism, the SNS is hypersensitive to stress, and some evidence that clonidine (which lessens central NE function) has been effective in treating autism (Frankhauser, Karumanchi, German, Yales, & Karumanchi, 1992). Studies have shown that NE levels are increased on measures of acute response in individuals who have autism (Lake, Ziegler, & Murphy, 1977; Leboyer et al., 1992; Levanthal. Cook, Morford, & Ravitz, 1990), but not on measures on basal functioning (Launay, Bursztejn, Ferrari, & Dreux, 1987; Martineau, Barthelemy, Jouve, & Muh, 1992; Minderaa, Anderson, Volkmar, & Akkerhuis, 1994). This last finding suggests that there is little alteration in baseline sympathetic functioning in individuals who have autism when compared to normal controls. The differences seem to be more at the level of acute response rather than baseline functioning.

HYPOTHALAMIC–PITUITARY FUNCTIONING (HPF) Studies on hypothalamic–pituitary functioning (HFP) and autism have concentrated on cortisol secretion,

SYMPATHETIC NERVOUS SYSTEM (SNS)

The part of the nervous system that controls the fight-or-flight response.

thyroidism, and sex hormones, because these all play a role in the stress response and are closely related to the sympathetic nervous system.

Cortisol Cortisol is released from the adrenal cortex in response to stress. Some studies have not shown a significant difference in cortisol levels in individuals with autism on a measure of baseline functioning (Nir et al., 1995; Sandman, Barron, Chicz-Demet, & DeMet, 1990; Tordjman et al., 1997), but others have indicated a decreased level in autism (Curin et al., 2003; Hoshino et al., 1984; Jensen, Realmuto, & Garfinkel, 1985). Some evidence has suggested that individuals with low-IQ autism have more difficulty suppressing cortisol than those with higher IQ's (Buitelaar, van Engeland, van Ree, & de Wied, 1990), leading to the hypothesis that cortisol secretion in people who have autism must be viewed as a continuous variable.

Hypothyroidism Congenital hypothyroidism (underactive thyroid function) has been found in a number of patients who have autism (Gillberg & Coleman, 1992; Gillberg, Gillberg, & Koop, 1992; Ritvo et al., 1990). Because samples sizes in these studies have been small, it is not yet clear whether the finding of hypothyroidism is coincidental or poses a major risk factor for the development of autism. More research is needed before it can be considered a significant factor.

Sex Hormones Concerning a possible inhibited release of sex hormones in people who have autism, one study (Tordjman, Anderson, McBride, & Hertzig, 1995) found no differences in sex hormones between autistic and control groups. Currently, there are no known reports of the therapeutic effect of increasing sex-related hormones in autistic individuals.

In conclusion, Anderson and Hoshino (2005) highlighted how few replicated studies have supported differences in neurochemical risk factors in individuals who have autism. The most robust and replicated support exists for the increase in serotonin among those who have autism. Although there may be abnormalities in other neurochemicals, none of these can be considered a significant risk factor until more research is able to provide more replicated results.

Neurological Risk Factors

In recent decades, magnetic resonance imaging (MRI) has made possible the study of the cognitive and brain bases of autism and related disorders. Studies of autopsied brains of individuals who had autism have revealed an increase of brain volume and brain weight (Bailey, Luthert, Bolton, Le Couteur, & Rutter, 1993; Carper, Moses, Tigue, & Courchesne, 2002; Courchesne et al., 2001; Herbert et al., 2004). Although most individuals who have autism are born with normal head circumferences, head growth appears to accelerate dramatically during the preschool years (Lainhart, Piven, Wzorek, & Landa, 1997). The area of the brain that increases the greatest appears to be white matter in the frontal lobe. Also, studies have shown that for those aged 13 or less, brain weight is heavier than expected by 100 to 200 grams, in contrast to those over the age of 21, whose brains were lighter in weight than expected (Bauman & Kemper, 1997).

Brain studies related to autism indicate that it is a neural system disorder that affects information processing/integration and whose onset is at about 30 weeks of gestation (Minshew, Sweeney, Bauman, & Webb, 2005). These problems in neuronal connectivity appear together with later abnormal brain weight and volume.

Brain Function

In contrast to traditional MRI, functional magnetic resonance imaging (fMRI) allows studies of the brain dynamically, while it is at work. Such studies of individuals who have autism have assumed a great deal of importance in the last few years, because fMRI can detect functional aberrance. fMRI studies of people who have ASD have concentrated in the areas of language/communication dysfunction, social dysfunction, and stereotyped repetitive behaviors.

LANGUAGE/COMMUNICATION DYSFUNCTION   At least five fMRI studies have examined language dysfunction (Boddaert et al., 2003; Gervais et al., 2004; Herbert et al., 2002; Just, Cherassky, Keller, & Minshew, 2004; Muller et al., 1999). The studies consistently showed deficiencies in left temporal lobe language regions as the likely cause for language dysfunction. Gervais et al. (2004) found, more specifically, that subjects with AD, when compared with controls, failed to activate voice-selective regions of the brain in response to vocal sounds in contrast to nonvocal sounds. In a study of participants with HFA, Just et al. (2004) found more activation in **Wernicke's area** and less activation in **Broca's area**, which could explain why those with AD tend toward overanalysis and hyperlexia, but have greater difficulties integrating words into a coherent whole, which results in poorer conceptual comprehension.

WERNICKE'S AREA

A portion of the left posterior temporal lobe of the brain, involved in the ability to understand words.

BROCA'S AREA

A portion of the frontal lobe of the brain, usually of the left cerebral hemisphere, and associated with the motor control of speech.

SOCIAL DYSFUNCTION   To understand the cause of social dysfunction in individuals who have ASD, studies have concentrated on social perception and social cognition.

Face Perception   Face perception forms the basis of the social perception studies. To function socially, an individual must be able to recognize identity through the structural features of another person's face and to perceive the internal state of another through the shape and changes of the face (Schultz & Robins, 2005). Numerous studies have shown that those who have ASD have an impaired ability to recognize facial identity (Davies, Bishop, Manstead, & Tantum, 1994; Deruelle, Rondan, Gepner, & Tardif, 2004; Grelotti, Gauthier, & Schultz, 2002; Hauck, Fein, & Maltby, 1999; Joseph & Tanaka, 2003). Recently, fMRI studies have attempted to examine the cause of this impaired ability.

The area of the brain that is responsible for face selectivity is in a portion of the fusiform gyrus knows as the fusiform face area (FFA), a small region in the underside of the temporal lobe. This area of the brain is responsible for the second aspect of social perception, the interpretation of social signals in the form of changing aspects of the face and body. Schultz et al. (2000) showed that among a group of fourteen participants who had ASD, the FFA area of the brain was hypoactive. This hypoactivity was compensated for by overactivity in another area of the brain, the inferior temporal gyrus, which is responsible for object differentiation. Hypoactivity of the FFA has been replicated in numerous other studies (see, e.g., Critchley et al., 2000; Hall, Szechtman, & Nahmias, 2003; Hubi et al., 2003; Pierce Muller, Ambrose, Allen, & Courchesne, 2001; Piggot et al., 2004; Wang, Dapretto, Hariri, Sigman, & Bookheimer, 2004). Only two studies thus far failed to show hypoactivity in the FFA among those who have ASD (Hadjikhani et al., 2004; Pierce, Haist, Sedaghat, & Courchesne, 2004). At present, the evidence seems to be more in the direction that impairment of face recognition of those who have ASD is the result of hypoactivity of the FFA.

Social Cognition   Studies on the prefrontal region, the part of the brain that is responsible for social cognition (i.e., thinking about others' thoughts, feelings, and intentions) have shown dysfunction among those who have ASD (Castelli, Frith, Happe, & Frith, 2002; Ernst, Zametkin, Matochik, Pascualvaca, & Cohen, 1997; Haznedar et al., 2000). More specific studies have concentrated on the amygdala, the part of the brain responsible for processing emotional information and emotional arousal. Those who have ASD, when assigned tasks that require the recognition of facial expression, had hypoactivity of the amygdala (Baron-Cohen et al., 1999; Castelli et al., 2002; Pierce et al., 2001; Wang et al., 2004).

Environmental Factors

Being a monozygotic twin, obstetric complications, and vaccinations have all been considered possible risk factors in the development of ASDs. There is little evidence, to date, that being a monozygotic twin is a major risk factor. Some studies have shown an association between autism and obstetric complications (Tsai, 1987). Bolton, Murphy, Macdonald, and Whitlock (1997), after a systematic review, concluded that the association between obstetric complications and ASDs was a consequence of a genetically abnormal fetus. The association, therefore, represents an epiphenomenon—a secondary phenomenon resulting from the condition—rather than a primary causal factor.

In recent years there has been much talk about vaccinations, particularly the measles–mumps–rubella (MMR) vaccination, as a cause of ASDs. The origin of this hypothesis was the temporal association between the time of the MMR vaccination and the first manifestation of ASD. Studies have not been able to confirm the temporal association (Farrington, Miller, & Taylor, 2001; Taylor et al., 1999). Furthermore, Japan discontinued the use of the MMR vaccination, which did not affect the rates of autism. A related concern has been the effects of thimerosal, a vaccine preservative containing ethyl mercury, as a cause of ASDs (Bernard, Enayati, Redwood, Roger, & Binstock, 2001). This causal hypothesis is based on studies that have shown mercury in high doses can cause neurodevelopmental abnormalities (Stratton, Gable, & McCormick, 2001). Some recent studies have tested this causal hypothesis and found little evidence to support it. Denmark, for example, discontinued the use of thimerisol, but there was no decrease in the reported number of ASDs (Hviid, Stellfeld, Wohlfahrt, & Melbye, 2003). Other factors, such as maternal and congenital hypothyroidism, and maternal cocaine and alcohol abuse, have also been considered in the etiology of

ASDs. Although such factors may play contributory roles, there is little evidence to suggest that they are common causal factors.

In summary, current research indicates that ASD is a complex genetic disorder with interaction effects on brain development. The previous sections have reviewed the research regarding the genetic and neurological causes of ASD. Research continues, especially with fMRI studies of the brain function of those who have ASD. With larger sample sizes and more sophisticated laboratory equipment, future studies should shed more light on the etiology and development of ASD.

ASSESSMENT OF AUTISM SPECTRUM DISORDERS

Because of the recent rise in diagnosed rates of ASDs and the more favorable outcomes for early intervention, numerous assessment instruments are available for individuals from infancy through adulthood. For our purposes, we will confine ourselves to instruments that are appropriate for a school-aged population and divide them into three groups: screening rating scales, diagnostic interviews, and observation scales.

Screening Measures

Screening scales are the most numerous assessments instruments for ASDs and can be divided into two types: those that screen individuals from within the general population and those that screen individuals from those at risk for other developmental disorders.

***AUTISM BEHAVIOR CHECKLIST* (ABC; KRUG, ARICK, & ALMOND, 1980a, 1980b)** The ABC is rating scale of fifty-seven items that assesses behavior in five areas: sensory, relating, body and object use, language and social interaction, and self-help. It was originally intended to be completed by teachers for purposes of educational planning. The ABC takes about 20 minutes to complete, and the authors recommend that the informant have known the individual for at least 3 to 6 weeks. It can be used for any individual 18 months or older.

The ABC has been used widely and has the advantage of easy administration and scoring. More recently, its psychometric properties have been questioned. For example, Sturmey, Matson, and Sevin (1992) found some of the **alphas** of the subscales to be quite low. The ABC subscales were not empirically formulated but grouped according to face validity. As a result, factor analysis of the ABC has not supported the subscale grouping of items (Miranda-Linne & Melin, 2002; Wadden, Bryson, & Rodger, 1991). Interrater reliability has ranged from 95 percent (Krug et al., 1980b) to less than 70 percent (Volkmar, Cicchetti, Dykens, & Sparrow, 1988). Some have suggested that the number of items on the ABC be reduced and that the cutoff score be revised to increase sensitivity (Oswald & Volkmar, 1991). Presently, the best use of the ABC appears to be with older children and adults (Coonrod & Stone, 2005).

ALPHA

Also known as Cronbach's alpha, it is the measure of a scale's reliability through the correlation of scores on a test–retest or split half, where one half of the test is correlated with the second half.

CHILDHOOD AUTISM RATING SCALE (CARS; SCHOPLER, REICHLER, & RENNER, 1988)

The CARS is one of the most well known, widely used, and best documented rating scales for screening behaviors associated with ASD (Lord & Corsello, 2005). It consists of fifteen items designed to discriminate between children with AD and those with other developmental disorders. Minimal training is required to administer the CARS. Items are scored on a continuum from 1 to 4, with 30 being a suggested cutoff score for mild to moderate autism; 37 and above suggests more severe autism. The CARS should be used with individuals 4 years of age or older.

Psychometric properties are reportedly quite good. Interrater reliability for an individual item is generally greater than 0.50, and correlations from different sources (e.g., parent informant and observation) were greater than 0.80. Sensitivity of the CARS is also quite high; 92 percent of an adult sample who had a cutoff score of 30 also met the DSM-III criteria for AD (Sevin, Matson, Coe, & Fee, 1991). Subsequent studies have shown less sensitivity, but that can be regained with a cutoff score of 32 (Lord, 1995, 1997). Total scores on the CARS are internally consistent (Kurita, Kita, & Miyake, 1992). A factor analysis of the CARS yielded five factors: social communication, emotional reactivity, social orienting, cognitive and behavioral consistency, and odd sensory explanation (Stella, Mundy, & Tuchman, 1999).

The CARS can be used for clinical observation, by parents and teachers, and also as part of a parent interview. The ease of scoring and administration, along with its appropriateness for the educational system, make the CARS a highly desirable instrument for screening for ASDs.

GILLIAM AUTISM RATING SCALE (GARS; GILLIAM, 1995)

The GARS consists of fifty-six items grouped into four domains: early development, stereotyped behaviors, communication skills, and social interaction. Items are rated on a four-point scale ranging from "Never Observed" to "Frequently Observed." It is designed for individuals ages 3 to 22, takes about 10 minutes, and can be completed by anyone who is familiar with the child's behavior, although the early development part is most appropriately filled out by the primary caretaker. In addition to screening, the GARS can also help in planning treatment goals and measuring responses to interventions (Coonrod & Stone, 2005).

Reliability of the GARS, both internal and interrater, is quite high. In general, the initial report of the GARS psychometric properties was quite good (Gilliam, 1995). However, subsequent analysis of the GARS found that it produced a high number of false negatives (South et al., 2002). Revisions of the GARS continue, and it promises to be a valuable instrument. Presently, it is recommended that it be used in conjunction with other measures to diagnose AD (Lord & Corsello, 2005).

SOCIAL RESPONSIVENESS SCALE (SRS; CONSTANTINO, 2002)

Formerly known as the *Social Responsivity Scale,* the SRS is a 65-item questionnaire to be completed by an adult (e.g., teacher or parent) who observes the child in a social situation. It is designed to measure an individual's capacity for reciprocal social interaction, and the sixty-five items load on three dimensions: communication (six items), social interactions (thirty-five items), and repetitive and stereotyped behaviors and interests (twenty items). Items are rated on a scale of 0 (not true) to 3 (almost always true) according to frequency. Interrater reliability between parents and teachers ranged from 0.73 to 0.75; test–retest reliabilities ranged from 0.83 to 0.88, and internal consistency had a reported alpha of 0.97 (Constantino et al., 2004). The SRS can be a useful and reliable instrument if the intention is to measure difficulties in social reciprocity and odd behaviors (Lord & Corsello, 2005).

CHILDREN'S SOCIAL BEHAVIOR SCALE (CSBQ; LUTEIJN, LUTEIJN, VOLKMAR, JACKSON, & MINDERAA, 2000)   The CSBQ is a 96-item questionnaire to be completed by parents for individuals between the ages of 4 and 18. Items require the respondent to focus on behaviors within the last 2 months and to rate them from 0 (does not describe the child) to 2 (clearly applies to the child). The CSBQ has five factors: acting out, social contact problems, social insight problems, anxious/rigid, and stereotypical. Except for the stereotypical scale, the subscales have adequate internal consistency, as well as test–retest reliability.

The CSBQ can be helpful in discriminating, AD from other PDDs. Preliminary analyses show that children with PDD-NOS scored higher on the acting-out scale than did children with AD. Because it is fairly new, investigations continue of the CSBQ, but it promises to be a helpful screening measure, especially for purposes of differential diagnosis.

Diagnostic Interviews

Presently, there are two diagnostic interview schedules for ASDs worthy of review: the *Autism Diagnostic Interview–Revised* (ADI-R) and the *Diagnostic Interview for Social and Communication Disorders* (DISCO).

ADI-R (LORD, RUTTER, & LeCOUTEUR, 1994)   The ADI-R is a revision of the *Autism Diagnostic Interview* (ADI; LeCouteur, Rutter, Lord, & Rios, 1989) that grew out of the need to include a broader range of children. The ADI-R is a semistructured interview for caregivers of children and adults suspected of having an ASD or a PDD-NOS. The instrument consists of ninety-three items and takes about 2 hours to complete. Some training is required to administer the ADI-R, which can be acquired through video materials. The ADI-R has been translated into many languages and is considered to be one of the most valuable instruments for the diagnosis of ASDs. Interrater reliability, internal consistency, and convergent validity are all excellent. Factor analyses have produced varying patterns (Constantino & Todd, 2003; Tadevosyan-Leyfer et al., 2003; Tanguay, Robertson, & Derrick, 1998). The ADI-R is clearly designed for diagnostic purposes and is not used to measure change. Its most appropriate use is in the hands of an experienced clinical interviewer, which can limit its use, but the ADI-R is perhaps the most reliable instrument for making a diagnosis of AD.

DISCO 9 (WING, LEEKAM, LIBBY, GOULD, & LARCOMBE, 2002)   The DISCO has undergone nine revisions since the original *Handicaps, Behaviors, and Skills*

(HBS) schedule (Wing & Gould, 1978, 1979). Up until 2002, the use of the DISCO was limited to school-aged children, and the primary purpose was to aid in educational planning. The latest version of the DISCO goes beyond the school-age years and is designed not so much for diagnosis as to assess the pattern of development over an extended period of time, in order to help with appropriate placements and interventions for those who have ASD (Leekam, Libby, Wing, Gould, & Taylor, 2002). The interview covers the areas of social interaction, communication, imagination, and repetitive activities, as well as daily living skills appropriate to developmental level. DISCO 10 is already in the planning stages, as the authors are constantly trying to improve its reliability. For purposes of appropriate treatment planning, placement, and interventions, the DISCO is a very valuable interview schedule in the hands of a trained interviewer.

Observation Scales

Unlike the previous reviewed instruments, which rely on information provided by a third party (teacher, parent, etc.), these next instruments assess the child through direct observation. As with other observation instruments, they can be time-consuming but provide more reliable information than that obtained from a third party.

***AUTISM DIAGNOSTIC OBSERVATION SCHEDULE* (ADOS; LORD, RUTTER, DILAVORE, & RISI, 1999)**   The ADOS is the combined product of two previous instruments: the ADOD-G, designed for use with those who have fluent speech; and the PL-ADOS, designed for preschool children with little or no expressive language who are suspected of having an ASD. The combined instrument allows for a standardized protocol for the observation of social and communicative behaviors. The ADOS provides a series of presses to initiate the child's social interaction, play, and communication. Immediately after the administration of a press, the behavior is coded and later scored. The context in which the behavior occurs is changed, which permits an assessment across different situations. Administration takes about 45 minutes, and it requires some training.

Internal consistency and interrater reliability for the ADOS is excellent (Lord & Corsello, 2005). Several studies have found three factors in the ADOS that account for upward of 70 percent of the variance: joint attention, affective reciprocity, and **theory of mind** (Robertson, Tanguay, L'Ecuyer, Sims, & Waltrip, 1999; Tanguay et al., 1998). One advantage of the ADOS is its potential to differentiate ASDs and PDD-NOS, because observations are based on a standardized protocol and context. The information generated by the ADOS about the social and communicative functioning of the child can be particularly valuable to parents, clinicians, and teachers (Lord & Corsello, 2005).

***PSYCHOEDUCATIONAL PROFILE—REVISED* (PEP-R; SCHOPLER, REICHLER, BASHFORD, LANSING, & MARCUS, 1990)**   Based on the original *Psychoeducational Profile* (PEP; Schopler & Reichler, 1979), the PEP-R is a developmental and diagnostic measure for assessing children with ASDs. It has wide dissemination and has been translated into several languages. Its most appropriate use is with children ages 3 to 7. The PEP-R rates the following characteristics of autism:

THEORY OF MIND

In recent years, refers to the ability to attribute mental states to oneself and others and to understand that others have beliefs, desires, and intentions that are different from one's own.

response to material (eight items), language (eleven items), affect and development of relationships (twelve items), and sensory modalities (twelve items).

Unfortunately, much of the available psychometric information is for the original PEP. The PEP-R is reported to have good **convergent validity** and **discriminate validity** (Lam & Rao, 1993) and high internal consistency (Steerneman, Muris, Merckelbach, & Willems, 1997). Both the PEP and the PEP-R have been used extensively in research. They have also been used in clinical and educational settings, but to a lesser extent.

Instruments for Asperger Syndrome

Currently, two instruments are specifically tailored to the diagnosis of AS.

ASPERGER'S SYNDROME (AND HIGH-FUNCTIONING AUTISM) DIAGNOSTIC INTERVIEW (ASDI; GILLBERG, GILLBERG, RASTAM, & WENTZ, 2001) The ASDI is a structured interview administered to anyone who knows the child's present functioning, as well as his or her early development. It consists of twenty items that operationalize the diagnostic criteria for AS: social, interests, routines, verbal/speech, communication, and motor. The interviewer elicits as much information as possible regarding the different items and then rates them on a three-point scale. Interrater and test–retest reliability for the ASDI are reportedly very high, as is convergent validity.

AUSTRALIAN SCALE FOR ASPERGER'S SYNDROME (ASAS; GARNETT & ATTWOOD, IN ATWOOD, 1997) The ASAS is a popular instrument because it first appeared in a widely read book, *Asperger's Syndrome: A Guide for Parents, Professionals, People with Asperger's Syndrome and Their Partners* (Atwood, 1997). Parents and educational systems are the most frequent users of the instrument. There is little peer-reviewed literature, however, on the psychometric properties of the ASAS. The ASAS has nineteen items that deal with the five symptom areas typically associated with AS: social and emotional difficulties, cognitive skills deficits, communication skills deficits, specific interests, and motor clumsiness. Scoring is according to a seven-point Likert scale ranging from "rarely" (0) to "frequently" (6). A parent or teacher typically completes the ASAS. Because of the lack of good psychometric data, it is recommended at this time that the ASAS be used more as a screening instrument and less as a diagnostic tool.

TREATMENT STRATEGIES

In recent years, treatment interventions for ASD have focused on curriculum and classroom structure, behavioral interventions to promote learning and adaptive functioning, developing early language and communication, developing social communication skills (especially for HFA and AS), models of educational intervention, working with families, and psychopharmacology. It is beyond the scope of this book to deal with all of these interventions. Appropriate to the purpose of this book, we focus on behavioral interventions,

---

CONVERGENT VALIDITY

The degree to which a scale is similar to (converges on) other scale(s) that theoretically measure the same construct.

DISCRIMINATE VALIDITY

The degree to which a scale diverges from a scale(s) that theoretically measures a dissimilar construct.

developing social communication skills, and psychopharmacology, but do not include interventions more relevant to academic instruction.

Behavioral Interventions for Aberrant Behaviors

Behavioral interventions for people who have ASD have emphasized the role of antecedents, consequences, and skill acquisition.

ANTECEDENTS Although behavioral interventions have always highlighted the role of consequences, the role of antecedents in working with individuals who have ASD has been emphasized more and more (Reeve & Carr, 2000). Antecedents can be either remote or immediate. Remote antecedents usually deal with the setting in which the problem behavior occurs, with the understanding that certain environmental factors are responsible for the problem behavior. Modification of these factors can play a significant role in achieving the targeted behaviors. For example, studies have supported that when young children who have autism are in closer proximity to normally developing peers, there is a reduction in aberrant behaviors (McGee, Paradis, & Feldman, 1993). Another example is the role of physical exercise. Several studies have shown support for the benefits of vigorous exercise as an antecedent to reducing aggressive behaviors in children who have autism (Elliott, Dobbin, Rose, & Soper, 1994; Koegel & Koegel, 1989).

Studies have also supported the role of immediate antecedents in effecting targeted treatment. For example, Kennedy and Itkonnen (1993) found that by oversleeping in the morning, individuals who have autism set up a chain of events that resulted in more behavioral problems at school. Another example is the use of high-probability requests as antecedents to achieve a low-probability request, that is, one that has been resisted in the past. Several studies have supported the effective use of high-probability requests as immediate antecedents (Davis, Brady, Williams, & Hamilton, 1992; Houlihan, Jacobson, & Brandon, 1994; Mace, Hock, Lalli, & West, 1988).

CONSEQUENCES The importance of the role of consequences in the learning of new behaviors and the unlearning of old ones is universally accepted. The most effective use of consequences is in the form of a *reinforcer:* "a stimulus event that increases the probability that the response that immediately precedes it will occur again" (Gladding, 2001, p. 103).

Reinforcement *Differential reinforcement* (i.e., reinforcement provided in some situations and not in others) has been employed on a wide scale in working with children who have autism. The most common form of differential reinforcement used with ASD children is *differential reinforcement of other behaviors* (DRO). DRO is designed to reinforce any response other than the targeted (i.e., problematic) behaviors. It has been successfully employed in reducing stereotypy (Haring, Breen, Pittts-Conway, & Gaylord-Ross, 1986), severe aggression and self-injury (Wong, Floyd, Innocent, & Woolsey (1992), and hand flapping (Ringdahl et al., 2002). Token economies have also proven successful in dealing with an array of aberrant behaviors in children who have autism (Kennedy & Haring, 1993).

Punishment Research has shown the use of punishment as a consequence to be less effective than the use of reinforcement. Nevertheless, punishment is still widely used and in many cases is the result of a spontaneous reaction to the child's provocative behaviors. Mild punishments (i.e., verbal reprimand, overcorrection, time-out, denial of privileges) are acceptable and have proven effective in reducing the throwing of objects (Charlop, Burgio, Iwata, & Ivancic, 1988), self-injury (Mulick & Meinhold, 1994), and hair pulling (Holttum, Lubetsky, & Eastman, 1994).

Behavioral Interventions to Promote Learning

Aside from the use of more traditional interventions to reduce negative behaviors, behavioral interventions to promote the learning of social skills and other adaptive behaviors in children who have autism are being used more and more. Since the 1960s, it has been widely accepted that children who have autism can learn. Behavioral interventions to promote learning in children who have autism have included structured interventions, naturalistic interventions, self-management strategies, and video instruction.

DISCRETE TRIAL TRAINING (DT)

An intensive treatment designed to assist individuals who have developmental disabilities, such as autism. It involves directly training a variety of skills that individuals who have disabilities may not pick up naturally. Discrete trial training is conducted using intensive drills of selected materials. A specific behavior is prompted or guided, and children receive reinforcement for proper responses.

STRUCTURED BEHAVIORAL INTERVENTIONS Lovaas (1987) developed structured behavioral interventions that are known as ***discrete trial training*** **(DT)**. The following explanation of discrete trial training is reproduced from Arick, Krug, Fullerton, Loos, and Falco (2005, p. 1004):

> Skills are taught in a logical sequence building on previously learned skills. Concepts to be taught are identified and then broken down into specific program elements for instruction. Each instructional session consists of a series of discrete trials. A discrete trial consists of a four-step sequence: (1) instructional cue, (2) child response, (3) consequence (generally a positive reinforcer) and, (4) pause. Data is collected to monitor the child's progress and to help determine when a pre-set criteria has been reached.

More recently, DT has been used to develop nonacademic skills such as play and peer interaction (Schreibman & Ingersoll, 2005). It is important to note that in DT, the teaching materials are selected by an adult and rarely varied. Research has consistently supported the effectiveness of DT in teaching children who have autism a variety of important behaviors (Lovaas, 1987; Miranda-Linne & Melin, 1992). The Lovaas (1982) study found that 47 percent of those who had received 40 hours per week of intensive DT during a 2-year period had reached normal intellectual and educational functioning, compared to 2 percent who received less intensive instruction. Critics of DT say that its highly structure methods prevent learning from generalizing to more natural environments, and strict stimulus control prevents the spontaneous use of the learned behaviors (Schreibman & Ingersoll, 2005).

NATURALISTIC BEHAVIORAL INTERVENTIONS In contrast to DT, naturalistic behavioral interventions are, as the name implies, more natural and child-centered.

This class of interventions has undergone evolution since the late 1960s, when it was originally developed by Hart and Risley (1968). In spite of the variety of techniques and interventions now used, naturalistic behavioral interventions all share certain basic components, which are listed in Table 9.2.

One of the more well known and popular naturalistic interventions is **paradigm/pivotal response training (PRT)**. This training is also based on a four-step sequence: cue, child response, consequence, and pause. However, trials in PRT are incorporated into the environment in a functional context. During PRT, the child chooses the activity or object and the reinforcer is a natural consequence to the behaviors being rewarded. The nature of this strategy makes it possible to engage the child throughout all activities and locations throughout the day (Arick et al., 2005, p. 1004).

PRT's significance is its use of teaching skills that go beyond language to include symbolic play (Stahmer, 1995) and joint attention (Whalen & Schreibman, 2003).

Studies comparing naturalistic techniques and more structured techniques generally have found that the former result in more generalized and spontaneous use of skills (Charlop-Christy & Carpenter, 2000; Delprato, 2001; Miranda-Linne & Melin, 1992). Other studies have found that employing the techniques of PRT has led to reduced stress and more happiness among both parents and children (Koegel, Bimbela, & Schreibman, 1996).

VIDEO INSTRUCTION In light of research supporting the notion that children who have autism are visual learners and respond better to interventions that rely on visual stimuli, video instruction has become a recognized learning intervention for this population. Studies have found that modeling provided through video instruction is effective in developing skills in conversational speech (Sherer et al., 2001), daily living skills (Shipley-Benamou, Lutzker, & Taubman, 2002), verbal responding (Buggey, Tombs, Gardener, & Cervetti, 1999), and emotional understanding (Schwandt et al., 2002). **Video modeling** has also proven effective with self-management techniques such as self-monitoring, self-delivery of reinforcement, and self-evaluation of performance (Thiemann &

PIVOTAL RESPONSE TRAINING (PRT)

A program of incidental teaching procedures that aims to increase a child's motivation to learn, monitoring of his or her own behavior, and initiation of communication with others. These changes are described as pivotal because they are viewed as helping the child learn a wide range of other skills. PRT was previously referred to as the *natural language paradigm*.

VIDEO MODELING

Showing a videotape of a person actually demonstrating a behavior for a child to imitate. For persons with autism spectrum disorders, video modeling may result in faster acquisition and better generalization than in-vivo (live) modeling, possibly because it does not require social interaction during learning.

TABLE 9.2 Components of Naturalistic Behavioral Interventions

- The learning environment is loosely structured.
- Teaching occurs during ongoing interactions between the child and the adult.
- The child initiates the teaching episode by indicating interest in an item or activity.
- Teaching materials are selected by the child and varied often.
- The child's production of the target behavior is explicitly prompted.
- A direct relationship exists between the child's response and the reinforcer.
- The child is reinforced for attempts to respond.

Source: From "Behavioral Interventions to Promote Learning in Individuals with Autism" by L. Schreibman and B. Ingersoll in *Handbook of Autism and Pervasive Developmental Disorders: Vol 2. Assessment, Interventions, and Policy* (3rd ed., p. 883), by F. R. Volkmar, R. Paul, A. Klin, and D. Cohen (Eds.), 2005, New York: Wiley. Copyright 2005 by Wiley Publishers. Reprinted with permission.

Goldstein, 2001). Self-monitoring techniques are more appropriate for individuals with HFA, about which we will have more to say in a later section.

Researchers have also been interested in what kind of models (self versus other, video versus live) is most effective with autism. While research is just beginning in this area, Charlop-Christy, Le, & Freeman (2000) found that video modeling resulted in faster acquisition and more generalization of new behaviors than in-vivo (live) modeling. Schreibman and Ingersoll (2005) cautioned, however, that video instruction should not be used to the exclusion of other behavioral interventions that are more social in nature. Overuse of video modeling would remove children who have autism from social demands that should be included in the treatment plan.

RECENT TRENDS   Exploration of better and more sophisticated ways to teach children who have autism is ongoing. For example, experts now believe that children who have autism are capable of learning more sophisticated behaviors such as joint attention (Whalen & Schreibman, 2003), symbolic play (Stahmer, 1995), theory of mind (Garfinkle, 2000), and reciprocal imitation (Ingersoll & Schreibman, 2001). In addition, teaching through the use of **social stories** and picture schedules developed by the progenitors of Treatment and Education of Autistic and Related Communication-Handicapped Children (TEACCH) is becoming more and more popular. These newer pedagogies are in need of empirical support, a dimension that has always favored the stricter behavioral approaches that emphasize data collection and validation. The inclusion of family members and peers has become more emphasized in recent years. These newer approaches demand stronger collaboration among school, home, and community. Therefore, the selection of treatment intervention should carefully consider variables not only in the child but also in the family and school personnel in order to select what is most appropriate and has the greatest chance of success.

SOCIAL STORIES

A social story describes a situation, skill, or concept in terms of relevant social cues, perspectives, and common responses in a specifically defined style and format. The goal is to share accurate social information in a patient and reassuring manner that is easily understood by its audience.

Higher-Functioning Autism and Asperger Syndrome: Enhancing Social Competence

Although there are differences between the challenges of those who have HFA and those who have AS, research has shown that positive long-term outcomes for both groups are correlated to the degree of social communicative competence (Marans, Rubin, & Laurent, 2005). Table 9.3 highlights the differences in learning style between HFA and AS and their implications.

Aside from the differences listed in Table 9.3, HFA and AS share the difficulty of understanding the emotional states of social partners and their intentions, as well as difficulty recognizing social conventions across different contexts. These shared difficulties imply that both groups will benefit from interventions that create more awareness of the intentions and emotions of social partners and increase the predictability of unfamiliar social events (Marans et al., 2005). The goals of intervention designed to increase social and emotional competence should include:

1. Increasing the individual's acquisition of conventional verbal and nonverbal communication forms for requesting assistance and/or organizing supports

TABLE 9.3   Differences in Learning Style Between High-Functioning Autism (HFA) and Asperger Syndrome (AS) and Their Implications

High-Functioning Autism	Asperger Syndrome
Strengths in visual-spatial perception and visual memory	Weaknesses in visual-spatial perception and visual memory
Preference for nontransient or static information	Strengths in expressive and receptive language and verbal memory
Weaknesses in expressive and receptive language and verbal memory	
Implications:	*Implications:*
The provision of static visual cues is an appropriate accommodation when supporting individuals who have HFA in their awareness of social conventions. Verbal mediation strategies, although often helpful with individuals who have AS, may prove to be less effective for individuals who have HFA, secondary to the transient and language-based nature of this modality of learning.	The strong verbal abilities skills characteristic of AS often provide an ideal modality for intervention, as the use of verbal mediation can be incorporated throughout the individual's day. This refers to the use of explicit, verbal instruction to facilitate awareness of the subtleties of social and emotional behavior that unaffected individuals typically learn incidentally through ongoing observations of nonverbal social cues in their environment.

Source: From "Addressing Social Communication Skills in Individuals with High-Functioning Autism and Asperger Syndrome: Critical Priorities in Educational Programming" by W. D. Marans, E. Rubin, and A. Laurent in *Handbook of Autism and Pervasive Developmental Disorders: Vol 2. Assessment, Interventions, and Policy* (3rd ed., p. 985), by F. R. Volkmar, R. Paul, A. Klin, and D. Cohen (Eds.), 2005, New York: Wiley. Copyright 2005 by Wiley Publishers. Reprinted with permission.

2. Increasing the individual's ability to use specific vocabulary or conversational devices to express emotional state and arousal level
3. Increasing the ability to identify and express emotional state and arousal level, as well as using regulating strategies, with and without the use of visual supports
4. Increasing social understanding and social expectations through language-based strategies (Marans et al., 2005, p. 986)

In order for interventions to succeed, those who have HFA and AS must enjoy interpersonal support from peers, teachers and other school professionals, family, and community, as well as appropriate educational and learning supports. The very nature of a social disability involves other people, and these other people are critical in providing successful outcomes and improving social competence in those who have HFA and AS.

INTERPERSONAL SUPPORTS   In spite of their lack of social competence, people who have HFA and AS greatly desire friendships. When attempts at friendship fail, they often turn toward adults and/or age-inappropriate peers for relationship. If age-appropriate peers are not included in the treatment, their lack of understanding for those who have HFA and AS will result in further rejection of these individuals. A number of programs are available to help peers modify some of their own forms of communication and gain reassurance about the difficulties they experience in interacting with those who have HFA and AS. Some of these support programs include the integrated play group model (Wolfberg, 2003), play organizers (Odom et al., 1999), the buddy skills training program (English, Goldstein, Shafer, & Kaczmarek, 1997), the I LAUGH program (Winner, 2002), and Navigating the Social World (McAfee, 2002). Older peers can benefit from a more conceptual explanation of the disability.

For school personnel, a first step in supporting those who have HFA and AS is to use communication that is clear and explicit. Sarcastic and idiomatic subtleties, the use of nonverbal social cues (e.g., frowning to show surprise), and, in the case of HFA, the use of verbal language without visual cues may hamper successful communication (Marans et al., 2005). Not all school personnel will be able to provide the necessary supports. Interventions should target teachers, bus drivers, cafeteria workers, recess monitors, and others whose natural temperament makes them ideal candidates for training that provides communicative support across various environments within the school.

Families that include a member with a social disability can experience a good deal of stress when misunderstandings and arguments become the norm. Family support for those who have HFA and AS should include members understanding the nature of the disability and modifications they can make in their own communicative style. Emotional support for family members is also an important intervention, as is helping the family modify its goals and expectations not only for the individual who has HFA or AS, but for the family as a whole. For example, it may not be advisable to abruptly change a plan that had previously been made and communicated clearly to the individual.

Community activities for those who have HFA and AS should be carefully selected. Parents may want their children who have HFA and AS to participate in team activities (e.g., sports) like many other children. However, team sports require social awareness and good motor skills, which are often deficient in those who have HFA and AS. More individual activities, such as swimming, martial arts, skiing, horseback riding, or golf, may be more appropriate.

LEARNING AND EDUCATIONAL SUPPORTS As discussed previously, individuals who have HFA and AS differ in their verbal language and visual-spatial abilities. Their common strength, however, is in processing the written word (Rourke & Tsatsanis, 2000; Wetherby, Prizant, & Schuler, 2000). To enhance their communication skills, dialogue scripts are a preferred intervention (Krantz & McClannahan, 1998). Such scripts will include the content of social conversations and may be in the form of comic scripts, video modeling, or video replay. Written schedules, especially about unfamiliar events that have yet to unfold, can be particularly helpful, along with the use of social stories (Gray & Garand, 1993) to provide strategies for appropriate social conversation and emotional regulation (Hagiwara

& Myles, 2001). As a learning support, social stories are designed to help those who have HFA and AS

- Understand their own social difficulties
- Pay careful attention to the social context
- Select the most important aspects of a social situation
- Identify appropriate behaviors and responses
- Identify the social partner's perspective
- Understand the consequences of a particular positive behavior (Marans et al., 2005)

As they are more able to understand and anticipate the sequence of events in a social situation, individuals who have HFA and AS will become more socially competent.

Psychopharmacological Treatment

Although psychopharmacological intervention appears to be quite common for children who have ASD and PDD-NOS, there is relatively little empirical support for its effectiveness. Empirical studies have generally suffered from methodological flaws such as small sample sizes, **open label**, and lack of replication (Scahill & Martin, 2005). The three most common categories of drugs used to treat children who have autism and other PDDs are atypical antipsychotics, SSRIs, and stimulants.

OPEN LABEL

A type of study in which both the health providers and the patients are aware of the drug or treatment being given, in contrast with blind and double blind studies, in which one or both of the constituents do not know what drug or treatment is being given.

ATYPICAL ANTIPSYCHOTICS Clozapine (Clozaril), risperidone (Ripserdol), olanzapine (Zyprexa), quetiapine (Seroquel), ziprasidone (Geodon), and aripiprazole (Abilify) are known as atypical antipsychotics (AAPs) that have come to replace the more traditional antipsychotics such as Haldol and Prolixin.

Clozapine Clozapine, which was the first AAP introduced in the United States, is used in very low doses for fear of side effects, most notably seizures. Zuddas, Ledda, Fratta, Muglia, and Cianchetti (1996) reported that two of three children with symptoms of hyperactivity and aggression were treated successfully with clozapine; Chen, Bedair, McKay, Bowers, and Mazure (2001) reported that a 17-year-old male who had autism was treated successfully with clozapine for aberrant behaviors including repetitive motions.

Risperidone Risperidone has been the most widely studied AAP, with multisite trials conducted in 2002 by the Research Units on Pediatric Psychopharmacology (RUPP) Autism Network. The two-phase study included 101 children in the first phase and 63 in the second phase, all of whom had autism with severe tantrums, aggression, and self-injurious behavior. Compared to the placebo group, the risperidone group showed significant lower levels of irritability, social withdrawal, stereotypy, hyperactivity, and inappropriate speech as measured by the *Aberrant Behavior Checklist*. The biggest difference between the two groups was on the irritability scale. Relapse rate was also significantly higher in the placebo group. Side effects, considered transient and mild in the risperidone groups, included increased appetite along with weight gain, fatigue, drowsiness, tremors, and drooling.

To date, no double-blind, placebo-controlled studies have been done for the other AAPs, and they have been used in very limited cases. There have been individual reports supporting moderate success, but potential side effects in children continue to be a major concern. For example, there have been reports of drug-induced diabetes in adults taking olanzapine, and therefore its use in children is suspect (Scahill & Martin, 2005). In a report about quetiapine, Hirsch, Link, Goldstein, and Arvanitis (1996) found that only two of six boys (ages 6 to 15) who had autism and mental retardation were responders. In a study of twelve participants (nine who had autism and three who had PDD-NOS) medicated with ziprasidone, 50 percent were rated *much improved* or *very much improved* on the *Clinical Global Impression Scale*.

SSRIs   Fluoxetine (Prozac), fluvoxamine (Luvox), setraline (Zoloft), paroxetine (Paxil) and mirtzapine (Remeron) have all been used in the treatment of autism and PDD-NOS.

Fluoxetine   Several reports have documented the successful use of Prozac in young children who have autism (Cook, Rowlett, Jaselskis, & Leventhal, 1992; DeLong, Teague, & McSwain-Kamran, 1998). In the Cook et al. (1992) report, a greater percentage of those 15 or older were responders (nine of twelve) compared to those younger than 15 (six of eleven). In the DeLong et al. (1998) study, twenty-two of thirty-seven young children improved in core symptoms of autism.

Fluvoxamine   One of the concerns regarding Luvox is behavioral activation (hyperactivity, disinhibition, insomnia, and aggression), which occurred in twelve of sixteen subjects treated with fluvoxamine (Scahill & Martin, 2005). In a follow-up study, lower doses of fluvoxamine resulted in only three of eighteen participants experiencing behavioral activation, but there was a lack of efficacy for the group as a whole (Martin, Koenig, Anderson, & Scahill, 2003). One difficulty with this study was that the sample was heterogeneous—children and adolescents who had PDD and anxiety disorder.

Other SSRIs   Most of the studies with setraline and paroxetine have been with adults. One study with Remeron as the drug of choice found that nine of twenty-six participants with PDD were either *much improved* or *very much improved* as measured on the CGI (Posey, Guenin, Kohn, Swiezy, & McDougle, 2001).

The SSRIs are currently used carefully with children and adolescents because of reports of an increase in suicidality. There is limited evidence of the effectiveness of SSRIs in treating children who have autism and PDD. The more rigorous studies have been done with adults, and it appears that positive outcomes for this population are not always the same for children and adolescents.

STIMULANTS   The effectiveness of stimulants in the treatment of attention-deficit hyperactivity disorder (ADHD) in children and adolescents is well documented. Their efficacy and safety in the treatment of autism and PDD is less studied, but their use with this population appears to be quite common, according to community and clinic-surveys (Aman, Collier-Crespin, & Lindsay, 2000; Martin, Koenig, Scahill, & Bregman, 1999). In a review of the literature, Aman, Buican, & Arnold (2003) concluded that the positive response rate to stimulants among those who have developmental disabilities is lower and side effects seem to be higher than in ADHD. Although a number of studies have been done on stimulant intervention for individuals who have been diagnosed with both ADHD and mental retardation, only one study of the use of stimulants for autism (Quintana, Birmaher, Stedge, & Lenon, 1995) and one study of those diagnosed with PDD and ADHD (Handen, Johnson, & Lubetsky, 2000) exist. Research has suggested that, overall, stimulant medication can be effective in treating children who have developmental disabilities and ADHD symptoms (Scahill & Martin, 2005), but it is not clear at this time whether such medication is effective in treating symptoms of hyperactivity associated with autism.

SCHOOL-BASED INTERVENTIONS

The preceding review of the characteristics, causes, and treatment options for autism spectrum disorders has provided a solid foundation from which we can select the most relevant research-based intervention for both Carmen, who has autistic disorder, and James, who has Asperger syndrome. In both cases, accurate assessments to determine the behaviors most detrimental to academic and social functioning are critical. Likewise, for both students, a functional behavioral assessment is appropriate and useful in identifying the target or problem behaviors and the purpose they serve for the student. Model assessment processes and appropriate behavioral intervention plans are described below for both Carmen and James.

Assessing the Problem: Carmen

A functional assessment for Carmen derived from the model developed by Barnhill (2005) might look something like the following example.

The first step is *identifying and describing the problem or target behavior(s)*. Clearly, Carmen's most challenging behaviors include: (1) tantruming associated with sudden changes in routine, (2) interference with intersubjectivity or joint attention (the ability to share an object or event with another person), (3) the lack of eye gaze with someone trying to communicate, and (4) an inability to communicate or express feelings and emotions, or to engage in or sustain a dialogue or conversation. We will address each of these problem behaviors later in this section.

The second step in the process is *collecting baseline data and academic performance information* to substantiate our behavioral hypotheses and to help determine Carmen's present level of performance, as well as the negative impact of these problem behaviors. Accordingly, using the *Childhood Autism Rating Checklist* (CARS; Schopler et al., 1988), the *Autism Behavior Checklist* (ABC; Krug et al., 1980a, 1980b), and the *Autism Diagnostic Observation Schedule* (ADOS; Lord et al., 1999), together with teacher and parent observations and interviews and curricular-based measures, significant deficits were substantiated in all four target areas identified above.

The third step is *identifying the environmental and setting demands* that might instigate and fuel each of the target behaviors. In this case, Carmen's teachers found that, consistent with his diagnosis of AD, any deviation from his "schedule" or change in his environment causes frustration that triggers a tantrum in which he screams, throws things, kicks and punches persons or objects in his proximity, and engages in moderately self-injurious behavior (e.g., he bites his hand and slaps his head).

A confirmatory step is *direct observation of Carmen's behavior across settings* (i.e., in the classroom, on the playground, in the lunchroom, at activities such as gym and art, and at home). Carmen was observed in several settings (e.g., school, home, and clinic) over several weeks by various caregivers and practitioners, including his parents, his teachers at Metamorphosis School, and his clinical psychologist. An analysis of their observations identified the following behavioral trends:

1. Carmen is consistently frustrated by sudden changes to his daily routine, the sequence of steps followed in accomplishing a particular task, a change in staff or caregiver, or, in short, anything outside the familiar.
2. Carmen has significant difficulty maintaining eye gaze and intersubjectivity, even with persons with whom he is very familiar.
3. Carmen seems unable to initiate or sustain verbal communication with another. He is currently incapable of engaging in a conversation.
4. Carmen appears to receive some form of gratification in self-stimulation, such as hand flapping and the noncreative manipulation of objects.

Based on analyses of systematic observations of the target behaviors, the following *hypotheses* were developed regarding the purpose or function served by the target behaviors:

1. Carmen needs a schedule routine to reduce anxiety created by change and unstructured activity. He takes comfort in the familiar and predictable. Thus, a viable routine is critical for his success in school, and any changes or modifications to that routine need to be introduced gradually to minimize anxiety and aid his adjustment.
2. Carmen clearly lacks the interpersonal skills that facilitate interaction and the development of meaningful peer and adult relationships. These social and communication skills must be taught in a very authentic context and, like every other competency taught to Carmen, must be introduced incrementally in measurable steps. Approximations of the target behavior must be reinforced positively.
3. Carmen receives some gratification through self-stimulation behaviors such as hand flapping, twirling his hair, and the repetitive manipulation of objects such as coins. His teachers and clinicians must try to help Carmen initially reduce, and ultimately stop, engaging in these aberrant behaviors. This will be accomplished most effectively through the gradual replacement of these egocentric behaviors with more socially interactive ones.

The final step in the functional behavioral assessment is to test the validity of the hypothesis by assessing the effectiveness of the behavioral intervention plan developed expressly to address each of the proposed hypotheses. Based on the degree to which this plan is successful in reducing or transforming the target behaviors, appropriate modifications and adjustments will be made.

Developing an Effective Intervention Plan: Carmen

As suggested by Horner et al. (1999–2000), any effective behavioral intervention plan should include six essential components: (1) an understanding of the student's perception of antecedent events and her environment, (2) an investment in preventing reoccurrences of the target behavior, (3) the use of effective teaching as a powerful deterrent to the undesired behavior, (4) an accurate understanding of the purpose served by the undesired behavior for the individual, (5) an emphasis on positive reinforcement of appropriate behavior, and (6) a contingency plan to address more severe behavioral issues, as well as reoccurrences of targeted undesirable behavior.

Carmen's behavioral intervention plan should address each of the target behaviors with an effective, research-based treatment. The following plan represents a possible set of interventions appropriate for each of the target behaviors identified for Carmen.

TARGET 1: TANTRUMING ASSOCIATED WITH CHANGES IN ROUTINE An appropriate daily routine for the classroom should be developed and implemented. This routine should be modified when necessary, and any resulting changes in the established routine should be introduced gradually over a period of several days if feasible. Each time Carmen does *not* tantrum in response to these incremental changes, he should receive positive reinforcement, referred to as "differential reinforcement of other behaviors" (DRO). The reinforcer can be primary, such as food, or secondary, such as a token that may be exchanged later for a tangible reward. The important aspect of DRO is that the teacher, clinician, or caregiver must ensure that she is reinforcing a *desired* behavior and not inadvertently reinforcing the target behavior.

TARGET 2: INTERFERENCE WITH INTERSUBJECTIVITY OR JOINT ATTENTION A naturalistic behavioral intervention; specifically, paradigm/pivotal response training (PRT), will be employed to address these interpersonal skills deficits. As noted earlier in the chapter, PRT is very effective in helping students who have AD develop joint attention. The advantage of PRT compared with discrete trial training (DT) is that it has been shown to result in greater spontaneous use and generalizability of the skills. Furthermore, PRT is less structured than DT and is generally preferred by teachers for that reason.

TARGET 3: LACK OF EYE GAZE WITH SOMEONE TRYING TO COMMUNICATE Like target 2, this targeted behavior deficit will be effectively addressed using pivotal response training (PRT).

TARGET 4: INABILITY TO INITIATE OR SUSTAIN A CONVERSATION A recommended intervention for this skills deficiency is video instruction. As noted earlier, video instruction provides effective modeling of conversational speech skills, as well as verbal responding and facilitates the acquisition of these skills more quickly than in-vivo (live) modeling.

TARGET 5: ENGAGES IN SELF-STIMULATING BEHAVIORS SUCH AS HAND FLAPPING AND THE NONCREATIVE MANIPULATION OF OBJECTS AND STEREOTYPY In addressing this problem, the most effective nonpunitive approach is to identify preferred reinforcers for Carmen, such as food or tokens, withhold these and ignore self-stimulation episodes, then provide the preferred reinforcement only after the self-stimulating behavior has stopped or in the complete absence of the self-stimulating behavior. An alternative approach is to use either DT or PRT to teach an appropriate alternative behavior to the self-stimulation and then provide reinforcement only for the appropriate behavior. Finally, research has also supported the efficacy of differential reinforcement of other behaviors (DRO) to provide reinforcement for any appropriate response other than the target behavior (i.e., self-stimulation, stereotypy, etc.).

Lastly, once the various interventions to address the target behavior have been implemented for a reasonable period of time, at minimum 5 or 6 weeks, those with oversight of the BIP should evaluate the efficacy of each of the component treatments, as well as a "good contextual fit" between the elements of the plan, the skill-level and personalogical characteristics of the plan implementers, the quality of environmental supports, and the compatibility of the child and caregiver. If any aspect of the plan is seen as ineffective, then an alternative plan must be developed and implemented as soon as possible.

Assessing the Problem: James

In accordance with the model we have been using throughout this book, we will assess and determine the probable purpose or goal associated with James's target behaviors. Once again, the first step is *identifying and describing the problem or target behavior(s)*. A primary area of concern regarding James's well-being is his occasional depression, which can generate suicidal ideation and threats of suicide. With the help of his therapist, James has been able to understand that he becomes depressed when he is unsuccessful in attracting and retaining same-age friends. It is the behavior that interferes with this desired outcome that needs to be targeted for change.

Based on the results of the *Asperger's Syndrome Diagnostic Interview* (ASDI; Gillberg, Gillberg, Rastam, & Wentz, 2001), as well as the observations of James's teachers, parents, and psychologist, the key target behaviors include the following.

1. ***Verbosity and egocentric focus in communication that impede learning and socialization.*** For example, James talks incessantly about the upcoming mid-term congressional elections and extols the virtues of the Democratic Party's candidates while vilifying their Republican Party opponents. This perseverating behavior interferes with his ability to focus

on the topic at hand and alienates peers who are simply not interested in his pedantic diatribe.

2. ***An inability to appreciate the perspectives of social partners.*** For example, when James is actually able to engage another student in a political discussion, he typically "filibusters" his social partner's attempts to interject her impressions, ignoring her protests. He also doesn't seem to be able to "hear," let alone consider, another's viewpoint. This seeming disregard for the opinions of others usually results in a "disconnect," whereupon the conversational partner withdraws from the dialogue and avoids James altogether, adding to James's sense of alienation.

3. ***Lack of empathy as a consequence of poor insight regarding the emotions of other people.*** For example, on one occasion, a student was sharing a very poignant story concerning the recent loss of a grandparent with the class; James, unable to provide empathy through active listening, abruptly cut off the student to share his knowledge of the Holocaust and how much greater was the loss and human suffering represented by that act of genocide. In so doing, he showed his lack of appreciation for the pain experienced by the speaker and her personal loss, as well as the courage she displayed in sharing such a painful experience. The teacher and, later, several classmates rebuked him for his lack of sensitivity.

The next recommended action involves *collecting baseline data and academic performance information*. As noted, the results of the ASDI, as well as observation reports collected from James's teachers, parents, and clinical psychologist substantiate the diagnosis of Asperger syndrome. Similarly, James's academic performance in subjects that are not of interest to him, specifically, math, science, and language arts, is substandard, whereas he excels in the subjects that interest him. He is also very articulate and precocious in his use of advanced vocabulary, a characteristic of students who have Asperger syndrome.

Once sufficient data have been collected, the team must investigate and describe the *environmental and setting demands* that may instigate or sustain the problem behaviors. In this regard, James appears to be trapped in a cycle of self-destructive behavior. He clearly wants to be liked and to receive social acceptance from his peers; however, he dominates social interactions and fails to acknowledge the contributions of social partners. This behavior alienates potential friends and further confirms his reputation as a narcissistic "crank."

Because James, like most students who have AS, is sociable and craves interpersonal attention, he constantly inserts himself into social situations in which he is unwelcome. Invariably, he sets himself up for further rejection and ridicule. Occasionally, James reacts angrily to this rejection and shouts obscenities at his perceived adversary. This behavior only escalates the abuse and denigration. On one occasion, James felt so hurt and angry at being rejected that he ran away from school, eluding staff and the police who were summoned, and walked all the way to his home—a distance of eight miles.

The next step is *completing a direct observation* of the student. The observations of James's parents and teachers have provided invaluable data for the assessment process. James's parents are divorced and living separately, although in the same town. Both parents are well educated and professionally employed. His mother is attending law school at a local university at night and tends to be more involved in James's education and treatment. She has been conscientious about journalizing James's behavior in her home. According to his mother, James displays a similarly pedantic style in communicating with her and his younger brother. She notes that he usually secludes himself in his bedroom, where he reads books on U.S. political themes or watches science fiction movies, another passion. He rarely interacts with his mother; she believes this is partly caused by her absence from the home to attend law school, but she also notes that James has expressed that she "doesn't understand him" or appreciate his "interests." He and his brother have little in common: she ascribes this, in part, to their disparity in age.

James's schoolteachers have been recording any episodes involving perseverating behavior, such as unidirectional conversation and lack of reciprocity, as well as "acting-out" events and "escalating" or provocative behavior such as verbal insults and threats.

Dr. Simmons, the resident psychiatrist at the special school James attends, has reviewed all this anecdotal information and determined that it is consistent with AS and exacerbated by other factors including adolescent development.

A necessary next step in the assessment process is *developing a hypothesis* about the purposes or functions served by James's problem behaviors. After reviewing the available data on James's behavior in the classroom, the IEP team advanced the following hypotheses.

1. James clearly seeks social interaction with classmates and wants to develop lasting friendships.
2. Unfortunately, his pedantic verbosity and egocentric focus prohibit reciprocity and tend to alienate potential social partners.
3. James is dramatically affected by this alienation, which he interprets as rejection due to prejudice, jealousy, or misunderstanding on the part of his classmates.
4. James frequently experiences depression as a consequence of this rejection and sometimes entertains thoughts of suicide.
5. Occasionally, James exhibits inappropriate behaviors such as rude gestures, verbal aggression and insults, and self-injurious actions. These episodes typically end with James overturning his desk, throwing notebooks and pens at persons he deems to be his "tormentors," and running out of class. He then needs to be subdued and calmed by the crisis intervention team.

The final step in the process is *testing the hypothesis* by assessing the effectiveness of the resulting behavioral intervention plan. Accordingly, a behavioral intervention plan was developed and implemented, based on the results of the functional behavioral assessment and resulting hypotheses. The effectiveness of the BIP in addressing the target behaviors will be carefully evaluated, and any necessary modifications or adjustments will be made.

Developing an Effective Intervention Plan: James

Applying the components of an effective behavioral intervention plan as recommended by Horner et al. (1999–2000; 2005) to the case example of James might result in the following interventions. (As with previous case examples, it is important that interventions be developed to address *each* of the target behaviors identified in the behavioral assessment.)

TARGET 1: EGOCENTRIC FOCUS OF CONVERSATION WITH NO INTEREST IN RECIPROCITY AND SUBJECT OBSESSION James has been scheduled to participate in weekly group meetings involving the psychiatrist, the speech-language pathologist, and other students at the school who have AS. The focus of this group is to teach appropriate socialization skills such as turn taking in conversations, active listening, employing related verbal and nonverbal communication skills, appreciating another's perspective, and understanding and responding to social cues such as those apparent in body language and facial expression. The skills taught in the group have been disseminated to all of James's teachers, who will act as coaches to provide positive feedback and encouragement when he employs the appropriate social skills.

TARGET 2: DEPRESSION AND SUICIDAL IDEATION James has been prescribed an antidepressant that has been helpful in stabilizing his moods and reducing suicidal ideation; nevertheless, teachers should provide encouragement and positive reinforcement whenever James displays appropriate interpersonal behavior or attempts to engage in recursive (two-way) communication. Teachers and other school professionals should continue to monitor James's affect and demeanor in school and take all threats of self-injury seriously, regardless of the context.

TARGET 3: "ACTING OUT" USING VERBAL AND PHYSICAL AGGRESSION In the event that James's behavior escalates to a point where he abruptly leaves or must be escorted from the classroom, a crisis intervention plan should be in place. This plan should conform to the school-wide policy for handling episodes of extreme and potentially dangerous behavior. As a minimum, all teachers should be familiar with these procedures. Typically, the teacher who is present should initiate the process, which usually begins with a call to the general office or the crisis intervention team leader. A designated, well-trained crisis intervention team then deploys rapidly to the site, providing effective intervention in the crisis, as well as bystander control. Following the event, the affected teacher or staff member completes an incident report, which is filed in the school office. The members of the crisis intervention team prepare a joint report that indicates the time and date of the incident and details their course of action, as well as the perceived emotional state and actions of the student in crisis. These reports, along with the accounts of student and staff eyewitnesses, are critical in identifying antecedent events that precipitated the crisis, as well as the consequences of the problem behavior.

Ideally, teachers and school staff should be aware of the triggers that instigate James's acting-out behaviors. Often, students exhibit behavioral warning signs that signal the escalation of aggression. If the trigger can be neutralized, by removing either the instigator or the student in crisis, then a more severe and potentially serious situation can be averted. In James's case, perhaps the most importunate signal is the onset of verbal threats and denigration directed toward his perceived tormentor. Teacher intervention at this point is crucial to helping James regain self-control and to deescalating a volatile situation.

Information about the behavioral intervention plan must be included in the student's IEP. It is the responsibility of the multidisciplinary team to disseminate this information to each of James's teachers. The best way to do this is to schedule a meeting at the beginning of the school year that includes all James's teachers and related services providers. A copy of the behavioral intervention plan can then be distributed to all the stakeholders, intervention protocols can be discussed, and the school psychologist can address any questions about the execution of the plan. Lastly, a contingency or crisis intervention plan should be clearly articulated to ensure that all staff members know the procedures to follow in the event of a behavioral crisis. This plan should identify key persons to be notified, as well as the actions and responsibilities of each of the responders.

After it has been in place for 5 or 6 weeks, the plan should be reviewed to determine its effectiveness. If the plan as a whole, or any aspect of the plan, is producing less than desired results, that feature of the plan or the entire plan itself should be modified or replaced.

 FROM THE FIELD

Mary McDonald, Ph.D.

Mary McDonald is an assistant professor in the Special Education Program at Hofstra University and directs Eden II Programs' Outreach and Consultation Program. She has nearly 20 years experience directing programs for students with autism spectrum disorder. She completed her Ph.D. in Learning Theory at the CUNY Graduate Center and is a Board Certified Behavior Analyst. Dr. McDonald presents both locally and nationally. She has published articles in the areas of self-management and social reciprocity in children who have autism. Her current research interests include the use of video modeling to teach social and vocational skills and the promotion of response to intervention in education.

Currently there is a great deal of controversy and speculation about the dramatic increase in the incidence of ASD among school-age children. Can you provide a plausible explanation or explanations for this phenomenal increase?

It is true that there has been a dramatic increase in the number of students diagnosed with autism spectrum disorders over the past 15 or so years. It is most plausible that there are a variety of reasons for this increase. In particular, Asperger's was only added to the DSM [Diagnostic and Statistical Manual] in 1994 and this change would in effect itself lead to an increase in diagnosis. In addition, there has been a great emphasis on educating the public about autism spectrum disorders, and through education we have seen a greater number of students referred for evaluation sooner. Pediatricians are also becoming more educated about autism spectrum disorders, and autism screening is now occurring along with the general developmental screenings to ensure early detection. Lastly, although there are many specific factors that have likely led to an increase in diagnosis, the level of increase (approximately 800 percent over the past 10 years in the United States) is of epidemic proportions. Because we are unsure of the causes of autism spectrum disorders, it is impossible to know why the numbers might be increasing; there are many theories, such as the idea that thimerosol in vaccines is the cause of autism. Current research shows that there is a genetic component to ASD, and we know that it is more likely in siblings. Research is continuing to determine the causes of autism, as it is believed that there is a genetic predisposition and then an environmental influence that may be the cause.

Clearly, one of the greatest challenges for both students with ASD and their teachers is the impact of the disorder on the development of social skills. Can you address this issue in light of current research?

The three main areas in which characteristics of ASD are included are communication, social skills, and behavior. Each of the areas listed may affect the social ability of an individual with ASD. For example, a student who lacks the ability to communicate verbally, to understand and respond to nonverbal social behaviors of a peer, who engages in repetitive behavior to the exclusion of any other more appropriate behaviors will have difficulty interacting with others socially. The lack of ability to engage in appropriate social behaviors and have social understanding of the world around them is a hallmark of the ASD diagnosis. The research focuses on both theories related to the social deficits in autism, including theory of mind (Baron-Cohen, 1988), the enactive mind model (Klin, Jones, Schultz, & Volkmar, 2003), executive functioning (Yerys, Hepburn, Pennington, & Rogers, 2008), and the effective behavioral teaching approaches to social skills (Jones, Feeley & Takacs, 2007; Scattone, 2008). The research is promising, and many students with ASD are benefiting from the use of specific teaching methods (e.g., video modeling).

Current research is even examining high-tech options such as the use of virtual reality models to teach social skills to individuals with ASD, but we still have a long way to go.

Specifically, as this question relates to students with high-functioning autism and Asperger syndrome, what are the implications of research relative to helping them develop the social skills needed for success in life?

The research for students with HFA and Asperger's is focused on understanding how students with ASD understand the social world. Specifically, areas such as eye gaze and perception are being studied to determine how students with ASD look at a social situation both physically (where do they look with their eyes, what are they focused on in a picture or social situation) and what are they thinking when they see a social situation (what are their perceptions) about what is ensuing. The research is still in the somewhat early stages but thus far has shown us that individuals with ASD are not looking at the same things their neurotypical peers are and they are not perceiving situations as being social in the way their peers would. Therefore, people with ASD are missing crucial pieces of information that would allow them to understand social situations and act accordingly.

Given that social skills or "people skills" are clearly the most important ones in the quest for greater independence for students with autism spectrum disorders, what are some strategies that teachers can use to facilitate the acquisition of these skills by students in their classrooms who have ASD?

Students with ASD need to learn what to do in the social situation and then they need to be shown how to do it and then they need many opportunities to practice the skill and receive feedback. Teachers should first conduct a social skills assessment on their students to be sure they address the areas in need. Second, teachers should develop clear objectives related to social behavior. Third, teachers must task analyze the social skills so they can be taught to the students. Fourth, teachers should determine what teaching method to use to teach the skill, based on three factors: the research, the student's learning style, and the student's history of learning. Teachers can use some basic strategies such as reinforcing appropriate social behavior when it occurs—"catch 'em being social"—provide prompts to encourage appropriate social interactions, model appropriate social behavior for students, or use peer models in the classroom. There are a number of research-based strategies for teaching social skills, such as written or audio scripts, video modeling, or social stories. Teachers can look to the Association for Science in Autism Treatment to assist them in deciding which interventions may be based on science at this time (www.asatonline.org).

Could you share with our readers the results of any current research you have conducted in this area, or, for that matter, that your contemporaries may have conducted that you consider to be important to teachers and other stakeholders in working more effectively with students who have ASD?

One of my recent research projects focused on increasing creativity in play with young students with ASD through the provision of instructions and reinforcement. Students who had difficulty engaging in creative play prior to intervention were able to play more creatively, and the social validity data showed that they were able to reach levels similar to those of their peers when their play was judged by a general education teacher. A second research project involved promoting appropriate work-related social behaviors in adolescents with ASD through the use of video modeling. The students learned how to engage in appropriate work-related behaviors by observing them performed for them on a video. This allowed adolescents with ASD to be more independent in a work setting. I do believe it is most important for teachers to get to know their students and look to the research to guide them in their teaching of students with autism.

Finally, could you provide a personal anecdote that describes a "success story," an example of a student who, through effective teacher and parent intervention, was able to make significant social and academic gains on the journey toward greater independence?

Only one? Yes, I have had many success stories, but one in particular stands out to me at this time. There is one student with ASD who I met when she was only 3 years old. She did not have the skills that her typical peers did, she did not engage in eye contact, she was not able to imitate simple actions, she did not play appropriately with toys, she was not speaking or imitating spoken language, and she also engaged in some challenging behaviors due to her lack of ability to communicate her needs. We began a home-based program based on the principles of applied behavior analysis, and the child who seemed to not be able to learn was learning at a rapid speed. By the time she was 4 years old, we wanted her to have more structured opportunities with her peers, so in addition to the home-based services, she began attending a local preschool. In preschool, we provided her with a supported inclusion program (a staff member trained in the principles of applied behavior analysis accompanied her to a general education class). While she was in the class the shadow (staff member) provided her with reinforcers (including praise) for appropriate behavior and prompts as needed to interact with her teachers and peers. Through the years and countless hours of hard work by her behavioral therapists and her parents, she began to gain a number of important skills. Slowly over the years, she began speaking, she was playing with toys, she began to initiate language for the first time. As the years passed we stayed focused on her needs, and our focus changed often as she developed. She continued to attend inclusion classes with typical peers throughout her educational career. She is now in high school and she is able to have a conversation with me about just about any topic, she is very involved in her school and community as she acts in school plays, she sings in a singing group, and she attends dance class and performs in recitals. This summer for the first time she is participating in an internship work program at a local aquarium (her future goal is to be an animal trainer at Sea World). She went on the interview (that in and of itself is an accomplishment) and she was awarded the internship. She was so excited about it that she called me to let me know that she had gotten the "job." I believe that she is an amazing person. I have learned so much from her and I am proud to know her. I hope teachers can feel that way about all their students and know what an impact you can make on someone's life. Effective early intervention is crucial for children with ASD. I know she will continue to do great things in the future and it is because of the foundation she was provided early on.

Summary

In this chapter, we have examined autism spectrum disorder, with a focus on autistic disorder and Asperger syndrome. An examination of the characteristics and etiology of these disorders revealed three key indicators: (1) impairments in social interaction, (2) impairments in communication, and (3) restricted repetitive and stereotyped patterns of behavior. Both AS and AD share all but one of these characteristics—impairments in communication. Children and youth who have Asperger syndrome typically display precocious vocabulary development and are generally articulate and talkative.

Although experts agree that the diagnosis of ASD has increased dramatically in the last decade, the possible reasons for this exponential growth are controversial. Some researchers have suggested that the proliferation of environmental toxins and the use of biotic material in infant vaccinations might be a contributor, whereas others have maintained that the use of more sophisticated and discriminating diagnostic instruments and criteria helps to account for the drastic increase in diagnosis. Nevertheless, at present, the most promising etiological studies seem to point in the direction of genetic influences that affect neurological development.

One of the most reliable and best-documented instruments for assessment is the *Childhood Autism Rating Scale* (CARS; Schopler, Reichler, & Renner, 1988). This instrument is most effective for use with individuals 4 years of age or older. Another reliable assessment instrument, the *Gilliam Autism Rating Scale* (GARS; Gilliam, 1995) is useful in helping to identify autism spectrum disorders in persons aged 3 years and older. Lastly, the *Children's Social Behavior Scale* (CSBQ; Luteijn et al., 2000), another relatively reliable screening instrument, can be useful in making a differential diagnosis. Diagnostic interviews and observation scales such as the *Autism Diagnostic Observation Schedule* (ADOS; Lord et al., 1999) can provide valuable information to help in the identification of autism spectrum disorder. Similarly, the *Asperger's Syndrome Diagnostic Interview* (ASDI; Gillberg et al., 2001) has been shown to be both a reliable and a valid assessment tool for Asperger syndrome.

Effective interventions for students who have ASD include behavioral ones, such as discrete trial training (Lovaas, 1987) that reinforces behavioral approximations; naturalistic behavioral interventions, such as paradigm response training (PRT; Arick et al., 2005), which helps develop symbolic play (Stahmer, 1995); joint attention (Whalen & Schreibman, 2003); cognitive therapies, including video modeling (Thiemann & Goldstein, 2001); and social stories (Gray & Garand, 1993) that can be used to teach social skills such as identifying affect, understanding the consequences of a particular behavior, under-standing another's perspective, and, most important, recognizing socially inappropriate behaviors and replacing those with more appropriate, pro-social ones. Finally, there appears to be little evidence to support the efficacy of pharmacological interventions used to treat children and youth who have ASD.

Tips for Teachers

1. Be sure to obtain and review the IEP for a student assigned to your classroom who has ASD, particularly the behavioral intervention plan. If you need clarification or guidance, contact your school psychologist or special education chairperson and arrange to review the IEP together.

2. Provide visual-pictorial reminders of students' schedules using picture exchange communication systems (PECS) for students who are nonverbal or unable to read; provide a written one for students who are literate and post the schedule near their desks or in a conspicuous spot that can be easily viewed as they come into the classroom.

3. Try to avoid sudden changes in students' schedules; instead, introduce them gradually. Most students who have ASD find sudden changes in routine disconcerting and often react with displeasure and frustration, occasionally tantruming when faced with a change in schedule. If an unannounced change is necessary, have a contingency plan ready to help the agitated student cope with the anxiety and frustration imposed by the change. To the extent possible, ensure that all other activities in the student's schedule remain unaltered, and provide reminders of the schedule change throughout the day to help the student adapt to the new routine.

4. Use a naturalistic behavioral intervention, such as PRT, to help increase intersubjectivity and improve joint attention, and use it consistently. Also, conscientiously record the number of approximations, as well as the frequency in the student's achievement of the behavioral objective. Be sure that these successes receive positive reinforcement.

5. Students who have Asperger syndrome often experience difficulty initiating and/or sustaining a dialogue with a social partner. You can use video instruction to provide nonthreatening modeling of successful behavior. Also, be sure that you comply with the strategies outlined in the student's BIP that address social and interpersonal skills issues.

6. Be sure that you have a crisis intervention or crisis management plan established in the event of a serious behavioral incident, and know and follow the prescribed procedures.

7. Use prearranged cues to remind students who have Asperger syndrome when they are engaged in pedantic speech, are dominating a discussion, or fail to consider the perspective of a social partner.

8. Become familiar with the triggers that incite a student who has AS and diffuse the volatile situation by removing the affected student or antagonist or by redirecting the adversarial interaction.

9. Use social stories when feasible in lessons, or use the "teachable moment" to provide an opportunity to conduct a "social autopsy" on an ineffective or inappropriate social behavior, and then teach the correct behavioral response.

10. Reduce self-stimulating behavior and stereotypy by providing differential reinforcement for other behaviors (DRO)—ones that are more appropriate substitutes for the target behaviors.

Focus Questions Revisited

1. Suppose you are going to be Carmen's classroom teacher next year. What would you want to know about his classroom performance and about his learning and behavioral needs as provided by his current teacher?

A Sample Response

I would need to have a copy of Carmen's current IEP, complete with a behavioral intervention plan that would help me understand his present level of performance in the academic curriculum, as well as the strategies that are effective in helping him achieve his current goals. I would also ask to see samples of Carmen's academic work products in order to better understand how his academic strengths and weaknesses are manifest in the classroom. Finally, I would want to know the interpersonal strategies that facilitate Carmen's participation in the classroom, as well as ones that elicit engagement in learning and social activities.

2. Similarly, imagine that you will be teaching James next year. What would be important for you to know about James's classroom performance to be fully prepared to help him learn and develop?

A Sample Response

As for Carmen, I would want to review James's current IEP, noting especially his strengths and weaknesses, as well as his current goals, both academic and behavioral. I would also study his behavioral intervention plan to learn effective strategies for helping James cope with the social and behavioral challenges he experiences as a result of his AS. Furthermore, I would ask to see samples of his work both in the content areas in which he is successful and those in which he is struggling, so as to develop an effective academic support plan. Lastly, I would want to interview his current teachers to learn about the approaches they found helpful in improving James's social skills, as well as his academic performance.

3. Research the *theory of mind* and describe what insights it provides about the functional understanding of students who have autistic disorder.

A Hint for Your Response

The theory of mind suggests that individuals who have autistic disorder experience difficulty in understanding the perspective of another because of a brain anomaly (Garfinkle, 2000).

4. As Carmen's teacher, what are some important academic considerations to facilitate his acquisition of skills?

A Sample Response

Some important academic considerations might include the following.

a. Be very clear and organized about everything you teach, especially when giving instructions. Any confusion will only create further anxiety, conflict, and tension for both you and the student.

b. Establish routine patterns: Spatial routines associate specific locations with specific activities—for example, a pictorial chart used as a daily schedule. Temporal routines associate time with an activity and make the beginning and ending of an activity visually apparent. Instructional routines associate specific social and communication behaviors.

c. Initiate one-on-one interactions frequently throughout the day to help increase the student's eye contact.

d. Break tasks down into simple parts. This will help the student achieve greater success while avoiding unnecessary frustration.

e. Repeat, repeat, repeat instructions to help the child stay focused on the task at hand.

f. Enhance the student's understanding of instructional and environmental structure by providing routines and visual aids in forms other than written language. For example, learn a few American Sign Language signs to signal transitions, such as the sign for snack or lunchtime.

g. Minimize the time spent waiting to begin activities. Have all materials prepared and handy when starting a lesson. Teaching that is "scattered" and disorganized upsets a student who has autism or another form of pervasive developmental disorder.

h. Teach appropriate social skills through modeling behavior role playing, the use of social stories, and video instruction. Remember, however, to be patient, regularly taking time to help the child learn how to act in various situations. Extending this effort can be difficult, especially if the ASD is severe, but it will achieve positive results.

i. Arrange for a peer to guide and cue the student through social situations. The affected student may be more willing to model her own behavior after that of a peer than that of a teacher.

j. When the student is refraining from aggressive or inappropriate behavior, or employing a more appropriate alternative one, provide positive reinforcement that is both realistic and genuine.

k. The student may not understand what may seem to you to be social common sense because of the ASD or AS, or simply a lack of experience. Therefore, initially, take a more direct approach to teaching social skills rather than allowing the student to learn through trial and error. Specifically, the student may need help interpreting social situations and developing appropriate responses. For example, you might help the student understand how to take turns with a toy (Adapted with permission from Pierangelo & Giuliani, 2001).

5. Suppose you have a student who has Asperger syndrome and a behavioral profile similar to James's. This student has begun to dominate a discussion involving a controversial topic in current events: He is not allowing another student, with a different perspective, to express her views. A third classmate, frustrated by the lack of reciprocity on the part of the student who has AS, reproaches him, threatening him with physical violence. The student who has AS, feeling rejected, hurt, and afraid, abruptly runs from the classroom, hurling epithets at you and the other students while simultaneously throwing books, chalk, and an eraser at his adversary as he flees. What can you do to ensure the safety of this student and restore order to the classroom?

A Sample Response

You should have already established a crisis intervention plan for just such emergencies. Typically, without a plan, teachers either (a) allow the student in crisis to flee, unescorted, in order to maintain classroom control and then later address the student's departure with parents and administrators, or (b) chase after the fleeing student, leaving the other students to discuss the possible outcomes for the student in crisis or to take advantage of the lack of supervision to "act up."

An effective crisis intervention plan will let the teacher signal for assistance using a prearranged method—perhaps via a classroom telephone or intercom. This signal will alert a designated, trained emergency response or crisis intervention team to quickly converge on the location of the incident and either provide the necessary intervention there, or gather information from the teacher who signaled for help about the antecedent events and probable location of the student or students in crisis. The teacher can then restore order to the classroom, write an eyewitness account of the incident using the designated form, and use the "teachable moment" to help the class understand the cause of the incident and help prevent its recurrence.

The teacher is also able, thereby, to avoid participating in a physical restraint, should that become necessary. This helps the child with ASD or AS continue to see the teacher as an ally, not an adversary, and preserves the therapeutic relationship between teacher and student.

6. Explain discrete trial training.

A Sample Response

In discrete trial training, the student who has AD is taught skills presented in a logical sequence that builds on previously acquired ones. Concepts to be taught are identified and then broken into steps using task analysis. Each instructional session consists of a series of discrete trials. These trials involve a focus-step sequence: (a) instructional cue, (b) student response, (c) consequence (generally a positive reinforcer), and (d) pause. Information is collected and analyzed to help monitor the student's progress and determine when a preset behavioral objective has been achieved (Arick et al., 2005, p. 1004).

7. What is paradigm/pivotal response training (PRT), and why is it often preferred over more structured techniques such as discrete trial training?

A Sample Response

Like discrete trial training, PRT is based on a four-step sequence: (a) cue, (b) student response, (c) consequence, and (d) pause. The principal difference between the two behavioral approaches is that trials in PRT are incorporated into the environment in a functional context. For example, in PRT, the student selects the activity or object and the reinforcer is a natural consequence to the behaviors being rewarded, making it possible to engage the student throughout all activities and locations in the course of the day (Arick et al., 2005, p. 1004).

Research comparing naturalistic techniques such as PRT and more structured ones such as DT has demonstrated that PRT resulted in more generalized and spontaneous use of skills (Charlop-Christy, Le, & Freeman, 2000; Delprato, 2001; Miranda-Linne et al., 1992). Furthermore, additional studies revealed that PRT helped reduce stress and increase a sense of well-being among both children with AD and their family members (Koegel et al., 1996).

8. Describe video modeling and what its therapeutic implications are for children who have AD or AS?

A Sample Response

Video modeling, as opposed to in-vivo (live) modeling, refers to a therapeutic approach that involves the videotaping of "actors" or "role models," who demonstrate socially appropriate behaviors in conversational speech, verbal responding, daily living or adaptive behavior skills, and emotional empathy or understanding. Researchers have found that children who have AD acquire these skills with greater rapidity and generalize them to different contexts to a greater degree through video modeling than through in-vivo modeling, perhaps because the video characterizations are less intimidating and more visually stimulating (Charlop-Christy, Le, & Freeman, 2000).

In contrast, students who have AS or high-functioning autism benefited more from in-vivo modeling (Schreibman & Ingersoll, 2005) and were able to use video-modeling to learn self-management techniques such as self-monitoring, self-delivery of reinforcement, and self-evaluation of performance (Thiemann & Goldstein, 2001).

9. What are "social stories," and how are they used to help students who have Asperger syndrome or higher-functioning autism (HFA) acquire strategies for appropriate social conversation and emotional regulation?

A Sample Response

Social stories are just that, stories that involve students similar to those with AS and HFA who are learning from them. These "stories" or "social scripts" depict a hypothetical social situation in which the protagonist makes ineffective choices. The teacher, parent, or therapist uses this safe hypothetical situation to teach the appropriate social response or choice and then allows the teacher and student to assume the roles and read the script, choosing the correct behavioral response in a particular social context.

Social stories are designed to help those with HFA and AS understand their own social difficulties, pay careful attention to the social context, select the most important aspects of a social situation, identify appropriate behavioral responses, identify the social partner's perspective, and understand the consequences of a particular positive behavior (Edelson, 2005; Marans et al., 2005).

10. Suppose you are a classroom teacher in a public elementary school and, because you are regarded as somewhat knowledgeable about autism spectrum disorder (having thoroughly read and understood this chapter), you are approached by some colleagues about the enigmatic behaviors exhibited by a new student for whom they share instruction.

To help confirm their suspicions about the type of disorder that may be affecting this child, they ask you to assemble a list of behavioral characteristics typically observed in an individual who has autism spectrum disorder. What are some key characteristics you could provide?

A Sample Response

Some of the following characteristics may be evident in mild to severe forms of autism:

1. Apparent insensitivity to pain
2. Avoidance of touching others
3. Unprovoked aggression
4. Communication problems
5. Difficulty relating to people
6. Difficulty dealing with changes in routines
7. Does not smile at familiar people
8. Echolalia (repeats words or phrases instead of using normal language)
9. Picky eating habits
10. Hyper- or hyposensitivity (over-or undersensitivity to sensory stimuli)
11. Inappropriate attachment to objects
12. Inappropriate emotional response to situations
13. Lack of imagination or inability to pretend
14. Limited, if any, eye contact
15. Limited range of interests
16. Little interest in making friends
17. Perseverating behavior (excessive concentration on a single person, item, or idea)
18. Disdain for physical contact (may seem cold and unaffectionate)
19. Volatile temperament resulting in tantrums
20. Apparent fearlessness
21. Self-injurious behavior
22. Unresponsive to verbal cues (seems deaf)
23. Hyper- or hypoactivity
24. Gesticulates instead of using speech
25. Preference for being alone (isolation)
26. Repetitive behavior patterns and body movements
27. Self-stimulating behavior ("stimming")
28. Sustained odd play
29. Uneven gross and fine motor skills
30. Unresponsiveness to standard teaching methods (Pierangelo & Giuliani, 2001)

11. Devon is a student who has Asperger's syndrome. Using what you have learned in the chapter about this type of ASD and assuming that he is enrolled in the grade that you teach or will be certified to teach, respond to each of the following:

- What other related service professionals could help you develop a behavioral intervention plan or coach you to work more effectively with Devon?
- Suggest one or two approaches that, in conjunction with other affected teachers and related service providers, you could reasonably use in the classroom to help improve Devon's academic performance in his least preferred and most challenging subject: English language arts. Briefly describe your plan for implementing these approaches.
- Suggest one or two behavioral interventions that, in collaboration with the appropriate related service provider(s), could help Devon to improve his social behaviors in the classroom, thereby increasing his social network and peer relations. Again, briefly describe your plan for employing these interventions.

A Sample Response

Devon, a sophomore in high school who has Asperger's syndrome, struggles in English class because he dislikes writing, especially creative writing. Moreover, Devon manifests behaviors that are considered narcissistic and bizarre by his peers and teachers, which frequently result in his social alienation and consequently cause him to feel lonely and depressed.

(a) In Devon's case, the related service professionals with whom I would seek to collaborate include the school psychologist, Dr. Schwartz, and the speech language pathologist, Ms. Marber. I also would work with Devon's English teacher, Mr. Black, to determine a way that we might increase his engagement in the class and facilitate his production in the creative writing component of the course.

(b) In response to the academic concern; specifically, Devon's reticence to participate in creative writing, we have decided to allow Devon to submit poems, a genre in which he displays some talent and interest, in order to satisfy the course requirement that he provide written products reflecting compositional creativity in both fiction and non-fiction literature. In addressing the later requirement, Mr. Black has agreed to allow Devon to produce an additional research paper on a topic of interest and that has relevance to the course. Devon and Mr. Black have agreed that he will compose a comprehensive paper on the work of Herman Hesse, one of Devon's favorite authors. I will reinforce his research as well as the development of the initial drafts of this assignment during his resource period.

(c) In order to effectively address Devon's social skills deficits, I have enlisted the help of Dr. Schwartz, the school psychologist, and Ms. Marber, the speech language pathologist in developing an intervention plan that I, as well as Devon's other teachers, can realistically implement in the classroom. After conducting a functional behavioral assessment, I met with both of these professionals to draft a classroom-based behavioral intervention plan that would effectively address Devon's two most debilitating social skills deficits: his apparent self-absorption evident in his tendency to "lecture" instead of converse with others, *and* his inability to initiate and sustain social discourse that is accompanied by appropriate eye contact and a friendly demeanor.

In addressing the latter behavior, Ms. Marber is working with Devon, both individually in his speech sessions as well as in her "conversation group," which includes several other students who, like Devon, display social skills deficits. I am simply reminding Devon to use those skills when he reverts to old behavior patterns in the classroom. Also, I am recording the frequency of his use of the desired replacement behaviors to provide Ms. Marber with feedback she can use in her therapy sessions with Devon.

Devon's tendencies to appear self-absorbed together with his lack of reciprocity in conversations are issues that I continually monitor, as well. Both Ms. Marber and Dr. Schwartz have addressed these issues in their individual and group sessions with Devon. They also have asked that I use the "teachable moment" to gently remind Devon that he needs to give others a chance to respond to his comments and that he needs to stay on topic in his reply. I also discreetly remind his classmates that Devon is working very hard on these conversational skills and that they need to be patient and supportive of his efforts. Devon has also been provided with a checklist identifying both the target behaviors mentioned, including those that he wants to eliminate as well as those prosocial ones that he wants to acquire. In this way, Devon is a collaborator in his own social development.

Chapter 10

At-Risk Behaviors and Emotional Disturbance

Peggy Gans

FOCUS QUESTIONS

1. What are the four substances that are most commonly abused by children and adolescents, and why do they pose such a threat?

2. The National Institute on Drug Abuse provides six guidelines in selecting an effective school-based drug-abuse prevention program: What are they?

3. Identify the school professionals who serve as resources for teachers who have concerns about a student at risk for or engaged in substance abuse.

4. What are two key factors that increase the risk of acquiring a sexually transmitted disease (STD) for adolescents who have emotional disturbances?

5. Of the three sex education program types described in this chapter, identify the one that you consider to be most effective, and explain why you consider it so.

6. As a new high school teacher, you notice that some of your students wear distinctive clothing and behave in ways that are unusual and a bit unsettling. What are some of the characteristics or warning signs that you might look for to confirm your suspicions of their gang affiliation?

7. In developing a school-wide approach to prevent gang membership and gang activity, what are some critical elements to include?

This chapter examines four behaviors (substance use, at-risk sexual activity, violence, and gang membership) in which those who have emotional disturbances have a higher risk of participation. The organization of this chapter is different than that of the preceding ones in that it does not pretend to give an in-depth overview of each of the problems, but rather enough information to sensitize school personnel to these at-risk behaviors and suggestions to access appropriate interventions.

SUBSTANCE USE AND ABUSE

CASE EXAMPLE: Michael R.

Michael R., a high school senior, is completing his last academic course in summer school and looks forward to starting classes at a local community college in the fall. He eventually wants to become a meteorologist and has always enjoyed studying and observing weather. He is now poised to realize this life-long dream.

Two years ago, however, Michael's prospects looked very bleak: He was failing every subject in school and was drinking excessive amounts of alcohol, smoking marijuana, and using cocaine, Vicodin, OxyContin, and any other available substance to get "high." Michael's parents had divorced a year before he began using, but were both very supportive of him and had tried, unsuccessfully, on two occasions to get him into rehab. The administration in his school was seeking to expel him because of his extensive truancy and absenteeism. Essentially, Michael was falling through the cracks. The final straw came late in his sophomore year, when he overdosed on Vicodin and alcohol at a rave and would have died were it not for the quick and effective action of the detox-intensive care unit at a nearby hospital.

As it turned out, however, this near-death experience proved to be a turning point in Michael's life. While he was still recovering in the hospital, a clinical social worker found him a placement in a special residential treatment facility not too far from his home. Here, he could go to school and be enrolled in a reputable outpatient rehabilitation program. His progress on the road to "clean and sober" would be carefully monitored by Alan G., the institution's drug awareness counselor. Alan, a clinical social worker with special certification in substance-abuse counseling, had worked successfully with several other students at the school, and he became Michael's lifeline and safety net. At any time during the day, Michael could call Alan at his confidential phone service and leave a message requesting a session; typically within the hour, one was arranged. A similar contingency plan was established for night-time emergencies or struggles. After several months of halting gains and heart-breaking relapses, Michael was finally able to acquire the coping skills to enable him to remain drug- and alcohol-free.

That breakthrough occurred almost 2 years ago, and, thanks to the support network provided by school staff, Alan G., rehabilitation center counselors, and Michael's parents, he will be graduating with a high school diploma in only a few weeks.

Introduction

Data strongly indicate that adolescents who use substances have high rates of psychiatric disorders. Henggeler et al. (1986) found that among participants in a drug-abuse intervention program 35 percent met the criteria for conduct disorder, 19 percent met the criteria for social phobia, 12 percent for oppositional defiant disorder, and 9 percent for major depression. In another study, 89.8 percent had a history of delinquent behavior, 29.7 percent met the criteria for disorders of anxiety and depression, and 27.3 percent had attention problems (Waldron, Slesnick, Brody, Charles, & Peterson, 2001). A third study found that 55 percent met the criteria for an externalizing disorder, 39 percent for conduct disorder, 18 percent for attention-deficit hyperactivity disorder (ADHD), 22 percent for depression, and 26 percent for an anxiety disorder (Kaminer, Burleson, & Goldberger, 2002). Together, these studies make it abundantly clear that those who have emotional disturbances are very much at risk for turning to substances as a means of coping.

Most experts agree that substance use evolves into substance abuse and dependence through a complex interaction of multiple factors that include genetic, psychological, familial, and nonfamilial environments (O'Brien et al., 2005). Therefore, not all those who have emotional disturbances will abuse substances, but it must be considered a significant factor. The more risk factors a student possesses, the greater is the risk for substance abuse. Table 10.1 lists the groups of children research has identified as being at risk for substance abuse.

Because most adolescents experiment with drugs in one form or another, how does one assess the seriousness of drug use? When does drug use become abuse? Which students should schools be especially concerned about? The DSM-IV-TR (American Psychiatric Association, 2000) has established criteria for substance abuse and dependence but does not make any

TABLE 10.1 Children at Risk for Substance Abuse

- Children engaged in early alcohol or drug experimentation
- Children of substance-dependent parents
- Children with substance-abusing siblings
- Children with conduct disorder
- Children with psychiatric disorders
- Children with deviant and substance-abusing peers
- Children temperamentally seeking high sensation
- Children with impulse and self-control problems
- Children under poor parental supervision
- Children living in heavy-drug-use neighborhoods
- Children with school problems
- Children with social skills deficits
- Children of parents with poor parenting skills
- Children who are victims of trauma, abuse, and neglect

Source: From "Substance Use Disorders" by C. P. O'Brien, J. C. Anthony, K. Carroll, A. R. Childress, C. Dackis, G. Diamond et al. in *Treating and Preventing Adolescent Mental Health Disorders* (p. 416) by D. L. Evans, E. B. Foa, R. E. Gur, H. Hendin, C. P. O'Brien, M. E. P. Seligman et al., 2005, New York: Oxford University Press. Copyright 2005 by Oxford University Press. Reprinted with permission.

distinctions for children and adolescents. In the DSM-IV-TR, substance dependence is an addiction that involves the physiological processes of **tolerance** and **withdrawal**. *Substance abuse* refers to the use of substances in a way that interferes with social, school, or occupational functioning. The implication of the DSM-IV-TR criteria is that substances can be used in ways that are not pathological. Value judgments about the use of substances are made according to who takes them, for what purposes they are taken, when and where they are taken, and how much and how frequently they are taken (Robinson, 1989). For example, a drink after work for a middle-aged man is not viewed as much of a problem, as it is for an adolescent who, upon returning home after school, has a drink (Gloria & Robinson-Kurpius, 2000). Youngsters who begin experimenting with tobacco and alcohol at a very young age (e.g., between 9 and 12 years) offer more cause for concern than those who experiment much later.

One way of understanding and assessing drug use among adolescents is through the drug use continuum (Muisener, 1994) and the adolescent chemical use experience as outlined in Table 10.2. Although most adolescents will not progress beyond social use, those who do require help. With the help of the drug use continuum, teachers and other school personnel can make distinctions among the many adolescent substance users and intervene accordingly.

TOLERANCE

In relation to substance use or abuse, refers to a need for increased amounts of a substance to achieve the desired effect and a noticeably diminished effect from use of the same amount of the substance.

WITHDRAWAL

In relation to substance use or abuse, refers to physiological and or mental readjustment symptoms following discontinued use of a substance. A person suffering from withdrawal may also use the substance to avoid symptoms of withdrawal.

Drugs of Choice Among Adolescents

The four most common substances used and abused by children and adolescents are alcohol, nicotine, marijuana, and inhalants.

TABLE 10.2 The Drug Use Continuum

1. *Experimental Use.* Experimental use recognizes that many adolescents try a certain drug because of peer pressure, wanting to have fun, curiosity, or feeling bored (Jalali, Jalali, Crocetti, & Turner, 1981). Experimenters never settle into a drug-using pattern (Miziker-Gonet, 1994), understand the difference between fun and danger, and typically use only alcohol and marijuana (Gloria & Robinson-Kurpius, 2000). Experts disagree as to the number of trials that constitute the maximum for experimental use. Some have proposed ten or fewer experiences (Avis, 1990), others have proposed four or five (Miller, 1989).

2. *Social use.* Adolescents at this stage seek the mood swing derived from substances that was experienced during the experimental phase. They use drugs regularly in certain situations (e.g., a weekend party). Misuse and overindulgence in these situations cause concern that more serious drug use might occur. Social use does not imply acceptable use. It is termed such as a means for assessing the seriousness of the adolescent's use of drugs.

3. *Operational use.* Muisener's (1994) operational use is synonymous with abuse and is marked by a preoccupation with the mood swing. There are two types of operational users: the "pleasure-pursuant user," who seeks to feel good through the drug; and "the pain-avoidant" or "compensatory" user, who uses drugs to avoid painful feeling or to cope with difficult situations. The compensatory user is at greater risk for developing a more serious drug problem, because drugs have become a coping mechanism.

4. *Dependent use.* According to Muisener (1994), these adolescents engage in compulsive drug use and urgently seek the mood swing created by drugs. Much of the adolescent's time and energy is spent getting drugs and getting high. Compulsive users derive their identity from drugs, and they become a subculture in relation to the mainstream, nonabusing population.

ALCOHOL   The use of alcohol is pervasive in U.S. society. For every person in the United States, 24 gallons of beer, 2 gallons of distilled spirits, and more than 2 gallons of wine are sold each year (Gloria & Robinson-Kurpius, 2000). Youth between the ages of 13 and 15 are at risk to begin drinking. According to the *2006 Monitoring the Future Study* (Johnston, O'Malley, Bachman, & Schulenberg, 2006), nearly 73 percent of today's teenagers have consumed alcohol by the end of high school, and 41 percent have done so by eighth grade. In addition, 56 percent of twelfth-graders and 20 percent of eighth-graders report having been drunk at least once in their life. The good news is that in 2006 alcohol use nationwide continued to decline among twelfth-graders and leveled off for eighth-graders, but the bad news was that alcohol use increased among tenth-graders (Johnston et al., 2006). Forty-five percent of children who start drinking before the age of 15 will become alcoholics at some point in their lives. If the onset of drinking is delayed by 5 years, a child's risk of serious alcohol problems is decreased by 50 percent (Grant & Dawson, 1997). For many youth, what begins as experimental will develop later into uncontrollable drinking.

NICOTINE   In the last 10 years, the perceived risk of cigarette smoking among youth has increased and resulted in significant decreases in the rates of smoking among eighth-, tenth-, and twelfth-graders (Johnston et al., 2006). Nevertheless, approximately 47 percent of youth have tried cigarettes by the grade 12, and 22 percent of twelfth-graders identify themselves as smokers. Among eighth-graders, 25 percent have tried cigarettes, and 9 percent are habitual smokers. Nicotine abuse is clearly a problem that begins in youth. Males are more likely to smoke than females: 36.5 percent of males ages 12 and older smoke, compared to 24.3 percent of females. Males are much more likely to use smokeless tobacco. American Indians and Alaska Natives are more likely to smoke than any other racial or ethnic group.

MARIJUANA Marijuana is the most widely used illicit drug in the United States and is usually the first illicit drug that adolescents use (Gloria & Robinson-Kurpius, 2000). There are many street names for marijuana, including "pot," "weed," "Mary Jane," "herb," and "boom," among others. Research on the effects of marijuana is still in its early stages, and scientists have not been able to determine whether marijuana is physiologically addictive. However, the psychological addiction to marijuana is indisputable and very powerful. More than 120,000 people per year seek treatment for their addiction to marijuana (National Institute on Drug Abuse, 2000). There has been a slight, nonsignificant decline among youth in the use of marijuana, as there has been with all illicit drugs. However, the rates of marijuana use remain high. In 2006, the prevalence rate of marijuana was just under 12 percent among eighth-graders, 25 percent among tenth-graders, and 32 percent among twelfth-graders (Johnston et al., 2006).

Longitudinal research has also shown negative social consequences for heavy users of marijuana. For those below college age, marijuana use has been associated with:

- Lower achievement
- High levels of delinquent and aggressive behavior
- Greater rebelliousness
- Poor relationships with parents
- Having delinquent friends (Johnston et al., 2006)

Curbing marijuana use is a challenging task. Many adolescents experiment with marijuana and enjoy its positive effects. Because it increases sensory perception, listening to music and smoking marijuana is a frequent combination for adolescents. Though it is illegal, marijuana is readily available and its use justified because it is less dangerous than other illicit drugs. These factors must be considered in trying to prevent marijuana abuse among adolescents.

INHALANTS Inhalants are the fourth most commonly used substance among youth and the most commonly used among eighth-grade students. Most adults are exposed daily to chemical vapors in homes and workplaces. Because these substances are not meant to be inhaled, the average person may have difficulty considering these vapors as drugs. Inhalants are "breathable chemical vapors that produce psychoactive (mind-altering) effects" (National Institute on Drug Abuse, 2001, p. 1). They are popular among young people because they are readily available, inexpensive, and can be used in a nonsuspicious fashion. Table 10.3

TABLE 10.3 Categories of Inhalants

1. Solvents

(a) Industrial or household solvents, including paint thinners, degreasers, gasoline, and glues

(b) Art or office supply solvents, including correction fluids, felt-tip marker fluid, and electronic contact cleaners

2. Gases

(a) Gases in household or commercial products, including butane lighters, propane tanks, whipping cream aerosols or dispensers, and refrigerant gases

(b) Household aerosol propellant, including solvents in spray paints, hair or deodorant sprays, and fabric protector sprays

(c) Medical anesthetic gases, including ether, chloroform, halothane, and nitrous oxide

3. Nitrates

(a) Aliphatic nitrites, including cyclohexyl nitrite, available to the general public; amyl nitrite, available by prescription; and butyl nitrite, now an illegal substance

Source: From *Inhalants* by the National Institute of Drug Abuse, 2001. *Inhalants.* Retrieved from http://www.drugabuse.gov/inhalants/html.

describes the different categories of inhalants. Inhalant use has been on the rise in recent years and perceived risk among eighth- and tenth-graders has fallen steadily in the last 5 years, which indicates that inhalant use will continue to increase. In 2005, approximately 36 percent of twelfth-graders had used inhalants, compared to 23 percent of tenth-graders and 11 percent of eighth graders.

OTHER DRUGS Besides the four most commonly used substances we have described so far, teenagers also use a smorgasbord of other drugs. The 2005 *Monitoring the Future Study* divides these drugs into three categories: drugs that are decreasing in use, drugs that are holding steady, and drugs that are showing signs of increased use.

- Drugs that are decreasing in use include hallucinogens, amphetamines, methamphetamines, and sedatives.
- Drugs that are holding steady include LSD (lysergic acid diethylamide), powder cocaine, crystal methamphetamine ("ice"), heroin, narcotics, tranquilizers, anabolic steroids, and "club" drugs (ketamine, rohypnol, and GHB [gamma-hydroxybutyric acid]).
- Drugs that are increasing in use include ecstasy (3,4-methylene-dioxymethamphetamine or MDMA), OxyContin, and Vicodin.

Treatment of Substance Abuse

Treatment of substance abuse has been for the most part psychosocial in nature and consists of four different approaches: short-term (4 to 6 weeks) inpatient, outpatient, therapeutic community, and outward bound-type or life skills training programs (O'Brien et al., 2005). Most of the research on program evaluation and effectiveness, however, has been done with inpatient programs, and those that have been done on other programs often do not include comparison or control groups. Because most adolescent substance abusers receive outpatient services for their problems, there is a serious need for more research into their effectiveness.

Outpatient approaches typically have employed behavioral, cognitive-behavioral, family, and multisystemic approaches. Though relatively new and not so extensive, research into the effectiveness of treatment for adolescents with substance abuse has revealed the following:

- Well-defined structured approaches are better than no treatment at all.
- Treatments that focus on broad aspects of functioning seem to produce the best results.
- Those who complete treatment have the best results.
- Inclusion of family members increases retention and outcomes.
- Contingency management through behavioral therapy, which has been successful with adults, is beginning to show promise with adolescents.
- Cognitive-behavioral therapies also show promise, especially when used in conjunction with family therapy.
- Group approaches have produced mixed results, and there exists the possibility of deviant peers together escalating the problem (O'Brien et al., 2005).

TREATMENT OF COMORBIDITIES Because of the high rates of comorbidity between substance abuse and emotional disturbance, treating dually diagnosed adolescents can be especially challenging. In general, these adolescents have poorer outcomes, and if the co-occurring disorder is left untreated, the probability of retention and completion in a drug intervention program is dramatically lessened (Grella, Hser, Joshi, & Rounds-Bryant, 2001; Lohman, Riggs, Hall, Mikulich, & Klein, 2002). Pharmacological treatment for dually diagnosed adolescents can be risky. Current research is investigating pharmacological agents with low abuse liability that can be used in substance-abusing adolescents with ADHD, bipolar disorder, depression, or anxiety disorders.

Prevention of Substance Abuse

Fortunately, much more research has been done on the effectiveness of drug prevention programs for children and adolescents. Programs that do *not* work include:

- Information-only programs
- Scare tactics
- One-shot programs
- Values-clarification programs

The National Institute on Drug Abuse (1999) has established the following principles as guides in adopting effective school-based prevention programs.

1. School based programs should extend from kindergarten through high school. At the very least, they should reach children in the critical middle school and high school years.

2. Programs should employ well-tested, standardized interventions with detailed lesson plans and student materials.
3. Programs should employ age-appropriate interactive teaching methods (e.g., modeling, role playing, discussion, group feedback, reinforcement, and extended practice).
4. Programs should foster pro-social bonding to both the school and the community.
5. Program components should include teaching social competence (i.e., communication, self-efficacy, assertiveness) and drug resistance skills that are culturally and developmentally appropriate; promoting positive peer influence; promoting antidrug social norms; emphasizing skills training teaching methods; and include an adequate "dosage" (ten to fifteen sessions in a year).
6. Programs should be periodically evaluated to determine their effectiveness (National Institute on Drug Abuse, 1999, p. 12).

Research has identified four goals associated with successful prevention programs: increasing students' self-esteem, social skills, decision-making/problem-solving skills, and ability to resist the influence of peers (Botvin, 1986; Bradley, 1988). In addition, programs more recently have included alternative activities, such as adventure recreation and education, to substitute for the lure of risk-taking behaviors associated with drug use (McWhirter, 2007).

Numerous commercially-driven, school-based programs exist for the prevention of adolescent substance abuse. It is not within the scope of this chapter to review these programs. School personnel who wish to implement a prevention program are cautioned to make an informed decision after reviewing the independent research regarding the effectiveness of such programs and their suitability for a particular school.

AT-RISK SEXUAL BEHAVIORS

A Study in Contrasts: Two Stories

CASE EXAMPLE: Miriam

Miriam, a 17-year-old high school senior and honor student, comes from an intact, middle-class family living in a comfortable home in suburban Minneapolis. Her father is the pastor of a local congregation and her mother teaches in a school affiliated with the church. Miriam and her siblings, two older sisters and a younger brother, have always taken an active part in the church: Miriam teaches a Sunday school class for very young children, attends Wednesday night Bible study, and helps organize activities for the youth group that meets on Friday evenings.

In school, Miriam is a model student, active in the debating society and drama club, and participating as a soloist with the school chorale. In short, Miriam's free time is very limited, and her parents like it that way. They have extolled the virtues of serving others and staying viable through engagement in worthwhile pursuits, especially those relevant to her faith. To those around her, even those who know her well, Miriam is regarded in every way as an exemplary young woman: an ideal American teenager, the "girl next door."

That is why it came as such a shock to her family, friends, and classmates when, quite unexpectedly, Miriam's school counselor informed her parents that she was two months pregnant!

CASE EXAMPLE: Elisha

In contrast to Miriam, Elisha comes from a poor family living in a poor neighborhood near Seattle's busy marketplace. Surrounded by drug addicts and prostitutes, Elisha and her family members take risks every day just walking to school or the local grocery store. Elisha's father, an itinerant laborer, left their home when she was 2, and her mother, a recovering addict, has tried unsuccessfully to support the family through the tips and wages she receives as a waitress, supplemented by public assistance.

Elisha began to engage in risk-taking behaviors at an early age. For example, she began smoking cigarettes at age 7, drinking alcohol at 9, smoked her first "joint" at the age of 11, and eventually tried "hard" drugs a year or two later. Although she has never been to "rehab" and does not consider herself dependent on drugs or alcohol, she relishes life on the street, replete with risks, dangers, and the "pay off": excitement!

Not surprisingly, she had her first sexual experience at the age of 12 with one of her mother's many short-term boyfriends, who subsequently violated her several more times. A few years later, after spending 6 months in "juvy" (juvenile detention) for petty theft, vagrancy, and drug possession, one of her former "boyfriends" confronted her about giving him the "clap," specifically, genital herpes. After weeks of prodding from a few concerned friends, Elisha went to an STD (sexually transmitted disease) clinic and discovered from the results of blood tests that she had not only contracted genital herpes but was also HIV positive. Upon receiving this news, Elisha felt as though she had just been given a death sentence.

Two young women, two different stories; however, their personal crises can be better appreciated both in nature and need after reading the following section.

Introduction

It is difficult to think of a topic that stimulates more interest and, at the same time, more controversy in schools than issues related to sexuality. Other than the most benign sex education done through health education classes, material about safer sex and pregnancy prevention is bound to cause a reaction even in not so conservative school districts of the United States. Sexual development is an overwhelmingly important characteristic of adolescence; therefore, its presence in the school setting is unavoidable. And because sexual awakening brings with it a host of problems (romantic attachments and breakups, peer conflicts and jealousies, sexual harassment, unsafe sex, struggles with sexual orientation, and teenage pregnancy/ motherhood), it is inconceivable that schools could be competent at their jobs without being knowledgeable about and feeling comfortable with sex-related matters.

Emotional disturbance is considered a risk factor for sexual victimization (Raghavan, Bogart, Elliott, Vestal, & Schuster, 2004; Varia, 2006). Those with mental disability can be either victims or perpetrators of inappropriate sexual activity. This section, therefore, deals with at-risk sexual behaviors and covers such topics as HIV/AIDS, STDs, and teen pregnancy/parenthood.

Unprotected Sexual Activity: The Risk of HIV/AIDS

Adolescents, like any others who are sexually active, are at-risk for acquiring sexually transmitted diseases, especially acquired immune deficiency syndrome (AIDS). More than 3 million teens acquire an STD every year, making the United States the country with the highest adolescent STD rate in the developed world (Centers for Disease Control, 2005). The most common STD in the United States is chlamydia, but gonorrhea, genital warts, herpes, and syphilis are also common (McWhirter, 2004). In June 2005, the Centers for Disease Control reported that 5309 individuals between the ages of 15 and 19 had been diagnosed with AIDS. However, this number is misleading because of the high incidence of HIV infection and the long asymptomatic period (up to 10 years). In 2005, 44,168 Americans were diagnosed with AIDS (Centers for Disease Control, 2005), and it is believed that most of these individuals contracted HIV during their teen years (Gray, House, & Champeau, 2000). The number of teens who account for all AIDS in this country doubles every year (McWhirter, 2004).

The most common routes for acquiring HIV are unprotected sexual contact with infected persons and sharing a needle with an infected person during intravenous drug use (Gray et al., 2000). School personnel should realize that all students, male or female, gay, straight, or bisexual, are at risk for contracting HIV if they engage in unprotected sexual behaviors that allow for the sharing of body fluids. Statistics vary, but in 2005, 63 percent of high school students reported using a condom the last time they had sexual intercourse, up from 54 percent in 1995 (Kaiser Family Foundation, 2006). The data are somewhat confounding in that adolescents are more aware and use more condoms, but the incidence of oral and anal sex has increased. The fact that adolescents experiment and use drugs and alcohol on a regular basis contributes to the risk of unprotected sex. One-quarter of sexually active high school students admitted to using alcohol or drugs during their most recent sexual encounter (Kaiser, 2006). Being under the influence of drugs or alcohol impairs judgment and increases the probability of engaging in risky sexual behaviors and the sharing of needles if drugs are used intravenously (Gray et al., 2000).

There is some positive news about the AIDS epidemic in that both knowledge and the practice of safer sex have increased among adolescents. However, they continue to be at risk for contracting HIV and other STDs. Research has shown that those who are most at risk (those adolescents who have multiple partners, abuse drugs and alcohol, and generally participate in delinquent behaviors) are the least likely to practice safer sex (McCarthy, Brack, Laygo, Brack, & Orr, 1997). Among adolescents, HIV/AIDS occurs across race, socioeconomic status, gender, and sexual orientation. Therefore, school personnel need to be very knowledgeable about HIV/AIDS and willing to initiate and support prevention efforts in their schools.

HELPING STUDENTS WHO ARE HIV-POSITIVE   Everyone infected with HIV/AIDS is at increased risk for depression and suicide. They may manifest somatic complaints, anhedonia (the inability to experience pleasure), withdrawal, and irritability perhaps evidence of an underlying depression (Cobia, Carney, & Waggoner, 1998). Other emotional reactions can include sadness, confusion, anxiety, fear of isolation, rejection, loss of friends, and death (Cobia et al., 1998; Spiegel & Mayers, 1991). A child's emotional difficulties may manifest more aggressively, in fighting and classroom disruption (Pizzo & Wilfert, 1991). Most important, the school needs to provide the child with an opportunity to express any and all of the above emotions within an environment that is safe and nurturing. In addition, school personnel can focus on self-esteem building, problem solving, conflict resolution, and the development of self-efficacy (Cobia et al., 1998; Levinson & Mellins, 1992). Play therapy is a recommended modality for children suffering from HIV infection (Weiner & Septimus, 1991). Because many providers will be involved in the life of an HIV-infected child, an important part of the school's job is environmental engineering—keeping track of the services the child receives, avoiding duplication of services, and advocating for the child whenever a needed service is lacking.

Many of the above guidelines for working with HIV-infected children are also applicable to working with HIV-infected adolescents. In addition, schools need to consider the formation of intimate meaningful relationships, issues of sexual orientation, safer sex practices, as well as other risky behaviors. Depression and suicide are a very real threat for HIV-positive adolescents. The dynamics of loss have to be considered when working with HIV-positive adolescents, because they may perceive themselves as being unable to enjoy a life like their peers in terms of intimate relationships, physical ability, and so on. They may also suffer from guilt, especially if the disease was contracted through unprotected sex or intravenous drug use (Cobia et al., 1998). As with children, the emotional reactions can be quite varied. By showing empathy, support, and unconditional acceptance, teachers and other school personnel can play a vital role in the lives of HIV-infected adolescents.

Teenage Pregnancy and Motherhood

In the United States, 750,000 teenage women aged 15 to 19 become pregnant every year (Guttmacher Institute, 2006). The good news is that during the 1990s teen birth rates declined by nearly a third, from 61.8 per 1,000 females aged 15 to 19 to 41.1 per 1,000 in 2004. Hispanics have the highest teen birth rates—81.5 per 1,000 females aged 15 to 19. In 2005, 82.8 percent of births to females aged 15 to 19 occurred to unmarried women.

A TYPOLOGY OF ADOLESCENT PREGNANCY Adolescent pregnancy and motherhood is the result of a complex interplay of social, cultural, economic, family, and biological factors (Brewster, Billy, & Grady, 1993; Sherwood-Hawes, 2000). To understand this complexity, it may be helpful to distinguish three categories of adolescent pregnancy: intentional, accidental, and uninformed (MacFarlane, 1995).

Intentional Pregnancy This group of adolescents actually wants to become pregnant. Within this group, there are two subtypes: one whose culture accepts and even rewards early pregnancy; the other whose psychological

---

TABLE 10.4   Psychological Needs Fulfilled by an Intentional Pregnancy

1. *Power.* Teens may perceive that pregnancy will enhance their power to make choices in their lives by giving them "adult" status.

2. *Control.* Teens may use pregnancy to control other people. The adolescent may use the pregnancy to force a boyfriend to marry her or compel her parents to comply with her wishes or desires.

3. *Intimacy.* Teens may equate sex with intimacy. Instead of developing intimacy and then becoming sexually active, teenagers may have the misunderstanding that sexual involvement creates emotional intimacy. Teens often believe that having a baby will create more intimacy with their sexual partner. Likewise, adolescent girls may feel that their child will help meet their needs for intimacy.

4. *Escape.* Teens may view pregnancy as an avenue of escape. Adolescents who are experiencing difficulties at home or who want to move out of their parents' homes may believe that pregnancy will allow them to move into another household or to establish a household of their own. Pregnancy may also allow teenagers to escape the expectations others have for them concerning achievement and status.

5. *Rebellion.* Pregnancy may also be a means of rebelling against parental authority. If teenagers know that their parents dislike their sexual partners, or are opposed to them being sexually active or becoming pregnant, a pregnancy is the ultimate "in your face" act for a teenager.

6. *Purpose.* Pregnancy can be an avenue to form a relationship with someone who will love them and give them a sense of purpose in life.

7. *Procreation.* Teens may see pregnancy as a way to pass on part of themselves to the next generation. The infant becomes a symbol of making a lasting legacy or contribution.

Source: From *All About Sex: The School Counselor's role to Handling Tough Adolescent Problems* (pp. 43–44) by L. J. Bradley, E. Harchow, and B. Robinson, 1999, Thousand Oaks, CA: Corwin Press. Copyright by Corwin Press. Reprinted with permission.

needs are fulfilled through having a baby. As an example of the first group, Sciarra & Ponterotto (1998) found that early pregnancy and motherhood restored a sense of balance and stability to low-income Hispanic families. These were families living in areas of urban blight, and many of the adolescents' mothers felt that by having a child their daughter would remain off the street because of her duties and responsibilities to the newborn child. Table 10.4 lists and describes the psychological needs that adolescents among the second subtype may seek to fulfill through an intentional pregnancy. How accurately one can determine the number of intentional or desired pregnancies is difficult to know. Many adolescents will consider their pregnancy intended or desired after the fact rather than admit it was a mistake; others might covertly desire the pregnancy and overtly deny it. This may be especially true in cases in which the adolescent decides to bring the pregnancy to term.

Accidental Pregnancy   This appears to be the most common category of adolescent pregnancy. These adolescents know and understand the proper use of contraceptives, but take risks by using them haphazardly or not at all (MacFarlane, 1995). Sometimes drugs or alcohol are involved, which cloud judgment, cause impulsiveness, and prevent the proper use of contraception.

Uninformed (Misinformed) Pregnancy This group of pregnant teens reports that if proper contraception information had been provided to them, they would not have become pregnant (MacFarlane, 1995). This group may not even have thought about pregnancy, because their ignorance allows them to believe that it can't happen if they have sex only once, or if it's their first time. Their knowledge is limited and often inaccurate.

RISK FACTORS ASSOCIATED WITH ADOLESCENT PREGNANCY AND MOTHERHOOD All of the following have been found to increase the risk of bearing children during adolescence:

1. Having a parent who was also a teenage parent
2. Having a sibling who is (was) a teenage parent
3. Coming from a single-parent family
4. Coming from a family marked by marital strife, instability, and poor communication
5. Lower educational and career opportunities
6. Poor school performance
7. Ethnicity
8. Low socioeconomic status

When several of these factors are present in a single individual, the risk for adolescent childbearing is significantly increased. No one can underestimate the influence of poverty on adolescent motherhood, because the overwhelming majority of adolescent mothers are from poor and low-income families. Those adolescents who choose to abort their pregnancy are more likely to come from higher socioeconomic environments, be more successful in school, have parents and friends with positive attitudes toward abortion, reside in communities that provide accessible publicly funded abortions, and tend to have fewer friends or relations who are adolescent parents (Furstenberg, Brooks-Gunn, & Chase-Landsdale, 1989; Sherwood-Hawes, 2000).

CONSEQUENCES OF EARLY CHILDBEARING The factors associated with early childbearing can appear so cogent that one may wonder to what extent it is preventable. Yet the consequences of early childbearing are so overwhelmingly negative that one cannot easily relinquish prevention efforts. Adolescent mothers suffer significant socioeconomic, educational, health-related, and family development consequences (McWhirter, 2004).

Socioeconomic Consequences An adolescent mother is much more likely to live in poverty than her older counterpart. Moore et al. (1993) found the that average family income of girls who became mothers at age 16 or younger was 25 percent that of families whose mothers became pregnant in their late 20s. Adolescent mothers receive a disproportionate share of public assistance (Medicaid, food stamps, etc.) (McWhirter, 2004) and are more likely to live in inadequate housing, suffer poor nutrition and health, be unemployed or underemployed, out of school, and have inadequate career training (Robinson, Watkins-Ferrell, Davis-Scott, & Ruch-Ross, 1993). If adolescent mothers come from poor and low-income backgrounds, their own childbearing will continue the cycle of poverty.

Educational Consequences Teen mothers are three times more likely to drop out of school than those who delay childbearing until their 20s (McWhirter, 2004). Many schools have begun to provide alternative schools or programs for adolescent mothers. These initiatives are more than likely responsible for the increase in teen mothers who complete high school. However, only a small percentage attends college. The teen mother's lack of education has consequences for her children, who evidence more behavioral problems in school (Thomson, Hanson, & McLanahan, 1994), poor attendance, low grade-point averages, lower scores on standardized tests, and lower expectations for attending college (Astone & McLanahan, 1991).

Health-Related Consequences Pregnant teens have more prenatal, peri-natal, and postnatal problems than older mothers (McWhirter, 2004). Only one in five pregnant teens under the age of 15 receives any prenatal care during the first trimester. Teen mothers are more likely to have complications related to prematurity, which increases the likelihood of delivering a low-birth-weight child (under 5.5 pounds), and low-birth-weight children are two to ten times more likely to have academic or behavioral problems (Furstenberg, Morgan, Moore, & Peterson, 1987). Children born to mothers under the age of 17 have higher rates of injury, illness, and sudden infant death syndrome (SIDS) (Morris, Warren, & Aral, 1993). African American and Hispanic teen mothers are more likely to receive late or no prenatal care than their European American counter-parts (McWhirter, 2004).

Family Development As mentioned earlier, more than 75 percent of adolescent child bearers are not married. Many teenage fathers relinquish their responsibilities and do little to provide a secure emotional and financial environment for their children (Kiselica, 1995; Sciarra & Ponterotto, 1998). Single-mothers who do work are forced to work long hours at low-paying jobs because of their lack of education. The stress of trying to raise children and be the sole economic provider is overwhelming for many adolescent mothers and makes the potential for child abuse greater (Becker-Lausen & Rickel, 1995). If they do marry, teen mothers are more likely to divorce within 5 years. In short, there is a great deal more likelihood that children born to teen mothers will grow up in families marked by greater conflict and instability.

WORKING WITH THE ADOLESCENT MOTHER-TO-BE Table 10.5 lists suggestions for helping the pregnant teen who has made the decision to bring her pregnancy to term. With regard to continuing her education, one adolescent mom had this to say about her education:

TABLE 10.5 Suggestions for Working with the Adolescent Mother-to-Be

1. *Assess the client's immediate needs*. Many pregnant teens may be confused about prenatal care. School personnel can help them see the importance of such care and direct them to places where they can receive it. If the adolescent is afraid to tell her parents and/or boyfriend, school personnel can help her to work through these fears, because avoiding such disclosure is not going to improve the situation.

2. *Decide whom to notify*. Depending on state regulations and school polices, the teen's parent may have to be notified. If the student wants to tell her parents and/or boyfriend but does not know how, the teacher can offer to be part of the meeting with the parent. The teacher can also do some role-plays with the student to anticipate the reactions of the other party and strategize how to deal with such reactions.

3. *Identify supportive relationships*. A student who becomes pregnant may experience the rejection of her peers or feel isolated because of her situation. Many community agencies run support groups for pregnant teens, and the school can refer the student.

4. *Consider long-term options*. As the pregnancy advances, the school should help the adolescent plan her educational future. A decision should be made as to whether the pregnant teen will attend the same school or an alternative school. Child care arrangements should also be discussed, so the adolescent can continue to attend school after the birth. Many alternative schools provide day care in the school building. Although the data regarding education and adolescent motherhood are not encouraging, schools should help the pregnant teen understand that she can have her baby and also continue her education. Schools can also help with other long-term needs by making sure the adolescent receives any public assistance for which she qualifies, especially from the Special Supplemental Food Program for Women Infants, and Children (WIC).

Source: Adapted from *All About Sex: The School Counselor's Role to Handling Tough Adolescent Problems* by J. J. Bradley, E. Harchow, and B. Robinson, 1999.

> Well, you know, I thought, if I'm being bad like this and am pregnant and am gonna be a mother, I need to give example to other kids. . . . I changed so I could be an example, a good example. Then when my baby be born, you know, she grows up, they could talk good things about me, not bad. When I wasn't pregnant, I used to not care. But now, you know, 'cause I have a baby, I have to give an example to her, you know, and to other kids, get an education for the baby. So when the baby asks her [the mother] something, she'll know what to answer. Or if not, if she don't finish school, she'll be a dropout, the baby's gonna be a dropout. She'll tell her mother, "You were a dropout. Why can't I be too? If you left school, why can't I leave too?" (Sciarra & Ponterotto, 1998, p. 759).

When suggesting services to a pregnant teen or adolescent mother, the school should consider the following issues:

1. Is transportation available? Is there a bus route or a friend with a car?

2. How many hours will it likely take to apply? How long until the application is approved? What can be done in the meantime?

3. What verification (of income, hours, and caring arrangements) must be provided? Can you make copies for the student? What is the deadline for submitting verification?

4. Does the student have a Social Security card? Does the student have official birth certificates for her- or himself and for the baby? How does the student get them? (Scherman, Korkanes-Rowe, & Howard, 1990, p.140)

WORKING WITH TEEN FATHERS   Often, the teenage father is forgotten about in the discussion of adolescent pregnancy and motherhood. Kiselica and Scheckel (1995) suggested that teenage fathers are susceptible to the *couvade syndrome,* the presence of physical symptoms that occur in male partners or husbands of pregnant women. These symptoms can include indigestion, colic, gastritis, nausea, vomiting, increased or decreased appetite, diarrhea, constipation, headache, dizziness, and cramping (Bogren, 1986). In his research on teen fathers, Goodyear (2002) found that they clustered into two groups. One group was more predatory, less loving and committed to their partners, less responsible as fathers, and more likely to view the pregnancy as an indication of their masculinity. The other group was found to be the opposite: less predatory, more loving and committed, more responsible, and less inclined to view the pregnancy as a symbol of masculinity. Cultural factors may also be involved in the teen father's seeming lack of involvement in the pregnancy and birth of his child (Sciarra & Ponterotto, 1998). In a national survey, school counselors were found to be more likely to refer teen mothers than teen fathers for health and basic living services (Kiselica, Gorcynski, & Capps, 1998). If schools are reluctant to include teen fathers as part of their interventions with teen mothers, they perhaps exclude a source of support for the well-being of the adolescent mothers and their children, especially if these fathers belong to the less predatory group.

As part of the couvade syndrome, teen fathers may avoid the women they have impregnated. Schools can play a critical role in mitigating this avoidance, especially if the teen father is also a student at the school. Teen fathers should not be allowed to shirk their responsibility. Teachers and other school professionals can help them understand the consequences of their actions and the responsibility that accompanies fathering a child.

Approaches to Sex Education

In the literature, three basic programs in schools can be identified to promote safer sex and prevent pregnancy:

1. Abstinence-only programs (or delay of sexual activity) that do not discuss contraception

2. Programs that discuss abstinence and contraception, with concrete information about the different kinds of contraception

3. Comprehensive programs that provide information about abstinence, contraception, clinical services, and reproductive health education topics (McWhirter, 2004)

ABSTINENCE-ONLY PROGRAMS   Abstinence-only programs of sex education are usually provided as part of a health education curriculum that requires teaching about the physiological aspects of sex and reproduction. Normally, in these programs, abstinence is discussed as the only acceptable way of preventing pregnancy and STDs. These programs avoid dealing with controversial issues such as contraception and homosexuality, often because school personnel fear the reaction of parents and other members of the community. There is no research to support the effectiveness of abstinence-only programs in delaying first intercourse or preventing teen pregnancy. However, some abstinence-only programs have been found to promote stronger abstinence attitudes (Kirby et al., 1994) and do increase knowledge about reproduction and the biological aspects of sexuality (Barth, Fetro, Leland, & Volkan, 1992; Hofferth, 1991).

KNOWLEDGE OF AND ACCESS TO CONTRACEPTION   These programs provide all the information of traditional programs but also discuss contraception and how to get it. Research has been inconclusive about the effectiveness of such programs, because knowledge alone is only weakly related to behavior (Kirby, 1999, 2001). Some of these programs have been found to change both behavior and attitudes, whereas others have not (Kirby et al., 1994). Neither knowledge alone nor access alone seems to be an effective approach in changing sexual behavior. On the other hand, there is no evidence to suggest that a contraception component in sex education programs increases sexual activity (Franklin, Grant, Corcoran, Miller, & Bultman, 1997; Kirby, 2001; Sellers, McGraw, & McKinlay, 1994).

Some evidence has supported school-based clinics that offer comprehensive family planning and health services, including the dispensation of contraception, as having succeeded in lowering pregnancy rates and delaying the initiation of intercourse (Dryfoos, 1994). According to Kirby (1999), "most studies that have been conducted during the past 20 years have indicted that improving access to contraception did not significantly increase contraceptive use or decrease teen pregnancy (p. 92)." Although the last 10 years have seen a decrease in the number of programs that include access to contraceptives, their use among adolescents has increased significantly without a correlated decrease in pregnancy or HIV infection. It may be that simply providing access is not sufficient but it must occur within a more comprehensive, multicomponent approach to preventing teenage pregnancy and HIV infection.

LIFE SKILLS/LIFE OPTIONS APPROACH   This category designates comprehensive prevention programs that include aspects of the other two programs along with attitude and skill-building themes intended to promote more responsible decisions about sexual activity. These programs encourage abstinence and/or delay of sexual activity, provide concrete knowledge about contraception, and deal with nonsexual factors, such as self-esteem building, decision-making skills, assertiveness training, and delineating a clear vision of a successful and self-sufficient future (McWhirter, 2004). Much of the information imparted in these programs is applied to the student's personal situation through discussion, role plays, behavior simulation, and drama. These programs promote self-understanding through the examination of sexual attitudes and behaviors. Besides dealing with sexual matters, the life skills/life options programs also include a career component designed to help at-risk adolescents become more aware of job opportunities and promote a clearer vision of the future. Some programs even provide a part-time work experience along with remedial education in reading and math.

The research on these comprehensive prevention programs has supported their effectiveness. For example, participants in the Youth Incentive Entitlement Employment Program (YIEPP) had higher levels of knowledge about sexual reproduction and contraception, a greater tendency to delay sexual activity, and were more likely to use contraception when compared to non-program participants (Hofferth, 1991; Olsen & Farkas, 1990). Other programs, such as the Teen Outreach Program (TOP), the American Youth and Conservation Corps, the Seattle Social Development Program, and the Quantum Opportunities Program, have all been shown to be effective in reducing pregnancy and childbearing and promoting safer sex (Allen, Philliber, Herrling, & Kuperminc, 1997; Catalano, Hawkins, Kosterman, Abbott, & Hill, 1998; Hahn, Levitt, & Aaron, 1994; Jastrzab, Masker, Blomquist, & Orr, 1996).

SCHOOL VIOLENCE

CASE EXAMPLES: Eric Harris and Dylan Klebold

In Littleton, Colorado, April 20, 1999, promised to be just another day for the people of this Heartland community, one replete with good, law-abiding citizens, good schools, good values, and good students. At 11:19 A.M., however, as many students in the local high school were in the cafeteria eating lunch, two young men, clothed in black trench coats and carrying a duffle bag and a back pack, but otherwise unremarkable, proceeded to create havoc for hundreds of innocent students and teachers and changed forever the notion that school is a sanctuary—a safe place to learn and grow.

After the carnage, during which 188 rounds of ammunition and many small home-made bombs were expended or detonated, twelve students and one teacher lay dead and twenty-five others had been wounded. The perpetrators, two seniors, Eric Harris and Dylan Klebold, subsequently committed suicide. This seminal event in the annals of school violence represents a disturbing turning point. Whereas the incidence of school violence has declined over the last 20 years, the lethality of its consequences has sharply increased, as demonstrated by the carnage meted out by Harris and Klebold.

At first, school officials, as well as the media, portrayed these two young men as aberrations, misfits who seemed harmless enough. School officials, law enforcement officers, and parents defended themselves against assignations of blame by insisting they could never have predicted such a devastating outcome, based on the two boys' conduct and demeanor right up to their murderous spree. These stakeholders maintained that the boys had played their parts very well and thus obscured their true feelings and intentions.

And yet, a closer examination of the facts reveals an entirely different profile of the two perpetrators. Both young men demonstrated a penchant for violence, had advocated and eagerly anticipated the annihilation of humankind in poetical and prosaic rants on the Internet, and had engaged in vandalizing homes, as well as breaking and entering and theft. The county record is available to the public and clearly details the nature of the offense for which both boys received 10 months in the juvenile diversion program, which required that they perform community service and attend counseling sessions, as well as anger-management training. In fact, Harris and Klebold had so thoroughly convinced the diversion officer assigned to them of their successful rehabilitation that on their release from the program, he noted optimistically that "Eric is a bright young man who is likely to succeed in life. Dylan is a very bright young man who has a great deal of potential." However, the juvenile justice system and the school apparently missed the fact that the boys had been stockpiling weapons and constructing bombs in their own homes for months prior to the execution of their homicidal plan. Likewise, they missed the fact that Harris had been in therapy and was taking Luvox to combat depression (Bai, 1999; Cullen, 2003).

It is our contention that both boys clearly displayed sociopathic tendencies that should, at minimum, have prompted teachers and administrators to recommend them for special education services under the classification, "emotionally disturbed." The services provided to students who have been so diagnosed typically include counseling, which might have helped to avert this terrible tragedy. Sadly, this never happened.

In responding to incidents of school violence like that at Columbine and increasing concerns about the rising incidence of bullying in schools, teachers and school professionals will benefit from the important information that follows.

Introduction

According to the Center for the Prevention of School Violence (CPSV) (2000), school violence is "any behavior that violates a school's educational mission or climate of respect or jeopardizes the intent of the school to be free of aggression against person or property, drugs, weapons, disruptions, and disorder" (p. 2). Within this definition, bullying, sexual harassment, abuse directed against gay and lesbian students must be included. This section is written from the perspective that any student behavior that creates a hostile school environment for another student is considered school violence. In one report, 12 percent of teens said the behavior of students in their school was a positive influence, while 40 percent said it interfered with their performance, and almost one in five students reported being threatened with a beating (State of Our Nation's Youth, 2000). Table 10.6 summarizes important data on school violence and safety.

The chapter on conduct disorder (Chapter 2) discussed at length the many factors that research has implicated in the etiology of violence and aggression. Recent research allows us to conclude that certain factors are stronger predictors than others, and a factor's strength depends on the age of the child. To reiterate, risk factors involved in youth violence create a complicated picture. Some factors are stronger predictors at a certain age than at another age. The most significant factors appear to be

- Parental attitudes that are favorable towards violence
- Parental criminality
- Poor family management practices
- Low commitment to schooling
- Having delinquent friends
- Sensation seeking and involvement in drug selling
- Gang membership
- Hyperactivity or attention deficits

TABLE 10.6 Summary of Data on School Violence

Crime at school	• The most common criminal incidents in school are theft, larceny, and physical attacks/fights without a weapon.
	• Younger students (ages 12–14) are more likely than older students to be victims of crime at school.
	• The percentage of students reporting theft declined between 2003 and 2005, from 4% to 3%, while the percentage reporting serious violent crime during the same period similarly declined from 2.8% to 2.2% from 2003–2004, but rose again to 2.4% in 2005.
Teacher victimization	• Secondary school teachers were more likely than elementary school teachers to have been threatened with injury by a student. However, elementary school teachers were more likely than secondary school teachers to report having been physically attacked.
	• Approximately 80% of crimes against teachers are neither violent nor serious; 66% of the crimes are theft.
	• More male than female teachers report having been threatened with injury, but female teachers were more likely than their male counterparts to have been physically attacked.
	• Central-city teachers are more likely to be victims of violent crime than urban fringe, suburban, and rural teachers.
School environment	• The percentage of public schools experiencing one or more violent incidents was 81%.
	• An estimated 160,000 students skip school daily for fear of physical harm.
	• Black and Hispanic students fear more for their safety than white students.
	• The percentage of students who reported that street gangs were present at their schools was 24%.
	• In recent years, the percentage of students carrying a weapon, such as a gun, knife, or club to school has been about 10%.
	• Bullying and sexual harassment are by far the most common forms of school violence reported by students. Seventy-five percent of students report having been bullied at some point in their schooling, and 81% of female students report some form of sexual harassment in school or on school grounds.
	• Gay and lesbian students are the most frequent victims of hate crimes at school and skip school at a rate five times greater than heterosexual students because of personal safety concerns.
	• About 13% of students experience hate-related words in school, and 38% report having seen hate-related graffiti in school.

Source: From *Indicators of School Crime and Safety* by the U.S. Departments of Education and Justice, 2006. Retrieved from http://nces.ed.gov/programs/crimeindicators/crimeindicators2006.

TABLE 10.7   The Sixteen Early Warning Signs of Aggressive and Violent Behavior

1. Social withdrawal
2. Excessive feelings of isolation and being alone
3. Excessive feelings of rejection
4. Being a victim of violence
5. Feeling picked on and persecuted
6. Low school interest and poor academic performance
7. Expression of violence in writings and drawings
8. Uncontrolled anger
9. Patterns of impulsive and chronic hitting, intimidating, and bullying behaviors
10. History of discipline problems
11. History of violent and aggressive behaviors
12. Intolerance for differences and prejudicial attitudes
13. Drug use and alcohol use
14. Affiliation with a gang
15. Inappropriate access to, possession of, and use of firearms
16. Serious threats of violence

Source: From *Early Warning, Timely Response: A Guide to Safe Schools* (pp. 14–17) by K. Dwyer, D. Osher, and C. Warger, 1998. Washington, DC: U.S. Department of Education.

The more risk factors a student possesses, the greater is the potential for violent behavior.

EARLY WARNING SIGNS   In 1998, the U.S. Department of Education and the U.S. Department of Justice published a well-received document entitled, *Early Warning, Timely Response: A Guide to Safe Schools* (Dwyer, Osher, & Warger, 1998). The document began by listing sixteen early warning signs of aggressive and violent behavior. Schools might consider posting these warning signs on the walls of offices or creating a handout to be available to students, teachers, and parents in the literature rack in classrooms and offices. Table 10.7 lists these sixteen early warning signs of violent behavior.

IMMINENT WARNING SIGNS   Imminent warning signs mean that a student is close to behavior that is dangerous to himself or herself and others (Dwyer et al., 1998). These signs require an immediate response on the part of the school and the student's family. Imminent warning signs include:

• Serious physical fighting with peers or family members
• Severe destruction of property
• Severe rage for seemingly minor reasons
• Detailed threats of lethal violence
• Possession and/or use of firearms and other weapons
• Other self-injurious behaviors or threats of suicide (Dwyer et al., 1998, p. 11)

TABLE 10.8   Checklist of Characteristics of Youth Who Have Caused School-Associated Violent Deaths

1. _____ Has a history of tantrums and uncontrollable angry outbursts
2. _____ Characteristically resorts to name calling, cursing, or abusive language
3. _____ Habitually makes violent threats when angry
4. _____ Has previously brought a weapon to school
5. _____ Has a background of serious disciplinary problems at school and in the community
6. _____ Has a background of drug, alcohol, or other substance abuse or dependency
7. _____ Is on the fringe of his or her peer group, with few or no close friends
8. _____ Is preoccupied with weapons, explosives, or other incendiary devices
9. _____ Has previously been truant, suspended, or expelled from school
10. _____ Displays cruelty to animals
11. _____ Has little or no supervision and support from parents or a caring adult
12. _____ Has witnessed or been a victim of abuse or neglect in the home
13. _____ Has been bullied and/or bullies or intimidates peers or younger children
14. _____ Tends to blame others for difficulties and problems that he causes himself
15. _____ Consistently prefers TV shows, movies, or music that expresses violent themes and acts
16. _____ Prefers reading materials that deal with violent themes, rituals, and abuse
17. _____ Reflects anger, frustration, and the dark side of life in school essays or writing projects
18. _____ Is involved with a gang or an antisocial group on the fringe of peer acceptance
19. _____ Is often depressed and/or has significant mood swings
20. _____ Has threatened or attempted suicide

Source: From *Checklist of Characteristics of Youth Who Have Caused School-Associated Violent Deaths* by the National School Safety Center, 1998. Retrieved from http://www.schoolsafety.us/Checklist-of-Characteristics-of-Youth-Who-Have-Caused-School-Associated-Violent-Deaths-p-7.html. Used with permission.

Law enforcement should be called to the school when a student is carrying a weapon and has threatened to use it, and/or has presented a detailed plan (i.e., a designated time, place, and method) to harm or kill others. If imminent signs other than these two are present, school personnel should immediately inform the parents and help arrange for assistance from appropriate agencies, such as child and family services and community mental health. Table 10.8 is a checklist from the National School Safety Center to help schools assess a student's potential for violence.

Evaluating and Responding to Threats of Violence

In schools, the number of threats of violence far surpasses the number of violent incidents. On the one hand, this is fortunate, because the risk of lethal violence in schools is very low; on the other hand, threats of violence are quite common and are potentially a problem in any school. Therefore, schools need an informed way of dealing with threats. Much of what follows in this section is based on *The School Shooter: Threat Assessment Perspective*, published by the National Center for the Analysis of Violent Crime (NCAVC) (2001). The document is the result of studying eighteen schools throughout the country. At fourteen of these schools, actual shootings occurred; at the other four, a student(s) made significant preparations but was detected and preempted by law enforcement officers. The NCAVC defines a threat as "an expression of intent to do harm or act out violently against someone or something. A threat can be spoken, written, or symbolic—for example, motioning with one's hands as though shooting another person" (p. 6). Much like those who threaten suicide, those who threaten violence are not all equal and therefore each threat must be assessed for its own seriousness.

Threats can be direct ("I'm going to place a bomb on the top shelf in the reference section of the library"), indirect ("If I wanted to, I could blow this place up"), veiled ("This place would be much better off if you weren't a teacher here"), or conditional ("If you call my parents, I'm gonna shoot you"). Threats are more serious if they contain specific plausible detail, the emotional state of the threatener is questionable, and there are identifiable precipitating stressors. According to the NCAVC (2001), threats can be divided into three levels of risk: low (threat poses minimal risk to the victim and public safety), medium (a threat that could be carried out), and high (a threat that poses an imminent and serious danger to the safety of others. Table 10.9 lists the characteristics for each level of risk. An example of a high-level of threat would be "Tomorrow at 7:30 in the morning, I'm going to shoot Mrs. Wilson because at that time she is always in her homeroom by herself. I have a 9-mm. Believe me, I'm gonna do it. I'm sick and tired of the way she treats me." The parallels to the assessment process for suicide risk are obvious: The more direct and detailed the plan, the more serious is the risk. Personality, family, school, and social factors (as outlined earlier in this chapter) need to be considered in order to properly assess the student making the threat and to better judge its seriousness.

Threat Management in Schools

To properly manage threats in a school, the NCACV recommended the following guidelines.

- *Inform students and parents of school policies.* Schools should publicize a threat response and intervention policy at the beginning of each school year. The school's policy should detail how the school evaluates threats and responds to them. Students and parents should receive a clear message that any threat will be reported, investigated, and dealt with in an efficient and uncompromising fashion.

TABLE 10.9 Characteristics of Low, Medium, and High Levels of Threat

Low Level of Threat

• The threat is vague and indirect.
• Information in the threat is inconsistent, implausible, or lacks detail.
• The threat lacks realism.
• The content of the threat suggests the person is unlikely to carry it out.

Medium Level of Threat

• The threat is more direct and more concrete than a low-level threat.
• The wording of the threat suggests that the threatener has given some thought to carrying out the act.
• There may be a general indication of a possible place and time.
• There is no strong indication that the threatener has taken preparatory steps, although there may be some veiled reference or ambiguous or inconclusive evidence pointing to that possibility—an allusion to a book or movie that shows the planning of a violent act, or a value, general statement about the availability of weapons.
• There may be a specific statement seeking to convey that the threat is not empty: "I'm serious" or "I really mean this."

High Level of Threat

• The threat is direct, specific, and plausible.
• The threat suggests that concrete steps have been taken toward carrying it out—for example, a statement indicating that the threatener has acquired or practiced with a weapon or has had the victim under surveillance.

Source: From *The School Shooter: A Threat Assessment Perspective* (pp. 8–9) by the National Center for the Analysis of Violent Crime, 2001. Retrieved from www.fbi.gov/library/schools/school2.

• *Designate a threat assessment coordinator.* This person, having received appropriate threat assessment training, should oversee and coordinate the school's response to all threats. Any student who makes a threat should be referred to the coordinator, who will assess the level of threat, evaluate the threatener, plan and monitor interventions, and maintain close relationships with community resources, especially in terms of getting help with a high-level threat that requires the involvement of law enforcement officers.

• *Facilitate leakage.* "Leakage" refers to students who reveal threats made by another student to the proper authorities. Students are in the best position to see and hear signs of potential violence, and schools must help and support them in breaking the "code of silence." In the same way that students are taught to reveal their friends who are in trouble (thinking of suicide, suffering physical or sexual abuse, etc.), they should understand the importance of revealing threats. A common strategy is for students to imagine the threatened scenario taking place: "If so and so really did such and such, you knew about it and didn't tell anyone, think for a minute the burden you would carry for the rest of your life. True friends help and protect other friends from endangering themselves and others."

- *Consider forming a multidisciplinary team.* In addition to the threat assessment coordinator, schools can form teams drawn from school staff and other professionals in mental health and law enforcement. The team can review threats, consult with experts, and provide recommendations and advice to the coordinator and/or school administration. These functions can be part of a general crisis response team that deals with other problems such as suicide. Proper intervention must go beyond disciplinary action to deal with the emotional turmoil that causes a student to make threats. The NCACV (2001) described succinctly the role of disciplinary action:

> It is especially important that a school not deal with threats by simply kicking the problem out the door. Expelling or suspending a student for making a threat must not be a substitute for careful threat assessment and a considered, consistent policy of intervention. Disciplinary action alone, unaccompanied by any effort to evaluate the threat or the student's intent, may actually exacerbate the danger—for example, if a student feels unfairly or arbitrarily treated and becomes even angrier and more bent on carrying out a violent act. (NCACV, 2001, p.26)

Effective and Ineffective Approaches to School Violence

ZERO-TOLERANCE POLICIES AND STUDENTS WHO HAVE DISABILITIES   Currently, little research has supported the effectiveness of zero-tolerance policies in preventing school violence (McAndrews, 2001; Skiba & Peterson, 1999; Smothers, 2000). In the case of students who have disabilities who transgress school discipline policies and are removed from school, there is a required course of action that involves the development of a functional behavioral assessment (FBA) from which a positive behavioral intervention plan or positive behavior supports (PBS) plan is implemented, regardless of the cause of the removal. Such a plan should ideally include multiple strategies that include teaching pro-social behaviors and do not rely on coercion and punishment to affect such change (Dunlap & Koegel, 1999; Yell, Rozalski, & Drasgow, 2001). Moreover, behavioral plans that simply describe the misconduct and its consequences are out of compliance with the federal Individuals with Disabilities Education Act (IDEA, 1997; Gorn, as cited in Yell et al., 2001). In addition, the IDEA (1997) further legislates that school personnel responsible for the education of students displaying problem behaviors receive adequate training in both the development of an FBA, as well as the implementation of effective behavioral interventions (Gartin & Murdick, 2001). Such a shift in focus from intolerance to intervention should obviate the need for a school culture based on consequences. What the literature has recommended, in contrast to ineffective zero-tolerance policies, are programs that seek to provide an understanding of the conditions that incubate school violence and thus preempt their development at the very earliest stages (Braddock, 1999; Knoster & Kincaid, 1999; Stein & Davis, as cited in Gartin & Murdick, 2001). The following is a synthesis of some of the best practices endorsed by research as being effective in helping prevent school violence.

EFFECTIVE APPROACHES TO SCHOOL VIOLENCE A comprehensive examination of the research that supports the most effective practices in preventing violence in schools revealed that most could be organized according to discrete categories, including: (1) the effective use of functional behavioral analysis and behavioral intervention plans, (2) screening for risk factors, (3) teaching acceptance of diversity, (4) self-esteem building and social skills training, (5) conflict resolution through peer mediation, (6) the importance of family and community involvement, and (7) the classroom as community. Ideally, schools should incorporate as many of these components as possible in the development of their school-wide violence prevention programs. An overview of each of the recommended components follows.

Effective Use of Functional Behavioral Assessment First, in accordance with IDEA (1997), students who show a tendency toward the commission of violent acts should be prescribed a functional behavioral analysis (FBA) to determine the various antecedents that may have some bearing on the cause, as well as the purpose of the behavior. Once a cause or purpose has been identified, then an appropriate behavioral intervention plan (BIP) must be developed to help the student learn an alternate and pro-social means of obtaining his or her goal. The BIP must be effectively implemented and monitored by all stakeholders, which presumes that school personnel have received training in both the creation and use of this behavior-change technique (Gartin & Murdick, 2001; Leone, Mayer, Malmgren, & Meisel, 2000; Yell, Rozalski, & Dragow, 2001).

Screening for Risk Factors Effective prevention through screening for various predisposing factors that suggest the potential for violent behavior has also been recommended in the literature (e.g., Burns, Dean, & Jacob-Timm, 2001; Hazler & Carney, 2000; Morrison & Skiba, 2001). Research has led to recommendation of several approaches that have shown some predictive reliability in identifying students who are most likely to commit violent acts (Burns et al., 2001). The most promising of these include: (1) informal early-warning checklists and "profiling" characteristics and conditions (Hazler & Carney, 2000; Sandhu, 2000; Spivak & Prothrow-Stith, 2001); (2) the *Systematic Screening for Behavior Disorders* (SSBD) checklist (Walker & Severson, as cited in Burns et al., 2001); (3) the *My Worst School Experience Scale* (MWSES; Hyman, Berna, Kohr, & DuCette, as cited in Burns et al., 2001); and (4) the *Pathways of Ideas and Behaviors* approach (Borum et al., as cited in Burns et al., 2001).

The goal of the first two of these predictive instruments, informal checklists and profiling characteristics and the SSBD, is to identify students who may engage in violent behaviors for the purpose of providing primary intervention. The limitation inherent in assembling a checklist or profile is always the tendency to overidentify relative to the rather generalized quality of the characteristics. Further, it is difficult to establish predictive validity for checklists based on characteristics apparent in violent students. Nevertheless, the SSBD shows promise as a predictive instrument, principally because it is based on the antecedent behaviors of at-risk students. Research has suggested that previous behavior is the most reliable predictor of future behavior (e.g., Burns et al., 2001).

The MWSES is derived from scales that assess educator-induced posttraumatic stress disorder. While reliability levels are reported as being relatively high, the newness of the scale has resulted in limited data from which to assess construct validity. However, researchers are optimistic about its usefulness in the early identification of students who are at risk for violent behavior. The concept of a "threat assessment" approach, which bypasses profiling characteristics in favor of the determination of a behavioral "process" leading to violence, represents a promising preventative measure. One version of this approach employs a ten-question survey, which helps the assessor determine whether the student has sufficient predisposing factors for the commission of a violent act, as well as the means to do so (access to a weapon, a viable plan, a support system, etc.).

Other predictive systems involve reconceptualizing threat assessment as "risk management" (Mulvey & Cauffman, 2001). This perspective acknowledges that risk for violent behavior is a dynamic process requiring an ongoing evaluation of the factors that increase such risk for children and youth who have been categorized as high-risk Thus, the process starts with a risk assessment of the individual, which identifies high- or low-risk status, followed by close monitoring of changes that might signal a violent episode.

Some researchers caution that no one method of risk assessment for the commission of violence is defensibly superior because of the low base rate of violent acts committed in schools; however, an array of effective risk assessment and management strategies is clearly recommended as a preemptive measure (Burns et al., 2001). In addition, any risk screening instrument used by schools should meet two criteria: (1) It must produce reliable assessment; and (2) it must provide quality data that facilitate the development of an effective intervention. Finally, effective risk assessment should consider the effect of a school's ability to provide early intervention, as well as the existing climate and discipline policy in the school.

Violence prevention programs are proliferating in schools across the United States; however, more valuable to the practitioner than specific program descriptions is a delineation of the components that make them effective. The following is a discussion and synthesis of some of the more promising themes repeated in many of the programs.

Teaching Acceptance of Diversity An important aspect of any violence prevention program is helping students to appreciate diversity across the spectrum of difference that encompasses race, ethnicity, learning, and gender (Perlstein, 2000). This can be accomplished best by teaching children at an early age to celebrate and understand diversity. The current trend toward inclusive education represents a positive move in that direction. Similarly, placing diverse students in learning groups helps to reduce stigmatization and prejudice, which are especially prevalent among very young students. Finally, teaching students social and self-management skills, as well as providing them with a vocabulary that facilitates a meaningful discussion of diversity issues is critical to this process (Edwards, 2001; Hunter, Elias, & Norris, 2001; Lantieri & Patti, 1998; Poland, 1994; Willert & Willert, 2000).

Self-Esteem Building and Social Skills Training   The *Resolving Conflict Creatively Program* (RCCP) prescribes a K–12 classroom curriculum that incorporates the skills of empathy, active listening, assertiveness, the expression of feeling in appropriate ways, perspective-taking, cooperation, and negotiation (Aber, Jones, Brown, Chaudry, & Samples, 1998; Lantieri, 1998). In a related study, students who had emotional disorders (ED) acted as student trainers to teach appropriate social interactions to peers who had ED. The results showed that both peer trainers and student trainees derived benefit from such a program, displaying improved social skills that were maintained and generalized across settings (Blake, Wang, Cartledge, & Gardner, 2000). Similar programmatic research has suggested that effective antiviolence interventions involve teaching students alternative ways to express anger and frustration, how to make effective nonviolent choices rather than simply reacting to emotional stimuli, and, through modeling, how to deal proactively with feelings of anger, frustration, and impatience (Curwin, 1995; Sauerwein, 1995; Willert & Willert, 2000).

Furthermore, in their 5-factor model for violence and suicide reduction, Speaker and Petersen (2000) noted the importance of creating in students a "success identity" that flows from a sense of responsibility for one's self and one's environment. According to Leone et al. (2000), and Skiba and Peterson (2000), a sense of self-esteem and self-worth is linked to the development of the awareness of one's potential for success and contributes significantly to reduced participation in violent acts.

Similarly, Edwards (2001) stated that children should be provided opportunities to develop **resilience** within the school curriculum. Resilience has been shown to help students deal positively with disruptive circumstances at home or in school that might otherwise result in misbehavior and violence. A further benefit of resilience is its correlation to the development of ancillary strengths, such as social competence, problem-solving skills, a critical consciousness, responsible autonomy, and a sense of purpose (Christle, Jolivette, & Nelson, 2000; Edwards, 2001).

Likewise, embedded in social competence are empathy, communication skills, flexibility, responsiveness, and a sense of humor. Problem-solving skills refer to the ability to make meaningful plans, be resourceful, and think creatively. A critical consciousness involves the intrinsic awareness of the sources of oppression in one's life such as abusive parents, unreasonable teachers, and an elitist student culture. Students who are autonomous have succeeded in developing an internal locus of control and, ultimately, a sense of **self-efficacy**. Therefore, resilient students are not influenced by destructive criticism, nor are they victims of pathological relationships (Edwards, 2001). They are therefore less likely to engage in violent or antisocial behaviors as a means of retaliation.

RESILIENCE

The positive capacity of people to cope with stress and catastrophe. It is also used to indicate a characteristic of resistance to future negative events. In this sense, *resilience* corresponds to cumulative *protective factors* and is used in opposition to cumulative *risk factors*.

SELF-EFFICACY

People's beliefs about their capabilities to produce designated levels of performance that exercise influence over events that affect their lives. Self-efficacy beliefs determine how people feel, think, motivate themselves, and behave. Such beliefs produce these diverse effects through four major processes: cognition, motivation, affect, and selection.

Conflict Resolution Through Peer Mediation A significant component of many violence prevention programs is conflict resolution, most typically accomplished using some form of peer mediation (Garibaldi, Blanchard, & Brooks, 1996; Lantieri, 1998; Lovell & Richardson, 2001; Skiba & Peterson, 2000; Speaker & Petersen, 2000; Vail, 1995). Peer mediation is described in both the RCCP (Lantieri, 1998) and the *S.T.O.P. the Violence* (Lovell & Richardson, 2001) programs. The rationale that supports the value of peer mediation has evolved from a growing belief that students should be included in the school as participants in policymaking and community building. As such, they should have a role in the development of a nonviolent inclusive atmosphere (Curwin, 1995; Edwards, 2001; Kohn, 1996).

The function of a peer mediator is simply to provide fair and impartial arbitration in an atmosphere that requires a civil and nonviolent presentation of both sides of a disputed issue. The value of this student-chaired mediation is that it facilitates an open and unabridged meeting of the two disputants without the fear of disciplinary repercussions, provided the rules of mediation are followed. The success rate of this intervention in defusing potentially violent student confrontations is remarkably good (Garibaldi, Blanchard, & Brooks, 1996).

The Importance of Family and Community Involvement Two of the five critical factors identified in one study as the principal causes of school violence were (1) a decline in family structure and (2) family violence and drug use (Poland, 1994; Speaker & Petersen, 2000). Thus, if the family is a catalyst of violence that can generalize to the school, it seems prudent to include its constituents in any prevention program. Further, besides acting as a clearinghouse for essential family services such as health care and family counseling, schools should provide opportunities for families to be involved during instructional time, as well as in after-school activities (e.g., parent volunteers for various in-school duties and after-school tutoring, and as chaperones for special events).

Violence prevention plans are most effective when they involve all the key stakeholders: families, administrators, teachers, and students, as well as the community. Because research has suggested a correlation between violence committed by youth in the community, as well as in the school, students who commit violent acts in the community are more likely to do the same in school and vice versa (Leone, Mayer, Malmgren, & Meisel, 2000). Therefore, partnerships between local law enforcement, business, social service agencies, teachers, administrators, and families create a sense of shared purpose and collaboration in reducing both school and community violence.

The Classroom as Community Finally, an essential component of any violence prevention program is *community building*. Earlier studies have supported the notion of the importance of developing a positive school climate; one that honors diversity, provides a forum for dissidence, and values the contributions of every student (Poland, 1994). Similarly, educators need to address the purpose of classroom management. In an innovative approach to this issue, Kohn

(1996) has suggested that teachers determine whether their goal is to inculcate compliance or encourage democratic skills engendered through partnership with and empowerment of their students.

The principles espoused by Dewey (1969) are not out of step with the issues of violence prevention facing schools at the dawn of the twenty-first century. Nor is it anachronistic to describe schools as moral communities in which the constituents care for each other, where acceptance is unconditional, and where the struggles of the individual member become the concerns of all (Edwards, 2001; Fenstermacher & Soltis, 1992; Rasicot, 1999). Indeed, according to Dewey (1969) and others, schools should have the same imperatives as a democratic society, where individual freedoms are safeguarded and the rights of the majority of students and faculty are protected. Similarly, students who feel that they are valued members of a community of learners may experience the power of choice derived from an internal locus of control and thus will be more likely to eschew violence and antisocial behavior (Austin, 2003a; Edwards, 2001; Furman-Brown, 2002; Kohn, 1996).

Bullying

One of the leading researchers on bullying is the Norwegian Dan Olweus. According to Olweus (1992), a student is bullied or victimized "when he or she is exposed, repeatedly and over time to negative actions on the part of one of more other persons" (p. 101). These negative actions are understood as intentionally inflicting or attempting to inflict injury or discomfort on another. Behaviors perpetrated toward the victim may be physical (e.g., hitting, kicking, pushing, choking), verbal (e.g., name calling, taunting, malicious teasing, threatening, spreading nasty rumors), or other types, such as obscene gestures, making faces, or keeping someone isolated from a group (Olweus, 2004). These latter, more subtle forms are referred to as *indirect bullying*, in contrast to *direct bullying*, which denotes more active attacks on the victim. Bullying is found among both boys and girls, although among girls the forms of bullying tend to be more subtle.

It may be difficult for parents and school personnel to distinguish between normal teasing and bullying. Table 10.10 poses a series of questions to help educators make this distinction. If the agent's behavior is in the direction of age-inappropriate, negative, intense, and frequent, then it is better understood as bullying rather than teasing.

The effects of bullying on the victim are both short- and long-term. The short-term effects include unhappiness, pain and humiliation, confusion, distress, loss of self-esteem, anxiety, insecurity, loss of concentration, and refusal to go to school. Some victims develop psychosomatic complaints, such as headaches and stomachaches. The psychological consequences of being bullied are serious, as victims begin to feel stupid, ashamed, and unattractive, and see themselves as failures (Olweus, 2004). Regarding long-term effects, Olweus (1993) found that young adults at the age of 23 who had been bullied in grades 6 through 9 were more depressed and suffered lower self-esteem than their nonvictim counterparts.

TABLE 10.10   How to Distinguish Bullying from Normal Teasing

1. What is the nature of the behavior in question? Is it age-appropriate? To whom is it directed? Is it specific to one gender or both? Is it directed toward vicinity-aged peers or those younger or older in age? What is the content of the behavior?

2. What is the level of intensity of the behavior? What are the specifics of the behavior? Is the behavior verbal, physical, or psychological? Is the behavior seemingly done in a humorous fashion or with anger, harshness, or malicious intent by the agent?

3. How often does the behavior occur? Is this a frequent occurrence or an isolated incident? Are there times when the behavior occurs more often?

4. How does the target of the agent's behavior respond? Is the target upset of offended by the behavior? Does the target understand the behavior? Does the target reciprocate in kind to the agent? How does the agent respond to the target's attempts at self-defense against the behavior?

Source: From "the Bully as Victim: Understanding Bully Behaviors to Increase the Effectiveness of Interventions in the Bully-Victim Dyad," by W. B. Roberts and A. A. Morotti, 2000, *Professional School Counseling, 4*, p. 150. Copyright 2000 by the American School Counselor Association. Reprinted with permission.

WHO BULLIES AND WHY   Bullies tend to possess certain characteristics. However, the seriousness and pervasiveness of their bullying depends on environmental factors, such as the school's tolerance for such behaviors, teacher attitudes, the arrangement of break periods, and so on. As indicated in the previous section on predictors of violence, the influence of the early home environment cannot be underestimated. Bullies learn their behaviors early in life and tend to come from home environments that are quite harsh (Craig, Peters, & Konarski, 1998; Pepler & Sedighdellami, 1998), where punishment is usually physical and capricious. The home environment is filled with criticism, sarcasm, and put-downs (Greenbaum, Turner, & Stephens, 1989), and there is a general absence of warmth and nurturing. As a result, a personality is formed around the belief and justification that intimidation and force are the ways to deal with life's challenges (Roberts & Morotti, 2000). Through the dynamics of projective identification, the bully tends to prey on the less powerful, who remind the bully of his or her own vulnerability. "Bullies, through attacking the weaknesses of others, are striking out against the shame and humiliation they feel for their own inability to defend themselves against their abusers" (Roberts & Morotti, 2000, p. 151).

Unfortunately, the bully's behavior is often reinforced by parents, peers, and the media. The bully's parents often defend their child's behaviors as sticking up for himself. Because the parents themselves have modeled such behaviors, they find it hard to disapprove of it. Some of the bully's peers may take delight in seeing another student victimized and encourage the bully to continue the victimization. Figure 10.1 is a curvilinear depiction of possible student roles and reactions in a bullying situation. The media is also guilty of portraying behaviors common to the bully as appropriate ways to deal with difficult and challenging situations.

FIGURE 10.1 The Bullying Circle: Students' Reactions to Bullying

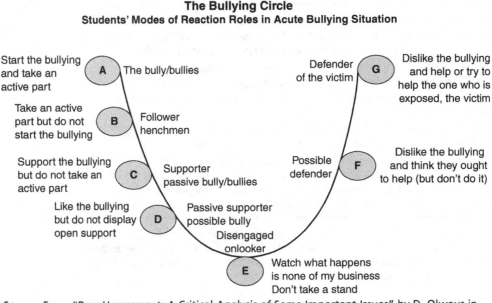

The Bullying Circle
Students' Modes of Reaction Roles in Acute Bullying Situation

Start the bullying and take an active part — **A** The bully/bullies

Take an active part but do not start the bullying — **B** Follower henchmen

Support the bullying but do not take an active part — **C** Supporter passive bully/bullies

Like the bullying but do not display open support — **D** Passive supporter possible bully

Disengaged onlooker — **E** Watch what happens is none of my business Don't take a stand

Possible defender — **F** Dislike the bullying and think they ought to help (but don't do it)

Defender of the victim — **G** Dislike the bullying and help or try to help the one who is exposed, the victim

Source: From "Peer Harassment: A Critical Analysis of Some Important Issues" by D. Olweus in *Peer Harassment in School* (p. 15) by J. Juvonen and S. Graham (Eds.), 2001. New York: Guilford Press. Copyright by D. Olweus. Reprinted with permission.

WHO GETS BULLIED AND WHY Because bullying affects a large number of students, it is somewhat difficult to profile the typical victim. Hanish and Guerra (2000a) examined the variables of children at risk for victimization along four dimensions: demographic characteristics, behavioral characteristics, peer group dynamics, and school structure influences.

Demographic Characteristics Younger children are more vulnerable to peer victimization than older children, because younger children are less apt to have developed protection skills. Bullying in elementary school, however, is generally transient and relatively untargeted. Fewer older children are victimized, but when bullying does occur, it remains more stable over time (Hanish & Guerra, 2000a). There are also gender differences in the type of victimization experienced. Boys are more likely to be physically victimized, whereas girls are more likely to be sexually and relationally victimized (i.e., gossiped about, excluded from activities, and sexually harassed) (Crick & Bigbee, 1998). In terms of race and ethnicity, Hanish and Guerra (2000b) found that among a sample of elementary school students living in disadvantaged communities, Whites and African Americans were more likely to be victimized than Latinos. More research is needed to determine to what degree race and ethnicity are significant variables in school victimization.

Behavioral Characteristics Some children are victimized because they are perceived as being unable to defend themselves. They may be physically weak, submit easily to peer demands, be rejected by peers, and have few friends

(Hodges, Boivin, Vitaro, & Bukowski, 1999; Hodges, Malone, & Perry, 1997; Olweus, 1993). Also, aggressiveness has been found to increase the likelihood of being victimized (Hodges et al., 1997; Schwartz, McFayden-Ketchum, Dodge, Pettit, & Bates, 1999). Aggressive behaviors can annoy and alienate others, leaving the student without support and therefore vulnerable to bullies. Students who are socially withdrawn, shy, or unsure of themselves are also at risk of being victimized. Social withdrawal is a stronger risk factor among older children (Younger & Boyko, 1987; Younger Schwartzman, & Ledingham, 1985). Contrary to popular belief, there is little empirical support that students who are fat, wear glasses, speak with an unusual dialect, or have a different ethnic background are more likely to be bullied (Olweus, Limber, & Mihalic, 1999).

Peer Group Dynamics   As mentioned earlier, peers can display a spectrum of reactions to bullying. Estimates are that peer protection occurs in less than 15 percent of bullying incidents (Atlas & Pepler, 1998). Peers may be distressed by the bullying, but active defense against the bully is relatively uncommon. On the contrary, peers may encourage the bullying. Bullying can be the result of wanting to attain or maintain a position of influence and power among peers in the school (Adler & Adler, 1995). If the bullied one does not have an active support group, the victimization will remain more stable over time and therefore have more significant consequences for the victim.

School Structure Influences   Unfortunately, schools provide environmental influences that can be conducive to bullying. Unsupervised time allows the bully opportunities to prey on victims and causes most incidents to happen in hallways, during change of classes, and on the playground (Atlas & Pepler, 1998). In addition, victims are reluctant to report the bully's behavior for fear of reprisal (Smith & Thompson, 1991). Bullying, therefore, can occur even on a large scale without the knowledge of school officials.

THE VICTIM-TURNED-AGGRESSOR   Because bullying by its very definition is intense and sustained, the victim finds it impossible to be indifferent to the harassment. Although many victims will manifest negative symptoms (withdrawal, depression, truancy, dropping out of school, and even suicide), some will turn aggressor and, in some rare instances, commit deadly school violence. A significant number of school shooters have had a history of being bullied, and therefore the victim-turned-aggressor has become a concern in many schools. Several experts on violence have suggested that suicide and deadly revenge are the result of the same psychodynamics operating within the victim (see, e.g., Carney, 2000; Olweus, 1997; Rigby & Slee, 1999). In other words, the risk factors for the level of aggression against the self and others are the same. Hazler and Carney (2000) have categorized these risk factors as biological, psychological, cognitive, and environmental.

Biological Risk   Reaching the age of puberty increases the risk level for victims turned aggressors. Hormonal fluctuations along with rapid physical and psychological changes can increase the individual's level of hostility and desire for revenge.

Psychological/Cognitive Risk   If the victim is severely depressed, a sense of hopelessness and negative self-evaluation increases the risk level for serious aggression. The victim may reason: "Since life is not worth living, what's the difference if I kill myself and those who have been tormenting me?" Often, an accompaniment to depression is cognitive rigidity, an example of which is seeing revenge as the only option, and which can lead a victim to serious aggression against others. Michael Carneal, after killing three of his fellow students in Paducah, Kentucky, cried out: "Kill me now. Shoot me."

Environmental Risk   Both family factors and poor peer relationships can elevate the risk of violent aggression. Families with poor problem-solving skills that do not encourage assertiveness make it hard for the victim to learn alternative ways of dealing with conflict (Hazler & Carney, 2000). Isolation from peers also increases the risk of perpetrating deadly violence (Hazler, 1996; Olweus, 1996). Many school shooters could not rely even on one friend to provide a safety net and prevent tragedy from occurring.

BULLYING AND STUDENTS WHO HAVE DISABILITIES   Students who have disabilities, particularly those who have emotional or behavioral disorders, appear more likely to be either bullies or victims of bullying than the normal student population. Although this is a logical inference, we support this contention with the findings of several studies. For example, Pepler and Craig (2000) found that bullies typically engaged in higher rates of substance abuse, negative peer interactions, delinquency, gang involvement, depression, and suicidal ideation than the normal population. In addition, they were found to be much more predisposed to committing criminal acts, as well as participating in domestic violence (Pepler & Craig, 2000). In further support of these findings, Olweus (1993) found that approximately 60 percent of boys identified as bullies in grades 6 through 9 had one criminal conviction by the time they reached 24 years of age. Similarly, targets of bullying were found to experience higher rates of anxiety, depression, withdrawal, suicide, and aggression, as well as physical health problems. Individuals who exhibited both behavioral characteristics seemed to be most affected and were, consequently, the most rejected by peers (Olweus, 1993; Pepler & Craig, 2000). Clearly, these behavioral outcomes represent characteristics present in many students who are diagnosed with emotional or behavioral disorders.

As noted earlier in the chapter, students engage in bullying for a variety of reasons, and their targets, either excessively vulnerable or aggressive and proactive, have psychosocial characteristics that mark them as such and define their roles in school. Similarly, as noted, the role of the bystander witness clearly influences the bullying process. In addition, teachers, administrators, and parents significantly affect the dynamic and pathological relationship between bully and target or targets. It is essential, therefore, that any effective intervention plan address the influences of these actors in its development and design.

Thanks to the work of investigators such as Olweus (1993), as well as others in the field, several effective approaches have been established and represent helpful options in addressing bullying as a school-wide issue. We will describe a few of the more promising approaches later in this section, but these programmatic solutions share some basic characteristics:

1. Enlist the school principal's commitment and involvement.
2. Have ongoing educational teacher discussions.
3. Use a multifaceted, comprehensive approach that includes establishing a school-wide policy, which addresses indirect bullying (e.g., social exclusion), as well as direct bullying (e.g., physical aggression); provide guidelines for actions that teachers, other staff, and students should take if bullying is observed; educate and involve parents; adopt specific intervention strategies to deal with bullies, their targets, and bystanders; develop strategies to deal with bullying that occurs in specific settings by providing increased supervision, and conduct postintervention surveys to assess the efficacy of the strategy in reducing bullying.
4. Create a positive, school-wide, "violence-free" environment.
5. Establish class rules and conduct meetings on a weekly basis to review the effects of these rules (explicit in these class rules is one that specifically repudiates bullying and enlists the help of all students in eliminating it and helping defend the target).
6. Implement formative consequences that take away a desired activity and replace it with one that is restorative and promotes awareness and empathy (e.g., the bully must come up with a way to provide assistance or support to the target).
7. Train targets and bullies in social skills (e.g., empathy, self-regulation, anger management and awareness, tolerance, respect for others, initiating and maintaining a conversation, as well as understanding the hidden curriculum).
8. Involve parents (e.g., inform the parents of both the bully and the target of the bullying and make them aware of bullying prevention policies, as well as the consequences associated with the behavior) (Heinrichs, 2003; Sampson, 2002).

SPECIFIC INTERVENTIONS TO REDUCE BULLYING IN SCHOOLS Four research-based interventions that have demonstrated success in reducing bullying in schools are (1) the Olweus Bullying Prevention Program, (2) A General Semantics Approach to School-Age Bullying, (3) A Human Rights Approach to Bullying Prevention, and (4) A Change the School Approach (Employing the Peace-Able Place Program, currently known as the Too Good for Violence Program). We will, in turn, briefly outline the important characteristics of each of these programs.

The Olweus Bullying Prevention Program First, the Olweus Bullying Prevention Program (Olweus, 1993; Olweus, Limber, & Mihalic, 1999) is widely considered one of the most effective and comprehensive interventions for use in schools. The program operates with interventions targeting three levels: (1) the school, (2) the classroom, and (3) the individual (including the bully, the target, and the parents of both). At the school-level, the program is initiated with the administration of a questionnaire that anonymously assesses students' perceptions of bullying in their school. Next, a bully prevention co-ordinating committee is established that consists of teachers, parents, and school administrators. In-service training is provided to staff on a systematic basis, and school-wide rules against bullying are developed and posted conspicuously throughout the school. Finally, staff members are posted strategically throughout the school to increase effective student supervision during break periods.

Classroom-level interventions involve regular teacher-led classroom meetings about bullying and peer relations, as well as class parent meetings. Finally, individual-level interventions include individual meetings with children who bully, meetings with children who are targets of bullying, and meetings with affected parents (Olweus et al., as cited in The Brown University Child and Adolescent Behavior Letter, April 2005).

The General Semantic Approach to School-Age Bullying This approach to bullying prevention focuses on specifics rather than generalities (e.g., encouraging students, teachers, administrators, and other school staff to describe their personal bullying experiences), grounding them in real-life issues and solutions. In so doing, it reminds us that we are all complex, multifaceted individuals who operate within the world, creating experiences that are unique to each of us. Another aspect of this approach is the "indexing" of types of bullying (e.g., physical abuse differs from relational abuse), which helps to target the intervention to the context of the behavior.

The next step in this approach is to use the imperative "No!" as a consistent countermeasure when confronted with or observing an act of bullying. Consistently applied, this sends a message to the individual who bullies that his or her behavior is unacceptable and will not accomplish whatever function is intended. Furthermore, the authors exhort students and adults to refrain from "intentional" responses to the bully that can become too personal and exacerbate the situation, actually encouraging further retaliation. Instead, students and teachers should keep statements neutral and factual. For example, an extensional response to someone who engages in bullying behavior might be to say, "Bullying causes problems for everyone, including you—stop it now so we can work things out." Confrontations like this, however, should only be conducted with the support of a group, to minimize risk to the speaker.

Step three of this approach involves training in self-management or anger management techniques for students and teachers. The rationale for this is that if individuals, target or bystander, who are affected by bullying can leave to delay their reactions and manage their emotions and behavior, they can effectively neutralize the intended effect of the bully—that is, a "knee-jerk reaction" to the bullying. To accomplish this, the program teaches participants Ellis's "ABC's" of "Rational-Emotive-Behavior Therapy," in which the A represents an **A**ctivating event, the B, **B**eliefs" or thoughts about an event, and the C, the emotional **C**onsequences of one's beliefs. The idea here is that if teachers and students can learn to use self-talk to help process the experience, they can defuse their emotional response to a situation. The key to its effective use is the ability to replace absolutes or "allness" statements with more general ones. For example, in a situation in which a bully has called a child a bad name, the child might be tempted to react with, "I won't let him talk to me that way. It makes me feel hurt and angry!" According to the ABC approach, a better response is to replace the absolutes with generalities, that is, "I'd rather he didn't talk to me that way. It's unpleasant and annoying!"

The final step in the general semantic approach is the use of empathy. The authors contend that, when dealing with a bully, before administering correction or discipline, it is best to offer empathy first. For example, using the words "I understand" or "I think I can understand," followed by an appraisal of what might have provoked or initiated the bullying behavior, leads the child who bullies to feel understood or acknowledged; this feeling will predispose him to accept the corrective action and listen to your admonition, as opposed to becoming hostile and unreceptive (Liepe-Levinson & Levinson, 2005).

A Human Rights Approach to Bullying Prevention As Greene (2006) noted, the most important step in developing a school-based bullying prevention program involves gaining the support of administrators, teachers, parents, auxiliary school staff, and partners in establishing intervention and prevention programs and policies (p. 73).

Some states, such as Idaho, have adopted a K–12 Human Rights curriculum that is an integral part of the social studies curriculum. Greene (2006) pointed out that the strength of these curricula rests on their emphasis on creating a classroom and school-wide dialogue about what constitutes bullying and harassment and what the rights and expectations of every student should be vis-à-vis respect and civil treatment (p. 75).

Furthermore, to educate students about human rights and human rights infractions, teachers provide assignments that require them to investigate instances of human rights abuses and develop meaningful ways to address them. Similarly, teachers and administrators should be provided ongoing professional development in the area of bullying identification and prevention techniques. Moreover, research supports that teachers who express caring attitudes towards their students, are confident in their craft, monitor academic work and social behavior, and intervene swiftly when problems occur tend to have fewer problems with bullying (Roland & Galloway, 2002).

A Change in the School Approach to Bullying In accordance with the recommendations provided by many researchers, the first step in this, and any effective bullying prevention program, is to establish a school-wide committee to determine the prevalence of bullying in the school. Next, based on the results of this investigation, the committee disseminates these findings to the school faculty and administration, identifying key goals for helping to prevent bullying. These goals then serve as the focus of any preventative approach. Inherent in any good prevention plan are core values, acknowledged school-wide. Any viable plan should endeavor to reinforce these "desirable" values or traits in students, while eliminating interventions or approaches that are not compatible with them. For example, one school identified "verbal aggression" as a frequent antecedent to bullying and consequently established it as a primary goal to be addressed by its prevention program.

The "change the school" approach to reducing or eliminating bullying and other forms of school violence involves three components: (1) modify the school norms and policies to create a positive school environment, (2) educate the students, and (3) train teachers who are not compatible with these values (Orpinas & Horne, 2006). Accordingly, we will briefly discuss each of these.

1. **Create a positive environment.** Schools are encouraged to follow Curwin and Mendler's (1997) four steps to create a positive environment that is free of violence and bullying: (a) identify the school's core values, (b) create rules and consequences based on these values, (c) model these values, and (d) eliminate behaviors and interventions that are not synchronous with these values.

2. **Educate students.** One recommended program that teaches students skills that militate against violence and bullying is "Too Good for Violence" (Mendez Foundation, 1995). Essentially, this program provides students with training in anger management, conflict resolution, respect for self and others, and effective communication. The training format for each of these skill areas typically consists of experiential learning, cooperative groups, and role-playing. The keys to the success of this program are twofold: the quality of the training, and time commitment.

3. **Train teachers.** Teacher training incorporates school-wide strategies for bullying and aggression prevention, including conflict-resolution strategies, character education, and behavior management approaches. In addition, such training should be flexible enough to permit adaptations and modifications as required by the teacher and the relevant contexts.

To conclude, although the occurrence of school violence has declined in recent years, incidents of bullying, in contrast, continue to rise. For example, according to the U.S. Department of Justice, one out of every four children will be bullied by a peer in school this month (Liepe-Levinson & Levinson, 2005), and approximately 1.6 million students in grades 6 through 10 in the United States are bullied at least once a week (Ericson, 2001).

The effects of bullying are profound for both the bully and the target of the bullying behavior. Targets of bullying experience loneliness, have difficulty making social and emotional adjustments, and suffer humiliation, insecurity, and a loss of self-esteem. As adults they are at greater risk of experiencing depression, as well as other mental disorders including schizophrenia, and they are more likely to commit suicide.

Bullies, on the other hand, typically engage in other forms of antisocial behavior, including destruction of property, theft, truancy, fighting, dropping out of school, and substance abuse. Furthermore, bullies are more likely to participate in criminal activities as adults and, similarly, to be convicted of at least one crime (Ericson, 2001).

Fortunately, there are things that schools and school personnel can do to reduce the incidence of bullying. The following are the key elements that should be included in any effective preventive program: (1) enlist the involvement and commitment of school administrators, (2) schedule ongoing teacher discussions, (3) develop a multifaceted, comprehensive approach that includes establishing a school-wide policy and provide guidelines for teachers and administrators, (4) create a positive school environment, (5) establish class rules regarding bullying, (6) develop and implement specific consequences for bullying behavior, (7) provide students with social skills training and self-awareness/self-regulation strategies, and (8) involve parents in the bullying prevention plan, as well as enforcement procedures (Orpinas & Horne, 2006).

Lastly, there are a variety of effective, research-based programs that are designed to reduce and, ideally, prevent bullying in schools. The following represent a few of the most recommended of these that have been described in greater detail earlier in this section: (1) The Olweus Bullying Prevention Program, (2) A General Semantic Approach to School-Age Bullying, (3) A Human Rights Approach to Bullying Prevention, and (4) A "Change the School" Approach to Bullying.

It is our hope that the preceding information will help teachers become actively engaged in one of these vital preventive programs; the consequences of bullying are simply too damaging to the affected students and their families for teachers to remain uninformed and uninvolved.

GANG MEMBERSHIP AND RELATED ACTIVITIES

CASE EXAMPLE: A Personal Anecdote: Matteo

I (Vance Austin) had been a classroom teacher in a school for children and youth who have emotional or behavioral disorders for 2 years when, in the middle of the school year, a young man from "the city" (New York) was admitted to my class. Matteo (not his real name) was 16 years old and had been living in the Fordham section of the Bronx before being referred to my school. As I read his case file I realized that this was a young man who had never received a "break" and was long overdue for one. I was eager to do what ever I could to make a difference in this young man's life and had visions, as do most young teachers, of being instrumental in his redemption and future success.

However, as the days and weeks passed, I began to understand that it would take a good deal more than the best intentions of a young white teacher from Canada to provide Matteo with an epiphany. I frequently drove to town to "retrieve" Matteo from the streets, ran interference for him when he ran afoul of other teachers, community members, and the local police, and tried to provide him with the "fatherly" advice and attention I perceived he was sorely missing and which, I was convinced, was the key to his reformation. I was wrong.

First of all, as Matteo firmly pointed out one day after I once again intervened in an altercation involving another teacher, he was beyond redemption and certainly didn't want to be "saved" if it meant becoming "white" or "establishment" like me. Although he was respectful to me and appreciated all that I was trying to do to help him, he made it very clear that I was neither his father nor a member of his neighborhood "family." Undaunted, I set about, more fervently than ever, to prove him wrong. I accompanied him to his cottage after school and provided an hour of extra tutoring, I assembled review materials to help him prepare for the state comprehensive exams, and I continued to be an advocate in both the school and the community. I even went as far as to obtain special permission to bring Matteo to my home for Thanksgiving dinner. Matteo genuinely appreciated this opportunity and thoughtfully presented my wife and me with a box of chocolates to show it.

In my naiveté, I thought I was making progress, winning Matteo over, transforming a life; I had much to learn about Matteo and Matteo's world. My enlightenment, however, was swiftly approaching. In May of that year, I had my epiphany. I had just returned from lunch and was preparing to teach my students in English 11 a lesson about, interestingly, the themes of war, power, and human conflict represented in Henry V, when I heard what sounded like a riot just outside the classroom window. The students and I ran to the window in time to see Matteo swinging a baseball bat at five older boys—on further investigation, these "boys" were armed with "shivs" (knives) and handguns. Someone from the principal's office had already called the police, and before I could run outside, foolishly, to intervene, they had the five other boys and Matteo in custody.

After school, I drove to the police headquarters where Matteo and the other boys were confined and learned the full story from Matteo. According to Matteo, these five young men were from his "hood" but were members of a rival gang. They claimed that Matteo had been implicated in a beating inflicted on one of their members that was so severe, he was left seriously injured and would be maimed for life. Matteo denied taking part in the beating but admitted that he was a member of a rival gang, the Black Aces, and was subsequently taken to the Juvenile Offenders wing of Rikers' Island Detention Center to await trial (the police found a gun and a bag of "ice" [crystal methamphetamine] on him during their body search).

I did not know about gangs and gang behavior before working with Matteo. The only gangs I had knowledge of were the Sharks and the Jets from *West Side Story*. After this experience, I researched as much information about gangs as I could find and discovered two glaring oversights in my dealings with Matteo. First, he was trying to explain that he had a family that was his neighborhood, a code or euphemism for the gang, and that this "family" gave him everything he needed. Second, he had been initiated into the Black Aces at the age of 13, a rite of passage that was typical for many young men in his community. His biological father was a member of the gang and even presided over his "initiation," which involved participation in a brazen, premeditated attack on members of a rival gang.

Third, I had missed the telltale signs and signals that are very clearly displayed by gang members; for example, Matteo always wore a black-and-white bandanna, which he carefully stuffed in a back pocket of his jeans, allowing a corner to hang, obtrusively, from it. I had noticed that he wore the bandanna around his head occasionally, when he was off school grounds. Finally, Matteo showed me a "tag" (gang graffiti) that he used to mark books, notebooks, and even (much to my chagrin) the stalls in the boys' bathroom at school. I learned that this "tag" was used by gang members to mark their turf, or as a challenge to a rival gang.

GANGS

Groups of individuals, juvenile and/or adult, who associate on a continuing basis, form an allegiance for a common purpose, and participate in delinquent or criminal activities. Gangs may range from a loose-knit group of individuals who associate and commit crimes together to a formal organization with a leader or ruling council, gang colors, gang identifiers, and a gang name.

Youth Gangs in the United States: Current Data

According to a survey conducted in 2000 by the National Youth Gang Center (NYGC), an affiliate of the federal Office of Juvenile Justice and Delinquency Prevention (OJJDP), there are more than 24,000 active **gangs** in the United States. The overall membership in these gangs exceeded 760,800 in 2004 (Egley, Howell, & Major, 2006). Whereas this number represents a decline of 5 percent from the previous year, in cities with a population of 25,000 or more, the number of gang members actually increased by 2 percent. Similarly, 91 percent of cities with a population of more than 25,000 reported at least one gang-related homicide from 1999 to 2000. This statistic represents an increase in the number of gang-related homicides for 47 percent of these cities. In addition, researchers have noted that gang-related homicides account for approximately one-fourth of all homicides in the 173 U.S. cities that have a population of 100,000 or more. In two of these cities, Los Angeles and Chicago, the number of gang-related homicides exceeded 50 percent of the total number of homicides.

Furthermore, researchers noted that as many as 48 percent of the youth involved in gangs arguably could be considered emotionally disturbed (Valedez, Kaplan, & Codina, 2000). Similarly, Grant, Van Acker, Guerra, Duplechain, and Coen (1998) acknowledged a significant link between emotional or behavioral disorders and at-risk behaviors, particularly school violence and gang membership. In further support of the predisposition of youth with emotional and behavioral disorders toward gang involvement are the results of a study conducted by Wood et al. (1997).

Another study of youth in detention, in which a majority met the diagnostic criteria for one or more psychiatric disorders—most commonly, conduct disorder—revealed that nearly 60 percent of males and 75 percent of females were involved in or affiliated with a gang. Also, delinquency, which correlates to conduct disorder, is highly represented in youth who are gang members. Moreover, depression is also more prevalent in youthful gang members than in same-age peers who are not affiliated with gangs (Teplin et al., 2006).

These and other studies support our contention that youth who have emotional or behavioral disorders are at risk for gang involvement at a rate that is significantly higher than the normal population. Such findings highlight the need for teachers to be knowledgeable about the characteristics of gang membership and behavior, the functions served by gang membership, typical gang-related activities, the impact of gang membership on schools, and interventions that may help reduce gang membership and its potentially devastating consequences.

Gang Impact in Schools

One report found that between 1989 and 1995, the presence of gangs in schools nearly doubled. Furthermore, this study identified a strong correlation between the presence of gangs in schools and an increase in the prevalence of guns and drugs (Howell & Lynch, 2000). Evidence has also supported the significant role that gangs have played in the widespread increase in school violence (Egley, 2000; Thornberry, 1998; Wallach, 1994). Rates of violence are significantly higher in schools where gangs are present and, conversely, the victimization rate in schools that do not report the presence of gangs is lower (Snyder & Sickmund, 1999).

Furthermore, although gangs may not be directly responsible for all school violence, their very presence can create a "tenacious framework" that incubates it (Gaustad, 1991, p. 24). In response to the perceived presence of gangs, many youth are arming themselves, which increases the potential for shootings—either offensive, in connection with criminal activity, or in defense against or revenge for such acts. Several studies have revealed that because gangs frequently engage in drug trafficking and weapons sales, their presence in schools invariably means that these undesirable commodities will be more prevalent and available (Bodinger-deUriarte, 1993; Trump, 1993). In addition, students in schools that have gangs are twice as likely to report that they fear being a victim of violence as their peers at schools without gangs (Trump, 1993).

Another unanticipated and insidious effect of gangs in schools is their use of schools as sites for gang recruitment and socialization (Arthur & Erikson, 1992; Bodinger-deUriarte, 1993). One study even found that gang members who had dropped out or been expelled from school often returned to it clandestinely in order to socialize with gang members who were still attending the school (Boyle, 1992).

Characteristics of Gangs in Schools

Howell and Lynch (2000) surveyed high school students to determine their awareness of the characteristics of gangs and gang members in their schools. Through the results of this survey, they were able to identify five indicators of gang presence: (1) a recognized name of the gang, (2) "tagging" or marking turf with graffiti, (3) time spent with other gang members, (4) violence, and (5) clothing or other identifying items. This study further determined that gang presence in schools appeared to be correlated with several factors, especially:

1. The size of the community (increased presence in schools in communities of up to 50,000 population).
2. Drug availability: As expected, gangs were more prolific where drugs were more accessible.
3. Security steps: Schools with more elaborate and extensive security procedures were more likely to have gangs.
4. The level of victimization at school: The higher the frequency of victimization, the greater was the prevalence of gangs in the school (Howell & Lynch, 2000).

These factors might be explained as follows.

1. First, the size of communities reporting increased gang presence is becoming progressively smaller, apparently because gangs are now becoming very much a part of small cities and suburbs as the population in large cities migrates to less expensive metropolitan areas, such as the boroughs, suburbs, and surrounding small communities.
2. Drugs have traditionally been associated with criminal activity, given the demand, their illicit nature, and, consequently, the opportunity to make a huge profit very quickly. Gangs, by their very nature and organizational structure, are uniquely positioned to benefit from the drug trade, and they can achieve a monopoly in schools as a result of their willingness to use violence to intimidate competitors and control the market.
3. Heightened security procedures in schools are an indirect predictor of increased gang presence, because these measures are usually implemented in urban schools located in high-crime neighborhoods, and gangs tend to incubate in these conditions.

4. Similarly, although victimization at school may not be related directly to the presence of gangs, schools in which victimization rates are high are typically located in high-crime neighborhoods in which gangs flourish. Students in these schools tend to associate gangs either directly or indirectly with increased victimization, whether such association is justified or not. It seems fair to assume that at least some of the school-related victimization and violence can be attributed to gangs, because analyses of gang arrests show that violent gang crimes begin to escalate early in the school day and peak in the early afternoon (Howell & Lynch, 2000).

Purpose Served by Gang Membership

The two key predictors of gang membership are residence in a gang-infested neighborhood and having an older sibling who is a member of a gang (Hixon, 1999). According to Spergel (1995), there is no specific personality type that predisposes youth to gang membership.

Sanchez Jankowski (1991) suggested several reasons for joining a gang, after systematically debunking some popular misperceptions such as the deleterious effect of a "broken home"; the untenable nature of a dysfunctional family that leads the child to seek out a more stable, "safe," accepting environment; the constraints on employment options based on dropping out of school; and finally, the "Pied Piper" effect—that is, succumbing to the seduction of the romanticized gang life represented by high-status older peers.

In contrast to these unsubstantiated reasons, Sanchez Jankowski (1991) and Molidor (1996) proposed several empirically supported ones: (1) material incentives, (2) recreation, (3) a place of refuge and camouflage, (4) physical protection, (5) an opportunity to resist living lives like one's parents, and (6) commitment to one's community.

Relative to the school, Parks (1995) advanced several possible incentives. The first is the notion that in some cases negative teachers may help turn some children and youth to seek acceptance and values in a gang (Padilla, 1992). Likewise, school administrators who establish arbitrary and oppressive rules, exact capricious punishments, and enforce them inconsistently may inadvertently contribute to a student's decision to turn to a gang for succor (Miller, 1992).

Finally, the structure of the school may also contribute to gang membership. Huff (1996) reported the alienating effect of harsh disciplinary measures, consistent academic failure, unresponsive teachers, and an irrelevant curriculum. Similarly, Harootunian (1986) noted that labeling, stereotyping, tracking, and other discriminatory practices of school staff may also help to make gang membership more appealing.

In addition, according to Sanchez Jankowski (1991), several key factors are integral to the formation of youth gangs:

1. Youth experience a sense of alienation and helplessness because traditional supports (family, school) are missing and a gang fills this void.
2. Gangs provide a sense of identity, power, and control, and serve as an outlet for anger.

3. The control of "turf" is critical to the survival and well-being of the gang and is therefore zealously defended.

4. Finally, the gang must recruit successfully, filling its ranks with willing and unwilling members, in order to survive and be relevant in the school and community.

Profile of an Adolescent Gang Member

In the United States, the typical gang member tends to be a young man of color, 13 to 24 years of age, from the urban underclass (Parks, 1995). Although there are exceptions, gangs tend to be composed of individuals from the same race or ethnicity and often display their membership through distinctive styles of dress, referred to as "colors," and through specific activities and patterns of behavior. Furthermore, gang members typically show great loyalty to their community or neighborhood and often demarcate their "turf" with representative graffiti, referred to as "tagging." This graffiti is also displayed on school walls, usually in the bathrooms, as well as on exterior walls and windows (Sanchez Jankowski, 1991).

As noted earlier, gang members are usually youth who feel particularly vulnerable as a result of living in a dangerous, gang-infested neighborhood, who seek the family they don't have, or who look for the power and prestige that has eluded them often because of prejudice and discrimination.

Female gang members, while fewer than their male counterparts, make up about 10 percent of gangs and share some characteristics similar to those of male members. Their ages range from 13 to 18, and they are becoming more like their male counterparts in the level and type of violent acts and crimes that they commit. Female gang members, like male members, tend to be individuals who have grown up in gang-infested and impoverished neighborhoods. They also reflect a pattern of failure in school and have frequently been suspended from school for fighting drug or weapon possession. Unlike the young male gang members, however, they typically have been and continue to be victims of sexual abuse. Usually, after they have been suspended, these girls drop out of school or are truant so often that they fail. Furthermore, there appears to be little, if any, school or parent follow-up once these girls stop attending school. While they were attending, the majority of gang-involved females carried a knife or a gun for a "boyfriend," because women are less frequently and thoroughly searched by school security personnel. Finally, like the boys in gangs, female members are most frequently African American or Latina and come from lower-socioeconomic households in neighborhoods defined as "urban poor" (Molidor, 1996).

Combating Gang Activities in Schools

After reviewing the literature about preventing or reducing gang-related behavior in schools, three themes become apparent: (1) the need for pro-social and constructive alternatives to supplant the benefits provided by gang membership; (2) finding positive ways to address students' needs for validation and self-esteem; and (3) instituting these measures in elementary and middle schools, because research has indicated that gangs begin recruiting future members at these early levels (Arnette & Walsleben, 1998; Hixon, 1999; McEvoy, 1990; Molidor, 1996; Parks, 1995; Wallach, 1994; Wood & Huffman, 1999). We discuss these themes in this section.

Wallach (1994) and others have identified several approaches that have been shown to be effective strategies in themselves, or combined in various ways, can form the basis for a school-wide approach:

1. Target students who are vulnerable to gang recruitment for special assistance, particularly through the use of peer counselors and support groups.
2. Establish moral and ethical education, values clarification, and conflict resolution as important components of the school curriculum.
3. Create an inviting school climate in which every student feels valued.
4. Educate all school staff, including support staff, about how gangs develop and how to respond to them.
5. Using a culturally sensitive approach, offer special programs for parents about gangs and how to deal with them as parents.
6. Monitor youths who are at risk for gang involvement, such as those who have been diagnosed with emotional or behavioral disorders, and offer educational programs that provide information about the destructiveness of gang involvement.
7. Monitor youths who are not enrolled in the school but who loiter around the school during the daytime.
8. Provide opportunities for students to discuss their school experiences, as well as constructive and productive plans for the future.

McEvoy (1990) reported that the development and promotion of intramural sports has proven to be a very effective alternative to the need for competition and physical interaction that gang membership provides. Such involvement has deterred many at-risk youth from joining gangs. Involvement in intramural sports and other extracurricular groups encourages new friendships and loyalties, increases an individual's attachment to the school while simultaneously helping to improve academic performance, as well as providing opportunities for success both within the classroom setting and beyond.

Furthermore, engaging gang leaders in peer mediation helps them to learn to use their leadership skills to serve peers in a pro-social, constructive way. McEvoy (1990) also suggested that schools provide alternative outreach programs to educate gang members in more accessible venues and at times that accommodate conflicting work schedules.

In another vein, in schools in which rival gangs are feuding, school officials are encouraged to communicate with both groups and negotiate a "truce" to ensure that the educational process is neither threatened nor disrupted (McEvoy, 1990).

Another relevant study, conducted by Wood and Huffman (1999), identified some key implications for schools, administrators, and teachers regarding the prevention of gang activities in the school. Most noteworthy among them is the need for staff and administrator training in developing a school safety management plan. In conjunction with the development of this plan, the authors stress the importance of staff development for teachers and the community, including police officers, probation officers, and staff members, and addressing school safety, gang activity, and violence.

All students should be made aware of policies and rules, as well as the rationale behind their implementation. In addition, teachers should be selected for their concern for individual students, their willingness to mentor students, and their ability to work as part of a team beyond their command of the subject matter. Furthermore, teachers should receive training in crisis intervention and classroom management techniques, both as an integral part of the teacher preparation program and in ongoing staff development. One very effective program, called *therapeutic crisis intervention* (TCI), has been widely used to train school and residential treatment staff to defuse potentially violent situations and intervene using minimal and well-orchestrated restraints. The goal of TCI and similar crisis intervention training is to help staff establish a solid rapport and mutually respectful relationship with students. Parents should also be included, where possible, in student activities, staff development, and behavior management training with their students. Research has supported the importance of including even estranged and dysfunctional parents in these processes, with the understanding that stronger family systems can help reduce the attraction of gangs, which often serve as surrogate families (Wood & Hufman, 1999).

Because research has supported the need for a comprehensive approach to the prevention of gang-related activities in schools (Miller, 1992), schools might consider the model proposed by Green and Kreuter (1992), called "Precede-Proceed." This model proposes that three types of factors influence the growth and development of gangs: predisposing factors, enabling factors, and reinforcing or support factors. These authors suggested that any effective intervention/prevention approach should address each of these three factors.

1. ***Predisposing Factors.*** Research has identified teen-aged African American and Hispanic males as the most-represented racial/ethnic group among gang members. Because many of these young men come from single-parent homes in which that parent is most often the mother, it is reasonable to hypothesize that strong male mentoring might be effective, such as that provided by male teachers. Similarly, because these at-risk young men look to gangs to provide honor, respect, and power, as well as to instill courage, after-school intramural sports programs might help to satisfy these needs in a pro-social way.

2. ***Enabling Factors.*** According to Green and Kreuter (1992), the major factors that must be addressed to prevent school gang violence are the school, the community, and racism. For many children, especially those of color, schools are irrelevant and discriminatory institutions. This perception is furthered by the dearth of teachers and administrators of color, the lack of culturally relevant curricula, and distinctly lower expectations for minority children. Such awareness can be discouraging for at-risk youth and may, consequently, predispose them to gang influence and membership (Miller, 1992; Parks, 1995). In response, schools must begin to actively recruit male teachers of color, develop curricula that incorporate and value a multicultural perspective, provide viable after-school

programs, and train teachers to be more culturally sensitive and inclusive as they plan and implement units and lessons.

Furthermore, other investigators believe that in-school gang mediation is effective in helping to prevent and significantly reduce the incidence of gang-related violence (Sanchez & Anderson, 1990). This approach solicits the participation of gang leaders, trains them in effective peer mediation techniques, and then involves them as mediators in gang-related disputes. Participants in the mediation process must do so voluntarily and submit to very explicit rules of conduct and procedures laid out by the mediator. The keys to successful mediation are respect for the mediator and the mediator's ability to facilitate and sustain open and productive dialogue between the disputants (Sanchez & Anderson, 1990).

Perhaps the most subtle yet significant factor in the perpetuation of gang-related violence is racism. Schools, as noted earlier, can inadvertently contribute to this problem through the perpetuation of racial stereotyping relative to learning and academic success (e.g., African American and Hispanic students typically perform less well than white and Asian American students). Teachers and administrators must guard against subtle and sometimes unconscious attitudes and behaviors that might be perceived as racist or discriminatory by their students. One way to counter these unhealthy attitudes and prejudices is to celebrate diversity and multicultural identity in the classroom and the school through a multicultural fair, or by observing a specific national or ethnic holiday (Kwanzaa, Chinese New Year, Cinco de Mayo, Puerto Rican Day, Martin Luther King Day, Black History Month, etc.)

3. ***Reinforcing or Support Factors.*** Family, friends, peers, employers, teachers, administrators, and other stakeholders can have a powerful influence on the perpetuation or suppression of gang violence. Preeminent among them are parents, families, and teachers (Green & Kreuter, 1992). According to Arthur and Erickson (1992), teachers need to strive to acquire the following skills, through either in-service or preservice training programs: (a) how to connect with "tough" inner-city youth, (b) knowledge of students' cultures, (c) effective interpersonal skills, (d) active (and sincere) listening, and (e) cross-cultural communication.

An Example of a Successful Prevention Program

One very effective program in helping curb gang membership is called *Gang Resistance Is Paramount* (G.R.I.P.). The success of this program is due to the combined effect of its three major components: (1) neighborhood meetings that provide parents with support, resources, and tangible assistance as they work to keep their children out of gangs; (2) a 15-week course for fifth-grade students and a 10-week program for second-grade students that addresses everything from "tagging" to "tattoos" and includes discussions about drug abuse, the effect of gang involvement on the family, and peer pressure, as well as attractive, pro-social activities and opportunities; and (3) a school-based follow-up program for ninth-graders that helps build self-esteem, takes an unequivocal look at the consequences of a criminal lifestyle, and examines the undeniable benefits of an education and the career opportunities that it provides. An exit survey determined that of 3,612 former program participants, all of whom were considered at risk for gang membership, 96 percent were not identified as gang members (Ostos, as cited in Arnette & Walsleben, 1998).

Conclusion

The case of the young man profiled at the beginning of this section is, unfortunately, not unique. Matteo's story is far from over, but he will need extensive help and support once he is released from detention to stay free of the "gang life." Unfortunately, without the intensive intervention of teachers, family members, and community stakeholders, it will be almost impossible for Matteo to break his connection to the Black Aces.

In this section we have examined the structure and characteristics of gangs and their connection with the school. We have also examined their detrimental effects on the school and its constituents. To understand better the pressures exerted on young men like Matteo, we also considered the purpose that gang membership serves, as well as its seductive effect on young men of color living in poor urban neighborhoods.

Finally, in a more optimistic vein, we learned about various effective, field-tested interventions that help students who are at risk for gang involvement to resist its allure and thus avoid becoming perpetrators of gang violence in the school. It is our hope that this information may help teachers become effective agents of intervention to help save a young man or woman from a life of crime.

FROM THE FIELD

Bryan Mulvihill, LCSW

Bryan Mulvihill is a drug awareness counselor at the Apex School, a residential program and day school for adolescents who have emotional and adjustment difficulties.

Tell us about the students you typically work with.

The students that I work with come from all over the New York City metro area and as far away as upstate New York. The students are referred by their home school district, usually because of emotional or behavioral problems. These problems can range from depression, bipolar disorder, and pervasive developmental disorders to truancy, conduct, and oppositional problems. The students end up at the Apex School because their home district can no longer provide the appropriate level of education. By the time students arrive at the Apex School, most, but not all, have been through psychiatric hospitalizations, some form of drug treatment, other residential or day school programs, and/or home schooling provided by the district. Inherent with students like this is substance abuse. The level of substance use can range from experimentation to abuse to dependence. The students that I work with are generally good kids that just happen to have a long list of unfortunate circumstances. Some have difficult family lives. Some get mixed up on the streets, and some have organic predisposition to substance use and/or psychiatric disorders. Most of the substance abuse students that I work with have co-occurring disorders, meaning that they have a psychiatric disorder, as well as a substance use disorder. Substance use is often their attempt to manage their problems.

What approach or approaches have you used that have proven effective in connecting with or "getting through" to your students?

Be honest and direct with the students. You don't have to disclose personal information in an attempt to relate or connect with them. If you do, chances are that they will still say, "You don't know what it's like." If you are honest and direct with them, they will see you for who you are and that's where the connection is made. Avoid falling into the trap of asking twenty questions or accusatory questions. Students will immediately get suspicious and shut down. Start with a normal conversation or with a check-in type of conversation. This will help promote a relaxed environment and not the sense that they are in trouble. Try to avoid jumping right into the topic or incident at hand. In most cases the student will bring up the incident at some point during the conversation. Allowing the students to bring it up on their terms helps to put you in a more supportive role rather then an authoritative role. Also, avoid taking sides. The more you argue or try to convince them that what they are doing is wrong, the more they will try to defend their actions.

What practical advice would you offer a teacher who suspects that one of her students is coming to class "high?"

Speak with the student one-on-one. Let them know your concerns and that you will have to speak with the appropriate school staff. The student will more than likely be upset, but you will be doing them a greater service in the long run. Ignoring the behavior will only enable it and the student will look at their behavior as okay or that you don't mind. How to confront the student and who to tell will all depend on the student and their family. I would be cautious to reach out to the family unless you have a working relationship with them. You never know how a family will react. Some could appreciate your call, while another could be angry with you for meddling in their business.

Tell us some of the not-so-effective ways in which you or other school professionals you know have been inclined to address the issue of a student coming to school under the influence. Why did they seem like good approaches at the time? Why were they not as effective as you or others had hoped?

I think one of the more common mistakes that someone can make is to keep it between the student and themselves. I think at the time it might seem like a good approach because they don't want to betray the student's trust or maybe they feel the student has enough problems in their life and they don't want to add to them by getting them in trouble. Clearly, approaching it this way does nothing to address or resolve the problem. Therefore, the problem will continue. Another mistake is not involving the student and telling them what is happening. The student needs to be part of the process, whether they are happy with it or not. In some cases this may not be appropriate (i.e., the student needs to be sent to the emergency room). I think some people avoid involving the student because they don't want to confront the student for fear of how they may react. The reality is that if a student is coming to school under the influence, then they need to be confronted. They need to understand that coming to school under the influence is not an acceptable behavior. This kind of situation is a big opportunity to have a successful intervention. Some students will learn their lesson, while others will blow it off and continue to do what they want. In these kinds of situations you can only reach the ones that want to be reached. By not involving the student you miss the opportunity for them to take responsibility for their actions.

How about a brief anecdote about a successful experience you've had "reaching" a student who was abusing?

First, you have to decide how you would define success. Success for each student will be different. For one student it might be them reducing the amount of their use. For another, it might be them becoming sober. A successful experience that I had working with a student was with a student named Elan. Elan was referred to our program by her local school district after long-term school difficulties, ongoing conflictual relationships with her family, and extensive drug use. Her drug of choice was marijuana, which she was using on a daily basis. She had also experimented with cocaine, ecstasy, mushrooms, and Special K [ketamine hydrochloride, an anesthetic]. Elan had a history of two hospitalizations. One related to drug use and the other related to her mood swings. She was later diagnosed as having bipolar disorder. Upon her arrival at the Apex School Elan continued to use drugs despite repeated consequences. Her drug use was affecting her personal life, her family, socially, and academically. Elan's drug use only made her more anxious and her moods more volatile. Eventually, she was referred to an outpatient drug treatment program. After 3 months she signed herself out of that program. I continued to see her for individual drug counseling and in a drug group on campus. One day she just decided to stop completely. She made her mind up that she had had enough. She no longer liked the high or the feeling of being out of control. By the time she graduated from the Apex School she was 3 years sober. I think what helped me reach her was that I listened to her and didn't pass judgment about what she said. She was the kind of student that you couldn't tell her what she should or shouldn't do. Instead, she needed to find her own way. My role was just to guide her in the more positive direction.

Summary

There is significant evidence that students who have emotional or behavioral disorders, especially disruptive behaviors, such as those associated with ADHD and conduct disorder, are at greater risk of engaging in certain destructive behaviors. The most common and pernicious of these are substance use and abuse, risky sexual behaviors, school violence, and gang membership and related activities.

Substance abuse among children and youth with emotional or behavioral disorders continues to proliferate, despite the best attempts to intervene and slow the process. This risk-taking behavior is particularly onerous because of the volatile interaction of abused drugs with prescribed ones, as well as the unpredictable effects of nonprescribed drugs on individuals with serious psychiatric disorders. Intervention and effective rehabilitation are critical to help affected young people who have emotional or behavioral disorders continue to comply with their behavioral intervention plans.

Risky sexual behaviors are more frequent among students who have emotional or behavioral disorders because of the impulsivity of many of these individuals, their apparent lack of concern for the consequences of their actions, and their tendency toward narcissism. The risk of detrimental outcomes for these behaviors has increased today as a result of the prevalence of sexually transmitted diseases, the most serious of which is HIV/AIDS. Another related issue is the increased likelihood of accidental, intentional, and uninformed pregnancy, which carries significant health and emotional consequences, as well as socioeconomic implications. Key interventions used to counter risky, impulsive, and irresponsible sexual behavior include abstinence-only programs, knowledge of and access to contraception, and life skills/life options approaches such as that provided by the Teen Outreach Program and Quantum Opportunities Program, to name two.

Despite its drop in the last decade or so, the severity of school violence, and its sometimes lethal results, have generated much attention. Schools should have clear and comprehensive plans for responding to these rare, but frequently catastrophic, events, and teachers, students, and administrators must be proactive in recognizing the early warning signs and following crisis intervention protocols. One form of school violence, however, continues to increase: the ubiquitous bullying phenomenon. Many studies have been conducted in the course of the last decade that have examined the etiology of bullying, the characteristics of the bully and the target of bullying, the possible repercussions

if the bullying is not addressed, and programs that have shown progress in reducing and preventing bullying and its potentially devastating consequences.

Finally, in this chapter, we examined youth gangs and their effects on schools. Our investigation revealed the characteristics of youth gangs, the typical profile of a gang member, the effects of gangs on schools and their constituents, as well as some effective prevention and intervention strategies.

We hope that the information in this chapter will be both illuminating and helpful to teachers working with students who have emotional and behavioral disorders, who, by the very nature of these disorders, are at greater risk for engaging in drug abuse, sexually promiscuous behaviors, school violence, bullying, and gang related activities.

Tips for Teachers

For Students Who Are Substance Abusers

1. Because substance abuse, if it involves a controlled substance, involves the potential for criminal prosecution, teachers may want to refer students of concern to the appropriate school counselor (e.g., the drug awareness counselor), with whom they have a level of confidentiality and privilege. Teachers should avoid accusing any student specifically of abusing drugs and/or alcohol or speaking publicly or privately about the problem with the student because of lack of professional qualification and potential legal implications.

2. Students who come to school "high" or intoxicated should be intercepted at the door or in homeroom and parents or caregivers contacted to take the individual home.

3. Students who abuse drugs or alcohol during the school day and are suspected of being "high" or intoxicated in class should be escorted to the nurse's office for evaluation, and both school administration and the student's parents or caregivers should be noti-

fied and asked to take the individual home for further evaluation.

4. Students who voluntarily share a concern about a personal struggle with abuse or that of another student should be referred to the appropriate school counselor or drug awareness counselor for assistance and follow-up.

5. It is the job of the drug awareness counselor or psychologist, in conjunction with the parents and the affected student, to discuss the need for and options regarding effective rehabilitation programs. It is beyond the purview of teachers to engage in these conversations with the student, and such unwarranted discussion can have serious legal implications. Simply put; teachers should always act as referents for students suspected of substance abuse or who voluntarily disclose substance abuse. Therefore, teachers need to know the referral procedures: who to contact, and how to follow up to ensure the student receives the help he or she needs.

For Students Who Engage in Risky Sexual Behaviors

1. Clearly, teachers are not trained to deal with the issues surrounding teen pregnancy or sexually promiscuous behaviors that occur outside the school; however, as with substance abusers, they should refer an affected student to the school counselor or health professional, who can then provide the individual with helpful resources.

2. Although teachers should not engage in discussion about sexual or reproductive issues, they should be supportive of students' concerns and encourage students to speak with their parents, medical practitioner, school counselor, or health care professional about their concerns.

3. Teachers should avoid sharing a particular philosophy about sexual behavior, whether they favor abstinence or safe sex. Teachers should ensure that students receive appropriate sex education as part of the health curriculum and that student issues or concerns are treated confidentially and respectfully, and are addressed quickly by appropriate school personnel.

4. Teachers' primary concerns in matters involving student sexual behaviors should be for the health and safety of the student and the prevention of unwanted pregnancy and sexually transmitted disease.

For Students Who Perpetrate School Violence and Engage in Bullying

1. Do not tolerate bullying: allowing seemingly harmless behavior to continue unaddressed can be viewed by children who bully as an indication of tolerance or acceptance.

2. Set rules for behavior in your classroom and ensure that students share in their development and enforcement, as well as specific consequences and restitutions for breaking them.

3. Learn and teach both conflict-resolution and anger-management skills. An example of a free online training program that teaches these skills is the New Jersey Education Association (NJEA) program called *Peer Mediation and Conflict Resolution Program* (available online at: www.njsbf.com/njsbf/student/conflictres/conflictres.cfm).

4. Learn and watch for the warning signs of violence; these include social withdrawal, feelings of rejection, rage, expressions of violence in writings or drawings, gang affiliation, and making serious threats of violence.

5. Know your school resources for dealing with students who engage in threats or in violent behavior (e.g., school counselor, school psychologist, crisis intervention team and plan).

6. Enforce school policies that seek to reduce the risk of violence (e.g., keep an eye on hallways between periods, check on students in recess areas or the school cafeteria during recess or lunch breaks).

7. Help implement a safe school plan. If one doesn't exist, organize other concerned teachers and approach the administration about establishing one.

8. Report safety threats or legitimate concerns about potential violence to the school administration, immediately.

9. Encourage and support student-led violence prevention programs. Examples of these programs include peer mediation, teen courts, and violence prevention training.

10. Take time to get to know your students' parents or caregivers. It is possible that many of the more recent and lethal episodes of school violence might have been averted had teachers been alerted to the possibility by family members (Adapted from Druck & Kaplowitz, 2005).

For Students Who Are Involved in Gangs and Gang Violence

Seven Warning Signs of Gang Involvement

1. The student suddenly has a new group of friends.
2. The student has a new nickname.
3. The student shows a lack of interest in studies and school activities.
4. The student has truancy problems and performs poorly in school.

5. The student is frequently late or is unaccounted for at times during the school day.
6. The student wears specific theme colors or has a particular style of dress.
7. This student has tattoos and wears clothing with distinctive logos or insignias (Adapted from Hixon, 1999).

What Teachers Can Do to Help

1. Learn the characteristics of local gangs.
2. Heed the preceding seven warning signs of gang involvement.
3. Listen to the concerns of your students. Discuss gangs, drug use, and the criminal justice system with them, and, when possible, invite community experts, such as representatives of the local police, to share in the discussion of these issues.

4. Build self-esteem in your students.
5. Encourage membership in school-sponsored teams and clubs.
6. Supervise your students and routinely check both isolated and obscure school locations, as well as the activities of large gatherings of students (during school breaks or lunch time).
7. Work hard to prevent students from dropping out of school.
8. Report suspected gang activity to the school administration.
9. Promote gun safety programs.
10. Organize a gang task force in the school (Adapted from Hixon, 1999).

Focus Questions Revisited

1. What are the four substances that are most commonly abused by children and adolescents, and why do they pose such a threat?

A Sample Response

The four most commonly abused substances are alcohol, nicotine, marijuana, and inhalants (solvents, gases, and nitrates). They present a real problem for youth and those who wish to prevent substance use and abuse because three of them are sold "over the counter" and are therefore readily available to children and youth. The fourth, marijuana, though it is a controlled substance, is nonetheless ubiquitous and is easily obtained from sources in the community.

2. The National Institute on Drug Abuse provides six guidelines in selecting an effective school-based drug-abuse prevention program: What are they?

A Sample Response

1. School-based programs should extend from kindergarten through high school. At the very least, they should reach children in the critical middle school and high school years.

2. Programs should employ well-tested, standardized interventions with detailed lesson plans and student materials.
3. Programs should employ age-appropriate interactive teaching methods (e.g., modeling, role playing, discussion, group feedback, reinforcement, and extended practice).
4. Programs should foster pro-social bonding to both the school and the community.
5. Program components should include (a) teaching social competence (i.e., communication, self-efficacy, assertiveness) and drug resistance skills that are culturally and developmentally appropriate; (b) promoting positive peer influence; (c) promoting antidrug social norms; (d) emphasizing skills training teaching methods; and (e) include an adequate "dosage" (ten to fifteen sessions in a year).
6. Programs should be evaluated periodically to determine their effectiveness. (National Institute on Drug Abuse, 1999b, p. 12)

3. Identify the school professionals who serve as resources for teachers who have concerns about a student at risk for or engaged in substance abuse.

A Sample Response

Teachers should know that most schools now employ a drug awareness counselor, or assign a school counselor with appropriate training to that position.

4. What are two key factors that increase the risk of acquiring an STD for adolescents who have emotional disturbances?

A Sample Response

There are two key risk factors that predispose adolescents who have emotional disturbances to the acquisition of an STD: (a) the higher incidence of substance abuse, including intravenous use, in youth who have emotional disturbances, and (b) the behavioral tendency toward risk-taking, impulsive behaviors that is characteristic of many individuals who have emotional disturbances. Note: Although the most commonly abused substances are not taken intravenously, the altered state produced by these substances, i.e., alcohol and marijuana, can impair judgment regarding safe sex practices.

5. Of the three sex education program types described in this chapter, identify the one that you consider to be most effective, and explain why you consider it so.

A Sample Response

In my opinion, the most effective type of sex education program is a comprehensive approach. For example, the Life Skills/Life Options Approach combines, in my opinion, the critical elements of the other major approaches, including encouraging abstinence or delay of sexual activity, providing concrete knowledge about contraception, and offering strategies for building self-esteem, decision-making skills, and developing a clear vision of a successful and independent future (McWhisten, 2004).

6. For each of the following scenarios involving instances of school bullying and violence or the potential for violence, provide a viable intervention that could be employed by a classroom teacher to mitigate the problem.

(*Hint*: Use this chapter as a source for possible research-based solutions.)

a. Devon is a new student in your grade 8 class. He exhibits very oppositional and defiant behavior toward you and other authority figures. He refuses to comply with any of your requests, preferring to respond with barely audible insults or threats. The class is really becoming affected by his inappropriate remarks and intimidating gestures. He has begun to threaten other students who complain about his behavior. You are at your wits' end and notice that you are beginning to avoid him. Learning is seriously jeopardized by his behavior. What should you do short of removing him from class?

b. John has borrowed money from a classmate and is overdue in repaying the loan. John has assured Dustin, the classmate, several times that he would repay the money on a specific date; each time John has had a different excuse for not having the money. This most recent excuse was, for Dustin, the "last straw." You observe Dustin approach John as your students enter the classroom, witness a brief verbal exchange, and see Dustin punch John in the mouth, which precipitates a fistfight. Several members of the class begin to shout encouragement for one combatant or the other, while the rest of the class are shocked spectators frozen into inaction. Blood has begun to flow from John's mouth and nose, as well as from a cut above Dustin's right eye. Two of the larger boys are holding back students who seem intent on helping to break up the fight. What do you do and what resources do you employ to regain control, stop the fight, and give appropriate consequences to the students involved in the melee?

c. Maria and Chantelle are attending the seventh-grade dance. The girls used to be "best friends," but they have been at odds over the attentions of a certain boy. You are a chaperone for the dance and have been assigned hallway patrol outside the boys' and girls' bathrooms. As you pass the girls' lavatory, you hear an animated conversation between Maria and Chantelle. The volume and intensity escalates until you observe Maria run out into the hallway pursued by Chantelle, who says, "Listen b——, if I see you anywhere near Marcus I will f— you up, you hear me!" When you try to ask Chantelle to explain the reason for her inappropriate outburst, she turns to you and says loudly and in front of a group of students attracted by the commotion, "Why don't you stay out of my business? Nobody asked you to butt in, b——!" What is your response?

d. Evan, a quiet, gifted student in your fifth-grade homeroom, has become rather morose of late, ever since the transfer in of Billy, a new student who has a reputation as a "tough guy." You have observed the change in Evan's demeanor whenever Billy enters the room or passes by Evan's desk. Evan avoids eye contact with Billy and appears to be intimidated by Billy's size and aggressive behaviors. One day you overhear a conversation between the two boys in which Billy threatens Evan if he does not agree to share his answers to an important homework assignment. When you confront Billy and Evan about the incident, Billy laughs and says he was just "playing" with Evan. Evan, glancing quickly at Billy, agrees. Shortly after this incident, however, two of your most conscientious students approach you and report that Billy is constantly threatening Evan, occasionally punching him in the chest or arm or tackling him in the schoolyard. Evan is really afraid of Billy. . . too afraid to tell his teachers or parents for fear of retaliation. What do you do to help Evan, deal effectively with Billy, and address the bullying?

e. Ten-year-old Mandy passes Urdu's desk and hold her nose. "Someone smells bad around here," she announces to the class.

The classroom erupts in laughter. Another classmate, Bryan, chimes in, "It's all the curry and stuff they eat—they all stink! Get some air fresheners, quick!" Again the class roars. After speaking privately to Bryan and Mandy about their hurtful behavior, you notice that Urdu is silent, using her textbook to hide the tears that she is unable to suppress. What do you do to help Urdu become more accepted by the class? What are the appropriate consequences for Mandy, Bryan, and the rest of the class? How can such prejudice and rejection be prevented in the future?

f. You are asked by the principal of your school to cover a grade 8 class that has a particularly ominous reputation for misbehavior. As the substitute, you want to do things right and, with your background in special education, you feel confident that you can "handle' the assignment. During the morning's math lesson, you notice a brief exchange between two of the boys in the back of the class. You observe a large, surly boy toss a crumpled piece of looseleaf paper onto the desk of a small, frail-looking boy, who seems clearly fearful and intimidated. In order to avoid an embarrassing confrontation, you say nothing, but you pick up the discarded paper after the class is dismissed. A note scribbled on the paper reads:

"Jeff you —! If you don't want to get beat you better have my money for me after school. Meet me out back by the maintenance shed before the buses come. You better show up with the money or u no what will happen! P.S. Don't tell anyone or yore ded!!!"

You toss the note in your desk drawer and contemplate your next move. You must think fast, because the class will return from gym in 10 minutes and then will be dismissed for the day. What are your options? What is your best course of action?

7. As a new high school teacher, you notice that some of your students wear distinctive clothing and behave in ways that are unusual and a bit unsettling. What are some of the characteristics or warning signs that you might look for to confirm your suspicions of their gang affiliation?

A Sample Response

There are several characteristics that I would look for to help confirm my suspicions about the students' gang involvement and prompt me to report my concerns to the appropriate administrator and/or to law enforcement officials. The following are highly correlated ones: (a) the students have new "nicknames," (b) the students show a lack of interest in studies and school activities, (c) the students have developed chronic truancy problems and are performing poorly in school, (d) the students are frequently late for class or are unaccounted for during the school day, (e) the students wear specific theme colors and have a particular style of dress, and (f) the students have tattoos and wear clothing with distinctive logos or insignias (Hixon, 1999).

8. In developing a school-wide approach to prevent gang membership and gang activity, what are some critical elements to include?

A Sample Response

The following are eight critical elements for inclusion in any effective school-wide gang prevention program:

a. Target students who are vulnerable to gang recruitment for special assistance.

b. Establish values clarification and character education as part of the school curriculum.

c. Create an inviting school climate in which every student feels valued.

d. Educate all school staff, including support staff, about how gangs recruit and develop and how to respond to them.

e. Offer special programs for parents about gangs and how to deal with their influence on their children.

f. Monitor youths who have been identified as being at risk for gang involvement.

g. Monitor youths who are not enrolled in the school, but who loiter around the school while it is in session.

h. Provide opportunities for students to engage in after-school activities, such as clubs and intramural sports teams.

Peggy Gans

FOCUS QUESTIONS

1. What are some of the variables that contribute to maladaptive behaviors in children and youth?

2. List three important contributions that teachers can make to students who have emotional and behavioral disorders.

3. In preparing to work effectively with students who exhibit maladaptive behaviors, the teacher must understand three things about them and the undesirable behaviors. What are they?

4. Identify the key implications of IDEA (2004) for students who have emotional and behavioral disorders.

5. How would you define *meaningful learning* as it relates to students who have emotional and behavioral disorders? What can a teacher do to ensure that these students are learning meaningful and relevant skills in the classroom?

6. What is meant by the term *trigger child?*

7. How important is developing a positive relationship with students who have emotional and behavioral disorders, and how is this best accomplished?

8. What are the dangers of stereotyping in working with students who misbehave? How can we avoid the pitfalls of misperception and subsequent misidentification that are frequently based on our own prejudices and cultural ignorance?

9. How can we work collaboratively with caregivers and family members to improve the classroom and social performance of children who have emotional and behavioral disorders?

RETROSPECTIVE AND OVERVIEW

When the present authors were students, eons ago, teaching was a very explicit, well-defined task: Disperse knowledge, test to evaluate, and promote or retain. There was nothing in the teacher's job description that involved social skills instruction or, for that matter, any involvement or concern with the student's social-emotional state or with life outside the classroom. In many cases, even today, there are teachers, administrators, and parents who prefer this view of the teacher's job description. One teacher I spoke with a few years ago reflected this perception when he basically told me that he was being paid to teach and was not a social worker or a psychologist. If teaching was well executed, he contended, there would be little time for anything else; and if students were alone held accountable for their performance, many of the behavior problems currently encountered in the classroom would simply disappear. Although I believe my friend shared a popularly held view that has some merit, I don't think it is a very realistic one. I compare this view to the one held about drug and alcohol addiction by many in society today. For them, addiction represents narcissism at its worst and is simply caused by a series of poor choices made by very lazy, weak, or undisciplined people. Some are very skeptical of the "disease model" used to understand and treat the disorder and consequently consider rehabilitation treatments or the 12-step programs originally associated with alcoholics anonymous to be essentially flawed. They support this belief with examples of persons who have been in and out of rehabilitation programs for years and have never been successful at living entirely independent of drugs or alcohol.

Similarly, many parents, teachers, and administrators consider the majority of students who have chronic behavior problems to simply need "a firm hand" at home and in school. They attribute the maintenance of these misbehaviors to a permissive social culture, one that is quick to "pathologize" laziness, irresponsibility, and bad behavior, thereby excusing the maladoptive behavior. For many, zero-tolerance policies and strictly enforced disciplinary procedures represent the best approach to dealing with chronic misbehavior. Those students who display more serious emotional or behavioral disorders (EBD) are the purview of the school psychologist or outside professionals, and if they cannot be sustained by these measures, many believe that these children should be placed in a more intensive treatment facility.

Clearly, the authors of this book do not subscribe to that perspective. We believe, after more than 50 years of experience between us, that, much like physical diseases, emotional and behavioral disorders have defining characteristics that facilitate treatment and intervention. The purpose of these varied diagnostic categories is not to stigmatize or stereotype an individual, but actually to help caregivers and professionals provide more effective interventions—ones that are ultimately individualized to serve the specific needs of a child. Our intention, in developing each chapter, was to provide exemplary cases, based on the experiences of actual children and youth. These cases were then used to provide a systematic approach to identifying and treating the behavioral problems displayed by a child who exhibits a set of characteristics that correlate to a particular disorder. However, we have tried to be clear, even in our discussion of these case examples, that each child is unique, with problems that are very individual and, consequently, so must the interventions be. Furthermore, we remind the reader that every child's behavioral problems are a function of several critical and intersecting variables that include, but are not limited to, (1) environment, (2) antecedent events, (3) personalogical variables, (4) the function a behavior serves, and (5) the factors that contribute to and sustain it.

The reader will have noticed that we recommend a **multisystemic approach** in the treatment of the disorders we address. This multisystemic method is the approach that has been most often recommended in the literature and, we believe, offers the student the best chance for successful remediation of the problem. Many behavioral disorders are simply manifestations of years of physical, psychological, or emotional abuse, ineffective parenting, and pathological family systems. The affected children growing up in these circumstances may either "learn" or acquire the destructive behaviors of the caregivers, or they may develop coping skills that manifest as antisocial or disruptive behaviors. These undesirable behaviors are then transferred to the classroom, with the result that the teacher is often substituted for the parent. In these cases, teachers

MULTISYSTEMIC APPROACH

A multiple-system treatment approach to many emotional and behavioral disorders that typically combines family therapy with individual and peer-oriented therapies, acknowledging the importance of affecting behavior change in all these important milieus.

can implement behavioral interventions that involve a positive reinforcement system to help reduce the undesired behaviors while reinforcing and encouraging more pro-social ones. However, it is dangerous to assume that children learn, by osmosis, these more appropriate replacement behaviors—it is therefore incumbent on the teacher to "teach" these skills. Furthermore, for most students who misbehave or who are experiencing emotional problems, it is not sufficient simply to teach reactive responses to various behavioral stimuli. If we want these behaviors to generalize to other social contexts and settings, we must also teach these students more pro-social and effective ways of thinking about and approaching a problem (problem-solving skills). Thus, for students who engage in defiant, aggressive, or destructive behaviors, teaching some sort of pro-social cognitive-behavioral response is highly recommended.

For students who have EBD and who are not cognitively intact (e.g., those with low-functioning autism), interventions that are exclusively behavioral, such as discrete trial training, appear to be the most effective.

To return to a point discussed earlier, namely, that teachers should not be expected to engage in professional activities other than teaching, we remind the reader that, in many cases, teachers have more sustained contact with students during the course of a typical day than parents do (Cavin, 1998). Thus it is imperative that teachers use that opportunity to effect positive change in their students, both academic and social. In a similar vein, studies of "resilience" have revealed that children who grow up in abusive, disruptive households and dangerous communities and who do not succumb to these destructive influences do so for two reasons: (1) a higher level of innate resilience and (2) someone in their lives who believes in them and provides support (Rosenberg et al., 2004; Wickes-Nelson & Israel, 2005). In many cases, the role of "supporter" falls to the teacher.

Indeed, our students notice everything we say but don't do, and idealize but fail to live out. As teachers, we have a profound influence on our students' lives and, as a result, we are obliged to use our influence to help students develop as learners, as well as members of a civil society. In the preceding chapters in this book we have provided examples of how teachers may help their students develop social skills and acquire more pro-social behaviors, in conjunction with the support of parents and professionals, such as the school psychologist or school counselor. These approaches have demonstrated success, but not without the key initiatives on the part of the teacher of (genuine) *empathy, reality,* and *support.* We refer to *empathy* as the feeling of genuine compassion for the welfare of another or the act of sharing another's feelings; *reality* is used here to mean that, like a mirror, we reflect back to the student the real effects of her behavior on herself and others; and by *support* we imply the extent to which a teacher, given her resources and opportunities, provides emotional and physical help to a student in trouble. Psychologists have acknowledged that, ultimately, these three contributions are all we can really give anyone, but they are essential in the development of a positive rapport with students who have EBD (Connolly, 2006).

Another important characteristic of many children who have EBD is their tendency to feel that they are not and cannot be protected. The role of the teacher in combating this misperception is as a "protector"—though this is not to suggest that the teacher is a superhero who can protect the child from all the forces of evil that threaten the child (including the child himself), but that the teacher can model ways in which a healthy, resilient individual protects himself; sometimes with words, sometimes with actions, and sometimes through intentionally avoiding and ignoring or "running away."

Nevertheless, neither teachers nor caregivers can provide the interventions and support that a child needs unless they fully appreciate the history, context, and functions of the child's problem behavior. This book has highlighted these aspects in each chapter and provided concrete examples of how teachers can ascertain these factors. Thus, once again, truly effective intervention is wholly dependent on accurate and thorough assessment of the child and the problem behavior.

Whether prepared or unprepared, willing or unwilling, today's classroom teachers are as much players in a child's social-emotional development as they are in the child's academic growth. Not being prepared to provide empathy, reality, and support is abdicating both a teacher's principal responsibility and privilege. Refusing to understand the student's social milieu and accept the multivariate roles of teachers in working with students is to miss a wonderful opportunity to make a difference in the lives of children.

Next, we examine the impact of the newly reauthorized federal Individuals with Disabilities Education Act (IDEA, 2004) on students who have emotional or behavioral disorders and their parents.

IMPLICATIONS OF IDEA (2004) REGULATIONS FOR STUDENTS WHO HAVE EMOTIONAL OR BEHAVIORAL DISORDERS

First, the provisions of IDEA that require a functional behavioral assessment and a behavioral intervention plan that were established in the 1997 reauthorization of the act continue to be mandated in IDEA 2004; however, there have been a few changes to the 1997 regulations regarding discipline that could have a profound impact on the educational and, consequently, the social outcomes for students who have EBD.

The first of these relates to the **"stay put" provision**, which previously was denied only to students with disabilities who are involved in drug sales or possession, the possession of weapons, or engagement in dangerous behavior, specifically regarded as the commission of violent acts. Under the new regulations, the right of a student who has a disability to "stay put" in his or her current educational placement pending an appeal is eliminated. The ramifications of this change for students who have EBD and their families are grave. For example, one immediate effect is the threat to such a child's assurance of a free and appropriate public education in the least restrictive environment, two of the key principles of IDEA. We have learned in this book that, for most students who have EBD, predictability with minimal disruption to routine is critical to academic success. Furthermore, under the No Child Left Behind Act (2002), children who are transferred to alternative settings during the course of the school year are not required to be included in the reporting of Adequate Yearly

"STAY PUT" PROVISION

The former right of a student who has a disability to "stay put" in his or her current educational placement pending an appeal, which was eliminated in IDEA (2004).

Progress (AYP). This exclusion of challenging students by removing them to alternative settings might provide school administrators with a convenient solution to the deleterious effect of students who have EBD on AYP reports. Ostensibly, such an option might encourage the proliferation of disciplinary actions against these and other students who have disabilities.

Prior to the recent reauthorization, the burden of proof in determining that a student's behavior was not a manifestation of the child's disability, before standard sanctions could be imposed, fell on the school district. Under IDEA 2004, the burden of proof rests squarely with the child's parents. This is often a lop-sided battle because, without expert council or familiarity with the law, most parents do not know the procedures for collecting and presenting appropriate supporting data. Furthermore, the language requiring the Individualized Education Plan (IEP) team to consider whether the child's disorder impaired his ability to control or fully understand the consequences of his misbehavior has been deleted. Similarly, the language that required the multidisciplinary or IEP team to consider whether the IEP was appropriate has also been deleted. The possible implications of these omissions should be apparent to the reader.

In addition, a very important change affecting teachers is the revised standard for a basis of knowledge for children who are not yet eligible for special education and related services. Essentially, a local education agency (LEA) should be considered to have knowledge that a child has a bona-fide disability if, before the behavior that precipitated the disciplinary action occurred, a teacher of that child expressed concern in writing directly to either a school administrator or the director of special education that she "has specific concerns about a pattern of behavior demonstrated by the child" [U.S. Department of Education, 2004, 615(K)(5)(B)].

A minor change involves the 45-calendar-day limit on the removal of a student for school code violations. Effective in 2005, this removal limit has been extended to forty-five school days, which translates to 9 weeks without participation in the school curriculum—a further impediment for students who are already struggling academically.

What are the implications of these changes for students who have emotional and behavioral disorders? These changes reflect a growing intolerance for "acting out" or dangerous behaviors on the part of society in general. Recent school shootings and the lingering war in Iraq and Afghanistan as publicized in the media have helped to sensitize the American public to acts perceived as violent or antisocial. Adults and even children who engage in such behaviors receive little compassion these days, and tolerance for defiance and aggression is extremely low. If you were careful in your reading of the previous few pages, you will have noticed that this growing intolerance of antisocial acts among the general public is reflected in the amendments to the disciplinary statutes that once protected the rights of students who have EBD and their parents, placing the responsibility for determining the behavioral implications of a bona fide emotional disturbance on school district officials. In 2004, however, the responsbility was reassigned from the school to the parents of the affected child. The problem with such a transfer is that parents typically lack the knowledge and legal expertise to argue effectively in support of their child's right to remain in the school. Furthermore, we know from research that change is exceptionally difficult for students who have EBD and can simply exacerbate their behavior problems (Cullinan, 2002). This modification to IDEA will most assuredly aggravate these problems by increasing the likelihood that more students who have EBD will remain in alternative placements.

Similarly, the 2004 change in the language relative to the **45-day removal policy** from calendar days to school days means that students awaiting a manifestation determination will be out of their home school for an additional 2 weeks. The possible negative effects of this extension are the same as those previously discussed.

What can we do, in light of these changes to IDEA, to ensure that we continue to serve as advocates for our students who have disabilities and their parents? First, we need to ensure that we employ behavioral interventions that are effective in helping to decrease the misbehavior of our students who have EBD. Second, we must ensure that the parents of these children understand their rights and responsibilities under IDEA 2004 and its changes regarding disciplinary procedures. This requires that we provide them with not only access to this information, but also that we explain some of the more technical aspects in a way that facilitates their understanding of the act, as well as its implications for their child. Third, we have to convey these changes to the students they might affect in a way that is clear and concise. It is important that the students understand the consequences of violations of school rules and policies in light of the changes that have been made to the discipline provisions of IDEA (2004).

Finally, there is one modification that is supportive of the implication of a child's disability relative to a misbehavior or act that results in disciplinary intervention or punishment, namely, that *parents* and *teachers* can establish a "basis for knowledge" that a child committing a school code violation does or can be construed to have a disability as long as the parents or teachers have expressed "specific concern in writing about a pattern of behavior demonstrated by the child" or that the child is in need of special education services to the appropriate administrative personnel of the school or agency [615(K)(5)(B)]. As long as a parent or teacher of the affected child has done this, then the school has a basis of knowledge for suggesting that the misbehavior is a manifestation of an existing disorder, that is, an emotional or behavioral disorder and, providing the child did not engage in "dangerous behavior" that includes the sale or possession of drugs or weapons, or has not inflicted serious bodily injury to himself or others, the school must provide a valid rationale for the removal of the child for more than ten consecutive days from his current educational placement.

More constructively, in the following section we examine the positive effects of technology and good instruction on the prognosis for students who have EBD.

FORTY-FIVE-DAY REMOVAL POLICY

Refers, effective 2004, to the IDEA regulation that students awaiting a manifestation determination may be removed from their home school for forty-five school days (the regulation previously specified forty-five *calendar* days).

POSITIVE EFFECTS OF TECHNOLOGY AND MEANINGFUL LEARNING EXPERIENCES

Research has supported the benefit of meaningful learning experiences for students who have emotional and behavioral disorders (Walker, 2004). By *meaningful* we mean the teaching of skills that the *student* perceives as useful. If a student, with or without a behavior disorder, asks you, "Why do I have to learn that?" and you can't provide a valid rationale, perhaps the "skill" *isn't* worth learning. Clearly, as teachers, we must address the skills and topics mandated by the curriculum and prepare our students to take standardized tests; however, it is incumbent upon us to ensure that all of our students are engaged in some purposeful learning activity that prepares them for life and not just to be able to successfully complete tests (Popham, 2007). The definition of *meaningful learning* is just that: skills and knowledge that prepare our students to live successful and independent lives, not simply as voyeurs or consumers of services, but also as participants and contributors. Is this an overly ambitious goal for teachers? We don't think so, because we know that self-efficacy is a critical component of self-esteem, and self-esteem correlates with ownership, value, and self-worth. When individuals feel that they have a stake in the outcome of things, as well as in the rewards, they tend to develop a sense of ownership and are less likely to engage in behavior that jeopardizes their success. Therefore, they are less inclined to act out, misbehave, steal, fight, vandalize, or engage in the destructive behaviors that society abhors.

That is not to say that providing meaningful learning activities will serve as a panacea for behavioral disorders. On the contrary, there will continue to be students who have been so affected by their unwholesome environment that they simply cannot integrate or use the skills learned in the classroom in productive ways and may continue to practice destructive behavior patterns. However, there is evidence that much of the antisocial behavior observed in schools can be significantly reduced by engaging the students in meaningful learning activities.

A Word on the Use of Computers

The proliferation of computers in schools and in society at large is no longer a phenomenon but an expectation. Given the versatility of computers, combined with access to the Internet and all the resources that such a connection provides, the usefulness of computers as an educational resource is clear. Furthermore, as a result of the larger class sizes in today's schools, the personal computer can often provide individualized instruction that the harried teacher cannot.

The advent of "learner-centered software" represents a paradigm shift in the pedagogical use of the computer. The unique benefits of this innovative software include: (1) offering students a choice in selecting the goal of the activity, thus empowering students who have emotional or behavioral disorders, who typically feel disenfranchised in the learning process (Healy, 1999); (2) providing feedback that is informational and nonjudgmental; and (3) encouraging estimation and approximation, which reinforce the importance of understanding the process whereby a solution is achieved and not focusing solely on providing the correct response (Mokros & Russell, 1986). Similarly, word processing software encourages students to write more and, ultimately, better, because typewritten drafts are easier to edit and thus facilitate revision, as well as compensating for some students' illegible handwriting.

Regardless of which academic interventions we use to help improve the educational performance of students who have EBD, the fact remains that we must acknowledge the recursive relationship between a child's learning set and misbehavior that impedes it. Academic achievement is highly correlated with engagement, so interventions that increase the latter have a higher probability of success. An example of one such approach is **direct instruction** (Walker et al., 1995), which emphasizes the structure, sequencing, and pacing of instruction, as well as the opportunity to receive feedback and practice.

Other effective practices include **class-wide peer tutoring (CWPT)** (Delquadri et al., 1986) and **reciprocal peer tutoring (RPT)** (Falk & Wehby, 2001; Fantuzo, King, & Heller, 1992). Both of these approaches have been shown to increase students' academic engagement and rates of responding. The success realized as a result of employing either of these tutoring formats is attributed to the effects of group-oriented contingencies. In both programs, the student is reinforced through the praise and encouragement generated by a more skilled peer, as well as by the opportunity for immediate error correction and reinforcement.

Yet another effective behavioral intervention that we have acknowledged several times throughout this book is **self-monitoring**, also frequently referred to self-management or self-recording (Agran, 1998). This strategy improves the academic performance of students who have EBD by teaching these students systematic procedures for observing, evaluating, and recording their own behavior at specific times during the school day. The benefit of this practice for the student is the improvement in his rate of on-task behavior and, consequently, an increase in academic productivity. Similarly, continuous monitoring of student performance is a very effective practice in improving academic performance. This is especially true in conjunction with **curricular-based measurement (CBM)**, which uses performance scores on criterion-referenced tests to inform instructional decisions.

Next, we turn our attention to the pragmatics of classroom management and how to teach those students who are the most personally challenging. We refer to them as the "trigger children" because they seem so adept at finding and exploiting our vulnerabilities.

HOW TO WORK EFFECTIVELY WITH THE TRIGGER CHILD

A *trigger child* is a child who seems to have a real capacity for inciting anger and outrage and provoking "nontherapeutic" responses from teachers and other caregivers. These children typically have the disruptive disorders we described in Chapters 2 and 3, conduct disorder and oppositional defiance disorder; however, children who have anxiety disorders, such as obsessive-compulsive disorder (see Chapter 6), can also fall in this category. In truth, any child whose behaviors cause professional educators, caregivers, or parents to respond in kind—that is, in an unprofessional manner—constitutes, for that individual, a "trigger child."

First, as we discussed earlier, it is important to find a reason to "like" the trigger child. Sometimes this can be accomplished through conscientious effort on the teacher's part. For example, initiating conversation with the child on a topic in which he is interested, praising the child for some small accomplishment,

DIRECT INSTRUCTION

A general term for the explicit teaching of a skill set using lectures or demonstrations of the material rather than exploratory models such as inquiry-based learning. Emphasizes the structure, sequencing, and pacing of instruction, as well as the opportunity to receive feedback and practice.

CLASS-WIDE PEER TUTORING (CWPT)

A peer-assisted instructional strategy designed to be integrated with most existing reading curricula. This approach provides students with increased opportunities to practice reading skills by asking questions and receiving immediate feedback from a peer tutor. Pairs of students take turns tutoring each other to reinforce concepts and skills initially taught by the teacher. The teacher creates age-appropriate peer teaching materials for the peer tutors; these materials take into account tutees' language skills and disabilities.

RECIPROCAL PEER TUTORING (RPT)

A collaborative approach that embeds assessment in a formalized learning process to facilitate student involvement with course content and improve achievement. Students engaging in RPT are paired and given explicit instruction on how to construct multiple-choice questions for different types of statistical content knowledge.

or asking about her well being can foster compassion. Learning about the child's history, engaging the parents in a collaborative discussion about the child's school experience, as well as behavior displayed at home, recreational preferences, likes and dislikes, can provide the teacher with valuable insights into the child and his behavioral repertoire.

A Word About Relationship

In our experience, there is no single intervention that surpasses the benefit of relationship. Establishing one with a child who has an emotional or behavioral disorder is not a guarantee that the undesired behavior will disappear or even diminish, but without one, the behaviors will probably continue and likely escalate, at least in your classroom. By *relationship* we do not imply that the teacher need compete with parents, relatives, or best friends. We are instead referring to a healthy, affirming pro-social human connection. Most children who have EBD experience a real challenge in making friends with peers, let alone establishing relationships with authority figures. Your efforts in that endeavor will improve your classroom climate, make interactions with the child more positive, preclude or reduce defiant and confrontational behaviors while simultaneously providing the affected individual with a wonderful model for establishing and sustaining relationships in the future. Developing relationships with these students is a risky business because, many times, the child's disorder almost compels him to try to scuttle them. Children who have EBD are generally so used to rejection that they simply don't have any experience in establishing and maintaining relationships. Likewise, they often don't have any examples of healthy, reciprocal relationships to draw on. Furthermore, establishing a relationship with one of these children requires a "leap of faith" on the part of the teacher, because one cannot truly enter into a relationship with another individual without trust, and trust requires a certain level of self-disclosure. Relationship, like dialogue, is a shared experience, one that demands reciprocity. The best way to start developing a relationship with one of your students is simply to be yourself. That is sometimes more difficult than it sounds because, as teachers, we often play an expected role, one that was modeled for us by our mentor-teachers and was typically devoid of relationship—except for those few special teachers who made a difference in our appreciation of school and, subsequently, of life. If we were able to analyze the interpersonal skills employed by our favorite teachers, we would find, invariably, that they were just being themselves and generously shared the best of who they were with us, their students. Why take such risks, you might ask; isn't such behavior crossing the line demarcating professionalism? The answer is an unqualified "No." How else can children learn to connect with the world and enjoy interacting in a positive and pro-social way with others?

Knowing others and being known by them is beneficial to students who have EBD on three levels: first, by simply sharing feelings, experiences, or personal anecdotes, we bring our students closer and let them know that personal sharing is welcome; second, opportunities to engage in polite discourse such as teachers provide may not be experienced in other contents of the students' lives and can enable them to engage in the kind of reciprocal communication that will be helpful to them in life; third, the process of "unpacking"—that is, letting oneself be known and, likewise, learning about others, is a step toward better mental health, a deeper sense of **"belongingness"** (Kohn, 1996) and an enrichment of one's self-esteem.

Another strategy that has potential in changing defiant, disruptive student behaviors is simply to avoid reacting to such behavior and meeting anger and hostility with kindness. There is an aphorism in the Bible that reads, "A soft answer turns away wrath (Proverbs 15:1)," and this is a very poignant maxim for teachers working with a trigger child. This does not mean we don't impose consequences for rule breaking and insubordinate behavior; it simply means that our demeanor and behavioral response is not influenced by the child's maladaptive behavior. By avoiding the temptation to react in kind, we free ourselves to try alternatives that avoid the struggle for power and teach the student ways of resolving conflict appropriately, without "losing face."

Likewise, humor, if appropriate to the circumstances, can help defuse a potentially explosive situation. Also, a humorous anecdote, strategically interjected, can be a wonderful stress reliever. It can teach a lesson in a way that is nonthreatening and far more palatable than an exposition about "right" versus "wrong." In this vein, I am reminded of the teacher who, noticing one of her newest students standing alone at one end of the soccer field while her classmates frolicked farther down the field, asked how she was feeling. The student, appearing rather distracted, shot back a terse, "Fine, thank you, Ma'am." This raised the level of concern of the teacher, a special educator, who was nonplussed and emboldened to inquire further: "Do you have any friends?" The student, once again, responded cryptically, "Lots!" Finally, the teacher, inspired to take action, sidled up to the alienated child and asked sincerely, "Would you like me to be your friend?" Exasperated, the young girl looked at the teacher and said, "Yes, Ma'am, but could you please get off the soccer field, we're playing a game here and I'm the goalie!" In recounting this humorous anecdote, we are reminded of the old adage, "Laughter is the best medicine," and often when working through crises in the classroom, so it is!

Another important strategy in working with the trigger child is engaging in nonjudgmental conversation, what can also be referred to as **active listening**. Often, as teachers, we are so used to providing solutions that we feel we must do so even when our most troubled students express a concern, fear, or problem. However, many times this is not what the student wants; she just needs a sympathetic ear, someone who will not judge her disclosure. "Confession is good for the soul," the saying goes, and sharing sensitive or troubling issues is cathartic and requires great courage and trust; being able to just listen and not offer unsolicited advice builds such trust. Children who have EBD often have real issues about trusting adults, and by engaging in nonjudgmental conversation, teachers demonstrate that some adults are trustworthy, thus increasing the likelihood that these children will confide in them in the future.

"BELONGINGNESS"

Being a part or member of a group, whether it is family, friends, career, or sports affiliations. People have a desire to belong and be an important part of something A motive to belong is the need for strong, stable relationships with other people.

ACTIVE LISTENING

An intent to "listen for meaning," in which the listener checks with the speaker to see that a statement has been correctly heard and understood. The goal of active listening is to improve mutual understanding.

AVOIDING THE PITFALLS OF STEREOTYPING

While we acknowledge that, as special educators, we work within the framework of IDEA and the thirteen categories of disability that are encompassed therein, nevertheless, we do not advocate the arbitrary classification of students who have emotional or behavioral issues without applying early and prereferral interventions to mitigate the stigma of the "emotionally disturbed" label. It is our conviction, however, that students who truly meet the criteria and do not respond to prereferral intervention should be appropriately classified in order to receive the benefit of the full array of special education services available to them.

We contend that often, a far more destructive outcome of the classification "emotionally disturbed" is represented in the "rush to judgment" and the misperceptions and outright fallacies it engenders in the unenlightened. Too often children who have been classified as "emotionally disturbed" are assumed to be defiant, antisocial, violent, or disruptive. This assumption is frequently incorrect because, as we know from reading this book, many students receive this classification because of an anxiety or mood disorder, and these children rarely display the types of behaviors that teachers find either threatening or disruptive. It is therefore incumbent on teachers to help reduce the stigma that is associated with the classification "emotionally disturbed" by educating their students and their parents about the nature of the disorder and its various typologies. Books such as this one help teachers do just that by providing current and complete information about the various disorders encompassed within this broad category.

UNDERSTANDING DIVERSITY AND ITS RELEVANCE TO IDENTIFICATION AND INTERVENTION

First, we want to remind teachers of the significant studies conducted in the latter half of the 1990s and continuing today that establish the disproportionate identification of children and youth of color as recipients of special education. Whereas African Americans make up about 12 percent of the U.S. population, they constitute a disproportionate 24 percent of children receiving special education services. Research has revealed that much of this overidentification is related to racial stereotyping and discriminatory practices. In addition to African Americans, research has also demonstrated a similar disproportionate representation of Latino and Native American children (U.S. Department of Education, 2006). In fact, over the past three decades, research has continued to reveal a pattern of overrepresentation of all three ethnic groups, particularly in the more stigmatizing categories of mental retardation, emotional disturbance, and communication disorder (Harry, 1994; Heller, Holtgmon, & Messick, 1982; Maheady, Algozzine, & Ysseldyke, 1984; Meier, Stewart, & England, 1990; Wright & Santa Cruz, 1983). Furthermore, to dispel another misperception that is frequently held by the majority culture, poverty is *not* a significant contribution to **disproportionality** in special education—in fact; recent studies have demonstrated that race continues to be the single most significant correlate (Skiba, Poloni-Staudinger, Simmons, Fegins-Azziz, & Chung, 2005).

DISPROPORTIONALITY

The disproportionate representation of minority students in special education.

In response to this patent inequity, IDEA (2004) has required, effective July 1, 2005, the collection and examination of data from each state to determine if significant disproportionality, based on race and ethnicity, is occurring within state and local education agencies (SEAs & LEAs) with respect to:

1. The identification of children as children who have disabilities in accordance with a particular impairment as described in Section 602 (3);
2. The placement in a particular educational setting of such children; and
3. The incidence, duration, and type of disciplinary actions, including suspensions and expulsions [618(d)(1)].

The reauthorization of IDEA has established specific requirements that must be followed when reviewing policies and procedures of states or LEAs in the case of a determination of significant disproportionality with respect to the identification of children who have disabilities.

In such cases, the state must provide for review and, if appropriate, a revision of policies, procedures, and practices that may have caused the overrepresentation, require any such LEA to provide comprehensive early intervention services for all children in the LEA, particularly children from overidentified groups, and require the LEA to report on the revised policies, practices, and procedures (U.S. Department of Education, 2006). Relative to the disproportionate representation of minority populations, particularly in the category of "emotionally disturbed," teachers should implement a solution-focused approach to early intervention (Watkins & Kurtz, 2001). Such an approach addresses the potential for prejudice among the students' teachers and related services personnel, helping them to be more understanding and supportive, focusing on the affected child's behavioral strengths rather than his shortcomings (i.e., nonpathologizing versus problem-saturated perspective). Integral to this solution-focused approach is allowing the student to be the "expert" in developing solutions to his behavior issues rather than viewing the child as "the problem." Examples of questions that a teacher can use to help the student who is at risk for referral become the "expert" in developing some effective solutions include the following:

- "Tell me about a time when you could have easily blown up but instead you kept your cool."
- "How did you deal with the urge to blow up?"
- "What advice would you give to someone your age who's having a hard time controlling his temper?"

A second phase of the solution-focused approach is to create a portfolio or "book" with the at-risk student that documents the individual's strengths and improvements and also contains a classroom-based contingency management plan that is based on a points-reward system.

Another way that teachers can help to reduce the incidence of misidentification or overidentification of "minority-categorized" children is by learning to appreciate the different ways that parents from diverse cultures interact with school personnel and the traditions of the school. This knowledge may help teachers appreciate the various ways that their students approach the school and its teachers, which may reflect cultural norms that differ from those of the dominant society. In other words, teachers need to ask themselves, "Is the child's behavior truly mal-adaptive, or am I simply reacting to behavioral norms that are different from mine and projecting my cultural expectations on this child?"

Because teachers are the primary source of referral for special education services, and 75 to 80 percent of children who are referred for evaluation are classified, it is critical these teachers ensure that their reasons for referral are based on scientific evidence and are not influenced by cultural or ethnic bias. This requires honest self-reflection and thoughtful consideration of a holistic evaluation of the child's problem behaviors and their context—in other words, a conscientiously applied functional behavioral assessment (Artiles & Harry, 2006).

In short, if a student from an ethnic minority group (e.g., African American, Latino, or Native American) is legitimately identified as needing special education services, the interventions, provided they are based on a sound and thorough FBA and are research-based, should prove as successful as they would for a similarly identified child from the majority cultural group. The real challenge is ensuring that teachers strive to provide effective early intervention that is scientifically based and appropriate for the individual *before* referring the child for formal evaluation by the multidisciplinary team (MDT). Likewise, it is important that teachers examine their own cultural biases when working with a child from another race or culture who presents behavior problems to ensure that, to the extent possible, these innate biases do not influence their perception of the child and her behavioral purposes (Artiles & Harry, 2006).

WORKING COLLABORATIVELY WITH THE FAMILIES OF STUDENTS WHO HAVE EMOTIONAL AND BEHAVIORAL DISORDERS

IDEA (2004) requires that parents receive notification and are included in all aspects of their child's special education experience; nonetheless, the benefits of parent involvement appear to be self-evident. Christenson and Cleary (1990) provide a list of some of the most frequently identified benefits of parent involvement: (1) students' grade and test scores improve, they complete more homework, and they are more involved in classroom activities; (2) teachers are perceived as having better interpersonal and teaching skills, are given higher teacher evaluation scores by principals, and report greater job satisfaction; (3) parents show better understanding of school functions, enjoy better communication with their children and teachers relative to school work, and are more involved in their children's homework; and (4) parents regard school as more effective in providing successful programs.

Robinson and Fine (1994) noted that parent-teacher collaboration produces significant beneficial effects for teachers as well. Specifically, research has determined that teachers' self-efficacy is positively correlated with parent involvement in conferences, volunteering, and home tutoring. Likewise, teachers with high self-efficacy tend to see parents as significant contributors to the academic success of their students (Hoover-Demsey, Bassler, & Brissie, 1992). Based on these and other findings, it would seem to be to the school's advantage to develop greater parent involvement through approaches that facilitate increased parent participation in the education of their children.

Barriers to the collaborative process between parents and teachers include: (1) lack of consistent and personal contact, e.g., via weekly newsletters, bulletins, or notes; (2) the tendency to use **disprivileging speech** that alienates parents, such as when teachers employ professional jargon or acronyms like IEP, CSE, IDEA, or LRE without explanation; (3) patronizing speech that places parents in a "one-down" or subservient role to teachers; (4) planning IEP meetings, annual reviews, or parent–teacher conferences at times that accommodate the teachers but represent a scheduling challenge for working parents; and (5) failure to make the parent feel valued and important to the process; as well as (6) not recognizing that parental resistance or hostility may represent a historic distrust of schools and the school system (Robinson & Fine, 1994).

These barriers can be removed, according to Fine (1991), by: (1) including parents in the decision-making process for their child; (2) educating these parents regarding their rights under IDEA and as bona-fide members of the decision-making team; and (3) empowering them thorough the development of trust and mutual respect. In short, parents should feel that they share a mandate with the multidisciplinary team; that is, to make educational decisions and design effective interventions that are in the best interests of their child.

The following represent some of the ways that teachers can facilitate the involvement of parents as collaborators in their child's education. First, teachers can help to educate parents about child and adolescent developmental characteristics so that parents will have reasonable expectations for child behavior and learning across grade levels. Second, teachers can use a variety of means to communicate with parents on a routine basis; for example, they can send progress reports home, call parents to remind them about upcoming classroom activities and parent–teacher meetings and workshops, and, where appropriate, schedule meetings with parents not just in the school but, where feasible, in a variety of conducive locations. Third, parents can be encouraged to volunteer in the school. As volunteers, they can assist with class trips, help with individual tutoring, assist with projects and crafts, and read aloud to small groups. Fourth, parents can provide valuable oversight for homework. To facilitate this, some schools provide "college in the classroom" workshops after school in which the children's teachers instruct parents about the content skills currently taught in the classroom, thus providing parents with the knowledge necessary to be a valuable at-home tutor. Fifth, parents can and should be involved in decision-making, governance, and advocacy through membership in one or more parent–teacher organizations and committees (e.g., PTA; SEPTA). Finally, parents should be informed by the school about various community support groups that can provide outside resources in support of their child (i.e., child care, health care, and cultural activities).

Lastly, both teachers and parents need to be well versed in the skills that are prerequisite for effective communication and collaboration. Robinson and Fine (1994) have identified four such skills: (1) accurate listening that reflects back to the listener both content and emotion, and is committed to understanding the speaker's message as the speaker intended; (2) appreciating the other person's

DISPRIVILEGING SPEECH

The intended or unintended effects of using technical or professional terminology to effectively disenfranchise a nonaffiliated individual or group unfamiliar with such language.

frame of reference, that is, the individual's knowledge of the issues, as well as any prejudices or orientations in conjunction with that person's emotional investment in the outcomes; (3) introducing ideas noncompetitively—avoiding their "win–lose" quality—for example, present ideas as suggestions, not mandates; and (4) avoid off-topic conversations that prove a distraction rather than a solution; instead, approach any parent-teacher conflict using a "solution-oriented" process whereby both stakeholders reach agreement on what they want to happen, relative to the affected child, and what needs to occur to realize that goal.

Recent research has also produced recommendations for both the preservice and in-service teacher. In the case of preservice teachers, the research asks them to: (1) consider their own perceptions and beliefs about parents and parent involvement, (2) understand the parents' perspective relative to their support for the teacher's educational goals, (3) investigate parent–school practices, (4) review studies on parent–teacher interaction, (5) participate in role-playing activities to help prepare for actual communication with parents, (6) engage in actual parent conferences as an integral part of field experience, (7) candidly assess the quality of communication with parents, and (8) develop a parent collaboration plan that complements the teacher's personality, experience, and teaching goals (Lazar & Slostad, 1999).

Similarly, Lazar and Slostad (1999) urged schools to provide workshops in which teachers share their successful collaborative experiences with parents. They proposed that these workshops also specifically address the development of teacher–parent collaboration skills, effective communication techniques, and shared governance with parents. Finally, they contended that teachers need opportunities to employ collaborative practices involving parents and then assess these practices to determine the most effective ones.

THE LAST WORD

In concluding, we hope that the reader will appreciate the importance we place on conducting good assessment in the case of students who misbehave and demonstrate emotional and behavioral disorders. Target behaviors must be carefully identified and measured for two reasons: to establish a baseline on which to base intervention goals; and to assess the effectiveness of interventions with an eye to achieving the maximum benefit for the student. Simply put, teachers cannot provide effective interventions that produce meaningful and lasting improvements without conducting sound, measurable assessment using reliable and valid instruments. That is not to say that every aspect of the child's maladaptive behavior can be measured using a schedule or checklist; some of the elements that form pathological behavior patterns, such as **personalogical variables** like temperament, are not easily quantified. In acknowledgement of this, Kauffman (2005) noted, "Teaching is much more than measurement. A mechanical approach to teaching that excludes affective concerns is no more justifiable than an approach that neglects cognitive and behavioral goals" (p. 440). He added, "If the student's most important behavioral characteristics are not monitored, however, then it will be almost impossible

PERSONALOGICAL VARIABLES

Inherent or inborn traits and behavioral characteristics that help define the "personality" of an individual.

for the teacher to communicate anything of substance about the student's progress to the youngster or to anyone else" (p. 440).

It is important that teachers understand that, despite all the rhetoric about "one size fits all" programs and new "research-based" interventions, there are truly only four things they can provide a student who has an emotional or behavioral disorder: caring (empathy), honesty (reality), support (academic and emotional), and consistency. It is essential that teachers find a reason to *care* for each of their students, and the reason must be founded. We can all do that! Caring does not mean that we don't provide relevant consequences, and it does not imply that we should allow students to dodge accountability through excuses. What it does mean is that we recognize the capacity for kindness and civility that is inherent in every human being and nurture the humanity in every student we teach.

Furthermore, we must be *honest* with our students and with ourselves. Our students are constantly observing us and unconsciously measuring the degree to which our actions support our words. Does their scrutiny disclose our hypocrisy or our integrity? Children and youth who have EBD need us to be honest in our communications about both their deficiencies and their strengths. Compliments need to be founded on real accomplishments, not on empty pronouncements about their "potential". The child in our class who has conduct disorder may never be the CEO of a major corporation, but he can achieve a quality of life that includes happy times with family and friends, satisfying work, and financial stability.

Support is the one thing that most teachers are eager and willing to provide to each of their students. However, support for a child with an emotional or behavioral disorder does not include watering down the curriculum, extending a due date because the student made excuses, or allowing that student to meet an inferior standard. On the contrary, research has supported that all students, particularly those with emotional and behavioral disorders, respond to higher standards in kind (Kohn, 1996; Walker et al., 2004). Thus, academic support and, for the most part, emotional support, needs to be "scaffolded" and follow the notion of "proximal development" espoused by Vygotsky (1978) and others. To borrow an aphorism attributed to Thomas Jefferson, "[Teachers] should not do for students what they can do for themselves." Struggle is good, as Kauffman (2005) observed: "The teacher's task is to choose at first just manageable tasks for students and then gradually allow them to set their own goals as they become attuned to their true capabilities and desires" (p. 442).

Lastly, teachers need to provide consistency for their students who have emotional or behavioral challenges. If you establish a classroom rule, you must enforce it and provide the stated consequences every time it is broken. Be very careful about making promises and threats: Whatever you promise must be actualized, because your credibility is at stake. As we have learned, students who have emotional and behavioral disorders thrive on consistency; they typically have been exposed to models of inconsistency and whimsy at home and, thus, frequently look to teachers to provide the stability and predictability they need.

We offer the following anecdote to highlight the importance of this characteristic. As a weekly behavioral incentive, one of the authors typically provides his high school students with a breakfast of cream cheese and bagels every Friday morning. On one such Friday, he was running late and decided not to stop at the bagel shop on his way to school. When he got to school, however, he discovered that his students had not forgotten, and they were clearly disappointed; some even said that they counted on their Friday bagel as breakfast for the day. Seeing how important this ritual was to the students, the author requisitioned a van and took them to the bagel shop, after which they resumed normal classroom activities, appeased and gratified that an important expectation had been met. To the extent possible, teachers must be dependable and model consistent behaviors.

Finally, one of the characteristics of many of our children and youth who have EBD that we have not stressed in this book is the need to feel and be "safe." This is not exclusive to these children; it is, of course, an essential human need identified by Maslow (1948) and others. Nevertheless, many of them are extremely vulnerable individuals and don't know how to be or feel safe. Often, their homes and communities are fearful places in which they are neither physically nor emotionally safe. Teachers can help these children feel secure by modeling "safe" behaviors.

Safe behaviors are the antithesis of risk-taking ones; students who have EBD are frequently consummate risk takers, but they seldom know how to avoid dangers and reduce the risks that imperil their young lives on many levels. The modeling of "safe" behavior can be accomplished when teachers make choices that are healthy, such as pursuing a hobby, playing a team sport, eating a salad instead of a hamburger, and avoiding unhealthy behaviors such as smoking, drinking excessively, and not using epithets or slurs to denigrate a colleague or student. Teachers also model "safe" behavior when they avoid provocation and remain calm in a crisis. Lastly, teachers model "safe" behavior when they follow the rules they espouse and adhere to a personal philosophy that values integrity and honesty but does not neglect fun and sharing a good laugh with others. Ironically, many times, students who have EBD engage in risk-taking behavior either consciously or unconsciously to "prove" to us that we *can't* keep them safe, and they are usually right! However, we can help them learn to make the kinds of choices that will, in time, ensure that they can take responsibility for their own well-being.

We close this chapter and the book with a passage written by Clark Cavin, a very committed special educator; from his article, *Maintaining Sanity in an Insane Classroom:*

> If teachers are to maintain their sanity when working with students who have emotional and behavioral disorders, they must keep their toolboxes full. They must know how to recognize and defuse the violence cycle. They must know how to de-escalate volatile situations. And, finally, they must maintain their own mental health.
>
> Working with kids with behavior problems and severe emotional disturbance is indeed a special calling. I certainly am not reaching as

many of the students who pass through my doors as I want. . . . Above all, remember that these kids with all of their problems, their criminal records, their probation officers, their idiosyncrasies, their unlovable characteristics, and their strange families are still kids. They need someone to care. They need someone to accept them. They need to know they are somebody. If you are willing to provide these ideals, you can be the connection that bridges the gap from dropout to diploma.

Working with students who have behavioral disorders and emotional disturbances is the most challenging undertaking in education. If you are searching for rewards and accolades, teach gifted and talented or one of the fine arts. If you teach because you love the subject matter, choose English, history, Spanish, math or whatever subject excites you. If you want to work with neat kids who really care and want to better themselves, work in honors, athletics or student government. But, if you want to set up camp a few feet outside the gates of hell and try to rescue a few just before they tumble in, join me in this place. Few will praise you. Colleagues may look on you as a second-class citizen. Most of the kids will not appreciate you. You won't get Christmas gifts or thank-you letters. Your deepest satisfaction comes from knowing that Chris and Nick would not have graduated without you, that Marvin would have been expelled without you, that Eric ran away from home and would not give his new phone number to anyone but you. With a whole lot of love, prayer, and hard work, you did the impossible. And, tomorrow morning, when the bell rings at 8:00, you will have the opportunity to do the impossible again. (Cavin, 1994, 1995, as cited in Cavin, 1998, p. 384)

We sincerely hope that tomorrow morning, when the bell rings, you will be there, in your classroom, ready to teach these troubled and troubling students who desperately need you, whether they know it or not.

FROM THE FIELD

Nina Zaragoza, Ph.D.

From the beginning of her career to the present, Nina Zaragoza has worked in urban environments as an early childhood teacher, elementary school teacher, special education teacher, English teacher, professor of education, and director of education for a nonprofit organization focused on children. Her professional journey has taken her from Buffalo to Miami, to Vladimir, Russia, to Brooklyn, and the South Bronx, and has enabled her to work with children, youth, teachers, and community youth workers of varying ethnicities and backgrounds. In the past few years, she has served as a special education teacher in Brooklyn, an adjunct professor at local colleges, and a consultant with children, teachers, community workers, and families in New York City and abroad. Dr. Zaragoza is presently the president of Creative Curriculum Connections, Inc.

As someone who has been a classroom teacher, as well as a researcher, author, and college professor, you have had the benefit of several vantage points from which to view and "experience" the development of the field of special education. Because this book is *primarily* concerned with students who have emotional and behavioral disorders, can you share your insights and a personal experience or two relative to IDEA (2004) and its implications for them?

The IDEA's emphasis on high expectations and its focus on ensuring all students the foundation and opportunity to pursue further education have powerful implications for students and teachers. Because of IDEA, teachers now have the privilege of looking beyond traditional assumptions about academic proficiency and access because of behavioral and emotional difficulties. IDEA supports all students' right to receive the dignity and respect they deserve, no matter what their label. Now, with the support of IDEA, teachers must provide purposeful, relevant work, which enables all students to progress and strive toward continued and life-long learning. In fact, IDEA helps teachers and students break the debilitating chains of low-expectations and look beyond to healthy work and relationships.

As a classroom teacher of children labeled "special education," I often notice that my students do much more than expected by the administration and their other teachers. These low expectations deeply sadden me, but I hope that the work of my students will inspire others to look beyond the labels. Indeed, my students' performances of poetry, self-authored drama productions, and purposeful work in the community (i.e., visiting senior homes, contributing writing to local libraries, etc.) confirm the belief that all students can and want to learn.

I saw this same confirmation in the glowing faces of twelve high schoolers with emotional and behavioral difficulties when they read their own stories to children at a neighboring elementary school. These high school students worked through feelings of helplessness, anxiety, and fear of public speaking to serve as reading models to the younger children. Yes, there were difficulties for the teacher and students during the writing, finding pictures to the text, and book binding. And it was even more difficult to convince these students, who have already met with so much failure academically, emotionally, and behaviorally, to step out and share. But because we persevered with diligence and faith, we will always remember the success symbolized by Andre, a 15-year-old who, upon leaving the elementary school, kissed his book and said, "I won't ever forget this!"

Based on your professional experiences and insights, how has the proliferation of technology improved learning and achievement for students who have emotional and behavioral disorders, among others with disabilities?

I think that technology in these classrooms can have varying effects depending on how and when the teacher encourages its use. Technology used as a part of purposeful work, i.e., writing, publication, and some electronic communication, serves to ease some of the obstacles that have previously hindered many of our students. For example, difficulties with spelling and grammar can be eased with the various spell and grammar check programs available.

I often see, though, that excessive use of computer-assisted instruction and assessment has negative effects on academic and social growth. Learning happens within relationships, and the necessary time needed to form and strengthen these teaching and learning relationships should be paramount. When children are placed in front of computers to learn concepts that can be done within relationships, valuable lessons of community and connections are lost.

I also think that technology such as television, computers, and hand held games permeate many of the homes of our students. Too often parents place their children in front of the TV to manage and control them. Too often children sit before the computer screen for hours playing games, interacting with WebKins, My Space, etc. I do not support any justification of this excessive use and, in fact, because of the prominent place of television/computer programs in the home, we as teachers must limit such use in the classroom. Whether television /computer programs exhibit educational value, this is not justification enough to deny children the real social interaction so necessary for academic and emotional growth.

In this chapter, we use the term _trigger child_ to refer to students in our classrooms, both with and without emotional disturbances, who "push our buttons" or present significant challenges to our teaching. What insights or suggestions can you provide our readers, based on your own experiences, that might help them work more effectively with these difficult students?

Frankly, the term "trigger child" deeply offends me. This term immediately puts the blame and responsibility of "disturbances" solely on the child. This is analogous to saying "learning-disabled child" versus "child with learning disabilities." I also think that the label "trigger child" negatively colors perceptions. Just as negative and low-expectations many times serve as self-fulfilling prophesies, this label can perpetuate behavior or actually magnify low levels of disruptiveness. Sadly, this label, like most others, follow students on to other teachers.

Before I discuss concrete examples and specific suggestions, I'd like to note that my suggestions focus on teacher thinking and behavior. We can complain endlessly about student behavior, lack of administrative support, lack of parental concern, poor living conditions, etc., etc., and while we might want to address these areas in different ways at different times, we often do not have control over them. So we can either choose to allow these factors to block us and paralyze us to bitter inaction or we can decide to look at what we can do and what we can change within our own area of influence. We each have the power to look at the underlying reasons for our responses toward these "difficult" children. We, indeed, have the power to not react negatively and decide to change our perceptions of the student and of the behavior. Let's get on to some real scenarios for clarity.

As an educational consultant, many schools call me to work in classrooms to help support teachers and students. I am sometimes asked to follow students seen as troublesome and disruptive so that I can give suggestions to help improve the situation. These are the students seen loitering in high school hallways because they don't care to enter the classroom, or they have been sent out of the classroom because of inappropriate behavior. While some variation in behavior occurs depending on the teacher, some common teacher behaviors/practices are usually evident across classrooms. For example, because teachers expect negative, disruptive behavior from these students, they notice every little movement made. I saw this recently in one high school English classroom. When John called out or turned to his friend to talk, an immediate reprimand followed. When another student exhibited the same disruptive behavior, it was ignored. In every class, teachers were either hypervigilant in regard to John or totally ignored him for the entire period and allowed him to come and go as he pleased. These extremes came from good intentions but need to be examined more deeply.

Let's think about the messages we send John and his classmates through these behaviors. Of course, everyone knows, John included, that John is a "marked" man, i.e., a "trigger child." This already colors the messages that teachers send. Therefore, everyone expects John to be either negatively singled out or allowed to get away with murder. Whether one or the other happens usually depends on the mood and energy of the teacher. This unpredictability wreaks havoc in any classroom and actually does the same internally to the students and teachers involved. We all need to feel emotionally safe and secure before any learning happens.

While ignoring inappropriate behavior definitely has its place, it must occur within a context of positive recognition. Therefore, while I often suggest ignoring a behavior until it is extinguished, this technique will be totally ineffective and actually harmful if the student does not also receive recognition for positive work and interactions. Yes, I can already hear some of you thinking, "But he/she never does anything positive!" You know what? I don't believe this. I believe that you have allowed this child to drain you so that you cannot see the small, positive interactions that happen right before your eyes. He/she sits and waits patiently for 5 minutes before class begins. He turns to the right page. He raises his hand without calling out. He enters the room and says, "Hello, Miss." Do you say hello back, or do you answer with something sarcastic (also mislabeled "humor"). Can you say, "Thank you, John, I see you raised your hand and haven't called out." Or "I'm sorry we didn't start right away but I noticed, John, you were waiting patiently for us to begin." This kind of recognition and appreciation needs to be part of our classroom culture. But sadly, in almost every classroom I visit, it is not. (For more details, see Shanika's story in Zaragoza [2002]).

Let me point out, though, ignoring doesn't mean that we allow a student to sit and not complete the required work because, "at least he/she is quiet." These low expectations send the clear message, whether intentional or not, that you do not care about this student's progress. The message sent, whether intentional or not, clearly states that this student means less to you than the others. The message states that you do not have faith in this student and that you do not care. Yes, I know these words sound harsh, but think about the harshness of the messages you inadvertently send. Teaching is a high calling and a serious responsibility. Do we need to be perfect? Of course not. Must we reflect continually on our words and actions? Most definitely.

Clear, appropriate consequences need to be in place for all students to address incomplete or missing work. But it actually isn't difficult to understand why so many of our students do not complete the work given. For a minute,

let's put ourselves in their places. Look at the actual tasks you require. Would you like to complete them? Do they really hold any value in the big picture? Answer the questions after the passage, write a summary, color in the right bubble. Why? If you answer, "Because that's what we're told to do," then I beseech you to rethink what you are doing and why. Did you become a teacher to push papers or to have a positive impact on the next generation? If you answer the latter, then you know teaching and learning is much more than filling in the blank and test prep. You know that it is about purpose, joy, and service to others. Students involved in work that has a purpose and impact on an audience (i.e., drama, poetry, community project) will complete it. (For more details, see "Project Orientation" at www.ninazaragoza.com.)

Finally, let me encourage you as you reflect upon your responses to your students to take care of your own emotional health. We all have issues that in certain contexts negatively color our thoughts and interactions. For example, if we have a psychological need to be in a position of authority, this might hinder us from enabling our students to have authority and ownership over their own work and choices. If we have a tendency to note what we lack instead of acknowledging our own strengths, than we will more times than not first see the deficits in others before seeking to understand their strengths. I ask that you open your heart to yourself and your students. For in the end, real teaching and learning happens within caring, connected relationships.

In your books and publications, you discuss the importance of appreciating diversity in its many connotations. Based on your experience, how can teachers ensure that they consider cultural, language, and learning differences when working with students who engage in maladaptive and/or disruptive behaviors?

To ensure that all students in our classes are appreciated and honored for who they are, we need to set up a noncompetitive, nurturing classroom community so that all members feel safe to be who they are and who they are becoming. Appreciating diversity is not about designating a special month for this or that culture but about giving voice to the personal story of each student and teacher. Therefore, in my classrooms, Langston Hughes' poetry permeates the curriculum all year—not just in February. We study Jose Marti, Nikki Giovanni, Toni Morrison over the year as students are enabled to make choices to connect to a variety of authors. I also encourage and enable (through library, museum visits, guest speakers, etc.) my students and families to share aspects of their cultures so that we continue classroom and cultural connections throughout the year.

Curriculum decisions also honor diversity. For example, when students have some choice about their reading material, writing topics, long-term projects, and response to material covered, we continue to learn about who they are and what they care about. Indeed, we begin to know each other, and what better way to show honor but to know and deeply care about each individual heart.

Another theme in this chapter that is addressed in your writing relates to working collaboratively with parents and families of students who have disabilities. Because, frequently, the parents of students who have emotional and behavioral disorders, as well as those of children who have other disabilities feel a sense of alienation from the school and are, consequently, reluctant to approach teachers for help. Could you share some ways that you have engaged them as collaborators in their child's learning?

Again, in the end (and the beginning!), it's a matter of the heart. When families begin to understand that you care about their children, they themselves begin to feel cared for. So we, as teachers, must grow to care about each and every child. If we do not care about our students, then we have already lost our families. Why

would a parent want to connect to a teacher who either openly or subtly dislikes their child? I ask you to put yourself in their place. I ask that you do whatever inner work necessary to build love and compassion for each one of your students no matter how difficult they may be and no matter how many you have. Yes, this is deep, serious, and difficult. But it must be part of the teaching and learning process.

I hear from many teachers that it is difficult to care about certain children, that some children are unlikeable. This grieves me. Perhaps we dislike the behavior of a student, but the student's behavior is not the student. Sadly, so many forget to keep the label separated from the child and have children designated as "favorites." I hear, "But it's normal to have favorites. That's just human nature." I do not accept this dangerous belief that divides students against students. We have a duty to view each and every one of our students with eyes of compassion, eyes that look beyond labels, culture, socioeconomic status, and, yes, beyond behavior. We have the duty to, indeed, see a positive, healthy vision for this student and set up respectful classroom environments that support this vision.

How will families know that you care? They will know because you:

- Smile when you see them
- Respect their knowledge by asking for suggestions and insight about their child
- Write consistent notes with positive news about their child
- Translate all written material, workshop information, etc., into their first language
- Send appropriate homework that exhibits that you have taken the time to teach the homework concepts
- Give appropriate notice and sufficient guidance for long-term projects so as not to add stress to family
- Make regular phone calls (even in middle school and high school) to report on progress
- Arrange workshops at various times to allow for different work schedules and younger siblings

Finally, I ask that you have compassion for your families. Perhaps they do things that you totally disagree with. Perhaps these behaviors negatively influence their children's progress. Perhaps you're right. But remember, parents love their children and do the best they can with what they know and what they have. Show compassion and treat their children the way that you would want your own treated. (See Zaragoza [2005] for more detail.)

Is there a success story from your considerable experience in the field relative to a student who has an emotional or behavioral disorder that negatively affects his or her learning that you could share with our readers, which might provide them with an additional insight or intervention strategy?

I will always hold dear the story I shared above about the twelve high schoolers who worked through writing and publication to read their own stories to elementary school children. I will never forget their faces that showed confidence and satisfaction in an important job finished and well done. The following day the teacher sent me an email saying, "That was amazing. Best part of the year for myself and my students. Thank you so much for everything!"

In fact, part of this success story includes this teacher who, throughout the year, voiced discouragement about his students' extremely disruptive behavior and language, poor attitude, and lack of motivation. This teacher, too, doubted his ability to handle it all. But with consistent coaching about noting the small improvements, setting up a positive classroom structure, allowing students more academic choice, and striving toward more project-oriented work, the classroom environment slowly changed for the better. (See "Suggestions for Teachers" at www.ninazaragoza.com for more detail.)

As you can probably tell even from these few responses, I do not believe that decontextualized strategies or recipes have a place in the teaching and learning process. Decisions need to be made within the context of a philosophy of education that honors the strengths and abilities of all classroom members. We all have varying abilities and emotional profiles, but we also all have similar needs that when filled will enable us to grow optimally. We all need to feel safe, respected, cared for, and given opportunities to care for others. We need to know that our life matters. We need to engage in productive, purposeful work that impacts ourselves and others in a deep and meaningful way. To enable a community that will address these needs requires deep, ongoing reflection, conversation, and support. It is serious work that will impact the hearts of a generation.

Focus Questions Revisited

1. What are some of the variables that contribute to maladaptive behaviors in children and youth?

A Sample Response

Some of the critical and intersecting variables that foster and sustain maladaptive behaviors in children and youth include, but are not limited to: (a) environment, (b) antecedent events, (c) personalogical variables, (d) the function a behavior serves, and (e) the factors that contribute to and sustain it. Many behavioral disorders are simply manifestations of years of physical, psychological, or emotional abuse, ineffective parenting, and pathological family systems. The affected children growing up in these circumstances may either "learn" or acquire the destructive behaviors of the caregivers, or may develop coping skills that manifest as antisocial or disruptive behaviors. These undesirable behaviors are then transferred to the classroom, with the result that the teacher is often substituted for the parent.

2. List three important contributions that teachers can make to students who have emotional and behavioral disorders.

A Sample Response

Three important contributions a teacher can make to students who have emotional and behavioral disorders are (genuine) empathy, reality, and support. Empathy is feeling genuine compassion for the welfare of another or sharing another's feelings; reality can be understood as a mirror, by which the teacher reflects back to the student the real effects of her behavior on both herself and others; support refers to the extent to which a teacher, given her resources and opportunities, provides emotional and physical help to a student who is in trouble. Psychologists have acknowledged that, ultimately, these three contributions are all we can really give anyone, but they are essential in the development of a positive rapport with students who have emotional and behavioral disorders (Connolly, 2006).

3. In preparing to work effectively with students that exhibit maladaptive behaviors, the teacher must understand three things about them and the undesirable behaviors. What are they?

A Sample Response

Three things that teachers must understand about students who have emotional and behavioral disorders with whom they work are the history, context, and functions of the child's problem behavior.

4. Identify the key implications of IDEA (2004) for students who have emotional and behavioral disorders.

A Sample Response

The first key implication relates to the "stay put" provision, which previously was denied only to students with disabilities who are involved in drug sales or possession, the possession of weapons, or engagement in dangerous behavior, specifically regarded as committing violent acts. Under the new regulations, the right of a student who has a disability to "stay put" in his or her current educational placement pending an appeal is eliminated.

In addition, under IDEA 2004, the burden of proof relative to the manifestation determination rests squarely with the child's parents. This is often a lop-sided battle because, without expert council or familiarity with the law, most parents do not know the procedures for collecting and presenting such supporting data. Furthermore, the language requiring the IEP team to consider whether the child's disorder impaired his ability to control or fully understand the consequences of his misbehavior has been deleted. The possible implications of these omissions should be apparent. Even more disturbing is the determination that a local education agency (LEA) should be considered to have knowledge that a child has a bona fide disability if, before the behavior that precipitated the disciplinary action occurred, a teacher of that child expressed concern in writing directly to either a school administrator or the director of special education that she "has specific concerns about a pattern of behavior demonstrated by the child." [U.S. Department of Education, 2004, 615(K)(5)(B)]. Finally, the 2004 change in the language relative to the 45-day removal policy from calendar days to school days means that students awaiting a manifestation determination will be out of their home school for an additional 2 weeks. Similarly, effective in 2005, this removal limit has been extended to 45 school days, which translates to 9 weeks without participation in the school curriculum, a further impediment for students who are already struggling academically.

5. How would you define *meaningful learning* as it relates to students who have emotional and behavioral disorders? What can a teacher do to ensure that these students are learning meaningful and relevant skills in the classroom?

A Sample Response

Meaningful learning refers to the teaching of knowledge and skills that the student perceives as useful. If a student, with or without a behavior disorder, asks you, "Why do I have to learn that?" and you can't provide a valid justification, perhaps the "skill" *isn't* worth learning. Clearly, as teachers, we must address the skills and topics mandated by the curriculum and prepare our students to take standardized tests; however, it is incumbent upon us to ensure that all of our students are engaged in some purposeful learning activity that prepares them for life and not just to be able to successfully complete tests (Popham, 2001). The definition of meaningful learning is just that: skills and knowledge that prepare our students to live successful and independent lives, not simply as voyeurs or consumers of services, but also as participants and contributors.

6. What is meant by the term *trigger child?*

A Sample Response

A trigger child is a child who seems to have a real capacity for inciting anger and outrage and provoking "nontherapeutic" responses from teachers and other caregivers. These children typically have disruptive disorders such as oppositional defiance disorder and conduct disorder; however, children who have anxiety disorders such as obsessive-compulsive disorder can also fall in this category. In truth, any child whose behaviors cause professional educators, caregivers, and parents to respond in kind—that is, in an unprofessional manner—constitutes, for that individual, a *trigger child.*

7. How important is developing a positive relationship with students who have emotional and behavior disorders, and how is this best accomplished?

A Sample Response

By "relationship," the inference is to a healthy, affirming pro-social human connection. Most children who have emotional or behavioral disorders experience a real challenge in making friends with peers, let alone establishing relationships with authority figures. Teachers' efforts in that endeavor will improve their classroom climate, make interactions with the child more positive, preclude or reduce defiant and confrontational behaviors while simultaneously providing the affected individual with a model for establishing and sustaining relationships in the future.

8. What are the dangers of stereotyping in working with students who misbehave? How can we avoid the pitfalls of misperception and subsequent misidentification that are frequently based on our own prejudices and cultural ignorance?

A Sample Response

Too often, children who are classified as "emotionally disturbed" are assumed to be defiant, antisocial, violent, or disruptive. This assumption is frequently incorrect, because many students receive this classification because of an anxiety or mood disorder, and these children rarely display the types of behaviors that teachers find either threatening or disruptive. It is therefore incumbent on teachers to help reduce the stigma that is associated with the classification "emotionally disturbed" by educating their students and their parents about the nature of the disorder and its various typologies. Books such as this one help teachers do just that, by providing current and complete information about the various disorders encompassed within this broad category.

9. How can we work collaboratively with caregivers and family members to improve the classroom and social performance of their children who have emotional and behavioral disorders?

A Sample Response

The following are some of the ways that teachers can facilitate the involvement of parents as collaborators in their child's treatment.

1. Teachers can help to educate parents about child and adolescent developmental characteristics so that parents will have reasonable expectations for child behavior and learning across grade levels.

2. Teachers can use a variety of means to communicate with parents on a routine basis; for example, they can send progress reports home, call parents to remind them about upcoming classroom activities and parent–teacher meetings and workshops, and, where appropriate, schedule meetings with parents not just in the school but, where feasible, in a variety of conducive locations.

3. Parents can be encouraged to volunteer in the school. As volunteers, they can assist with class trips, help with individual tutoring, assist with projects and crafts, and read aloud to small groups.

4. Parents can provide valuable oversight for homework. To facilitate this, some schools provide "college in the classroom" workshops after school in which the children's teachers instruct parents about the content skills currently taught in the classroom, thus providing parents with the knowledge necessary to be a valuable at-home tutor.

5. Parents can and should be involved in decision making, governance, and advocacy through membership in one or more parent–teacher organizations and committees (e.g., PTA, SEPTA).

6. Parents should be informed by the school about various community support groups that can provide outside resources in support of their child (i.e., child care, health care, and cultural activities).

References

Zaragoza, N. (2002). *Rethinking language arts: Passion and practice.* New York: RoutledgeFalmer.

Zaragoza, N. (2005). Including families in the teaching and learning process. In J. Kincheloe (Ed.), *Classroom teaching: An introduction.* New York: Peter Lang.

REFERENCES

1900–1970, U.S. Public Health Service, *Vital Statistics of the United States,* annual, Vol. I and Vol. II; 1971–2001, U.S. National Center for Health Statistics, *Vital Statistics of the United States,* annual; *National Vital Statistics Report (NVSR;* formerly *Monthly Vital Statistics Report).*

Abella, E., Feliu, E., Granada, I., Milla, F., Oriol, A., Ribera, J., et al. (2002). Bone marrow changes in anorexia nervosa are correlated with the amount of weight loss and not with others clinical findings. *American Journal of Clinical Pathology, 118,* 582–588.

Aber, J. L., Jones, S. M., Brown, J. L., Chaundry, N., & Samples, F. (1998). Resolving conflict creatively: Evaluating the developmental effects of a school-based violence prevention program in neighborhood and classroom contexts. *Developmental Psychopathology, 10,* 187–213.

Abolt, T., & Thyer, B. A. (2003). Social work assessment of children with oppositional defiant disorder: Reliability and validity of the Child Behavior Checklist. *Social Work in Mental Health, 1*(1), 73–84.

Achenbach, T. M. (1991a). *Manual for the Child Behavior Checklist/4-18 and 1991 profile.* Burlington: University of Vermont, Department of Psychiatry.

Achenbach, T. M. (1991b). *Manual for the teachers report form and 1991 profile.* Burlington: University of Vermont, Department of Psychiatry.

Achenbach, T. M. (1991c). *Manual for the youth self-report form and 1991 profile.* Burlington: University of Vermont, Department of Psychiatry.

Achenbach, T. M. (1992). *Manual for the Child Behavior Checklist/2-3 and 1992 profile.* Burlington: University of Vermont, Department of Psychiatry.

Achenbach, T. M. (2001a). *Manual for the Achenbach system of empirically based assessment school-age forms & profiles.* Burlington: University of Vermont, Department of Psychiatry.

Achenbach, T. M. (2001b). *Manual for the Achenbach system of empirically based assessment pre-school forms & profiles.* Burlington: University of Vermont, Department of Psychiatry.

Achenbach, T. M., & Edelbrock, C. S. (1991). *Child Behavior Checklist and Youth Self Report.* Burlington, VT: Author.

Adamson, L. B. (1995). *Communication development during infancy.* Madison, WI: Brown & Benchmark.

Adler, P. A., & Adler, P. (1995). Dynamics of inclusion and exclusion in preadolescent cliques. *School Psychology Quarterly, 58,* 145–162.

Agran, M. (1998). Teaching self-monitoring, self-evaluation, and self-reinforcement strategies. In M. Wehmeyer & D. J. Sands (Eds.), *Making it happen: Student involvement in educational planning, decision making, and instruction* (pp. 355–377). Baltimore: Paul H. Brookes.

Agras, W. (2001). The consequences and costs of the eating disorders. *Psychiatric Clinics of North American, 24,* 371–379.

Agras, W. S., Crow, S. J., Halmi, K. A., Mitchell, J. E., Wilson, G. T., & Kraemer, H. C. (2000). Outcome predictors for the cognitive behavior treatment of bulimia nervosa: Data from a multisite study. *American Journal of Psychiatry, 157*(8), 1302–1308.

Agras, W. S., Schneider, J. A., Arnow, B., Raeburn, S. D., & Telch, C. F. (1989). Cognitive-behavioral and response-prevention treatments for bulimia nervosa. *Journal of Consulting and Clinical Psychology, 57*(2), 215–221.

Agras, W. S., Telch, C. F., Arnow, B., Eldredge, K., Detzer, M. J., Henderson, J., et al. (1995). Does interpersonal therapy help patients with binge eating disorder who fail to respond to cognitive-behavioral therapy? *Journal of Consulting and Clinical Psychology, 63*(3), 356–360.

Ainsworth, M. S., Blehar, M. C., Waters, E., & Wall, S. (1978). *Patterns of attachment: A psychological study of the strange situation.* Oxford, England: Erlbaum.

Albano, A. M., & Hayward, C. (2004). Social anxiety disorder. In T. H. Ollendick & J. S. March (Eds.), *Phobic and anxiety disorders in children and adolescents: A clinician's guide to effective psychosocial and pharmacological interventions* (pp. 198–235). New York: Oxford University Press.

Albano, A. M., Knox, L. S., & Barlow, D. H. (1995). Obsessive-compulsive disorder. In A. R. Eisen, C. A. Kearney, & C. E. Schaefer (Eds.), *Clinical handbook of anxiety disorders in children and adolescents* (pp. 282–316). Lanham, MD: Jason Aronson.

Albano, A. M., Marten, P. A., Holt, C. S., & Heimberg, R. G. (1995). Cognitive-behavioral group treatment for social phobia in adolescents: A preliminary study. *Journal of Nervous and Mental Disease, 183*(10), 649–656.

Alberto, P. A., & Troutman, A. C. (2003). *Applied behavior analysis for teachers* (6th ed.). Upper Saddle River, NJ: Merrill/Prentice Hall.

Alexander, J. F., Robbins, M. S., & Sexton, T. L. (2000). Family-based interventions with older, at-risk youth: From promise to proof to practice. *Journal of Primary Prevention, 21*(2), 185–205.

Alexander, K., & Alexander, M. D. (1992). *American public school law*. St. Paul, MN: West Publishing Company.

Allen, J. P., Philliber, S., Herrling, S., & Kuperminc, G. P. (1997). Preventing teen pregnancy and academic failure: Experimental evaluation of a developmentally based approach. *Child Development, 68*(4), 729–742.

Allen, K. M., Thombs, D. L., Mahoney, C. A., & Daniel, E. L. (1993). Relationships between expectancies and adolescent dieting behaviors. *Journal of School Health, 63,* 176–181.

Aman, M. G., Arnold, L. E., McDougle, C. J., Vitiello, B., Scahill, L., Davies, M., et al. (2005). Acute and long-term safety and tolerability of risperidone in children with autism. *Journal of Child and Adolescent Psychopharmacology, 15*(6), 869–884.

Aman, M. G., Buican, B., & Arnold, L. E. (2003). Methylphenidate treatment in children with borderline IQ and mental retardation: Analysis of three aggregated studies. *Journal of Child and Adolescent Psychopharmacology, 13*(1), 29–40.

Aman, M. G., Collier-Crespin, A., & Lindsay, R. L. (2000). Pharmacotherapy of disorders in mental retardation. *European Child & Adolescent Psychiatry, 9,* I/98–I/107.

Ambrosini, P. J. (2000). Historical development and present status of the Schedule for Affective Disorders and Schizophrenia for School-Age Children (K-SADS). *Journal of the American Academy of Child & Adolescent Psychiatry, 39*(1), 49–58.

Ambrosini, P. J., Wagner, K. D., Biederman, J., Glick, I., Tan, C., Elia, J., et al. (1999). Multicenter open-label sertraline study in adolescent outpatients with major depression. *Journal of the American Academy of Child & Adolescent Psychiatry, 38*(5), 566–572.

American Medical Association. (2005). Featured report: Recommendations for physician and community collaboration on the management of obesity (A-05).

Retrieved February 5, 2008, from http://www.ama-assn.org/ama/pub/category/15495.html

American Psychiatric Association Steering Committee on Practice Guidelines. (2000). *American Psychiatric Association practice guidelines for the treatment of psychiatric disorders: Compendium 2000.* Washington, DC: American Psychiatric Association.

American Psychiatric Association. (1994). *Diagnostic and statistical manual of mental disorders* (4th ed.). Washington, DC: Author.

American Psychiatric Association. (1996). *Practice guidelines*. Washington, DC: Author.

American Psychiatric Association. (2000). *Diagnostic and statistical manual of mental disorders* (text rev.). Washington, DC: Author.

Andersen, A. E., Bowers, W., & Evans, K. (1997). Inpatient treatment of anorexia nervosa. In D. M. Garner & P. E. Garfinkel (Eds.), *Handbook of treatment for eating disorders* (2nd ed., pp. 327–353). New York: Guilford Press.

Anderson, D. A., & Maloney, K. C. (2001). The efficacy of cognitive-behavioral therapy on the core symptoms of bulimia nervosa. *Clinical Psychology Review, 21*(7), 971–988.

Anderson, G. M., & Hoshino, Y. (2005). Neurochemical studies of autism. In F. R. Volkmar, R. Paul, A. Klin, & D. Cohen (Eds.), *Handbook of autism and pervasive developmental disorders: Vol. 1. Diagnosis, development, neurobiology, and behavior* (3rd ed., pp. 453–472). Hoboken, NJ: John Wiley & Sons, Inc.

Anderson, R. N., & Smith, B. L. (2003). Death: Leading causes for 2001. *National Vital Statistics Report, 52*(9), 1–19.

Andrews, G., Stewart, G., Allen, R., & Henderson, A. S. (1990). The genetics of six neurotic disorders: A twin study. *Journal of Affective Disorders, 19*(1), 23–29.

Angold, A., & Costello, E. J. (1993). Depressive comorbidity in children and adolescents: Empirical, theoretical, and methodological issues. *American Journal of Psychiatry, 150*(12), 1779–1791.

Angold, A., & Costello, E. J. (1996). The relative diagnostic utility of child and parent reports of oppositional defiant behaviors. *International Journal of Methods in Psychiatric Research, 6*(4), 253–259.

Angold, A., & Costello, E. J. (2000). The Child and Adolescent Psychiatric Assessment (CAPA). *Journal of the American Academy of Child & Adolescent Psychiatry, 39*(1), 39–48.

Anzai, N., Lindsey-Dudley, K., & Bidwell, R. J. (2002). Inpatient and partial hospital treatment for adolescent eating disorders. *Child and Adolescent Psychiatric Clinics of North America, 11*(2), 279–309.

Arick, J. R., Krug, D. A., Fullerton, A., Loos, L., & Falco, R. (2005). School-based programs. In F. R. Volkmar, R. Paul, A. Klin, & D. Cohen (Eds.), *Handbook of autism and pervasive developmental disorders: Vol. 2. Assessment, interventions, and policy* (3rd ed., pp. 1003–1028). Hoboken, NJ: John Wiley & Sons, Inc.

Arnette, J. L., & Walsleben, M. C. (1998, April). Combating fear and restoring safety in schools. *Juvenile Justice Bulletin.* Retrieved November 19, 2008, from http://www.ojjdp.ncjrs.org/jjbulletin/9804/contents.html

Arroyo, W., & Eth, S. (1995). Assessment following violence-witnessing trauma. In E. Peled, P. G. Jaffe, & J. L. Edleson (Eds.), *Ending the cycle of violence: Community responses to children of battered women* (pp. 27–42). Thousand Oaks, CA: Sage.

Arthur, R., & Erickson, E. (1992). *Gangs and schools.* Holmes Beach, FL: Learning Publications. (ERIC Document Reproduction Service No. ED358204)

Artiles, A., & Harry. B. (2006). Issues of overrepresentation and educational equity for culturally and linguistically diverse students. *Intervention in School and Clinic, 41*(4), 228–232.

Asarnow, J. R., & Carlson, G. A. (1988). Childhood depression: Five-year outcome following combined cognitive-behavior therapy and pharmacotherapy. *American Journal of Psychotherapy, 42*(3), 456–464.

Astone, N. M., & McLanahan, S. S. (1991). Family structure, parental practices and high school completion. *American Sociological Review, 56*(3), 309–320.

Atlas, R. S., & Pepler, D. J. (1998). Observations of bullying in the classroom. *Journal of Educational Research, 92*(2), 86–99.

Attia, E., Mayer, L., & Killory, E. (2001). Medication response in the treatment of patients with anorexia nervosa. *Journal of Psychiatric Practice, 7*(3), 157–162.

Attwood, T. (1997). *Asperger's syndrome: A guide for parents and professionals.* London: Jessica Kingsley.

August, G. J., Lee, S. S., Bloomquist, M. L., Realmuto, G. M., & Hektner, J. M. (2004). Maintenance effects of an evidence-based prevention innovation for aggressive children living in culturally diverse urban neighborhoods: The Early Risers effectiveness study. *Journal of Emotional and Behavioral Disorders, 12*(4), 194–205.

August, G. J., Realmuto, G. M., Hektner, J. M., & Bloomquist, M. L. (2001). An integrated components preventive intervention for aggressive elementary school children: The Early Risers program. *Journal of Consulting and Clinical Psychology, 69*(4), 614–626.

Austin, V. L. (2001). Teachers' beliefs about co-teaching. *Remedial and Special Education (2001), 22*(4), 245–255.

Austin, V. L. (2003a). Fear and loathing in the classroom: A candid look at school violence and the policies and practices that address it. *Journal of Disability Policy Studies, 14*(1), 17–22.

Austin, V. L. (2003b). Pharmacological interventions for students with ADD. *Intervention in School and Clinic, 38*(5), 289–296.

Avis, H. (1990). *Drugs and life.* Dubuque, IA: Brown.

Bacaltchuk, J., Hay, P., & Mari, J. J. (2000). Antidepressants versus placebo for the treatment of bulimia nervosa: A systematic review. *Australian and New Zealand Journal of Psychiatry, 34*(2), 310–317.

Bacon, A. L., Fein, D., Morris, R., Waterhouse, L., & Allen, D. (1998). The responses of autistic children to the distress of others. *Journal of Autism and Developmental Disorders, 28*(2), 129–142.

Bai, M. (1999, May 3). Anatomy of a massacre. *Newsweek,* 24–31.

Bailer, U., & Kaye, W. (2003). A review of neuropeptide and neuroendocrine dysregulation in anorexia and bulimia nervosa. *Current Drug Targets—CNS and Neurological Disorders, 2,* 53–59.

Bailey, A., Le Couteur, A., Gottesman, I., & Bolton, P. (1995). Autism as a strongly genetic disorder: Evidence from a British twin study. *Psychological Medicine, 25*(1), 63–77.

Bailey, A., Luthert, P., Bolton, P., Le Couteur, A., & Rutter, M. (1993). Autism and megalencephaly. *Lancet, 34,* 1225–1226.

Baker, P. H. (2005). Managing student behavior: How ready are teachers to meet the challenge? *American Secondary Education, 33*(3), 51–64.

Bandura, A. (1973). *Aggression: A social learning analysis.* Oxford, England: Prentice Hall.

Bandura, A. (1977). *Social learning theory.* New York: General Learning Press.

Bandura, A. (1986). *Social foundations of thought and action: A social cognitive theory.* Englewood Cliffs, NJ: Prentice Hall.

Bandura, A., Blanchard, E. B., & Ritter, B. (1969). Relative efficacy of desensitization and modeling approaches for inducing behavioral, affective, and attitudinal changes. *Journal of Personality and Social Psychology, 13*(3), 173–199.

Bandura, A., & Menlove, F. L. (1968). Factors determining vicarious extinction of avoidance behavior through symbolic modeling. *Journal of Personality and Social Psychology, 8*(2), 99–108.

Barabasz, A. F. (1973). Group desensitization of test anxiety in elementary school. *Journal of Psychology: Interdisciplinary and Applied, 83*(2), 295–301.

Barkley, R. A. (2003). Issues in the diagnosis of attention-deficit/hyperactivity disorder in children. *Brain and Development, 25*(2), 77–83.

Barkley, R. A., DuPaul, G. J., & McMurray, M. B. (1990). A comprehensive evaluation of attention deficit disorder with and without hyperactivity as defined by research criteria. *Journal of Consulting and Clinical Psychology, 58,* 775–789.

Barkley, R. A., & Murphy, K. R. (1998). *Attention-deficit hyperactivity disorder: A clinical workbook.* New York: Guilford.

Barlow, D., & Durand, V. (2005). *Abnormal psychology: An integrative approach* (4th ed). Belmont, CA: Wadsworth.

Barnhill, G. P. (2005). Functional behavioral assessment in schools. *Intervention in School and Clinic, 40*(3), 131–144.

Baron-Cohen, S., Leslie, A. M., & Frith, U. (1986). Mechanical, behavioural and intentional understanding of picture stories in autistic children. *British Journal of Developmental Psychology, 4*(2), 113–125.

Baron-Cohen, S., Ring, H. A., Wheelwright. S., Bullmore, E. T., Brammer, M. J., Simmons, A., et al. (1999). Social intelligence in the normal and autistic brain: An fMRI study. *European Journal of Neuroscience, 11,* 1891–1898.

Barrett, P., Dadds, M., & Rapee, R. (1996). Family treatment of childhood anxiety: A controlled study. *Journal of Consulting and Clinical Psychology, 64,* 333–342.

Barrett, P. M. (1998). Evaluation of cognitive-behavioral group treatments for childhood anxiety disorders. *Journal of Clinical Child Psychology, 27*(4), 459–468.

Barrett, P. M., Rapee, R. M., Dadds, M. M., & Ryan, S. M. (1996). Family enhancement of cognitive style in anxious and aggressive children. *Journal of Abnormal Child Psychology, 24*(2), 187–203.

Barrios, B. A., & Hartmann, D. P. (1997). Fears and anxieties. In E. J. Mash & L. G. Terdal (Eds.), *Assessment of childhood disorders* (3rd ed., pp. 230–327). New York: Guilford Press.

Barth, R. P., Fetro, J. V., Leland, N., & Volkan, K. (1992). Preventing adolescent pregnancy with social

and cognitive skills. *Journal of Adolescent Research, 7*(2), 208–232.

Battin, S. R., Hill, K. G., Abbott, R. D., Catalano, R. F., & Hawkins, J. D. (1998). The contribution of gang membership to delinquency beyond delinquent friends. *Criminology, 36,* 93–115.

Bauer, A. M. (1987). A teacher's introduction to childhood depression. *Clearing House, 61,* 81–84.

Bauman, M. L., & Kemper, T. L. (1997). Is autism a progressive process? *Neurology, 48*(Suppl. 2), A285.

Beardslee, W. R., Versage, E. M., & Gladstone, T. R. G. (1998). Children of affectively ill parents: A review of the past 10 years. *Journal of the American Academy of Child & Adolescent Psychiatry, 37*(11), 1134–1141.

Beck, A. T. (1967). *Depression.* New York: Harper & Row.

Beck, A. T., Rush, A. G., Shaw, B. F., & Emery, G. (1979). *Cognitive therapy for depression.* New York: Guilford Press.

Beck, A. T., & Steer, R. A. (1993). *Beck Depression Inventory.* San Antonio, TX: Psychological Corporation.

Beck, A. T., Ward, C. H., Mendelson, M., Mock, J., & Erbaugh, J. (1961). An inventory for measuring depression. *Archives of General Psychiatry, 4,* 561–571.

Becker-Lausen, E., & Rickel, A. U. (1995). Integration of teen pregnancy and child abuse research: Identifying mediator variables for pregnancy outcome. *Journal of Primary Prevention, 16*(8), 39–53.

Behan, J., & Carr, A. (2000). Oppositional defiant disorder. In A. Carr (Ed.), *What works with children and adolescents?: A critical review of psychological interventions with children, adolescents and their families* (pp. 102–130). Florence, KY: Taylor & Frances/Routledge.

Beidel, D. C., Morris, T. L., & Turner, M. W. (2004). Social phobia. In J. S. March (Ed.), *Anxiety disorders in children and adolescents* (2nd ed., pp. 141–163). New York: Guilford Press.

Beidel, D. C., & Turner, S. M. (1988). Comorbidity of test anxiety and other anxiety disorders in children. *Journal of Abnormal Child Psychology, 16*(3), 275–287.

Beidel, D. C., Turner, S. M., & Morris, T. L. (1999). Psychopathology of childhood social phobia. *Journal of the American Academy of Child & Adolescent Psychiatry, 38*(6), 643–650.

Beidel, D. C., Turner, S. M., & Morris, T. L. (2000). Behavioral treatment of childhood social phobia. *Journal of Consulting and Clinical Psychology, 68*(6), 1072–1080.

Bender, W. N. (1997). *Understanding ADHD: A practical guide for teachers and parents.* Upper Saddle River, NJ: Merrill.

Ben-Tovim, B., Walker, K., Gilchrist, P., Freeman, R., Kalucy, R., & Esterman, A. (2001). Outcome in patients with eating disorders: A five-year study. *Lancet, 357,* 1254–1257.

Berghold, K. M., & Lock, J. (2002). Assessing guilt in adolescents with anorexia nervosa. *American Journal of Psychotherapy, 56*(3), 378–390.

Bernal, M. E., Klinnert, M. D., & Schultz, L. A. (1980). Outcome evaluation of behavioral parent training and client-centered parent counseling for children with conduct problems. *Journal of Applied Behavior Analysis, 13*(4), 677–691.

Bernard, S., Enayati, A., Redwood, L., Roger, H., & Binstock, T. (2001). Autism: A novel form of mercury poisoning. *Medical Hypotheses, 56,* 462–471.

Bernstein, G. A., Borchardt, C. M., Perwien, A. R., Crosby, R. D., Kushner, M. G., Thuras, P. D., et al. (2000). Imipramine plus cognitive-behavioral therapy in the treatment of school refusal. *Journal of the American Academy of Child & Adolescent Psychiatry, 39*(3), 276–283.

Bernstein, G. A., Crosby, R. D., Perwien, A. R., & Borchardt, C. M. (1996). Anxiety Rating for Children—Revised: Reliability and validity. *Journal of Anxiety Disorders, 10*(2), 97–114.

Biederman, J., Faraone, S. V., & Lapey, K. (1992). Comorbidity of diagnosis in attention-deficit hyperactivity disorder. In G. Weiss (Ed.), *Child and adolescent psychiatric clinics of North America: Attention-deficit hyperactivity disorder* (pp. 335–360). Philadelphia: Saunders.

Biederman, J., Faraone, S. V., Milberger, S., & Jetton, J. G. (1996). Is childhood oppositional defiant disorder a precursor to adolescent conduct disorder? Findings from a four-year follow-up study of children with ADHD. *Journal of the American Academy of Child & Adolescent Psychiatry, 35*(9), 1193–1204.

Biederman, J., Faraone, S., Mick, E., & Moore, P. (1996). Child Behavior Checklist findings further support comorbidity between ADHD and major depression in a referred sample. *Journal of the American Academy of Child & Adolescent Psychiatry, 35*(6), 734–742.

Biederman, J., Rosenbaum, J. F., Bolduc-Murphy, E. A., & Faraone, S. V. (1993). A 3-year follow-up of children with and without behavioral inhibition. *Journal of the American Academy of Child & Adolescent Psychiatry, 32*(4), 814–821.

Biederman, J., Rosenbaum, J. F., Chaloff, J., & Kagan, J. (1995). Behavioral inhibition as a risk factor for anxiety disorders. In J. S. March (Ed.), *Anxiety disorders in children and adolescents* (pp. 61–81). New York: Guilford Press.

Biederman, J., Rosenbaum, J. F., Hirshfeld, D. R., & Faraone, S. V. (1990). Psychiatric correlates of behavioral inhibition in young children of parents with and without psychiatric disorders. *Archives of General Psychiatry, 47*(1), 21–26.

Bird, H. R., Gould, M. S., Yager, T., & Staghezza, B. & Canino (1989). Risk factors for maladjustment in Puerto Rican children. *Journal of the American Academy of Child & Adolescent Psychiatry, 28*(6), 847–850.

Birmaher, B., Bridge, J. A., Williamson, D. E., Brent, D. A., Dahl, R. E., Axelson, D. A., et al. (2004). Psychosocial functioning in youths at high risk to develop major depressive disorder. *Journal of the American Academy of Child & Adolescent Psychiatry, 43*(7), 839–846.

Birmaher, B., Khetarpal, S., Brent, D., & Cully, M. (1997). The Screen for Child Anxiety Related Emotional Disorders (SCARED): Scale construction and psychometric characteristics. *Journal of the American Academy of Child & Adolescent Psychiatry, 36*(4), 545–553.

Birmaher, B., Ryan, N. D., Williamson, D. E., & Brent, D. A. (1996). Childhood and adolescent depression: A review of the past 10 years, Part I. *Journal of the American Academy of Child & Adolescent Psychiatry, 35*(11), 1427–1439.

Birmaher, B., Waterman, G. S., Ryan, N., & Cully, M. (1994). Fluoxetine for childhood anxiety disorders. *Journal of the American Academy of Child & Adolescent Psychiatry, 33*(7), 993–999.

Blake, C., Wang, W., Cartledge, G., & Gardner, R. (2000). Middle school students with serious emotional disturbances serve as social skills trainers and reinforcers for peers with SED. *Behavioral Disorders, 25,* 280–298.

Boddaert, N., Belin, P., Chabane, N., Poline, J. B., Barthélémy, C., Mouren-Simeoni, M. C., et al. (2003). Perception of complex sounds: Abnormal pattern of cortical activation in autism. *American Journal of Psychiatry, 160*(11), 2057–2060.

Bodfish, J. W., Symons, F. J., Parker, D. E., & Lewis, M. H. (2000). Varieties of repetitive behavior in autism: Comparisons to mental retardation. *Journal of Autism and Developmental Disorders, 30*(3), 237–243.

Bodinger-deUriarte, C. (1993). *Membership in violent gangs fed by suspicion, deterred through respect.* Los Alamitos, CA: Southwest Regional Educational Laboratory. (ERIC Document Reproduction Service No. ED358399)

Boer, F. (1998). Anxiety disorders in the family: The contribution of heredity and family interactions. In P. D. A. Treffers (Ed.), *Emotional disorders and somatoform disorders in children and adolescents: The current state of research* (pp. 109–114). Leiden, Netherlands: Boerhaave Comissie.

Bogren, L. Y. (1986). The couvade syndrome. *International Journal of Family Psychiatry, 7*(2), 123–136.

Bolton, P., Macdonald, H., Pickles, A., & Rios, P. (1994). A case-control family history study of autism. *Journal of Child Psychology and Psychiatry, 35*(5), 877–900.

Bolton, P. F., Murphy, M., Macdonald, H., & Whitlock, B. (1997). Obstetric complications in autism: Consequences or causes of the condition? *Journal of the American Academy of Child & Adolescent Psychiatry, 36*(2), 272–281.

Borduin, C. M., Henggeler, S. W., Blaske, D. M., & Stein, R. J. (1990). Multisystemic treatment of adolescent sexual offenders. *International Journal of Offender Therapy and Comparative Criminology, 34*(2), 105–113.

Borduin, C. M., Mann, B. J., Cone, L. T., Henggeler, S. W., Fucci, B. R., Blaske, D. M., et al. (1995). Multisystemic treatment of serious juvenile offenders: Long-term prevention of criminality and violence. *Journal of Consulting and Clinical Psychology, 63*(4), 569–578.

Borduin, C. M., Schaeffer, C. M., & Ronis, S. T. (2003). Multisystemic treatment of serious antisocial behavior in adolescents. In C. A. Essau (Ed.), *Conduct and oppositional defiant disorders: Epidemiology, risk factors, and treatment* (pp. 299–318). Mahwah, NJ: Erlbaum.

Borduin, C. M., & Schaeffer, C. M. (2001). Multisystemic treatment of juvenile sex offenders. A progress report. *Journal of Psychology & Human Sexuality, 13*, 25–42.

Botvin, G. J. (1986). Substance abuse prevention efforts: Recent developments and future directions. *Journal of School Health, 56*, 369–374.

Bower, B. (2003). ADHD's brain trail: Cerebral clues emerge for attention disorder. *Science News Online.* Retrieved March 10, 2008, from http://www.sciencenews.org/20031129/fob1.asp

Bowers, W. A. (2001). Basic principles for applying cognitive-behavioral therapy in anorexia nervosa. *Psychiatric Clinics of North America, 24*(2), 293–303.

Bowers, W. A., & Andersen, A. E. (2007). Cognitive-behavior therapy with eating disorders: The role of medication in treatment. *Journal of Cognitive Psychology, 21*, 16–27.

Bowlby, J. (1969). Disruption of affectional bonds and its effects on behavior. *Canada's Mental Health Supplement, 59*, 1–12.

Boyle, K. (1992). *School's a rough place: Youth gangs, drug users, and family life in Los Angeles.* Washington, DC: Department of Education, Office of Educational Research and Improvement. (ERIC Document Reproduction Service No. ED360435)

Boyles, M. H., & Pickles, A. R. (1998). Strategies to manipulate reliability: Impact on statistical associations. *Journal of the American Academy of Child and Adolescent Psychiatry, 37*(10), 1077–1084.

Braddock, D. (Ed.). (1999). *Positive behavior support for people with developmental disabilities: A research synthesis.* Washington, DC: American Association on Mental Retardation.

Bradley, D. F. (1988). Alcohol and drug education in the elementary school. *Elementary School Guidance & Counseling, 23*(2), 99–105.

Bradley, L. J., Jarchow, E., & Robinson, B. (1999). *All about sex: The school counselor's role to handling tough adolescent problems.* Thousand Oaks, CA: Corwin Press.

Bradley, M. C., & Mandell, D. (2005). Oppositional defiant disorder: A systematic review of evidence of intervention effectiveness. *Journal of Experimental Criminology, 1*(3), 343–365.

Bradlyn, A. S. (1982). *The effects of a videotape preparation package in reducing children's arousal and increasing cooperation during cardiac catheterization.* Unpublished doctoral dissertation, University of Mississippi.

Brady, E. U., & Kendall, P. C. (1992). Comorbidity of anxiety and depression in children and adolescents. *Psychological Bulletin, 111*(2), 244–255.

Breiner, S. (2003). An evidence-based eating disorder program. *Journal of Pediatric Nursing, 18*, 75–80.

Brent, D. A., Perper, J. A., Moritz, G., & Liotus, L. (1995). Posttraumatic stress disorder in peers of adolescent suicide victims: Predisposing factors and phenomenology. *Journal of the American Academy of Child & Adolescent Psychiatry, 34*(2), 209–215.

Brent, D. A., Roth, C. M., & Holder, D. P. (1996). Psychosocial interventions for treating adolescent suicidal depression: A comparison of three psychosocial interventions. In D. J. Kolko, E. D. Hibbs, & P. S. Jensen (Eds.), *Psychosocial treatments for child and adolescent disorders: Empirically based strategies for clinical practice* (pp. 187–206). Washington, DC: American Psychological Association.

Brestan, E. V., & Eyberg, S. M. (1998). Effective psychosocial treatments of conduct-disordered children and adolescents: 29 years, 82 studies, and 5,272 kids. *Journal of Clinical Child Psychology, 27*(2), 180–189.

Breton, J. J., Bergeron, L., Valla, J. P., Berthiaume, C., Gaudet, N., Lambert, J., et al. (1999). Quebec Child Mental Health Survey: Prevalence of *DSM-III—R* mental health disorders. *Journal of Child Psychology and Psychiatry, 40*(3), 375–384.

Brewerton, T. D. (1995). Toward a unified theory of serotonin dysregulation in eating and related disorders. *Psychoneuroendocrinology, 20*(6), 561–590.

Brewster, K. L., Billy, J. O., & Grady, W. R. (1993). Social context and adolescent behavior: The impact of community on the transition to sexual activity. *Social Forces, 71*(3), 713–740.

Bridge, J. A., Iyengar, S., Salary, C. B., Barbe, R. P., Birmaher, B., Pincus, H. A., et al. (2007). Clinical response and risk for reported suicidal ideation and suicide attempts in pediatric antidepressant treatment: A meta-analysis of randomized controlled trials. *Journal of the American Medical Association, 297,* 1683–1696.

Briggs-Gowan, M. J., Horwitz, S. M., Schwab-Stone, M. E., Leventhal, J. M., & Leaf, P. J. (2000). Mental health in pediatric settings: Distribution of disorders and factors related to service use. *Journal of the American Academy of Child & Adolescent Psychiatry, 39*(7), 841–849.

Brower, M. C., & Price, B. H. (2001). Neuropsychiatry of frontal lobe dysfunction in violent and criminal behavior: A critical review. *Journal of Neurology, Neurosurgery and Psychiatry, 71,* 720–726.

Brown, M. B. (2000). Diagnosis and treatment of children and adolescents with attention-deficit/hyperactivity disorder. *Journal of Counseling and Development, 78*(2), 195–203.

Brown, T. E. (1996). *Brown Attention Deficit Disorder Scales manual.* San Antonio, CA: Psychological Corporation.

Brown, T. L., Henggeler, S. W., Schoenwald, S. K., Brondino, M. J., & Pickrel, S. G. (1999). Multisystemic treatment of substance abusing and dependent juvenile delinquents: Effects on school attendance at posttreatment and 6-month follow-up. *Children's Services: Social Policy, Research, & Practice, 2*(2), 81–93.

Brown University Child and Adolescent Behavior Letter (April 2005). Is your child being bullied? Tips for parents, 21(s4), 9–10. DOI: 10.1002/cbl.20502111. Wiley Periodicals.

Bruch, M. A., & Heimberg, R. G. (1994). Differences in perceptions of parental and personal characteristics between generalized and nongeneralized social phobics. *Journal of Anxiety Disorders, 8*(2), 155–168.

Bruner, J., & Feldman, C. (1993). Theories of mind and the problem of autism. In S. Baron-Cohen, H. Tager-Flusberg, & D. J. Cohen (Eds.), *Understanding other minds: Perspectives from autism.* Oxford, England: Oxford University Press.

Brunner, R. L., Maloney, M. J., Daniels, S., & Mays, W. (1989). A controlled study of Type A behavior and psychophysiologic responses to stress in anorexia nervosa. *Psychiatry Research, 30*(2), 223–230.

Buck, G. H., Polloway, E. A., Kirkpatrick, M. A., Patton, J. R., McConnell Fad, K. (2000). Developing behavioral intervention plans: A sequential approach. *Intervention in School and Clinic, 36*(1), 3. Retrieved March 5, 2008, from Wilson Education Abstracts database. (Document ID No. 59160207)

Buck, R. (2000). Conceptualizing motivation and emotion. *The Behavioral and Brain Sciences, 23*(2), 195–203.

Buggey, T., Toombs, K., Gardener, P., & Cervetti, M. (1999). Training responding behaviors in students with autism: Using videotaped self-modeling. *Journal of Positive Behavior Interventions, 1*(4), 205–214.

Buitelaar, J. K., van Engeland, H., van Ree, J. M., & de Wied, D. (1990). Behavioral effects of Org 2766, a synthetic analog of the adrenocorticotrophic hormone (4–9), in 14 outpatient autistic children. *Journal of Autism and Developmental Disorders, 20*(4), 467–478.

Bulik, C. M. (2002). Eating disorders in adolescents and young adults. *Child and Adolescent Psychiatric Clinics of North America, 11*(2), 201–218.

Bulik, C. M. (2004). Genetic and biological risk factors. In J. K. Thompson (Ed.), *Handbook of eating disorders and obesity* (pp. 3–16). Hoboken, NJ: John Wiley & Sons, Inc..

Bulik, C. M., Sullivan, P. F., Carter, F. A., McIntosh, V. V., & Joyce, P. R. (1998). The role of exposure with response prevention in the cognitive-behavioural therapy for bulimia nervosa. *Psychological Medicine, 28*(3), 611–623.

Bulik, C., Sullivan, P., Wade, T., & Kendler, K. (2000). Twin studies of eating disorders: A review. *International Journal of Eating Disorders, 27,* 1–20.

Burke, J. D., Loeber, R., & Birmaher, B. (2002). Oppositional defiant disorder and conduct disorder: A review of the past 10 years, part II. *Journal of the American Child and Adolescent Psychiatry, 41,* 1275–1293.

Burns, M. K., Dean, V. J., & Jacob-Timm, S. (2001). Assessment of violence potential among school children: Beyond profiling. *Psychology in Schools, 38,* 239–246.

Burt, S. A., Krueger, R. F., McGue, M., & Iacono, W. G. (2001). Sources of covariation among attention-deficit/hyperactivity disorder, oppositional defiant disorder, and conduct disorder: The importance of shared environment. *Journal of Abnormal Psychology, 110*(4), 516–525.

Campbell, M., Adams, P. B., Small, A. M., & Kafantaris, V. (1995). Lithium in hospitalized aggressive children with conduct disorder: A double-blind and placebo-controlled study. *Journal of the American Academy of Child & Adolescent Psychiatry, 34*(4), 445–453.

Campbell, S. B. (1995). Behavior problems in preschool children: A recent review of the research. *Journal of Child Psychology, 36,* 113–149.

Canino, G., Shrout, P. E., Rubio-Stipec, M., Bird, H. R., Bravo, M., Ramirez, R., et al. (2004). The *DSM-IV* rates of child and adolescent disorders in Puerto Rico. *Archives of General Psychiatry, 61*(1), 85–93.

Cantwell, D. P., & Baker, L. (1989). Stability and natural history of *DSM-III* childhood diagnoses. *Journal of the American Academy of Child & Adolescent Psychiatry, 28*(5), 691–700.

Capaldi, D. M., & Paterson, G. R. (1996). Can violent offenders be distinguished from frequent offenders? Prediction from childhood to adolescence. *Journal of Research in Crime and Delinquency, 33,* 206–231.

Caplan, R., Guthrie, D., Shields, W. D., & Yudovin, S. (1994). Communication deficits in pediatric complex partial seizure disorder and schizophrenia. *Development and Psychopathology, 6*(3), 499–517.

Capps, L., Losh, M., & Thurber, C. (2000). "The frog ate the bug and made his mouth sad": Narrative competence in children with autism. *Journal of Abnormal Child Psychology, 28*(2), 193–204.

Caputo, A. A., Frick, P. J., & Brodscky, S. L (1999). Family violence and juvenile sex offending: Potential mediating roles of psychopathic traits and negative attitudes toward women. *Criminal Justice and Behavior, 26,* 338–356.

Capuzzi, D., & Gross, D. R. (2000). I don't want to live: The adolescent at risk for suicidal behavior. In D. Capuzzi & D. R. Gross (Eds.), *Youth risk: A prevention resource for counselors, teachers, and parents* (3rd ed., pp. 319–352). Alexandria, VA: American Counseling Association.

Carey, G. (1990). Genes, fears, phobias, and phobic disorders. *Journal of Counseling & Development, 68*(6), 628–632.

Carlson, G. A., & Abbott, S. F. (1995). Mood disorders and suicide. In H. I. Caplan & B. J. Sadock (Eds.), *Comprehensive textbook of psychiatry* (4th ed., pp. 2367–2391). Baltimore, MD: Williams & Wilkins.

Carney, J. V. (2000). Bullied to death: Perceptions of peer abuse and suicidal behaviour during adolescence. *School Psychology International, 21*(2), 213–223.

Carper, R. A., Moses, P., Tigue, Z. D., & Courchesne, E. (2002). Cerebral lobes in autism. Early hyperplasia and abnormal age effects. *Neuroimage, 16,* 1038–1051.

Carrion, V. G., & Steiner, H. (2000). Trauma and dissociation in delinquent adolescents. *Journal of the American Academy of Child & Adolescent Psychiatry, 39*(3), 353–359.

Carrion, V. G., Weems, C. F., Ray, R., & Reiss, A. L. (2002). Toward an empirical definition of pediatric PTSD: The phenomenology of PTSD symptoms in youth. *Journal of the American Academy of Child & Adolescent Psychiatry, 41*(2), 166–173.

Carter, A. S., Davis, N. O., & Klin, A. (2005). Social development in autism. In F. R. Volkmar, R. Paul, A. Klin, & D. Cohen (Eds.), *Handbook of autism and pervasive developmental disorders: Vol. 1. Diagnosis, development, neurobiology, and behavior* (3rd ed., pp. 312–334). Hoboken, NJ: John Wiley & Sons, Inc.

Carter, A. S., Ornstein-Davis, N., Klin, A., & Volkmar, F. R. (2005). Social development in autism. In F. R. Volkmar, R. Paul, A. Klin, & D. Cohen (Eds.), *Handbook of autism and pervasive developmental disorders: Vol. 1. Diagnosis, development, neurobiology, and behavior* (3rd ed., pp. 312–334). Hoboken, NJ: John Wiley & Sons, Inc.

Carter, F. A., McIntosh, V. V. W., Joyce, P. R., Sullivan, P. F., & Bulik, C. M. (2003). Role of exposure with response prevention in cognitive-behavioral therapy for bulimia nervosa: Three-year follow-up results.

International Journal of Eating Disorders, 33(2), 127–135.

Cash, T. F. (1994). Body-image attitudes: Evaluation, investment, and affect. *Perceptual and Motor Skills, 78*(3), 1168–1170.

Casper, R. C. (2002). How useful are pharmacological treatments in eating disorders? *Psychopharmacology Bulletin, 36,* 88–104.

Casper, R. C., & Troiani, M. (2001). Family functioning in anorexia nervosa differs by subtype. *International Journal of Eating Disorders, 30*(3), 338–342.

Cassidy, J. (1995). Attachment and generalized anxiety disorder. In D. Cicchetti & S. L. Toth (Eds.), *Emotion, cognition, and representation* (pp. 343–370). Rochester, NY: University of Rochester Press.

Castellanos, F. X., Giedd, J. N., Eckburg, P., Marsh, W. L. (1994). Quantitative morphology of the caudate nucleus in attention deficit hyperactivity disorder. *The American Journal of Psychiatry, 151*(12), 1791–1796.

Castellanos. F. X., & Swanson. J. (2002). Biological underpinnings of ADHD. In S. Sandberg (Ed.), *Hyperactivity and attention disorders of childhood* (2nd ed., pp. 336–366). Cambridge, England: Cambridge University Press.

Castelli, F., Frith, C., Happé, F., & Frith, U. (2002). Autism, Asperger syndrome and brain mechanisms for the attribution of mental states to animated shapes. *Brain: A Journal of Neurology, 125*(8), 1839–1849.

Caster, J. B., Inderbitzen, H. M., & Hope, D. (1999). Relationship between youth and parent perceptions of family environment and social anxiety. *Journal of Anxiety Disorders, 13,* 237–251.

Catalano, R. F., Hawkins, J. D., Kosterman, R., Abbott, R. D., & Hill, K. G. (1998). *Long term effects of the Seattle Social Development Project: Implications for theory and practice.* Paper presented at the annual meeting of the Society for Research on Adolescence, San Diego, CA.

Cautela, J., Cautela, J., & Esonis, S. (1983). *Forms for behavior analysis with children.* Champaign, IL: Research Press.

Cavin, C. (1998). Maintaining sanity in an insane classroom: How a teacher of students with emotional disturbances can keep from becoming an emotionally disturbed teacher. *Education & Treatment of Children, 21*(3), 370–384.

Center for the Prevention of School Violence. (2000). *Stats 2000: Selected school violence research findings.* Available at http://www.cpsv.org

Centers for Disease Control. (2005). *Trends in reportable sexually transmitted diseases.* Atlanta, GA: Author.

CHADD Fact Sheet No. 3. (2000). *Medical management of children and adults with AD/HD.* Retrieved April 24, 2002, from http://63.102.85.98/fs/fs3.htm

CHADD.org (2008). Home page. Retrieved March 4, 2008, from http://www.chadd.org/content/CHADD/understanding/researchstudies/defaulthtm

Chamberlain, L. L. (1995). Strange attractors in patterns of family interaction. In R. Robertson & A. Combs (Eds.), *Chaos theory in psychology and life sciences.* Hillsdale, NJ: Erlbaum.

Chamberlain, P., & Patterson, G. R. (1995). Discipline and child compliance in parenting. In M. H. Bornstein (Ed.), *Handbook of parenting: Vol. 4. Applied and practical parenting* (pp. 205–225). Hillsdale, NJ: Erlbaum.

Charlop, M. H., Burgio, L. D., Iwata, B. A., & Ivancic, M. T. (1988). Stimulus variation as a means of enhancing punishment effects. *Journal of Applied Behavior Analysis, 21*(1), 89–95.

Charlop-Christy, M. H., & Carpenter, M. H. (2000). Modified incidental teaching sessions: A procedure for parents to increase spontaneous speech in their children with autism. *Journal of Positive Behavior Interventions, 2*(2), 98–112.

Charlop-Christy, M. H., Le, L., & Freeman, K. A. (2000). A comparison of video modeling with in vivo modeling for teaching children with autism. *Journal of Autism and Developmental Disorders, 30*(6), 537–552.

Chartier, M. J., Walker, J. R., & Stein, M. B. (2001). Social phobia and potential childhood risk factors in a community sample. *Psychological Medicine, 31*(2), 307–315.

Chatfield, J. (2002). AAP guideline on treatment of children with ADHD. *American Family Physician, 65,* 726–728.

Chemtob, C., Hamada, R., & Nakashima, J. (1996). *Psychosocial intervention for post-disaster trauma symptoms in elementary school children: A controlled field study.* Unpublished manuscript, University of Hawaii.

Chemtob, C., Nakashima, J., & Carlson, J. (2002). Brief treatment for elementary school children with disaster-related posttraumatic stress disorder. A field study. *Journal of Clinical Psychology, 58,* 99–112.

Chen, N. C., Bedair, H. S., McKay, B., Bowers, M. B., Jr., & Mazure, C. (2001). Clozapine in the treatment of aggression in an adolescent with autistic disorder. *Journal of Clinical Psychiatry, 62*(6), 479–480.

Chilcoat, H. D., & Breslau, N. (1998). Investigations of causal pathways between PTSD and drug use disorders. *Addictive Behaviors, 23*(6), 827–840.

Christensen, A., Johnson, S. M., Phillips, S., & Glasgow, R. E. (1980). Cost effectiveness in behavioral family therapy. *Behavior Therapy, 11*(2), 208–226.

Christenson, S. L., & Cleary, M. (1990). Consultation and the parent–educator partnership: A perspective. *Journal of Educational and Psychological Consultation, 1,* 219–241.

Christle, C. A., Jolivette, K., & Nelson, C. M. (2000). *Youth aggression and violence: Risk, resilience, and prevention* (ERIC Digest No. E602, Report No. EDO-EC-00-11). Arlington, VA: ERIC Clearinghouse on Disabilities and Gifted Education. (ERIC Document Reproduction Service No. ED449632)

Church, C., Alisanski, S., & Amanullah, S. (2000). The social, behavioral, and academic experiences of children with Asperger syndrome. *Focus on Autism and Other Developmental Disabilities, 15*(1), 12–20.

Clarizio, H. F. (1985). Cognitive-behavioral treatment of childhood depression. *Psychology in the Schools, 22*(3), 308–322.

Clark, D. B., Bukstein, O. G., Smith, M. G., & Kaczynski, N. A. (1995). Identifying anxiety disorders in adolescents hospitalized for alcohol abuse or dependence. *Psychiatric Services, 46*(6), 618–620.

Clarke, G. N., DeBar, L. L., Lewinsohn, P. M., Kazdin, A. E., & Weisz, J. R. (2003). Cognitive-behavioral group treatment for adolescent depression. In *Evidence-based psychotherapies for children and adolescents* (pp. 120–134). New York: Guilford Press.

Clarke, G. N., Rohde, P., Lewinsohn, P. M., Hops, H., & Seeley, J. R. (1999). Cognitive-behavioral treatment of adolescent depression: Efficacy of acute group treatment and booster sessions. *Journal of the American Academy of Child & Adolescent Psychiatry, 38*(3), 272–279.

Clarke, R. A., Murphy, D. L., & Constantino, J. N. (1999). Serotonin and externalizing behavior in young children. *Psychiatry Research, 86,* 29–40.

Cloninger, C. R. (1986). A unified biosocial theory of personality and its role in the development of anxiety states. *Psychiatric Development, 3,* 167–226.

Cloninger, C. R. (1988). A unified biosocial theory of personality and its role in the development of anxiety states: A reply to commentaries. *Psychiatric Development, 2,* 83–120.

Cnattingius, S., Hultman, C. M., Dahl, M., & Sparén, P. (1999). Very preterm birth, birth trauma, and the risk of anorexia nervosa among girls. *Archives of General Psychiatry, 56*(7), 634–638.

Cobia, D. C., Carney, J. S., & Waggoner, I. M. (1998). Children and adolescents with HIV disease: Implications for school counselors. *Professional School Counseling, 1*(5), 41–45.

Cohen, D. J., Caparulo, B. K., Shaywitz, B. A., & Bowers, M. B. (1977). Dopamine and serotonin metabolism in neuropsychiatrically disturbed children. *Archives of General Psychiatry, 34*(5), 545–550.

Cohen, D. J., Shaywitz, B. A., Johnson, W. T., & Bowers, M. (1974). Biogenic amines in autistic and atypical children. *Archives of General Psychiatry, 31*(6), 845–853.

Cohen, J. A., Berliner, L., & Mannarino, A. P. (2000). Treating traumatized children: A research review and synthesis. *Trauma, Violence, & Abuse, 1*(1), 29–46.

Cohen, J. A., Deblinger, E., & Mannarino, A. P. (July, 2000). *A multisite randomized controlled treatment study for sexually abused children.* Paper presented at the annual meeting of the American Professional Society on the Abuse of Children, Chicago.

Cohen, J. A., & Mannarino, A. P. (1996). Factors that mediate treatment outcome of sexually abused preschool children. *Journal of the American Academy of Child & Adolescent Psychiatry, 35*(10), 1402–1410.

Cohen, J. A., & Mannarino, A. P. (1997). A treatment study for sexually abused preschool children: Outcome during a one-year follow-up. *Journal of the American Academy of Child & Adolescent Psychiatry, 36*(9), 1228–1235.

Cohen, J. A., & Mannarino, A. P. (2004). Posttraumatic stress disorder. In T. H. Ollendick & J. S. March (Eds.), *Phobic and anxiety disorders in children and adolescents: A clinician's guide to effective psychosocial and pharmacological interventions* (pp. 405–432). New York: Oxford University Press.

Cohen, J., Deblinger, E., Mannarino, A., & Steer, R. (2004). A multisite, randomized controlled trial for children with sexual abuse-related PTSD symptoms. *Journal of the American Academy of Child & Adolescent Psychiatry, 43,* 393–402.

Coie, J. D., & Dodge, K. A. (1998). Aggression and antisocial behavior. In W. Damon & N. Eisenberg (Eds.), *Handbook of child psychology: Social, emotional, and personality development* (pp. 779–862). Toronto: John Wiley & Sons, Inc.

Cole, D. A., & Carpentieri, S. (1990). Social status and the comorbidity of child depression and conduct disorder. *Journal of Consulting and Clinical Psychology, 58*(6), 748–757.

Coleman, M. C., & Webber, J. (2002). *Emotional and behavioral disorders: Theory and practice.* Boston: Allyn & Bacon.

Collins, R. L., & Ricciardelli, L. A. (2005). Assessment of eating disorders and obesity. In D. M. Donovan & G. A. Marlatt (Eds.), *Assessment of addictive behaviors* (2nd ed., pp. 305–333). New York: Guilford.

Comer, R. J. (1995). *Abnormal psychology* (2nd ed.). New York: W. H. Freeman.

Comings, D. E., Gade-Andavalu, R., Gonzales, N., Muhleman, D., Blake, H., & Dietz, G. (2000). Comparison of the role of dopamine, serotonin, and noradrenaline genes in ADHD, ODD and conduct disorder: Multivariate regression analysis of 20 genes. *Clinical Genetics, 57,* 178–196.

Compton, S. N., Grant, P. J., Chrisman, A. K., Gammon, P. J., Brown, V. L., & March, J. S. (2001). Sertraline in children and adolescents with social anxiety disorder: An open trial. *Journal of the American Academy of Child & Adolescent Psychiatry, 40*(5), 564–571.

Compton, S. N., Nelson, A. H., & March, J. S. (2000). Social phobia and separation anxiety symptoms in community and clinical samples of children and adolescents. *Journal of the American Academy of Child & Adolescent Psychiatry, 39*(8), 1040–1046.

Conners, C. K. (1998). *Conners Rating Scales—Revised.* North Tonawanda, NY: Multi-Health Systems.

Conners, C. K., Sitarenios, G., Parker, J. D. A., & Epstein, J. N. (1998). The revised Conners' Parent Rating Scale (CPRS-R): Factor structure, reliability, and criterion validity. *Journal of Abnormal Child Psychology, 26*(4), 257–268. Retrieved March 14, 2008, from Research Library database. (Document ID No. 32782601)

Connolly, P. (2006, September). *Bet you can't keep me safe! How to work effectively with adolescents with anxiety and mood disorders in a residential school setting.* Paper presented at the Fall 2006 Summit Staff Development Workshop, Nyack, NY.

Connor, D. F. (2002). *Aggression and antisocial behavior in children and adolescents: Research and treatment.* New York: Guilford Press.

Connor, D. F., Glatt, S. J., Lopez, I. D., Jackson, D., & Melloni, R. H., Jr. (2002). Psychopharmacology and aggression. I: A meta-analysis of stimulant effects on overt/covert aggression-related behaviors in ADHD. *Journal of the American Academy of Child & Adolescent Psychiatry, 41*(3), 253–261.

Constantino, J. N. (2002). *The Social Responsiveness Scale.* Los Angeles: Western Psychological Services.

Constantino, J. N., Gruber, C. P., Davis, S., Hays, S., Passante, N., & Przybeck, T. (2004). The factor structure of autistic traits. *Journal of Child Psychology and Psychiatry, 45,* 719–726.

Constantino, J. N., & Todd, R. D. (2003). Autistic traits in the general population: A twin study. *Archives of General Psychiatry, 60*(5), 524–530.

Cook, E. H., Rowlett, R., Jaselskis, C., & Leventhal, B. L. (1992). Fluoxetine treatment of children and adults with autistic disorder and mental retardation. *Journal of the American Academy of Child & Adolescent Psychiatry, 31*(4), 739–745.

Coonrod, E. E., & Stone, W. L. (2005). Screening for autism in young children. In F. R. Volkmar, R. Paul, A. Klin, & D. Cohen (Eds.), *Handbook of autism and pervasive developmental disorders: Vol. 2. Assessment, interventions, and policy* (3rd ed., pp. 707–729). Hoboken, NJ: John Wiley & Sons, Inc.

Corey, G. (2008). *Theory and practice of counseling and psychotherapy* (8th ed.). Belmont, CA: Brooks-Cole.

Cornwall, E., Spence, S. H., & Schotte, D. (1997). The effectiveness of emotive imagery in the treatment of darkness phobia in children. *Behavior Change, 13,* 223–229.

Correctional Association of New York. (2002, March). Rethinking juvenile detention in New York City: A report by the Juvenile Justice Project. Retrieved February 10, 2008, from http://www.correctionalassociation.org/publications/download/jjp/rethinking_detention.pdf

Costello, E. J., Angold, A., Burns, B. J., Stangl, D. K., Tweed, D. L., Erkanli, A., et al. (1996). The Great Smoky Mountains Study of youth: Goals, design, methods, and the prevalence of *DSM-III-R* disorders. *Archives of General Psychiatry, 53*(12), 1129–1136.

Council for Exceptional Children, Task Force on Children with ADHD. (1992). *Children with ADHD: A shared responsibility.* Reston, VA: Author.

Courchesne, E., Karns, C. M., Davis, H. R., Ziccardi, R., Carper, R. A., Tigue, Z. D., et al. (2001). Unusual brain growth patterns in early life in patients with autistic disorder: An MRI study. *Neurology, 57*(2), 245–254.

Coyle, J. T., Pine, D. S., Charney, D. S., Lewis, L., Nemeroff, C. B., Carlson, G. A., et al. (2003). Depression and Bipolar Support Alliance consensus statement on the unmet needs in diagnosis and treatment of mood disorders in children and adolescents. *Journal of the American Academy of Child & Adolescent Psychiatry, 42*(12), 1494–1503.

Craig, W. M., Peters, R. D., & Konarski, R. (1998). *Bullying and victimization among Canadian school children.* Available at http://www.hrdc-drhc.ca/arb/publications/research/abw-98-28e.html

Crick, N. R., & Bigbee, M. A. (1998). Relational and overt forms of peer victimization: A multiinformant approach. *Journal of Consulting and Clinical Psychology, 66*(2), 337–347.

Crick, N. R., & Dodge, K. A. (1996). Social information-processing mechanisms in reactive and proactive aggression. *Child Development, 67,* 993–1002.

Crick, N. R., Werner, N. E., Casas, J. F., O'Brien, K. M., Nelson, D. A., Grotpeter, J. K., et al. (1999). Childhood aggression and gender: A new look at an old problem. In D. Bernstein (Ed.), *The 45th Nebraska symposium on motivation: Gender and motivation* (pp. 75–141). Lincoln: Nebraska University Press.

Critchley, H. D., Daly, E. M., Bullmore, E. T., Williams, S. C. R., Van Amelsvoort, T., Robertson, D. M., et al. (2000). The functional neuroanatomy of social behaviour: Changes in cerebral blood flow when people with autistic disorder process facial expressions. *Brain: A Journal of Neurology, 123*(11), 2203–2212.

Croonenberghs, J., Findling, R. L., Reyes, M., & Karcher, K. (2005). Risperidone in children with disruptive behavior disorders and subaverage intelligence: A 1-year, open-label study of 504 patients: Dr. Croonenberghs et al. reply. *Journal of the American Academy of Child & Adolescent Psychiatry, 44*(10), 970–971.

Cueva, J. E., Overall, J. E., Small, A. M., & Armenteros, J. L. (1996). Carbamazepine in aggressive children with conduct disorder: A double-blind and placebo-controlled study. *Journal of the American Academy of Child & Adolescent Psychiatry, 35*(4), 480–490.

Culatta, R. A., Tompkins, J. R., & Werts, M. G. (2003). *Fundamentals of special education: What every teacher needs to know* (2nd ed.). Upper Saddle River, NJ: Merrill/Prentice Hall.

Cullen, D. (2003). Columbine report released (May 16, 2000). *Salon.com.* Retrieved January 23, 2008, from http://dir.salon.com/news/feature/2000/05/16/columbine/index.html?pn=1

Cullinan, D. (2002). *Students with emotional and behavioral disorders: An introduction for teachers and other helping professionals.* Upper Saddle River, NJ: Merrill/Prentice Hall.

Cummings, M., Waller, D., Johnson, C., Bradley, K., Leatherwood, D., & Guzzetta, C. (2001). Developing and implementing a comprehensive program for children and adolescents with eating disorders. *Journal of Child and Adolescent Psychiatric Nursing, 14,* 167–178.

Cunningham, C. E., Bremner, R., & Boyle, M. (1995). Large group community-based parenting programs for families of preschoolers at risk for disruptive behaviour disorders: Utilization, cost effectiveness, and outcome. *Journal of Child Psychology and Psychiatry, 36*(7), 1141–1159.

CureAutismNow.org (2008). http://www.Autismspeaks.org/science/research/index.php

Curin, J. M., Terzic, J., Petkovic, Z. B., Zekan, L., Terzic, I. M., & Susnjara, I. M. (2003). Lower cortisol and higher ACTH levels in individuals with autism. *Journal of Autism and Developmental Disorders, 33*(4), 443–448.

Curwin, R. L. (1995, February). A humane approach to reducing violence in schools. *Educational Leadership, 52*(5), 72–75.

Curwin, R. L., & Mendler, A. N. (1997). *As tough as necessary: Countering violence, aggression, and hostility in our schools.* Alexandria, VA: Association for Supervision and Curriculum Development.

Dadds, M. R., & McHugh, T. A. (1992). Social support and treatment outcome in behavioral family therapy for child conduct problems. *Journal of Consulting and Clinical Psychology, 60*(2), 252–259.

Dadds, M. R., Sanders, M. R., Behrens, B. C., & James, J. E. (1987). Marital discord and child behavior problems: A description of family interactions during treatment. *Journal of Clinical Child Psychology, 16*(3), 192–203.

Dare, C., & Eisler, I. (1997). Family therapy for anorexia nervosa. In D. M. Garner & P. E. Garfinkel (Eds.), *Handbook of treatment for eating disorders* (2nd ed., pp. 307–324). New York: Guilford Press.

Dare, C., & Szmukler, G. (1991). Family therapy of early-onset, short-history anorexia nervosa. In D. B. Woodside & L. Shekter-Wolfson (Eds.), *Family approaches in treatment of eating disorders* (pp. 23–47). Washington, DC: American Psychiatric Association.

Davidson, J. (1993, March). *Childhood histories of adults' social phobias.* Paper presented at the Anxiety Disorders Association annual convention, Charleston, SC.

Davidson, J. R., Kudler, H. S., Saunders, W. B., & Erickson, L. (1993). Predicting response to amitriptyline in posttraumatic stress disorder. *American Journal of Psychiatry, 150*(7), 1024–1029.

Davies, S., Bishop, D., Manstead, A. S. R., & Tantam, D. (1994). Face perception in children with autism and Asperger's syndrome. *Journal of Child Psychology and Psychiatry, 35*(6), 1033–1057.

Davis, C. A., Brady, M. P., Williams, R. E., & Hamilton, R. (1992). Effects of high-probability requests on the acquisition and generalization of responses to requests in young children with behavior disorders. *Journal of Applied Behavior Analysis, 25*(4), 905–916.

DeBellis, M. D., Chrousos, G. P., Dorn, L. D., Burke, L., Helmers, K., Kling, M. A., et al. (1994). H-P-A axis dysregulation in sexually abused girls. *Journal of Clinical Endocrinology and Metabolism, 78,* 249–255.

Deblinger, E., Lippmann, J., & Steer, R. (1996). Sexually abused children suffering post-traumatic stress symptoms: Initial treatment outcome findings. *Child Maltreatment, 1,* 310–321.

DelBello, M. P., Kowatch, R. A., Warner, J., Schwiers, M. L., Rappaport, K. B., Daniels, J. P., et al. (2002). Adjunctive topiramate treatment for pediatric bipolar disorder: A retrospective chart review. *Journal of Child and Adolescent Psychopharmacology, 12*(4), 323–330.

de Haan, E., Hoogduin, K. A. L., Buitelaar, J. K., & Keijsers, G. P. J. (1998). Behavior therapy versus clomipramine for the treatment of obsessive-compulsive disorder. *Journal of the American Academy of Child & Adolescent Psychiatry, 37*(10), 1022–1029.

DeLong, G. R., Teague, L. A., & McSwain-Kamran, M. M. (1998). Effects of fluoxetine treatment in young children with idiopathic autism. *Developmental Medicine & Child Neurology, 40*(8), 551–562.

Delprato, D. J. (2001). Comparisons of discrete-trial and normalized behavioral intervention for young children with autism. *Journal of Autism and Developmental Disorders, 31*(3), 315–325.

Delquadri, J., Greenwood, C. R., Whorton, D., Carta, J. J., & Hall, R. V. (1986). Classwide peer tutoring. *Exceptional Children, 52,* 535–542.

Depue, R. A., Krauss, S., Spoont, M. R., & Arbisi, P. (1989). General behavior inventory identification of unipolar and bipolar affective conditions in a nonclinical university population. *Journal of Abnormal Psychology, 98*(2), 117–126.

Deruelle, C., Rondan, C., Gepner, B., & Tardif, C. (2004). Spatial frequency and face processing in children with autism and Asperger syndrome. *Journal of Autism and Developmental Disorders, 34*(2), 199–210.

Deschenes, C., Ebeling, D. G., & Sprague, J. (1994). *Adapting curriculum and instruction in inclusive classrooms: A teacher's desk reference.* Bloomington, IN: The Center for School and Community Integration Institution for the Study of Developmental Disabilities.

Devlin, M. J. (1996). Assessment and treatment of binge-eating disorder. *Psychiatric Clinics of North America, 19*(4), 761–772.

Dewey, J. (1969). *The school and society.* Chicago: University of Chicago Press.

DeWit, D. J., Ogborne, A., Offord, D. R., & MacDonald, K. (1999). Antecedents of the risk of recovery from DSM-III-R social phobia. *Psychological Medicine, 29*(3), 569–582.

deZwaan, M. (2001). Binge eating disorder and obesity. *International Journal of Obesity and Related Metabolic Disorders, 25*(Supp. 1), S51–S55.

Dierker, L., Merikangas, K., & Szatmari, P. (1999). Influence of parental concordance for psychiatric disorders on psychopathology in offspring. *Journal of the American Academy of Child and Adolescent Psychiatry, 38,* 280–289.

Dingemans, A. E., Bruna, M. J., & van Furth, E. F. (2002). Binge eating disorder: A review. *International Journal of Obesity, 26*(3), 299–307.

Dishion, T. J., French, D. C., & Patterson, G. R. (1995). The development and ecology of antisocial behavior. In D. Cicchetti & D. J. Cohen (Eds.), *Developmental psychopathology: Vol. 2. Risk, disorder, and adaptation* (pp. 421–471). Oxford, England: Wiley.

Dmitrieva, T. N., Oades, R. D., Hauffa, B. P., & Eggers, C. (2001). Dehydroepiandrosterone sulphate and corticotrophin levels are high in young male patient with conduct disorder: Comparison for growth factor, thyroid, and gonadal hormones. *Neuropsychobiology, 43,* 134–140.

Dobson, K. S., & Dozois, D. J. A. (2004). Attentional biases in eating disorders: A meta-analytic review of Stroop performance. *Clinical Psychology Review, 23*(8), 1001–1022.

Dodge, K. A. (1980). Social cognition and children's aggressive behavior. *Child Development, 51*(1), 162–170.

Dodge, K. A., & Coie, J. D. (1987). Social-information-processing factors in reactive and proactive aggression in children's peer groups. *Journal of Personality and Social Psychology, 53*(6), 1146–1158.

Dodge, K. A., Price, J. M., Bachorowski, J. A., & Newman, J. P. (1990). Hostile attributional biases in severely aggressive adolescents. *Journal of Abnormal Psychology, 99*(4), 385–392.

Dowdy, C. A., Patton, J. R., Smith, T. E. C., & Polloway, E. A. (1998). *Attention deficit/hyperactivity disorder in the classroom: A practical guide for teachers.* Austin, TX: Pro-Ed.

Druck, K., & Kaplowitz, M. (2005). Setting up a no-bully zone. *Virginia Journal of Education, 98*(4), 6–10.

Drug Enforcement Administration (DEA), National Drug Threat Assessment. (2008). http://www.usdoj.gov/dea/concern/18862/2008.pdf

Dryfoos, J. G. (1990). *Adolescents at risk: Prevalence and prevention.* New York: Oxford University Press.

Dryfoos, J. G. (1994). *Full-service schools: A revolution in health and social services for children, youth, and families.* San Francisco: Jossey-Bass.

Dunlap, G., & Koegel, R. L. (1999). Welcoming introduction. *Journal of Positive Behavior Interventions, 1,* 2–3.

Dunn, R. S., Thies, A. P., & Honigsfeld, A. (2001). *Synthesis of the Dunn and Dunn Learning-Style Model research: Analysis from a neuropsychological perspective.* Jamaica, NY: St. John's University, Center for the Study of Learning and Teaching Styles.

DuPaul, G. J., Power, T. J., Anastopoulos, A. D., & Reid, R. (1999). *The ADHD Rating Scale–IV: Checklists, norms, and clinical interpretation.* New York: Guilford.

DuPaul, G. J., & Stoner, G. (1994). *ADHD in the schools: Assessment and intervention strategies.* New York: Guilford.

Dwyer, K., Osher, D., & Warger, C. (1998). *Early warning, timely response: A guide to safe schools.* Washington, DC: U.S. Department of Education.

Eaves, L., Rutter, M., Silberg, J. L., Shillady, L., Maes, H., & Pickles, A. (2000). Genetic and environmental causes of covariation in interview assessments of disruptive behavior in child and adolescent twins. *Behavior Genetics, 30*(4), 321–334.

Eaves, L. J., Silberg, J. L., Maes, H. H., Simonoff, E., Pickles, A., Rutter, M., et al. (1997). Genetics and developmental psychopathology: 2. The main effects of genes and environment on behavioral problems in the Virginia Twin Study of Adolescent Behavioral Development. *Journal of Child Psychology and Psychiatry, 38*(8), 965–980.

Eddy, K. T., Keel, P. K., Dorer, D. J., Delinsky, S. S., Franko, D. L., & Herzog, D. B. (2002). Longitudinal comparison of anorexia nervosa subtypes. *International Journal of Eating Disorders, 31*(2), 191–201.

Edelson, M. G. (2005). A car goes in a garage like a can of peas goes in the refrigerator: Do deficits in real-world knowledge affect the assessment of intelligence in individuals with autism? *Focus on Autism and Other Developmental Disabilities, 20*(1), 2–9.

Edwards, C. H. (2001). Student violence and the moral dimensions of education. *Psychology in the Schools, 38,* 249–257.

Edwards, L., & Chard, D. J. (2000). Curricular reform in a residential treatment program: Establishing academic expectations for students with emotional and behavioral disorders. *Behavioral Disorders, 25*(3), 259–263.

Egley, A. (2000). *Highlights of the 1999 National Youth Gang Survey: OJJDP fact sheet.* Washington, DC: U.S. Department of Justice, Office of Justice Programs, Office of Juvenile Justice and Delinquency Prevention.

Egley, A., Jr., Howell, J. C., and Major, A. K. (2006). *National Youth Gang Survey: 1999–2001.* Washington, DC: U.S. Department of Justice, Office of Juvenile Justice and Delinquency Prevention.

Eisen, A. R., & Silverman, W. K. (1993). Should I relax or change my thoughts? A preliminary examination of cognitive therapy, relaxation training, and their combination with overanxious children. *Journal of Cognitive Psychotherapy, 7*(4), 265–279.

Eisen, A. R., & Silverman, W. K. (1998). Prescriptive treatment for generalized anxiety disorder in children. *Behavior Therapy, 29*(1), 105–121.

Eisler, I., Dare, C., Hodes, M., Russell, G., Dodge, E., & Le Grange, D. (2000). Family therapy for adolescent anorexia nervosa: The results of a controlled comparison of two family interventions. *Journal of Child Psychology and Psychiatry, 41*(6), 727–736.

Elkins, I. J., Iacono, W. G., Doyle, A. E., & McGue, M. (1997). Characteristics associated with the persistence of antisocial behavior: Results from the recent longitudinal research. *Aggressive Violent Behavior, 2,* 101–124.

Elliott, D. S. (1994). Serious violent offenders: Onset, developmental course, and termination. The American Society of Criminology 1993 presidential address. *Criminology, 32,* 1–21.

Elliott, R. O., Dobbin, A. R., Rose, G. D., & Soper, H. V. (1994). Vigorous, aerobic exercise versus general motor training activities: Effects on maladaptive and stereotypic behaviors of adults with both autism and mental retardation. *Journal of Autism and Developmental Disorders, 24*(5), 565–576.

Elliot, S. N., & Gresham, F. M. (1991). *Social skills intervention guide: Practical strategies for social skills training.* Circle Pines, MN: American Guidance Service.

Elliott, S. N., Witt, J. C., Kratochwill, T. R., & Stoiber, K. C. (2002). Selecting and evaluating classroom interventions. In M. R. Shinn, H. M. Walker, and G. Stoner (Eds.), *Interventions for academic and behavior problems II: Preventive and remedial approaches* (pp. 275–294). Bethesda, MD: National Association of School Psychologists.

Ellis, E. S. (1992). LINCS: *A starter strategy for vocabulary learning.* Lawrence, KS: Edge Enterprises.

Emslie, G. J., Kennard, B. D., & Kowatch, R. A. (1995). Affective disorders in children: Diagnosis and management. *Journal of Child Neurology, 10*(1), S42–S49.

Emslie, G. J., Rush, A. J., Weinberg, W. A., & Gullion, C. M. (1997). Recurrence of major depressive disorder in hospitalized children and adolescents. *Journal of the American Academy of Child & Adolescent Psychiatry, 36*(6), 785–792.

Emslie, G. J., Rush, A. J., Weinberg, W. A., Kowatch, R. A., Carmody, T., & Mayes, T. L. (1998). Fluoxetine in child and adolescent depression: Acute and maintenance treatment. *Depression and Anxiety, 7,* 32–39.

Emslie, G. J., Rush, J., Weinberg, W. A., Kowatch, R. A., Hughes, C. W., Carmody, T., et al. (1997). A double-blind, randomized, placebo-controlled trial of fluoxetine in children and adolescents with depression. *Archives of General Psychiatry, 54*(11), 1031–1037.

Emslie, G. J., Weinberg, W. A., Rush, A. J., & Adams, R. M. (1990). Depressive symptoms by self-report in adolescence: Phase I of the development of a questionnaire by self-report. *Journal of Child Neurology, 5*(2), 114–121.

English, K., Goldstein, H., Shafer, K., & Kaczmarek, L. (1997). Promoting interactions among preschoolers with and without disabilities: Effects of a buddy skills training program. *Exceptional Children, 63,* 229–243.

Erford, B. T. (1993). *Disruptive behavior rating scale (DBRS).* East Aurora, NY: Slosson Educational Publications.

Ericson, N. (2001). *Addressing the problem of juvenile bullying: OJJDP fact sheet 27.* Washington, DC: U.S. Department of Justice, Office of Juvenile Justice and Delinquency Prevention.

Ericsson, M., Poston, W. S. C., & Foreyt, J. P. (1996). Common biological pathways in eating disorders and obesity. *Addictive Behaviors, 21*(6), 733–743.

Ernst, M., Cookus, B. A., & Moravec, B. C. (2000). Pictorial Instrument for Children and Adolescents

(PICA-III-R). *Journal of the American Academy of Child & Adolescent Psychiatry, 39*(1), 94–99.

Ernst, M., Zametkin, A. J., Matochik, J. A., Pascualvaca, D., & Cohen, R. M. (1997). Reduced medial prefrontal dopaminergic activity in autistic children. *Lancet, 350,* 638.

Eskes, G. A., Bryson, S. E., & McCormick, T. A. (1990). Comprehension of concrete and abstract words in autistic children. *Journal of Autism and Developmental Disorders, 20*(1), 61–73.

Everill, J. T., & Waller, G. (1995). Reported sexual abuse and eating psychopathology: A review of the evidence for a causal link. *International Journal of Eating Disorders, 18*(1), 1–11.

Eyberg, S. M., & Pincus, D. (1999). *Eyberg Child Behavior Inventory & Sutter Eyberg Student Behavior Inventory: Professional manual.* Lutz, FL: Psychological Assessment Resources.

Eyberg, S. M., & Robinson, E. A. (1983). Conduct problem behavior: Standardization of a behavioral rating scale with adolescents. *Journal of Clinical Child Psychology, 12*(3), 347–354.

Fabreg, J. H., Ulrich, R., & Mezzich, J. E. (1993). Do caucasian and black adolescents differ at psychiatric intake? *Journal of the American Academy of Child and Adolescent Psychiatry, 32,* 407–413.

Fabrega, H., Ulrich, R., & Mezzich, J. (1993). Do Caucasian and Black adolescents differ at intake? *Journal of the American Academy of Child & Adolescent Psychiatry, 32*(2), 407–413.

Fad, K. M., Patton, J. R., & Polloway, E. A. (1998). *Behavioral intervention planning: Completing a functional behavioral assessment and developing a behavioral intervention plan.* Austin, TX: Pro-Ed.

Fairbanks, J. M., Pine, D. S., Tancer, N. K., Dummit, E. S., III, Kentgen, L. M., Martin, J., et al. (1997). Open fluoxetine treatment of missed anxiety disorders in children and adolescents. *Journal of Child and Adolescent Psychopharmacology, 7,* 17–29.

Fairburn, C. G. (1980). Self-induced vomiting. *Journal of Psychosomatic Research, 24*(3), 193–197.

Fairburn, C. G., & Beglin, S. J. (1994). Assessment of eating disorders: Interview or self-report questionnaire? *International Journal of Eating Disorders, 16*(4), 363–370.

Fairburn, C. G., & Cooper, Z. (1993). The Eating Disorder Examination (12th edition). In G. T. Wilson (Ed.), *Binge eating: Nature, assessment, and treatment* (pp. 317–360). New York: Guilford Press.

Fairburn, C. G., Cooper, Z., Doll, H. A., Norman, P., & O'Connor, M. (2000). The natural course of bulimia nervosa and binge eating disorder in young women. *Archives of General Psychiatry, 57*(7), 659–665.

Fairburn, C. G., & Harrison, P. J. (2003). Eating disorders. *Lancet, 361*(9355), 407–416.

Fairburn, C. G., Shafran, R., & Cooper, Z. (1999). A cognitive behavioural theory of anorexia nervosa. *Behaviour Research and Therapy, 37*(1), 1–13.

Fairburn, C. G., Stice, E., Cooper, Z., Doll, H. A., Norman, P. A., & O'Connor, M. E. (2003). Understanding persistence in bulimia nervosa: A 5-year naturalistic study. *Journal of Consulting and Clinical Psychology, 71*(1), 103–109.

Falk, K. B., & Wehby, J. H. (2001). The effects of peer-assisted learning strategies on the beginning reading skills of young children with emotional or behavioral disorders. *Behavioral Disorders, 26,* 344–359.

Fantuzzo, J. W., King, J. A., & Heller, L. R. (1992). Effects of reciprocal peer tutoring on mathematics and school adjustment: A component analysis. *Journal of Educational Psychology, 84,* 331–339.

Faraone, S. V., Biederman, J., & Mick, E. (2006). The age-dependent decline of attention deficit hyperactivity disorder: A meta-analysis of follow-up studies. *Psychological Medicine, 36,* 159–165.

Faraone, S. V., & Doyle, A. E. (2003). The nature and heritability of attention-deficit/hyperactivity disorder. *Child Adolescent Psychiatric Clinician in North America 10*(2): 299–316.

Faraone, S. V., Spencer, T., Aleardi, M., Pagano, C., & Biederman, J. (2004). Meta-analysis of the efficacy of methylphenidate for treating adult attention-deficit/hyperactivity disorder. *Journal of Clinical Psychopharmacology, 24,* 24–29.

Farmer, E. M. Z., Compton, S. N., Burns, J. B., & Robertson, E. (2002). Review of the evidence base for treatment of childhood psychopathology: Externalizing disorders. *Journal of Consulting and Clinical Psychology, 70*(6), 1267–1302.

Farrington, C. P., Miller, E., & Taylor, B. (2001). MMR and autism: Further evidence against a causal association. *Vaccine, 19,* 3632–3635.

Farrington, D. P. (1989). Early predictors of adolescent aggression and adult violence. *Violence and Victims, 4,* 79–100.

Farrington, D. P. (1995). The development of offending and antisocial behavior from childhood: Key findings from the Cambridge study in delinquent development. *Journal of Child Psychology and Psychiatry, 36,* 929–964.

Farrington, D. P. (1997). Early prediction of violent and nonviolent youthful offending. *European Journal on Criminal Policy and Research, 5,* 51–66.

Farroni, R., Csibra, G., Simion, F., & Johnson, M. (2002). Eye contact detection in humans from birth. *Proceedings of the National Academy of Sciences, 99,* 9602–9695.

Feather, N. T. (1985). Masculinity, femininity, self-esteem, and subclinical depression. *Sex Roles, 12*(5), 491–500.

Fein, G. G., Gariboldi, A., & Boni, R. (1993). Antecedents of maternal separation anxiety. *Merrill-Palmer Quarterly, 39*(4), 481–495.

Feindler, E. L., Ecton, R. B., Kingsley, D., & Dubey, D. R. (1986). Group anger control training for institutionalized psychiatric male adolescents. *Behavior Therapy, 17,* 109–123.

Feingold, B. F. (1975). Hyperkinesis and learning disabilities linked to artificial food flavors and colors. *The American Journal of Nursing, 75*(5), 797–803.

Feldman, C., Bruner, J., & Kalmar, D. (1993). Plot, plight, and dramatism: Interpretation at three ages: Reply. *Human Development, 36*(6), 346–349.

Fenstermacher, G. D., & Soltis, J. F. (1992). *Approaches to teaching.* New York: Teachers College Press.

Ferro, T., Carlson, G. A., Grayson, P., & Klein, D. N. (1994). Depressive disorders: Distinctions in children. *Journal of the American Academy of Child & Adolescent Psychiatry, 33*(5), 664–670.

Feshbach, N. (1983) Learning to care: A positive approach to child training and discipline. *Journal of Clinical Child Psychology, 12,* 266–271.

Finch, A. J., Nelson, W. M., & Hart, K. J. (2006). Conduct disorder: Description, prevalence, and etiology. In W. M. Nelson, A. J. Finch, & K. J. Hart (Eds.), *Conduct disorders: A practitioner's guide to comparative treatments* (pp. 1–13). New York: Springer.

Findling, R. L., McNamara, N. K., Branicky, L. A., Schluchter, M. D., Lemon, E., & Blumer, J. L. (2000). A double-blind pilot study of risperidone in the treatment of conduct disorder. *Journal of the American Academy of Child & Adolescent Psychiatry, 39*(4), 509–516.

Findling, R. L., McNamara, N. K., Gracious, B. L., Youngstrom, E. A., Stansbrey, R. J., Reed, M. D., et al. (2003). Combination lithium and divalproex sodium in pediatric bipolarity. *Journal of the American Academy of Child & Adolescent Psychiatry, 42*(8), 895–901.

Fine, M. J. (Ed.). (1991). *Collaboration with parents of exceptional children.* Brandon, VT: Clinical Psychology.

Firestone, P., Kelly, M. J., & Fike, S. (1980). Are fathers necessary in parent training groups? *Journal of Clinical Child Psychology, 9*(1), 44–47.

First, M. B., Frances, A., & Pincus, H. A. (2002). DSM-IV-TR *handbook of differential diagnosis.* Washington, DC: American Psychiatric Publishing.

Fischer, M., & Newby, R. F. (1998). Use of the restricted academic task in ADHD dose-response relationships. *Journal of Learning Disabilities, 31*(6), 608–612.

Fisher, M., Golden, N. H., Katzman, D. K., & Kreipe, R. E. (1995). Eating disorders in adolescents: A background paper. *Journal of Adolescent Health, 16*(6), 420–437.

Flament, M. F., Rapoport, J. L., Berg, C. Z., & Sceery, W. (1989). Obsessive-compulsive disorder in adolescence: An epidemiological study. *Annual Progress in Child Psychiatry & Child Development,* 499–515.

Flannery-Schroeder, E. C. (2004). Generalized anxiety disorder. In T. L. Morris & J. S. March (Eds.), *Anxiety disorders in children and adolescents* (2nd ed., pp. 125–140). New York: Guilford Press.

Flannery-Schroeder, E. C., & Kendall, P. C. (2000). Group and individual cognitive-behavioral treatments for youth with anxiety disorders: A randomized clinical trial. *Cognitive Therapy and Research, 24*(3), 251–278.

Foa, E. B., Johnson, K. M., Feeny, N. C., & Treadwell, K. R. H. (2001). The Child PTSD Symptom Scale: A preliminary examination of its psychometric properties. *Journal of Clinical Child Psychology, 30*(3), 376–384.

Fombonne, E. (2003). The prevalence of autism. *Journal of the American Medical Association, 289,* 87–89.

Fombonne, E. (2005). Epidemiological studies of pervasive developmental disorders. In F. R. Volkmar, R. Paul, A. Klin, & D. Cohen (Eds.), *Handbook of autism and pervasive developmental disorders: Vol. 1. Diagnosis, development, neurobiology, and behavior* (3rd ed., pp. 42–69). Hoboken, NJ: John Wiley & Sons, Inc.

Ford, J. D., Racusin, R., Ellis, C. G., Daviss, W. B., Reiser, J., Fleischer, A., et al. (2000). Child maltreatment, other trauma exposure and posttraumatic symptomatology among children with oppositional defiant and attention deficit hyperactivity disorders. *Child Maltreatment, 5*(3), 205–217.

Foreyt, J. P., & Mikhail, C. (1997). Anorexia nervosa and bulimia nervosa. In E. J. Mash & L. G. Terdal (Eds.), *Assessment of childhood disorders* (3rd ed., pp. 683–716). New York: Guilford Press.

Francis, G., Last, C. G., & Strauss, C. C. (1987). Expression of separation anxiety disorder: The roles of age and gender. *Child Psychiatry & Human Development, 18*(2), 82–89.

Frankhauser, M. P., Karumanchi, V. C., German, M. L., Yales, A., & Karumanchi, S. D. (1992). A double-blind placebo controlled study of the efficacy of transdermal clonidine in autism. *Journal of Clinical Psychiatry, 53,* 77–82.

Franklin, C., Grant, D., Corcoran, J., Miller, P. O. D., & Bultman, L. (1997). Effectiveness of prevention programs for adolescent pregnancy: A meta-analysis. *Journal of Marriage & the Family, 59*(3), 551–567.

Franklin, M. E., Foa, E., & March, J. S. (2003). The pediatric obsessive-compulsive disorder treatment study (POTS): Rationale, design, and methods. *Journal of Child and Adolescent Psychopharmacology, 13*(Suppl 1), S39–S51.

Franklin, M. E., Rynn, M. A., Foa, E. B., & March, J. S. (2004). Pediatric obsessive-compulsive disorder. In T. H. Ollendick (Ed.), *Phobic and anxiety disorders in children and adolescents: A clinician's guide to effective psychosocial and pharmacological interventions* (pp. 381–404). New York: Oxford University Press.

Franklin, M. E., Rynn, M., March, J. S., & Foa, E. B. (2002). Obsessive-compulsive disorder. In M. Hersen (Ed.), *Clinical behavior therapy: Adults and children* (pp. 276–303). Hoboken, NJ: John Wiley & Sons, Inc.

Frederick, B. (1999). *Factors contributing to recidivism among youth placed with the New York State Division for Youth* (Research Report). Albany, NY: Office of Justice Systems Analysis, New York State Division of Criminal Justice Services.

Freeman, K. A., & Hoganson, J. M. (2006). Conduct disorders. In M. Hersen (Ed.), *Clinician's handbook of child behavioral assessment* (pp. 477–501). Boston: Elsevier.

Frick, P. J., Bodin, S. D., & Barry, C. T. (2000). Psychopathic traits and conduct problems in community and clinic-referred samples of children: Further development of the psychopathology screening device. *Psychological Assessment, 12,* 382–393.

Frick, P. J., Cornell, A. H., Bodin, S. D., Dane, H. A., Barry, C. T., & Loney, B. R. (2003). Callous-unemotional traits and developmental pathways to severe conduct problems. *Developmental Psychology, 39,* 246–260.

Frick, P. J., Kamphaus, R. W., Lahey, B. B., Loeber, R., Christ, M. G., Hart, E. L., et al (1991). Academic underachievement and the disruptive behavior disorders. *Journal of Consulting & Clinical Psychology, 59,* 289–294.

Frick, P. J., Lahey, B. B., Applegate, B., & Kerdyck, L. (1994). *DSM-IV* field trials for the disruptive behavior disorders: Symptom utility estimates. *Journal of the American Academy of Child & Adolescent Psychiatry, 33*(4), 529–539.

Frick, P. J., Lahey, B. B., Loeber, R., & Stouthamer-Loeber, M. (1991). Oppositional defiant disorder and conduct disorder in boys: Patterns of behavioral covariation. *Journal of Clinical Child Psychology, 20*(2), 202–208.

Frick, P. J., Lahey, B. B., Loeber, R., Stouthamer-Loeber, M., Christ, M. A. G., & Hanson, K. (1992). Familial risk factors to oppositional defiant disorder and conduct disorder: Parental psychopathology and maternal parenting. *Journal of Consulting and Clinical Psychology, 60*(1), 49–55.

Frick, P. J., Lilienfeld, S. O., Ellis, M. L., Loney, B. R., & Silverthorn, P. (1999). The association between anxiety and psychopathy dimensions in children. *Journal of Abnormal Psychology, 27,* 381–390.

Friedman, A. S. (1989). Family therapy vs. parent groups: Effect on adolescent drug abusers. *American Journal of Family Therapy, 17,* 335–347.

Funderburk, B. W., Eyberg, S. M., Newcomb, K., McNeil, C. B., Hembree-Kigin, T., & Capage, L. (1998). Parent-child interaction therapy with behavior problem children: Maintenance of treatment effects in the school setting. *Child & Family Behavior Therapy, 20*(2), 17–38.

Furman, L. (2005). What is attention-deficit hyperactivity disorder (ADHD)? *Journal of Child Neurology, 20,* 994–1002.

Furman-Brown, G. (Ed.). (2002). *School as community: From promise to practice.* New York: SUNY Press.

Furstenberg, F. F., Brooks-Gunn, J., & Chase-Lansdale, L. (1989). Teenaged pregnancy and childbearing. *American Psychologist, 44*(2), 313–320.

Furstenberg, F. F., Morgan, S. P., Moore, K. A., & Peterson, J. L. (1987). Race differences in the timing of adolescent intercourse. *American Sociological Review, 52*(4), 511–518.

Garber, J., & Kaminski, K. M. (2000). Laboratory and performance-based measures of depression in children and adolescents. *Journal of Clinical Child Psychology, 29*(4), 509–525.

Garfinkel, P. E., Lin, E., Goering, P., & Spegg, C. (1995). Bulimia nervosa in a Canadian community sample: Prevalence and comparison of subgroups. *American Journal of Psychiatry, 152*(7), 1052–1058.

Garfinkel, P. E., Lin, E., Goering, P., & Spegg, C. (1996). Purging and nonpurging forms of bulimia nervosa in a community sample. *International Journal of Eating Disorders, 20*(3), 231–238.

Garfinkle, A. N. (2000). *Using theory-of-mind to increase social competence in young children with autism: A model for praxis in early childhood special education.* Ann Arbor, MI: ProQuest Information & Learning.

Garfinkle, A. N., & Schwartz, I. S. (2002). Peer imitation: Increasing social interaction in children with autism and other developmental disabilities in inclusive preschool classrooms. *Topics in Early Childhood Special Education, 22*(1), 26–38.

Garibaldi, A., Blanchard, L., & Brooks, S. (1996). Conflict resolution training, teacher effectiveness, and student suspension: The impact of a health and safety initiative in the New Orleans public schools. *Journal of Negro Education, 65*(4), 408–413.

Garner, D. M. (1991). *The Eating Disorder Inventory-2: Professional manual.* Odessa, FL: Psychological Assessment Resources.

Gartin, B. C., & Murdick, N. L. (2001). A new IDEA mandate: The use of functional assessment of behavior and positive behavior supports. *Remedial and Special Education, 22,* 344–349.

Gaustad, J. (1991). Schools respond to gangs and violence. Eugene, OR: Oregon School Study Council. (ERIC Document Reproduction Service No. ED337909)

Geddes, J., & Butler, R. (2002). Depressive disorders. In S. Barton (Ed.), *Clinical evidence mental health* (pp. 61–76). Williston, VT: BMJ Books.

Geller, B., & Luby, J. (1997). Child and adolescent bipolar disorder: A review of the past 10 years. *Journal of the American Academy of Child & Adolescent Psychiatry, 36*(9), 1168–1176.

Geller, B., Tillman, R., Craney, J. L., & Bolhofner, K. (2004). Four-year prospective outcome and natural history of mania in children with a prepubertal and early adolescent bipolar disorder phenotype. *Archives of General Psychiatry, 61*(5), 459–467.

Geller, B., Williams, M., Zimerman, B., Frazier, J., Beringer, L., & Warner, K. L. (1998). Prepubertal and early adolescent bipolarity differentiate from ADHD by manic symptoms, grandiose delusions, ultra-rapid or ultradian cycling. *Journal of Affective Disorders, 51*(2), 81–91.

Geller, B., Zimerman, B., Williams, M., Bolhofner, K., & Craney, J. L. (2001). Bipolar disorder at prospective follow-up of adults who had prepubertal major depressive disorder. *The American Journal of Psychiatry, 158*(1), 125–127. Retrieved March 29, 2008, from Research Library database. (Document ID No. 66452262)

Geller, D. A., Hoog, S. L., Heiligenstein, J. H., Ricardi, R. K., Tamura, R., Kluszynski, S., et al. (2001). Fluoxetine treatment for obsessive-compulsive disorder in children and adolescents: A placebo-controlled clinical trial. *Journal of the American Academy of Child & Adolescent Psychiatry, 40*(7), 773–779.

Gerlinghoff, M., Gross, G., & Backmund, H. (2003). Eating disorder therapy concepts with a preventive goal. *European Child & Adolescent Psychiatry, 12*, I/72–I/77.

Gervais, H., Belin, P., Boddaert, N., Leboyer, M., Coez, A., Sfaello, I., et al. (2004). Abnormal cortical voice processing in autism. *Nature Neuroscience, 7*(8), 801–802.

Ghaziuddin, M. (2002). Asperger syndrome: Associated psychiatric and medical conditions. *Focus on Autism and Other Developmental Disabilities, 17*(3), 138–144.

Giaconia, R. M., Reinherz, H. Z., Silverman, A. B., & Pakiz, B. (1995). Traumas and posttraumatic stress disorder in a community population of older adolescents. *Journal of the American Academy of Child & Adolescent Psychiatry, 34*(10), 1369–1380.

Giancola, P. R. (1995). Evidence for dorsolateral and orbital prefrontal cortical involvement in the expression of aggressive behavior. *Aggressive Behavior, 21,* 431–450.

Gilbert, S., & Thompson, J. K. (1996). Feminist explanations of the development of eating disorders: Common themes, research findings, and methodological issues. *Clinical Psychology: Science and Practice, 3*(3), 183–202.

Gillberg, C., & Coleman, M. (1992). *The biology of the autistic syndromes* (2nd ed.). London: Mac Keith Press.

Gillberg, C., Gillberg, C., Rastam, M., & Wentz, E. (2001). The Asperger syndrome (and high-functioning autism) diagnostic interview (ASDI): A preliminary study of a new structured clinical interview. *Autism, 5*(1), 57–66.

Gillberg, C., & Svennerholm, L. (1987). CSF monoamines in autistic syndromes and other pervasive developmental disorders of early childhood. *British Journal of Psychiatry, 151,* 89–94.

Gillberg, C., Svennerholm, L., & Hamilton-Hellberg, C. (1983). Childhood psychosis and monoamine

metabolites in spinal fluid. *Journal of Autism and Developmental Disorders, 13*(4), 383–396.

Gillberg, I. C., Gillberg, C., & Kopp, S. (1992). Hypothyroidism and autism spectrum disorders. *Journal of Child Psychology and Psychiatry, 33*(3), 531–542.

Gilliam, J. E. (1995). *Gilliam Autism Rating Scale.* Austin, TX: ProEd.

Gilmour, J., Hill, B., Place, M., & Skuse, D. H. (2004). Social communication deficits in conduct disorder: A clinical and community survey. *Journal of Child Psychology and Psychiatry, 45*(5), 967–978.

Ginsburg, G. S., & Walkup, J. T. (2004). Specific phobia. In T. H. Ollendick & J. S. March (Eds.), *Phobic and anxiety disorders in children and adolescents: A clinician's guide to effective psychosocial and pharmacological interventions* (pp. 175–197). New York: Oxford University Press.

Gladding, S. T. (2001). *The counseling dictionary.* Upper Saddle River, NJ: Merrill.

Glasser, W. (1965). *Reality therapy: A new approach to psychiatry.* New York: Harper & Row.

Gloria, A. M., & Robinson-Kurpius, S. E. R. (2000). I can't live without it: Adolescent substance abuse from a cultural and contextual framework. In D. Capuzzi & D. R. Gross (Eds.), *Youth risk: A prevention resource for counselors, teachers, and parents* (3rd ed., pp. 409–439). Alexandria, VA: American Counseling Association.

Goenjian, A. K., Karayan, I., Pynoos, R. S., Minassian, D., Najarian, L. M., Steinberg, A. M., & Fairbanks, L. M. (1997). Outcome of psychotherapy among early adolescents after trauma. *American Journal of Psychiatry, 154,* 536–542.

Goldbloom, D. S., Olmsted, M., Davis, R., Clewes, J., Heinmaa, M., Rockert, W., et al. (1997). A randomized controlled trial of fluoxetine and cognitive behavioral therapy for bulimia nervosa: Short-term outcome. *Behaviour Research and Therapy, 35*(9), 803–811.

Goldstein, D. J., Wilson, M. G., Thompson, V. L., Potvin, J. H., & Rampey, A. H. (1995). Long-term fluoxetine treatment of bulimia nervosa. *British Journal of Psychiatry, 166*(5), 660–666.

Gonet, M. M. (1994). *Counseling the adolescent substance abuser: School-based intervention and prevention.* Thousand Oaks, CA: Sage.

Goodman, R., & Stevenson, J. (1989). A twin study of hyperactivity—I. An examination of hyperactivity scores and categories derived from Rutter teacher and parent questionnaires. *Journal of Child Psychology and Psychiatry, 30*(5), 671–689.

Goodyear, R. K. (2002). A concept map of male partners in teenage pregnancy: Implications for school counselors. *Professional School Counseling, 5*(3), 186–193.

Gotestam, K. G., & Agras, W. S. (1995). General population-based epidemiological study of eating disorders in Norway. *International Journal of Eating Disorders, 18,* 119–126.

Gowen, L. K., Hayward, C., Killen, J. D., Robinson, T. N., & Taylor, C. B. (1999). Acculturation and eating disorder symptoms in adolescent girls. *Journal of Research on Adolescence, 9*(1), 67–83.

Grant, B. F., & Dawson, D. A. (1997). Age at onset of alcohol use and its association with *DSM-IV* alcohol abuse and dependence: Results from the national longitudinal alcohol epidemiologic survey. *Journal of Substance Abuse, 9,* 103–110.

Grant, S. H., Van Acker, R., Guerra, N., Duplechain, R., & Coen, M. (1998). A school and classroom enhancement program to prevent the development of antisocial behavior in children from high-risk neighborhoods. *Preventing School Failure, 42,* 121–127.

Grave, R. D., Ricca, V., & Todesco, T. (2001). The stepped-care approach in anorexia nervosa and bulimia nervosa: Progress and problems. *Eating and Weight Disorders, 6*(2), 81–89.

Gray, C. A., & Garand, J. D. (1993). Social stories: Improving responses of students with autism with accurate social information. *Focus on Autistic Behavior, 8*(1), 1–10.

Gray, L. A., House, R. M., & Champeau, D. A. (2000). A future in jeopardy: Adolescents and AIDS. In D. Capuzzi & D. R. Gross (Eds.), *Youth at risk: A prevention resource for teachers, parents, and counselors* (pp. 281–317). Alexandria, VA: American Counseling Association.

Graziano, A. M., & Mooney, K. C. (1980). Family self-control instruction for children's nighttime fear reduction. *Journal of Consulting and Clinical Psychology, 48*(2), 206–213.

Green, L. W., & Kreuter, M. W. (1992). CDC's planned approach to community health as an application of PRECEDE and an inspiration for PROCEED. *Journal of Health Education, 23,* 140–147.

Greenbaum, S., Turner, B., & Stephens, R. (1989). *Set straight on bullies.* Malibu, CA: National School Safety Center.

Greene, R. W. (2006). Oppositional defiant disorder. In R. T. Ammerman (Ed.), *Comprehensive handbook of personality and psychopathology: Vol. 3.* (pp. 285–298). Hoboken, NJ: John Wiley & Sons, Inc.

Greene, R. W., & Ablon, J. S. (2005). *Treating explosive kids: The collaborative problem-solving approach.* New York: Guilford Press.

Greene, R. W., Biederman, J., Zerwas, S., Monuteaux, M., Goring, J. C., & Faraone, S. V. (2002). Psychiatric comorbidity, family dysfunction, and social impairment in referred youth with oppositional defiant disorder. *American Journal of Psychiatry, 159*(7), 1214–1224.

Greene, R. W., & Doyle, A. E. (1999). Toward a transactional conceptualization of oppositional defiant disorder: Implications for assessment and treatment. *Clinical Child and Family Psychology Review, 2*(3), 129–148.

Greenhill, L. L., Halperin, J. M., & Abikoff, H. (1999). Stimulant medications. *Journal of the American Academy of Child and Adolescent Psychiatry, 38,* 503–512.

Greenhill, L. L., Solomon, M., Pleak, R., & Ambrosini, P. (1985). Molindone hydrochloride treatment of hospitalized children with conduct disorder. *Journal of Clinical Psychiatry, 46*(8), 20–25.

Grella, C. E., Hser, Y.-I., Joshi, V., & Rounds-Bryant, J. (2001). Drug treatment outcomes for adolescents with comorbid mental and substance use disorders. *Journal of Nervous and Mental Disease, 189*(6), 384–392.

Grelotti, D. J., Gauthier, I., & Schultz, R. T. (2002). Social interest and the development of cortical face specialization: What autism teaches us about face processing. *Developmental Psychobiology, 40*(3), 213–225.

Gresham, F. M. (2004). Current status and future directions of school-based behavioral interventions. *School Psychology Review, 33,* 326–343.

Gresham, F. M. (2005). Response to intervention: An alternative means of identifying students as emotionally disturbed. *Education & Treatment of Children, 28*(4), 328–344. Retrieved March 5, 2008, from Wilson Education Abstracts database. (Document ID No. 933826921)

Gresham, F. M. (2007). Response to intervention and emotional and behavioral disorders. *Assessment for Effective Interventions, 32*(4), 214–222.

Gresham, F. M., Watson, T. S., & Skinner, C. H. (2001). Functional behavioral assessment: Principles, procedures, and future directions. *School Psychology Review, 30*(2), 156–172.

Gullone, E., & King, N. J. (1992). Psychometric evaluation of a revised fear survey schedule for children and adolescents. *Journal of Child Psychology and Psychiatry, 33*(6), 987–998.

Gunewardene, A., Huon, G. F., & Zheng, R. (2001). Exposure to Westernization and dieting: A cross-cultural study. *International Journal of Eating Disorders, 29*(3), 289–293.

Gushue, G. V. (2004). Race, color-blind racial attitudes, and judgments about mental health: A shifting standards perspective. *Journal of Counseling Psychology, 51,* 398–407.

Gushue, G. V., Constantine, M. G., & Sciarra, D. T. (2008). The influence of culture, self-reported multicultural counseling competence, and shifting standards of judgment on perceptions of family functioning of White family counselors. *Journal of Counseling & Development, 86,* 85–94.

Guttmacher Institute. (2006). *Facts on American teens' sexual and reproductive health.* Retrieved July 15, 2007, from http://www.guttmacher.org/pubs/fb_ATSRH.html

Hadjikhani, N., Chabris, C. F., Joseph, R. M., Clark, J., McGrath, L., Aharon, I., et al. (2004). Early visual cortex organization in autism: An fMRI study. *Neuroreport: For Rapid Communication of Neuroscience Research, 15*(2), 267–270.

Hagiwara, R., & Myles, B. S. (2001). A multimedia social story intervention: Teaching skills to children with autism. *Focus on Autism and Other Developmental Disabilities, 2,* 82–95.

Hahn, A., Leavitt, T., & Aaron, P. (1994). *Evaluation of the Quantum Opportunities Program (QOP): Did the program work?* Waltham, MA: Center for Human Resources.

Hale, J. B., Hoeppner, J. B., DeWitt, M. B., Coury, D. L., Ritacco, D. G., & Trommer, B. (1998). Evaluating medication response in ADHD: Cognitive, behavioral, and single-subject methodology. *Journal of Learning Disabilities, 31*(6), 595–607.

Hall, G. B. C., Szechtman, H., & Nahmias, C. (2003). Enhanced salience and emotion recognition in autism: A PET study. *American Journal of Psychiatry, 160*(8), 1439–1441.

Hallahan, D. P., Lloyd, J. W., Kauffman, J. M., Weiss, M., & Martinez, E. A. (1996, 1999, 2005). *Learning disabilities: Foundations, characteristics, and effective teaching* (3rd ed.). Boston: Allyn & Bacon.

Halperin, J. M., McKay, K. E., Grayson, R. H., & Newcorn, J. H. (2003). Reliability, validity, and preliminary normative data for the children's aggression scale—teacher version. *Journal of the*

American Academy of Child & Adolescent Psychiatry, 42*(8), 965–971.

Hamilton, D. I., & King, N. J. (1991). Reliability of a behavioral avoidance test for the assessment of dog phobic children. *Psychological Reports, 69*(1), 18.

Hamilton, M. (1959). The assessment of anxiety states by rating. *British Journal of Medical Psychology, 32,* 50–55.

Hamilton, S. B., & MacQuiddy, S. L. (1984). Self-administered behavioral parent training: Enhancement of treatment efficacy using a time-out signal seat. *Journal of Clinical Child Psychology, 13*(1), 61–69.

Handen, B. L., Johnson, C. R., & Lubetsky, M. (2000). Efficacy of methylphenidate among children with autism and symptoms of attention-deficit hyperactivity disorder. *Journal of Autism and Developmental Disorders, 30*(3), 245–255.

Hanish, L. D., & Guerra, N. G. (2000a). Children who get victimized at school: What is known? What can be done? *Professional School Counseling, 4*(2), 113–119.

Hanish, L. D., & Guerra, N. G. (2000b). The roles of ethnicity and school context in predicting children's victimization by peers. *American Journal of Community Psychology, 28*(2), 201–223.

Haring, T. G., Breen, C. G., Pitts-Conway, V., & Gaylord-Ross, R. (1986). Use of differential reinforcement of other behavior during dyadic instruction to reduce stereotyped behavior of autistic students. *American Journal of Mental Deficiency, 90*(6), 694–702.

Harned, M. S. (2000). Harassed bodies: An examination of the relationships among women's experiences of sexual harassment, body image and eating disturbances. *Psychology of Women Quarterly, 24*(4), 336–348.

Harned, M. S., & Fitzgerald, L. F. (2002). Understanding a link between sexual harassment and eating disorder symptoms: A mediational analysis. *Journal of Consulting and Clinical Psychology, 70*(5), 1170–1181.

Harootunian, B. (1986). School violence and vandalism. In S. J. Apter & A. P. Goldstein (Eds.), *Youth violence: Programs and prospects.* Elmsford, NY: Pergamon Press.

Harry, B. (1994). *The disproportionate representation of minority students in special education: Theories and recommendations.* Alexandria, VA: National Association of State Directors of Special Education.

Hart, B. M., & Risley, T. R. (1968). Establishing use of descriptive adjectives in the spontaneous speech of disadvantaged preschool children. *Journal of Applied Behavior Analysis, 1*(2), 109–120.

Hart, S. L. (1991). Childhood depression: Implications and options for school counselors. *Elementary School Guidance & Counseling, 25*(4), 277–289.

Hattie, J., Biggs, J., & Purdie, N. (1996). Effects of learning skills interventions on student learning: A meta-analysis. *Review of Educational Research, 66*(2), 99. Retrieved March 7, 2008, from Wilson Education Abstracts database. (Document ID No. 10006263)

Hauck, M., Fein, D., & Maltby, N. (1999). Memory for faces in children with autism. *Child Neuropsychology, 4,* 187–198.

Hawkins, J. D., Arthur, M. W., & Catalano, R. F. (1995). Preventing substance abuse. In M. Tonry & D. P. Farrington (Eds.), *Building a safer society: Strategic approaches to crime prevention: Vol. 19. Crime and justice: A review of research* (pp. 343–427). Chicago: University of Chicago Press.

Hayward, C., Gotlib, I. H., Schraedley, P. K., & Litt, I. F. (1999). Ethnic differences in the association between pubertal status and symptoms of depression in adolescent girls. *Journal of Adolescent Health, 25*(2), 143–149.

Hayward, C., Varady, S., Albano, A. M., Thienemann, M., Henderson, L., & Schatzberg, A. F. (2000). Cognitive-behavioral group therapy for social phobia in female adolescents: Results of a pilot study. *Journal of the American Academy of Child & Adolescent Psychiatry, 39*(6), 721–726.

Hazell, P. (2002). Depression in children. *British Medical Journal, 325*(7358), 229–230.

Hazler, R. J. (1996). *Breaking the cycle of violence: Interventions for bullying and victimization.* Washington, DC: Accelerated Development.

Hazler, R. J., & Carney, J. V. (2000). When victims turn aggressors: Factors in the development of deadly school violence. *Professional School Counseling, 4*(2), 105–112.

Haznedar, M. M., Buchsbaum, M. S., Wei, T. C., Hof, P. R., Cartwright, C., Bienstock, C. A., et al. (2000). Limbic circuitry in patients with autism spectrum disorders studied with positron emission tomography and magnetic resonance imaging. *American Journal of Psychiatry, 157*(12), 1994–2001.

Healy, J. M. (1999). *Failure to connect: How computers affect our children's minds—and what we can do about it.* New York: Touchstone.

Heinrichs, R. (2003). A whole-school approach to bullying: Special considerations for children with exceptionalities. *Intervention in School and Clinic, 38*(4), 195–204.

Heller, K. A., Holtzman, W. H., & Messick, S. (Eds.). (1982). *Placing children in special education: A strategy for equity.* Washington, DC: National Academy Press.

Hendren, R. L., & Mullen, D. J. (2006). Conduct disorder and oppositional defiant disorder. In M. K. Dulcan & J. M. Wiener (Eds.), *Essentials of child and adolescent psychiatry* (pp. 357–387). Washington, DC: American Psychiatric Publishing.

Henggeler, S. W. (1991). Multidimensional causal models of delinquent behavior and their implications for treatment. In R. Cohen & A. W. Siegel (Eds.), *Context and development* (pp. 211–231). Hillsdale, NJ: Erlbaum.

Henggeler, S. W., Borduin, C. M., Melton, G. B., Mann, B. J., Smith, L., Hall, J. A., et al. (1991). Effects of multisystemic therapy on drug use and abuse in serious juvenile offenders: A progress report from two outcome studies. *Family Dynamics of Addiction Quarterly, 1,* 40–51.

Henggeler, S. W., Cunningham, P. B., Pickrel, S. G., & Schoenwald, S. K. (1996). Multisystemic therapy: An effective violence prevention approach for serious juvenile offenders. *Journal of Adolescence, 19*(1), 47–61.

Henggeler, S. W., Melton, G. B., & Smith, L. A. (1992). Family preservation using multisystemic therapy: An effective alternative to incarcerating serious juvenile offenders. *Journal of Consulting and Clinical Psychology, 60*(6), 953–961.

Henggeler, S. W., Pickrel, S. G., & Brondino, M. J. (1999). Multisystemic treatment of substance abusing and dependent delinquents: Outcomes, treatment fidelity, and transportability. *Mental Health Services Research, 1,* 171–184.

Henggeler, S. W., Rodick, J. D., Borduin, C. M., Hanson, C. L., Watson, S. M., & Urey, J. R. (1986). Multisystemic treatment of juvenile offenders: Effects on adolescent behavior and family interaction. *Developmental Psychology, 22*(1), 132–141.

Henry, D. B., Tolan, P. H., & Gorman-Smith, D. (2001). Longitudinal family and peer group effects on violence and nonviolent delinquency. *Journal of Clinical Child Psychology, 30*(2), 172–186.

Herbert, M. R., Harris, G. J., Adrien, K. T., Ziegler, D. A., Makris, N., Kennedy, D. N., et al. (2002). Abnormal asymmetry in language association cortex in autism. *Annals of Neurology, 52*(5), 588–596.

Herbert, M. R., Ziegler, D. A., Makris, N., Filipek, P. A., Kemper, T. L., Normandin, J. J., et al. (2004). Localization of white matter volume increase in autism and developmental language disorder. *Annals of Neurology, 55,* 530–540.

Herpertz-Dahlmann, B., Müller, B., Herpertz, S., Heussen, N., Hebebrand, J., & Remschmidt, H. (2001). Prospective 10-year follow-up in adolescent anorexia nervosa: Course, outcome, psychiatric comorbidity, and psychosocial adaptation. *Journal of Child Psychology and Psychiatry, 42*(5), 603–612.

Herzog, D. B., Dorer, D. J., Keel, P. K., Selwyn, S. E., Ekeblad, E. R., Flores, A. T., et al. (1999). Recovery and relapse in anorexia and bulimia nervosa: A 7.5-year follow-up study. *Journal of the American Academy of Child & Adolescent Psychiatry, 38*(7), 829–837.

Herzog, D. B., Greenwood, D. N., Dorer, D. J., Flores, A. T., Ekeblad, E. R., Richards, A., et al. (2000). Mortality in eating disorders: A descriptive study. *International Journal of Eating Disorders, 28*(1), 20–26.

Hewitt, J. K., Silberg, J. L., Rutter, M., Simonoff, E., Meyer, J. M., Maes, H., et al. (1997). Genetics and developmental psychopathology: 1. Phenotypic assessment in the Virginia Twin Study of Adolescent Behavioral Development. *Journal of Child Psychology and Psychiatry, 38*(8), 943–963.

Heyne, D., King, N. J., & Tonge, B. (2004). School refusal. In T. H. Ollendick & J. S. March (Eds.), *Phobic and anxiety disorders in children and adolescents: A clinician's guide to effective psychosocial and pharmacological interventions* (pp. 236–271). New York: Oxford University Press.

Hill, J. H., Liebert, R. M., & Mott, D. E. (1968). Vicarious extinction of avoidance behavior through films: An initial test. *Psychological Reports, 22*(1), 192.

Hinshaw, S. P. (1991). Stimulant medication and the treatment of aggression in children with attentional deficits. *Journal of Clinical Child Psychology, 20*(3), 301–312.

Hinshaw, S. P. (1994a). *Attention deficits and hyperactivity in children.* Thousand Oaks, CA: Sage.

Hinshaw, S. P. (1994b). Conduct disorder in childhood: Conceptualization, diagnosis, comorbidity, and risk status for antisocial functioning in adulthood. In D. C. Fowles, P. Sutker, & S. H. Goodman (Eds.), *Progress in experimental personality and psychopathology research* (pp. 3–44). New York: Springer.

Hinshaw, S. P., Klein, R. G., & Abikoff, H. (1998). Childhood attention deficit hyperactivity disorder: Nonpharmacological and combination treatment.

In P. E. Nathan & J. M. Gorman (Eds.), *A guide to treatments that work* (pp. 26–41). New York: Oxford University Press.

Hirsch, S. R., Link, C. G. G., Goldstein, J. M., & Arvanitis, L. A. (1996). ICI 204,636: A new atypical antipsychotic drug. *British Journal of Psychiatry, 168*(29), 45–56.

Hixon, A. L. (1999). Preventing street gang violence. *American Family Physician, 59*(8), 2121-2, 2125, 2132.

Hodges, E. V. E., Boivin, M., Vitaro, F., & Bukowski, W. M. (1999). The power of friendship: Protection against an escalating cycle of peer victimization. *Developmental Psychology, 35*(1), 94–101.

Hodges, E. V. E., Malone, M. J., & Perry, D. G. (1997). Individual risk and social risk as interacting determinants of victimization in the peer group. *Developmental Psychology, 33*(6), 1032–1039.

Hodges, K., Kline, J., Stern, L., Cytryn, L., & McKnew, D. (1982). The development of the child assessment interview for research and clinical use. *Journal of Abnormal Child Psychology, 10,* 173–189.

Hoek, H. W. (1993). Review of the epidemiological studies of eating disorders. *International Review of Psychiatry, 5*(1), 61–74.

Hoek, H. W., & van Hoeken, D. (2003). Review of the prevalence and incidence of eating disorders. *International Journal of Eating Disorders, 34*(4), 383–396.

Hoff, K. E., Ervin, R. A., & Friman, P. C. (2005). Refining functional behavioral assessment: Analyzing the separate and combined effects of hypothesized controlling variables during ongoing classroom routines. *School Psychology Review, 34*(1), 45–57.

Hofferth, S. L. (1991). Programs for high risk adolescents: What works? *Evaluation and Program Planning, 14*(1), 3–16.

Hogan, A. E. (1999). Cognitive functioning in children with oppositional defiant disorder and conduct disorder. In H. C. Quay & A. E. Hogan (Eds.), *Handbook of disruptive behavior disorders* (pp. 317–335). New York: Kluwer Academic/Plenum.

Hohlstein, L. A., Smith, G. T., & Atlas, J. G. (1998). An application of expectancy theory to eating disorders: Development and validation of measures of eating and dieting expectancies. *Psychological Assessment, 10*(1), 49–58.

Holttum, J. R., Lubetsky, M. J., & Eastman, L. E. (1994). Comprehensive management of trichotillomania in a young autistic girl. *Journal of the American Academy of Child & Adolescent Psychiatry, 33*(4), 577–581.

Hoover-Dempsey, K. V., Bassler, O. C., & Brissie, J. S. (1992). Parent efficacy, teacher efficacy, and parent involvement: Explorations in parent–school relations. *Journal of Educational Research, 85,* 287–294.

Horatio Alger Association of Distinguished Americans. (2005). *State of our nation's youth.* Available at http://www.horatioalger.com/pdfs/state05.pdf

Horner, R. H., Sugai, G., Todd, A. W., & Lewis-Palmer, T. (1999–2000). Elements of behavior support plans: A technical brief. *Exceptionality, 8,* 205–215.

Horner, R. H., Sugai, G., Todd, A. W., & Lewis-Palmer, T. (2005). School-wide positive behavior support: In L. Bambara & L. Kern (Eds.), *Individualized supports for students with problem behaviors: Designing positive behavior plans* (pp. 359–390). New York: Guilford Press.

Horrigan, J. (1998, December 18). Risperidone appears effective for children and adolescents with severe PTSD. *Psychiatric News,* p. 8.

Hoshino, Y., Watanabe, M., Tachibana, R., Watanabe, M., Murata, S., Yokoyama, F., et al. (1984). Serotonin metabolism and hypothalamic-pituitary function in children with infantile autism and minimal brain dysfunction. *Japanese Journal of Clinical Psychiatry, 26,* 937–945.

Houlihan, D., Jacobson, L., & Brandon, P. K. (1994). Replication of a high-probability request sequence with varied interprompt times in a preschool setting. *Journal of Applied Behavior Analysis, 27*(4), 737–738.

Howell, J. C., & Lynch, J. (2000, August). *Juvenile justice bulletin* (#NCJ183015). Washington, DC: U.S. Department of Justice.

Howell, K. W., Fox, S. L., & Morehead, M. K. (1993). *Curriculum-based evaluation.* Pacific Grove, CA: Brooks/Cole.

Howlin, P., Goode, S., Hutton, J., & Rutter, M. (2004). Adult outcome for children with autism. *Journal of Child Psychology and Psychiatry, 45*(2), 212–229.

Hubi, D., Bolte, S., Feineis-Matthews, S., Lanfermann, H., Federspeil, A., Strik, W., et al. (2003). Functional imbalance of visual pathways indicates alternative face processing strategies in autism. *Neurology, 61,* 1232–1237.

Hudson, J. L., & Rapee, R. M. (2002). Parent-child interactions in clinically anxious children and their siblings. *Journal of Clinical Child and Adolescent Psychology, 31*(4), 548–555.

Huff, C. R. 1996. The criminal behavior of gang members and nongang at-risk youth. In C. R. Huff (Ed.), *Gangs in America* (2nd ed., pp. 75–102). Thousand Oaks, CA: Sage.

Humphrey, L. L. (1986). Family relations in bulimic-anorexic and nondistressed families. *International Journal of Eating Disorders, 5*(2), 223–232.

Humphrey, L. L. (1987). Comparison of bulimic-anorexic and nondistressed families using structural analysis of social behavior. *Journal of the American Academy of Child & Adolescent Psychiatry, 26*(2), 248–255.

Hunter, L., Elias, M. J., & Norris, J. (2001). School-based violence prevention: Challenges and lessons learned from an action research project. *Journal of School Psychology, 39,* 161–175.

Hviid, A., Stellfeld, M., Wohlfahrt, J., & Melbye, M. (2003). Association between thimerosal-containing vaccine and autism. *Journal of the American Medical Association, 290,* 1763–1766.

Hyman, I. A., Wojtowicz, A., Lee, K. D., Haffner, M. E., Fiorello, C. A., Storlazzi, J. J., et al. (1998). School-based methylphenidate placebo protocols: Methodological and practical issues. *Journal of Learning Disabilities, 31*(6), 581–594, 614.

Ialongo, N. S., Horn, W. F., Pasco, J. M., Greenberg, G., Packard, T., Lopez, M., et al. (1993). The effects of a multimodal intervention with attention-deficit hyperactivity disorder children: A 9-month follow-up. *Journal of the American Academy of Child and Adolescent Psychiatry, 32*(1), 182–189.

IDEAdata.org (2007). ASD assessment rate. Retrieved February 9, 2008, from https://www.ideadata.org/IDEA618DataTables.asp

Individuals with Disabilities Education Act Amendments of 1997, 20 U.S.C. § 1401 (26).

Ingersoll, B., & Schreibman, L. (2001, November). *Training spontaneous imitation in children with autism using naturalistic teaching strategies.* Paper presented at the annual meeting of the International Meeting for Autism Research, San Diego, CA.

Ingersoll, B., Schreibman, L., & Stahmer, A. (2001). Brief report: Differential treatment outcomes for children with autistic spectrum disorder based on level of peer social avoidance. *Journal of Autism and Developmental Disorders, 31*(3), 343–349.

Ingram, K., Lewis-Palmer, T., & Sugai, G. (2005). Function-based intervention planning: Comparing the effectiveness of FBA indicated and contra-indicated intervention plans. *Journal of Positive Behavior Interventions, 7,* 224–236.

Insel, T. R. (1992). Toward a neuroanatomy of obsessive-compulsive disorder. *Archives of General Psychiatry, 49*(9), 739–744.

Insel, T. R., & Akiskal, H. S. (1986). Obsessive-compulsive disorder with psychotic features: A phenomenologic analysis. *American Journal of Psychiatry, 143*(12), 1527–1533.

Institute of Educational Sciences, U.S. Department of Education. (2006). National Center for Educational Statistics, Digest of Educational Statistics. Retrieved February 2, 2008, from http://nces.ed.gov/programs/digest/d06/tables/dt06-106.asp

Is your child being bullied? Tips for parents. (April 2005). *Brown University Child and Adolescent Behavior Letter 21*(4), 9–10.

Jaberghaderi, N., Greenwald, R., Rubin, A., Dolatubadim, S., & Zand, S. O. (2002). *A comparison of CBT and EMDR for sexually abused Iranian girls.* Unpublished manuscript, Allame Tabatabee University, Tehran, Iran.

Jackson, C. T., Fein, D., Wolf, J., Jones, G., Hauck, M., Waterhouse, L., et al. (2003). Responses and sustained interactions in children with mental retardation and autism. *Journal of Autism and Developmental Disorders, 33*(2), 115–121.

Jacobi, C., Hayward, C., de Zwaan, M., Kraemer, H. C., & Agras, W. S. (2004). Coming to terms with risk factors for eating disorders: Application of risk terminology and suggestions for a general taxonomy. *Psychological Bulletin, 130*(1), 19–65.

Jacobson, S. W., & Frye, K. F. (1991). Effect of maternal social support on attachment: Experimental evidence. *Child Development, 62*(3), 572–582.

Jalali, B., Jalali, M., Crocetti, G., & Turner, F. (1981). Adolescents and drug use: Toward a more comprehensive approach. *American Journal of Orthopsychiatry, 51*(1), 120–130.

Jastrzab, J., Masker, J., Blomquist, J., & Orr, L. (1996). *Evaluation of national and community service programs: Impacts of service. Final report on the evaluation of the American Youth and Conservation Service Corps.* Cambridge, MA: Abt Associates.

Jenkins, E. J., & Bell, C. C. (1994). Violence among inner city high school students and post-traumatic stress disorder. In S. Friedman (Ed.), *Anxiety disorders in African Americans* (pp. 76–88). New York: Springer.

Jensen, J. B., & Garfinkel, B. D. (1990). Growth hormone dysregulation in children with major depressive disorder. *Journal of the American Academy of Child & Adolescent Psychiatry, 29*(2), 295–301.

Jensen, J. B., Realmuto, G. M., & Garfinkel, B. D. (1985). The dexamethasone suppression test in infantile autism. *Journal of the American Academy of Child Psychiatry, 24*(3), 263–265.

Jensen, M. M. (2005). *Introduction to emotional and behavioral disorders: Recognizing and managing problems in the classroom.* Upper Saddle River, NJ: Pearson Education.

Jensen, P. S., Martin, D., & Cantwell, D. (1997). Comorbidity in ADHD: Implications for research, practice, and *DSM-IV. Journal of the American Academy of Child Adolescent Psychiatry, 36*(8), 1065–1079.

Jerome, L., Gordon, M., & Hustler, P. (1994). Comparison of American and Canadian teachers' knowledge and attitudes towards attention deficit hyperactivity disorder (ADHD). *Canadian Journal of Psychiatry, 39,* 563–566.

Johnson, J. G., Cohen, P., Kasen, S., & Brook, J. S. (2002). Eating disorders during adolescence and the risk for physical and mental disorders during early adulthood. *Archives of General Psychiatry, 59*(6), 545–552.

Johnston, C., & Ohan, J. L. (1996). The importance of parental attributions in families of children with attention-deficit/hyperactivity and disruptive behavior disorders. *Clinical Child and Family Psychology Review, 8,* 167–182.

Johnston, L. D., O'Malley, P. M., Bachman, J. G., & Schulenberg, J. E. (2006). *Monitoring the future: National results on adolescent drug use.* Bethesda, MD: National Institute on Drug Abuse.

Jones, V., Dohrn, E., & Dunn, C. (2004). *Creating effective programs for students with emotional and behavior disorders: Interdisciplinary approaches for adding meaning and hope to behavior change interventions.* Boston: Pearson Education.

Jordan, D. R. (1998). *Attention deficit disorder: ADHD and ADD syndromes* (3rd ed.). Austin, TX: Pro-Ed.

Joseph, R. M., & Tanaka, J. (2003). Holistic and part-based face recognition in children with autism. *Journal of Child Psychology and Psychiatry, 44*(4), 529–542.

Just, M. A., Cherkassky, V. L., Keller, T. A., & Minshew, N. J. (2004). Cortical activation and synchronization during sentence comprehension in high-functioning autism: Evidence of underconnectivity. *Brain: A Journal of Neurology, 127*(8), 1811–1821.

Kaczynski, J., Denison, H., Wiknertz, A., Ryno, L., & Hjalmers, N. (2000). Structured care program yielded good results in severe anorexia nervosa. *Lakartidningen, 97,* 2734–2737.

Kafantaris, V., Coletti, D. J., Dicker, R., Padula, G., & Kane, J. M. (2003). Lithium treatment of acute mania in adolescents: A large open trial. *Journal of the American Academy of Child & Adolescent Psychiatry, 42*(9), 1038–1045.

Kagan, D. M. (1990). How schools alienate students at risk: A model for examining proximal classroom variables. *Educational Psychologist, 25*(2), pp. 105–125.

Kagan, J., Reznick, J. S., & Gibbons, J. (1989). Inhibited and uninhibited types of children. *Child Development, 60*(4), 838–845.

Kaiser Family Foundation. (2006). *National survey of teens on HIV/AIDS*. Available at http/www.kff.org

Kalafat, J. (1990). Adolescent suicide and the implications for school response programs. *School Counselor, 37*(5), 359–369.

Kaminer, Y., Burleson, J. A., & Goldberger, R. (2002). Cognitive-behavioral coping skills and psychoeducation therapies for adolescent substance abuse. *Journal of Nervous and Mental Disease, 190*(11), 737–745.

Kamphaus, R. W., Reynolds, C. R., & Hatcher, N. M. (1999). Treatment planning and evaluation with the BASC: The Behavior Assessment System for Children. In M. E. Maruish (Ed.), *The use of psychological testing for treatment planning and outcomes assessment* (2nd ed., pp. 563–597). Mahwah, NJ: Erlbaum.

Kane, M. T., & Kendall, P. C. (1989). Anxiety disorders in children: A multiple-baseline evaluation of a cognitive-behavioral treatment. *Behavior Therapy, 20*(4), 499–508.

Kanfer, F. H., Karoly, P., & Newman, A. (1975). Reduction of children's fear of the dark by competence-related and situational threat-related verbal cues. *Journal of Consulting and Clinical Psychology, 43*(2), 251–258.

Karoly, P., & Rosenthal, M. (1977). Training parents in behavior modification: Effects on perceptions of family interaction and deviant child behavior. *Behavior Therapy, 8*(3), 406–410.

Kasari, C., Sigman, M. D., Baumgartner, P., & Stipek, D. J. (1993). Pride and mastery in children with autism. *Journal of Child Psychology and Psychiatry, 34*(3), 353–362.

Kashani, J. H., & Orvaschel, H. (1990). A community study of anxiety in children and adolescents. *American Journal of Psychiatry, 147*(3), 313–318.

Kauffman, J. M. (2005). *Characteristics of emotional and behavioral disorders of children and youth* (8th ed.). Upper Saddle River, NJ: Pearson Education.

Kaufman, J., Birmaher, B., Brent, D., & Rao, U. (1997). Schedule for affective disorders and schizophrenia for school-age children—Present and lifetime version (K-SADS-PL): Initial reliability and validity data. *Journal of the American Academy of Child & Adolescent Psychiatry, 36*(7), 980–988.

Kay, S. R., Wolkenfield, F., & Murrill, L. M. (1988). Profiles of aggression among psychiatric patients: I. Nature and prevalence. *Journal of Nervous Mental Disorders, 176*, 539–546.

Kaye, W. H., & Weltzin, T. E. (1991). Neurochemistry of bulimia nervosa. *Journal of Clinical Psychiatry, 52*, 21–28.

Kazdin, A. E. (1973). The effect of suggestion and pretesting on avoidance reduction in fearful subjects. *Journal of Behavior Therapy and Experimental Psychiatry, 4*(3), 213–221.

Kazdin, A. E. (1995). Child, parent and family dysfunction as predictors of outcome in cognitive-behavioral treatment of antisocial children. *Behaviour Research and Therapy, 33*(3), 271–281.

Kazdin, A. E. (1998). Psychosocial treatments for conduct disorder in children. In P. E. Nathan & J. M. Gorman (Eds.), *A guide to treatments that work* (pp. 65–89). New York: Oxford University Press.

Kazdin, A. E. (2001). Treatment of conduct disorders. In J. Hill & B. Maughan (Eds.), *Conduct disorders in childhood and adolescence* (pp. 408–448). New York: Cambridge University Press.

Kazdin, A. E. (2005). Child, parent, and family-based treatment of aggressive and antisocial child behavior. In E. D. Hibbs & P. S. Jensen (Eds.), *Psychosocial treatments for child and adolescent disorders: Empirically based strategies for clinical practice* (2nd ed., pp. 445–476). Washington, DC: American Psychological Association.

Kazdin, A. E. (2005). *Parent management training: Treatment for oppositional, aggressive, and anti-social behavior in children and adolescents*. New York: Oxford University Press.

Kazdin, A. E., Bass, D., Siegel, T., & Thomas, C. (1989). Cognitive-behavioral therapy and relationship therapy in the treatment of children referred for antisocial behavior. *Journal of Consulting and Clinical Psychology, 57*(4), 522–535.

Kazdin, A. E., Esveldt-Dawson, K., French, N. H., & Unis, A. S. (1987). Problem-solving skills training and relationship therapy in the treatment of antisocial child behavior. *Journal of Consulting and Clinical Psychology, 55*(1), 76–85.

Kazdin, A. E., Siegel, T. C., & Bass, D. (1992). Cognitive problem-solving skills training and parent management training in the treatment of antisocial behavior in children. *Journal of Consulting and Clinical Psychology, 60*(5), 733–747.

Kazdin, A. E., & Wassell, G. (2000). Therapeutic changes in children, parents, and families resulting from treatment of children with conduct problems. *Journal of the American Academy of Child & Adolescent Psychiatry, 39*(4), 414–420.

Keenan, K., & Shaw, D. (1997). Developmental and social influences on young girls' early problem behavior. *Psychological Bulletin, 12,* 95–113.

Keller, M. B., Ryan, N. D., Strober, M., Klein, R. G., Kutcher, S. P., Birmaher, B., et al. (2001). Efficacy of paroxetine in the treatment of adolescent major depression: A randomized, controlled trial. *Journal of the American Academy of Child & Adolescent Psychiatry, 40*(7), 762–772.

Kelly, S. J., Day, N., & Streissguth, A. P. (2000). Effects of prenatal alcohol exposure on social behavior in humans and other species. *Neurotoxicology and Teratology, 22*(2), 143–149.

Kempes, M., Matthys, W., de Vries, H., & van Engeland, H. (2005). Reactive and proactive aggression in children: A review of theory, findings and the relevance for child and adolescent psychiatry. *European Child & Adolescent Psychiatry, 14*(1), 11–19.

Kendall, P. C. (1991). Guiding theory for therapy with children and adolescents. In P. C. Kendall (Ed.), *Child and adolescent therapy: Cognitive-behavioral procedures* (pp. 3–22). New York: Guilford Press.

Kendall, P. C. (1992). *Copy cat workbook.* Ardmore, PA: Workbook Publishing.

Kendall, P. C. (1994). Treating anxiety disorders in children: Results of a randomized clinical trial. *Journal of Consulting and Clinical Psychology, 62*(1), 100–110.

Kendall, P. C., Flannery-Schroeder, E., Panichelli-Mindel, S. M., Southam-Gerow, M., Henin, A., & Warman, M. (1997). Therapy for youths with anxiety disorders: A second randomized clinical trial. *Journal of Consulting and Clinical Psychology, 65*(3), 366–380.

Kendall, P. C., Panichelli-Mindel, S. M., Sugarman, A., & Callahan, S. A. (1997). Exposure to child anxiety: Theory, research, and practice. *Clinical Psychology: Science and Practice, 4*(1), 29–39.

Kendall, P. C., & Pimentel, S. S. (2003). On the physiological symptom constellation in youth with generalized anxiety disorder (GAD). *Journal of Anxiety Disorders, 17*(2), 211–221.

Kendall, P. C., Pimentel, S., Rynn, M. A., Angelosante, A., & Webb, A. (2004). Generalized anxiety disorder. In T. H. Ollendick & J. S. March (Eds.), *Phobic and anxiety disorders in children and adolescents: A clinician's guide to effective psychosocial and pharmacological interventions* (pp. 334–380). New York: Oxford University Press.

Kendler, K. S. (2001). Twin studies of psychiatric illness: An update. *Archives of General Psychiatry, 58*(11), 1005–1014.

Kendler, K. S., Neale, M. C., Kessler, R. C., & Heath, A. C. (1992). The genetic epidemiology of phobias in women: The interrelationship of agoraphobia, social phobia, situational phobia, and simple phobia. *Archives of General Psychiatry, 49*(4), 273–281.

Kennedy, C. H., & Haring, T. G. (1993). Combining reward and escape DRO to reduce the problem behavior of students with severe disabilities. *Journal of the Association for Persons with Severe Handicaps, 18*(2), 85–92.

Kennedy, C. H., & Itkonnen, T. (1993). Effects of setting events on the problem behavior of students with severe disabilities. *Journal of Applied Behavioral Analysis, 26,* 321–327.

Kent, R. N., & O'Leary, K. D. (1976). A controlled evaluation of behavior modification with conduct problem children. *Journal of Consulting and Clinical Psychology, 44*(4), 586–596.

Kessler, R. C., McGonagle, K. A., Zhao, S., & Nelson, C. B. (1994). Lifetime and 12-month prevalence of *DSM-III-R* psychiatric disorders in the United States: Results from the National Comorbidity Study. *Archives of General Psychiatry, 51*(1), 8–19.

Kessler, R. C., Sonnega, A., Bromet, E., Hughes, M., & Nelson, C. B. (1995). Posttraumatic stress disorder in the National Comorbidity Survey. *Archives of General Psychiatry, 52*(12), 1048–1060.

Kim, M. S., Kim, J. J., & Kwon, J. S. (2001). Frontal P300 decrement and executive dysfunction in adolescents with conduct problems. *Child Psychiatry & Human Development, 32*(2), 93–106.

Kimonis, E. R., & Frick, P. J. (2006). Conduct disorder. In R. T. Ammerman (Ed.), *Comprehensive handbook of personality and psychopathology: Vol 3. Child psychopathology* (pp. 299–315). Hoboken, NJ: John Wiley & Sons, Inc.

King, N. J., Cranstoun, F., & Josephs, A. (1989). Emotive imagery and children's night-time fears: A multiple baseline design evaluation. *Journal of Behavior Therapy and Experimental Psychiatry, 20*(2), 125–135.

King, N. J., Gullone, E., & Ollendick, T. H. (1992). Manifest anxiety and fearfulness in children and adolescents. *Journal of Genetic Psychology, 153*(1), 63–73.

King, N. J., Muris, P., & Ollendick, T. H. (2004). Specific phobia. In T. L. Morris & J. S. March (Eds.), *Anxiety disorders in children and adolescents* (2nd ed., pp. 263–279). New York: Guilford Press.

King, N. J., Muris, P., & Ollendick, T. H. (2005). Childhood fears and phobias: Assessment and treatment. *Child and Adolescent Mental Health, 10*(2), 50–56.

King, N. J., Ollendick, T. H., & Murphy, G. C. (1997). Assessment of childhood phobias. *Clinical Psychology Review, 17*(7), 667–687.

Kirby, D. (1999). Reflection on two decades of research on teen sexual behavior and pregnancy. *Journal of School Health, 69,* 89–94.

Kirby, D. (2001). *Emerging answers: Research findings on programs to reduce teen pregnancy* (Summary). Washington, DC: National Campaign to Prevent Teenage Pregnancy.

Kirby, D., Short, L., Colins, J., Rugg, D., Kolbe, L., Howard, M., et al. (1994). School-based programs to reduce sexual risk behaviors: A review of effectiveness. *Public Health Report, 109,* 339–360.

Kiselica, M. S. (1995). *Multicultural counseling with teen fathers: A practical guide.* Newbury Park, CA: Sage.

Kiselica, M. S., Gorcynski, J., & Capps, S. (1998). Teen mothers and fathers: School counselor perceptions of service needs. *Professional School Counseling, 2*(2), 146–152.

Kiselica, M. S., & Scheckel, S. (1995). The couvade syndrome (sympathetic pregnancy) and teenage fathers: A brief primer for school counselors. *School Counselor, 43*(1), 42–51.

Kjelgaard, M. M., & Tager-Flusberg, H. (2001). An investigation of language impairment in autism: Implications for genetic subgroups. *Language and Cognitive Processes, 16*(2), 287–308.

Klin, A. (1994). Asperger syndrome. *Child and Adolescent Psychiatry Clinic of North America, 3,* 131–148.

Klin, A., McPartland, J., & Volkmar, F. R. (2005). Asperger syndrome. In F. R. Volkmar, R. Paul, A. Klin, & D. Cohen (Eds.), *Handbook of autism and pervasive developmental disorders: Vol. 1. Diagnosis, development, neurobiology, and behavior* (3rd ed., pp. 88–125). Hoboken, NJ: John Wiley & Sons, Inc.

Klinteberg, B. A., Andersson, T., Magnusson, D., & Stattin, H. (1993). Hyperactive behavior in childhood as related to subsequent alcohol problems and violent offending: A longitudinal study of male subjects. *Personality and Individual Differences, 15,* 381–388.

Knoster, T., & Kincaid, D. (1999). Effective school practice in educating students with challenging behaviors. *TASH Newsletter, 11*(25), 8–11.

Kochanska, G., & Aksan, N. (1995). Mother-child mutually positive affect, the quality of child compliance to requests and prohibitions, and maternal control as correlates of early internalization. *Child Development, 66*(1), 236–254.

Koegel, L. K., & Koegel, R. L. (1989). Autism. In M. Hersen (Ed.), *Innovations in child behavior therapy* (pp. 395–428). New York: Springer.

Koegel, R. L., Bimbela, A., & Schreibman, L. (1996). Collateral effects of parent training on family interactions. *Journal of Autism and Developmental Disorders, 26*(3), 347–359.

Kohn, A. (1996). *Beyond discipline: From compliance to community.* Alexandria, VA: Association for Supervision and Curriculum Development.

Kollins, S. H., Barkley, R. A., & DuPaul, G. J. (2001). Use and management of medications for children diagnosed with attention deficit hyperactivity disorder (ADHD). *Focus on Exceptional Children, 33*(5), 1–23.

Kondas, O. (1967). Reduction of examination anxiety and stage-fright by group desensitization and relaxation. *Behaviour Research and Therapy, 5*(4), 275–281.

Koning, C., & Magill-Evans, J. (2001). Social and language skills in adolescent boys with Asperger syndrome. *Autism, 5*(1), 23–36.

Kornhaber, R. C., & Schroeder, H. E. (1975). Importance of model similarity on extinction of avoidance behavior in children. *Journal of Consulting and Clinical Psychology, 43*(5), 601–607.

Kovacs, M. (1985). The Children's Depression Inventory (CDI). *Psychopharmacological Bulletin, 21,* 995–998.

Kovacs, M., Akiskal, H. S., Gatsonis, C., & Parrone, P. L. (1994). Childhood-onset dysthymic disorder: Clinical features and prospective naturalistic outcome. *Archives of General Psychiatry, 51*(5), 365–374.

Kovacs, M., & Paulaukas, S. L. (1984). Developmental stage and the expression of depressive disorders in children: An empirical analysis. *New Directions for Child Development, 26,* 59–80.

Kowatch, R. A., Emslie, G. J., & Kennard, B. D. (1997). Mood disorders in children and adolescents. In D. P.

Parmelee (Ed.), *Child and adolescent psychiatry for the clinician* (pp. 121–140). Philadelphia: Mosby.

Kowatch, R. A., Emslie, G. J., Wilkaitis, J., & Dingle, A. D. (2005). Mood disorders. In S. B. Sexson & R. B. David, *Child and adolescent psychiatry* (pp. 132–153). Malden, MA: Blackwell.

Kowatch, R. A., Suppes, T., Carmody, T. J., Bucci, J. P., Hume, J. H., Kromelis, M., et al. (2000). Effect size of lithium, divalproex sodium, and carbamazepine in children and adolescents with bipolar disorder. *Journal of the American Academy of Child & Adolescent Psychiatry, 39*(6), 713–720.

Krantz, P. J., & McClannahan, L. E. (1998). Social interaction skills for children with autism: A script-fading procedure for beginning readers. *Journal of Applied Behavior Analysis, 31*(2), 191–202.

Krautter, T. H., & Lock, J. (2004). Treatment of adolescent anorexia nervosa using manualized family-based treatment. *Clinical Case Studies, 3*(2), 107–123.

Kruesi, M. J. P., Casanova, M. F., Mannheim, G., & Johnson-Bilder, A. (2004). Reduced temporal lobe volume in early onset conduct disorder. *Psychiatry Research: Neuroimaging, 132*(1), 1–11.

Kruesi, M. P., Hibbs, E. D., Zahn, T. P., Keysor, C. S., Hamburger, S. D., Bartko, J. J., et al. (1992). A two-year perspective follow-up study of children and adolescents with disruptive behavior disorders: Prediction by cerebrospinal fluid 5-hydroxyin-doleacetic acid, homovanillic acid, and autonomic measures. *Archives of General Psychiatry, 49*, 429–435.

Kruesi, M. P., Rapoport, J. L., Hamburger, S., Hibbs, E. D., Potter, W. Z., Lenare, M., et al. (1990). Cerebrospinal fluid monoamine metabolites, aggression, and impulsivity in disruptive behaviors of children and adolescents. *Archives of General Psychiatry, 47*, 419–426.

Krug, D. A., Arick, J., & Almond, P. (1980a). *Autism screening instrument for educational planning.* Austin, TX: ProEd.

Krug, D. A., Arick, J., & Almond, P. (1980b). Behavior checklist for identifying severely handicapped individuals with high levels of autistic behavior. *Journal of Child Psychology and Psychiatry, 21*(3), 221–229.

Kurita, H., Kita, M., & Miyake, Y. (1992). A comparative study of development and symptoms among disintegrative psychosis and infantile autism with and without speech loss. *Journal of Autism and Developmental Disorders, 22*(2), 175–188.

Kuroda, J. (1969). Elimination of children's fears of animals by the method of experimental desensitization:

An application of learning theory to child psychology. *Psychologia: An International Journal of Psychology in the Orient, 12*(3), 161–165.

Kutcher, S. P., & Marton, P. (1989). Parameters of adolescent depression: A review. *Psychiatric Clinics of North America, 12*(4), 895–918.

La Greca, A. M., Silverman, W. K., & Wasserstein, S. B. (1998). Children's predisaster functioning as a predictor of posttraumatic stress following Hurricane Andrew. *Journal of Consulting and Clinical Psychology, 66*(6), 883–892.

Lahey, B. B., Applegate, B., Barkley, R. A., & Garfinkel, B. (1994). *DSM-IV* field trials for oppositional defiant disorder and conduct disorder in children and adolescents. *American Journal of Psychiatry, 151*(8), 1163–1171.

Lahey, B. B., Loeber, R., Hart, E. L., Frick, P. J., Applegate, B., Zhang, Q., et al. (1995). Four year longitudinal study of conduct disorders: Patterns and predictors of persistence. *Journal of Abnormal Psychology, 104*, 83–93.

Lahey, B. B., Loeber, R., & Quay, H. C. (1998). Validity of the *DSM-IV* subtypes of conduct disorder based on age of onset. *Journal of American Academy of Child & Adolescent Psychiatry, 37*, 435–442.

Laine, C. J. (1991). Attitudes toward children by student teachers over the duration of their training. *Journal of the Ontario Institute for Studies in Education, 22*(3), 22–23.

Lainhart, J. E., Piven, J., Wzorek, M., & Landa, R. (1997). Macrocephaly in children and adults with autism. *Journal of the American Academy of Child & Adolescent Psychiatry, 36*(2), 282–290.

Lake, C. R., Ziegler, M. G., & Murphy, D. L. (1977). Increased norepinephrine levels and decreased dopamine-ß-hydroxylase activity in primary autism. *Archives of General Psychiatry, 34*(5), 553–556.

Lamberg, L. (2003). Advances in eating disorders offer food for thought. *Journal of the American Medical Association, 290*, 1437–1442.

Lam, M. K., & Rao, N. (1993). Developing a Chinese version of the Psychoeducational Profile (CPEP) to assess autistic children in Hong Kong. *Journal of Child Psychology and Psychiatry and Allied Disciplines, 37*, 785–801.

Lan, I. (2001). Pharmaceuticals: Conspiracy to increase Ritalin profits alleged. *The Journal of Law, Medicine, and Ethics, 29*(1), 100–102.

Lane, K. L., Gresham, F. M., & O'Shaughnessy, T. E. (2002). Serving students with or at-risk for emotional and behavior disorders: Future challenges. *Education and Treatment of Children, 25,* 507–521.

Lantieri, L., & Patti, J. (1998).Waging peace in our schools. *Journal of Negro Education, 65,* 356–368.

Lantzouni, E., Frank, G. R., Golden, N. H., & Shenker, R. I. (2002). Reversibility of growth stunting in early onset anorexia nervosa: A prospective study. *Journal of Adolescent Health, 31*(2), 162–165.

Last, C. G., Hansen, C., & Franco, N. (1998). Cognitive-behavioral treatment of school phobia. *Journal of the American Academy of Child & Adolescent Psychiatry, 37*(4), 404–411.

Last, C. G., Hersen, M., Kazdin, A. E., Finkelstein, R., & Strauss, C. (1987). Comparison of *DSM-III* separation anxiety and overanxious disorders: Demographic characteristics and patterns of comorbidity. *Journal of the American Academy of Child & Adolescent Psychiatry, 26*(4), 527–531.

Last, C. G., Perrin, S., Hersen, M., & Kazdin, A. E. (1992). *DSM-III-R* anxiety disorders in children: Sociodemographic and clinical characteristics. *Journal of the American Academy of Child & Adolescent Psychiatry, 31*(6), 1070–1076.

Last, C. G., Perrin, S., Hersen, M., & Kazdin, A. E. (1996). A prospective study of childhood anxiety disorders. *Journal of the American Academy of Child & Adolescent Psychiatry, 35*(11), 1502–1510.

Last, C. G., Phillips, J. E., & Statfeld, A. (1987). Childhood anxiety disorders in mothers and their children. *Child Psychiatry & Human Development, 18*(2), 103–112.

Last, C. G., & Strauss, C. C. (1990). School refusal in anxiety-disordered children and adolescents. *Journal of the American Academy of Child & Adolescent Psychiatry, 29*(1), 31–35.

Last, C. G., Strauss, C. C., & Francis, G. (1987). Comorbidity among childhood anxiety disorders. *Journal of Nervous and Mental Disease, 175*(12), 726–730.

Launay, J. M., Bursztejn, C., Ferrari, P., & Dreux, C. (1987). Catecholamines metabolism in infantile autism: A controlled study of 22 autistic children. *Journal of Autism and Developmental Disorders, 17*(3), 333–347.

Lavik, N. J., Clausen, S. E., & Pedersen, W. (1991). Eating behaviour, drug use, psychopathology and parental bonding in adolescents in Norway. *Acta Psychiatrica Scandinavica, 84*(4), 387–390.

LaVoie, R. (2005). *It's so much work to be your friend: Helping the child with learning disabilities find social success.* New York: Simon & Schuster.

Lazar, A., & Slostad, F. (1999, March/April). How to overcome obstacles to parent–teacher partnerships. *The Clearing House,* 206–210.

Lazarus, A. A., & Abramovitz, A. (1962). The use of "emotive imagery" in the treatment of children's phobias. *Journal of Mental Science, 108*(453), 191–195.

Le Blanc, M., & Kaspy, N. (1998). Trajectories of delinquency and problem behavior: Comparison of social and personal control characteristics of adjudicated boys on synchronous and nonsynchronous paths. *Journal of Quantitative Criminology, 14*(2), 181–214.

Leboyer, M., Bouvard, M. P., Launay, J. M., Tabuteau, F., Waller, D., Dugas, M., et al. (1992). A double-blind study of naltrexone in infantile autism. *Journal of Autism and Developmental Disorders, 22*(2), 309–319.

Leckman, J. F., Grice, D. E., Boardman, J., & Zhang, H. (1997). Symptoms of obsessive-compulsive disorder. *American Journal of Psychiatry, 154*(7), 911–917.

Leckman, J. F., Weisssman, M. M., Merikangas, K. R., Pauls, D. L., Prusoff, B. A., & Kidd, K. K. (1985). Major depression and panic disorder. A family study perspective. *Psychopharmacology Bulletin, 21,* 543–545.

Le Couteur, A., Bailey, A., Rutter, M., & Gottesman, I. (1989, August 3–5). *Epidemioloigcally based twin study of autism.* Paper presented at the First World Congress on Psychiatric Genetics, Cambridge, England.

Le Couteur, A., Rutter, M., Lord, C., & Rios, P. (1989). Autism diagnostic interview: A standardized investigator-based instrument. *Journal of Autism and Developmental Disorders, 19*(3), 363–387.

Lee, A., Hobson, R. P., & Chiat, S. (1994). I, you, me, and autism: An experimental study. *Journal of Autism and Developmental Disorders, 24*(2), 155–176.

Lee, S. (1995). Self-starvation in context: Towards a culturally sensitive understanding of anorexia nervosa. *Social Science & Medicine, 41*(1), 25–36.

Lee, S., Chan, Y. Y. L., & Hsu, L. K. G. (2003). The intermediate-term outcome of Chinese patients with anorexia nervosa in Hong Kong. *American Journal of Psychiatry, 160*(5), 967–972.

Leekam, S. R., Libby, S. J., Wing, L., Gould, J., & Taylor, C. (2002). The diagnostic interview for social and communication disorders: Algorithms for ICD-10 childhood autism and Wing and Gould autistic spectrum disorder. *Journal of Child Psychology and Psychiatry, 43*(3), 327–342.

Lefkowitz, M. M., & Tesiny, E. P. (1980). Assessment of childhood depression. *Journal of Consulting and Clinical Psychology, 48*(1), 43–50.

Leit, R. A., Pope, H. G., Jr., & Gray, J. J. (2001). Cultural expectations of muscularity in men: The evolution of Playgirl centerfolds. *International Journal of Eating Disorders, 29*(1), 90–93.

Leitenberg, H., & Callahan, E. J. (1973). Reinforced practice and reduction of different kinds of fears in adults and children. *Behaviour Research and Therapy, 11*(1), 19–30.

Lenz, B. K., & Hughes, C. A. (1990). A word identification strategy for adolescents with learning disabilities. *Journal of Learning Disabilities, 23*(3), 149–158, 163.

Leo, J. (2002, January/February). American preschoolers on Ritalin. *Society,* 52–60.

Leonard, D., & Mehler, P. S. (2001). Medical issues in the patient with anorexia nervosa. *Eating Behaviors, 2*(4), 293–305.

Leonard, H. L., Goldberger, E. L., Rapoport, J. L., & Cheslow, D. L. (1990). Childhood rituals: Normal development or obsessive-compulsive symptoms? *Journal of the American Academy of Child & Adolescent Psychiatry, 29*(1), 17–23.

Leonard, H. L., & Swedo, S. E. (2001). Paediatric autoimmune neuropsychiatric disorders associated with streptococcal infection (PANDAS). *International Journal of Neuropsychopharmacology, 4*(2), 191–198.

Leone, P. E., Mayer, M. J., Malmgren, K., & Meisel, S. M. (2000). School violence and disruption: Rhetoric, reality, and reasonable balance. *Focus on Exceptional Children, 33*(1), 1–20.

Lerner, J., Safren, S. A., Henin, A., Warman, M., Heimberg, R. G., & Kendall, P. C. (1999). Differentiating anxious and depressive self-statements in youth: Factor structure of the negative affect self-statement questionnaire among youth referred to an anxiety disorders clinic. *Journal of Clinical Child Psychology, 28*(1), 82–93.

Leventhal, B. L., Cook, E. H., Morford, M., & Ravitz, A. (1990). Relationships of whole blood serotonin and plasma norepinephrine within families. *Journal of Autism and Developmental Disorders, 20*(4), 499–511.

Levenson, R. L., & Mullins, C. A. (1992). Pediatric HIV diseases: What psychologists need to know. *Professional Psychology and Practice, 23,* 410–415.

Levine, M. P., & Piran, N. (2005). Eating disorders. In T. P. Gullotta & G. R. Adams (Eds.), *Handbook of adolescent behavioral problems: Evidence-based approaches to prevention and treatment* (pp. 363–386). New York: Springer Science+Business Media.

Lewczyk, C. M., Garland, A. F., Hurlburt, M. S., Gearity, J., & Hough, R. L. (2003). Comparing DISC-IV and clinician diagnoses among youths receiving public mental health services. *Journal of the American Academy of Child & Adolescent Psychiatry, 42*(3), 349–356.

Lewinsohn, P. M., Clarke, G. N., Hops, H., & Andrews, J. A. (1990). Cognitive-behavioral treatment for depressed adolescents. *Behavior Therapy, 21*(4), 385–401.

Lewinsohn, P. M., Clarke, G. N., & Rohde, P. (1994). Psychological approaches to the treatment of depression in adolescents. In W. M. Reynolds & H. F. Johnston (Eds.), *Handbook of depression in children and adolescents* (pp. 309–344). New York: Plenum Press.

Lewinsohn, P. M., Clarke, G. N., Rohde, P., Hops, H., & Seeley, J. R. (1996). A course in coping: A cognitive-behavioral approach to the treatment of adolescent depression. In E. D. Hibbs & P. S. Jensen (Eds.), *Psychosocial treatments for child and adolescent disorders: Empirically based strategies for clinical practice* (pp. 109–135). Washington, DC: American Psychological Association.

Lewinsohn, P. M., Gotlib, I. H., & Hautzinger, M. (1998). Behavioral treatment of unipolar depression. In V. E. Caballo (Ed.), *International handbook of cognitive and behavioural treatments for psychological disorders* (pp. 441–488). Oxford, England: Pergamon/Elsevier Science Ltd.

Lewinsohn, P. M., Klein, D. N., & Seeley, J. R. (1995). Bipolar disorders in a community sample of older adolescents: Prevalence, phenomenology, comorbidity, and course. *Journal of the American Academy of Child & Adolescent Psychiatry, 34*(4), 454–463.

Lewinsohn, P. M., Rohde, P., & Seeley, J. R. (1998). Major depressive disorder in older adolescents: Prevalence, risk factors, and clinical implications. *Clinical Psychology Review, 18*(7), 765–794.

Lewinsohn, P. M., Rohde, P., Seeley, J. R., & Hops, H. (1991). Comorbidity of unipolar depression: I. Major depression with dysthymia. *Journal of Abnormal Psychology, 100*(2), 205–213.

Lewis-Palmer, T., & Sugai, G. (2005). Function-based intervention planning comparing the effectiveness of FBA function-based and non-function-based intervention plans. *Journal of Positive Behavior Interventions, 7*(4), 224–236.

Lewis, S. (1974). A comparison of behavior therapy techniques in the reduction of fearful avoidance behavior. *Behavior Therapy, 5,* 648–655.

Liepe-Levinson, K., & Levinson, M. H. (2005). A general semantics approach to school-age bullying. *ETC: A Review of General Semantics, 62*(1), 4–17 PB.

Litner, B. (2003). Teens with ADHD: The challenge of high school. *Child & Youth Care Forum, 32,* 137–158.

Livingston, K. (1997). Ritalin: Miracle drug or cop-out? *The Public Interest, 127,* 3–18.

Lochman, J. E., & Dodge, K. A. (1994). Social-cognitive processes of severely violent, moderately aggressive, and nonaggressive boys. *Journal of Consulting and Clinical Psychology, 62*(2), 366–374.

Lochman, J. E., Powell, N. R., Jackson, M. F., & Czopp, W. (2006). Cognitive-behavioral psychotherapy for conduct disorder: The Coping Power program. In W. M. Nelson, III, A. J. Finch, Jr., & K. J. Hart (Eds.), *Conduct disorders: A practitioner's guide to comparative treatments* (pp. 177–215). New York: Springer.

Lochman, J. E., Powell, N. R., Whidby, J. M., & Fitzjerald, D. P. (2006). Aggressive children: Cognitive-behavioral assessment and treatment. In P. C. Kendall (Ed.), *Child and adolescent therapy: Cognitive-behavioral procedures* (3rd ed., pp. 33–81). New York: Guilford Press.

Lochman, J. E., Wayland, K. K., & White, K. J. (1993). Social goals: Relationship to adolescent adjustment and to social problem solving. *Journal of Abnormal Child Psychology, 21*(2), 135–151.

Lochman, J. E., & Wells, K. C. (2002). Contextual social-cognitive mediators and child outcome: A test of the theoretical model in the Coping Power program. *Development and Psychopathology, 14*(4), 945–967.

Lock, J., & Le Grange, D. (2001). Can family based treatment of anorexia nervosa be manualized? *Journal of Psychotherapy Practice & Research, 10*(4), 253–261.

Lock, J., & le Grange, D. (2006). Eating disorders. In D. A. Wolfe & E. J. Mash (Eds.), *Behavioral and emotional disorders in adolescents: Nature, assessment, and treatment* (pp. 485–504). New York: Guilford Press.

Lock, J., Reisel, B., & Steiner, H. (2001). Associated health risks of adolescents with disordered eating: How different are they from their peers? Results from a high school survey. *Child Psychiatry & Human Development, 31*(3), 249–265.

Loeber, R., Brinthaupt, V. P., & Green, S. M. (1990). Attention deficits, impulsivity, and hyperactivity with or without conduct problems: Relationships to delinquency and unique contextual factors. In R. J. McMahon & R. D. Peters (Eds.), *Behavioral disorders of adolescence: Research, intervention, and policy in clinical and school settings* (pp. 39–61). New York: Plenum Press.

Loeber, R., Burke, J. D., Lahey, B. B., Winters, A., & Zera, M. (2000). Oppositional defiant disorder and conduct disorder: A review of the past 10 years, part I. *Journal of the American Academy of Child and Adolescent Psychiatry, 39,* 1468–1482.

Loeber, R., Green, S. M., Keenan, K., & Lahey, B. B. (1995). Which boys will fare worse? Early predictors of the onset of conduct disorder in a six-year longitudinal study. *Journal of the American Academy of Child & Adolescent Psychiatry, 34*(4), 499–509.

Lohman, M., Riggs, P. D., Hall, S. K., Mikulich, S. K., & Klein, C. A. (2002, June). *Perceived motivations for treatment in depressed, substance-dependent adolescents with conduct disorder.* Paper presented at the College on Problems of Drug Dependence: 64th Annual Scientific Meeting, Quebec, Canada.

Loney, B. R., & Lima, E. N. (2003). Classification and assessment. In C. A. Essau (Ed.), *Conduct and oppositional defiant disorders: Epidemiology, risk factors, and treatment* (pp. 3–31). Mahwah, NJ: Erlbaum.

Loney, J., & Milch, R. (1985). Hyperactivity, aggression, and inattention in clinical practice. In M. Wollrach & D. Routh (Eds.), *Advances in developmental and behavioral pediatrics* (pp. 113–147). New York: JAI Press.

Long, N. J., & Morse, W. C. (1996). *Conflict in the classroom: The education of at-risk and troubled students.* Austin, TX: Pro-Ed.

Long, N. J., Wood, M. M., & Fecser, F. A. (2001). *Life space crisis intervention: Talking with students in conflict.* Austin, TX: Pro-Ed.

Long, P., Forehand, R., Weirson, M., & Morgan, A. (1994). Does parent training with young noncompliant children have long-term effects? *Behavior Research & Therapy, 32,* 101–107.

Looff, D., Grimley, P., Kuller, F., & Martin, A. (1995). Carbamazepine for PTSD. *Journal of the American Academy of Child & Adolescent Psychiatry, 34*(6), 703.

Lord, C. (1995). Follow-up of two-year-olds referred for possible autism. *Journal of Child Psychology and Psychiatry, 36*(8), 1365–1382.

Lord, C. (1997). Diagnostic instruments in autism spectrum disorders. In D. J. Cohen & F. R. Volkmar (Eds.), *Handbook of autism and pervasive developmental disorders* (2nd ed., pp. 460–483). New York: John Wiley & Sons, Inc.

Lord, C., & Corsello, C. (2005). Diagnostic instruments in autistic spectrum disorders. In F. R. Volkmar, R. Paul, A. Klin, & D. Cohen (Eds.), *Handbook of autism and pervasive developmental disorders: Vol. 2. Assessment, interventions, and policy* (3rd ed., pp. 730–771). Hoboken, NJ: John Wiley & Sons, Inc.

Lord, C., Rutter, M. L., DiLavore, P. C., & Risi, S. (1999). *Autism Diagnostic Observation Schedule–WPS* (WPS ed.). Los Angeles: Western Psychological Services.

Lord, C., Rutter, M., & Le Couteur, A. (1994). Autism Diagnostic Interview—Revised: A revised version of a diagnostic interview for caregivers of individuals with possible pervasive developmental disorders. *Journal of Autism and Developmental Disorders, 24*(5), 659–685.

Loukas, A., Fitzgerald, H. E., Zucker, R. A., & von Eye, A. (2001). Parental alcoholism and co-occurring antisocial behavior: Prospective relationships to externalizing behavior problems in their young sons. *Journal of Abnormal Child Psychology, 29,* 91–106.

Lovaas, O. I. (1982). Comments on self-destructive behaviors. *Analysis & Intervention in Developmental Disabilities, 2*(1), 115–124.

Lovaas, O. I. (1987). Behavioral treatment and normal educational and intellectual functioning in young autistic children. *Journal of Consulting and Clinical Psychology, 55*(1), 3–9.

Loveland, K., McEvoy, R. E., Tunali, B., & Kelley, M. L. (1990). Narrative story telling in autism and Down syndrome. *British Journal of Developmental Psychology, 8,* 9–23.

Loveland, K. A., & Tunali-Kotoski, B. (2005). The school-age child with an autistic spectrum disorder. In F. R. Volkmar, R. Paul, A. Klin, & D. Cohen (Eds.), *Handbook of autism and pervasive developmental disorders: Vol. 1. Diagnosis, development, neurobiology, and behavior* (3rd ed., pp. 247–287). Hoboken, NJ: John Wiley & Sons, Inc.

Loveland, K. A., Tunali-Kotoski, B., Chen, Y. R., Ortegon, J., Pearson, D. A., Brelsford, K. A., et al. (1997). Emotion recognition in autism: Verbal and nonverbal information. *Development and Psychopathology, 9*(3), 579–593.

Lovell, M. K., & Richardson, B. (2001). Family and consumer sciences educators can play significant roles in curbing school violence. *Journal of Family and Consumer Sciences, 93*(1), 24–29.

Lowe, M. R. (1993). The effects of dieting on eating behavior: A three-factor model. *Psychological Bulletin, 114*(1), 100–121.

Lucas, A. R., Beard, C. M., O'Fallon, W. M., & Kurland, L. T. (1991). 50-year trends in the incidence of anorexia nervosa in Rochester, Minn.: A population-based study. *American Journal of Psychiatry, 148*(7), 917–922.

Luteijn, E., Luteijn, F., Jackson, S., Volkmar, F., & Minderaa, R. (2000). The Children's Social Behavior Questionnaire for milder variants of PDD problems: Evaluation of the psychometric characteristics. *Journal of Autism and Developmental Disorders, 30*(4), 317–330.

Lyon, M. R., Cline, J. C., Zepetnek, J., Shan, J. J., & Pang, P. (2001). Effect of the herbal extract combination Panax quinquefolium and Ginko biloba on attention-deficit hyperactivity disorder: A pilot study. *Journal of Psychiatry and Neuroscience, 26*(3), 221–225.

Mace, F. C., Hock, M. L., Lalli, J. S., & West, B. J. (1988). Behavioral momentum in the treatment of noncompliance. *Journal of Applied Behavior Analysis, 21*(2), 123–141.

Macera, M. H., & Mizes, J. S. (2006). Eating disorders. In M. Hersen (Ed.), *Clinician's handbook of child behavioral assessment* (pp. 437–457). San Diego, CA: Elsevier Academic Press.

MacFarlane, R. M. (1995). Adolescent pregnancy. In M. W. O'Hara, R. C. Reiter, S. R. Johnson, A. Milburn, & J. Engeldinger (Eds.), *Psychological aspects of women's reproductive health* (pp. 248–264). New York: Springer.

Maguin, E., Hawkins, J. D., Catalano, R. F., Hill, K., Abbott, R., & Herrenkohl, T. (1995). *Risk factors measured at three ages for violence at age 17–18.* Paper presented at the American Society of Criminology, November, 1995, Boston, MA.

Maguin, E., Loeber, R., & LeMahieu, P. (1993). Does the relationship between poor reading and delinquency hold for different age and ethnic groups? *Journal of Emotional Behavioral Disorders, 1,* 88–100.

Maheady, L., Algozzine, B., & Ysseldyke, J. E. (1984). Minority over-representation in special education: A functional assessment perspective. *Special Services in the Schools, 1,* 5–20. (Reprinted in *Education Digest* [1985, September], 50–53).

Malley, J., Beck, M., & Adorno, D. (2001). Building an ecology for non-violence in schools. *International Journal of Reality Therapy, 21*(1), 22–27.

Malone, R. P., Delaney, M. A., Leubbert, J. F., Cater, J., & Campbell, M. (2000). A double-blind placebo-controlled study of lithium in hospitalized aggressive children and adolescents with conduct disorder. *Archives of General Psychiatry, 57*(7), 649–654.

Maloney, M. J., McGuire, J. B., & Daniels, S. R. (1988). Reliability testing of a children's version of the Eating Attitude Test. *Journal of the American Academy of Child & Adolescent Psychiatry, 27*(5), 541–543.

Manassis, K. (2001). Child-parent relations: Attachment and anxiety disorders. In W. K. Silverman & P. D. A. Treffers (Eds.), *Anxiety disorders in children and adolescents: Research, assessment and intervention* (pp. 255–272). New York: Cambridge University Press.

Manicavasagar, V., Silove, D., Curtis, J., & Wagner, R. (2000). Continuities of separation anxiety from early life into adulthood. *Journal of Anxiety Disorders, 14*(1), 1–18.

Mann, J., & Rosenthal, T. L. (1969). Vicarious and direct counterconditioning of test anxiety through individual and group desensitization. *Behaviour Research and Therapy, 7*(4), 359–367.

Marans, W. D., Rubin, E., & Laurent, A. (2005). Addressing social communication skills in individuals with high-functioning autism and Asperger syndrome: Critical priorities in educational programming. In F. R. Volkmar, R. Paul, A. Klin, & D. Cohen (Eds.), *Handbook of autism and pervasive developmental disorders: Vol. 2. Assessment, interventions, and policy* (3rd ed., pp. 977–1002). Hoboken, NJ: John Wiley & Sons, Inc.

March, J. S. (1999). Assessment of pediatric posttraumatic stress disorder. In P. A. Saigh & J. D. Bremner (Eds.), *Posttraumatic stress disorder: A comprehensive text* (pp. 199–218). Needham Heights, MA: Allyn & Bacon.

March, J. S., Amaya-Jackson, L., Murray, M. C., & Schulte, A. (1998). Cognitive-behavioral psychotherapy for children and adolescents with posttraumatic stress disorder after a single-incident stressor. *Journal of the American Academy of Child and Adolescent Psychiatry, 37*(6), 585–593.

March, J. S., Biederman, J., Wolkow, R., Safferman, A., Mardekian, J., Cook, E. H., et al. (2000). Sertraline in children and adolescents with obsessive-compulsive disorder: A multicenter randomized controlled trial: Correction. *JAMA, 283*(10), 1293.

March, J. S., Franklin, M. E., Leonard, H. L., & Foa, E. B. (2004). Obsessive-compulsive disorder. In T. L. Morris (Ed.), *Anxiety disorders in children and adolescents* (2nd ed., pp. 212–240). New York: Guilford Press.

March, J. S., & Mulle, K. (1995). Organizing an anxiety disorders clinic. In P. Stallings, D. Erhardt, & C. K. Conners (Eds.), *Anxiety disorders in children and adolescents* (pp. 420–435). New York: Guilford Press.

March, J. S., Mulle, K., & Herbel, B. (1994). Behavioral psychotherapy for children and adolescents with obsessive-compulsive disorder: An open trial of a new protocol-driven treatment package. *Journal of the American Academy of Child & Adolescent Psychiatry, 33*(3), 333–341.

March, J. S., Parker, J. D. A., Sullivan, K., & Stallings, P. & Conners (1997). The Multidimensional Anxiety Scale for Children (MASC): Factor structure, reliability, and validity. *Journal of the American Academy of Child & Adolescent Psychiatry, 36*(4), 554–565.

Marcotte, D. (1997). Treating depression in adolescence: A review of the effectiveness of cognitive-behavioral treatments. *Journal of Youth and Adolescence, 26*(3), 273–283.

Marks, I. M. (1969). *Fears and phobias.* Oxford, England: Academic Press.

Martin, A., Koenig, K., Anderson, G. M., & Scahill, L. (2003). Low-dose fluvoxamine treatment of children and adolescents with pervasive developmental disorders: A prospective, open-label study. *Journal of Autism and Developmental Disorders, 33*(1), 77–85.

Martin, A., Koenig, K., Scahill, L., & Bregman, J. (1999). Open-label quetiapine in the treatment of children and adolescents with autistic disorder. *Journal of Child and Adolescent Psychopharmacology, 9*(2), 99–107.

Martin, B. (1977). Brief family intervention: Effectiveness and the importance of including the father. *Journal of Consulting and Clinical Psychology, 45*(6), 1002–1010.

Martin, B., & Hoffman, J. (1990). Conduct disorders. In M. Lewis & S. Miller (Eds.), *Handbook of developmental psychopathology* (pp. 109–118). New York: Plenum.

Martineau, J., Barthélémy, C., Jouve, J., & Muh, J. P. (1992). Monoamines (serotonin and catecholamines) and their derivatives in infantile autism: Age-related changes and drug effects. *Developmental Medicine & Child Neurology, 34*(7), 593–603.

Mash, E. J., & Wolf, D. A. (2005). *Abnormal child psychology* (3rd ed.). Belmont, CA: Wadsworth.

Masia, C. L., & Morris, T. L. (1998). Parental factors associated with social anxiety: Methodological limitations and suggestions for integrated behavioral research. *Clinical Psychology: Science and Practice, 5*(2), 211–228.

Maslow, A. (1948). "Higher" and "lower" needs. *Journal of Psychology, 25,* 433–436.

Matthys, W., Cuperus, J. M., & Van Engeland, H. (1999). Deficient social problem-solving in boys with ODD/CD, with ADHD, and with both disorders. *Journal of the American Academy of Child & Adolescent Psychiatry, 38*(3), 311–321.

Maughan, B., Rowe, R., Messer, J., Goodman, R., & Meltzer, H. (2004). Conduct disorder and oppositional defiant disorder in a national sample: Developmental epidemiology. *Journal of Child Psychology and Psychiatry, 45*(3), 609–621.

Mawdsley, R. D. (1993). Supervisory standard of care for students with disabilities. *Education Law Reporter, 80,* 779–791.

May, M. (2000). Disturbing behavior: Neurotoxic effects in children. *Environmental Health Perspectives, 108*(6). Retrieved January 20, 2008, from http://www.ehponline.org/docs/2000/108-6/focus.html

Mazure, C. M., Halmi, K. A., Sunday, S. R., & Romano, S. J. (1994). The Yale-Brown-Cornell Eating Disorder Scale: Development, use, reliability and validity. *Journal of Psychiatric Research, 28*(5), 425–445.

McAfee, J. (2002). *Navigating the social world: A curriculum for individuals with Asperger's syndrome, high functioning autism, and related disorders.* Arlington, TX: Future Horizons.

McAndrews, T. (2001). *Zero tolerance policies.* (ERIC Digest No. 146, Report No. EDO-EA-01-03). Eugene, OR: ERIC Clearinghouse on Educational Management. (ERIC Document Reproduction Service No. ED451579)

McCarney, S. B. (2004). *Attention deficit disorders evaluation scale, 3rd ed. (ADDES-3).* Columbia, MO: Hawthorne Educational Services.

McCarthy, C. J., Brack, C. J., Laygo, R. M., Brack, G., & Orr, D. P. (1997). A theory based investigation of adolescent risk behaviors and concern about AIDS. *School Counselor, 44*(3), 185–197.

McCauley, E., Myers, K., Mitchell, J., & Calderon, R. (1993). Depression in young people: Initial presentation and clinical course. *Journal of the American Academy of Child & Adolescent Psychiatry, 32*(4), 714–722.

McCloskey, L. A., & Walker, M. (2000). Posttraumatic stress in children exposed to family violence and single-event trauma. *Journal of the American Academy of Child & Adolescent Psychiatry, 39*(1), 108–115.

McCluskey, K., & McCluskey, A. (1999). The agony and the empathy: A hyperactive child's journey from despair to achievement. *Reclaiming Children and Youth, 7,* 205–212.

McCord, J. (1991). Competence in long-term perspective. *Psychiatry, 54,* 227–237.

McEvoy, A. (1990). Combating gang activities in schools. *Education Digest, 56*(2), 31–34.

McGee, G. G., Paradis, T., & Feldman, R. S. (1993). Free effects of integration on levels of autistic behavior. *Topics in Early Childhood Special Education, 13*(1), 57–67.

McGee, R., Partridge, F., Williams, S., & Silva, P. A. (1991). A twelve-year follow-up of preschool hyperactive children. *Journal of the American Academy of Child and Adolescent Psychiatry, 30,* 224–232.

McGee, R., Williams, S., Share, D., Anderson, J., & Silva, P. (1986). The relationship between specific retardation, general reading backwardness and behavioral problems in a large sample of Duedin boys: A longitudinal study from five to eleven years. *Journal of Child Psychology and Psychiatry, 47,* 597–610.

McGee, R., Williams, S., & Silva, P. A. (1984). Background characteristics of aggressive, hyperactive, and aggressive-hyperactive boys. *Journal of the American Academy of Child Psychiatry, 23,* 280–284.

McGilley, B., & Pryor, T. (1998). Assessment and treatment of bulimia nervosa. *American Family Physician, 57,* 2743–2750.

McGuffin, P., & Katz, R. (1989). The genetics of depression: Current approaches. *British Journal of Psychiatry, 155*(6), 18–26.

McKinney, J. D., Montague, M., & Hocutt, A. M. (1993). Educational assessment of children with attention deficit disorder. *Exceptional Children, 60*(2), 125–131.

McKnight, C. D., Compton, S. N., & March, J. S. (2004). Posttraumatic stress disorder. In T. L. Morris (Ed.), *Anxiety disorders in children and adolescents* (2nd ed., pp. 241–262). New York: Guilford Press.

McNaughton, N., & Gray, J. A. (2000). Anxiolytic action on the behavioural inhibition system implies multiple types of arousal contribute to anxiety. *Journal of Affective Disorders, 61*(3), 161–176.

McNeil, B. J., & Nelson, K. R. (1991). Meta-analysis of interactive video instruction: A 10 year review of achievement effects. *Journal of Computer-Based Instruction, 18*(1), 1–6.

McWhirter, B. T., McWhirter, J. J., Hart, R. S., & Gat, I. (2000). Preventing and treating depression in children and adolescents. In D. Capuzzi & D. R. Gross (Eds.), *Youth risk: A prevention resource for counselors, teachers, and parents* (3rd ed., pp. 137–165). Alexandria, VA: American Counseling Association.

McWhirter, J. J. (2004). Teenage pregnancy and risky sexual behavior. In J. J. McWhirter, B. T. McWhirter, E. H. McWhirter, & R. J. McWhirter (Eds.), *At-risk youth: A comprehensive response* (3rd ed., pp. 133–155). Belmont, CA: Brooks/Cole.

McWhirter, J. J. (2007). *At-risk youth: A comprehensive response for counselors, teachers, psychologists, and human service professionals.* Belmont, CA: Thomson Brooks/Cole.

Mehlman, P. T., Higley, J. D., Faucher, I., Lilly, A. A., Taub, D. M., Vickers, J., et al. (1994). Low CSF 5-HIAA concentrations and severe aggression and impaired impulse control in nonhuman primates. *American Journal of Psychiatry, 151,* 1485–1491.

Mehlman, P. T., Higley, J. D., Faucher, I., Lilly, A. A., Taub, D. M., Vickers, J., et al. (1995). Correlation of CSF 5-HIAA concentration with sociality and the timing of emigration in free-ranging primates. *American Journal of Psychiatry, 152,* 907–913.

Meier, K., Stewart, J., Jr., & England, R. E. (1989). *Race, class, and education: The politics of second-generation discrimination.* Madison: University of Wisconsin Press.

Melamed, B. G., & Lumley, M. A. (1988). Dental subscale of the Children's Fear Survey Schedule. In M. Hersen & A. S. Bellack (Eds.), *Dictionary of behavioral assessment techniques* (p. 171). Oxford, U.K.: Pergamon.

Meltzoff, A., & Gopnik, A. (1994). The role of imitation in understanding persons and developing a theory of mind. In S. Baron-Cohen, H. Tager-Flusberg, & D. J. Cohen (Eds.), *Understanding other minds: Perspectives from autism* (pp. 335–366). New York: Oxford University Press.

Mendez Foundation. (1995). Retrieved January 20, 2008, from http://www.mendezfoundation.org

Mendler, A. (1992). *What do I do when . . .? How to achieve discipline with dignity in the classroom.* Bloomington, IN: National Education Service.

Mendlowitz, S. L., Manassis, K., Bradley, S., Scapillato, D., Miezitis, S., & Shaw, B. F. (1999). Cognitive-behavioral group treatments in childhood anxiety disorders: The role of parental involvement. *Journal of the American Academy of Child & Adolescent Psychiatry, 38*(10), 1223–1229.

Menzies, R. G., & Clarke, J. C. (1993). The etiology of childhood water phobia. *Behaviour Research and Therapy, 31*(5), 499–501.

Metha, A., Weber, B., & Webb, L. D. (1998). Youth suicide prevention: A survey and analysis of policies and efforts in the 50 states. *Suicide and Life-Threatening Behavior, 28*(2), 150–164.

Mezzacappa, E., Tremblay, R. E., & Kindlon, D., Saul, J. P., Arsenault, L., Seguin, J., et al. (1997). Anxiety, antisocial behavior, and heart rate regulation in adolescent males. *Journal of Child Psychiatry, 38,* 457–469.

Miles, D. R., & Carey, G. (1997). Genetic and environmental architecture on human aggression. *Journal of Personality and Social Psychology, 72*(1), 207–217.

Militerni, R., Bravaccio, C., Falco, C., Fico, C., & Palermo, M. T. (2002). Repetitive behaviors in autistic disorder. *European Child & Adolescent Psychiatry, 11*(5), 210–218.

Miller, G. E., & Prinz, R. J. (1990). Enhancement of social learning family interventions for childhood conduct disorder. *Psychological Bulletin, 108*(2), 291–307.

Miller, L. C., Barrett, C. L., & Hampe, E. (1974). Phobias of childhood in a prescientific era. In A. Davids (Ed.), *Child personality and psychopathology: Current topics.* Oxford, England: Wiley.

Miller, L. C., Barrett, C. L., Hampe, E., & Noble, H. (1972). Factor structure of childhood fears. *Journal of Consulting and Clinical Psychology, 39*(2), 264–268.

Miller, P. H. (1989). *Theories of developmental psychology* (2nd ed.). New York: W. H. Freeman/Times Books/ Henry Holt & Co.

Miller, W. B. (1992 [Revised from 1982]). *Crime by youth gangs and groups in the United States.* Washington, DC: U.S. Department of Justice, Office of Justice Programs, Office of Juvenile Justice and Delinquency Prevention.

Minden, J., Henry, D. B., Tolan, P. H., & Groman-Smith, D. (2000). Urban boys' social networks and school violence. *Professional School Counseling, 4,* 95–104.

Minderaa, R. B., Anderson, G. M., Volkmar, F. R., & Akkerhuis, G. W. (1994). Noradrenergic and adrenergic functioning in autism. *Biological Psychiatry, 36*(4), 237–241.

Miniño, A. M., Arias, E., Kochanek, K. D., Murphy, S. L., & Smith, B. L. (2002). Deaths: Final data for 2000. *National Vital Statistics Report, 50*(15), 1–119.

Minshew, N. J., Sweeney, J. A., Bauman, M. L., & Webb, S. J. (2005). Neurologic aspects of autism. In F. R. Volkmar, R. Paul, A. Klin, & D. Cohen (Eds.), *Handbook of autism and pervasive developmental disorders: Vol. 1. Diagnosis, development, neurobiology, and behavior* (3rd ed., pp. 473–514). Hoboken, NJ: John Wiley & Sons, Inc.

Mintz, L. B., O'Halloran, M. S., Mulholland, A. M., & Schneider, P. A. (1997). Questionnaire for eating disorder diagnoses: Reliability and validity of operationalizing *DSM–IV* criteria into a self-report format: Correction. *Journal of Counseling Psychology, 44*(2), 132.

Minuchin, S. (1974). *Families and family therapy.* Oxford, England: Harvard University Press.

Minuchin, S., Rosman, B. L., & Baker, L. (1978). *Psychosomatic families: Anorexia nervosa in context.* Oxford, England: Harvard University Press.

Miranda-Linné, F., & Melin, L. (1992). Acquisition, generalization, and spontaneous use of color adjectives: A comparison of incidental teaching and traditional discrete-trial procedures for children with autism. *Research in Developmental Disabilities, 13*(3), 191–210.

Miranda-Linné, F., & Melin, L. (2002). A factor analytic study of the Autism Behavior Checklist. *Journal of Autism and Developmental Disorders, 32*(3), 181–188.

Mitchell, J. E., deZwaan, M., & Roerig, J. (2003). Drug therapy for patients with eating disorders. *Current Drug Targets—CNS and Neurological Disorders, 2,* 17–29.

Mitchell, J. E., Myers, T., Swan-Kremeier, L., & Wonderlich, S. (2003). Psychotherapy for bulimia nervosa delivered via telemedicine. *European Eating Disorders Review, 11*(3), 222–230.

Mizes, J. S., Christiano, B., Madison, J., Post, G., Seime, R., & Varnado, P. (2000). Development of the Mizes Anorectic Cognitions Questionnaire—Revised: Psychometric properties and factor structure in a large sample of eating disorder patients. *International Journal of Eating Disorders, 28*(4), 415–421.

Modan-Moses, D., Yaroslavsky, A., Novikov, I., Segev, S., Toledano, A., Miterany, E., et al. (2003). Stunting of growth as a major feature of anorexia nervosa in male adolescents. *Pediatrics, 111,* 270–276.

Moffit, T. E. (2003). Life course persistent and adolescence-limited antisocial behavior: A 10-year research review and research agenda. In B. B. Lahey, T. E. Moffitt, & A. Caspi (Eds.), *Cause of conduct disorder and juvenile delinquency* (pp. 49–75). New York: Guilford Press.

Moffit, T. E., Caspi, A., Dickson, N., Silva, P., & Stanton, W. (1996). Childhood-onset versus adolescent-onset antisocial conduct problems in males: Natural history from ages 3 to 18 years. *Development and Psychopathology, 8,* 399–424.

Moffit, T. E., Gabrielli, W. F., Mednick, S. A., & Schulsinger, F. (1981). Socioeconomic status, IQ, and delinquency. *Journal of Abnormal Psychology, 90*(2), 152–156.

Moffit, T. E., Lynam, D. R., & Silva, P. A. (1994). Neuropsychological tests predicting male delinquency. *Criminology, 32,* 277–300.

Moffitt, T. E., & Silva, P. A. (1988a). IQ and delinquency: A direct test of the differential detection hypothesis. *Journal of Abnormal Psychology, 97*(3), 330–333.

Moffit, T. E., & Silva, P. A. (1988b). Neuropsychological deficit and self-reported delinquency in an unselected birth control cohort. *Journal of the American Academy of Child and Adolescent Psychiatry, 27,* 233–240.

Mokros, J. R., & Russell, S. J. (1986). Learner-centered software: A survey of microcomputer use with special needs students. *Journal of Learning Disabilities, 19*(3), 185–190.

Molidor, C. E. (1996). Female gang members: A profile of aggression and victimization. *Social Work, 41*(3), 251–260.

Mooney, K. C. (1985). Children's nighttime fears: Ratings of content and coping behaviors. *Cognitive Therapy and Research, 9,* 309–319.

Moore, K. A., Myers, D. E., Morrison, D. R., Nord, C. W., Brown, B., & Edmonston, B. (1993). Ages at first childbirth and later poverty. *Journal of Research on Adolescents, 3,* 393–422.

Morris, L., Warren, C. W., & Aral, S. O. (1993). Measuring adolescent sexual behaviors and related health outcomes. *Public Health Report, 108*(Suppl. 1), 31–36.

Morrison, G. M., & D'Incau, B. (1997). The web of zero-tolerance: Characteristics of students who are recommended for expulsion from school. *Education and Treatment of Children, 20,* 316–335.

Morrison, G., & Skiba, R. (2001). Predicting violence from school misbehavior: Promises and perils. *Psychology in the Schools, 38*(2), 173–184.

MTA Cooperative Group. (1999). A 14-month randomized clinical trial of treatment strategies for attention-deficit/hyperactivity disorder. *Archives of General Psychiatry, 56,* 1073–1086.

Mufson, L., & Fairbanks, J. (1996). Interpersonal psychotherapy for depressed adolescents: A one-year naturalistic follow-up study. *Journal of the American Academy of Child & Adolescent Psychiatry, 35*(9), 1145–1155.

Mufson, L., Moreau, D., Weissman, M. M., & Wickramaratne, P. (1994). Modification of interpersonal psychotherapy with depressed adolescents (IPT-A): Phase I and II studies. *Journal of the American Academy of Child & Adolescent Psychiatry, 33*(5), 695–705.

Mufson, L., Weissman, M. M., Moreau, D., & Garfinkel, R. (1999). Efficacy of interpersonal psychotherapy for depressed adolescents. *Archives of General Psychiatry, 56*(6), 573–579.

Muise, A. M., Stein, D. G., & Arbess, G. (2003). Eating disorders in adolescent boys: A review of the adolescent and young adult literature. *Journal of Adolescent Health, 33*(6), 427–435.

Muisener, P. P. (1994). *Understanding and treating adolescent substance abuse.* Thousand Oaks, CA: Sage.

Mulder, E. J., Anderson, G. M., Kema, I. P., De Bildt, A., Van Lang, N. D. J., Den Boer, J. A., et al. (2004). Platelet serotonin levels in pervasive developmental disorders and mental retardation: Diagnostic group differences, within-group distribution, and behavioral correlates. *Journal of the American Academy of Child & Adolescent Psychiatry, 43*(4), 491–499.

Mulick, J. A., & Meinhold, P. M. (1994). Developmental disorders and broad effects of the environment on learning and treatment effectiveness. In E. Schopler & G. B. Mesibov (Eds.), *Behavioral issues in autism* (pp. 99–128). New York: Plenum Press.

Müller, R. A., Behen, M. E., Rothermel, R. D., Chugani, D. C., Muzik, O., Mangner, T. J., et al. (1999). Brain mapping of language and auditory perception in high-functioning autistic adults: A PET study. *Journal of Autism and Developmental Disorders, 29*(1), 19–31.

Mulvey, E. P., & Cauffman, E. (2001). The inherent limits of predicting school violence. *American Psychologist, 56,* 797–802.

Muratori, F., Picchi, L., Bruni, G., Patarnello, M., & Romagnoli, G. (2003). A two-year follow-up of psychodynamic psychotherapy for internalizing disorders in children. *Journal of the American Academy of Child & Adolescent Psychiatry, 42*(3), 331–339.

Muriel, A. C., Bostic, J. Q., & Dolan, J. M. (2002). Mood disorders. In D. L. Kaye, M. E. Montgomery, & S. W. Munson (Eds.), *Child and adolescent mental health* (pp. 276–296). Philadelphia: Lippincott, Williams, & Wilkins.

Myers, K. M., Collett, B. R., & Ohan, J. L. (2003). Ten-year review of rating scales versus scales assessing attention-deficit hyperactivity disorder. *Journal of the American Academy of Child and Adolescent Psychiatry, 42*(9), 1015–1037.

Nader, K., Blake, D., Kriegler, J., & Pynoos, R. (1994). *Clinician Administered PTSD Scale for Children (CAPS-C), current and lifetime diagnosis version, and instruction manual.* Los Angeles: UCLA Neuropsychiatric Institute and National Center for PTSD.

Narayan, M., Srinath, S., Anderson, G. M., & Meundi, D. B. (1993). Cerebrospinal fluid levels of homovanillic acid and 5-hydroxyindoleacetic acid in autism. *Biological Psychiatry, 33*(8), 630–635.

Nation, K. (1999). Reading skills in hyperlexia: A developmental perspective. *Psychological Bulletin, 125*(3), 338–355.

National Center for Education Statistics, Institute of Educational Sciences. (2006, January). *Percentage distribution of disabled students 6 to 21 years old receiving education services for the disabled, by educational environment and type of disability: Fall 1989 through Fall 2004.* Retrieved March 4, 2008, from http://nces.ed.gov/programs/digest/d05/tables/dt05_051.asp

National Center for Health Statistics. (2007). *ASD growth rate.* Retrieved February 9, 2008, from http://www.cdc.gov/nchs/

National Center for Health Statistics. (2007). *Incidence of ASD.* Retrieved February 9, 2008, from http://www.cdc.gov/nchs/

National Center for the Analysis of Violent Crime. (2001). *The school shooter: A threat assessment perspective.* Available at http://www.fbi.gov/library/schools/school2

National Institute of Mental Health Home Page. (2007). *Eating disorders.* Retrieved December 30, 2007, from http://www.nimh.nih.gov/health/topics/eating-disorders/index.shtml

National Institute on Drug Abuse. (1999). *Preventing drug use among children and adolescents: A research-based guide.* Washington, DC: Author.

National Institute on Drug Abuse. (2000). *Marijuana* [On-line]. Available at http://www.drugabuse.gov/tobacco.html

National Institute on Drug Abuse. (2001). *Inhalants* [On-line]. Available at http://www.drugabuse.gov/inhalants/html

National Institute on Drug Abuse. (2006). Fact sheet. Retrieved January 12, 2008, from http://www.drugabuse.gov/Infofacts/ritalin.html

National Institutes of Health Consensus Statement. (1998). *Diagnosis and treatment of ADHD.* Retrieved March 4, 2008, from http://consensus.nih.gov/1998/1998AttentionDeficitHyperactivityDisorder110PDF.pdf

National School Safety Center. (1998). *Checklist of characteristics of youth who have caused school-associated violent deaths.* Retrieved March 21, 2008, from http://www.schoolsafety.us/Checklist-of-Characteristics-of-Youth-Who-Have-Caused-School-Associated-Violent-Deaths-p-7.html

National Youth Gang Center. (2000). *Frequently asked questions regarding gangs.* Retrieved February 20, 2008, from http://www.ir.com/nygc/fac.htm

Neary, D. (2000). *The effects of adolescent and young adult suicide on family and friends: A meta-analysis.* ProQuest Information & Learning.

Needleman, H. L., Riess, J. A., Tobin, M. J., Biesecker, G. E., & Greenhouse, J. B. (1996). Bone lead levels and delinquent behavior. *JAMA, 275,* 363–369.

New York State Division of Criminal Justice Services. (2003). *2002–2004 New York State Comprehensive Juvenile Justice Plan.* Retrieved March 4, 2008, from www.criminaljustice.state.ny.us/ofpa/pdfdocs/jj3yrplan.pdf

New York State Teacher Certification Examinations. (2006). *CST: Students with disabilities 060.* Albany, NY: National Evaluation Systems, Inc., New York State Education Department, Office of Teaching Initiatives.

Niec, L. N. (2004, November). *Assessing parent-child interactions across diagnoses: Validity of the dyadic parent-child coding system.* Chair of symposium presented at the annual convention for the Association of the Advancement of Behavior Therapy, New Orleans, LA.

Nigg, J. T., & Hinshaw, S. P. (1998). Parent personality and psychiatric history in relation to child antisocial behaviors in childhood ADHD. *Journal of Child Psychology and Psychiatry, 39,* 145–160.

Nir, I., Meir, D., Zilber, N., Knobler, H., Hadjez, J., & Lerner, Y. (1995). Circadian melatonin, thyroid-stimulating hormone, prolactin, and cortisol levels in serum of young adults with autism. *Journal of Autism and Developmental Disorders, 25*(6), 641–654.

Nixon, R. D. V., Sweeney, L., Erickson, D. B., & Touyz, S. W. (2003). Parent-child interaction therapy: A comparison of standard and abbreviated treatments for oppositional defiant preschoolers. *Journal of Consulting and Clinical Psychology, 71*(2), 251–260.

No Child Left Behind Act of 2001. (2002). Pub. L. No. 107-110, 115 Stat. 1425-2094.

Northup, J., & Gulley, V. (2001). Some contributions of functional analysis to the assessment of behaviors associated with attention deficit hyperactivity disorder and the effects of stimulant medication. *School Psychology Review, 30*(2), 227–234.

Northup, J., Gulley, V., Edwards, S., & Fountain, L. (2001). The effects of methylphenidate in the classroom: What dosage, for which children, for what problems? *School Psychology Quarterly, 16*(3), 303–310.

Obler, M., & Terwilliger, R. F. (1970). Pilot study on the effectiveness of systematic desensitization with neurologically impaired children with phobic disorders. *Journal of Consulting and Clinical Psychology, 34*(3), 314–318.

O'Brien, C. P., Anthony, J. C., Carroll, K., Childress, A. R., Dackis, C., Diamond, G., et al. (2005). Substance use disorders. In D. L. Evans, E. B. Foa, R. E. Gur, H. Hendin, C. P. O'Brien, M. E. P. Seligman, et al. (Eds.), *Treating and preventing adolescent mental health disorders* (pp. 335–429). New York: Oxford University Press.

Odom, S. L., McConnell, S. R., McEvoy, M. A., Peterson, C., Ostrosky, M., Chandler, L. K., et al. (1999). Relative effects of interventions supporting the social competence of young children with disabilities. *Topics in Early Childhood Special Education, 19*(2), 75–91.

Office of Special Education Programs. (2006). National Center for Education Statistics, Institute of Educational Sciences (IES). *Crime, violence, discipline, and safety in U.S. public schools: Finding from the school survey on crime and safety: 2005–2006.* Retrieved March 4, 2008, from http://nces.ed.gov/pubsearch/pusinfo.asp?pubid=2007361

Office of Statistics and Programming, Injury Center, National Center for Injury Prevention and Control, CDC. (2006). Retrieved February 2, 2008, from http://www.cdc.gov/ncipc/

Ogden, T., & Halliday-Boykins, C. A. (2004). Multisystemic treatment of antisocial adolescents in Norway: Replication of clinical outcomes outside of the U.S. *Child and Adolescent Mental Health, 9*(2), 77–83.

Olfson, M., Marcus, S., & Shaffer, D. (2006). Antidepressant drug therapy and suicide in severely depressed children and adults. *Archives of General Psychiatry, 63,* 865–872.

Olivardia, R., Pope, H. G., Mangweth, B., & Hudson, J. I. (1995). Eating disorders in college men. *American Journal of Psychiatry, 152*(9), 1279–1285.

Ollendick, T. H. (1983). Reliability and validity of the Revised Fear Survey Schedule for Children (FSSC-R). *Behaviour Research and Therapy, 21*(6), 685–692.

Ollendick, T. H., & King, N. J. (1991). Origins of childhood fears: An evaluation of Rachman's theory of fear acquisition. *Behaviour Research and Therapy, 29*(2), 117–123.

Ollendick, T. H., & King, N. J. (1994). Diagnosis, assessment, and treatment of internalizing problems in children: The role of longitudinal data. *Journal of Consulting and Clinical Psychology, 62*(5), 918–927.

Ollendick, T. H., & King, N. J. (1998). Empirically supported treatments for children with phobic and anxiety disorders: Current status. *Journal of Clinical Child Psychology, 27*(2), 156–167.

Ollendick, T. H., King, N. J., & Muris, P. (2002). Fears and phobias in children: Phenomenology, epidemiology, and aetiology. *Child and Adolescent Mental Health, 7*(3), 98–106.

Ollendick, T. H., & March, J. S. (2004). *Phobic and anxiety disorders in children and adolescents: A clinician's guide to effective psychosocial and pharmacological interventions.* New York: Oxford University Press.

Ollendick, T. H., Yang, B., Dong, Q., & Xia, Y. & Ling (1995). Perceptions of fear in other children and adolescents: The role of gender and friendship status. *Journal of Abnormal Child Psychology, 23*(4), 439–452.

Olsen, R. J., & Farkas, G. (1990). The effect of economic opportunity and family background on adolescent fertility among low-income blacks. *Journal of Labor Economics 8,* 341–362.

Olson, D. H., Bell, R., & Portner, J. (1982). *Family Adaptability and Cohesion Evaluation Scales II.* Minneapolis, MN: Life Innovations.

Olson, R. L., & Roberts, M. W. (1987). Alternative treatments for sibling aggression. *Behavior Therapy, 18*(3), 243–250.

Olweus, D. (1992). Bullying among school children: Intervention and prevention. In R. Peters, R. J. McMahon, & V. L. Quinsy (Eds.), *Aggression and violence throughout the life span* (pp. 100–125). Newbury Park, CA: Sage.

Olweus, D. (1993). Victimization by peers: Antecedents and long-term outcomes. In K. H. Rubin & J. B. Asendorpf (Eds.), *Social withdrawal, inhibition, and shyness in childhood* (pp. 315–341). Hillsdale, NJ: Erlbaum.

Olweus, D. (1996). Bully/victim problems at school: Facts and effective intervention. *Journal of Emotional and Behavioral Problems, 5,* 15–22.

Olweus, D. (1997). Tackling peer victimization with a school-based intervention program. In D. P. Fry & K. Bjorkqvist (Eds.), *Cultural variation in conflict resolution: Alternatives to violence* (pp. 215–234). Mahwah, NJ: Erlbaum.

Olweus, D. (2004). The Olweus Bullying Prevention Program: Design and implementation issues and a new national initiative in Norway. In P. K. Smith, D. J. Pepler, & K. Rigby (Eds.), *Bullying in schools* (pp. 13–36). Cambridge, UK: Cambridge University Press.

Olweus, D., Limber, S., & Mihalic, S. (1999). Bullying prevention program. In D. S. Elliot (Ed.), *Blueprints for violence prevention, book nine* (pp. 1–79). Golden, CO: Venture, C&M Press.

Olweus, D., Mattsson, A., Schalling, D., & Low, H. (1988). Circulating testosterone levels and aggression in adolescent males: A causal analysis. *Psychosomatic Medicine, 50,* 261–272.

Omizo, M. M., & Omizo, S. A. (1987). Group counseling with children of divorce: New findings. *Elementary School Guidance & Counseling, 22*(1), 46–52.

Orpinas, P., & Horne, A. M. (2006). *Bullying prevention: Creating a positive school climate and developing social competence.* Washington, DC: American Psychological Association.

Orsmond, G. I., Krauss, M. W., & Seltzer, M. M. (2004). Peer relationships and social and recreational activities among adolescents and adults with autism. *Journal of Autism and Developmental Disorders, 34*(3), 245–256.

Oswald, D. P., & Volkmar, F. R. (1991). Signal detection analysis of items from the Autism Behavior Checklist. *Journal of Autism and Developmental Disorders, 21*(4), 543–549.

Padilla, F. M. (1992). *The gang as an American enterprise: Puerto Rican youth and the American dream.* New Brunswick, NJ: Rutgers University.

Page, A. C. (1994). Blood-injury phobia. *Clinical Psychology Review, 14*(5), 443–461.

Palincsar, A. S., & Brown, A. L. (1986). Interactive teaching to promote independent learning from text. *The Reading Teacher, 39*(8), 771–777.

Palincsar, A. S., & Klenk, L. (1992). Fostering literacy learning in supportive contexts. *Journal of Learning Disabilities, 25*(4), 211–225, 229.

Pardini, D. A., & Lochman, J. E. (2003). Treatments for oppositional defiant disorder. In M. A. Reinecke, F. M. Dattilio, & A. Freeman (Eds.), *Cognitive therapy with children and adolescents: A casebook for clinical practice* (2nd ed., pp. 43–69). New York: Guilford Press.

Pardini, D. A., Lochman, J. E., & Frick, P. J. (2003). Callous/unemotional traits and social cognitive processes in adjudicated youth. *Journal of the American Academy of Child and Adolescent Psychiatry, 42,* 364–371.

Parks, C. (1995). Gang behavior in the schools: Reality or myth. *Educational Psychology Review, 7,* 41–68.

Paschall, M. J., & Hubbard, M. L. (1998). Effects of neighborhood and family stressors on African American male adolescents' self-worth and propensity for violent behavior. *Journal of Consulting and Clinical Psychology, 66*(5), 825–831.

Pastor, P. N., & Reuben, C. A. (2006). Identified attention-deficit/hyperactivity disorder and medically attended, nonfatal injuries: U.S. school-age children, 1997–2002. *Ambulatory Pediatrics, 6*(1), 38–44.

Patterson, G. R., Chamberlain, P., & Reid, J. B. (1982). A comparative evaluation of a parent-training program. *Behavior Therapy, 13*(5), 638–650.

Patterson, G. R., DeBaryshe, B. D., & Ramsey, E. (1989). A developmental perspective on antisocial behavior. *American Psychologist, 44*(2), 329–335.

Patterson, G. R., Dishion, T. J., & Chamberlain, P. (1993). Outcomes and methodological issues relating to treatment of antisocial children. In T. R. Giles (Ed.), *Handbook of effective psychotherapy* (pp. 43–88). New York: Plenum Press.

Patterson, G. R., Reid, J. B., & Dishion, T. J. (1992). *Antisocial boys: A social interactional approach* (Vol. 4). Eugene, OR: Castalia.

Patton, G. C., Selzer, R., Coffey, C., Carlin, J. B., & Wolfe, R. (1999). Onset of adolescent eating disorders: Population based cohort study over 3 years. *British Medical Journal, 318,* 765–768.

Pauls, D. L., Alsobrook, J. P., Goodman, W., & Rasmussen, S. (1995). A family study of obsessive-compulsive disorder. *American Journal of Psychiatry, 152*(1), 76–84.

Pauls, D. L., Mundo, E., & Kennedy, J. L. (2002). The pathophysiology and genetics of obsessive compulsive disorder. In K. L. Davis, D. Charney, J. T. Coyle, & C. Nemeroff (Eds.), *Neuropsychopharmacology.* Nashville, TN: American College of Neuropsychopharmacology.

PBS Frontline. (2001). *Medicating kids: Attention deficit hyperactivity disorder. The multimodal treatment study of children with attention deficit hyperactivity disorder.* Retrieved April 24, 2002, from http://www.pbs.org/wgbh/pages/frontline/shows/medicating/

PBS Frontline. (2008). *The medicated child: Six million American children are taking psychiatric drugs but most have never been tested on children. Is this good medicine—or an uncontrolled experiment?* Retrieved January 11, 2008, from http://www.pbs.org/wgbh/pages/frontline/medicatedchild/

Peach, L., & Reddick, T. L. (1991). Counselors can make a difference in preventing adolescent suicide. *School Counselor, 39*(2), 107–110.

Peed, S., Roberts, M., & Forehand, R. (1977). Evaluation of the effectiveness of a standardized parent training program in altering the interaction of mothers and their noncompliant children. *Behavior Modification, 1*(3), 323–350.

Pelham, W. E., Carlson, C., Sams, S. E., Vallano, G., Dixon, M. J., & Hoza, B. (1993). Separate and combined effects of methylphenidate and behavior modification on boys with attention deficit-hyperactivity disorder in the classroom. *Journal of Consulting and Clinical Psychology, 61*(3), 506–515.

Pepler, D. J., & Craig, W. (2000). *Report #60: Making a difference in bullying.* Available at http://www.arts.yorku.ca/lamarsh/pdf/Making_a_Difference_in_Bullying.pdf

Pepler, D. J., & Sedighdellami, F. (1998). *Aggressive girls in Canada.* Available online at http://www.hrdc.gc.ca/sp-ps/arb-drga/publications/research/abw-98-30e.shtml

Perlstein, D. (2000). Failing at kindness: Why fear of violence endangers children. *Educational Leadership, 56*(6), 76–79.

Perrin, S., & Last, C. G. (1992). Do childhood anxiety measures measure anxiety? *Journal of Abnormal Child Psychology, 20*(6), 567–578.

Perwien, A. R., & Bernstein, G. A. (2004). Separation anxiety disorder. In T. H. Ollendick & J. S. March (Eds.), *Phobic and anxiety disorders in children and adolescents: A clinician's guide to effective psychosocial and pharmacological interventions* (pp. 272–305). New York: Oxford University Press.

Piacentini, J., Jaffer, M., Bergman, R. L., McCracken, J., & Keller, M. (2001). *Measuring impairment in childhood OCD: Psychometric properties of the COIS.* Paper presented at the annual meeting of the American Academy of Child and Adolescent Psychiatry, Honolulu, HI.

Pierangelo, R., & Giuliani, G. A. (2000a). *Why your students do what they do and what to do when they do it: A practical guide for understanding classroom behavior (grades 6–12).* Champaign, IL: Research Press.

Pierangelo, R., & Giuliani, G. A. (2000b). *Why your students do what they do and what to do when they do it: A practical guide for understanding classroom behavior (grades K–5)*. Champaign, IL: Research Press.

Pierangelo, R., & Giuliani, G. A. (2001). *What every teacher should know about students with special needs: Promoting success in the classroom*. Champaign, IL: Research Press.

Pierce, K., Haist, F., Sedaghat, F., & Courchesne, E. (2004). The brain response to personally familiar faces in autism: Findings of fusiform activity and beyond. *Brain: A Journal of Neurology, 127*(12), 2703–2716.

Pierce, K., Müller, R. A., Ambrose, J., Allen, G., & Courchesne, E. (2001). Face processing occurs outside the fusiform "face area" in autism: Evidence from functional MRI. *Brain: A Journal of Neurology, 124*(10), 2059–2073.

Piggot, J., Kwon, H., Mobbs, D., Blasey, C., Lotspeich, L., Menon, V., et al. (2004). Emotional attribution in high-functioning individuals with autistic spectrum disorder: A functional imaging study. *Journal of the American Academy of Child & Adolescent Psychiatry, 43*(4), 473–480.

Pike, A., McGuire, S., Hetherington, E. M., Reiss, D., & Plomin, R. (1996). Family environment and adolescent depressive symptoms and antisocial behavior: A multivariate genetic analysis. *Developmental Psychology, 32*, 590–603.

Pike, K. M., Walsh, B. T., Vitousek, K., Wilson, G. T., & Bauer, S. (2004). Cognitive behavior therapy in post hospitalization treatment of anorexia nervosa. *American Journal of Psychiatry, 160*, 2046–2049.

Pillow, D. R., Pelham, W. E., Jr., Hoza, B., Molina, B. S. G., & Stultz, C. H. (1998). Confirmatory factor analyses examining attention deficit hyperactivity disorder symptoms and other childhood disruptive behaviors. *Journal of Abnormal Child Psychology, 26*(4), 293–309.

Piran, N., & Thompson, S. (2004). *Expanding the social model of disordered weight patterns*. Unpublished manuscript, OISE, University of Toronto, Canada.

Pisecco, S., Huzinec, C., & Curtis, D. (2001). The effect of child characteristics on teachers'acceptability of classroom-based behavioral strategies and psychostimulant medication for the treatment of ADHD. *Journal of Clinical Child Psychology, 30*(3), 413–421.

Pizzo, P. A., & Wilfert, C. M. (1991). *Pediatric AIDS: The challenge of HIV infection in infants, children,* *and adolescents*. Baltimore MD: Williams & Wilkins.

Pliszka, S. R. (1999). The psychobiology of oppositional defiant disorder and conduct disorder. In H. C. Quay & A. E. Hogan (Eds.), *Handbook of disruptive behavior disorders* (pp. 371–395). New York: Kluwer Academic/Plenum.

Poland, S. (1994). The role of school crisis intervention teams to prevent and reduce school violence and trauma. *School Psychology Review, 23*, 175–189.

Popham, W. J. (2007). *Classroom assessment: What teachers need to know* (7th ed.). Needham Heights, MA: Allyn & Bacon.

Posey, D. J., Guenin, K. D., Kohn, A. E., Swiezy, N. B., & McDougle, C. J. (2001). A naturalistic open-label study of mirtazapine in autistic and other pervasive developmental disorders. *Journal of Child and Adolescent Psychopharmacology, 11*(3), 267–277.

Powers, M. D., & Franks, C. M. (1988). Behavior therapy and the educative process. In J. Witt, S. Elliott, & F. Gresham (Eds.), *Handbook of behavior therapy in education* (pp. 3–36). New York: Plenum Press.

Powers, P. S., & Santana, C. A. (2002). Childhood and adolescent anorexia nervosa. *Child and Adolescent Psychiatric Clinics of North America, 11*(2), 219–235.

Prinz, R. J., & Jones, T. L. (2003). Family-based interventions. In C. A. Essau (Ed.), *Conduct and oppositional defiant disorders: Epidemiology, risk factors, and treatment* (pp. 279–298). Mahwah, NJ: Erlbaum.

Prizant, B. M., & Duchan, J. F. (1981). The functions of immediate echolalia in autistic children. *Journal of Speech & Hearing Disorders, 46*(3), 241–249.

Promising Practices Network. http://www.promisingpractices.net/

Puig-Antich, J. (1985). Biological factors in prepubertal major depression. *Psychiatric Annals, 15*(6), 390–397.

Puig-Antich, J., Perel, J. M., Lupatkin, W., & Chambers, W. J. (1987). Imipramine in prepubertal major depressive disorders. *Archives of General Psychiatry, 44*(1), 81–89.

Pynoos, R. S., Frederick, C., Nader, K., & Arroyo, W. (1987). Life threat and posttraumatic stress in school-age children. *Archives of General Psychiatry, 44*(12), 1057–1063.

Pynoos, R. S., Goenjian, A. K., & Steinberg, A. M. (1998). A public mental health approach to the postdisaster treatment of children and adolescents. *Child and Adolescent Psychiatric Clinics of North America, 7*(1), 195–210.

Quay, H. C., & Hogan, A. E. (1999). *Handbook of disruptive behavior disorders*. Dordrecht, Netherlands: Kluwer Academic Publishers.

Quintana, H., Birmaher, B., Stedge, D., & Lennon, S. (1995). Use of methylphenidate in the treatment of children with autistic disorder. *Journal of Autism and Developmental Disorders, 25*(3), 283–294.

Rachman, S. (1976). The passing of the two-stage theory of fear and avoidance: Fresh possibilities. *Behaviour Research and Therapy, 14*(2), 125–131.

Rachman, S. (1977). The conditioning theory of fear-acquisition: A critical examination. *Behaviour Research and Therapy, 15*(5), 375–387.

Raghavan, R., Bogart, L. M., Elliott, M. N., Vestal, K. D., & Schuster, M. A. (2004). Sexual victimization among a national probability sample of adolescent women. *Perspectives on Sexual and Reproductive Health, 36,* 225–232.

Raine, A., Brennan, P., & Mednick, S. A. (1997). Interaction between birth complications and early maternal rejection in predisposing individuals to adult violence: Specificity to serious, early-onset violence. *American Journal of Psychiatry, 154,* 1265–1271.

Raine, A., Venable, P. H., & Williams, M. (1990). Relationships between central and autonomic measures of arousal at age 15 years and criminality at age 24 years. *Archives of General Psychiatry, 47,* 1060–1064.

Ramsey, M. (1994). Student depression: General treatment dynamics and symptom specific interventions. *School Counselor, 41*(4), 256–262.

Rao, U., Ryan, N. D., Birmaher, B., & Dahl, R. E. (1995). Unipolar depression in adolescents: Clinical outcome in adulthood. *Journal of the American Academy of Child & Adolescent Psychiatry, 34*(5), 566–578.

Rapee, R. M. (1997). Potential role of childrearing practices in the development of anxiety and depression. *Clinical Psychology Review, 17*(1), 47–67.

Rapee, R. M., Barrett, P. M., Dadds, M. R., & Evans, L. (1994). Reliability of the *DSM-III-R* childhood anxiety disorders using structured interview: Interrater and parent-child agreement. *Journal of the American Academy of Child & Adolescent Psychiatry, 33*(7), 984–992.

Rapoport, J. L. (1989). The biology of obsessions and compulsions. *Scientific American, 260*(3), 83–89.

Rapoport, J. L., & Inoff-Germain, G. (2000). Treatment of obsessive-compulsive disorder in children and adolescents. *Journal of Child Psychology and Psychiatry, 41*(4), 419–431.

Rapoport, J. L., Inoff-Germain, G., Weissman, M. M., Greenwald, S., Narrow, W. E., Jensen, P. S., et al. (2000). Childhood obsessive-compulsive disorder in the NIMH MECA study: Parent versus child identification of cases. *Journal of Anxiety Disorders, 14*(6), 535–548.

Rasicot, J. (1999). The threat of harm. *American School Board Journal, 186*(3), 14–18.

Rasmussen, S. A., & Eisen, J. L. (1990). Epidemiology of obsessive compulsive disorder. *Journal of Clinical Psychiatry, 51*(2), 10–13.

Reeve, C. E., & Carr, E. G. (2000). Prevention of severe behavior problems in children with developmental disorders. *Journal of Positive Behavior Interventions, 2*(3), 144–160.

Rehm, L. P. (1977). A self-control model of depression. *Behavior Therapy, 8*(5), 787–804.

Reich, W. (2000). Diagnostic Interview for Children and Adolescents (DICA). *Journal of the American Academy of Child & Adolescent Psychiatry, 39,* 59–66.

Reichart, C. G. (2005). *Being a child of a bipolar parent: Psychopathology, social functioning, and family functioning.* Ridderkerk, Netherlands: Ridderprint.

Reichart, C. G., & Nolen, W. A. (2004). Earlier onset of bipolar disorder in children by antidepressants or stimulants? An hypothesis. *Journal of Affective Disorders, 78*(1), 81–84.

Reichart, C. G., Wals, M., & Hillegers, M. H. J. (2004). Psychopathology in the adolescent offspring of bipolar parents. *Journal of Affective Disorders, 78,* 67–71.

Reinecke, M. A., Ryan, N., & DuBois, D. L. (1998). Meta-analysis of CBT for depression in adolescents: Dr. Reinecke et al. reply. *Journal of the American Academy of Child & Adolescent Psychiatry, 37*(10), 1006–1007.

Reis, H. T. (2001). Relationship experiences and emotional well-being. In C. D. Ryff & B. Singer (Eds.), *Emotion, social relationships, and health.* New York: Oxford University Press.

Research Units on Pediatric Psychopharmacology Anxiety Study Group. (2001). Fluvoxamine for the treatment of anxiety disorders in children and adolescents. *New England Journal of Medicine, 344,* 1279–1285.

Research Units on Pediatric Psychopharmacology Autism Network. (2002). Risperidone in children with autism and serious behavioral problems. *New England Journal of Medicine, 347,* 314–321.

Rey, J. M., & Plapp, J. M. (1990). Quality of perceived parenting in oppositional and conduct disordered adolescents. *Journal of the American Academy of Child & Adolescent Psychiatry, 29*(3), 382–385.

Reynolds, C. R., & Kamphaus, R. W. (1992). *Behavioral assessment system for children.* Circle Pines, MN: American Guidance Service.

Reynolds, W. M. (1987*). RCDS manual.* Odessa, FL: Psychological Assessment Resources.

Reynolds, W. M. (1989). *RADS manual.* Odessa, FL: Psychological Assessment Resources.

Reynolds, W. M., & Johnston, H. F. (1994). *Handbook of depression in children and adolescents.* New York: Plenum Press.

Ricca, V., Mannucci, E., Zucchi, T., Rotella, C., & Faravelli, C. (2000). Cognitive-behavioral therapy for bulimia nervosa and binge eating disorder: A review. *Psychotherapy and Psychosomatics, 69,* 287–295.

Ricciardelli, L. A., & McCabe, M. P. (2004). A biopsychosocial model of disordered eating and the pursuit of muscularity in adolescent boys. *Psychological Bulletin, 130*(2), 179–205.

Riccio, C. A., Waldrop, J. M., Reynolds, C. R., & Lowe, P. (2001). Effects of stimulants on the continuous performance test (CPT): Implications for CPT use and interpretation. *The Journal for Neuropsychiatry and Clinical Neurosciences, 13*(3), 326–335.

Riddle, M. A., Reeve, E. A., Yaryura-Tobias, J. A., Yang, H. M., Claghorn, J. L., Gaffney, G., et al. (2001). Fluvoxamine for children and adolescents with obsessive-compulsive disorder: A randomized, controlled, multicenter trial. *Journal of the American Academy of Child & Adolescent Psychiatry, 40*(2), 222–229.

Rifkin, A., Karajgi, B., Dicker, R., & Perl, E. (1997). Lithium treatment of conduct disorders in adolescents. *American Journal of Psychiatry, 154*(4), 554–555.

Rigby, K., & Slee, P. (1999). Suicidal ideation among adolescent school children, involvement in bully-victim problems, and perceived social support. *Suicide and Life-Threatening Behavior, 29*(2), 119–130.

Rimland, B., & Baker, S. M. (1996). Brief report: Alternative approaches to the development of effective treatments for autism. *Journal of Autism and Developmental Disorders, 26*(2), 237–241.

Ringdahl, J. E., Andelman, M. S., Kitsukawa, K., Winborn, L. C., Barretto, A., & Wacker, D. P. (2002).

Evaluation and treatment of covert stereotypy. *Behavioral Interventions, 17*(1), 43–49.

Ritvo, E. R., Jorde, L. B., Mason-Brothers, A., & Freeman, B. J. (1990). The UCLA–University of Utah epidemiologic survey of autism: Recurrence risk estimates and genetic counseling. *Annual Progress in Child Psychiatry & Child Development,* 205–215.

Robb, A. S., & Dadson, M. J. (2002). Eating disorders in males. *Child and Adolescent Psychiatric Clinics of North America, 11*(2), 399–418.

Roberts, M. W., & Hope, D. A. (2001). Clinic observations of structured parent-child interaction designed to evaluate externalizing disorders. *Psychological Assessment, 13*(1), 46–58.

Roberts, W. B., Jr., & Morotti, A. A. (2000). The bully as victim: Understanding bully behaviors to increase the effectiveness of interventions in the bully-victim dyad. *Professional School Counseling, 4*(2), 148–155.

Robertson, J. M., Tanguay, P. E., L'Ecuyer, S., Sims, A., & Waltrip, C. (1999). Domains of social communication handicap in autism spectrum disorder. *Journal of the American Academy of Child & Adolescent Psychiatry, 38*(6), 738–745.

Robin, A. L., Gilroy, M., & Dennis, A. B. (1998). Treatment of eating disorders in children and adolescents. *Clinical Psychology Review, 18*(4), 421–446.

Robin, A. L., & Siegel, P. T. (1999). Family therapy with eating-disordered adolescents. In S. W. Russ & T. H. Ollendick (Eds.), *Handbook of psychotherapies with children and families* (pp. 301–325). Dordrecht, Netherlands: Kluwer Academic Publishers.

Robin, A. L., Siegel, P. T., Koepke, T., Moye, A. W., & Tice, S. (1994). Family therapy versus individual therapy for adolescent females with anorexia nervosa. *Journal of Developmental & Behavioral Pediatrics, 15*(2), 111–116.

Robinson, E. L., & Fine, M. J. (1994). Developing collaborative home-school relationships. *Preventing School Failure, 39*(1), 9–15.

Robinson, S. E. (1989). Preventing substance abuse among teenagers. A school and family responsibility. *Counseling and Human Development, 34,* 130–137.

Robinson, W. L., Watkins-Ferrell, P., Davis-Scott, P., & Ruch-Ross, H. S. (1993). Preventing teenage pregnancy. In D. S. Glenwick & L. A. Jason (Eds.), *Promoting health and mental health in children, youth, and families* (pp. 99–124). New York: Springer.

Robison, L. M., Sclar, D. A., Skaer, T. L., & Galin, R. S. (1999). National trends in the prevalence of attention-deficit/hyperactivity disorder and the prescribing of methylphenidate among school-age children: 1990–1995. *Clinical Pediatrics, 38*(4), 209–218.

Rogers-Adkinson, D., & Griffin, P. (1999). *Communication disorders and children with psychiatric and behavioral disorders*. San Diego, CA: Singular.

Rohde, P., Lewinsohn, P. M., & Seeley, J. R. (1991). Comorbidity of unipolar depression: II. Comorbidity with other mental disorders in adolescents and adults. *Journal of Abnormal Psychology, 100*(2), 214–222.

Roland, E., & Galloway, D. (2002). Classroom influences on bullying. *Educational Research, 44*(3), 299–312.

Rome, E., & Ammerman, S. (2003). Medical complications of eating disorders: An update. *Journal of Adolescent Health, 33*(6), 418–426.

Ronan, K. R., Kendall, P. C., & Rowe, M. (1994). Negative affectivity in children: Development and validation of a self-statement questionnaire. *Cognitive Therapy and Research, 18*(6), 509–528.

Rosenberg, M. S., Wilson, R. J., Maheady, L., & Sindelar, P. T. (2004). *Educating students with behavior disorders* (3rd ed.). Boston: Allyn & Bacon.

Ross, D. L., Klykylo, W. M., & Anderson, G. M. (1985). Cerebrospinal fluid indoleamine and monoamine effects in fenfluramine treatment of autism. *Annals of Neurology, 18*, 394.

Rourke, B. P., & Tsatsanis, K. D. (2000). Nonverbal learning disabilities and Asperger syndrome. In A. Klin, F. R. Volkmar, & S. S. Sparrow (Eds.), *Asperger syndrome* (pp. 231–253). New York: Guilford Press.

Rowe, R., Maughan, B., Costello, E. J., & Angold, A. (2005). Defining oppositional defiant disorder. *Journal of Child Psychology and Psychiatry, 46*(12), 1309–1316.

Russell, G. F., Szmukler, G. I., Dare, C., & Eisler, I. (1987). An evaluation of family therapy in anorexia nervosa and bulimia nervosa. *Archives of General Psychiatry, 44*(12), 1047–1056.

Russo, N. F., & Beidel, D. C. (1994). Comorbidity of childhood anxiety and externalizing disorders: Prevalence, associated characteristics, and validation issues. *Clinical Psychology Review, 14*, 199–221.

Rutgers, A. H., Bakermans-Kranenburg, M. J., van Ijzendoorn, M. H., & van Berckelaer-Onnes, I. A. (2004). Autism and attachment: A meta-analytic review. *Journal of Child Psychology and Psychiatry, 45*(6), 1123–1134.

Rutter, M. (2005). Genetic influences and autism. In F. R. Volkmar, R. Paul, A. Klin, & D. Cohen (Eds.), *Handbook of autism and pervasive developmental disorders: Vol. 1. Diagnosis, development, neurobiology, and behavior* (3rd ed., pp. 425–452). Hoboken, NJ: John Wiley & Sons, Inc.

Ryan, A. L., Halsey, H. N., & Matthews, W. J. (2003). Using functional assessment to promote desirable student behavior in schools. *Teaching Exceptional Children, 35*(5), 8–15.

Ryan, N. (2003). Medication treatment for depression in children and adolescents. *CNS Spectrum, 4*, 283–287.

Ryan, N. D., Dahl, R. E., Birmaher, B., & Williamson, D. E. (1994). Stimulatory tests of growth hormone secretion in prepubertal major depression: Depressed versus normal children. *Journal of the American Academy of Child & Adolescent Psychiatry, 33*(6), 824–833.

Sabatino, D. A., Webster, B. G., & Vance, H. B. (2001). Childhood mood disorders: History, characteristics, diagnosis and treatment. In A. Pumariega (Ed.), *Clinical assessment of child and adolescent behavior* (pp. 413–449). Hoboken, NJ: John Wiley & Sons, Inc.

Sachs, J. (1999). The hidden conspiracy in our nation's schools. *Behavioral Disorders, 25*(1), 80–82.

Saldana, L., & Henggeler, S. W. (2006). Multisystemic therapy in the treatment of adolescent conduct disorder. In W. M. Nelson, III, A. J. Finch, Jr., & K. J. Hart (Eds.), *Conduct disorders: A practitioner's guide to comparative treatments* (pp. 217–258). New York: Springer.

Salend, S. J. (2001). *Creating inclusive classrooms: Effective and reflective practices* (4th ed.). Columbus, OH: Merrill/Prentice Hall.

Salend, S. J. (2005). *Creating inclusive classrooms: Effective and reflective practices for all students* (5th ed.). Upper Saddle River, NJ: Merrill/Prentice Hall.

Sampson, R. (2002). Bullying in schools. In *Problem-oriented guides for police series: Guide no. 12*. Washington, DC: Office of Community Oriented Policing Services, U.S. Department of Justice.

Sanchez. F., and Anderson, M. L. (1990, May). Gang mediation: A process that works. *Principal Magazine, 69*(5), 59–61.

SanchezJankowski, M. S. 1991. *Islands in the street: Gangs and American urban society*. Berkeley: University of California Press.

Sandhu, D. S. (2000). Alienated students: Counseling strategies to curb school violence. *Professional School Counseling, 4*(2), 81–85.

Sandman, C. A., Barron, J. L., Chicz-DeMet, A., & DeMet, E. M. (1990). Plasma b-endorphin levels in patients with self-injurious behavior and stereotypy.

American Journal on Mental Retardation, 95(1), 84–92.

Sanson, A., Prior, M., & Smart, D. (1996). Reading disabilities with and without behavioral problems at 7–8 years: Prediction from longitudinal data from infancy to 6 years. *Journal of Child Psychology Psychiatry, 37,* 529–541.

Sansone, R. A., Levitt, J. L., & Sansone, L. A. (2005). The prevalence of personality disorders among those with eating disorders. *Eating Disorders: The Journal of Treatment & Prevention, 13*(1), 7–21.

Sansone, R. A., & Sansone, L. A. (2005). The eating disorders. In W. M. Klykylo & J. L. Kay (Eds.), *Clinical child psychiatry* (2nd ed., pp. 311–326). New York: John Wiley & Sons, Inc.

Sarason, S. B., Davidson, K. S., Lighthall, F. F., Waite, R. R., & Ruebush, B. K. (1960). *Anxiety in elementary school children.* Oxford, England: Wiley.

Sauerwein, K. (1995, March). Violence and young children. *The Executive Educator,* 23–26.

Scahill, L., Chappell, P. B., Kim, Y. S., & Schultz, R. T. (2001). A placebo-controlled study of guanfacine in the treatment of children with tic disorders and attention deficit hyperactivity disorder. *The American Journal of Psychiatry, 158*(7), 1067–1074.

Scahill, L., & Martin, A. (2005). Psychopharmacology. In F. R. Volkmar, R. Paul, A. Klin, & D. Cohen (Eds.), *Handbook of autism and pervasive developmental disorders: Vol. 2. Assessment, interventions, and policy* (3rd ed., pp. 1102–1117). Hoboken, NJ: John Wiley & Sons, Inc.

Scahill, L., Riddle, M. A., McSwiggin-Hardin, M., & Ort, S. I. (1997). Children's Yale-Brown Obsessive Compulsive Scale: Reliability and validity. *Journal of the American Academy of Child & Adolescent Psychiatry, 36*(6), 844–852.

Scahill, L., & Vitiello, B. (2002). Risperidone in children with autism and serious behavioral problems: Reply. *New England Journal of Medicine, 347*(23), 1891.

Schaeffer, C. M., & Borduin, C. M. (2005). Long-term follow-up to a randomized clinical trial of multisystemic therapy with serious and violent juvenile offenders. *Journal of Consulting and Clinical Psychology, 73*(3), 445–453.

Schaffer, D., Fisher, P., Dulcan, M. K., & Davies, M. (1996). The NIMH Diagnostic Interview Schedule for Children version 2.3 (DISC-2.3): Description, acceptability, prevalence rates and performance in the MECA study. *Journal of the American Academy of Child and Adolescent Psychiatry, 35,* 865–877.

Schaffer, D., Fisher, P., Lucas, C. P., Dulcan, M. K., & Schwab-Stone, M. E. (2000). The NIMH Diagnostic Interview Schedule for Children version IV (DISC-IV): Description, differences from previous versions, and reliability of some common diagnoses. *Journal of the American Academy of Child and Adolescent Psychiatry, 39,* 28–38.

Schain, R. J., & Freedman, D. X. (1961). Studies on 5-hydroxyindole metabolism in autistic and other mentally retarded children. *Journal of Pediatrics, 58,* 315–320.

Scheeringa, M. S., Peebles, C. D., Cook, C. A., & Zeanah, C. H. (2001). Toward establishing procedural, criterion, and discriminant validity for PTSD in early childhood. *Journal of the American Academy of Child & Adolescent Psychiatry, 40*(1), 52–60.

Scheeringa, M. S., Zeanah, C. H., Drell, M. J., & Larrieu, J. A. (1995). Two approaches to the diagnosis of posttraumatic stress disorder in infancy and early childhood: Erratum. *Journal of the American Academy of Child & Adolescent Psychiatry, 34*(5), 694.

Scherman, A., Korkanes-Rowe, D., & Howard, S. S. (1990). An examination of the living arrangements and needs expressed by teenage mothers. *The School Counselor, 38,* 133–141.

Schloss, P. J. (1983). Classroom-based intervention for students exhibiting depressive reactions. *Behavioral Disorders, 8*(4), 231–236.

Schlozman, S. C., & Schlozman, V. R. (2000). Chaos in the classroom: Looking at ADHD. *Educational Leadership, 58*(3), 28–33.

Schopler, E., & Reichler, R. J. (1979). *Individualized assessment and treatment for autistic and developmentally disabled children: Psychoeducational profile: Vol. 1.* Baltimore: University Park Press.

Schopler, E., Reichler, R. J., Bashford, A., Lansing, M. D., & Marcus, L. M. (1990). *Psychoeducational Profile—Revised.* Austin, TX: ProEd.

Schopler, E., Reichler, R. J., & Renner, B. R. (1988). *The Childhood Autism Rating Scale (CARS).* Los Angeles: Western Psychological Services.

Schreibman, L., & Ingersoll, B. (2005). Behavioral interventions to promote learning in individuals with autism. In F. R. Volkmar, R. Paul, A. Klin, & D. Cohen (Eds.), *Handbook of autism and pervasive developmental disorders: Vol. 2. Assessment, interventions, and policy* (3rd ed., pp. 882–896). Hoboken, NJ: John Wiley & Sons, Inc.

Schuhmann, E. M., Foote, R. C., Eyberg, S. M., Boggs, S. R., & Algina, J. (1998). Efficacy of parent-child interaction therapy: Interim report of a randomized trial with short-term maintenance. *Journal of Clinical Child Psychology, 27*(1), 34–45.

Schultz, R. T., Gauthier, I., Klin, A., Fulbright, R. K., Anderson, A. W., Volkmar, F., et al. (2000). Abnormal ventral temporal cortical activity during face discrimination among individuals with autism and Asperger syndrome. *Archives of General Psychiatry, 57*(4), 331–340.

Schultz, R. T., & Robins, D. L. (2005). Functional neuroimaging studies of autism spectrum disorders. In F. R. Volkmar, R. Paul, A. Klin, & D. Cohen (Eds.), *Handbook of autism and pervasive developmental disorders: Vol. 1. Diagnosis, development, neurobiology, and behavior* (3rd ed., pp. 515–533). Hoboken, NJ: John Wiley & Sons, Inc.

Schumann, G. G. (2006). Hypothalamic-pituitary-adrenal axis and substance use: So many questions—and we can answer them. *Addiction, 101*(11), 1538–1539.

Schur, E., Sanders, M., & Steiner, H. (1999). Body dissatisfaction and eating attitudes in young children. *International Journal of Eating Disorders, 27*, 74–82.

Schwandt, W. L., Pieropan, K., Glesne, H., Lundahl, A., Foley, D., & Larsson, E. V. (2002, May). *Using video modeling to teach generalized toy play.* Paper presented at the annual meeting of the Association for Behavior Analysis, Toronto, Canada.

Schwartz, D., McFadyen-Ketchum, S., Dodge, K. A., Pettit, G. S., & Bates, J. E. (1999). Early behavior problems as a predictor of later peer group victimization: Moderators and mediators in the pathways of social risk. *Journal of Abnormal Child Psychology, 27*(3), 191–201.

Sciarra, D. T., & Ponterotto, J. G. (1998). Adolescent motherhood among low-income urban Hispanics: Familial considerations of mother-daughter dyads. *Qualitative Health Research, 8*(6), 751–763.

Scott, S. (2006). Conduct disorders. In C. Gillberg, R. Harrington, & H. C. Steinhausen (Eds.), *A clinician's handbook of child and adolescent psychiatry* (pp. 522–556). Cambridge, U.K.: Cambridge University.

Seedat, S., Stein, D. J., Ziervogel, C., Middleton, T., Kaminer, D., Emsley, R. A., et al. (2002). Comparison of response to a selective serotonin reuptake inhibitor in children, adolescents and adults with posttraumatic stress disorder. *Journal of Child and Adolescent Psychopharmacology, 12*(1), 37–46.

Seguin, J. R., Boulerice, B., Harden, P. W., Tremblay, R. E., & Pihl, R. O. (1999). Executive functions and physical aggression after controlling for attention deficit hyperactivity disorder, general memory, and IQ. *Journal of Child Psychology Psychiatry, 40*, 1197–1208.

Seligman, M. E. (1974). Depression and learned helplessness. In R. J. Friedman & M. M. Katz (Eds.), *The psychology of depression: Contemporary theory and research.* Oxford, England: Wiley.

Sellers, D. E., McGraw, S. A., & McKinlay, J. B. (1994). Does the promotion and distribution of condoms increase teen sexual activity? Evidence from an HIV prevention program for Latino youth. *American Journal of Public Health, 84*(12), 1952–1959.

Seltzer, M. M., Krauss, M. W., Shattuck, P. T., Orsmond, G., Swe, A., & Lord, C. (2003). The symptoms of autism spectrum disorders in adolescence and adulthood. *Journal of Autism and Developmental Disorders, 33*(6), 565–581.

Serfaty, M. A., Turkington, D., Heap, M., Ledsham, L., & Jolley, E. (1999). Cognitive therapy versus dietary counselling in the outpatient treatment of anorexia nervosa: Effects of the treatment phase. *European Eating Disorders Review, 7*(5), 334–350.

Sevin, J. A., Matson, J. L., Coe, D. A., & Fee, V. E. (1991). A comparison and evaluation of three commonly used autism scales. *Journal of Autism and Developmental Disorders, 21*(4), 417–432.

Shaffer, D., Fisher, P., Dulcan, M. K., & Davies, M. (1996). The NIMH Diagnostic Interview Schedule for Children version 2.3 (DISC-2.3): Description, acceptability, prevalence rates, and performance in the MECA study. *Journal of the American Academy of Child & Adolescent Psychiatry, 35*(7), 865–877.

Shaffer, D., Fisher, P., Lucas, C. P., Dulcan, M. K., & Schwab-Stone, M. E. (2000). NIMH Diagnostic Interview Schedule for Children version IV (NIMH DISC-IV): Description, differences from previous versions, and reliability of some common diagnoses. *Journal of the American Academy of Child & Adolescent Psychiatry, 39*(1), 28–38.

Shaffer, R. (1984). *The child's entry into a social world.* London: Academic Press.

Sheinkopf, S. J., Mundy, P., Oller, D. K., & Steffens, M. (2000). Vocal atypicalities of preverbal autistic children. *Journal of Autism and Developmental Disorders, 30*(4), 345–354.

Sherer, M., Pierce, K. L., Paredes, S., Kisacky, K. L., Ingersoll, B., & Schreibman, L. (2001). Enhancing conversation skills in children with autism via video technology: Which is better, "self" or "other" as a model? *Behavior Modification, 25*(1), 140–158.

Sherrill, J. T., & Kovacs, M. (2000). Interview Schedule for Children and Adolescents (ISCA). *Journal of the American Academy of Child & Adolescent Psychiatry, 39*(1), 67–75.

Sherwood-Hawes, A. (2000). Children having children: Teenage pregnancy and parenthood. In D. Capuzzi & D. R. Gross (Eds.), *Youth risk: A prevention resource for counselors, teachers, and parents* (3rd ed., pp. 243–280). Alexandria, VA: American Counseling Association.

Sheslow, D. V., Bondy, A. S., & Nelson, R. O. (1983). A comparison of graduated exposure, verbal coping skills, and their combination in the treatment of children's fear of the dark. *Child and Family Behavior Therapy, 4*, 33–45.

Shinn, M. (1995). Best practices in curriculum based measurement and its use in a problem solving model. In A. Thomas & J. Grimes (Eds.), *Best practices in school psychology—III* (pp. 547–567). Washington, DC: National Association of School Psychologists.

Shipley-Benamou, R., Lutzker, J. R., & Taubman, M. (2002). Teaching daily living skills to children with autism through instructional video modeling. *Journal of Positive Behavior Interventions, 4*(3), 165–175.

Shippen, M. E., Simpson, R., & Crites, S. A. (2003). A practical guide to functional behavioral assessment. *Teaching Exceptional Children, 35*(5), 36–44.

Shoebridge, P. J., & Gowers, S. G. (2000). Parental high concern and adolescent-onset anorexia nervosa: A case-control study to investigate direction of causality. *British Journal of Psychiatry, 176*(2), 132–137.

Silove, D., Manicavasagar, V., O'Connell, D., & Morris-Yates, A. (1995). Genetic factors in early separation anxiety: Implications for the genesis of adult anxiety disorders. *Acta Psychiatrica Scandinavica, 92*(1), 17–24.

Silver, L. (1998). *Dr. Larry Silver's advice to parents on ADHD.* New York: Three Rivers Press.

Silver, L. B. (1999). Alternative (nonstimulant) medications in the treatment of attention-deficit/hyperactivity disorder in children. *Pediatric Clinics of North America, 46*(5), 965–975.

Silverman, W. K., & Albano, A. M. (1996). *Anxiety Disorders Interview Schedule for DSM-IV: Child and Parent Versions.* San Antonio, TX: Psychological Corporation.

Silverman, W. K., & Carmichael, D. H. (1999). Phobic disorders. In R. T. Ammerman, M. Hersen, & C. G. Last (Eds.), *Handbook of prescriptive treatments for children and adolescents* (2nd ed., pp. 172–192). Needham Heights, MA: Allyn & Bacon.

Silverman, W. K., & Dick-Niederhauser, A. (2004). Separation anxiety disorder. In T. L. Morris & J. S. March (Eds.), *Anxiety disorders in children and adolescents* (2nd ed., pp. 164–188). New York: Guilford Press.

Silverman, W. K., Kurtines, W. M., Ginsburg, G. S., Weems, C. F., Rabian, B., & Serafini, L. T. (1999). Contingency management, self-control, and education support in the treatment of childhood phobic disorders: A randomized clinical trial. *Journal of Consulting and Clinical Psychology, 67*(5), 675–687.

Silverman, W. K., & Rabian, B. (1995). Test-retest reliability of the *DSM-III-R* childhood anxiety disorders symptoms using the Anxiety Disorders Interview Schedule for Children. *Journal of Anxiety Disorders, 9*(2), 139–150.

Silverman, W. K., Saavedra, L. M., & Pina, A. A. (2001). Test-retest reliability of anxiety symptoms and diagnoses with Anxiety Disorders Interview Schedule for *DSM-IV:* Child and parent versions. *Journal of the American Academy of Child & Adolescent Psychiatry, 40*(8), 937–944.

Silverthorn, P., Frick, P. J., & Reynolds, R. (2001). Timing of onset and correlates of severe conduct problems in adjudicated girls and boys. *Journal of Psychopathology and Behavioral Assessment, 23*, 171–181.

Simonoff, E., Pickles, A., Meyer, J., Silberg, J., & Maes, H. (1998). Genetic and environmental influences on subtypes of conduct disorder behavior in boys. *Journal of Abnormal Child Psychology, 26*(6), 495–509.

Simpson, K. J. (2002). Anorexia nervosa and culture. *Journal of Psychiatric and Mental Health Nursing, 9*(1), 65–71.

Skiba, R. J., & Peterson, R. L. (2000). School discipline at the crossroads: From zero tolerance to early response. *Exceptional Children, 66*, 335–347.

Skiba, R., & Peterson, R. (1999). The dark side of zero tolerance: Can punishment lead to safe schools? *Phi Delta Kappan, 80*, 372–376, 381–382.

Skiba, R. J., Poloni-Staudinger, L., Simmons, A. B., Feggins-Azziz, L. R., & Chung, C. G. (2005). Unproven links: Can poverty explain ethnic disproportionality in special education? *Journal of Special Education, 39*, 130–144.

Skinner, B. F. (1969). *The technology of teaching*. New York: John Wiley & Sons, Inc.

Smith, D. D. (2007). *Introduction to special education: Making a difference*. Upper Saddle River, NJ: Pearson.

Smith, P. K., & Thomspon, D. (1991). Dealing with bully/victim problems in the U.K. In P. K. Smith & D. Thompson (Eds.), *Practical approaches to bullying* (pp. 1–2). London: Fulton.

Smith, T. E. C., Polloway, E. A., Patton, J. R., & Dowdy, C. A. (2006*). Teaching students with special needs in inclusive settings* (5th ed.). Boston: Allyn & Bacon.

Smolak, L., & Murnen, S. K. (2002). A meta-analytic examination of the relationship between child sexual abuse and eating disorders. *International Journal of Eating Disorders, 31*(2), 136–150.

Smothers, R. (2000). When school rules cheat kids. *Redbook, 195*(3), 88–91.

Snyder, H. N., & Sickmund, M. (1999). *Juvenile offenders and victims: 1999 national report*. Washington, DC: Office of Juvenile Justice and Delinquency Prevention.

Snyder, J., Schrepferman, L., & St. Peter, C. (1997). Origins of antisocial behavior: Negative reinforcement and affect dysregulation of behavior as socialization mechanisms in family interaction. *Behavior Modification, 21*(2), 187–215.

Sohlberg, S., & Strober, M. (1994). Personality in anorexia nervosa: An update and a theoretical integration. *Acta Psychiatrica Scandinavica, 89*(378), 16.

Sokol, M. (2000). Infection-triggered anorexia nervosa in children: Clinical description of four cases. *Journal of Child and Adolescent Psychopharmacology, 10*, 133–145.

South, M., Williams, B. J., McMahon, W. M., Owley, T., Filipek, P. A., Shernoff, E., et al. (2002). Utility of the Gilliam autism rating scale in research and clinical populations. *Journal of Autism and Developmental Disorders, 32*(6), 593–599.

Southam-Gerow, M. A. (2003). Child-focused cognitive-behavioral therapies. In C. A. Essau (Ed.), *Conduct and oppositional defiant disorders: Epidemiology, risk factors, and treatment* (pp. 257–277). Mahwah, NJ: Erlbaum.

Spaccarelli, S., Cotler, S., & Penman, D. (1992). Problem-solving skills training as a supplement to behavioral parent training. *Cognitive Therapy and Research, 16*(1), 1–17.

Spangler, D. L., & Stice, E. (2001). Validation of the Beliefs About Appearance Scale. *Cognitive Therapy and Research, 25*(6), 813–827.

Speaker, K. M., & Petersen, G. J. (2000). School violence and adolescent suicide: Strategies for effective intervention. *Educational Review, 52*(1), 65–73.

Speltz, M. L., DeKlyen, M., Greenberg, M. T., & Dryden, M. (1995). Clinic referral for oppositional defiant disorder: Relative significance of attachment and behavioral variables. *Journal of Abnormal Child Psychology, 23*(4), 487–507.

Spence, S. H. (1998). A measure of anxiety symptoms among children. *Behaviour Research and Therapy, 36*(5), 545–566.

Spence, S. H., Donovan, C., & Brechman-Toussaint, M. (2000). The treatment of childhood social phobia: The effectiveness of a social skills training-based, cognitive-behavioural intervention, with and without parental involvement. *Journal of Child Psychology and Psychiatry, 41*(6), 713–726.

Spencer, T., Biederman, J., Wilens, T., & Faraone, S. (2001). Efficacy of a mixed amphetamine salts compound in adults with attention deficit/hyperactivity disorder. *Archives of General Psychiatry, 58*(8), 775–782.

Spergel, I. A. 1995. *The youth gang problem*. New York: Oxford University Press.

Spiegel, L., & Mayers, A. (1991). Psychosocial aspects of AIDS in children and adolescents. *Pediatric Clinics of North America, 38*, 153–167.

Spirito, A., Plummer, B., Gispert, M., & Levy, S. (1992). Adolescent suicide attempts: Outcomes at follow-up. *American Journal of Orthopsychiatry, 62*(3), 464–468.

Spitzer, R., Endicott, J., Loth, J., McDonald-Scott, P., & Wasek, P. (1998). *Kiddie schedule for affective disorders and schizophrenia*. New York: Department of Research Assessment and Training.

Spivak, H., & Prothrow-Stith, D. 2001. The need to address bullying: An important component of violence prevention. *Journal of the American Medical Association, 285*(16), 2131–2132.

Spoont, M. R. (1992). Modulatory role of serotonin in neural information processing: Implications for human psychopathology. *Psychological Bulletin, 112*(2), 330–350.

Spring, B., Chiodo, J., & Bowen, D. J. (1987). Carbohydrates, tryptophan, and behavior: A methodological review. *Psychological Bulletin, 102*(2), 234–256.

Stahmer, A. C. (1995). Teaching symbolic play skills to children with autism using pivotal response training. *Journal of Autism and Developmental Disorders, 25*(2), 123–141.

Stallard, P., & Law, F. (1993). Screening and psychological debriefing of adolescent survivors of life-threatening events. *The British Journal of Psychiatry: The Journal of Mental Science, 163*, 660–665.

State of Our Nation's Youth. (2000). *The Horatio Alger Association of Distinguished Americans, 2000.* Available online at www.horatioalger.com/pubmat/surpro.htm

Steerneman, P., Muris, P., Merckelbach, H., & Willems, H. (1997). Brief report: Assessment of development and abnormal behavior in children with pervasive developmental disorders: Evidence for the reliability and validity of the Revised Psychoeducational Profile. *Journal of Autism and Developmental Disorders, 27*(2), 177–185.

Steffenburg, S., Gillberg, C., Hellgren, L., & Andersson, L. (1989). A twin study of autism in Denmark, Finland, Iceland, Norway and Sweden. *Journal of Child Psychology and Psychiatry, 30*(3), 405–416.

Steiger, H., Koerner, N., Engelberg, M. J., Israël, M., Ying Kin, N. M. K., & Young, S. N. (2001). Self-destructiveness and serotonin function in bulimia nervosa. *Psychiatry Research, 103*(1), 15–26.

Stein, D., Lilenfeld, L. R., Plotnicov, K., Pollice, C., Rao, R., Strober, M., et al. (1999). Familial aggregation of eating disorders: Results from a controlled family study of bulimia nervosa. *International Journal of Eating Disorders, 26*(2), 211–215.

Stein, M., & Davis, C. A. (2000). Direct instruction as a positive behavioral support. *Beyond Behavior, 10*(1), 7–12.

Steinberg, L. (April, 2000). Youth violence: Do parents and families make a difference? *National Institute of Justice Journal*, 30–38.

Steiner, H., Kwan, W., Shaffer, T. G., Walker, S., Miller, S., Sagar, A., et al. (2003). Risk and protective factors for juvenile eating disorders. *European Child & Adolescent Psychiatry, 12*, I/38–I/46.

Steiner, H., & Wilson, J. (1999). Conduct disorder. In R. L. Hendren (Ed.), *Disruptive behavior disorders in children and adolescents: Vol. 18, No. 2* (pp. 47–98). Washington, DC: American Psychiatric Association.

Steinhasuen, H. C. (1995). Treatment and outcome of adolescent anorexia nervosa. *Hormone Research, 43*, 168–170.

Steinhausen, H. C. (2002). The outcome of anorexia nervosa in the 20th century. *American Journal of Psychiatry, 159*(8), 1284–1293.

Steinhausen, H. C. (2006). Eating disorders: Anorexia nervosa and bulimia nervosa. In C. Gillberg & R. Harrington (Eds.), *A clinician's handbook of child and adolescent psychiatry* (pp. 272–303). New York: Cambridge University Press.

Steinhausen, H. C., Boyadjieva, S., Griogoroiu-Serbanescu, M., & Neumärker, K. J. (2003). The outcome of adolescent eating disorders: Findings from an international collaborative study. *European Child & Adolescent Psychiatry, 12*, I/91–I/98.

Steketee, G. (1994). Behavioral assessment and treatment planning with obsessive compulsive disorder: A review emphasizing clinical application. *Behavior Therapy, 25*(4), 613–633.

Stella, J., Mundy, P., & Tuchman, R. (1999). Social and nonsocial factors in the Childhood Autism Rating Scale. *Journal of Autism and Developmental Disorders, 29*(4), 307–317.

Stemberger, R. T., Turner, S. M., Beidel, D. C., & Calhoun, K. S. (1995). Social phobia: An analysis of possible developmental factors. *Journal of Abnormal Psychology, 104*(3), 526–531.

Stice, E. (2002). Risk and maintenance factors for eating pathology: A meta-analytic review. *Psychological Bulletin, 128*(5), 825–848.

Stice, E., & Ragan, J. (2002). A preliminary controlled evaluation of an eating disturbance psychoeducational intervention for college students. *International Journal of Eating Disorders, 31*(2), 159–171.

Stice, E., Telch, C. F., & Rizvi, S. L. (2000). Development and validation of the Eating Disorder Diagnostic Scale: A brief self-report measure of anorexia, bulimia, and binge-eating disorder. *Psychological Assessment, 12*(2), 123–131.

Stifter, C. A., Coulehan, C. M., & Fish, M. (1993). Linking employment to attachment: The mediating effects of maternal separation anxiety and interactive behavior. *Child Development, 64*(5), 1451–1460.

Stone, M. (1990). Abuse and abusiveness in borderline personality disorder. In P. S. Links (Ed.), *Family environment and borderline personality disorder* (pp. 133–148). Washington, DC: American Psychiatric Association.

Stone, W. L., & Caro-Martinez, L. M. (1990). Naturalistic observations of spontaneous communication in autistic children. *Journal of Autism and Developmental Disorders, 20*(4), 437–453.

Stone, W. L., Lemanek, K. L., Fishel, P. T., Fernandez, M. C., & Altemeier, W. A. (1990). Play and imitation skills in the diagnosis of autism in young children. *Pediatrics, 86*, 267–272.

Stone, W. L., Ousley, O. Y., & Littleford, C. D. (1997). Motor imitation in young children with autism:

What's the object? *Journal of Abnormal Child Psychology, 25*(6), 475–485.

Strand, P. S. (2000). Responsive parenting and child socialization: Integrating two contexts of family life. *Journal of Child and Family Studies, 9*(3), 269–281.

Stratton, K., Gable, A., & McCormick, M. C. (Eds.). (2001). *Immunization safety review: Thimerosal-containing vaccines and neurodevelopmental disorders.* Washington, DC: National Academy Press.

Strauss, C. C., & Last, C. G. (1993). Social and simple phobias in children. *Journal of Anxiety Disorders, 7*(2), 141–152.

Striegel-Moore, R. H., & Bulik, C. M. (2007). Risk factors for eating disorders. *American Psychologist, 62*(3), 181–198.

Striegel-Moore, R. H., & Franko, D. L. (2003). Epidemiology of binge eating disorder. *International Journal of Eating Disorders, 34,* S19–S29.

Striegel-Moore, R. H., Leslie, D., Petrill, S. A., Garvin, V., & Rosenheck, R. A. (2000). One-year use and cost of inpatient and outpatient services among female and male patients with an eating disorder: Evidence from a national database of health insurance claims. *International Journal of Eating Disorders, 27*(4), 381–389.

Strober, M., DeAntonio, M., Schmidt-Lackner, S., Freeman, R., Lampert, C., & Diamond, J. (1998). Early childhood attention deficit hyperactivity disorder predicts poorer response to acute lithium therapy in adolescent mania. *Journal of Affective Disorders, 51*(2), 145–151.

Strober, M., Lampert, C., Morrell, W., Burroughs, J., & Jacobs(1990). A controlled family study of anorexia nervosa: Evidence of familial aggregation and lack of shared transmission with affective disorders. *International Journal of Eating Disorders, 9*(3), 239–253.

Strober, M., Lampert, C., Schmidt, S., & Morrell, W. (1993). The course of major depressive disorder in adolescents: I. Recovery and risk of manic switching in a follow-up of psychotic and nonpsychotic subtypes. *Journal of the American Academy of Child & Adolescent Psychiatry, 32*(1), 34–42.

Stunkard, A. J., & Messick, S. (1985). The three-factor eating questionnaire to measure dietary restraint, disinhibition and hunger. *Journal of Psychosomatic Research, 29*(1), 71–83.

Sturmey, P., Matson, J. L., & Sevin, J. A. (1992). Analysis of the internal consistency of three autism scales. *Journal of Autism and Developmental Disorders, 22*(2), 321–328.

Sugai, G., Lewis-Palmer, T., & Hagan-Burke, S. (2000). Overview of the functional behavioral assessment process. *Exceptionality, 8*(3), 149–160.

Swanson, J. M., Kraemer, H. C., Hinshaw, S. P., Arnold, L. E., Conners, C. K., Abikoff, H. B., et al. (2001). Clinical relevance of the primary findings of the MTA: Success rates based on severity of ADHD and ODD symptoms at the end of treatment. *Journal of the American Academy of Child & Adolescent Psychiatry, 40*(2), 168–179.

Swedo, S. E., Leonard, H. L., Garvey, M., Mittleman, B., Allen, A. J., Perlmutter, S., et al. (1998). Pediatric autoimmune neuropsychiatric disorders associated with streptococcal infections: Clinical description of the first 50 cases. *American Journal of Psychiatry, 155*(2), 264–271.

Swedo, S. E., Rapoport, J. L., Leonard, H. L., & Lenane, M. (1989). Obsessive-compulsive disorder in children and adolescents: Clinical phenomenology of 70 consecutive cases. *Archives of General Psychiatry, 46*(4), 335–341.

Szymanski, M. L., & Zolotor, A. (2001). Attention-deficit/hyperactivity disorder: Management. *American Family Physician, 64*(8), 1355–1362.

Tadevosyan-Leyfer, O., Dowd, M., Mankoski, R., Winklosky, B., Putnam, S., McGrath, L., et al. (2003). A principal of components analysis of the Autism Diagnostic Interview–Revised. *Journal of the American Academy of Child & Adolescent Psychiatry, 42*(7), 864–872.

Tager-Flusberg, H. (1995). "Once upon a ribbit": Stories narrated by autistic children. *British Journal of Developmental Psychology, 13*(1), 45–59.

Tager-Flusberg, H., Paul, R.,& Lord, C. (2005). Language and communication in autism. In F. R. Volkmar, R. Paul, A. Klin, & D. Cohen (Eds.), *Handbook of autism and pervasive developmental disorders: Vol. 1. Diagnosis, development, neurobiology, and behavior* (3rd ed., pp. 335–364). Hoboken, NJ: John Wiley & Sons, Inc.

Tanguay, P. E., Robertson, J., & Derrick, A. (1998). A dimensional classification of autism spectrum disorder by social communication domains. *Journal of the American Academy of Child & Adolescent Psychiatry, 37*(3), 271–277.

Tannock, R. (1998). Attention deficit hyperactivity disorder: Advances in cognitive, neurobiological, and genetic research. *Journal of Child Psychology and Psychiatry & Allied Disciplines, 39*(1), 65–99.

Tannock, R., & Martinussen, R. (2001). Reconceptualizing ADHD. *Educational Leadership, 59*(3), 20–25.

Taylor, B., Miller, E., Farrington, C. P. Petropoulos, M. C., Favot-Mayand, I., Li, J., et al. (1999). Autism and measles, mumps, and rubella vaccine: No epidemiological evidence for a causal association. *Lancet, 353,* 2026–2029.

Taylor, E. (1994). Syndromes of attention deficit and overactivity. In M. Rutter, E. Taylor, & L. Hersov (Eds.), *Child and adolescent psychiatry: modern approaches* (pp. 285–307). Oxford, UK: Blackwell.

Teplin, L. A., Abram, K. M., McClelland, G. M., Mericle, A. A., Dulcan, M. K., & Washburn, J. J. (2006, April). Psychiatric disorders of youth in detention. *Juvenile Justice Bulletin.* Washington, DC: U.S. Department of Justice, Office of Juvenile Justice and Delinquency Prevention, NCJ210331.

Terr, L. (1990). *Too scared to cry: Psychic trauma in childhood.* New York: Harper & Row.

Terr, L. C. (1991). Childhood traumas: An outline and overview. *American Journal of Psychiatry, 148*(1), 10–20.

Terre, L., Poston, W. S. C., II, & Foreyt, J. P. (2006). Eating disorders. In E. J. Mash & R. A. Barkley (Eds.), *Treatment of childhood disorders* (3rd. ed., pp. 778–829). New York: Guilford Press.

Thelen, M. H., Mintz, L. B., & Vander Wal, J. S. (1996). The Bulimia Test—Revised: Validation with *DSM-IV* criteria for bulimia nervosa. *Psychological Assessment, 8*(2), 219–221.

Thiemann, K. S., & Goldstein, H. (2001). Social stories, written text cues, and video feedback: Effects on social communication of children with autism. *Journal of Applied Behavior Analysis, 34*(4), 425–446.

Thompson, J. K., Heinberg, L. J., Altabe, M., & Tantleff-Dunn, S. (1999). Interpersonal factors: Peers, parents, partners, and perfect strangers. In J. K. Thompson, L. J. Heinberg, M. Altabe, & S. Tantleff-Dunn (Eds.), *Exacting beauty: Theory, assessment, and treatment of body image disturbance* (pp. 175–207). Washington, DC: American Psychological Association.

Thompson-Brenner, H., Glass, S., & Western, D. (2003). A multidimensional meta-analysis of psychotherapy for bulimia nervosa. *Clinical Psychology: Science and Practice, 10*(3), 269–287.

Thomson, E., Hanson, T. L., & McLanahan, S. S. (1994). Family structure and child well-being: Economic resources vs. parental behaviors. *Social Forces, 73*(1), 221–242.

Thornberry, T. P. (1998). Membership in youth gangs and involvement in serious and violent offending. In R. Loeber and D. P. Farrington (Eds.), *Serious and violent offenders: Risk factors and successful interventions* (pp. 147–166). Thousand Oaks, CA: Sage.

Todd, R. D., Sitdhiraska, N., Reich, W., Ji, T. H., Joyner, C. A., Heath, A. C., & Neuman, R. J. (2002). Discrimination of *DSM-IV* and latent class attention-deficit/hyperactivity disorder subtypes by educational and cognitive performance in a population-based sample of child and adolescent twins. *Journal of the American Academy of Child and Adolescent Psychiatry, 41,* 820–828.

Topolski, T. D., Hewitt, J. K., Eaves, L. J., & Silberg, J. L. (1997). Genetic and environmental influences on child reports of manifest anxiety and symptoms of separation anxiety and overanxious disorders: A community-based twin study. *Behavior Genetics, 27*(1), 15–28.

Tordjman, S., Anderson, G. M., McBride, P. A., & Hertzig, M. E. (1995). Plasma androgens in autism. *Journal of Autism and Developmental Disorders, 25*(3), 295–304.

Tordjman, S., Anderson, G. M., McBride, P. A., Hertzig, M. E., Snow, M. E., Hall, L. M., et al. (1997). Plasma β-endorphin, adrenocorticotropin hormone, and cortisol in autism. *Journal of Child Psychology and Psychiatry, 38*(6), 705–715.

Treadwell, K. R. H., & Kendall, P. C. (1996). Self-talk in youth with anxiety disorders: States of mind, content specificity, and treatment outcome. *Journal of Consulting and Clinical Psychology, 64*(5), 941–950.

Treatment for Adolescents with Depression Study (TADS) Team. (2004). Fluoxetine, cognitive-behavioral therapy, and their combination for adolescents with depression: Treatment for Adolescents with Depression Study (TADS) randomized controlled trial. *JAMA, 292*(7), 807–820.

Trump, K. S. (1993, Spring). Youth gangs and school security. *School Intervention Report.* Holmes Beach, Florida: The Safe Schools Coalition, Inc.

Tsai, L. Y. (1987). Pre-, peri-, and neonatal factors in autism. In E. Schopler & G. B. Mesibov (Eds.), *Neurobiological issues in autism* (pp. 179–189). New York: Plenum Press.

Turner, S. M., Beidel, D. C., Roberson-Nay, R., & Tervo, K. (2003). Parenting behaviors in parents with anxiety disorders. *Behaviour Research and Therapy, 41*(5), 541–554.

Ultee, C. A., Griffioen, D., & Schellekens, J. (1982). The reduction of anxiety in children: A comparison of the effects of "systematic desensitization in vitro" and "systematic desensitization in vivo." *Behaviour Research and Therapy, 20*(1), 61–67.

U.S. Department of Education. (1997). *Nineteenth annual report to Congress on implementation of the Individuals with Disabilities Education Act.*

U.S. Department of Education. (2004). *Twenty-sixth annual report to Congress on implementation of the Individuals with Disabilities Education Act.*

U.S. Department of Education. (2006). Office of Special Education and Rehabilitative Services. Retrieved on February 23, 2007, from www.ed.gov/about/offices/list

U.S. Department of Education and Justice. (2006). *Indicators of school crime and safety, 2006.* Available online at http://nces.ed.gov/programs/crimeindicators/crimeindicators2006

U.S. Department of Health and Human Services. (1999). *Mental health: A report of the surgeon general.* Rockville, MD: U.S. Department of Health and Human Services, Substance Abuse and Mental Health Services Administration, Center for Mental Health Services, National Institutes of Health, National Institutes of Mental Health.

U.S. Department of Justice, Bureau of Justice Statistics (2004). Criminal Offender Statistics: Recidivism; Juvenile Delinquents in the Federal Criminal Justice System. Retrieved March 4, 2008, from www.ojp.usdoj.gov/bjs/crimoff.htm#data

Vail, K. (1995). An ounce of prevention. *American School Board Journal, 182*(9), 35–37.

Valdez, A., Kaplan, C. D., & Codina, E. (2000). Psychopathy among Mexican American gang members: A comparative study. *International Journal of Offender Therapy and Comparative Criminology, 44,* 46–58.

Valente, S. M. (2001). Treating attention deficit hyperactivity disorder. *Nurse Practitioner, 26*(9), 14–29.

Valla, J. P., Bergeron, L., & Smolla, N. (2000). The Dominic-R: A pictorial interview for 6- to 11-year-old children. *Journal of the American Academy of Child & Adolescent Psychiatry, 39*(1), 85–93.

Valleni-Basile, L. A., Garrison, C. Z., Jackson, K. L., & Waller, J. L. (1994). Frequency of obsessive-compulsive disorder in a community sample of young adolescents. *Journal of the American Academy of Child & Adolescent Psychiatry, 33*(6), 782–791.

van Goozen, S. H. M., Matthys, W., Cohen-Kettenis, P. T., Buitelaar, J. K., & van Engeland, H. (2000). Hypothalamic-pituitary-adrenal axis and autonomic nervous system activity in disruptive children and matched controls. *Journal of the American Academy of Child & Adolescent Psychiatry, 39*(11), 1438–1445.

van Strien, T., Frijters, J. E., Bergers, G. P., & Defares, P. B. (1986). The Dutch Eating Behavior Questionnaire (DEBQ) for assessment of restrained, emotional, and external eating behavior. *International Journal of Eating Disorders, 5*(2), 295–315.

Varia, S. (2006). *Dating violence among adolescents.* Retrieved June 20, 2007, from http://www.advocatesforyouth.org/publications/factsheet/fsdating.htm

Vitousek, K., & Manke, F. (1994). Personality variables and disorders in anorexia nervosa and bulimia nervosa. *Journal of Abnormal Psychology, 103*(1), 137–147.

Volden, J., & Lord, C. (1991). Neologisms and idiosyncratic language in autistic speakers. *Journal of Autism and Developmental Disorders, 21*(2), 109–130.

Volkmar, F. R. (1987). Diagnostic issues in the pervasive developmental disorders. *Journal of Child Psychology and Psychiatry, 28*(3), 365–369.

Volkmar, F. R., Cicchetti, D. V., Dykens, E., & Sparrow, S. S. (1988). An evaluation of the Autism Behavior Checklist. *Journal of Autism and Developmental Disorders, 18*(1), 81–97.

Volkmar, F. R., & Klin, A. (1994). Social development in autism: Historical and clinical perspectives. In S. Baron-Cohen, H. Tager-Flusberg, & D. J. Cohen (Eds.), *Understanding other minds: Perspectives from autism* (pp. 40–55). New York: Oxford University Press.

Volkmar, R. R., & Klin, A. (2005). Issues in the classification of autism and related conditions. In F. R. Volkmar, R. Paul, A. Klin, & D. Cohen (Eds.), *Handbook of autism and pervasive developmental disorders: Vol. 1. Diagnosis, development, neurobiology, and behavior* (3rd ed., pp. 5–41). Hoboken, NJ: John Wiley & Sons, Inc.

Vygotsky, L. S. (1978). *Mind in society.* Cambridge, MA: Harvard University Press.

Wadden, N. P., Bryson, S. E., & Rodger, R. S. (1991). A closer look at the Autism Behavior Checklist: Discriminant validity and factor structure. *Journal of Autism and Developmental Disorders, 21*(4), 529–541.

Wade, T. D., Bulik, C. M., Neale, M., & Kendler, K. S. (2000). Anorexia nervosa and major depression: Shared genetic and environmental risk factors. *American Journal of Psychiatry, 157*(3), 469–471.

Wagner, K. D., Ambrosini, P., Rynn, M., Wohlberg, C., Yang, R., Greenbaum, M. S., et al. (2003). Efficacy of sertraline in the treatment of children and adolescents with major depressive disorders. *JAMA, 290*(8), 1033–1041.

Wagner, K. D., Robb, A. S., Findling, R. L., Jin, J., Gutierrez, M. M., & Heydorn, W. E. (2004). A randomized, placebo-controlled trial of citalopram for the treatment of major depression in children and adolescents. *American Journal of Psychiatry, 161*(6), 1079–1083.

Wagner, K. D., Weller, E. B., Carlson, G. A., Sachs, G., Biederman, J., Frazier, J. A., et al. (2002). An open-label trial of divalproex in children and adolescents with bipolar disorder. *Journal of the American Academy of Child & Adolescent Psychiatry, 41*(10), 1224–1230.

Waisberg, J., & Woods, M. (2002). A nutrition and behavior change group for patients with anorexia nervosa. *Canadian Journal of Dietetic Practice and Research, 63,* 202–205.

Wakschlag, L. S., Lahey, B. B., Loeber, R., Green, S. M., Gordon, R. A., & Leventhal, B. L. (1997). Maternal smoking during pregnancy and the risk of conduct disorder in boys. *Archives of General Psychiatry, 54*(7), 670–676.

Waldron, H. B., Brody, J. L., Slesnick, N., & Monti, P. M. (2001). Integrative behavioral and family therapy for adolescent substance abuse. In S. M. Colby & T. A. O'Leary (Eds.), *Adolescents, alcohol, and substance abuse: Reaching teens through brief interventions* (pp. 216–243). New York: Guilford Press.

Waldron, H. B., Slesnick, N., Brody, J. L., Charles W. T., & Thomas R. P. (2001). Treatment outcomes for adolescent substance abuse at 4- and 7-month assessments. *Journal of Consulting and Clinical Psychology, 69*(5), 802–813.

Walker, H. M. (1995). *The acting-out child: Coping with classroom disruption* (2nd ed.). Longmont, CO: Sopris West.

Walker, H. M. (2004). Commentary: Use of evidence-based interventions in schools: Where we've been, where we are, and where we need to go. *School Psychology Review, 33*(3), 398–407. Retrieved March 5, 2008, from Wilson Education Abstracts database. (Document ID No. 724594001)

Walker, H. M., Ramsey, E., & Gresham, F. M. (2004). *Antisocial behavior in school: Strategies and best practices* (2nd ed.). Toronto, Ontario, Canada: Wadsworth.

Walker, H. M., & Severson, H. (1990). *Systematic Screening for Behavior Disorders (SSBD): User's guide and technical manual.* Longmont, CO: Sopris West.

Walker, H. M., & Severson, H. (2002). Developmental prevention of at risk outcomes for vulnerable anti-social children and youth. In K. L. Lane, F. M. Gresham, & T. E. O'Shaughnessy (Eds.), *Interventions for children with or at risk for emotional and behavioral disorders* (pp. 177–194). Boston: Allyn & Bacon.

Walkup, J., & Davies, M. (1999, October). The Pediatric Anxiety Rating Scale (PARS): A reliability study. *Scientific Proceedings of the 46th Annual Meeting of the American Academy of Child and Adolescent Psychiatry,* Chicago, p. 107 [abstract].

Wallach, L. (1994). Children coping with violence: The role of the school. *Contemporary Education, 65*(4), 182–184.

Waller, G. (1998). Perceived control in eating disorders: Relationship with reported sexual abuse. *International Journal of Eating Disorders, 23*(2), 213–216.

Walsh, B. T., & Devlin, M. J. (1995). Pharmacotherapy of bulimic nervosa and binge eating disorders. *Addictive Behaviors, 20*(6), 757–764.

Walsh, B. T., Wilson, G. T., Loeb, K. L., & Devlin, M. J. (1997). Medication and psychotherapy in the treatment of bulimia nervosa. *American Journal of Psychiatry, 154*(4), 523–531.

Walters, E. E., & Kendler, K. S. (1995). Anorexia nervosa and anorexic-like syndromes in a population-based female twin sample. *American Journal of Psychiatry, 152*(1), 64–71.

Wang, A. T., Dapretto, M., Hariri, A. R., Sigman, M., & Bookheimer, S. Y. (2004). Neural correlates of facial affect processing in children and adolescents with autism spectrum disorder. *Journal of the American Academy of Child & Adolescent Psychiatry, 43*(4), 481–490.

Warren, S. L., Huston, L., Egeland, B., & Sroufe, L. A. (1997). Child and adolescent anxiety disorders and early attachment. *Journal of the American Academy of Child & Adolescent Psychiatry, 36*(5), 637–644.

Waschbusch, D. A. (2002). A meta-analytic examination of comorbid hyperactive-impulsive-attention problems and conduct problems. *Psychological Bulletin, 128,* 118–150.

Watkins, A. M., & Kurtz, P. D. (2001). Using solution focused intervention to address African-American male overrepresentation in special education: A case study. *Children & Schools, 23*(4), 223–235.

Watson, J. B., & Rayner, R. (1920). Conditioned emotional reactions. *Journal of Experimental Psychology, 3,* 1–14.

Webster-Stratton, C. (1984). Randomized trial of two parent-training programs for families with conduct-disordered children. *Journal of Consulting and Clinical Psychology, 52*(4), 666–678.

Webster-Stratton, C. (1990). Enhancing the effectiveness of self-administered videotape parent training for families with conduct-problem children. *Journal of Abnormal Child Psychology, 18*(5), 479–492.

Webster-Stratton, C. (1992). Individually administered videotape parent training: "Who benefits?" *Cognitive Therapy and Research, 16*(1), 31–52.

Webster-Stratton, C. (2000). Oppositional-defiant and conduct-disordered children. In M. Hersen & R. T. Ammerman (Eds.), *Advanced abnormal child psychology* (2nd ed., pp. 387–412). Mahwah, NJ: Erlbaum.

Webster-Stratton, C., & Hammond, M. (1997). Treating children with early-onset conduct problems: A comparison of child and parent training interventions. *Journal of Consulting and Clinical Psychology, 65*(1), 93–109.

Webster-Stratton, C., & Reid, M. J. (2003a). Treating conduct problems and strengthening social and emotional competence in young children: The Dina Dinosaur treatment program. *Journal of Emotional and Behavioral Disorders, 11*(3), 130–143.

Webster-Stratton, C., & Reid, M. J. (2003b). Treating conduct problems and strengthening social and emotional competence in young children: The Dina Dinosaur treatment program. *Journal of Emotional and Behavioral Disorders, 11*(3), 130–143.

Webster-Stratton, C., & Reid, M. J. (2003c). The Incredible Years parents, teachers and children training series: A multifaceted treatment approach for young children with conduct problems. In A. E. Kazdin & J. R. Weisz (Eds.), *Evidence-based psychotherapies for children and adolescents* (pp. 224–240). New York: Guilford Press.

Webster-Stratton, C., Reid, M. J., & Hammond, M. (2004). Treating children with early-onset conduct problems: Intervention outcomes for parent, child, and teacher training. *Journal of Clinical Child and Adolescent Psychology, 33*(1), 105–124.

Weems, C. F., Hammond-Laurence, K., Silverman, W. K., & Ferguson, C. (1997). The relation between anxiety sensitivity and depression in children and adolescents referred for anxiety. *Behaviour Research and Therapy, 35*(10), 961–966.

Weinberg, W. A., & Emslie, G. J. (1991). Attention deficit hyperactivity disorder: The differential diagnosis. *Journal of Child Neurology, 6*, S23–S36.

Weiner, L., & Septimus, A. (1991). Psychological considerations and support for the child and family. In P. A. Pizzo & C. M. Wilfert (Eds.), *Pediatric AIDS: The challenge of HIV infection in infants, children, and adolescents* (pp. 577–594). Baltimore: Williams & Wilkins.

Weissman, M. M., Kidd, K. K., & Prusoff, B. A. (1982). Variability in rates of affective disorders in relatives of depressed and normal probands. *Archives of General Psychiatry, 39*(12), 1397–1403.

Weissman, M. M., Warner, V., Wickramaratne, P., & Kandel, D. B. (1999). Maternal smoking during pregnancy and psychopathology in offspring followed to adulthood. *Journal of the American Academy of Child & Adolescent Psychiatry, 38*, 892–899.

Weisz, J. R., Southam-Gerow, M. A., Gordis, E. B, & Connor-Smith , J. (2003). Primary and secondary control enhancement training for youth depression: Applying the deployment-focused model of treatment development and testing. In A. E. Kazdin & J. R. Weisz (Eds.), *Evidence-based psychotherapies for children and adolescents* (pp. 165–183). New York: Guilford Press.

Weller, E. B., Weller, R. A., & Danielyan, A. K. (2004a). Mood disorders in prepubertal children. In J. M. Wiener & M. K. Dulcan (Eds.), *The American Psychiatric Publishing textbook of child and adolescent psychiatry* (3rd ed., pp. 411–435). Washington, DC: American Psychiatric Publishing.

Weller, E. B., Weller, R. A., & Danielyan, A. K. (2004b). Mood disorders in adolescents. In J. M. Wiener & M. K. Dulcan (Eds.), *The American Psychiatric Publishing textbook of child and adolescent psychiatry* (3rd ed., pp. 437–481). Washington, DC: American Psychiatric Publishing.

Weller, E. B., Weller, R. A., Fristad, M. A., Rooney, M. T., & Schecter, J. (2000). Children's Interview for Psychiatric Syndromes (ChIPS). *Journal of the American Academy of Child & Adolescent Psychiatry, 39*(1), 76–84.

Wells, K. C., & Egan, J. (1988). Social learning and systems family therapy for childhood oppositional disorder: Comparative treatment outcome. *Comprehensive Psychiatry, 29*(2), 138–146.

Welner, Z., Reich, W., Herjanic, B., & Jung, K. G. (1987). Reliability, validity, and parent-child agreement studies of the Diagnostic Interview for Children and Adolescents (DICA). *Journal of the American Academy of Child & Adolescent Psychiatry, 26*(5), 649–653.

Weltzin, T. E., & Bolton, F. G. (1998). Bulimia nervosa. In V. Van Hasselt & M. Hersen (Eds.), *Handbook of psychological treatment protocols for children and adolescents* (pp. 435–465). Mahwah, NJ: Erlbaum.

Westby, C. (1999). Assessment of pragmatic competence in children with psychiatric disorders. In D. Rogers-Adkinson & P. Griffith (Eds.), *Communication disorders and children with psychiatric and behavioral disorders* (pp. 177–258). San Diego, CA: Singular.

Wetherby, A. M., Prizant, B. M., & Schuler, A. L. (2000). Understanding the nature of communication and language impairments. In A. M. Wetherby & B. M. Prizant (Eds.), *Autism spectrum disorders: A transactional developmental perspective* (pp. 109–141). Baltimore: Paul H. Brookes.

Weyandt, L. L. (2001). *An ADHD primer* (2nd ed.). Mahwah, NJ: Erlbaum.

Whalen, C., & Schreibman, L. (2003). Joint attention training for children with autism using behavior modification procedures. *Journal of Child Psychology and Psychiatry, 44*(3), 456–468.

Whaley, S. E., Pinto, A., & Sigman, M. (1999). Characterizing interactions between anxious mothers and their children. *Journal of Consulting and Clinical Psychology, 67*(6), 826–836.

Whelan, R. J. (1998). *Emotional and behavioral disorders: A 25-year focus.* Denver, CO: Love.

Whitaker, A., Johnson, J., Shaffer, D., & Rapoport, J. L. (1990). Uncommon troubles in young people: Prevalence estimates of selected psychiatric disorders in a nonreferred adolescent population. *Archives of General Psychiatry, 47*(5), 487–496.

Wicks-Nelson, R., & Israel, A. C. (1997). *Behavior disorders of childhood* (3rd ed.). Upper Saddle River, NJ: Prentice Hall.

Wicks-Nelson, R., & Israel, A. C. (2005). *Behavior disorders of childhood* (6th ed.). Upper Saddle River, NJ: Prentice Hall.

Wilens, T. E., Spencer, T. J., Biederman, J., & Girard, K. (2001). A controlled clinical trial of bupropion for attention deficit hyperactivity disorder in adults. *The American Journal of Psychiatry, 158*(2), 282–288.

Wilfley, D., Welch, R., Stein, R., Spurrell, E., Cohen, L., Saelens B., et al. (2002). A randomized comparison of group cognitive-behavioral therapy and group interpersonal psychotherapy for the treatment of overweight individuals with binge-eating disorder. *Archives of General Psychiatry, 59,* 713–721.

Willert, J., & Willert, R. (2000). An ignored antidote to school violence: Classrooms that reinforce positive social habits. *American Secondary Education, 29*(1), 27–33.

Williams, G. J., Power, K. G., Miller, H. R., & Freeman, C. P. (1994). Development and validation of the Stirling eating disorder scales. *International Journal of Eating Disorders, 16*(1), 35–43.

Williamson, D. A., Davis, C. J., Bennett, S. M., & Goreczny, A. J. (1989). Development of a simple procedure for assessing body image disturbances. *Behavioral Assessment, 11*(4), 433–446.

Williamson, D. A., Duchmann, E. G., Barker, S. E., & Bruno, R. M. (1998). Anorexia nervosa. In V. B. Van Hasselt & M. Hersen (Eds.), *Handbook of psychological treatment protocols for children and adolescents* (pp. 413–434). Mahwah, NJ: Erlbaum.

Williamson, D. A., Thaw, J. M., & Varnado-Sullivan, P. J. (2001). Cost-effectiveness analysis of a hospital-based cognitive-behavioral treatment program for eating disorders. *Behavior Therapy, 32*(3), 459–477.

Wilson, G. T., Eldredge, K. L., Smith, D., & Niles, B. (1991). Cognitive-behavioral treatment with and without response prevention for bulimia. *Behaviour Research and Therapy, 29*(6), 575–583.

Wilson, G. T., & Fairburn, C. G. (1993). Cognitive treatments for eating disorders. *Journal of Consulting and Clinical Psychology, 61*(2), 261–269.

Wilson, G. T., & Fairburn, C. G. (2002). Treatments for eating disorders. In P. E. Nathan & J. M. Gorman (Eds.), *A guide to treatments that work* (2nd ed., pp. 559–592). New York: Oxford University Press.

Wilson, G. T., & Pike, K. M. (2001). Eating disorders. In D. H. Barlow (Ed.), *Clinical handbook of psychological disorders: A step-by-step treatment manual* (3rd ed., pp. 332–375). New York: Guilford Press.

Wing, L., & Gould, J. (1978). Systematic recording of behaviors and skills of retarded and psychotic children. *Journal of Autism & Childhood Schizophrenia, 8*(1), 79–97.

Wing, L., & Gould, J. (1979). Severe impairments of social interaction and associated abnormalities in children: Epidemiology and classification. *Journal of Autism and Developmental Disorders, 9*(1), 11–29.

Wing, L., Leekam, S. R., Libby, S. J., Gould, J., & Larcombe, M. (2002). The Diagnostic Interview for Social and Communication Disorders: Background, inter-rater reliability and clinical use. *Journal of Child Psychology and Psychiatry, 43*(3), 307–325.

Winner, M. (2002). *Thinking about you thinking about me.* San Jose, CA: Author.

Wiseman, C., Sunday, S., Klapper, F., Klein, M., & Halmi, K. (2002). Short-term group CBT versus psycho-education on an inpatient eating disorder unit. *Eating Disorders: The Journal of Treatment & Prevention, 10,* 313–320.

Wiseman, C. V., Sunday, S. R., Klapper, F., Harris, W. A., & Halmi, K. A. (2001). Changing patterns of hospitalization in eating disorder patients. *International Journal of Eating Disorders, 30*(1), 69–74.

Wittchen, H. U., Stein, M. B., & Kessler, R. C. (1999). Social fears and social phobia in a community sample of adolescents and young adults: Prevalence, risk factors and co-morbidity. *Psychological Medicine, 29*(2), 309–323.

Wolfberg, P. (2003). *Peer play and the autism spectrum: The art of guiding children's socialization and imagination: Integrated Play Groups field manual.* Shawnee Mission, KS: Autism Asperger.

Wolpe, J. (1958). *Psychotherapy by reciprocal inhibition.* Stanford, CA: Stanford University Press.

Wonderlich, S. A. (1995). Personality and eating disorders. In K. D. Brownell & C. G. Fairburn (Eds.), *Eating disorders and obesity: A comprehensive handbook* (pp. 171–175). New York: Guilford Press.

Wonderlich, S. A., Brewerton, T. D., Jocic, Z., Dansky, B. S., & Abbott, D. W. (1997). Relationship of childhood sexual abuse and eating disorders. *Journal of the American Academy of Child & Adolescent Psychiatry, 36*(8), 1107–1115.

Wong, S. E., Floyd, J., Innocent, A. J., & Woolsey, J. E. (1992). Applying a DRO schedule and compliance training to reduce aggressive and self-injurious behavior in an autistic man: A case report. *Journal of Behavior Therapy and Experimental Psychiatry, 22,* 299–304.

Wood, M., Furlong, M. J., Rosenblatt, J. A., Robertson, L. M., Scozzari, F., & Sosna, T. (1997). Understanding the psychosocial characteristics of gang-involved youths in a system of care: Individual, family, and system correlates. *Education and Treatment of Children, 20,* 281–294.

Wood, S. F., & Huffman, J. B. (1999). Preventing gang activity and violence in schools. *Contemporary Education, 71*(1), 19–23.

Woodward, L., Taylor, E., & Dowdney, L. (1998). The parenting and family functioning of children with hyperactivity. *Journal of Child Psychology and Psychiatry, 39,* 161–169.

Wozniak, J., Biederman, J., Kiely, K., & Ablon, J. S. (1995). Mania-like symptoms suggestive of childhood-onset bipolar disorder in clinically referred children. *Journal of the American Academy of Child & Adolescent Psychiatry, 34*(7), 867–876.

Wright, P., & Santa Cruz, R. (1983). Ethnic composition of special education programs in California. *Learning Disability Quarterly, 6,* 387–394.

Yell, M. L., Rozalski, M. E., & Drasgow, E. (2001). Disciplining students with disabilities. *Focus on Exceptional Children, 33*(9), 1–20.

Young, R. C., Biggs, J. T., Ziegler, V. E., & Meyer, D. A. (1978). A rating scale for mania: Reliability, validity and sensitivity. *British Journal of Psychiatry, 133,* 429–435.

Younger, A. J., & Boyko, K. A. (1987). Aggression and withdrawal as social schemas underlying children's peer perceptions. *Child Development, 58*(4), 1094–1100.

Younger, A. J., Schwartzman, A. E., & Ledingham, J. E. (1985). Age-related changes in children's perceptions of aggression and withdrawal in their peers. *Developmental Psychology, 21*(1), 70–75.

Youngstrom, E. A., Findling, R. L., & Calabrese, J. R. (2004). Effects of adolescent manic symptoms on agreement between youth, parent, and teacher ratings of behavior problems. *Journal of Affective Disorders, 82,* S5–S16.

Zala, S. M., & Penn, D. J. (2004). Abnormal behaviours induced by chemical pollution: A review of the evidence and new challenges. *Animal Behaviour, 68*(4), 649–664.

Zangwill, W. M. (1983). An evaluation of a parent training program. *Child & Family Behavior Therapy, 5*(4), 1–16.

Zhu, A. J., & Walsh, B. T. (2002). In review: Pharmacologic treatment of eating disorders. *The Canadian Journal of Psychiatry/La Revue canadienne de psychiatrie, 47*(3), 227–234.

Zoccolillo, M. (1993). Gender and the development of conduct disorder. *Development and Psychopathology, 5,* 65–78.

Zonnevijlle-Bender, M. J. S., van Goozen, S. H. M., Cohen-Kettenis, P. T., van Elburg, A., & van Engeland, H. (2002). Do adolescent anorexia nervosa patients have deficits in emotional functioning: Erratum. *European Child & Adolescent Psychiatry, 11*(2), 99.

Zucker, K. J., Bradley, S. J., & Lowry Sullivan, C. B. (1996). Traits of separation anxiety in boys with gender identity disorder. *Journal of the American Academy of Child & Adolescent Psychiatry, 35*(6), 791–798.

Zuddas, A., Ledda, M. G., Fratta, A., Muglia, P., & Cianchetti, C. (1996). Clinical effects of clozapine on autistic disorder. *American Journal of Psychiatry, 153*(5), 738.

NAME INDEX

SUBJECT INDEX